The Social Work Experience

An Introduction to Social Work and Social Welfare

FOURTH EDITION

Mary Ann Suppes
Mount Mary College—Milwaukee, WI

Carolyn Cressy Wells
University of Wisconsin at Oshkosh

Boston   Burr Ridge, IL   Dubuque, IA   Madison, WI   New York   San Francisco   St. Louis
Bangkok   Bogotá   Caracas   Kuala Lumpur   Lisbon   London   Madrid   Mexico City
Milan   Montreal   New Delhi   Santiago   Seoul   Singapore   Sydney   Taipei   Toronto

McGraw-Hill Higher Education ⅋

A Division of The McGraw-Hill Companies

THE SOCIAL WORK EXPERIENCE
Published by McGraw-Hill, a business unit of The McGraw-Hill Companies, Inc., 1221 Avenue of the Americas, New York, NY, 10020. Copyright © 2003, 2000, 1996 by The McGraw-Hill Companies, Inc. All rights reserved. No part of this publication may be reproduced or distributed in any form or by any means, or stored in a database or retrieval system, without the prior written consent of The McGraw-Hill Companies, Inc., including, but not limited to, in any network or other electronic storage or transmission, or broadcast for distance learning.
Some ancillaries, including electronic and print components, may not be available to customers outside the United States.

This book is printed on acid-free paper.

3 4 5 6 7 8 9 0 DOW/DOW 0 9 8 7 6 5 4 3

ISBN 0-07-248597-3

Editorial director: *Phillip A. Butcher*
Senior sponsoring editor: *Carolyn Henderson Meier*
Senior marketing manager: *Daniel M. Loch*
Project manager: *Christina Thornton-Villagomez*
Production supervisor: *Carol Bielski*
Designer/cover design: *Jenny El-Shamy*
Media producer: *Shannon Rider*
Supplement producer: *Nathan Perry*
Photo research coordinator: *Jeremy Cheshareck*
Photo researcher: *Catherine Nance*
Typeface: *10.5/12 Times Roman*
Compositor: *Shepherd, Inc.*
Printer: *R. R. Donnelley & Sons Company*

Library of Congress Cataloging-in-Publication Data

Suppes, Mary Ann.
    The social work experience : an introduction to social work and social welfare / Mary Ann Suppes, Carolyn Cressy Wells.—4th ed.
        p. cm.
    Includes bibliographical references and index.
    ISBN 0-07-248597-3
    1. Social service—United States. 2. Social service—Vocational guidance—United States.
I. Wells, Carolyn Cressy. II. Title.
HV10.5 .S97 2003
361.3'2'02373—dc21   2002021935

www.mhhe.com

About the Authors

MARY ANN SUPPES brings an unusual breadth of teaching, practice, and professional experience to the writing of *The Social Work Experience*. She is currently a professor of social work at Mount Mary College in Milwaukee, Wisconsin, where she has served as director of the social work program for many years. She has provided curriculum consultation to numerous colleges and universities. A member of the Council on Social Work Education, the Association of Baccalaureate Social Work Program Directors (BPD), the National Association of Social Workers, and the Wisconsin Council on Social Work Education, she has served for many years on the CSWE Commission on Accreditation, currently serves on the CSWE Commission on Information Management and Research, is a member of the board of directors of BPD, has been treasurer of the Wisconsin Council on Social Work Education, and has chaired numerous CSWE site visits. Professor Suppes received both her undergraduate and graduate (MSW) degrees from the University of Wisconsin at Milwaukee and did postgraduate work at the University of Chicago.

CAROLYN CRESSY WELLS has recently become a professor of social work at the University of Wisconsin at Oshkosh. Previously she developed the social work program at Marquette University in Milwaukee, Wisconsin, where she served as the program director for many years. She is an active member of the Council on Social Work Education, the National Association of Social Workers, the Association of Baccalaureate Program Directors, and the Academy of Certified Social Workers, and has participated in a number of accreditation site visits for the Council on Social Work Education. She is author of three other social work texts: *Social Work Day to Day: The Experience of Generalist Social Work Practice; Social Work Ethics Day to Day: Guidelines for Professional Practice;* and *Stepping to the Dance: The Training of a Family Therapist.* She maintained a small private practice in individual, marital, and family counseling for many years. She received an undergraduate degree in anthropology from the University of California at Berkeley and an MSSW and PhD in child development and family relationships from the University of Wisconsin at Madison.

Foreword

Alejandro Garcia
Syracuse University

An introduction to the social work profession is a critical element in providing new social work students, as well as other students who are exploring an interest in social work, with a comprehensive understanding of the profession. Such an introduction must be provided in nonjargon language that college freshmen and sophomores can understand. In addition, the text must provide an accurate description of the breadth and depth of our dynamic profession. Mary Ann Suppes and Carolyn Cressy Wells, two social work educators with a total of over 50 years experience in directing undergraduate social work programs, have accomplished that task with distinction.

In 1989, on the eve of the publication of the second edition of *The Social Work Experience,* Ronald Federico, a noted authority on baccalaureate social work education, wrote that Mary Ann Suppes and Carolyn Wells had succeeded in developing a social work text that provided an introduction to the profession and provided an "integration of knowledge—from practice and from theory" in a creative and effective manner.

In the fourth edition, Suppes and Wells have maintained that creative approach and responded to a number of critical concerns and changing areas of social work and social policy. The new edition is organized into three areas. The first part addresses social work and its context and includes discussions of the professional social worker, theoretical perspectives for generalist practice, career opportunities, social welfare policy, and historical elements of the development of the profession as well as a discussion of poverty and populations at risk. The second part of the text provides excellent discussion of fields of services, including family and children's and elderly services, mental health, school social work, and social work in the workplace, in health care, and in criminal justice settings, as well as social work with persons with substance abuse problems. The final part looks toward the future and includes a number of major challenges for the profession.

A unique aspect of this book is the inclusion of "debate boxes" that contain a proposition regarding a current social welfare topic and then provide perspectives in favor of and against that proposition. The inclusion of these debate boxes should provoke much discussion among students of diverse issues of import to the social work profession. In each chapter, the authors also provide exhibits, key terms, websites, and discussion questions that help to illustrate and elaborate on the content and provide critical opportunities for students to integrate the content and to pursue further exploration.

Many of us in social work education have been concerned about the need for social work texts to respond to the growing multicultural nature of our society. This text contains a thoughtful integration of diversity content in chapter case studies and in the didactic content of the text. Each chapter begins with a case study, and many of these studies reflect human diversity. In a chapter on poverty and populations at risk, the authors question whether our society has achieved economic and social justice in light of the continuing, widespread existence of poverty, racism, sexism, ageism, and homophobia as well as handicapism. The book also includes ways in which our society has responded to these ubiquitous problems, as well as a provocative discussion on the current status of affirmative action in this country.

Suppes and Wells also updated a number of important social welfare areas in this text. These include excellent discussions of the 1996 welfare reform legislation and the Americans with Disabilities Act as well as the impact of the aging of the baby boomers on Social Security and Medicare in the near future. Other major problem areas that are updated include the feminization of poverty as well as the current increase of children and adolescents in poverty.

The authors' ability to integrate practice and social policy is excellent. One of the concerns that many of us who teach in the area of social policy have is that social work students are not provided with a balanced approach to practice and policy. Often, policy is an afterthought, and students continue through their social work education with a limited perspective on social policy. Suppes and Wells have done an impressive job of integrating social policy throughout this text. Not only is policy well addressed in terms of its importance to the social work profession, but current areas of import in social policy are discussed with a degree of clarity that reflects the authors' understanding of the level of sophistication of social work students at this level.

The first chapter in this text provides important information to the student beginning an examination of a career in social work. It anticipates questions students interested in making social work their profession may have, and it provides information on entry-level job searches, career paths, and job opportunities in the social work profession. It also provides important information on legal regulation as well as information on career facts and even employment projections. The second chapter, new for the fourth edition, provides social work students with introductory level theoretical approaches to generalist practice and also to the political spectrum that strongly impacts practice.

Suppes and Wells conclude their book by examining a number of issues that they believe will be important to society and the social work profession in the future. They draw from demographic trends, political forces, economic conditions, and technological advances to frame their view of the future. They examine the future of the profession, taking into consideration the changing multicultural nature of our society, as well as the graying of America and the continuing impact of immigrants and refugees. The changing nature of the

American family does not escape their assessments, and neither do technological advances in health care and the computerization of human services organizations.

The fourth edition of *The Social Work Experience* fulfills Suppes and Wells's commitment to develop a text that is generalist in orientation and that incorporates the ethics and values of the profession and human diversity issues. Suppes' extensive experience on the Council on Social Work Education's Commission on Accreditation and as a social work education consultant and Wells' extensive experience in social work education plus both authors' knowledge of the Council on Social Work Education's Educational Policy and Accreditation Standards are reflected in this text's incorporation of populations at risk, diversity, values and ethics, and generalist practice. This text is timely, provocative, and reflective of the contemporary nature of the social work profession in this increasingly complex society. It will provide new social work students, as well as those considering the social work profession for a career, with an exceptional understanding of the breadth and depth of the social work profession and the challenges it confronts on a daily basis in improving the social well-being of all elements of American society

Dr. Garcia is a professor in the School of Social Work at Syracuse University. He is also currently the Chair of the National Hispanic Council on Aging. He is the coeditor of *HIV Affected and Vulnerable Youth* (1999), *La Familia: Traditions and Realities* (1999), and *Elderly Latinos: Issues and Solutions for the 21st Century* (1993). He is an associate editor of the *Journal of Sociology and Social Welfare* and the book review editor of the *Journal of Ethnic and Cultural Diversity in Social Work*. He currently serves as a consulting editor of the *Journal of Social Work Education* and has served on the Board of Editors of the *Encyclopedia of Social Work,* 19th edition.

Preface

One beautiful, crisp fall day several years ago two friends, both experienced social work educators, set off by car for a conference 200 miles to the north. We were those friends, and our conversation during that drive sparked the ideas that resulted in *The Social Work Experience.* We were both teaching introductory courses in social work that semester and, because our roots were in social work practice, we were frustrated by the lack of well-developed, contemporary case study materials. Authentic, current case material, we were convinced, would help students to identify with the real people who are served by social workers across the United States, and with the social workers themselves.

It occurred to us that we could create those materials from our own professional practice experiences and from the field learning experiences of our students. Our case studies could portray diverse populations in both client and social worker roles. Some could illustrate baccalaureate social work students in field practicum settings. We could synthesize real-life situations of people we had known and thus avoid exact duplication of any actual cases. With these ideas and commitments, the book emerged.

THE FOURTH EDITION

In the preceding three editions of this text we designed case studies to illustrate generalist social work practice at different systems levels, carefully connecting case materials with theoretical content. Common themes were integrated into every chapter: generalist practice, social research, ethics and values, and human diversity. Beginning with the second edition we augmented the human diversity theme to include an examination of poverty, populations-at-risk, and social justice issues. Our concern for special issues relevant to women helped frame several of the case studies as well as the didactic content of the text. The development of major social welfare programs in the United States was traced. The history of the social work profession was presented within each field of practice, to acquaint students with the social and political context of the times and with the persons who provided strong leadership in the development of the profession. The primary focus of the book was entry-level generalist social work practice, but the linkage between generalist and specialist practice was also presented.

The common themes integrated into every chapter of the first three editions remain the same in the fourth edition. All information has been updated and augmented, however. The presentation of these materials has been enriched to include:

- New case studies, debate boxes, Internet sites, classroom exercises, research activities, and Internet research exercises
- An entirely new chapter, "Theoretical Perspectives for Social Workers," with introductory-level theoretical approaches to generalist practice and also to the political spectrum strongly impacting practice
- Ongoing examination of the effects of legislation on social welfare policy, social work practice, and the people served by social work practitioners, helping clarify the relationship of policy to practice
- Social work practice contributions addressing the effects of terrorist activities, both national and international
- Effects of welfare reform, the Earned Income Tax Credit, and other social programs designed to regulate the poor
- Documentation of the increasing diversity of the American population today, with discussion of potential ramifications

ORGANIZATION

All of the chapters in this text begin with case studies involving clients and social workers who are members of diverse groups. Case studies are provided to capture student interest and to provide appropriate context for the didactic material that follows. Each chapter includes content identified as important in the *Educational Policy and Accreditation Standards* of the Council on Social Work Education: generalist practice, social welfare policy, social systems, professional values and ethics, social research, human diversity, populations-at-risk, and social and economic justice. Human life span content is reflected in the case studies and also in the didactic content in many areas of the book.

Part One, "Social Work and Its Context," consists of four chapters. Chapter 1 introduces the generalist social worker, a professional who has earned the baccalaureate degree in social work from a program accredited by the Council on Social Work Education. Related professions are compared and contrasted; career opportunities are explored. Chapter 2 examines theoretical perspectives important to generalist practice, focusing on the ecosystems approach. It also explores political perspectives that shape social welfare policy. Chapter 3 presents social welfare policy development in historical perspective and discusses the history of the social work profession. Chapter 4 begins by examining one of the social work profession's core values: social and economic justice. Issues of poverty and prejudice are examined, and specific populations at greatest risk are identified.

Part Two, "Professional Practice Settings," examines nine fields of professional social work practice. These include family and children's services, social work in mental health settings, social work in health care, in the workplace, in the schools, in chemical dependency settings, in criminal justice settings, with older adults, and with people who have developmental disabilities. As discussed above, every chapter includes content identified as important by the Council on Social Work Education's *Educational Policy and Accreditation Standards.*

Part Three, "A Look at the Future," begins by looking at the remarkable human diversity that is rapidly changing the face of America. Next, the political scene is considered: how are strong political forces shaping the opportunity system for people, especially the poor? Recent dramatic shifts in economic conditions in the United States are reviewed. Then the impact of technology is explored: where are the biomedical technology breakthroughs taking us? What are the emerging ethical and moral implications? This part of the text also explores technological advances in computer usage in social work and the ethics of evolving technology for practice. Part Three also looks at the future of social work professional employment and discusses predicted employment opportunities.

PEDAGOGICAL AIDS

- Debate boxes are a unique pedagogical aid that contain a proposition regarding a current social welfare topic and then provide perspectives in favor of and against that proposition. The inclusion of these debate boxes should provoke much discussion among students regarding diverse issues of import to the social work profession.
- Exhibits included in every chapter provide information from original sources to help students better understand issues discussed in the body of the text. Some of these materials are didactic; others include political cartoons, poems, reflections on firsthand experience, and so forth.
- Key terms are highlighted in every chapter and further defined in an extensive glossary.
- Internet sites are included in every chapter that direct students to appropriate electronic data resources providing further information on various topics under consideration.
- Classroom exercises provide students with the opportunity to engage in small group discussion regarding various topics of interest to social work practitioners. A selection of these exercises is provided in every chapter.
- Every chapter includes research exercises designed to encourage the student to examine important contemporary issues in social work and social welfare outside of the classroom setting.
- Internet research exercises are included in every chapter to involve and familiarize the student in the use of Web-based source materials.

SUPPLEMENTS

As a full-service publisher of quality educational products, McGraw-Hill does much more than just sell textbooks. The company creates and publishes an extensive array of print, video, and digital supplements for students and instructors. This edition of *The Social Work Experience* is accompanied by an, *Instructor's Manual/Test Bank,* which includes chapter outlines, key terms, overviews, lecture notes, discussion questions, a complete test bank, and more. The *Instructor's Manual/Test Bank* is provided free of charge to instructors. Orders of new (versus used) textbooks help defray the cost of developing such supplements, which is substantial. Please contact your local McGraw-Hill representative for more information on the above supplement.

IN APPRECIATION

Today, as we put the finishing touches to the fourth edition, we wish to acknowledge and thank those who assisted us on this project. While the book is basically our own creation, it has been substantially enriched by the critiques and contributions of its editors and reviewers. Irving Rockwood, senior editor of the first edition, was instrumental in providing the transitional arrangements with McGraw-Hill that made the second and third editions possible. Ronald C. Federico's innovative ideas continue to shape the content of the book, in spite of his untimely death shortly after publication of the first edition.

For the fourth edition we wish to thank our editor Carolyn Henderson Meier for her assistance, and we are grateful to the following reviewers for their helpful critiques and comments: Gloria Duran Aguilar, Thomas College; Mary Ellen Elwell, Salisbury State University; Leonard Gibbs, the University of Wisconsin at Eau Claire; Waldo E. Johnson Jr., Loyola University, Chicago; Charles Jones, the University of Michigan at Flint; Teresa C. Jones, Michigan State University; Tim Kelly, The University of Georgia; Stephen M. Marson, The University of North Carolina at Pembroke; Taylor McGrawn, Rust College; John McNutt, Boston College; Dennis Myers, Baylor University; Andrew T. Nilsson, Eastern Connecticut State University; Kim-Anne Perkins, the University of Maine at Presque Isle; Jack Sellers, the University of North Alabama; Marjorie P. Steinberg, Western Connecticut State University; Stephanie Kissel, University of Wisconsin, Oshkosh; Dorthy Stucky Halley, Pittsburgh State University; E. Ann McGregor, Wichita State University; Minou Michlin, South Connecticut State University; Joan Elliott, Eastern Tennessee State University; Maureen Newton, Jacksonville State University; and Sharon Warren Cook, Winston-Salem State University.

Our gratitude is also expressed to those who provided materials for or helped to design our composite case studies: Luz Brugos, Isaac Christie, Joe Dooley, Jason Dietenberger, Michael George, Georgia Giese, Linda Ketcher Goodrich, Karen Greenler, Sandra Hill, David Kucej, Julie Kudick, Maureen Martin, Melissa Monsoor, Malcolm Montgomery, Jan Mowdy, Dolores Poole, Wanda Priddy, David Schneider, Sara Stites, Delores Sumner, Deborah Trakel, Jeanne West, Judith Wettengel, and Jodi Searl Wnorowski. We appreciate the exceptional library research assistance of Laurel Privatt at Mount Mary College and the Internet research of Dr. William Bunge. We are grateful to Roberta Allickson and Linda Van Groll for their technical asistance. We also wish to acknowledge and express special gratitude to Fritz Suppes for his "behind the scenes" contributions to library research, Internet exercises, photo selections, and countless technological consultations.

We are most indebted to the theorists and writers whose dream of generalist social work practice has inspired us. Along with hundreds of other social work educators, we are committed to keeping alive and strong the concept of generalist practice articulated by Betty L. Baer and Ronald C. Federico, among others. It is our sincere hope that faculty and students alike will find this book helpful in understanding and appreciating the context and practice of social work.

Mary Ann Suppes
Carolyn Cressy Wells

Contents in Brief

Contents

Part Two
PROFESSIONAL PRACTICE SETTINGS   159

Part Three
A LOOK AT THE FUTURE   543

PART ONE

Social Work and Its Context

Chapter 1 introduces the generalist social worker, a professional who has earned the baccalaureate degree in social work from a program accredited by the Council on Social Work Education. Major competencies required by the generalist social work practitioner are identified, and social work's purpose and tasks are compared with those of related disciplines. Social work values and ethics are outlined, and their central role to the profession is discussed.

Chapter 2 examines theoretical perspectives for social workers that impact both professional practice and the social welfare policies that strongly affect practice activities and options. Systems theory, as well as its relationship to social work, is introduced. The highly related ecosystems perspective is discussed in detail. Generalist social work practice theory is presented and discussed, with an emphasis on the importance of a strengths perspective. Then, political perspectives shaping social welfare policies are examined, including classical conservative, neoconservative, liberal, neoliberal, and radical. How the political spectrum impacts social welfare policy development is discussed.

Chapter 3 examines social welfare as a system or institution and explains the place of the profession of social work within this system. The institution of social welfare is central to the referral work of the generalist. In the United States it derived primarily from that existing in England when the first European settlers came to this continent. Hence, in order for students of social welfare to have some understanding of how the U.S. system developed, Old World history, especially English, will be explored.

An overview of social welfare history, highlighting major themes and trends, leads to an examination of major contemporary governmental social welfare programs. Although social workers today do not typically work in welfare agencies in roles providing financial and material aids, they need to know what the major programs are in order to provide adequate referral information to clients in need.

Chapter 4 explores issues of social and economic justice, poverty, and populations-at-risk, curriculum content areas required by the 2001 Educational Policy and Accreditation Standards of the Council on Social Work Education. Populations-at-risk often constitute the major clientele with whom professional social workers work: children, women, older adults, racial and ethnic minorities, people with disabilities, and gay and lesbian persons.

CHAPTER 1

The Social Work Profession

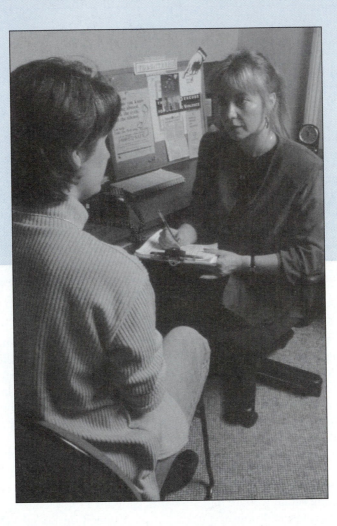

OUTLINE

SUSAN DUNN

The telephone rang shrilly at the women's shelter about 6:15 in the evening. The caller's voice was urgent, frightened, and intense, though little louder than a whisper. "I just called the crisis telephone line that was advertised on the radio," the woman began, "and the person who answered told me to try you. I need a safe place to stay, right now. Can you take me?"

"We may be able to," the social worker replied. "It depends on your situation. Our agency has been set up to help women who have been physically abused. Can you tell me something about yourself? What makes you need a place to stay just now?"

"I can't talk very long because I'm so afraid he'll come back soon," the caller responded, her voice slightly louder this time. "My husband just beat me up again, but he ran out when I threatened to call the police. The children saw the whole thing. I've decided I've had enough. But I don't know where to go. My friends are afraid to get involved. I've got two kids who have to go with me. I don't have any money of my own."

"Sounds like you're in a tough spot. My name is Pamela Wright. I'm a social worker here. Tell me if you need to stop talking. Call me back if you have to hang up. If you're in danger right at this moment, I can take your name and address and call the police for you."

"Oh no," the woman said. "The reason I didn't call the police in the first place is that I don't want to get my husband in trouble. I make him upset. Calling the police would embarrass the whole family. I couldn't possibly do that."

"You said your husband hurt you. Do you have injuries that may need immediate medical attention?"

"*When he hit my face I tried to defend myself. I didn't want my face covered with bruises again. I put my hands up to my face. My right arm hurts pretty badly now. I really don't think it's broken, though, because I can still use it and move my fingers. I don't think I need to go to the hospital. I just need to get away from here.*"

"*Do you feel it is safe for you to talk with me for a few minutes now?*"

"*Yes. The last time my husband got mad at me and left, he stayed away for a couple of hours. I'm pretty sure he'll do that again this time.*"

"*Well,*" Pamela Wright said gently, "*from what you say, this isn't the first time your husband has physically abused you. I take it that you want to be gone this time when he gets home?*"

"*Yes. He might come home drunk and hit me again. That's what happened last time. If it weren't for the children, I might take a chance and wait for him, because he might come home sorry and ready to make up. But the kids are awfully upset and scared. I want to get out of here this time.*"

"*Have you any relatives who might be able to take you and the children tonight? You might feel a lot better if you had some family members around you to support you and help with the kids this evening. We'd be happy to help you here even if you were staying somewhere else. You could come in tomorrow, in fact, to talk with one of our counselors about things you could think about doing to deal with the physical abuse by your husband.*"

"*I haven't got any family of my own around here. My parents live in another state, and so does my sister. They wouldn't want me to stay with them, anyway, with two little kids to worry about. My in-laws live near here, and they're good to me, but they would break down and tell my husband where I was. Then he'd come, and he might beat me up again. So I don't want anybody to know where I am.*"

Recognizing that this was an emergency situation Pamela Wright said quickly, "*We do have a room available in our shelter right now. I think that it is important for you to leave your home as quickly as possible. Will you be able to get yourself over here on your own if I give you the address?*"

"*That's another big problem. I don't think I can. My husband took the car. My arm really hurts. I don't think I can carry anything. My six-year-old can make it on her own, but the two-year-old is too much trouble to take on the bus the way my arm hurts. And I'll need to bring some clothes and things.*"

"*Have you any money at all right now?*" Pamela asked. "*We do have some special funds to send a cab in emergency situations, but those funds are very tight. Could you pay for a cab to get yourself and the kids over here?*"

"*Well, I have about $10 in my purse. My husband always keeps the checkbook with him, and he just gives me cash a little bit at a time. But if I spend what I have on a cab, I won't have any money at all to pay for my stay with you, or for anything else, for that matter.*"

"*Our services are free. We can supply you with a small room for yourself and your children. We also provide meals. You can stay with us for up to a month. We will help you to decide what to do next. There will be rules about sharing household tasks and some other things, but I can explain more when you get here. Do you think you want to come?*"

"*Yes, I do,*" the caller replied. "*Can I come with the kids right away?*"

"Certainly," Pamela said. "But how bad is your arm? Will you be able to manage?"

"I think I can. I'll just have to pack with one hand. My six-year-old can help. Is there anything in particular that we should bring?"

"We rely a lot on donations here, so anything you can bring would be appreciated. Bring the routine stuff—you know, toothbrushes, pajamas, toys, extra clothes, anything to keep you and the children as comfortable as possible."

"Okay. Thank you very much. I hope I'll be there soon."

"Fine. I'll give you our address. You are asked to tell it to no one but the cab driver, because for safety reasons we need to keep it secret." Pamela gave the woman the address of the shelter. "Now," she continued, "if your husband comes home before you get a chance to leave in the cab, do call the police right away, the minute you see him approaching. Or call us, and we'll call the police. Don't take the chance of another beating. Now, what is your name and address? I need to take your phone number too, just in case." The address that the caller, Susan Dunn, gave turned out to be from a neighborhood on the edge of the city generally considered middle to upper-middle class.

When Susan Dunn and her two children arrived at the shelter, their appearance betrayed some of their trouble. Susan's left eye was swollen and turning black. She held her sore arm awkwardly away from her side. The eyes of both children were red from crying. Their clothes, particularly Susan's, were rumpled; her blouse was torn. All three looked exhausted and tearful. Susan carried a small suitcase, and her six-year-old daughter was wearing a backpack that turned out to be full of school supplies.

The newcomers entered the shelter, a crowded house in a busy city neighborhood, quite hesitantly and looked anxiously about the first-floor hallway with its worn brown rug and cheerful, hopeful posters. A dark-eyed child of five or six ran up to greet them. Pamela Wright introduced herself and the child, waiting for Susan to introduce herself in turn, along with her own children: Martha and Todd.

Social niceties completed, Pamela Wright immediately asked Susan how her arm felt and if she would like to have a doctor look at it. The young mother shook her head. "My arm's pretty swollen but I'm sure it's not broken or badly injured," she said, wiggling her fingers for Pamela's benefit. "Right now, I just need a safe place where I can rest and calm down a little. Tomorrow, I'll think about seeing a doctor."

Pamela nodded slowly, and then took the exhausted family upstairs to their room. She gave them fresh bed linen and towels for the communal bathroom. Remembering Susan's injured arm, she made the beds for the family herself, talking with the mother and children informally to help them feel more at ease. She checked to find out if two-year-old Todd needed a crib; when Susan said he usually slept in one, Pamela found a crib that wasn't being used in another bedroom and solicited the help of a resident to move it.

Finally, with the family somewhat settled, Pamela called for a volunteer, a student named Becky, who attended a nearby college. Would Becky take charge of the youngsters so that Pamela could conduct an intake interview with the mother? Smiling, Becky took Todd by the hand and told Martha to follow them into the playroom, a cluttered little haven that had been a bedroom earlier in the history of the house. Here three other children were already playing, and under Becky's careful supervision, with toys as a common interest, the children began to get to know one another.

SOCIAL WORK: A UNIQUE PROFESSION

As the case study of Susan Dunn ends, you can probably imagine Pamela Wright's quick glance at Susan and Pamela's observation of the grim, anxious expression on Susan's face. In her professional practice this social worker had come to know well the terror and panic that threatened to overwhelm the women that arrived at the door of the shelter. Pamela's heart went out to Susan. She looked so frightened, so unsure of her decision. But, as a social worker, Pamela also understood the dynamics of domestic abuse and the vulnerability faced by adults and children in at-risk situations. Pamela would review quickly in her mind the information she would need to obtain from Susan. She would prepare to use her social work skills to listen to Susan's story and to offer Susan emotional support. The interview Pamela Wright was about to conduct with Susan Dunn would draw on Pamela's professional social work expertise. Pamela, a baccalaureate level social worker (**BSW**), was proud of her profession and confident in her ability to work with the people served by the shelter.

The Susan Dunn case was designed to introduce readers to this text and also to the profession of social work. Following Chapter 1, each of the chapters in the text will begin with a case study that will further illustrate the many dimensions of the profession, the diversity of the people social workers serve, and the social welfare system that forms the context for social work practice. We begin our exploration of this profession with a definition of **social work:**

> The major profession that delivers social services in governmental and private organizations throughout the world, social work helps people to prevent or to resolve problems in psychosocial functioning, to achieve life-enhancing goals, and to create a just society.

This definition underscores several important aspects of the profession. First, social work emerges out of the governmental and private organizations of nations; therefore, it is grounded in the human social welfare systems of countries. In conjunction with its focus on preventing and resolving problems in psychosocial functioning, the profession seeks to empower people and to identify and build on the strengths that exist in people and their communities. The ultimate goal of the social work profession is social justice.

While there are areas of overlap between social work and other human service professions, there are several ways in which social work is unique. Its dual focus on both the social environment and the psychological functioning of people differentiates social work from professions such as psychology and psychiatry. The social work approach, previously mentioned, of building on strengths within people and their communities further differentiates social work from these and other professions. The social work profession defines key values that, taken together, are unique among professions. The values guide and define the ethical practice of social workers. These values include the dignity and worth of all persons, commitment to service, and the ultimate goal of social justice, among others. The values appear in the *National Association of Social Workers Code of Ethics* (National Association of Social Workers, 1996). The code is referred to frequently throughout this book because it is so essential to social work practice.

Using this basic understanding of the uniqueness of the social work profession as a frame of reference, we will next explore the preparation needed to attain competence and expertise for social work practice. We will begin with the baccalaureate level. Because this book will emphasize social work at the baccalaureate level, more substantial information will be provided about this educational level than the other two levels, the master's (**MSW**) and doctorate degree levels of the profession.

Generalist BSW Social Workers

The BSW major can be completed in four years of college or university work, but it will take longer if the student is enrolled on a part-time basis. The BSW is the first or entry level into the social work profession. The degree is generally referred to in conversation as a BSW, but the actual degree awarded by colleges and universities ranges from a BA, BS, BSSW, to the BSW degree. All of these degrees are of equal value, assuming that the social work educational program in which the degree is earned is accredited by the Council on Social Work Education. The BSW social worker, like Pamela Wright in the chapter case study, is professionally prepared as a generalist. What is a generalist? The authors of this text define the **generalist social worker** as:

> A professional social worker who engages in a planned change process—discovering, utilizing, and making connections to arrive at unique, responsive solutions involving individual persons, families, groups, organizational systems, and communities. Generalist social workers respect and value human diversity. They identify and utilize the strengths existing in people and communities. Generalists seek to prevent as well as to resolve problems.

Another way of understanding generalist practice is to look at what it is not. A generalist social worker is not a specialist in psychotherapy (treatment of mental disorder) with individuals or families. Nor is she or he an expert in working with groups, nor primarily a community worker. Yet a generalist social worker must often counsel with individuals and families, will often facilitate groups, and must often track down and mobilize, or even create, appropriate community resources.

The Council on Social Work Education, the organization that accredits social work education programs in the United States, requires that baccalaureate programs prepare students to become entry level professionals in generalist practice. As a generalist with a four-year baccalaureate degree, there are certain competencies that Pamela Wright must have achieved.

The Expertise of the BSW Social Worker

BSW social workers are well prepared to begin practice when they graduate from college. The courses and fieldwork they complete provide them with knowledge and skills—expertise—in specific areas. These areas of competence are defined by the Council on Social Work Education (CSWE) in its 2001 Educational Policy Statement. CSWE states that graduates of baccalaureate social work programs must be able to:

1. Apply critical thinking skills within the context of professional social work practice.
2. Understand the value base of the profession and its ethical standards and principles, and practice accordingly.
3. Practice without discrimination and with respect, knowledge, and skills related to clients' age, class, color, culture, disability, ethnicity, family structure, gender, marital status, national origin, race, religion, sex, and sexual orientation.
4. Understand the forms and mechanisms of oppression and discrimination and apply strategies of advocacy and social change that advance social and economic justice.
5. Understand and interpret the history of the social work profession and its contemporary structures and issues.
6. Apply the knowledge and skills of generalist social work practice with systems of all sizes.
7. Use theoretical frameworks supported by empirical evidence to understand individual development and behavior across the life span and the interactions among individuals and between individuals and families, groups, organizations, and communities.
8. Analyze, formulate, and influence social policies.
9. Evaluate research studies, apply research findings to practice, and evaluate their own practice interventions.
10. Use communication skills differentially across client populations, colleagues, and communities.
11. Use supervision and consultation appropriate to social work practice.
12. Function within the structure of organizations and service delivery systems and seek necessary organizational change.

These competency areas are quite complicated. To better understand them, let's look at how Pamela Wright applied some of them. To begin with, the questions Pamela asked Susan in the telephone interview provided her with exactly the kind of information that Pamela needed, very quickly, to determine if Susan could be helped by the shelter. Using her critical, careful thinking skills (Competency 1), Pamela assessed Susan's crisis situation and determined that Susan could be admitted to the shelter. Notice how Pamela used communication skills (Competency 10). She communicated concern, caring, and respect yet she obtained necessary information. On the telephone and in welcoming Susan to the shelter, Pamela showed no discrimination based on Susan's age, class, culture, or any other factor (Competency 3). Pamela's generalist practice competence enabled her to understand the abuse and oppression that Susan had experienced as a woman (Competency 4). Her generalist social work knowledge and skills also enabled her to understand and respect other women at the shelter who were single parents, very poor, disabled, lesbian, or of diverse religions or cultures. Will Pamela Wright tell Susan to divorce her husband and never return to him again? Undoubtedly Pamela wants Susan and her children to be safe and to have a good

Counseling session in domestic violence shelter.

quality of life, but Pamela would be violating one of the ethics of the social work profession (Competency 2) if she took away Susan's right as a legally responsible adult to make her own decisions.

Pamela enjoyed working with families. Often she helped children and their mothers to find ways to talk to each other about what was happening in their lives. Discipline was a problem for many of the mothers at the shelter, and Pamela often helped family members to set new rules for the ways in which they interacted with each other. Each evening Susan conducted group sessions where the women talked about their day-to-day struggles and triumphs. Just being able to talk about her abuse with other women who understood gave Susan a sense of release. Susan was astounded to learn about the exciting ways other residents were building new lives around jobs, further education, and reconnecting to family members. Sometimes in group sessions issues emerged about the rules or procedures of the shelter. Pamela could advocate with the shelter's staff, executive director, or even the board of directors on behalf of the residents to get needed changes made. It was on the basis of her awareness of a growing number of Hispanic residents that special efforts were made to increase the Hispanic volunteers and staff members at the shelter and to develop educational materials on domestic violence in the Spanish language (Competency 12).

Pamela's social work practice, then, included much more than counseling with individuals and families. Groups, the shelter as an organizational system, and segments of the local community were also social systems (Competency 6) that Pamela continually worked with. The competence she needed to be effective in this broad range of responsibilities came from courses Pamela had taken in biology, sociology, and psychology as well as social work. The theories and knowledge from these courses helped Pamela to understand human behavior and the interactions between individual people and the other social systems in their lives (Competency 7).

Susan Dunn and the other residents were grateful that the shelter existed, but Pamela and the other staff were deeply concerned that their shelter often had to turn people away. Room was simply not available. Pamela and the agency director, an MSW social worker who was her supervisor (Competency 11), formed a committee to conduct research to identify factors related to the increase in domestic violence and possible solutions. Consideration was also being given to the possible need for a second shelter. Questions about the effectiveness of the current shelter program and the community domestic violence prevention programs were also researched (Competency 9). Pamela volunteered to study the changing social welfare policies that limited access to education for women receiving temporary financial assistance (Competency 8). The committee work excited Pamela. She could almost reach into the history of the social work profession and gain courage and insight from its activist pioneers (Competency 5).

Advanced Practice: Social Workers with MSW and PhD Degrees

Admission to an MSW program requires completion of a baccalaureate degree. An MSW can be completed in as little as one year for students who are awarded advanced standing because they have already completed a BSW. Usually, however, a master's degree is completed in two years of full-time coursework, longer for part-time study. The MSW prepares social workers for advanced professional practice in an area of concentration. Although they differ among MSW programs, concentrations include various methods of practice (such as group work, administration), fields of practice (clinical social work or health care), social problem areas (poverty, substance abuse), or special populations (older adults, a cultural group such as Hispanic Americans). Advanced generalist practice is also an area of concentration for some MSW programs.

An MSW social worker at the shelter for battered women, Amy Sacks, received specialized training in working with individuals, families, and groups. Such a concentration is fairly common at the graduate level and may be called direct practice, microlevel intervention, or clinical social work. Amy's role at the shelter is focused and scheduled; she does individual, family, and group therapy by appointment.

Amy is responsible for overseeing the shelter's program in crisis couple's counseling and for the batterers intervention program where she works with groups designed specifically for people like Susan Dunn's husband who abuse their partners. In batterers groups, which are sometimes court-ordered, members must confront their patterns of response to stress and explore new, nonviolent ways of expressing their needs and emotions. These group experiences may be difficult and extremely emotional and are sometimes confrontational; the group process is aimed primarily at personality change rather than at emotional support, which is the main goal for the evening women's groups at the shelter. In therapy groups and in couple's counseling, where personality change is a primary goal, specialized training for the leader or therapist is very important.

Pamela Wright's role at the shelter is broader and more flexible than Amy's. She too counsels individuals, families, and groups, but usually in a less formal manner, often as needed and not necessarily by appointment. In addition, she answers crisis calls, intervenes in problems among the residents, sees that children are cared for, trains volunteers, and supervises the myriad tasks involved in running a multifamily household. She does not live at the shelter but coordinates the schedules of evening staff and occasionally receives calls at night from staff for help during emergencies.

The fact that the BSW is educated to be a generalist does not mean that on occasion she or he does not develop or learn specialized skills in a particular field of practice (or, for that matter, that the MSW cannot be a generalist). In the real world, where funding may not provide the means to hire enough professionals to do a given job, both BSWs and MSWs may end up doing approximately the same thing; but the MSW curriculum provides its students with specialized knowledge in an area of concentration that allows them to work at an advanced practice level. MSWs are also more likely to be promoted to administrative positions, especially in larger organizations. The work of the BSW is usually more diverse and more flexible, and it usually involves mobilizing a wide variety of skills and resources.

Doctorate degrees are also offered in social work. Doctorates are the highest degrees awarded in education. In social work a doctorate could take three to five years to complete beyond the master's degree. The doctoral degree in social work. usually a PhD or a DSW, prepares people for teaching in colleges and universities, for specialized advanced practice, or for research and organizational administrative positions.

SOCIAL WORK PROFESSIONAL ROLES

At the opening of Chapter 1 a young mother and her family were assisted through a crisis situation by a BSW social worker. Her professional education had prepared Pamela Wright with skills and knowledge so that she knew how to function effectively. We will shortly take a look at baccalaureate social work education to see how this was accomplished, but first it might be interesting to examine briefly some of the roles and responsibilities that are the essence of social work practice. All of the skills and knowledge students learn through courses and fieldwork blend as they evolve into the practice roles. There are probably few professions that utilize as wide a variety of professional roles as social workers do.

What are roles? If we were looking at "role" from a sociological perspective, we would think of behaviors that are prescribed or defined by culture, society, and perhaps families. **Professional roles,** then, are the behaviors that are expected from persons who are sanctioned by society through education and legal certification to provide service in a specific profession. Most of us, for example, have a pretty good idea of what to expect from a doctor or a teacher. For social work, role expectations are not quite as clearly understood by the general public. Perhaps this is because there are so many professional roles in social work. The number and diversity of social work roles, however, provide opportunity for a great deal of creativity in practice. Just a sampling of the many professional roles available to social workers is provided here.

The role of **counselor** or **enabler** is probably the most frequently used role in social work. (The terms "counselor" and "enabler" tend to be used fairly interchangeably.) Empowering people and helping them to deal with feelings are characteristic of this role. Affirming personal strengths in clients helps them to find energy and motivation to tackle problems and to relinquish apathy and resistance. The counselor or enabler role focuses on improving "social functioning by modifying behaviors, relationship patterns, and social and physical environments" (Miley, O'Melia, & DuBois, 1998, p. 16). It is also used to help people cope with stress, crises, or changing life circumstances. Psychotherapy could be considered an advanced level of counseling, in which specially trained and certified professionals, including social workers, "help resolve symptoms of mental disorder, psychosocial stress, relationship problems, and difficulties in coping" (Barker, 1999, p. 389).

Another frequently used role is that of **advocate.** An advocate is someone who fights for the rights of others or fights to obtain needed resources. When a social worker, after lengthy phone calls and a rather difficult meeting, is finally able to convince the director of a shelter to keep a family for a week beyond the allotted time, the social worker was a successful advocate. Social workers advocate with doctors, teachers, judges, and even employers in their effort to obtain health care, special education, reduced sentencing, or employment accommodations for a disabled worker, for example. Advocacy efforts can be used on behalf of large populations of people, too, such as using the political process to create state or federal low-income housing programs.

The **broker** role is somewhat similar to the advocate role. Brokering, however, usually doesn't require strongly assertive action. Instead, the social worker uses the process of referral to link a family or person to needed resources. A new mother, for example, might be given information about doctors or clinics that will provide immunizations and health care for her baby. Effective brokers do not simply provide information; they also follow up to be sure that needed resources were actually obtained. For the broker role, social workers need knowledge of the location and quality of services that are available, eligibility requirements and fees, but they also need ability to help people make effective use of services (Kirst-Ashman & Hull, 2002).

Professional roles are often intertwined. The **case manager** role blends elements of all the roles previously mentioned and adds some new dimensions. Case management typically involves planning, locating, securing, and monitoring quality of services for people who are unable to do this because of ill health or frailties. Persons with chronic mental illness, infirm elderly persons, children with disabilities, or homeless families may all benefit from case management. Case management services may be brief, but often they are needed over a very long time, sometimes for a lifetime. Counseling is nearly always a component of case management, especially counseling that enables clients to achieve maximum benefit from the services they receive. Case management in social work should not be confused with the case management sometimes used in health care where the goal is to increase economic profits of a facility by denying access to care. Social work case management, instead, has a goal of increasing access and ensuring that good quality care is provided.

Do you think of social workers as teachers? Perhaps not, but in their role of **educator,** social workers do teach people about available resources, how to use services, how to communicate effectively, even how to budget or to discipline children safely and lovingly. A hospital social worker may help a physician to make a medical diagnosis understandable to a patient. When working with child neglect or abuse situations, social workers teach effective parenting skills. Coaching is an educational tool that may be used by a group worker to improve the socialization skills of lonely, insecure, socially immature adolescents. Speaking of groups, the **facilitator** role is prominent in social work with groups. As facilitators, social workers convene groups, introduce members, promote communication, and engage members in planning, decision making, and goal attainment.

In creating community change, the role of **organizer** is a powerful one. A social worker may, for example, bring representatives of several Native American social agencies together with members of environmental groups in an effort to build concerted, united opposition to legislation that proposes to open up forested reservation land to industrial exploitation. The organizer role could also be used to effect policy changes within a social agency, especially if the agency administrator or board of directors is resistant to the expressed needs of staff or clients.

Social workers create change. Professional roles shape and guide the action that generates change. Just a few of the many potential social work roles have been described here, but they offer some insight into how social workers practice their profession. Next we turn to an exploration of educational preparation for professional social work practice. Since this book's focus is on BSW social work, baccalaureate social work education will command our attention.

THE BACCALAUREATE SOCIAL WORK CURRICULUM

The Council on Social Work Education develops policy and sets standards for accreditation of bachelor's as well as master's degree social work education programs in the United States. In its 2001 accreditation standards, CSWE declared that BSW social work education includes a carefully designed course of study in the liberal arts and a professional foundation curriculum of course and fieldwork. This curriculum enables students to graduate with the expertise needed in order to begin their professional social work practice.

The professional foundation courses address eight content areas:

- Values and ethics
- Diversity
- Populations-at-risk and social and economic justice
- Human behavior and the social environment
- Social welfare policies and services
- Social work practice
- Research
- Field education

In order for a school's social work program to be accredited, the eight content areas must be provided, but not necessarily all in separate courses (Council on Social Work Education, 2001). Since these content areas are so important to the educational preparation of social workers, we will look at each area briefly.

Values and Ethics

This is the first of the professional foundation areas and one of critical importance in the professional life of social workers. Values can be thought of as the philosophical concepts that we cherish as individuals and within our families, our cultures, and our nation. The values of the profession can be found in the *National Association of Social Workers Code of Ethics.* They are shown in Exhibit 1 along with the ethical principles that flow from them.

Society in the United States and in many other countries holds contradictory values concerning the needy: some values revere the wealthy and downgrade the poor; other values teach that each person has worth regardless of material means. Some values found in society guide people toward helping the poor; others guide people away from helping the poor, either because poor people are viewed as unworthy or because they are viewed as potential competitors. Because we are all products of our society, an honest assessment of our own personal values may reveal that we have absorbed some quite negative values about certain people, the poor for example. Yet that clearly conflicts with the profession's valuing of social justice.

The reality is that not every social worker will agree totally and completely with all of the NASW values, but in order to be an effective social worker, we must believe that the values of the profession make sense overall. Probably persons who do not relate to these values will drop out of social work courses as students or will leave the profession early in their careers. A person who is racially

---

NASW Values and Ethical Principles

EXHIBIT 1

Value: Service

Ethical Principle: Social worker's primary goal is to help people in need and to address social problems.

Value: Social justice

Ethical Principle: Social workers challenge social injustice.

Value: Dignity and worth of the person

Ethical Principle: Social workers respect the inherent dignity and worth of the person.

Value: Importance of human relationships

Ethical Principal: Social workers recognize the central importance of human relationships.

Value: Integrity

Ethical Principal: Social workers behave in a trustworthy manner.

Value: Competence

Ethical Principal: Social workers practice within their areas of competence and develop and enhance their professional expertise.

Source: National Association of Social Workers (1996). *NASW Code of Ethics.* Washington, DC: National Association of Social Workers, pp. 5–6.

> ### *National Association of Social Workers Code of Ethics*
> *Six Major Sections of the Code of Ethics*
>
> EXHIBIT 2
>
> 1. Social Workers' Ethical Responsibilities to Clients
> 2. Social Workers' Ethical Responsibilities to Colleagues
> 3. Social Workers' Ethical Responsibilities in Practice Settings
> 4. Social Workers' Ethical Responsibilities as Professionals
> 5. Social Workers' Ethical Responsibilities to the Social Work Profession
> 6. Social Workers' Ethical Responsibilities to the Broader Society
>
> *Source:* National Association of Social Workers (1996). *NASW Code of Ethics.* Washington, DC: National Association of Social Workers, pp. 7–27.

discriminatory in his or her thinking is not likely to be comfortable in social work courses and may be denied admission to the social work major. Such persons are likely to "burn out" if they do succeed in graduating with a social work degree and, more importantly, they are very likely to harm others. By contrast, persons who value human diversity and respect the dignity of others are more likely to be good candidates for a career in social work.

Future chapters in this text will frequently refer to the *NASW Code of Ethics.* The entire code is reprinted in the Appendix at the back of this book. The six major sections of the *Code of Ethics* are shown in Exhibit 2.

Human Diversity

The United States is increasingly a home for diverse populations. The cultures and traditions brought by people from various lands greatly enrich our nation as a whole. Human diversity is a focus in social work education because practitioners must communicate with a wide variety of people. Social workers engage in problem-solving activities with people from quite different European American backgrounds as well as members of ethnic groups such as African Americans, Hispanics, Pacific Islanders, Native Americans, and many others. Social workers must work with women as well as men, with old people as well as young, with people who are gay and lesbian as well as those who are bisexual, transgendered, or heterosexual, and with people who have disabilities as well as those who do not. Human beings comprise a diverse lot indeed!

Courses students take help them to understand, affirm, and respect human diversity. Social workers must go beyond understanding cultural diversity. They must be able to actively explore diversity in practice because it affects every phase of the intervention process. Educational level, employment opportunities, and religious beliefs and values are among the factors that are crucial in forming a person's identity, and they strongly influence preferences, behaviors, and even the decision to trust a social worker. Our world is rapidly becoming more diverse as large numbers of people migrate away from areas that are poverty stricken or endangered by warfare. Even in historically monocultural countries such as Japan,

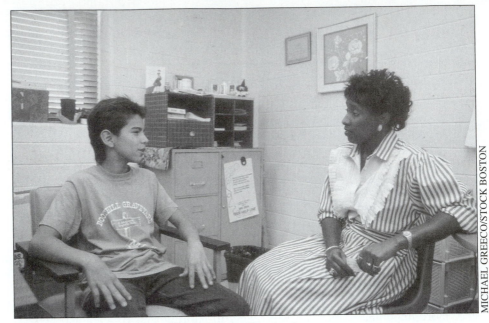

MICHAEL GRECO/STOCK BOSTON

BSW social worker interviews foster child at his school.

people are now learning to live alongside others whose culture is different from their own. In the United States immigrants and refugees in recent years have come from countries and from parts of the world that some U.S. citizens had never even heard of until recently: countries such as Afghanistan, Guatemala, and Ethiopia. Social workers of the future will need to be ready to learn about new cultures and traditions and to appreciate that differences lie not only between groups but also among people within specific cultures, religious denominations, age cohorts, or other defined groupings of people.

Populations-at-Risk and Social and Economic Justice

Since social justice is the ultimate goal of the profession, social work education provides special attention to populations that are most at risk of poverty, discrimination, and oppression. These are the most unloved people in our society. They are people that many other professionals prefer not to work with. They may be in poverty or discriminated against because of their skin color, spiritual values, physical disability, chronic mental illness, or sexual orientation. They may be frail and old, or on parole with a history of criminal convictions.

It is not enough, however, to learn of the existence of populations-at-risk. Social workers need to learn strategies that will be effective in assisting individuals, families, and whole communities of people to achieve their rights. The student social work case manager who battles with governmental agencies and obtains disability benefits for a chronically mentally ill woman, for example, may accomplish a significant improvement in the quality of that woman's life. In this case, intervention strategies learned in the classroom were effectively applied in the student's field placement. Advocacy strategies can be used to attain social and economic justice on an individual (**case advocacy**) basis or for whole groups of people (**cause advocacy**). Empowerment and other strategies are also available as tools for social work practice with populations-at-risk. Empowerment is one of the social work practice theories that will be explained in Chapter 2.

Human Behavior and the Social Environment

This area of the curriculum helps students to understand why people behave as they do. The *Code of Ethics* requires social workers to refrain from **judgmental thinking,** drawing quick and possibly negative conclusions about clients based on their behavior. Courses in the liberal arts such as biology, psychology, sociology, and even literature, history, philosophy also help students to gain a theoretical knowledge base in which to ground their growing understanding of human behavior. Social workers need sufficient understanding of the way human bodies function to recognize situations that require medical attention. If a mother reports that her 18-year-old son has taken an overdose of barbiturates and is acting strangely, the social worker needs to know that this is a life-threatening situation and medical help is urgently needed.

The phases of human development must also be understood. The biological, psychological, cultural, sociological, and spiritual components of human development are important components of social workers' knowledge base. Families sometimes seek help with parenting skills or come to the attention of agencies because of apparent child abuse or neglect. Social workers' understanding of healthy nurturing, of nonpunitive forms of discipline, and of appropriate physical touch between parents and children can help young families to thrive. The social work curriculum must provide course content that will enable students to understand all phases of the human life span, from the time of conception through old age and death.

In addition, social work programs prepare students to understand social systems theory. This includes the nature of systems, how energy ebbs and flows within and between systems, and the way that families, groups, organizations, and communities function as social systems. To work effectively with families, it is very helpful to understand how family systems operate. Parent-to-parent relationships, for example, differ in important ways from child-to-child or parent-to-child relationships. Similarly, communication patterns, decision making, and division of labor need to be understood by social workers if they wish to create change in organizational systems.

Social Welfare Policy and Services

In order to work effectively on behalf of the people they serve, social workers need to understand the basic structures of local, state, national, and even international social welfare systems. Because they understand systems theory, social workers know that all social systems, even social welfare systems, are constantly evolving and changing. If change is taking place, social workers will want to be a part of that change. **Policy practice** is the term used for the conscious effort to effect change in the laws, regulations, and provision of services of governmental and nongovernmental practices and policies. The kind of change in social policy that social workers seek is change that reflects the values of the social work profession.

Social Work Practice

The social work curriculum prepares students with the knowledge and skills that will help them to become effective practitioners. Students will learn how to interview clients and communicate effectively with a wide range of persons. Students will learn how to use the planned change process that is at the heart of generalist practice. The process begins with the social worker developing a professional relationship and engaging clients in change efforts. Uncovering strengths and resources in people and their environments is a powerful tool used by social workers. Students learn how to obtain information that will help them to assess the assets as well as the problems, issues, and needs that people have. Reaching once again into the values and ethics of the profession, social work students learn to work collaboratively with people, not to impose their own solutions on others. This text is not designed to teach social work practice skills; however, insights into social work practice will emerge in the chapter case studies. Generalist social work practice theory will also be further explained in Chapter 2.

Research

Research and practice are interwoven in the profession of social work. In all areas of practice, social workers are expected to produce research as well as use it in their practice. Students will learn how to use systematic approaches to gathering data from interviews, for example (**qualitative research**), or to use statistical, numerical data gathering and analysis to arrive at valid, reliable conclusions (**quantitative research**). They will learn to use computer technology, too, in their research. Additionally, the social work curriculum will engage students in the use of research to evaluate the effectiveness of their own work and to evaluate social programs.

Field Education

This is the part of the curriculum that students look forward to most eagerly. At last they will have an opportunity to apply what they have learned! BSW students spend a minimum of 400 hours working with clients in one or more supervised field placements. The settings selected are chosen to reinforce students' appreciation and understanding of the values and ethics of the social work profession. The placement settings range widely. They might include courts, hospitals, domestic violence shelters, prisons, schools, mental health facilities, nursing homes, and community planning sites. Under the supervision of credentialed social workers approved by the college or university's social work program, students engage in practice, consciously applying theoretical concepts and intervention skills learned in the classroom. Field education is carefully monitored and evaluated by social work faculty. BSW students generally do not enter field courses until the junior or senior year when they have achieved sufficient knowledge and skills to effectively serve others. When students complete field education, they are expected to be able to demonstrate all the competencies of the generalist social worker that were listed earlier in this chapter. In other words, they are ready to begin professional practice!

SELECTING A CAREER IN SOCIAL WORK

Selecting a career is surely one of life's most exciting and most difficult challenges. Fortunately, many resources are available to help with decisions about choice of career. Career counseling centers in colleges and universities offer a variety of aptitude and interest tests. The Internet and libraries offer resources such as the *Occupational Outlook Handbook* of the U.S. Bureau of Labor Statistics. Professors and advisers are yet another source of career advice and information. In the end, however, the choice is a very personal one.

You will find that every chapter in this text begins with a case study describing social workers in action. Here is a brief preview of the paths taken by several of those social workers as they launched their careers. Since this text is primarily focused on professional social work at the baccalaureate level, the three social work career tracks introduced are of BSW social workers. We will begin with Pamela Wright from this chapter's case study.

Pamela Wright

Pamela Wright entered college directly from high school. She had years of volunteer experience in the grade school where her mother was a teacher, and she knew the inner workings of hospitals through her father's employment as an accountant in a local hospital. Pamela knew that she wanted to be a social worker and, while in college, she selected elective courses in some of the liberal arts areas that would enhance her social work competence: courses in psychology, Spanish, and political science. Her senior year social work field placement was with an inner-city shelter for homeless families. As Pamela told her dorm roommate, she just loved her work at the shelter, especially her work with abused women and their children. Following graduation Pamela was immediately employed by the shelter that provided emergency care for Susan Dunn and her children.

Alan Martin

In Chapter 12 you will meet Jamie Sullivan's parole agent, Alan Martin. The two years Alan spent working on the family farm after high school convinced him that farming was not his calling in life. He enjoyed working outdoors, and the farm animals had always been a pleasant part of his life. When he took over after his father's death, Alan found that much of his time was spent on farm management. Accounting, bank financing, and crop planning necessitated a lot of paper work, allowing for minimal interaction with people. When Alan and his mother sold the farm and he enrolled at the state university branch campus, Alan was not sure what major to declare but he was sure that he wanted to work with people. Alan knew something about rural poverty. In his youth the family got by on the financial assistance provided because of his father's disability.

In his freshman year Alan considered several different majors. Still unsure at the start of his sophomore year, Alan enrolled in an Introduction to Social Work course. This course helped him to understand how social workers help people not just with their emotional problems but also with the problems that they experience with other people, with organizations, and within the community. A guest speaker for his class especially intrigued him. This social worker was a probation/parole agent for the state. When his junior year concluded and field placement planning began, however, Alan received a field placement in another area of interest to him: the substance abuse field. Just prior to receiving his BA degree in social work, Alan was hired by his field placement agency.

Several of his clients were on probation, and Alan's contacts with their probation agents reawakened his interest in the criminal justice system. Alan decided to take the exam for a probation/parole agent position. Six months and several interviews later Alan received notice that he had been approved for a position and, luckily, it was with the office that served the rural western part of the state. The best of both worlds! Alan really preferred living in a rural area. He also especially enjoyed working with youths. His new position was with the juvenile probation and parole unit. By the time Jamie Sullivan, the adolescent convicted of armed robbery, met with Alan for the first time, Alan had four years' experience in juvenile justice work.

Madeleine Johnson

Unlike Alan Martin, Madeleine Johnson grew up in a middle-class, primarily African American suburb of a large metropolitan city. Along with her two older sisters, Madeleine was involved in volunteer work with her church's youth groups. Madeleine's mother's volunteer service as a church nurse (assisting anyone who felt faint or persons who needed help with a wheelchair or walker) impressed Madeleine and was the impetus for her first career.

After completing a three-year nursing program, Madeleine worked in various hospitals and outpatient clinics for five years. Following her divorce and a period of personal unhappiness, Madeleine Johnson decided to pursue a second career. When she returned to college she found that it would take a total of three more years to earn a social work degree, but Madeleine was determined to do this. Her life experience proved to be a real asset, making courses in history, philosophy, and research much more interesting than she had expected. Madeleine really enjoyed the role play exercises in the social work courses; she could understand how clients might feel and yet she could also sense compatibility with the role of the social worker. Because of her nursing background, Madeleine was initially interested in a hospital field placement but was challenged by the social work faculty to explore new areas. After careful thought, a public social service agency was selected. Madeleine was given experience with nurturing groups for teen parents and with intensive, in-home services to families where child abuse had occurred. The panel that interviewed Madeleine when she applied for a position with the Salvation Army after graduation was impressed with her years of volunteer work, her experience as a nurse in health care, and her field placement with the public family and children's agency. You will learn about Madeleine Johnson's work with Dan Graves at the Salvation Army in Chapter 10.

The case studies introduce some social workers who struggled with career decisions, just as readers of this text may be struggling. "I want to help people. Which profession should I pursue? Am I in the right major?" These questions are asked over and over again by college students. Social work is an exciting career.

There are few "dull moments" in a day for social workers. It is a career that enables people to make a difference in the lives of others. It offers opportunities to transform the world. But it isn't the right profession for all people. College and university career counseling centers, libraries, or the Internet can all be valuable resources for further exploration of careers. Students are encouraged to talk with social workers, to do volunteer work, or perhaps to test their ability to work with others through a part-time job in the broad area of human services. Social work faculty members and advisers can also help sort out facts from the myths that exist about the profession. Taking an introductory course in social work or social welfare is a very useful way for students to further explore their suitability for a career in social work. We hope this book will increase our readers' understanding of social work as a profession. We hope, too, that it will give you a sense of the remarkable breadth of opportunities there are within this profession for people who sincerely want to make a difference in this world that we share.

EDUCATION AND THE SOCIAL WORK CAREER LADDER

In selecting a career, it is important for college students to understand the concept of the career ladder, which includes a progression of career advancement opportunities within a single, recognized profession. A **career ladder** is constructed of the steps one must take to progress upward and therefore to advance in a profession or occupation. The notion of a career ladder is based on the assumption that it is possible to begin at a low level and then to move from one position to another, continuously progressing toward the top of the ladder. In some occupations or professions, obtaining an entry degree enables a person to progress up the ladder without returning to school for graduate or postgraduate degrees. Advancement, then, is generally based primarily on performance. In other professions, the career-ladder concept is viable only if additional academic credentials are obtained. Social work reflects an interesting mix since there is quite a bit of overlap in roles, responsibilities, and opportunities among the professional levels. An experienced BSW, for example, may achieve an administrative position in a program that hires MSW and other professional disciplines. As Exhibit 3 shows, there are multiple educational levels within the profession. Each is explained below along with typical responsibilities.

At the lowest rung of the ladder is the preprofessional (also referred to as paraprofessional) human service aide. Although they do not have access to membership in NASW or to professional status, persons with bachelor's degrees in areas related to social work (psychology, sociology, and behavioral science majors, for example) and persons with associate degrees are employed in human services. They assist clients by helping with complicated paperwork or performing tasks such as assisting chronically mentally ill persons, frail elderly people, or persons with disabilities to obtain needed resources. Some preprofessional staff members are hired without regard for their academic credentials but, instead, for their extensive firsthand knowledge of the community served by the agency.

The BSW is the basic entry level. The academic credential for this category is precisely defined: bachelor's degree from a college or university social work program that is accredited by the Council on Social Work Education. The basic

The Social Work Career Ladder and Professional Education

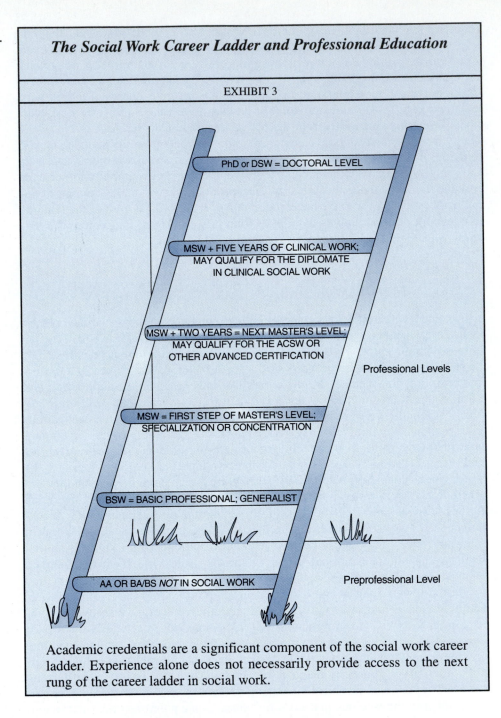

EXHIBIT 3

PhD or DSW = DOCTORAL LEVEL

MSW + FIVE YEARS OF CLINICAL WORK;
MAY QUALIFY FOR THE DIPLOMATE
IN CLINICAL SOCIAL WORK

MSW + TWO YEARS = NEXT MASTER'S LEVEL;
MAY QUALIFY FOR THE ACSW OR
OTHER ADVANCED CERTIFICATION

Professional Levels

MSW = FIRST STEP OF MASTER'S LEVEL;
SPECIALIZATION OR CONCENTRATION

BSW = BASIC PROFESSIONAL; GENERALIST

AA OR BA/BS *NOT* IN SOCIAL WORK

Preprofessional Level

Academic credentials are a significant component of the social work career ladder. Experience alone does not necessarily provide access to the next rung of the career ladder in social work.

professional level social worker has been prepared as a generalist and is able to engage in practice with individuals, families, groups, organizations, and communities. In this chapter a distinction is made between the responsibilities of Pamela Wright, the BSW, and those of Amy Sacks, who has an MSW degree. Pamela conducted intake interviews for the battered women's shelter, worked with the children and husband as well as the client herself, and ran group sessions with all the women in the shelter. As a recognized professional person, Pamela was able to engage clients, do an assessment of the problem, design and carry out an intervention plan, and then terminate and evaluate the intervention. Amy Sacks, in contrast, functioned at the MSW professional level.

The master's degree of the MSW level must be from a program accredited by the Council on Social Work Education. The curriculum of master's degree programs builds on generalist content to develop a concentration in a practice method or social problem area; some master's degrees focus on advanced generalist practice. The MSW social worker should be able to engage in generalist social work practice and also function as a specialist in more complex tasks. Amy Sacks, the MSW social worker at the shelter in the case study, received specialized graduate training in working with individuals, families, and groups. At the shelter Amy's role is more focused and the service she provides is in greater depth than Pamela Wright's. Amy does individual, family, and group therapy, usually by appointment.

At the top of the professional education classification system is the social work doctorate. Some doctoral programs have a research or teaching focus, whereas others prepare for advanced clinical practice. Although the number of doctoral programs has been growing, only 4.9 percent of NASW members in 1999 held social work doctorates (NASW, 1999).

EMPLOYMENT OPPORTUNITIES

Unfortunately, it is rather difficult to find research that accurately describes the full scope of employment of social workers. One very plausible reason for this is that social workers are so often employed under other titles. In some states, too, it is still possible for persons without degrees from accredited social work programs to obtain licensure or certification as social workers; research that included these persons would not provide a true picture of social work employment in that state. Researching the NASW membership base also fails to provide a clear picture of social work employment since not all social workers, whether BSWs or MSWs, hold membership in the social work national organization. While not providing a truly comprehensive survey of the profession, selected studies can provide useful data about employment in social work.

A Research Question: Where Do Social Work College Graduates Find Jobs?

Fortunately a valuable set of research data on employment of social work college graduates is available. It was collected by the Association of Baccalaureate Social Work Program Directors, Inc. (BPD), from over 10,000 BSW graduates beginning in 1990. This research was part of a nationwide effort to assess the outcomes of baccalaureate social work education and to determine if BSW programs were meeting the needs of program graduates as well as their employing agencies.

The graduates' responses about employment provide an answer to one of the most frequently asked questions about social work: Where do social work majors get jobs after graduation? As Exhibit 4 shows, child welfare settings accounted for the largest percentage (20.8%) of these social workers' primary employment practice settings, followed closely by mental health. An interesting pattern that emerged from this study was that no single type of employment setting accounted for much more than 20 percent of the social workers' practice settings. (This finding may reflect one of the purposes of baccalaureate social work education: to prepare generalist social workers who are competent to work in a wide variety of settings.) If clusters of similar settings are combined, it can be seen that close to one-third of BSW social workers were employed in child and family services (child welfare and family-focused practice) and a similar portion were employed in health care (mental health, medical, and chemical dependency) (Rogers et al., 1999).

The BPD survey findings related to fields of practice are not new. The surveys conducted by this organization have produced relatively similar findings for almost 10 years. It is also interesting to note that in 1990, Robert Teare, Barbara Shank, and Bradford Sheafor reported remarkably similar findings in a national

Primary Fields of Practice of BSWs	
EXHIBIT 4	
Public welfare	6.3%
Corrections	4.0
Disabilities (physical, intellectual, learning)	11.3
Family-focused practice	6.9
Child welfare	20.8
Mental health	14.2
Geriatrics	13.8
Chemical dependency	4.6
Medical social work	8.0
Other	10.0

Source: J. Rogers et al., (1999). Information about first social work job. *The revised BPD outcomes instruments report of findings: Total database (as of Oct. 1, 1999),* p. 5. Paper presented at the 17th Annual Program Meeting of the Association of Baccalaureate Social Work Program Directors, St. Louis, MO.

study of 1,345 BSWs. BPD initiated a new research project in 2000. Known as
BEAP (Baccalaureate Educational Assessment Package), this project will soon be
publishing findings on its website: http://www.bpdonline.org.

Another way of looking at jobs for BSWs is to consider the auspices, public
or private, of their employing organizations. The data from the BPD survey of
graduates shown in Exhibit 5 are interesting because they demonstrate that an
overwhelming portion of baccalaureate social workers are not employed by governmental agencies, as is often assumed. In fact, in the survey population, slightly
more than half (51.2%) of the graduates were employed by governmental agencies; the remainder (48.8%) worked for private sector social service organizations.
Interestingly, only 44.8 percent of these BSW social workers were in governmental positions for their first job; there was apparently some shifting from private
sector to government positions over time. Of all the employment auspices studied,
the private, nonsectarian sector (the American Red Cross would be one example)
consistently demonstrated hiring of the largest proportion of baccalaureate social
workers. The largest governmental employer in the BPD study proved to be state
government. When state, federal, federal-military, and local government employment figures were combined, it was found that 44.9 percent of social workers were
hired by governmental organizations and 55.2 percent were employed by private
organizations for their first professional social work position (Rogers et al., 1999).

Employment Patterns for MSWs

Research conducted by NASW in 2000 provides a picture of social work practice
of persons who hold primarily the MSW degree; 91 percent of the 2000 survey respondents had completed an MSW as their highest degree earned in social work
(NASW Practice Research Network, 2000). The NASW study has somewhat different categories, but it is interesting to compare Exhibit 6, the primary practice

Employment Auspices of BSWs: *First Professional Position Obtained*	
EXHIBIT 5	
Federal government (military-related)	1.0%
Federal government (civilian)	5.0
State government	23.9
County/municipal/town government	15.0
Private, church-related	12.2
Private, nonsectarian	43.0

Source: J. Rogers et al., (1999). Current social work job. *The revised BPD outcomes instrument report of findings: Total database (as of Oct. 1, 1999),* p. 9. Paper presented at the 17th Annual Program Meeting of the Association of Baccalaureate Social Work Program Directors, St. Louis, MO.

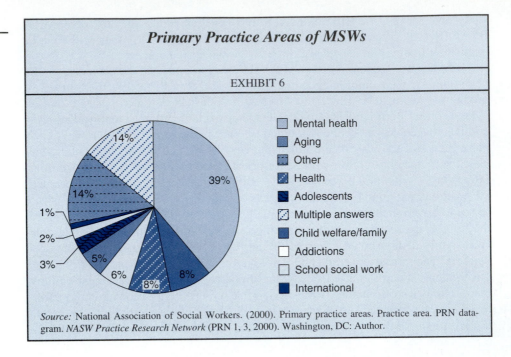

Primary Practice Areas of MSWs

EXHIBIT 6

- Mental health — 39%
- Aging
- Other — 14%
- Health — 14%
- Adolescents
- Multiple answers — 8%
- Child welfare/family — 8%
- Addictions — 6%
- School social work — 5%
- International

1%
2%
3%

Source: National Association of Social Workers. (2000). Primary practice areas. Practice area. PRN datagram. *NASW Practice Research Network* (PRN 1, 3, 2000). Washington, DC: Author.

areas of the MSW social workers, with Exhibit 4, which illustrates the primary practice areas of BSWs. The largest portion of BSWs were employed in child welfare and family-focused work, whereas the largest percentage of MSWs worked in mental health. Work with older adults attracted 20.8 percent of BSWs, but only 5 percent of MSWs. Both BSWs and MSWs were widely scattered across the many other areas of practice. Research focused on specific practice areas is somewhat difficult to conduct in social work because of the remarkably wide range of fields in which the profession is practiced.

An employment opportunity that was not incorporated into the BPD study but that appears in Exhibit 6 is that of the private for-profit sector. Private sector employment is growing significantly for BSW practitioners, although not as psychotherapists (a role that is appropriate only to MSWs or doctoral professionals). Counseling positions in mental health, house manager and group facilitation positions in group homes, telephone crisis and referral jobs in employee assistance programs—these are all examples of the kinds of for-profit employment opportunities that are available to baccalaureate social workers. If the trend toward privatization continues, the private for-profit sector will employ much greater numbers of social workers at all levels of the profession in the near future.

Salaries and Demand for Social Workers

During the 1990s there was a very uneven job market for social workers. In some urban areas of the United States it was difficult for social workers to find employment. At the same time, however, states such as Texas, Iowa, and Arkansas were seeking social workers. Rural areas employed uncredentialed people because they were unable to attract professionally trained social workers.

In more recent years, however, the job-search experiences reported in the BPD studies were quite positive. Although some BSW respondents had elected to go to graduate school after receiving their degrees and a small number sought employment in another field or were not successful in finding social work jobs, more than 75 percent consistently obtained social work employment. These recent graduates routinely provided information about their first social work job search for the annual BPD survey. In the 1999 survey findings, a considerable number, 27.1 percent, already had a social work job when they graduated from college, one that they had held before starting school or one they had obtained while they were in school. An additional 42 percent found social work positions within three months after graduation. By six months after graduation, 84.4 percent had taken a position in social work at the baccalaureate level (Rogers et al., 1999). This data is encouraging when one recognizes that sometimes people need time for themselves or their families and therefore delay a job search for weeks or even months.

Social work salaries vary immensely by region of the country, years of experience, practice setting and auspice, and highest degree earned. Commitment to vulnerable populations is a stronger motivation for some social workers than salary, and many accept employment with seriously underfunded organizations that pay extremely small salaries. This tends to skew the earnings data on social work employment and to give an impression of lower salaries than the salaries that may, in fact, be available from other organizations. The Bureau of Labor Statistics' *Occupational Outlook Handbook* is a good source for current general salary information. The median annual earnings for social workers in 1999 according to their sources was approximately $30,590 (2001).

The NASW study previously cited (NASW Practice Research Network, 2000) provides some interesting data about social work salaries for the year 1999. That year, the median income for the study group (comprised primarily of MSWs) was $45,660. Considering that some social workers choose to work in underfunded organizations because of the vulnerable populations they serve, it is not surprising that there were some fairly low salaries even among MSWs. What might be surprising for some people is the fact that some salaries exceeded $80,000. The range of MSW salaries is depicted in Exhibit 7.

Which organizational employers paid higher salaries? Exhibit 8 seeks to answer this question. Notice that figures are provided for two salary ranges: the highest 25 percent of salaries and the median salaries. Quite clearly, the new and rapidly growing private for-profit sector offered the highest incomes to MSWs in 1999 and the nonprofit sectarian sector provided the lowest salaries (NASW Practice Research Network, 2000). Unfortunately, comparable data are not currently available for BSW social workers, but it seems likely that nonprofit sectarian organizations are also among the lower salary employers of BSWs. Both MSW and BSW salaries tend to increase each year, though, so the salary information in these exhibits probably won't be a true representation of social work salaries when you read them, and they will be even less representative of social work salaries by the time you graduate. Salaries also vary considerably across the different geographic regions of the United States.

1999 Salaries of MSWs

EXHIBIT 7

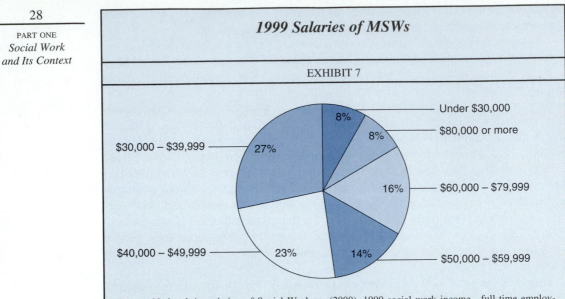

Source: National Association of Social Workers. (2000). 1999 social work income—full-time employment only. Social work income. PRN datagram *NASW Practice Research Network* (PRN 1, 1, 2000). Washington, DC: Author.

1999 MSW Salaries by Organizational Auspice

EXHIBIT 8

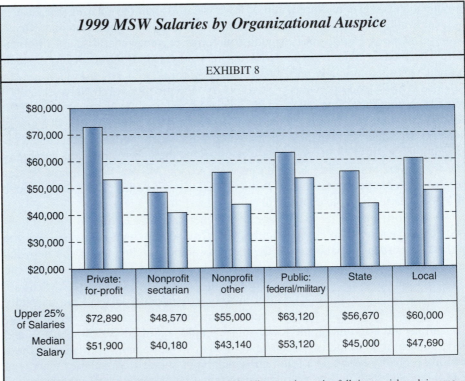

	Private: for-profit	Nonprofit sectarian	Nonprofit other	Public: federal/military	State	Local
Upper 25% of Salaries	$72,890	$48,570	$55,000	$63,120	$56,670	$60,000
Median Salary	$51,900	$40,180	$43,140	$53,120	$45,000	$47,690

Source: National Association of Social Workers. (2000). Nineteen ninety-nine full-time social work income by primary auspice. Social work income. PRN datagram *NASW Practice Research Network* (PRN 1, 1, 2000). Washington, DC: Author.

State Licensure and Certification

Can doctors practice their profession without being licensed? Can pharmacists? Dentists? How about social workers? While there are some situations in which doctors, pharmacists, and dentists may practice without a license, these are relatively few. Medicine, pharmacy, and dentistry were among the first professions to be legally regulated (Biggerstaff, 1995). **Legal regulation,** according to *The Social Work Dictionary,* is "the control of certain activities, such as professional conduct, by government rule and enforcement" (Barker, 1999, p. 273). Today doctors, pharmacists, and dentists are licensed by the states in which they practice.

Social workers, too, are legally regulated in all states in the United States. The first statute providing for legal regulation of social workers was passed in Puerto Rico in 1934 (Thyer & Biggerstaff, 1989). There are several different forms of legal regulation governing social work. In some states social workers are licensed, but often only at the MSW level. In other states social workers are certified, not licensed.

Licensure and certification are very similar. Both are created through passage of state law, so they are born out of the political process. State boards of regulation and licensing are responsible for administering licensing and certification of all professions. Only persons with appropriate credentials (usually degrees from CSWE accredited schools) are permitted to take the social work competency examinations that are required for licensure and for most state certification. A national organization, the Association of Social Work Boards (ASWB), provides examinations to the states; each state determines its own passing score. There is one important difference between certification and licensure. While certification protects the title "social worker," it doesn't prohibit uncertified people from practicing social work. They simply may not call themselves social workers. Certification is not considered to be as strong a form of legal regulation as licensure.

Although states determine the categories of social workers they will license or certify, the four categories most commonly seen and the academic degree and practice experience required are as follows:

Basic: a baccalaureate degree in social work

Intermediate: an MSW degree; no experience required

Advanced: MSW degree plus two years of experience

Clinical: MSW degree plus two years of clinical practice (Association of Social Work Boards, 2001)

Renewal of a state license or certification, which may occur every two years, usually requires documentation of completed continuing education. Earning a degree in social work is really not the end of a social worker's education!

NASW Certification of Professional Achievement

One challenge facing the profession is the growing demand of consumers and insurance companies for certification of experienced professionals beyond the entry level. NASW has met this challenge by creating specified credentials for social workers. NASW's certification is voluntary; it is not a form of governmental regulation such as licensing and certification.

The ACSW was the first advanced practice certification developed by NASW. The **ACSW** designates membership in the Academy of Certified Social Workers. This certification is available to members of NASW who have an MSW degree, two years of additional supervised social work practice, and who have passed the ACSW examination (NASW Online, 2001). The ACSW's considerable success over the years sparked the initiation in the early 1990s of a parallel form of certification for persons with a baccalaureate degree in social work, the ACSBSW. Sadly, it was discontinued in 1995 due to lack of widespread support by baccalaureate-level social workers.

Now, however, NASW has initiated a certification opportunity for BSWs who are NASW members: the **Certified Social Work Case Manager** (C-SWCM). Experience of one year in appropriately supervised case management work, state licensure or certification at the BSW level (including passage of the ASWB exam), and submission of supporting references are the requirements for the C-SWCM. An MSW-level case management certification has also been created, the Certified Advanced Social Work Case Manager (C-ASWCM). The requirements are similar to the BSW case manager certification except that state licensure or certification must be at the MSW level (NASW Online, 2001).

In addition to the case manager certifications, NASW has created several other specialized certification opportunities: Certified School Social Work Specialists (C-SSWS); Certified Clinical Alcohol, Tobacco and Other Drugs Social Workers (C-CATODSW); the Qualified Clinical Social Worker (QCSW); and the Diplomate in Clinical Social Work (QCSW). The QCSW and the Diplomate have been very successful. Both are advanced practice credentials; the Diplomate, which re-

Social workers attend NASW social policy forum in Washington, DC.

quires five years of post-MSW or postdoctorate clinical practice, is the highest professional level authorized by NASW. Information about any of these credentials is available online at http:www.naswdc.org (NASW Online, 2001). Credentials that testify to expertise in specialized areas of practice can provide a competitive advantage in the job market. They are also a way of alerting potential clients or referral sources to the knowledge and practice expertise of the social worker.

PROFESSIONAL SOCIAL WORK ORGANIZATIONS

This chapter has already referred to NASW and CSWE numerous times. Hopefully this signifies the remarkable importance of the two national social work organizations for the profession and for social workers. NASW and CSWE are, indeed, the most prominent, but many other professional social work organizations also exist.

The National Association of Social Workers

NASW has become the major professional membership organization in the United States. It was founded in 1955 when seven existing but quite separate social work organizations (such as the American Association of Medical Social Workers) joined together. The NASW has four major functions today:

1. Professional development
2. Professional action
3. Professional standards
4. Membership services

Graduates of schools of social work that are accredited by the Council on Social Work Education are eligible for full membership in the National Association of Social Workers. Students in CSWE-accredited programs are eligible for student membership at reduced rates. NASW's journal, *Social Work,* is a respected source for research findings in various fields of practice (useful for writing term papers). The monthly publication of the national office, *NASW News,* provides information regarding new developments, social policy discussions, and updates on legislation of interest to social workers and their clients; it also advertises social work professional positions. All 50 chapters publish newsletters keeping chapter members abreast of statewide developments. At the national level, NASW employs a lobbyist to represent members' views on policy issues known to Congress. Through PACE, the Political Action for Candidate Election wing of NASW, candidates for national as well as state offices are endorsed and information about their positions is disseminated. There are approximately 150,000 members of NASW (NASW Online, 2001).

NASW's strong commitment to service was dramatically evident in the overwhelming response of the national office, state chapters, and social workers across the United States following the terrorist attacks on September 11, 2001. Immediately following the attacks, the NASW national office provided information on its website, NASW Online, on how to help and where social workers' services could best be used. NASW Online also put up "numerous links to disaster-response organizations, victim's services and information on coping with trauma" (O'Neill, 2001, p. 14). Many NASW chapters across the United States acted as clearing-houses for social workers who wanted to help with disaster relief. The New York City and New York State NASW Chapters took leadership roles in disaster assistance work in New York City. The Metro Washington NASW Chapter targeted the Pentagon crash site. Pennsylvania Chapter members "participated in counseling and debriefings in Pittsburgh and the New York area and with members of the Secret Service" (O'Neill, 2001); they also operated a hotline, making referrals and providing information. NASW is an organization that social workers can be proud to support.

The Council on Social Work Education

Like NASW, the Council on Social Work Education (CSWE) is a private, non-governmental organization. Currently it has a membership of over 3,000 individuals plus 600 or more institutional memberships of colleges and universities. The mission of CSWE is to provide national leadership that will "ensure an adequate supply of competent social work professionals capable of addressing present and future social needs" (Beless, 1995, p. 633).

CSWE has accredited MSW programs since its creation in 1952. In 1974 accreditation was expanded to include baccalaureate programs. By 2001, 145 MSW programs and 428 BSW programs were accredited (Council on Social Work Education, 2001). To this day, doctoral programs in social work are not accredited by CSWE.

CSWE conducts a number of other activities in addition to accreditation. An annual conference, for example, showcases presentations of scholarly papers and current research. CSWE publishes books, a newsletter *(The Social Work Education Reporter),* and a scholarly journal (the *Journal of Social Work Education*). A recent and ongoing project aims at strengthening the competence of social workers for work with the growing population of older adults. Through its members the CSWE also seeks to influence social policy and funding, both governmental and private, to support social work education.

The National Association of Black Social Workers

The National Association of Black Social Workers (NABSW), like NASW, is a membership organization but unlike NASW its membership is open to any black person who is working in social work or human services; it does not specify academic credentials. NABSW was created in 1968 to address issues pertaining to the recruitment and education of black social workers and the delivery of social welfare services to black people (National Association of Black Social Workers, 1999).

Chapters of NABSW exist throughout the United States, and student units exist as well. The *Code of Ethics* speaks eloquently to the mission and purpose of this organization. It states, in part:

> I hold myself responsible for the quality and extent of service I perform and the quality and extent of service performed by the agency or organization in which I am employed, as it relates to the Black community.

I accept the responsibility to protect the Black community against unethical and hypocritical practice by any individuals or organizations engaged in social welfare activities.

I stand ready to supplement my paid or professional advocacy with voluntary service in the Black public interest.

I will consciously use my skills, and my whole being, as an instrument for social change, with particular attention directed to the establishment of Black social institutions. (National Association of Black Social Workers, 1999, p. 2)

Other Professional Organizations

There is a wealth of other professional organizations serving social workers. The National Association of Puerto Rican/Hispanic Social Workers, founded in 1971, advocates for Hispanic people and emphasizes human services issues that affect the Latino community. It advocates for public social policy to secure the well-being of Latino/Hispanic communities (Tourse, 1995).

Founded in 1970, the National Indian Social Workers Association seeks to support Native American people including Alaska Natives. It also provides consultation to tribal and other organizations. Other groups exist for gay and lesbian social workers, Asian American social workers, and American social workers who live and work in other countries. In addition there are practice-related organizations such as the National Association of Oncology Social Workers, the National Federation of Societies of Clinical Social Workers, and the North American Association of Christians in Social Work (Tourse, 1995).

International Social Work Organizations

Social workers in countries outside the United States have professional organizations as well. Some examples are the Australian Association of Social Workers, the Canadian Association of Social Workers, the Nederlands Instituut voor Zorg en Weizijn (The Netherlands), and the Israeli Association of Social Workers (Social Work Gateway, 2000).

Civil unrest, war, famine, and more recently terrorist attacks have led to an increased sense of global interdependence among social workers. Even before the terrorist attacks on the World Trade Center and the Pentagon, U.S. social workers had become involved in the refugee camps of Bosnia and with health organizations fighting the AIDS epidemic in Africa.

One social work organization, the International Federation of Social Workers (IFSW), was initiated in 1956 to help social workers learn about the experience of their counterparts in other countries. The IFSW represents half a million social workers around the world. Although membership in the IFSW is limited to national social work organizations, individuals may join the Friends of IFSW. The organization publishes a newsletter and quarterly journal to help keep membership informed about international issues (Johannesen, 1993). The purposes of the IFSW are listed in Exhibit 9.

Besides the IFSW, there are other international organizations, such as the International Association of Schools of Social Work and the International Council on Social Welfare. Effective regional organizations have also emerged in Africa, Asia,

Purposes of the International Federation of Social Workers (IFSW)

EXHIBIT 9

To promote social work as a profession through international cooperation and action, especially as regards professional values, standards, ethics, human rights, recognition, training and working conditions, and to promote the establishment of national associations of social workers where they do not yet exist;

To support national associations in promoting the participation of social workers in social planning, and the formulation of social policies, nationally and internationally, and the recognition of social work, enhancement of social work training as well as of values and professional standards in social work;

To encourage and facilitate co-operation between social workers of all countries and to provide means for discussion and the exchange of ideas and experience through meetings, study visits, research projects, exchanges, publications and other means of communication;

To establish and maintain relationships with, and to present and promote the view of social work to, international organizations relevant to social development and welfare.

Source: International Federation of Social Workers. (2001, July 17). *Aims*. Retrieved September 7, 2001, from http://www.ifsw.org.

Europe, and Latin America (Hokenstad, Khinduka, & Midgley, 1992). Hopefully the future will bring vastly increased cross-national and international social welfare development and advocacy efforts. What a challenge for the next generation of social workers!

COMPARING RELATED OCCUPATIONS

In order to meet the challenges of the present as well as the future, social workers need to understand and develop cooperative working relationships with the professions and occupational groups that work alongside us in the social welfare arena. Currently a lot of overlap exists in the responsibilities and tasks of professions. In hospitals, for example, nurses as well as social workers assist patients with discharge planning. In mental health the overlap appears even greater. Psychiatrists, psychologists, social workers, and professional counselors all engage in psychotherapy with individuals, groups, and families. Each profession, however, has its own area of expertise. This can be confusing. In the paragraphs that follow, we will try to identify and compare roles and responsibilites across several professions or occupations.

We will begin by looking at sociology, an academic area that is closely related to social work. In fact, social work students are likely to be required to take some sociology courses early in their social work major. Sociology is an academic discipline that examines society and the behavior and beliefs of specific groups in society. Sociologists study characteristics of all types of groups: ethnic minorities, families, children, men, women, gays, the elderly, juvenile delinquents, and many others. Sociologists also examine the class structure of society. Through careful research, they attempt to sort fact from fiction regarding the mythology surrounding various social groups. Sociologists develop theory regarding how and why people become what they are, and in particular they study the influence of the social environment on thought, behavior, and personality.

What students of sociology learn to do is to observe carefully, think systematically, develop theory, and do research to test theory. Sociological knowledge is useful to the social worker, and many social workers developed their initial interest in social work by taking sociology courses. Hence there is often confusion regarding the two disciplines. Also confusing is the fact that there are branches of sociology developing today called "applied" and "clinical" sociology. Applied sociology involves the use of sociological research methods for community needs assessment and program evaluation. Clinical sociology involves the application of sociological theory to social intervention. Their domains and methods are not yet clearly defined. Since sociologists specialize in the study of various types of groups, however, it is likely that applied and clinical sociologists will focus on the applications of sociological theory to behavior in groups, organizations, and communities.

Although they need to study sociology, social workers are expected to apply their knowledge to working with people to solve problems. Sociology normally teaches students to observe and to do research on social problems, but it is social work that teaches interpersonal skills and techniques and that provides an analytical approach to problem solving. Sociologists with advanced degrees often apply their education by doing research and teaching.

Psychology

Psychology is another field closely related to social work. Psychologists study individuals and try to understand how they develop as they do and the important internal factors that influence a person's mind and behavior. Many psychologists study perception and learning in the laboratory setting and try to understand the inner workings of the mind through experimental means. Like sociologists, many psychologists spend their careers doing research, testing theory, and teaching. One branch of psychology is applied, so that many psychologists also counsel individuals and families and conduct IQ tests, personality tests, and the like. Psychologists who wish to specialize in psychotherapy usually earn a doctorate degree.

Social workers must study both sociology and psychology. They must utilize information from both of these fields in order to assess the problems of their clients appropriately and to develop workable intervention plans. Social workers cannot focus solely on the individual, as psychologists tend to do, or on the social environment, as sociologists do. Instead, they must examine aspects of both, and how they interact, to engage in constructive problem solving.

The U.S. Department of Labor lists multiple specializations for psychology. The primary ones are licensed clinical psychologist and counseling psychologist. Both require a doctrate degree. Other specialization areas are school psychology; industrial-organizational psychology; developmental, social, and experimental or research psychology (Farr & Ludden, 2000). School psychologists may need only a master's degree. Yet another area of psychology, community psychology, overlaps social work in its interest in social issues and social institutions. Community psychologists are educated at both the master's and doctoral levels. Community psychology is said to have more of a research orientation than social work. It is also much less treatment focused than clinical psychology (Cook, 2001).

Counseling

Counseling is another profession that overlaps social work in many ways since counselors, too, serve the social and emotional needs of people in schools, mental health, and other settings where social workers are employed. Most counselors hold master's degrees from university programs in education or psychology, although some doctorates are also available in counseling. There is a confusing array of areas in this field, including professional or mental health counseling; educational, vocational, or school counseling; rehabilitation counseling; substance abuse and behavioral disorder counseling; and gerontological counseling. The vast majority of counselors, over 200,000 in 2000, were employed as educational, vocational, or school counselors (U.S. Department of Labor, 2001). Recent legislation allowing some counselors to be reimbursed by insurance companies has increased the growth of private practice among counselors. Like social workers, counselors work with people who have personal, family, or mental health problems; however, counselors often have special expertise in helping people with educational or career planning.

Marriage and Family Therapy

This is another professional area that is somewhat confusing because persons from a number of different professions can be certified as marriage and family therapists (MFTs). To qualify for certification in most states, evidence must be presented of completion of a master's or doctoral degree in marriage and family therapy or in a program with equivalent content. In addition, at least two years of clinical experience are required. MSW social workers, psychologists, psychiatrists, and some nurses may qualify. According to the American Association for Marriage and Family Therapy, MFTs treat a wide variety of personal and mental health problems. The focus, even for an interview with a single person, is on the relationships in which the person is most significantly involved (American Association for Marriage and Family Therapy, 2001). Marriage and family therapy emphasizes short-term treatment averaging 12 sessions.

Psychiatry

Psychiatry is related to social work, but psychiatry is a specialization of medicine. An MD (medical degree) must first be earned, and then the aspiring psychiatrist must complete a postdoctoral internship. Psychiatrists' primary focus on the inner person is grounded in their knowledge of physiology and medical practice. They may practice psychotherapy, but most do so very infrequently. Instead, their focus is on prescribing medications such as antidepressants and antipsychotics, the drugs used to treat psychoses (severe forms of mental illness). Psychiatrists frequently see people for 15-minute medication monitoring sessions.

Human Services

In its broadest definition, human services includes all occupations and professions seeking to promote the health and well-being of society: lawyers, firefighters, social workers, teachers, and so on. The narrower definition includes only those people who have completed an educational program with a major in human services or people who have been hired to work in the broad human services area without academic credentials. Human service academic programs generally offer a two-year associate degree, although sometimes they involve four-year degrees. While knowledge development is not ignored, the human service field emphasizes task completion and skill development. Graduates seek employment across multiple paraprofessional and professional job areas; these positions frequently offer only minimal opportunities for advancement.

In the 1980s, a National Commission for Human Service workers was initiated to credential and certify human service workers, but it has since disbanded. Currently, there is no national organization comparable to the NASW that establishes certification standards for human service workers (Woodside & McClam, 2002).

HOW PROFESSIONS RELATE

How might some of these professions become involved in a case such as that of the Dunn family? A sociologist might study the social problem of battered women or battering families; he or she might interview the Dunn family to learn what they have to say about the phenomenon from personal experience.

Through the counseling they receive from social workers while in crisis, Susan Dunn and her husband may decide there is enough hope for change for themselves that they will begin living together again. With encouragement, they may follow up on the MSW's recommendation that they attend longer-term marriage and family counseling with a family service agency. The Dunn's counselor at the family service agency might be either an MSW or a PhD psychologist. A consulting psychiatrist would be retained on the staff of the agency, to whom the Dunns could be referred if the primary counselor felt medication was required.

There could be several outcomes to this case. Let us say, for purposes of speculation, that as counseling progresses, Mr. Dunn voluntarily enters a group for batterers conducted by a professional counselor. Although he often feels like dropping out of the group, he continues with it as well as the family counseling. Over the months several episodes of angry outbursts occur, but there are no further episodes of physical abuse. Gradually both parents learn healthier ways of communicating with each other. Meantime, Susan Dunn has established a better relationship with her own family and begun to make routine visits back home. With the help of a vocational counselor she has enrolled in a computer class at the local community college and has acquired several women friends from class. Susan now has a safety plan involving family and friends, in the event that she should need it. If Mr. Dunn continues to work very hard with the batterers group and no longer uses violence as a way of dealing with his frustrations, the future looks reasonably promising for this couple.

What would happen if, instead, Susan Dunn remains in clear physical danger? Let us say, for example, that her husband refuses to attend any kind of counseling with her and openly threatens future abuse. Susan might still choose to go home, believing that, if she behaves more carefully, she will be able to avoid "causing" her husband to physically abuse her. She is likely to have at some point another crisis requiring her to flee again to the shelter. At least this time she will know where she is going. If her husband is drinking or becomes violent at work and loses his job, Susan may find herself becoming involved with her country's financial assistance program called Temporary Assistance for Needy Families (TANF). The staff she encounters there will probably not have professional training in social work. Their role is a more clerical one that may also involve some employment counseling and referral to other resources.

Although Susan Dunn comes from a middle-class background and has remained a member of the middle class because of her husband's occupation, once she leaves her husband she is at risk of poverty. Almost overnight she could become a poor, single mother. The social worker at the shelter might be able to help her locate an inexpensive apartment. She might also file a legal restraining order through the district attorney's office, prohibiting her husband from threatening or even contacting her. She might file for divorce and child support; however, legal action against her husband could be very difficult without money. If fortunate, she might be able to secure inexpensive legal assistance from a legal aid society. Waiting lists for such programs are often long, however. Susan's social worker will help her to assess her evolving situation and take whatever steps are necessary to ensure that Susan and her children are safe from harm. Susan's decisions, however, will be respected by the social worker.

The story of Susan Dunn and her family introduced readers of this chapter to the profession of social worker. The remainder of this text will delve into the work of social workers in much greater detail. Other social work clients will also be introduced as the chapters unfold. First, however, let us take a brief look at the history of the social work profession.

ORIGINS OF THE SOCIAL WORK PROFESSION

Social work is an evolving, relatively young profession. Three social movements arising in the late 1800s led to its birth. One major movement was the Charity Organization Society (COS); it began in England and took hold in Buffalo, New York, in 1877. Its most famous leader was Mary Richmond. Volunteers for the COS initially viewed the abject poverty of many urban dwellers, especially immigrants, to be the result of personal character defects. "Friendly visitors," usually wealthy women (just about the only people with time to spare) visited people in their homes to provide "moral uplift." Only as a last resort was material aid offered.

The second major movement leading to the birth of the social work profession was the settlement house movement, which, like the COS, began in England. In the United States, Jane Addams was its most famous leader. Addams established Hull House in Chicago in 1889. Settlement workers had a different view of poor people from the COS volunteers. They believed that poverty resulted from unjust and unfortunate social conditions. Settlement workers lived among the poor. They assisted in developing needed services such as day care for children of factory workers through mutual aid. They also advocated for better working conditions and protective legislation through various governmental bodies.

A third movement, more diffuse, was a child welfare movement. This began with the Children's Aid Society founded in New York in 1853, and was strengthened by the Society for the Prevention of Cruelty to Children that was founded in 1875, also in New York City (Popple, 1995).

A growing desire for professionalization emerged by the late 1890s. Charity organization work and settlement house work were increasingly salaried, but as yet there was no name for this profession. By the early 1900s the broad field of applied philanthrophy began to be called social work or social casework. The New York School of Philanthropy, established in 1904, was the first professional education program. Mary Richmond, leader of the Charity Organization Society (COS), was among the original faculty. The school is now known as the Columbia University School of Social Work (Popple, 1995).

With increasing confidence in their new profession, social workers invited Abraham Flexner to address the 1915 National Conference of Charities and Correction. Flexner's critique of the medical profession was renowned for dramatically improving that profession's status and quality of care. Flexner's pronouncement that social work was not yet a real profession startled the social work world but unleashed new energy directed at rectifying the deficiencies he identified (Popple, 1995).

As Flexner's criticisms were attended to, large numbers of persons flocked to the profession expanding social work practice into new areas such as schools and hospitals. The theory base of the profession was developed and research began to be published. Freudian theory was widely adopted in the 1920s. The Great Depression turned public attention to the economic and social forces causing poverty. The result was the passage of the Social Security Act in 1935, legislation in which social workers played a prominent role. From its earliest days, then, the profession of social work embodied emphases both in social reform and in the psychosocial problems of individuals, families, and communities.

World War I and II further increased social workers' involvement in mental health as psychiatric casualties of the wars brought large numbers of social workers into military social work. Social workers with master's degrees (MSWs) dominated the profession by the early 1950s, but they tended to work in specialization areas such as child welfare, medical social work, or psychiatric social work. In a remarkable move toward unity, seven specialty areas merged to found the National Association of Social Workers (NASW) in 1955. Until 1970, when baccalaureate social workers were added, NASW membership was exclusively limited to MSWs. The founding of NASW and enactment of the *NASW Code of Ethics* to ground the practice of all social workers firmly established social work as a profession.

In the years since the birth of the profession, social work has grown dramatically in numbers, in areas of practice, in the people it serves, and in status. In recent years it has achieved legal regulation (licensure or certification) in every state. The profession has struggled to retain its social reform legacy by lobbying against discriminatory legislation and by supporting social policies that promote human welfare and well-being. Social work and social welfare, therefore, remain intertwined today, as the next chapter in this text will explain. Because of its commitment to social and economic justice and its mission to work on behalf of people who are discriminated against, the profession of social work is sometimes not well understood nor even well accepted. Its values make social work a truly unique profession.

Contemporary social work practice makes increasing use of computer technology. The Internet has become a valuable resource for information that can be useful to practitioners and to the people they serve. So, as we conclude this chapter and before turning to the summary of Chapter 1, we encourage you to take a look at the following listing of Internet sites. They might be interesting to explore; all relate to the topics covered in this chapter, including a few sites related to domestic violence. You will find similar lists of Internet sites near the end of each chapter in this text. Following the summary, you will also find a list of key terms. They are the terms that have appeared in bold print within the chapter. If you aren't sure you understand them, you will find them in the glossary at the end of this text. The discussion questions and research activities may be used in class. The references are the source materials that the text authors used in writing this chapter. At the end of the chapter you will find several paragraphs entitled "For Further Reading." Here the authors provide several additional sources of information that might be of special interest to students. We hope that you will enjoy using this text!

INTERNET SITES

http://www.socialworkers.org	National Association of Social Workers
http://www.cswe.org	Council on Social Work Education
http://www.ifsw.org	International Federation of Social Workers
http://www.bpdonline.org.	Association of Baccalaureate Social Work Program Directors
http://uic.edu/jaddams/hull//hull_house.html	Hull House Museum
http://www.idbsu.edu/socwork/dhuff/XX.htm	The Social Work History Station

http://www.socialworker.com/
career.htm

The New Social Worker

41

CHAPTER 1
*The Social Work
Profession*

http://www.ncadv.org   National Coalition Against Domestic
Violence

http://www.vaw.umn.edu   Violence Against Women Online
Resources

http://www.abanet.org/domviol/   Commission on Domestic Violence—
home.html   American Bar Association

SUMMARY

The case of Susan Dunn and her family, who are in need of social services from a shelter following an episode of domestic violence, introduces the chapter and also the profession of social work. A definition of social work is offered. The ways in which social work is unique among human service professions, its strengths perspective, for example, are identified. Because the generalist perspective is a basic ingredient of all social work practice and lies at the heart of baccalaureate practice, the concept of generalist practice is explored. The generalist social worker is presented as one who engages in a systematic planned change process with a variety of social systems, including individual people, families, groups, organizations, and communities. Master's degree social workers are prepared for advanced practice within an area of concentration such as clinical social work or advanced generalist practice.

Social work educational programs prepare social workers at the baccalaureate (BSW), master's (MSW), and doctoral (PhD or DSW) levels. The chapter provided information about the curriculum at the baccalaureate level. Less information was presented about the MSW curriculum since it varies depending upon the area of concentration offered by the program.

Pamela Wright was the social worker who assisted Susan Dunn and her family in Chapter 1's case study. Each chapter in this text will begin with a case study showing how social workers engage people and work with them to solve problems across many different social agency and community practice settings. Most people who consider a career in social work do so because they want to help people. Like Pamela Wright, they want their lives to make a difference. The chapter offers information about career options and employment opportunities in social work.

The profession of social work, like most other professions, is legally regulated by state licensing boards and also offers opportunities for specialized practice certification. Unfortunately, there remains much work to be done to ensure that persons who deliver social services and claim to be social workers really are social workers. States' licensure laws vary considerably. Some states have no licensure or certification for BSW social workers. It is possible for persons without academic degrees in social work to obtain social work positions in other states. NASW, the National Association of Social Workers, has led the effort to achieve social work licensure at all levels and in all states. Chapter 1 explains some of the other ways in which NASW serves its members and also the best interests of their clients. Other social work professional organizations, such as the Council on Social Work Education and the International Federation of Social Workers, are also introduced in this chapter.

Social work is sometimes confused with other professions. Students often wonder, for example, whether they should major in psychology or social work, not knowing that social workers carry some of the same responsibilities for counseling and therapy as persons with degrees in psychology. Yet, while professions do overlap, all professions are unique and have their own areas of expertise. The chapter compares several related professions and highlights the uniqueness of the social work profession.

In the Chapter 2 case study you will meet another social worker, Stephanie Hermann, who applies her social work practice skills and knowledge to the problems faced by so many people that successful intervention required response from an entire community. The Stephanie Hermann case study leads to an exploration of the theories on which generalist social work practice is grounded. Inextricably connected to the theory of practice is an understanding of political perspectives and how they influence the well-being of people.

KEY TERMS

ACSW	facilitator
advocate	generalist social worker
BSW	judgmental thinking
broker	legal regulation
career ladder	MSW
case advocacy	organizer
case manager	policy practice
cause advocacy	professional roles
Certified Social Work Case Manager	qualitative research
counselor	quantitative research
educator	social work
enabler	

DISCUSSION QUESTIONS

1. What is the definition of social work given in this book? How would you explain social work to a friend?
2. What is a generalist social worker?
3. From what three social movements did the social work profession arise historically?
4. Name at least one person who contributed to the historical development of the social work profession. Explain that person's contribution.
5. How does the usual role of the baccalaureate-level social worker compare with that of the master's-level social worker?
6. There seems to be a common belief that the vast majority of social workers, especially BSWs, work for "the government." Is this true? What data are available to support your answer?

7. If your friend said to you, "There are no jobs in social work. Why are you going into this field?" what would you say? How would you substantiate your response to your friend?

8. Explain legal regulation of social work. How does licensure or certification protect the public? What are the benefits for social workers?

9. How does NASW provide recognition of special practice expertise? Identify at least one area for which NASW offers certification and explain how someone would qualify.

10. Describe the roles or purposes of professional social work organizations, including the National Association of Social Workers and the Council on Social Work Education. Can you name any additional professional social work organizations?

11. What is the purpose of the *Code of Ethics?* How do the values of the social work profession relate to the *Code of Ethics?*

12. Identify several professions related to social work. What characteristics distinguish social work from these other professions?

CLASSROOM EXERCISES

While not required, it is suggested that students break into small groups of three or four to discuss these exercises. It may be helpful to choose a scribe to record and report major points to the class after the group discussion.

1. Social work is regulated in all 50 states. However, regulations differ among the states. Compare and contrast licensure laws with certification. Which type of regulation do you believe best protects the public? Why?

2. Professional organizations such as the National Association of Social Workers (NASW) often provide recognition for various types of practice expertise. For example, the NASW offers the C-SWCM, or Certified Social Work Case Manager, to members who have baccalaureate degrees in social work and meet certain other requirements. Compare and contrast certification by a professional organization with state regulation that may include licensure or certification. What are the relative merits of each?

3. Undergraduate students who want to work with people often have difficulty choosing among related majors. Discuss the relative merits of majoring in sociology, psychology, human service, or social work if one's goal is to obtain a position working with people soon after graduation with a baccalaureate degree. Be sure to review information provided in the text while conducting this exercise.

RESEARCH ACTIVITIES

1. Conduct a series of interviews with a social worker, a sociologist, a psychologist, and another person from one of the human service professions. Compare and contrast their tasks and responsibilities.

2. Interview two baccalaureate-level social workers and two master's-level social workers. Compare and contrast their tasks and responsibilities.

3. Learn about your state NASW chapter. Where is it located? When, where, and how frequently does the chapter conduct meetings? Are students welcome to attend? What issues is your state chapter currently working on? Can students become involved?

4. Obtain information regarding legal regulation of social workers in your state. Does the law in your state provide for licensure, certification, or some other form of regulation? What levels of practice are regulated? What is the procedure that is required for licensure (or certification)? Is there an examination? How have graduates of your program fared with the state licensure exam?

5. Research your local area or state to determine the range of salaries paid to social workers. Compare differences in salaries by checking specific factors (variables) such as the practice setting—child welfare, school social work, mental health, aging, and probation and parole are just a few. Compare differences between BSW and MSW salaries. Entry-level salaries could also be compared with upper-range salaries paid for experienced, advanced practice.

INTERNET RESEARCH EXERCISES

1. One of the most interesting and informative social work sites on the Web is the Social Work History Station, http://www.idbsu.edu/socwork/dhuff/XX.htm.
   a. Go to the section on this site entitled "The Professionals." What can you learn from this site about the effect of World War I on social casework? ("Social casework" was the term commonly used at that time to refer to social work with individuals.)
   b. What was the second major event identified in "The Professionals" section that affected social casework?
   c. What does the author identify as the leading edge of social casework in the 1920s?
   d. Who were two prominent social workers active in the Roosevelt administration during the depression?

2. Many other countries, like the United States, have national professional organizations for the profession of social work. Go to the website http://www3.nf.sympatico.ca/nlasw, the site for the Newfoundland and Labrador Association of Social Workers. Find the page for "Mission and Goals."
   a. How does the NLASW mission differ from that of the National Association of Social Workers (NASW)?
   b. How similar are the goals of these two organizations?
   c. Go to the "Code of Ethics" page and read the philosophy. What is your impression? Could you live with this statement of philosophy?

3. When an individual wishes to advocate for specific issues, the World Wide Web offers numerous resources. An example would be EDUCAUSE (http://www.cause.org/).
   a. What is the primary cause that is espoused by this site?
   b. How is this site funded?
   c. One of the areas listed on the home page is "Cultural Issues." What sort of issues are addressed here?

REFERENCES

American Association for Marriage and Family Therapy. (n.d.). *FAQ's about MFT*. Retrieved December 21, 2001, from http://www.aamft.org/faqs/whatare.htm.

Association of Social Work Boards. (2001). *Licensing and certification*. Retrieved July 7, 2001, from http://www.aswb.org/licensing/license.html.

Barker, R. L. (1999). *The social work dictionary* (4th ed.). Washington, DC: NASW Press.

Beless, D. W. (1995). Council on Social Work Education. In *Encyclopedia of social work* (19th ed., Vol. 1, pp. 632–636). Washington, DC: NASW Press.

Biggerstaff, M. A. (1995). Licensing, regulation, and certification. In *Encyclopedia of social work* (19th ed., Vol. 2, pp. 1616–1624). Washington, DC: NASW Press.

Cook, M. J. (2001, December 7). *Community psychology . . . What is it?* Retrieved December 20, 2001, from http://www.communitypsychology.net/cmmtypsych.shtml.

Council on Social Work Education. (2001). *Directory of colleges and universities with accredited social work degree programs.* Alexandria, VA: Council on Social Work Education.

Council on Social Work Education. (2001, June 15). Educational policy and accreditation standards. Retrieved July 13, 2001, from http://www.cswe.org/accreditation/EPAS/epas.pdf.

Farr, J. M., & Ludden, L. L. (2000). *Enhanced occupational outlook handbook* (3rd ed.). Indianapolis, IN: JIST Publishing, Inc.

Hokenstad, M. C., Khinduka, S. K., & Midgley, J. (1992). The world of international social work. In M. C. Hokenstad, S. K. Khinduka, and J. Midgley (Eds.), *Profiles in international social work* (pp. 1–10). Washington, DC: NASW Press.

International Federation of Social Workers. (2001, July 17). *Aims.* Retrieved September 7, 2001, from http:/www.ifsw.org

Johannesen, T., "Historical roots, modern problems, and prospects of social work in Russia," Kolomna, Russia. Plenary Session, International Seminar. May 25, 1993.

Kirst-Ashman, K. K., & Hull, G. H. (2002). *Understanding generalist practice* (3rd ed.). Pacific Grove, CA: Brooks/Cole.

Miley, K. K., O'Melia, M., & DuBois, B. L. (1998). *Generalist social work practice: An empowering approach* (2nd ed.). Boston: Allyn and Bacon.

NASW Online. (2001, December 18). Credentials. Retrieved December 19, 2001, from http://www.naswdc.org/Default.htm.

National Association of Black Social Workers (NABSW). (1999, November 15). Retrieved July 11, 2001, from http://ssw.unc.edu/professional/NABSW.html.

National Association of Social Workers. (1996). *NASW Code of Ethics.* Washington, DC: NASW Press.

National Association of Social Workers. (1999). *NASW Membership Statistical Report. Nov., 1999.* Washington, DC: Author.

National Association of Social Workers. (2000). Practice area. PRN datagram. *NASW Practice Research Network* (PRN 1, 3, 2000). Washington, DC: Author.

National Association of Social Workers. (2000). Social work income. PRN datagram. *NASW Practice Research Network* (PRN 1, 1, 2000). Washington, DC: Author.

National Association of Social Workers. (2000). Ninteen ninety-nine full-time social work income by primary auspice. Social work income, PRN datagram. *NASW Practice Network* (PRN 1, 1, 2000). Washington, DC: Author.

Occupational outlook handbook. (2001, April 12). *Social workers.* Retrieved July 13, 2001, from http://stats.bls.gov/oco/ocos060.htm.

O'Neill, J. V. (2001). Chapters play helping role. *NASW News. 46* (10), 14.

Popple, P. R. (1995). Social work profession: History. In *Encyclopedia of social work* (19th ed., Vol. 3, pp. 2282–2291). Washington, DC: NASW Press.

Rogers, J., Smith, M., Ray, J., Hull, G., Pike, C., & Buchan, V. (1999). *The revised BPD outcomes instrument: report of findings: Total database (as of Oct. 1, 1999).* Paper presented at the 17th Annual Program Meeting of the Association of Baccalaureate Social Work Program Directors, St. Louis, MO.

Social Work Gateway, Center for Human Service Technology. (2000, June). Retrieved June 30, 2001, from http://www.chst.soton.ac.uk/webconn.ht.

Teare, R. J., Shank, B. W., & Sheafor, B. W. (1990, March). *The national undergraduate practitioner survey: Practice content and implications for education and certification.* Paper presented at the 36th Annual Program Meeting of the Council on Social Work Education, Reno, NV.

Thyer, B. A., & Biggerstaff, M. A. (1989). *Professional social work credentialling and legal regulation: A review of critical issues and an annotated bibliography.* Springfield, IL: Charles C. Thomas.

Tourse R. W. C. (1995). Special-interest professional associations. In R. L. Edwards (Ed.). *Encyclopedia of social work* (19th ed., Vol. 3, pp. 2314–2319). Washington, DC: NASW Press.

U.S. Department of Labor, Bureau of Labor Statistics. (2001). *Occupational outlook handbook: 2002–2003 edition.* Retrieved December 20, 2001 from http://www.bls.gov/oco.

Woodside, M., & McClam, T. (2002). *An introduction to human services* (4th ed.). Pacific Grove, CA: Brooks/Cole.

FOR FURTHER READING

Black, P. N., & Whelley, J. (1999, Winter). The social work licensure exam: Examining the exam through the lens of CSWE curriculum policy. *Arete. 23* (No. 1), 66–76.

Black and Whelley's article critiques the relationship between the national social work licensure exam and the Council on Social Work Education's educational policy. Although the CSWE curriculum document is the 1994 version and not the current 2001 revision, the critique remains essentially valid. Perhaps more important for the student reader, however, will be the tables that provide useful insight into the percentage of licensure exam questions related to each curriculum area. For example, while 70 percent of the exam questions pertained to social work practice, only 4 percent addressed ethics and values.

Christie, A., & Kruk, E. (1998, March). Choosing to become a social worker: Motives, incentives, concerns and disincentives. *Social Work Education. 17* (1), 21–34.

This journal article presents refreshing evidence of the wide differences in student motivations for entering social work programs. The article provides an international perspective as the study population is drawn from schools in Canada and the United Kingdom. Both qualitative and quantitative analyses are provided.

Ginsberg, L. H. (2001). *Careers in social work* (2nd ed.). Boston: Allyn and Bacon.

Ginsberg's paperback may prove to be one of the best investments made by the baccalaureate or master's degree student ready to initiate an employment search. A wealth of nitty-gritty, practical information is offered from tips on effective employment interviews and resumé preparation to handling of salary and compensation issues. Of special interest is the content on social work in smaller communities, in employee assistance programs, and in international settings; this information tends not to be well covered in most social work texts. Examples of state and federal employment application forms are welcome additions to the appendix.

Mayden, R. W., & Nieves, J. (2000). *Social work speaks: National Association of Social Workers policy statements 2000–2003* (5th ed.). Washington, DC: NASW Press.

The Delegate Assembly, an elected body of NASW members, meets every three years. One of its functions is to publicize social policy statements that reflect the values and the social action agenda of NASW. The current (5th) edition of *Social work speaks* reflects the policy statements that emerged from the 1999 Delegate Assembly and those that preceded it. The 57 topics are addressed in terms of background information, content describing the issues involved, and the NASW policy statement. Readings and references are provided. The topics covered are those frequently addressed in student term papers and research. A sampling of the topics includes adolescent pregnancy and parenting, AIDS, child abuse and neglect, correctional social work, family violence, homelessness, juvenile delinquency, mental health, racism, women's issues, and youth suicide.

Theoretical Perspectives for Social Workers

The case study for this chapter introduces a community-level problem requiring social work intervention and then describes how a particular person, Sandra McLean, is affected. It illustrates how persons and environments interact and how social welfare policy influences social work practice.

THE SEVERAL ROLES OF STEPHANIE HERMANN, BSW

Stephanie Hermann, BSW, waited impatiently for the mail that morning, for her boss had told her to expect an important memo. Stephanie worked as an assistant administrator in a regional office of the Division of Community Services, a part of her state's Department of Health and Social Services (DHSS). The office interpreted new DHSS policies pertaining to health and social service agencies in the region, both public and private. Stephanie consulted with agency administrators to clarify state policies and to document agency compliance.

Recently, the state DHSS office had received notice from the Federal Health Care Administration that people with developmental disabilities (DD) might lose eligibility for Medicaid funding in nursing homes. The intent of this policy was to encourage the development of community-based living settings for people with disabilities. A survey had been conducted around the state, and 2,025 adults with disabilities were found to be living in nursing homes. Among them was Sandra McLean, whose story will be a focus of this chapter.

This large number worried DHSS officials. They did not believe there were existing alternative community placement options that could care for anywhere near this number of people. Stephanie's boss had described the memo that was on its way as "at least trying to head us off from a bigger problem later."

The expected memo arrived: "The Department of Health and Social Services finds that an emergency exists. . . . This order amends the department's rules for nursing homes . . . to prohibit the admission of any person with a developmental disability, including mental retardation, to a nursing home for intermediate nursing care unless the nursing home is certified . . . as an intermediate care facility for the mentally retarded (ICF/MR)."

The memo explained that to obtain certification as an ICF/MR, a nursing home must identify staff skilled in working with persons with developmental disabilities and describe specific internal programs, supplementary services from other agencies, admissions policies, and individual care plans for each resident. The DHSS memo defined developmental disability as follows: "mental retardation or a related condition such as cerebral palsy, epilepsy, or autism, but excluding mental illness and the infirmities of aging."

Stephanie was excited by the new policy. She had long believed that most persons with disabilities should be placed in family-like settings. But few such places of residence currently existed. Adult family care homes (foster homes for adults) required families willing to take in persons with disabilities; small group homes required paid staff. Apartment living required monitoring and support. All required funding and neighbors willing to accept persons with disabilities.

BROCKTON MANOR

When Stephanie received the emergency order from the state DHSS, she decided to consult with every county in her region. Since at this point only new DD clients were prohibited from receiving Medicaid funding for nursing home care, Stephanie believed that new placement options could be developed gradually. She also consulted with nursing homes that were currently caring for persons with disabilities, to assist them in developing state-certified ICF/MR programs.

However, only two weeks after the state's emergency ruling, Brockton Manor, a large nursing home in Stephanie's region, decided to phase out its services for people with disabilities. Administrators believed they could easily fill their beds with elderly people, who are less costly to serve. Brockton Manor offered to cooperate with county and state officials in developing alternative living arrangements so that each of its 49 residents with developmental disabilities would have a place to go.

Now Stephanie had an immediate situation to deal with. A worst-case scenario would be 49 new street people. But fortunately, Medicaid regulations required individual assessments and specific discharge plans, including places to live and "active treatment." Active treatment involved individualized plans for training, therapy, and services to help achieve the highest possible level of functioning. But how did one find or develop such resources?

Stephanie determined that she would need to play several roles. The first would involve coordinating the efforts of various community agencies. Brockton Manor's major responsibility would be to provide individual plans of care for each DD resident; each county's primary responsibility would be to develop alternative living arrangements, and the state's responsibility would be to provide funding, with federal assistance through Medicaid.

A second community-organizing role would be to involve private voluntary organizations, such as the Association for Retarded Citizens (ARC), in planning efforts on behalf of Brockton Manor's DD clients. For example, the ARC might organize informational meetings and help locate alternative living settings.

Third, Stephanie knew she would have to mediate disputes among various county and state offices. Thirty-five of the 49 residents with developmental disabilities at Brockton Manor originally came from different counties. Their counties of origin were likely to refuse to resume responsibility because of the cost.

Fourth, Stephanie planned to help assess the needs of DD residents of Brockton Manor and to help develop appropriate discharge plans.

Stephanie began to carry out her organizing role immediately. She arranged a meeting of representatives from all the key agencies that would be involved in relocating the DD residents, including Brockton Manor staff, county officials responsible for finding new living arrangements, administrators from the state DHSS offices, and members of Stephanie's own regional office. A Subcommittee on Relocation was es-

tablished that met biweekly for over a year. The subcommittee set up teams to assess all residents with disabilities at Brockton Manor. It also conducted a study to determine the probable cost of **community placement** *for each resident.*

Funding complications soon became apparent. Besides encouraging development of more family-like settings, community placement was intended to cut costs. Medicaid thus funded community care at only 60 percent of the institutional-care reimbursement rate for the same DD person. Yet the money was supposed to cover active treatment as well as room, board, and assistance in daily living tasks. Many of the people at Brockton Manor required 24-hour supervision.

Still, the subcommittee pressed on. It organized a large "stakeholders" meeting for all agencies and individuals who might be willing to get involved. Videotapes of several residents were prepared to educate the community and to enhance the "human-interest" side of the story.

The meeting spearheaded a flurry of community activity. Voluntary organizations collected supplies for new apartments, the Kiwanis Club developed a proposal for public housing for people with disabilities, county departments of social service advertised for adult family care homes, and Brockton Manor solicited foster parents from its own staff. Two private social service agencies developed small group homes. Funding for these homes required creative planning; half the residents had to be taken from costly state institutions, because the Medicaid funding available for community placement for these persons was higher.

Through the development of small group homes and new **family care homes,** *15 of Brockton Manor's residents were soon placed into the community. One of these persons was Sandra McLean.*

SANDRA MCLEAN: THE EFFECTS OF INSTITUTIONALIZATION

Sandra McLean's mother had a long and difficult labor, and finally forceps were used in delivery. The forceps injured Sandra's skull. The result was mental retardation and grand mal epileptic seizures, commonly known as convulsions.

Mr. and Mrs. McLean raised Sandra at home until she was about eight years old, by which time she was toilet trained, could walk, and could say "Mama" and "Papa." Then they sent her to public school. This was before the days of special education, however, and they soon decided they could educate her better at home. They were able to teach the child to bathe, dress, and feed herself.

When Sandra was about 10, her parents had a second daughter, a normal, healthy infant named Susan. After Susan's arrival, the McLeans did not have quite so much time for Sandra, but by then she was more independent. When she was in her late teens, an activity center for people with disabilities was established in a nearby community. Sandra's middle-class parents could afford the moderate fee, and so she was enrolled. To the McLeans' delight, Sandra blossomed. She began to talk and smile more. She was a favorite among the staff.

The blow struck when Sandra was 27 years old. First, her father died of a heart attack. Shortly thereafter, her mother had a stroke. Partially paralyzed, the mother was no longer able to care for Sandra. Susan was ready to go to college, and Mrs. McLean did not want to hold her back. The family doctor suggested that Sandra be placed in a state institution. Mrs. McLean, seeing no other option, reluctantly agreed. At the institution, Sandra was medicated heavily to control her seizures. She spent her days strapped into a wheelchair, eyes glazed, drooling.

Several years later, Sandra was transferred to Brockton Manor, and several years after that, she was referred for community placement by Stephanie Hermann's team. Stephanie arranged for the mother, then very frail, to visit. The team listened with amazement as Mrs. McLean described Sandra as a young girl. Stephanie contacted Sandra's sister, Susan, and heard the same story. Mrs. McLean talked about the activity center Sandra had participated in years before, so staff there were contacted as well. A therapist who had known Sandra visited and was shocked to see her current condition. The therapist described the smiling person she used to know, who enjoyed socializing and could walk, talk, feed, and toilet herself.

Stephanie and the assessment team called in a physician who was skilled in working with people with disabilities. The physician was willing to prescribe different medications. The assessment team then held a joint meeting with all the professional staff at Brockton Manor who were involved with Sandra's care. They explained that Sandra might begin to have seizures again, and they discussed how to deal with them. They suggested that occasional grand mal seizures might not be too high a price to pay if the young woman were able to learn to walk again and to communicate with people, at least in a limited way. The nursing home staff agreed.

The plan worked. Sandra did begin to have seizures again, but they were not too difficult to handle. With physical therapy she learned to walk again, and with occupational therapy she learned to dress and feed herself. The nurses taught her how to toilet herself again. Sandra became a social person once more and began to use limited words. She clearly recognized her mother and sister. Everyone felt deeply rewarded. Now the time had come to develop community-based living arrangements.

Although Mrs. McLean would have loved to have her daughter return home, she was not physically able. Sandra's sister, Susan, explained to Stephanie Hermann, with obvious distress, that she worked full-time and had two children to care for. She frequently helped her mother with routine household chores. She did not feel able to take on her sister's care as well. But both mother and daughter welcomed the idea of a family care home for Sandra.

A potential home was located and licensed by social workers from the county Department of Social Services. The foster parents, a childless couple in their midthirties, had learned of the need through newspaper advertisements. They visited Sandra several times at Brockton Manor and took her home for a trial overnight visit before making a final decision. The Brockton Manor staff taught them about Sandra's special needs, especially about what to do during seizures.

Arrangements were made for Sandra to attend the local activity center for people with disabilities during the day, once she was living in her foster home. She enjoyed the social and recreational opportunities, such as exercise classes, educational games, and other small group activities very much. The placement worked out so well that her foster family took in a second adult with a disability.

Young adult with disability in family care home.

ONGOING CHALLENGES OF COMMUNITY PLACEMENT

An adult family care home was provided for Sandra McLean by the Department of Social Services because federal funding through Medicaid and Supplemental Security Income (to be discussed in Chapter 3) was sufficient to pay all her bills, including foster care and active treatment at the local activity center. However, funding was not sufficient to permit community placement of residents who needed more care, and eventually many of them had to be transferred to a different nursing home that met the new federal requirements.

SOCIAL WORK AND SYSTEMS THEORY

As illustrated by this chapter's case study, social work is a profession that requires working with systems of many sizes. For example, Stephanie Hermann was employed by a large state organization, the Department of Health and Social Services. The DHSS was, in turn, strongly impacted by the policies of an even larger organization, the federal government. Stephanie, by publicizing and interpreting new federal and state policies, affected the operations of the social service organizations and agencies in her entire region, both public and private. She provided professional assistance to help these organizations and agencies meet changing requirements. She also educated citizens' groups about new regulations and solicited their aid in developing new resources to meet community needs.

Besides working with larger systems, Stephanie worked with smaller ones. For example, she helped establish a formal task group, the Subcommittee on Relocation, which managed the job of finding and developing alternative living arrangements for disabled residents of Brockton Manor. She met with this group for more than a year. She also worked with a team of staff at Brockton Manor to assess the needs of each resident with a disability.

As part of her work in assessing the needs of individual residents at Brockton Manor, Stephanie worked with a yet smaller system, the individual named Sandra McLean (among others). To help gain a better understanding of Sandra's potential capabilities and needs, Stephanie met with Sandra's family members as well, Mrs. Mclean and Susan. These family meetings led Stephanie to contact another system or organization, the activity center that Sandra had attended many years before.

As is obvious from Sandra McLean's story, improving the life of just one person can involve skills in working with systems of many sizes. For this reason, social work is a complex practice. It requires the guidance of a broad theoretical framework to help organize and analyze large amounts of information. For many social workers, systems theory provides that theoretical framework. Systems theory helps the social worker attend to and understand the dynamic interactions among the many biological and social systems that affect ongoing practice (Shaefor, Horejsi, & Horejsi, 2000).

Applying systems theory requires familiarity with certain basic concepts. A few will be introduced here. The term **system** has been defined in many ways, but perhaps the simplest is that a system is a whole consisting of interacting parts. These parts are so interrelated that a change in any one part affects all the others.

Let us consider an example of a biological system, the human body. The body is composed of many interrelated, interacting parts, including the skeleton, muscles, blood, and so on. What happens when one part is disturbed in some way? Let's say a piece of the skeleton is broken. Every other part of the system is affected. Muscles tighten, and blood circulation increases in the area of the broken bone. Nerves carry impulses to the brain that are translated as pain, which affects every other part of the body.

Each of the major parts of the system called the human body can itself be considered a system: skeletal system, muscle system, blood system, nervous system, for example. These smaller systems are themselves made up of parts even smaller: organs, molecules, atoms, particles of atoms. Sometimes smaller systems within larger systems are called subsystems. Whether something is considered a system or a subsystem depends only on where the observer decides to focus attention. The important point to keep in mind with respect to systems theory is the concept of interrelationships: a change in one part of a system affects all the other parts in some way. Smaller systems that are parts of larger systems affect each other and the larger system as a whole. Any change in the larger system (or suprasystem) affects all the systems and subsystems within.

The human body is an example of a biological system, and humans, as biological organisms, are part of a larger physical environment. But people are also social systems and parts of larger social environments. Both physical and social environments are made up of systems of various sizes to which people must adapt.

Consider the human family. The family constitutes a certain type of social system, a whole consisting of interacting parts, so that while its form may vary, family members know who belongs and who does not. A change in one part affects all others: people cannot join or withdraw without other family members responding in

Important Systems for Social Workers	
EXHIBIT 1	
Change Agent System	Social workers and their agencies of employment
Client System	People who have requested social work services or who have entered into a formal or informal contract with a social worker
Target System	People who need to change in order for social work clients to meet their goals
Action System	All those who work cooperatively with the social worker to accomplish desired changes
Professional System	Social work education programs, professional organizations, and the social work professional culture, including values and ethics

some way. In the McClean case, having to send Sandra to an institution undoubtedly affected her mother's well-being in a negative way. Research has even shown that if one family member is physically injured in the presence of another, the physical body of the observer will be affected (stress hormones will be released, muscles will tighten, and so on). For this reason, systems theory has been adapted for use in medicine, social science, social work, and other professions (Wells, 1998).

Compton and Galaway (1999) have identified five systems of special importance to social workers: the change agent system, the client system, the target system, the action system, and the professional system. The change agent system includes social workers and their agencies of employment. The client system includes people who have requested social work services or who have entered into a formal or informal contract. The target system includes people who need to change in order for clients to meet their goals, and the action system includes all those who work cooperatively with the social worker to accomplish desired changes. The last system, the professional system, is made up of social work education programs, professional organizations, and the professional culture, including values and ethics (see Exhibit 1).

THE ECOSYSTEMS PERSPECTIVE

Social workers have long promoted a person-in-environment perspective. General systems theory, proposed by biologist Lugwig Von Bertalanffy in the late 1960s, was adopted by many social workers as an overall framework for practice very much because it was congruent with their ongoing experience. The theory helped social workers remember and pay attention to the interactions between larger and smaller systems and thus provided a useful framework for analysis. However, some theorists felt that systems theory was too abstract for practical use (Germain & Gitterman, 1995). They adopted instead a closely related outlook from biological science, the ecological or **ecosystems perspective,** which was derived from basic assumptions of systems theory (Sommer, 1995). Many social workers now use an ecosystems or ecological perspective to guide their practice.

The ecological perspective encourages social workers to maintain simultaneous focus on person and environment, much as workers have done since the birth of the profession. Now, however, the practice is supported and strengthened by a theoretical model. The ecosystems focus on interactions between person and environment is perhaps a simpler way of expressing systems concepts (such as the importance of interactional effects). The concept of "environment" from the ecosystems perspective is virtually synonymous with the concept of "suprasystem" from general systems theory; "person" is simply an example of a small system (see Exhibit 2).

Useful concepts for social workers who use an ecosystems perspective include person/environment fit, life stressors, and adaptation, among others. The person/environment fit is the actual fit between human wants and needs and the environmental resources available to meet them. Life stressors include issues and needs that exceed environmental resources. Adaptations are the processes people use to try to improve the fit between themselves and their environments (Germain & Gitterman, 1995).

To apply ecosystems concepts to the situation of Sandra McClean, consider how Sandra's environment affected her personally. Her life became completely different in the institutional setting from what it had been at home or at the activity center. Sandra's experience and behavior became so changed that she might as well have been a different person. The heavy dose of drugs that was administered to control her seizures acted as a physiological stressor that suppressed her capacity to adapt, and she essentially became a human vegetable. Only when federal policy changed,

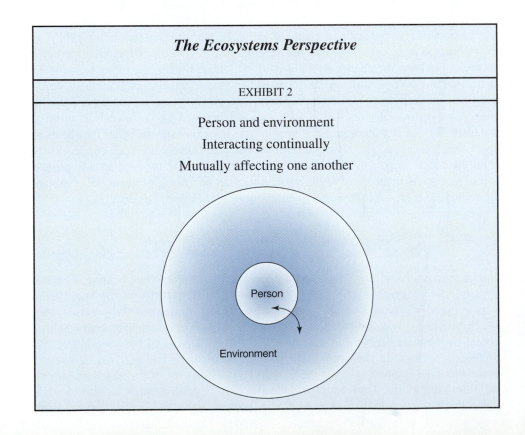

The Ecosystems Perspective

EXHIBIT 2

Person and environment
Interacting continually
Mutually affecting one another

Person

Environment

and Sandra was viewed as a whole person with human rights despite her disability, did she have a chance to live a more normal life. In her case, that required changes in state and local social policy, which led in turn to changes in the medical and social services available to her. Sandra couldn't live a reasonable life of her own until new opportunities were created in the wider environment by changed social policies, and by professional services committed to carrying out those policies.

Changes in Sandra herself also affected her environment. For example, her new abilities impacted various medical professionals, who were astounded at what she could accomplish and who then were willing to consider modifying medications for other people with disabilities as well. Sandra's new opportunities also affected the people who became her foster parents and those whom they later took in with her. Sandra's good fortune affected staff at the activity center, who rejoiced for her and developed new activities to assist in her recovery. Her mother and sister rejoiced also: a family tragedy had been transformed by what seemed like a miracle. (See Exhibit 3.)

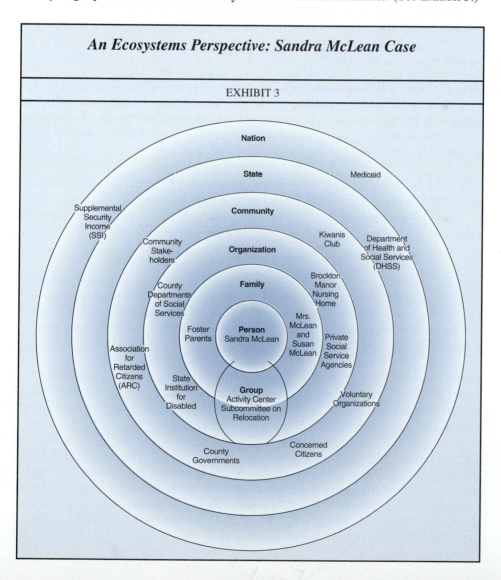

An Ecosystems Perspective: Sandra McLean Case

EXHIBIT 3

THE GENERALIST APPROACH

The **generalist approach** to social work practice is strongly rooted in systems theory. Guided by an ecosystems perspective, the generalist approach involves multiple **levels of intervention** and a systematic planned change process. While each CSWE-accredited baccalaureate social work program develops its own definition of generalist according to accreditation guidelines, the following is fairly typical:

> The generalist approach to social work practice, supported by concepts drawn from social systems theory and using an ecological perspective, is attentive to person and environment and their interactions. Generalist practice is based on research-guided knowledge and uses a planned change process to determine the level or levels of intervention—individual, family, group, organization, and/or community—appropriate to addressing the issues presented. It recognizes the profession's dual purpose and responsibility to influence social as well as individual change.

Levels of Intervention

Note that the definition above explains that the generalist approach involves not only an ecological perspective but a planned change process and the use of multiple "levels of intervention." The planned change process will be discussed further on. At this point, let us describe the various levels of intervention identified in the definition of generalist.

Individual   Working with individuals involves working one-on-one, either to help a person better adapt to his or her environment or to modify the environment so it better meets the needs of the person. In this chapter's case study, Stephanie Hermann worked with Sandra McLean individually to help assess her abilities and needs.

Family   Working with families may involve whole families or parts of a family, such as a mother and child or a pair of parents. Stephanie Hermann worked with members of Sandra's family in planning for her care. Some types of family work can be much more intensive. Family therapy, for example, assists families in overcoming conflicts and crises among members.

Group   Group work may involve many different types of groups. Stephanie Hermann developed and worked with a task group, the Subcommittee on Relocation, at Brockton Manor. The activity center where Sandra received services ran activity groups and support groups for its clients.

Organization   Working with organizations involves assessing needs within an organization and planning and coordinating efforts to meet those needs. For example, Stephanie alerted Brockton Manor about new federal regulations regarding care for residents with disabilities. When the nursing home administration decided not to serve these clients any longer, Stephanie planned and coordinated the organization's efforts to develop responsible discharge plans.

Social Work Levels of Intervention
EXHIBIT 4
Community Organization Group Family Individual

Community   Working with communities involves evaluating community needs and planning and coordinating efforts to meet those needs. Stephanie Hermann helped her region of the state to evaluate its capacity to provide family-like care for citizens with disabilities and coordinated the efforts to expand resources and options (please review Exhibit 3).

Some social workers prefer to talk of micro-, mezzo-, and macropractice rather than practice with individuals, families, groups, organizations, and communities. Professionals may differ, however, in their understanding of which levels of intervention these terms include. For example, Zastrow (1999) explains that micropractice involves work with individuals, mezzolevel involves families and groups, and macrolevel involves organizations and communities. Miley, O'Melia, and DuBois (1998), however, include families as well as individuals in microlevel intervention, organizations as well as groups in what they term midlevel intervention, and societies as well as communities in macrolevel intervention.

This text, to simplify, will refer to specific levels of intervention: individual, family, group, organization, and community. However, one must remember that as our world shrinks and we all become more interdependent, our concept of community must extend to include the whole planet (see Exhibit 4).

The Intervention Process

The third major component of the generalist approach, besides the ecosystems perspective and the use of multiple levels of intervention (as previously described), is the planned change process. This process has been known traditionally as the problem-solving process, and that terminology is still used by many social workers. The term "intervention" or "planned change process," however, tends to be preferred today because the concept is broader: it can more easily encompass the idea of preventive work. For example, parents who wish to maintain a safe and healthy neighborhood may request assistance in developing a community center where recreational activities can he provided for teens who might otherwise become involved in gangs.

Because it is very easy for a caring person to hear about a situation that needs change and immediately jump in to try to "do something," a careful **intervention process** is employed in professional social work practice. All too often, following one's first impulses only creates new problems. Acting after hearing just one person's side of a story neglects other people's experience and points of view. An explicit intervention process alerts responsible social workers to think carefully before acting and provides guidelines regarding how to think carefully. The process involves several steps, as described in CSWE Educational Policy and Accreditation Standards, (Section on Social Work Practice Council on Social Work Education, 2001, p. 10):

> Social work practice content is anchored in the purposes of the social work profession and focuses on strengths, capacities, and resources of client systems in relation to their broader environments. Students learn practice content that encompasses knowledge and skills to work with individuals, families, groups, organizations, and communities. This content includes engaging clients in an appropriate working relationship; identifying issues, problems, needs, resources, and assets; collecting and assessing information; and planning for service delivery. It includes using communication skills, supervision, and consultation. Practice content also includes identifying, analyzing, and implementing empirically based interventions designed to achieve client goals; applying empirical knowledge and technological advances; evaluating program outcomes and practice effectiveness; developing, analyzing, advocating, and providing leadership for policies and services; and promoting social and economic justice.

Obviously, this process is involved and requires expertise! To translate somewhat for beginning students, the generalist social worker begins with a situation in which change is desired, engages the client system, and carefully identifies the issues involved. The worker then gathers and assesses as much relevant data as possible. Once data have been collected from a variety of sources (such as the people or organizations bringing the concern, involved families or groups, community professionals, agency records, etc.), the worker then, in collaboration with the client system, identifies possible plans of action, develops a formal or informal contract, and goes on to assist in implementing mutually determined courses of action using the best knowledge and technological advances available. This process may involve leadership in developing new resources for oppressed populations. The worker then monitors and evaluates outcomes. When the situation has been improved to the clients' satisfaction, the social worker formally terminates his or her involvement.

The planned change process helps the generalist social worker determine which level or levels of intervention to involve in resolving the issue or concern. Generalist intervention may involve working only with an individual or with an entire family. It may involve working with a group, with an organization, or with a community. It may involve working with an individual, family, group, organization, and community all at the same time. The important point is that the plan of action determined by the generalist worker depends on the nature of the circumstance and vigilant implementation of the planned change process. The plan of action is not determined according to a method that simply happens to be preferred by the worker—for example, one-on-one counseling or group work (see Exhibit 5).

The Strengths Perspective: Resilience and Empowerment

Dennis Saleebey (1997) reminds social workers that it is of great importance to seek and identify strengths in all client systems. Focusing only on problems and deficits tends to discourage workers and clients alike. Saleebey notes that despite

The Intervention Process
EXHIBIT 5
Engaging the client system
Identifying and defining important issues
Gathering and assessing data
Identifying plans of action
Contracting
Implementing plans of action
Evaluating outcomes
Terminating

the difficulties our clients may have experienced, they have also developed many skills and attributes that have helped them to meet and overcome difficult challenges. People often exhibit remarkable resiliency in the face of adversity. Consider the example of Sandra McLean. Despite being warehoused in institutions for many years, this remarkable woman rebounded courageously when given a chance. She relearned how to walk, talk, feed, and toilet herself.

Assisting clients to discover and honor their own strengths and powers of **resilience** may be our very best service to them as individuals. In addition, many external environments, even seemingly the poorest and most harsh, offer important resources that can make a difference in our clients' lives. The practitioner's challenge is to help find these resources and assist clients to utilize them.

A **strengths perspective** leads naturally to the idea of empowering clients; recognizing and honoring strengths is a firm foundation for **empowerment.** According to Miley, O'Melia, and Dubois (1998), empowerment involves both personal and political aspects. *Personal* empowerment involves one's own sense of competence, control, mastery, and the like. *Political* empowerment involves resource accessibility and the power to make choices. Genuine options must be available in the wider environment, and people need the power to choose them (or not) in order to have political empowerment.

POLITICAL PERSPECTIVES

Whether people have the power to make choices in American society frequently depends on their economic status. And not every American has the economic means to secure enough resources to meet basic needs, much less to satisfy personal wants.

Karger and Stoesz (1998) explain that Americans, while assured of important political rights through the Constitution, have no similar document that ensures economic rights. Thus, the United States may be described as a "democratic-capitalist"

Preschool children from economically deprived families learn new skills at Head Start Center.

nation. While democratic institutions are built into American law, the economy of the nation relies largely on competitive forces in a free market. No one has a constitutional guarantee to sufficient economic resources to survive.

For many people, allowing the marketplace to determine the economic well-being of American citizens is simply the way things are. That there are other points of view and other policies in effect elsewhere in the world is either unknown or considered quite peculiar. Yet many people in America, and probably the majority in Europe, believe that governments should intervene in market activities for the public good: for example, to create jobs for people out of work or to provide day care services for children who have working parents.

Many Americans vote faithfully as good citizens without much understanding of the economic policies their party of choice promotes or how these policies might affect their personal lives. They vote instead for candidates of a particular party out of habit or family loyalty. As an example, a college professor compared the positions of each presidential candidate for a social work class shortly before the last election. The candidates differed markedly on important issues directly affecting American social welfare policy and social work practice. The National Association of Social Workers' political action committee (PACE) had strongly endorsed (formally recommended) one of them. The professor described the positions of each candidate carefully on many issues and explained why PACE had made its endorsement. Soon afterward, the best student in the class, a young woman who aspired to become a social worker, proudly reported registering and voting for the first time. But she had voted for the presidential candidate who opposed virtually every policy supported by the social work profession, the candidate whom PACE had not endorsed—because her family always voted for candidates of his party.

> ### *Up for Debate*
> *Proposition: Should the federal government develop
> programs designed to assist poor people?*
>
> | Yes | No |
> |---|---|
> | People are naturally industrious and will use such assistance responsibly to better their lives | People are naturally lazy, and government assistance will only make them more lazy and irresponsible |
> | Environmental conditions such as discrimination may hold a person back unless government assists to "level the playing field" | Individuals are autonomous and achieve according to their inborn talents; they have complete free will |
> | Government programs are necessary to help meet basic human needs for all | The free market economy is the best way to fulfill individual needs |
> | A free market economy needs intervention and regulation by government to ensure that competition is fair | Government's role should be to support, not regulate, the free market |

To help students begin to make more thoughtful voting choices, this chapter will introduce the political perspectives known as **conservative, liberal,** and **radical.** It will also briefly describe **neoconservative** and **neoliberal** views. The discussion here will be very basic; students are encouraged to read as much as possible from additional sources and to examine the "Up for Debate" box. Suggestions for further reading can be found at the end of the chapter.

The Political Spectrum

It is probably fairly common for people to vote as their families, friends, or neighbors do early in their voting careers. That is certainly the easiest way to decide for whom to vote. But candidates take different positions on many important issues impacting social welfare policy and social work practice. Those elected will usually try to accomplish whatever positions they promoted during their campaigns. So it makes good sense for voters to inform themselves about the positions that candidates take and to vote accordingly.

Learning about political parties can begin to help voters select candidates intelligently because the parties themselves take different positions on important issues. That is what party "platforms" are about. The platform tells the position of the party on many public issues such as health care, education, affirmative action, women's reproductive rights, social security, and the like.

Political parties in the United States today fall along a political spectrum, described as "right" to "left." Those on the "right" are considered relatively "conservative"; those on the "left" are relatively "liberal." The major conservative political party in the United States today is the Republican party, and the major liberal party is the Democratic party. There are parties even further "right" (or more conservative) than the Republican, however, and parties further "left" than the Democratic.

People who fall on different ends of the political spectrum (conservative versus liberal) tend to have different attitudes toward change; different views of individual behavior, human nature, and the family; different views toward the social system; and different perspectives on the proper role of government with respect to the economic market (Popple & Leighninger, 1999). We will discuss some of these differences below.

Conservative Perspectives

People who are conservative tend to resist change, to want to keep things as they are. The word "conservative" is actually derived from the verb "to conserve" or "to save." While probably everyone resists change to some degree—no matter how bad things are, at least they are known—political conservatives tend to exhibit this characteristic relatively strongly. In particular, conservatives want to keep the political and economic system unchanged, as is.

Are people naturally "bad" or "good" by nature? Philosophers and theologians have argued this question for centuries. Probably there is some merit in either stance. But in general, conservatives tend to take the pessimistic view, that people are born lazy, self-centered, and corrupt and, thus, must be pushed into working or taking responsibility for their own lives.

Are people fully autonomous, or shaped and fashioned by their environment? This is another question that has been argued through the ages by scholars and sages. The conservative perspective is that individuals are fully autonomous units who have total free will. Whatever a person achieves or does not achieve in life, therefore, is the direct result of his or her own efforts.

In accord with the tendency to want to conserve and a pessimistic view of human nature, conservatives desire to preserve the traditional free market economic system. They believe that government should not interfere with the market forces of supply and demand, but rather that supply and demand should be entirely self-regulating. Economists of this orientation argue that economic insecurity for individuals and families is *necessary* to motivate people to work (Karger & Stoesz, 1998). Otherwise, they will not make the effort. It follows that since people are naturally lazy and yet fully autonomous, if they are poor it is their own fault.

Conservatives do not believe that government should use its powers to try to help poor people, because, from this perspective, income inequality is necessary. It provides the economic incentive to work hard at jobs most needed by society. Social welfare programs to help poor people simply increase human laziness and dependency and should be abolished. If there is to be any government intervention at all, it should favor tax breaks for the rich because wealthy people invest money in the economic market. New investment leads to new jobs for poor people, who will be better off with more work. This perspective is popularly known as the "trickle down theory" or, more formally, as "supply-side economics."

The conservative orientation goes beyond economics. Preservation of social traditions such as the nuclear family is also strongly promoted. Thus, political conservatives generally oppose such potential public services as government day care programs since, from this perspective, child care should be provided only by a wife within the family household. Single-parenthood, sex outside of marriage, abortion, homosexuality, and so on, are also generally opposed by conservatives (Ginsberg, 1998) because these practices are not considered traditional. This type of conservatism, sometimes called **cultural conservatism,** results in major contradictions, however. While conservatives insist that government take a hands-off (laissez-faire) position with respect to intervention in the economic market, many conservatives push hard for government intervention restricting reproductive choice, access to sex education in the schools, and the like.

The major conservative political party in the United States today is the Republican party, as mentioned earlier: that of Presidents Nixon, Ford, Reagan, George and George W. Bush. Other conservative parties include the Traditionalists, who believe that Christian doctrine should become the law of the state, and the Libertarians, who oppose virtually all government regulation (including taxation) except when one individual threatens the physical safety of another (Karger & Stoesz, 1998).

Classical Conservatism versus Neoconservatism

Karger and Stoesz (1998) contrast classical conservative thought with that of today's neoconservatives and cultural conservatives. Classical conservatives believe strongly in separation of church and state, and believe that government has no right to intervene in the private lives of individuals. Hence, classical conservatives tend to be pro-choice with respect to reproductive rights and to favor extending privacy and civil rights to homosexuals.

A neoconservative movement arose in the mid-1970s, however. It opposed government welfare programs for the poor and advocated ending entitlements to welfare assistance for poor people (in particular, poor children and their parents). It advocated transferring any surviving public social welfare programs from federal to state control and from public to private ownership. It opposed public welfare programs because they might conceivably limit corporate profits or global competitiveness by offering people possible alternatives to low-wage labor.

The neoconservative movement merged with the cultural conservative movement that was gaining power at the same time. The cultural conservative movement, like classical conservatism, opposed government intervention in the economic market but, paradoxically, promoted government intrusion into the personal lives of individual citizens through restricting reproductive choice, homosexual rights, and so on.

A coalition of neoconservative and cultural conservative politicians won both houses of Congress in 1994. Over 300 Republican members of the House of Representatives signed the "Contract with America" that year, the agenda of the neo- and cultural conservatives. The same coalition won the White House in the 2000 election.

Liberal Perspectives

The liberal **worldview** is quite different from the conservative. First of all, the conception of human nature is more optimistic. Liberals believe that people are born naturally good and do not need to be controlled or forced to work. Rather,

Unemployed worker interviews at job placement service.

they need to be protected from corrupting influences in the wider environment (Popple & Leighninger, 1999). Liberals believe that people are industrious by nature and will take pleasure in hard work and personal accomplishment if conditions are humane.

While liberals do not deny human autonomy and free will totally, they believe that conditions in the social environment strongly affect people's chances to develop their talents and achieve a fulfilling life. From this viewpoint, if people are poor, it is in large part due to lack of opportunity, discrimination, oppression, and the like—problems that lie in the external environment.

It only makes sense that worldview affects political perspectives. Liberals, believing in the inherent goodness of people and the fact that unfavorable conditions in the wider environment may cause harm, support government intervention in the workings of the economic market to try to level the playing field for groups they believe are disadvantaged. For example, liberals tend to support government social welfare programs that provide monetary assistance to poor children and their families. They tend to support affirmative action programs to provide better access to jobs for women and ethnic minorities. They support national programs such as Head Start, which provides early environmental and educational enrichment for poor children to give them a better chance to fully develop their inborn talents (see Exhibit 6).

The major political party in the United States today that supports a liberal perspective is the Democratic party, that of Presidents Kennedy, Johnson, Carter, and Clinton. There are other parties more liberal than the Democratic in the United States; they are much smaller, however. The Green Party is an example. It pro-

The Political Spectrum	
EXHIBIT 6	
Liberal Perspectives	**Conservative Perspectives**
Change can make the world a better place	Change should be resisted; tradition should be maintained
People are born naturally good and industrious	People are born naturally lazy, corrupt, and self-centered
People are strongly influenced and shaped by their environment	People are autonomous and guided entirely by free will
Family is an evolving institution; family forms may change	The traditional family should be upheld; programs designed to help nontraditional families should be opposed
The social system needs regulating; government should intervene in the economic market to assist disadvantaged populations	The social system functions correctly as is; government regulation threatens individual liberty and smooth functioning of the economic market

motes environmental sustainability, community-based economics, grassroots democracy, nonviolence, respect for diversity, feminism, and social justice, among other progressive policies. The party began in Germany and is now a worldwide movement (Karger & Stoesz, 1998).

Neoliberalism

Traditional liberals have viewed government as the best way of bringing **social justice,** or fair access to resources for all, to the many Americans struggling outside the mainstream, However, continuing defeats of Democratic presidential candidates beginning in the late 1960s, all of whom represented liberal positions, forced many other candidates of that persuasion to reconsider their orientation (Karger & Stoesz, 1998). Conservative Republicans who defeated the liberal Democrats campaigned on platforms advocating lower taxes and decreased government spending. To explain the loss of influence of liberal perspectives in the national arena, Mimi Abramovitz (2000, p. 19) writes:

> To convince the public that it stood to gain from a smaller government and weaker social programs, the (conservative) reformers had to undermine the longstanding belief that government should play a large role in society. To this

end, they equated tax-and-spend policies with big government and portrayed popular movements as greedy "special interests" that wanted "too much democracy." Civil rights gains were called reverse discrimination and the victories of the women's and gay rights movements were seen as a threat to "family values."

Voters were urged to "get the government's hand out of their pockets" by voting for conservative candidates, who pledged to lower taxes. The argument apparently appealed to the self-interest of many voters, and increasing numbers of conservative candidates were elected.

In order to survive in this political climate, the Democratic Leadership Council was established in the late 1980s by politicians who became known as neoliberals. Among the founders were Bill Clinton and Albert Gore, elected president and vice president of the nation, respectively, in 1992. Neoliberals distanced themselves from traditional liberals by expressing more favorable attitudes toward big business and more caution about the role of big government (Karger & Stoesz, 1998). They tended to question the value of government aid to poor people. Thus, their overall political stance was to the "right" of traditional liberals. Much of the neoliberal economic agenda, in fact, paralleled that of the neoconservative, although their beliefs in these areas were not to the same degree, and neoliberals generally did not support the cultural agenda of the neoconservatives. In effect, politics as a whole in the United States shifted to the "right" in the final decades of the twentieth century.

Radical Perspectives

The radical perspective, which may be described as "left" of the liberal, is held by a much smaller number of people in this country than either the conservative or liberal, but it is still influential. The radical view of human nature parallels that of the liberal—that people are inherently good and naturally industrious. They will work hard and take pride in their achievements given reasonable working conditions. Like liberals, people who take a radical perspective believe that environmental influences may prevent people from achieving their full potential. But while liberals believe that the environment can potentially be made fair *within* the capitalist system by enlightened government intervention, radicals believe that an elite group of wealthy and powerful people actually makes the important decisions on national policy, so that "the interest group politics that preoccupies liberals is only a sideshow" (Popple & Leighninger, 1999, p. 10).

Since this wealthy and powerful elite make decisions that further their own interests at the expense of others, according to the radical point of view, fairness is not seen as possible under the present capitalist system. Instead, society must be entirely restructured to redistribute wealth and power among all the people. For some radicals, society can be restructured by incremental change; others believe a revolution will be needed.

Probably the major party in the United States today that most nearly reflects the radical perspective is the Socialist party, although it is very small in this country.

The Political Spectrum and Social Welfare Policy

Liberal and conservative positions fall toward opposite ends of the political spectrum, as described above. Conservatives oppose government intervention in the workings of the free market, except to bolster big business, and liberals support intervention to correct imbalances and empower citizens who fall outside the mainstream. As pointed out by Segal and Brzuzy (1998), politics toward the end of the twentieth century were polarized. These authors believe that the political debate involving issues of social welfare must change from "right versus wrong" to what actually benefits the most people. They suggest that a new dialogue must somehow be introduced between people of liberal and conservative persuasions. Otherwise, they fear that the well-being of many unfortunate people will be sacrificed in the ideological battle.

The terrifying events of September 11, 2001, when the World Trade Center and the Pentagon were attacked, seemed to instigate that very possibility: the beginning of a new dialogue. Politicians on both ends of the political spectrum suddenly seemed willing to work together to promote policies that would benefit large numbers of people, at least those affected by the tragedy. Massive federal dollars were directed toward disaster relief. Conservative President George W. Bush agreed to federalize airport security systems in the interest of greater public safety, contrary to his prior insistence that private industry manage these operations. Bipartisan legislation was introduced in Congress to expand Americorps, in an attempt to make it the largest national service program since Franklin Roosevelt's Civilian Conservation Corps during the Great Depression. President Bush supported this legislation, calling Americorps recruits "the perfect foot soldiers in the domestic battle against terrorism" (Stern, 2001). His support reversed former conservative opposition to the program, initiated in 1993 by the Democratic Clinton administration. Applications to Americorps surged by 30 percent after the terrorist attacks as the program became more visible to concerned citizens who wanted to help their beleaguered nation. On the other hand, in response to an economic downturn exacerbated by the terrorist attacks, tax cuts were passed by the House of Representatives returning enormous sums of money to huge corporations rather than to ordinary citizens, clearly in line with the political leanings of its conservative majority. The more liberal Senate attempted to pass a tax plan that aimed more to assist ordinary citizens, for example, by extending unemployment benefits. Both plans were defeated by the end of 2001.

Regarding a politically powerless but personally plucky individual like Sandra McLean, would there be any way that people from both ends of the political spectrum might be willing to assist her? It was a policy change at the *national* level that prompted reassessment of her care in the *local* nursing home and her subsequent rehabilitation and foster home placement. What could a conservative approach have done for Sandra? Under what conditions might the free market have had an interest in helping her? Or should Sandra have been helped even if the free market had no interest in her, given that she was unable to work? If so, why? If not, why not? Students are requested to keep such questions in mind as they read further in this text and others.

INTERNET SITES

http://www.democrat.org/party/dnc	The Democratic National Committee
http://www.rnc.org	The Republican National Committee
http://www.greens.org	The Green Parties of North America
http://www.lp.org	The Libertarian Party
http://liberated.tao.ca/links.htm	Links for Anarchists and Other Radicals
http://www.policyalternatives.ca/	Canadian Centre for Policy Alternatives
http://congress.org	Current issues, votes, debates
http://www.hudson.org/wpc/	Welfare Policy Institute
http://www.cna.org/isaac/Glossb.htm	Nonlinear Dynamics and Complex Systems Theory: Glossary of Terms
http://www.acm.asn.au/what/ strengthsperspective.htm	The Strengths Perspective—Seeing the Potential Instead of the Problem
http://www.projectresilience.com/	Project Resilience
http://homepage.dtn.ntl.com/ terence.p/barefoot/crisis.htm	The Crisis in Social Work: The Radical Solution

SUMMARY

This chapter begins with the case study of Sandra McLean, a young woman who suffered a head injury at birth and could not live independently. Sandra's situation is used to help illustrate the importance of two major types of theoretical perspectives necessary for competent social work practice: those that guide daily practice and those that guide social welfare policy decisions which strongly impact practice.

With respect to social work practice theory, the chapter discusses the influence of systems theory and an ecosystems perspective on today's generalist approach to practice. Levels of intervention included in the generalist approach are discussed as well as the systematic planned change or intervention process that is fundamental as well. The importance of a strengths-based orientation and recognition of client resilience is discussed.

The chapter then discusses basic political theory to help social work students understand different views on government action that will strongly impact practice with clients, who often fall outside the mainstream. Conservative perspectives are contrasted with liberal and radical viewpoints. Neoconservative, cultural conservative, and neoliberal points of view are discussed.

The chapter concludes with a discussion of the political spectrum and how it impacts social welfare policy decisions. Social work students are challenged to think about which political perspective might best assist their clients and to attempt to find ways to encourage people who fall on opposite ends of the political spectrum to work together to improve the lives of all.

KEY TERMS

active treatment
community placement
conservative
cultural conservative
ecosystems perspective
empowerment
family care home
generalist approach
intervention process
levels of intervention

liberal
neoconservative
neoliberal
radical
resilience
social justice
strengths perspective
system
worldview

DISCUSSION QUESTIONS

1. Considering the story of Sandra McLean provided in this chapter, can you think of ways in which social welfare policy may affect social work practice? Can you think of ways in which social welfare policy may directly affect the lives of people such as Sandra?

2. How is the "generalist approach" to social work practice defined in this text? Is this the only way the concept can be defined? What are the three main components of the generalist approach as identified in our definition?

3. Compare classical conservatism with neoconservatism and cultural conservativism.

4. Compare neoliberalism with liberalism. What factors may have led to the development of the neoliberal political movement? What recent president and vice president of the United States helped create this movement?

5. Define the concept of "system." How is the concept of system reflected in the ecosystems perspective? How can a systems approach or ecosystems perspective be helpful to social workers?

6. Describe and discuss the worldview of political conservatives. How does the worldview of conservatives lead people of this persuasion to promote a free market but no government intervention to try to make a better world? Which major American political party can be described as conservative?

7. Describe and discuss the worldview of political liberals. How does the worldview of liberals lead people of this persuasion to promote government intervention to try to make a better world? Which major American political party can be described as liberal?

8. Describe and discuss the worldview of political radicals. Why do they believe that using the regular political process to improve conditions in the United States will not work?

9. From reading about the political spectrum of the United States as briefly described in this text, where do you believe that you personally fit on this spectrum? Would you say that you occupy the same place on the spectrum as your parents? Your siblings? Your friends? Why or why not?

10. Identify and discuss the steps of the planned change or intervention process as identified by the Council on Social Work Education. Why is it important that social workers use a systematic process in their work?

11. What are the levels of intervention that are involved in the generalist approach to social work practice?

12. Which political perspective do you believe can best assist people like Sandra McLean in this chapter's case study? Please give your reasons.

CLASSROOM EXERCISES

While not required, it is suggested that students break into small groups of three or four to discuss these exercises. It may be helpful to choose a scribe to record and report important points to the class after the group discussion.

1. Think about an issue that has been troubling you in your own life, an issue that you are willing to share with your classmates. How much of the issue seems located in the wider environment (beyond your person)? How much seems personal only? How do person and environment interact to produce or maintain this issue? How do you think they will need to interact to best resolve it?

2. If a social worker were to become involved in assisting you to resolve your issue, what levels of intervention do you believe the worker should employ? Why?

3. Many ordinary people are assisted by government social welfare programs, even while they mistakenly believe that these programs only help "other" people. Tax deductions for home mortgages, social security benefits, and student loans are common examples of government welfare programs that help many of us. Identify those that may have helped you or your family now or in the past.

4. Sometimes people are categorized as "haves" or "have-nots," meaning that some people have plenty of resources at their disposal and some do not. Suppose that you are "have-not." Which political philosophy, conservatism or liberalism, do you believe will work best on your behalf? Why?

RESEARCH ACTIVITIES

1. Read your local newspaper to find out what social-welfare-related issues are active in your area. For example, perhaps a controversy exists over the location of a low-income housing project in your city or town, or over a zoning variance required to establish a group home for people with disabilities in your neighborhood.

2. Visit the local offices of the Democratic and Republican parties and examine their literature. Find out the types of policies these parties support on issues of concern to you.

3. Attend a session of your state legislature and observe the political debate process. If you live too far from your state capital, find out where a local governing body meets and attend a meeting

4. Talk with your family and friends about their political affiliations and ask them to tell you the reasons they have made their choices.

INTERNET RESEARCH EXERCISES

1. The National Alliance for the Mentally Ill has a very informative website. They have reported on a Supreme Court decision relative to community placement (http://nami.org/legal/990828c.html).
   a. What was at issue in this case?
   b. What did Justice Ginsberg equate to "unjustified institutional isolation"?
   c. On what two underlying principles was the majority position based?

2. The strengths perspective is a very powerful concept. An interesting paper discussing a practical use of this method was published by the University of Natal in Durban, South Africa (http://www.und.ac.za/und/cadds/Crisp/Mel Gray-Report2.htm).
   a. What was the aim of the CRISP project?
   b. D. Saleebey is cited in the paper. How did he describe the strengths perspective?
   c. Compare the medico-scientific description of a client to that using a strengths perspective approach.

3. One of the great benefits of the Internet is the ease with which groups can work together regardless of their physical location. An example of this is found at http://tiss.zdv.uni-tuebingen.de/webroot/spsba01_W98_1/USA2.htm.
   a. In the paper cited, how does the author compare the welfare systems in the United States with those in Germany?
   b. How does the author compare the approaches to poverty and welfare between Republicans and Democrats?
   c. What is the goal of the social welfare system as seen by what the author identifies as radicals?

REFERENCES

Abramovitz, M. (2000). *Under attack: Fighting back: Women and welfare in the United States.* New York: Monthly Review Press.

Compton, B., & Galaway, B. (1999). *Social work processes* (6th ed.). Pacific Grove, CA: Brooks/Cole.

Council on Social Work Education. (2001). *Educational Policy and Accreditation Standards.* Alexandria, VA: Council on Social Work Education.

Germain, C. B., & Gitterman, A. (1995). Ecological perspective. In *Encyclopedia of social work* (19th ed., pp. 816–822). Washington, DC: NASW Press.

Ginsberg, L. (1998). *Conservative social welfare policy, a description and analysis.* Chicago: Nelson-Hall.

Karger, J. K., & Stoesz, D. (1998). *American social welfare policy, a pluralist approach* (3rd ed). New York: Longman.

Miley, K. K., O'Melia, M., & DuBois, B. L. (1998). *Generalist social work practice* (2nd ed.). Boston: Allyn and Bacon.

Popple, P. R., & Leighninger, L. (1999). *Social work, social welfare and American society* (4th ed). Boston: Allyn and Bacon.

Saleebey, D. (1997). *The strengths perspective in social work practice* (2nd ed). New York: Longman.

Segal, E., & Brzuzy, S. (1998). *Social welfare policies, programs, and practice.* Itasca, IL: Peacock Publishers.

Shaefor, B. W., Horejsi, C. R., & Horejsi, G. A. (2000). *Tactics and guidelines for social work practice* (5th ed.). Boston: Allyn and Bacon.

Sommer, V. L. (1995). The ecological perspective. In M. J. Macy, N. Flax, V. L. Sommer, & R. Swaine, *Directing the baccalaureate social work program, an ecological perspective* (pp. 1–15). Jefferson City, MO: Association for Baccalaureate Social Work Program Directors.

Stern, S. (2001, November 20). New duties, new recruits fuel youth corps. *The Christian Science Monitor,* 4.

Wells, C. (1998). *Stepping to the dance: The training of a family therapist.* Pacific Grove, CA: Brooks/Cole.

Zastrow, C. H. (1999). *The practice of social work* (6th ed). Pacific Grove, CA: Brooks/Cole.

FOR FURTHER READING

Abramovitz, M. (2000). *Under attack: Fighting back: Women and welfare in the United States.* New York: Monthly Review Press.

This excellent little book describes American women's long history of struggle for economic rights. Abramovitz shows clearly that the 1996 Personal Responsibility and Work Opportunity Act, which ended entitlement for government aid for poor mothers and their children, was simply another setback in a long struggle for equality and respect for women's rights in this country.

Compton, B., & Galaway, B. (1999). *Social work processes* (6th ed.). Pacific Grove, CA: Brooks/Cole.

A classic text on social work practice that has survived through several editions, this is an excellent source of information on systems theory and how it can be used in social work practice.

Germain, C. B., & Gitterman, A. (1995). Ecological perspective. In *Encyclopedia of social work* (19th ed., pp. 816–822). Washington, DC: NASW Press.

Germain and Gitterman describe their concept of the ecological perspective in detail in this article. They outline and define multiple concepts that are important in this perspective, including ones that have been newly added by contemporary theorists.

Ginsberg, L. (1998). *Conservative social welfare policy: A description and analysis.* Chicago: Nelson-Hall.

Ginsberg provides a detailed historical perspective on the development of American social welfare policies and identifies persistent themes. He then examines how political orientation shapes perception of those themes. He examines conservative political policies and their impact on social welfare legislation, and the impact of conservative economic perspectives on social policy.

Karger, J. K., & Stoesz, D. (1998). *American social welfare policy: A pluralist approach* (3rd ed.). New York: Longman.

A very readable text on social welfare policy, this book examines the American political economy and describes the impact of the American political continuum on social welfare policy in the first chapter. Further discussion of the impact of multiple political perspectives on American social welfare policy is found throughout the book.

Popple, P., & Leighninger, L. (1999). *Social work, social welfare and American society* (4th ed.). Boston: Allyn and Bacon.

This text provides an in-depth discussion of competing perspectives of social welfare in the first chapter. The worldview of conservatives, liberals, and radicals is explained in depth, including attitudes toward change, views of human nature, views of the family, and views of government and the economic system. Further discussion of these topics is found throughout the book.

Social Welfare Policies and the Birth of the Profession: Historical Highlights

JUANITA CHAVEZ

Juanita cheered when she was offered the job as a social worker at Urban Neighborhood Center. A recent BSW graduate, Juanita knew she was competing for the position with more experienced workers. But she had an important skill: She spoke both Spanish and English fluently. Moreover, as part of the requirements of her social work major, she had served her senior-year field placement in an alternative school where Spanish was the first language of many of the students. Urban Neighborhood Center was located in an area where many residents were of Hispanic origin. Juanita hoped her bilingual abilities would help her get the job. They did.

Juanita had now been working for several months. She felt she was developing a broad understanding of the needs of the neighborhood as a whole that surrounded the agency. As part of her job, she was expected to help identify major needs of community residents, to inform residents about the services available at the center, and to provide them with information as appropriate concerning community resources that might help meet their needs. The Center provided after-school recreational programs for school-age children, limited tutoring services, and a food pantry staffed by volunteers. Lately, however, the food pantry had been short on supplies and hungry people had been sent home empty-handed.

Juanita liked the fact that her position gave her a broad perspective of the neighborhood in which she worked—indeed of the midsized city of which the neighborhood was a part. That knowledge could be disturbing, however. For example, the city had recently implemented a new program for poor parents called **Temporary Assistance for Needy Families (TANF),** *as required under the 1996 federal Personal Responsibility and Work Opportunity Act (PRWOA). TANF replaced the former program called Aid to Families with Dependent Children (AFDC) and required most parents to enter the paid job market or in some cases to attend job training programs.*

Juanita's first crisis call on the job related to TANF, and she remembered it well. A volunteer helping supervise a recreational program had called Juanita just as the new social worker was trying to organize her tiny office. Two children much too young for the agency's after-school programs, and much too young to be out on the streets alone, had been brought in by a school-age child who regularly came to the agency. The child said she had found the toddlers on the sidewalk, crying and apparently lost. Juanita soon encountered the young children, ages approximately two and three, who said their names were Tomas and Tomacita. They could not provide an address. They said they had been put to bed for a nap by their mother, but when they awakened, she was gone. Frightened, they began to search for her.

77

Juanita decided that she would have to call Protective Services to report abandoned children. Because the situation was not perceived as an emergency by the city's overburdened department, however, no worker arrived at Urban Neighborhood Center for several hours. Toward the end of the day, one of the longtime agency social workers returned after having made some home visits. By good fortune, this worker recognized Tomas and Tomacita and knew that they were siblings of a teenage girl who sometimes attended tutoring programs at the agency. There was a family telephone number on file. A call was made immediately, and a distraught mother answered. She had had to report to job training that day under the rules of the TANF program, she explained. Her older daughter, who usually babysat, was involved in an after-school field trip, and the neighbor who had promised to substitute had been unavailable at the last minute. The children's mother didn't dare miss her job training as she could then be eliminated from the TANF program. That would take away her only source of money for food and rent. She knew people who had missed a single day of training due to lack of child care who had already been dismissed. So Tomas and Tomacita's mother had opted to take a serious risk, hoping her children would remain asleep.

The children's mother and the protective services worker arrived at Urban Neighborhood Center at almost the same moment. Only the advocacy of the agency social worker who knew the mother prevented the children from being taken into the foster care system then and there. Had that happened, months might have passed before Tomas and Tomacita were returned home. Their mother promised, of course, never to leave the children again without a babysitter. The protective services worker scolded her for not taking advantage of child care that was supposed to be provided by the TANF program. The mother explained that she had applied for child care months before but that it hadn't come through yet.

Juanita learned later that child care, while theoretically available to poor mothers enrolled in TANF, in reality involved a long waiting list in her city. Soon Tomas and Tomacita's older sister was missing school regularly so that the mother could attend job training. The ability to secure a pay check to purchase food and shelter was naturally perceived by this family as more important than education. Juanita soon became aware of many other families who lived near Urban Neighborhood Center who were in the same situation. Many parents, languishing somewhere on TANF waiting lists for child care, depended on older children to babysit so they could go to work. Others with regular jobs earned wages too low to afford child care and also depended on their older children, especially teenage girls, to babysit. These helpful teens risked truancy proceedings, adding to family difficulties.

Juanita was beginning to collect data on a number of high school girls in her area who were routinely missing school to babysit for younger siblings. She hoped eventually to influence legislators to appropriate more funds for child care. Juanita also hoped to see a Spanish-speaking day care center established, because none yet existed in the city. She even approached her agency's board of directors to ask them to consider establishing one at Urban Neighborhood Center. She was excited when the board appointed a committee to study the situation and appointed Juanita a member. Juanita was now involved in conducting a door-to-door survey to find out how many families would take part in such a service if it were available.

79

CHAPTER 3
*Social Welfare
Policies and the
Birth of the
Profession:
Historical
Highlights*

As Juanita walked up the steps of a tiny, single-family cottage one day collecting data for her survey, she noticed that one of the special school vans that transport students with disabilities was pulling up to the door. The driver honked, and then asked Juanita to knock, since he needed to deliver a child. No one answered the door, however, and the driver explained that he would have to take the child back to school. Juanita could see the sad face of a little girl peering out of the side window of the bus. Her head was misshapen and too large for her features. The driver muttered something about irresponsible mothers, shook his head, and drove away.

Juanita returned to the cottage later that day. This time her knock was answered by a young woman who appeared to be in her early twenties. Juanita explained who she was and why she had dropped by earlier. The woman looked blank, and then said in a heavy accent, "I no speak English." Juanita then greeted the young woman in Spanish. Her reward was an enormous, engaging smile. When Juanita mentioned the incident with the bus, however, the young woman's face took on an alarmed expression. She invited Juanita inside. She introduced herself as Carla Romero. "You say you are a social worker from Neighborhood Center?" she asked in Spanish. Juanita nodded. "Maybe you can help me, then." Carla continued.

"Tell me how I can assist," Juanita replied in Spanish, and the young woman began her story.

Carla told Juanita that her young daughter, Maria, was physically and cognitively disabled due to complications of birth that had resulted in permanent swelling of the brain. Now six years old, Maria functioned at a 12-month level. She had to be constantly supervised. But Carla had to work to support herself and the child. Her exhusband, father of the child, kept in touch but had returned to Puerto Rico from where the couple had come. Child support checks were few and far between. Carla went to work when Maria began public school at the age of three. The little girl received skilled service at school: occupational, physical, and speech therapy. Lately, however, there had been an embarrassing problem. The school nurse had sent Maria home with head lice. Carla had bought a number of products from the neighborhood pharmacy and used them carefully, but a few nits, or eggs, seemed to persist no matter what Carla did. The child continued to be sent home.

Carla, since she could not speak English, had already had a neighbor call the school to explain that she was doing all she could. The neighbor asked politely if the child could remain in school in spite of a few nits because her mother, Carla, had to work to provide food and shelter for the family. But the school nurse insisted that Maria could not attend school unless she was nit-free. The next day Juanita called the nurse. She got the same story: No exceptions. Juanita called the health department for assistance. There she learned that certain strains of lice were currently resisting all remedies available in the store. The health department had effective treatments, a nurse there told her, but due to funding cuts, the staff could no longer provide services to help with this problem. Lice were no longer considered a "communicable disease" under current funding definitions! The nurse suggested taking the child to a doctor and fumigating the house.

Carla was fortunate in that, while her job was very low wage and did not provide any benefits such as health insurance, she was nevertheless able to take her daughter to the doctor and to save enough money to pay for fumigating the house. That was be-

cause Maria qualified for both Medicaid and Supplemental Security Income (programs authorized under the Social Security Act) as a severely disabled child. The doctor told the young mother, however, that he did not know of any better treatment for lice or nits than the over-the-counter remedies she was already purchasing in the local stores. Carla then bought another standard treatment at the neighborhood pharmacy. She also had the house fumigated. But the problem continued.

Carla called Juanita at Urban Neighborhood Center in desperation after her daughter was sent home from school for the third month in a row. Her neighbor was babysitting regularly now, but she was not happy about it and the cost was taking up most of Carla's food budget. The young mother frequently had to turn to Neighborhood Center's food pantry, but sometimes even the pantry was out of supplies. Juanita called the health department again, explaining that Carla had done everything she could but still her child was being sent home from school. The department continued to insist that they had no staff to deal with the problem. In desperation, Carla shaved Maria's head. Even that did not work! Tiny nits persisted, and Maria continued to be sent home. Juanita had angry words with the school nurse, explaining that the little girl, through no fault of her own, was missing out on valuable therapies at school and that her physical condition was deteriorating as a result. But the nurse, perhaps understandably, was unmovable.

Then Juanita had an inspiration. She called the social worker at the school Maria attended. That worker was aware of the problem and had already tried to intervene with the school nurse, but to no avail. But this worker and Juanita agreed that they would both make impassioned pleas to the health department. The health department refused once more, pleading budget cuts. Finally, the school social worker had her supervisor call the health department. That worked. At last, a public health nurse visited the Romero home. Juanita was present at the appointment, serving as translator and family advocate. The nurse promptly diagnosed Maria's strain of lice precisely and provided an effective remedy. Little Maria went back to school. But she had lost out on four months of education and therapy at an important developmental stage.

The Romero family's problem was not unique, of course. In Juanita's rounds of the neighborhood to collect information for her survey, she found that little Maria was not the only child missing school because of resistant strains of head lice. She also found several teenage girls at home taking care of babies, sometimes their younger siblings but sometimes their own children. Unable to afford the child care that would have enabled them to stay in school, they dropped out. They were lucky if their parents let them continue to live at home, because most jobs available to people without high school degrees paid too low a wage to cover rent, food, and clothing.

Juanita also found several children in the neighborhood who stayed out on the streets after school because their parents had to work long hours and could not be home to supervise. Local schools offered a few sports programs for boys, but programs for girls were lacking. She also learned to her surprise that many of the families who used the agency's food pantry included full-time workers; some of the larger families included two full-time working parents yet still could not make ends meet. Wages were simply too low to cover expenses for a family, so cupboards stood empty at times.

Juanita decided to take the results of her survey back to Urban Neighborhood Center's board of directors. Perhaps with a number of caring minds working on the problems she documented, effective solutions might be generated, including ways to raise new funds to finance new programs. As a social work professional, Juanita believed she could make a difference, especially if she could combine her problem-solving efforts and energies with those of other dedicated people committed to the agency and the surrounding community.

THE INSTITUTION OF SOCIAL WELFARE

We live in a complicated society. For example, while certain societal policies such as social and economic discrimination tend to create poverty in the first place, other societal efforts attempt to alleviate poverty. Many of the families living near Urban Neighborhood Center were poor, for example, as described in the preceding case study, possibly due to discrimination against people of ethnic minority background. A few public programs assisted them to some degree: the TANF program in which Tomas and Tomacita's mother was enrolled, and Supplemental Security Income (SSI) and Medicaid for which Maria Romero qualified as a severely disabled child. TANF is a cash benefit program run by the county (established under state law according to federal guidelines). SSI is a cash benefit program for certain categories of poor people administered by the federal government, and Medicaid is a federal program administered by the state that provides medical care for certain categories of poor people. These programs are all part of our nation's system or institution of social welfare.

What is "**social welfare**"? The *Social Work Dictionary* (Barker, 1987, p. 154) defines it as "a nation's system of programs, benefits, and services that help people meet those social, economic, educational and health needs that are fundamental to the maintenance of society." Is social welfare the same as social work? Not exactly, although the two are certainly related.

Social work, as described in Chapter 1, is a profession with the purpose of assisting people to improve their lives. Social welfare, in contrast to social work, is a system or institution (set of established practices) within a given nation. The purpose of this institution is not only to help individual people meet their basic needs but also to help the nation as a whole maintain stability. Social work is really only one profession among many that can be considered part of our nation's institution of social welfare. Other professions that also contribute to helping people meet social, economic, educational, and health needs are medicine, education, library science, and law, to name only a few. Because many of the decisions and referrals a social worker makes rely on familiarity with the various programs available within the social welfare system, we will focus on them before turning to the fields of practice explored in Part Two of this book.

Social Welfare Concepts: Residual versus Institutional

Wilensky and Lebeaux (1965) pointed out almost 50 years ago that our country holds two dominant conceptions of social welfare: residual and institutional. These distinctions seem valid today.

Those who endorse the residual approach to social welfare believe that people should normally be able to meet all their needs through their own family or through the job market. Only after the family and the job market have "failed" should the formal social welfare system get involved. Under these circumstances the assistance is considered "residual"; it is activated only as a temporary, emergency measure. Services are accompanied by the stigma of "charity," as they imply personal failure. The intent is that they be short-term, lasting only for the duration of the emergency.

Under the institutional conception, social welfare services are viewed as "normal, first line functions of modern industrial society" (Wilensky and Lebeaux, p. 138). According to the institutional view, social welfare services should be offered routinely as part of normal, nonemergency problem-solving processes; they should be available without stigma to help prevent further problems. This approach assumes that in a complex society everyone needs assistance at times. For example, even the best workers may lose their jobs when a company downsizes.

The social welfare system in the United States today reflects both the residual and the institutional approaches. Historically, the residual approach is older. Developments during and after the Great Depression of the 1930s pulled the social welfare system strongly toward the institutional concept, however. Then, during the 1970s, conservative politicians and presidential administrations began to pull it back toward the residual approach. This pull continues today. The two concepts of social welfare are outlined in Exhibit 1.

Now, let us examine the historical roots of the social welfare system in the United States, because what happened in the past has shaped what the system looks like today.

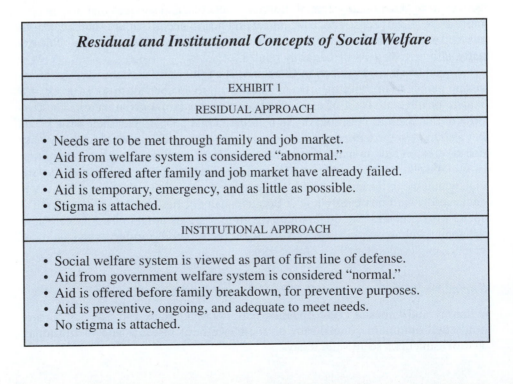

Residual and Institutional Concepts of Social Welfare

EXHIBIT 1

RESIDUAL APPROACH

- Needs are to be met through family and job market.
- Aid from welfare system is considered "abnormal."
- Aid is offered after family and job market have already failed.
- Aid is temporary, emergency, and as little as possible.
- Stigma is attached.

INSTITUTIONAL APPROACH

- Social welfare system is viewed as part of first line of defense.
- Aid from government welfare system is considered "normal."
- Aid is offered before family breakdown, for preventive purposes.
- Aid is preventive, ongoing, and adequate to meet needs.
- No stigma is attached.

Old-World Historical Roots

83

CHAPTER 3
*Social Welfare
Policies and the
Birth of the
Profession:
Historical
Highlights*

Social welfare policy is controversial today, and perhaps it always has been. Questions inevitably arise about who to help and how much. We may think we want to help our neighbor, but how much? And are we interested in helping a stranger at all?

The earliest form of assistance for the needy was probably mother caring for child. Mutual aid among adults familiar with each other would be another example of help for the needy in early times, when reciprocal helping roles were provided by extended family members or members of one's tribe.

Only when more formal institutions had developed could a concept like "aid to the stranger" arise. One of the earliest known forms of aid to the stranger was provided by religious groups. In Judeo-Christian tradition, almsgiving was commonly practiced. The commandment "Love thy neighbor," accentuated in the New Testament but based on early scripture, motivated people to give of what they had. Many believed that aiding the needy would provide a means of salvation in the next world. Some religious groups established formal tithes, with a portion of the money raised being used for assistance to the poor. Such assistance was certainly residual in nature, since it was offered as temporary charity in times of emergency.

England provided the model for social welfare provisions in its colonies in America, and so we will focus on the social welfare history of that country. Responsibility for the poor in England remained primarily a function of the church until the arrival of the Black Death (bubonic plague) from continental Europe in 1348. So many people died that a labor shortage resulted. In 1349, a law was passed called The Statute of Laborers, which forbade able-bodied people to leave their parishes and required them to accept any work available. Alms were forbidden to the able-bodied (Karger & Stoesz, 1998). Such a law clearly reflected the interests of the ruling class. Since the time of the plague, many secular laws relating to the poor have been designed to control the labor supply at least as much as to relieve the suffering of the destitute.

Throughout the 1500s the Commercial Revolution grew, and feudalism declined. Tenants were evicted from the land, sometimes in order to make room for sheep, whose wool was increasingly valuable in the manufacture of cloth. Large numbers of destitute people went looking for work in the cities, where they found themselves crowding into urban slums. The resulting poverty and social need led to government assumption of more responsibility for social welfare. In England, legislation culminated in the famous Elizabethan Poor Law of 1601 (Whitaker & Federico, 1997). The Elizabethan Poor Law was brought by the first colonists to America. Its concepts still influence current thinking about provisions for the poor in this country and, hence, affect current law.

The Elizabethan Poor Law and the Act of Settlement

The Elizabethan Poor Law of 1601 was the first public legislation establishing a governmental system to meet the needs of the poor. The law established which unit was responsible to assist whom. By establishing which categories of people were eligible for what kind of assistance, the law also was geared toward social control (Segal and Brzuzy, 1998).

The local governmental unit, usually the parish (a geographic area similar to a county), was to maintain its own poor, and taxes could be levied for this purpose. An overseer of the poor—a public official, not a member of the clergy—was to be appointed. Families were to take care of their own (reflecting the residual concept of social welfare). Whenever possible, grandparents were responsible to care for children and grandchildren, and similarly, children and grandchildren were responsible for parents and grandparents.

Poor people were divided into categories, and relief was provided according to the category. Two of the categories, the impotent poor and dependent children, were considered "deserving" and so were offered aid. Children were to be indentured, or placed in the service of whoever would charge the parish the least amount of money for their care (the "lowest bidder"). The impotent poor (the old, the blind, and people otherwise disabled) were to be either put into an **almshouse (indoor relief)** or offered aid in their own homes (**outdoor relief**), depending on which plan would be least expensive to the parish.

The category of able-bodied poor was not considered deserving. These people were treated punitively. Alms were prohibited. People who came from outside the parish (**vagrants**) were to be sent away. Able-bodied poor who were residents were to be forced to go to a **workhouse,** where living conditions were hard and work was long and tedious. If they refused, they were to be whipped or jailed or put in stocks (Johnson, 1995; Federico, 1984).

The intent of the Elizabethan Poor Law of 1601 was that almshouses and workhouses should be separate institutions, with the almshouses meeting the special needs of the "deserving" sick and infirm. In practice, most communities that built such facilities combined them into one building for the sake of expense. Records indicate that people dreaded going into such places (see Exhibit 2).

Minor adjustments to the law were made over the years; an important change in 1662 increased parish control over poor people. Quadagno (1982, p. 95) writes that "overseers, conscious of the desire of ratepayers to keep rates down, did all they could to prevent paupers from becoming chargeable to the parish." The Settlement Act of 1662 required every person to be enrolled as a resident in some parish somewhere. Procedures establishing residency were complex. Persons who could not prove legal residence in the parish where they were living could be declared vagrants and sent away, in order that they not become financial burdens on the parish in the future.

New Concepts in Poor Law

Two acts were passed in England in 1795 that temporarily improved the condition of the poor. One act forbade parishes to drive nonresidents away unless they actually applied for relief. The other, the Speenhamland Act, introduced new concepts into poor law. This act was a humane response to rising prices of wheat. Rather than force poor able-bodied people into workhouses after they were destitute, the law established a wage supplement to help prevent destitution. The size of the supplement was determined according to both the number of children in a family and the price of bread.

Improvement of the condition of the poor was temporary under this act because the law did not include a requirement for a minimum wage. The gentry tended to lower the wages they paid, and the difference was picked up through the wage supplement that was financed by taxes paid by small farmers (Quadagno, 1982). Hence, before long, taxpayers strongly opposed the law.

85

CHAPTER 3
*Social Welfare
Policies and the
Birth of the
Profession:
Historical
Highlights*

A Workhouse Experience

EXHIBIT 2

Q: And, in your opinion, many of the old people in your union would rather die than go to the workhouse?

A: Very many of them; they would rather, sir. . .

Q: Did you find that work severe?

A: No, not severe; monotonous. You did not know what to do. You could not go out to write a letter, or to read, or to do anything: you had no time of your own; in fact, it was a place of punishment, and not relief. . . .

Q: Would you state any other objections you have to the treatment of the aged poor?

A: I think the taskmaster is very much more severe than he should be.

Q: In what way?

A: Well, when you go to dine, or to breakfast, or anything like that, he says, "come quicker," and pushes you partly into the seat; that is a very trifling thing. I had a sore throat, and he objected to my wearing a scarf around my throat and he said, "I will pull those rags off you when you come back here again." That is, if I went back again. "You must not wear such things as this." I said, "I have a sore throat," and he says, "I don't care whether you and your father and your grandfather had sore throats." My father died of starvation through his throat growing together, and he suffered with sore throat. I suffered with sore throat, but not much; still, sufficient.

Q: Did you complain to the master of the workhouse of the language and treatment by the man you call the taskmaster?

A: No, my lord, not the slightest good in doing that.

Q: Why?

A: Whatever the taskmaster wished the master to say, the master would say. They were all under one control, even the doctor, and everybody was the same.

Source: Quoted from Jill Quadagno. (1982). *Aging in early industrial society: Work, family, and social policy in nineteenth century England.* New York: Academic Press, 107–110.

In 1834 the New Poor Law reinstated most of the provisions of the Elizabethan Poor Law and introduced a new principle known as **less eligibility.** This was based on the idea that "pauperism was willful and the condition of the pauper who was relieved should be worse than the condition of the poorest, independent, self-supporting laborer" (Quadagno, 1982, pp. 97–98).

Today, as a similar example, our nation has a minimum wage law, but the minimum wage leaves a family of three (e.g., husband, wife, and child) below the poverty level. A full-time worker with a family thus may qualify for public relief such as food stamps. Taxpayers' anger tends to focus on people who receive such assistance rather than on employers who profit from low wages.

POOR RELIEF IN THE UNITED STATES

Each colony in America enacted its own version of the Elizabethan Poor Law of 1601; Plymouth Colony was the first, in 1642. Ideas such as settlement and less eligibility, although codified under English law after the original colonization of America, continued to influence colonial attitudes.

After the American Revolution, the U.S. Constitution separated functions of state and federal governments, and assistance to the poor became a state prerogative. The federal government did not become involved until the end of the Civil War, in 1865, when the first national agency for social welfare was established: the Freedmen's Bureau. Through the Freedmen's Bureau, federal taxes supported free educational programs and financial assistance for former slaves for a few short years (Lieby, 1987). The bureau was disbanded in 1872 as a result of political infighting.

Values

Values strongly affected American poor law, and like the law itself, the major religious and cultural values of the United States originated in the Old World. Religious doctrines of various traditions taught that rich and poor alike should give what they could for others, motivated by love and compassion, not fear.

During the Protestant Reformation of the sixteenth century, many of these teachings were questioned. A Protestant ethic of salvation by hard work challenged the older notion of salvation by helping people in need. Puritan Calvinists, for example, "decreed one either saved or damned, a member of the elect or not. Charitable works could not alter this decision, for it was made eternally by God. One could, however, find out or at least seek indications of one's future celestial status" (Tropman, 1989). While no one could know for sure, many people came to believe that prosperity indicated one was among the elect and that poverty meant one was not among the elect. From this point of view, why help the poor?

Also in conflict with older religious and humanitarian ideals to help the unfortunate were new ideas from philosophy and economics. In *The Wealth of Nations* (1776), Adam Smith argued in favor of the principle that became known as laissez-faire: that government should not interfere in the "natural functioning" of the market by imposing interference such as taxes. The market should be allowed to perform solely according to the influences of supply and demand. Taxation to support poor people interfered with the rights of the wealthy and only created dependency among the poor, according to Smith's argument.

Thomas Malthus, an economic philosopher and clergyman, published *An Essay on the Principle of Population* in 1798. In it, he argued that relief for the poor contributed to overpopulation and that surplus population would result in disaster. Also contributing to reluctance to help the poor was Herbert Spencer's philosophy known as social Darwinism. Influenced by biological theories of evolution discussed in Charles Darwin's book *On the Origin of Species* (1859), Spencer preached that only the fittest people should survive. Poor people should be allowed to perish as they are demonstrably unable to compete (Karger and Stoesz, 1998). Such an argument overlooked the fact that no individual member of the human species could survive without the cooperation, as opposed to the competition, of others. For example, not a single person could survive infancy without the assistance and cooperation of others.

Do any of these arguments for or against aid to poor people sound familiar? Although some are centuries old, these ideas and values still affect societal responses to poor people today. Obviously, the value base underlying the social welfare system is complicated and conflicting. Conflicting values in social and political arenas affect what happens in social welfare legislation; in turn, social welfare legislation affects the resources available to social work practitioners and their clients.

87

CHAPTER 3
*Social Welfare
Policies and the
Birth of the
Profession:
Historical
Highlights*

The Charity Organization Society and the Settlement House Movement

The effects of values on approaches to social welfare in the United States are seen particularly clearly in two movements in private charity that strongly affected relief measures beginning in the 1880s. These movements, the Charity Organization Society and the Settlement Movement, have been introduced in Chapter 1 and will be discussed more fully here because they, along with a more diffuse child welfare movement to be discussed in Chapter 5, led to the birth of the social work profession. The two movements differed markedly in philosophy and methods.

The Charity Organization Society (COS) began in England in 1869; its first office in the United States opened in Buffalo, New York, in 1877 (Popple, 1995). Leaders of the COS believed that many poor people were unworthy, so that applicants for aid should be carefully investigated. Records were to be kept about each case, and a central registry was developed to ensure that no person received aid from more than one source. The principal form of help to be offered should be "moral uplift," which was to be provided by "friendly visitors." Most of the visitors were women recruited from the upper class. Not only were these the persons who had the most time to volunteer, but, due to the patriarchal nature of the era, church-related, unpaid work was among the few outlets for their talents.

The methods developed by the COS were used as models for local public agencies; organization, investigation, and written records proved very useful in welfare work. Mary Richmond, a well-known leader of the COS movement in the United States, taught in the first social work training school, the New York School of Philanthropy (now the Columbia University School of Social Work), begun in 1898. The COS replaced most friendly visitors with paid staff by the early 1900s, partly because there were not enough volunteers and partly because volunteers were found to lack appropriate expertise (Popple, 1995).

The settlement movement, in contrast, involved concepts of self-help and mutual aid rather than moral uplift. Jane Addams, one of the movement's most famous leaders, established Hull House in Chicago in 1889. Settlement work arose in response to continuing pressures of the Industrial Revolution, which brought large numbers of immigrants to American cities, where they were forced to work long hours in factories under dangerous, unhealthful conditions.

Settlement houses brought idealistic young people, including many women of upper-class background, into the slums to live and work with less-fortunate people. Settlement staff assisted immigrants in organizing into self-help groups and established **mutual aid** services ranging from day nurseries to garbage collection

Children enjoy social activities at a neighborhood center.

to organization of cultural events. In addition, settlement house staff and neighborhood participants became involved in political processes, advocating for better working conditions in the factories, better sanitation in the cities, and protective legislation for women and children.

Birth of the Social Work Profession: A Brief History

Although differing in philosophy and approach, the Charity Organization Society and the settlement movement cooperated to work on common causes. For example, records kept by COS workers often provided written evidence for settlement workers to use in advocating for social reform. They documented that poverty often resulted not from "unworthiness" but from low wages, illness, and injury on the job. In effect, COS workers were the first modern social case workers, focusing their change efforts on individuals and families. Settlement workers were the first modern social group workers, community organizers, and social activists (Lieby, 1987; Brieland, 1995) (see Exhibit 3).

The casework individual-cure approach that was characteristic of the Charity Organization Society was strongly shaped by residual thinking (as described earlier in this chapter). The settlement movement, in contrast, was an early manifestation of the institutional approach. Most social workers today are influenced by both residual and institutional thinking. Instead of moral uplift as the basis for casework services, however, personal development is a more characteristic goal.

Education for social work began, as described earlier, with the commencement of the summer training program in New York in 1898, run by the Charity Organization Society, which eventually became the New York School of Philan-

89

CHAPTER 3
*Social Welfare
Policies and the
Birth of the
Profession:
Historical
Highlights*

Charity Organization Society and Settlement Movement Compared

EXHIBIT 3

COS	Settlement Movement
LEADER	
Mary Richmond	Jane Addams
TYPE OF WORKER	
"Friendly visitors"	Volunteers who lived among poor
TYPE OF AID OFFERED	
Central registry of poor	Mutual aid
Short-term charity	Self-help
Moral uplift	Social and political action
PRIMARY LEVEL OF INTERVENTION	
Casework with individuals and families	Group work; work with organizations and communities

thropy. Other social work education programs were established soon afterwards—for example, the Chicago Institute of Social Science in 1903 and the School for Social Workers in Boston in 1904. New fields of work for social workers followed. Medical social work began at Massachusetts General Hospital in 1905, sponsored by Dr. Richard C. Cabot, and public schools began to use social workers in 1906 (Popple, 1995). A profession was forming, although with many different branches.

In 1915, Abraham Flexner made an influential report declaring that social work was not yet a full profession, in that he believed it lacked sufficient "educationally communicable technique." Flexner's report led to a preoccupation with psychiatrically oriented casework, because many social workers believed this function to be more "professional" according to his criteria. The preoccupation lasted through the 1920s to the neglect of settlement work, group work, and community work (Popple, 1995). Nevertheless, the Milford Conference in the mid-1920s identified eight generic aspects of casework across separate fields and "defined the distinguishing concern of social casework as the capacity of individuals to structure their social activities within a given environment" (Brieland, 1995, p. 2250). Thus, there was some recognition even in the 1920s that social work intervention should include an environmental component.

After the Great Depression struck in 1929, many social workers became government workers in Roosevelt's New Deal programs. However, most government social workers were baccalaureate-level and were not considered professionals or accepted into social work professional organizations of the time. After the Depression, during the 1940s through the 1960s, MSWs reasserted their dominance, and the profession concentrated again on mental health and techniques of working with individuals (Popple, 1995).

In 1952, the Council on Social Work Education (CSWE) was formed, replacing the American Association of Schools of Social Work (representing graduate education) and the National Association of Schools of Social Administration (representing undergraduate education). Unfortunately, the CSWE initially accredited graduate programs only; this policy continued for nearly 20 years. In effect, undergraduate-trained social workers were eliminated from the profession in the 1950s and 1960s. When the National Association of Social Workers (NASW) was formed in 1955, combining seven previous social work organizations, BSWs were not allowed membership (Popple, 1995).

In 1957, Earnest Greenwood published a classic article, "Attributes of a Profession." In it, he identified several major attributes of a profession, and offered the conclusion that social work was now a full profession according to these attributes. Social work had apparently "made it."

However, social work had narrowed its focus primarily to psychiatric case work to gain the status of profession. Events of the 1960s were to widen the attention of the profession again. President Lyndon Johnson's War on Poverty brought many social workers into the national effort to empower the poor. Baccalaureate workers especially became involved, raising their visibility. Social work's historical interest in the poor was rekindled. Schools broadened their curricula to include courses on planning, administration, and research (Popple, 1995). In 1970, NASW decided to allow BSWs from "approved" baccalaureate education programs to become full members of the organization. In 1974, the Council on Social Work Education began to accredit baccalaureate education programs for the first time. Currently, the educational model is that BSW students and first-year master's students are prepared to become generalists, and second-year MSW students study various concentrations (Brieland, 1995).

Currently there are over 400 baccalaureate education programs in the United States, four times the number of graduate programs. BSW and MSW programs have roughly equal influence within the CSWE. The BSW is viewed as the entry-level professional degree, while the MSW provides advanced training (Popple, 1995).

SOCIAL LEGISLATION IN THE TWENTIETH CENTURY

The history of social welfare in the United States in the twentieth century revealed, according to James Lieby, an increasing role over time for both public and private nonsectarian agencies (agencies not affiliated with particular religious groups). Lieby believes that "it is helpful to analyze this general trend in three periods: 1900–1930, when the action was at the level of local and state governments and local private agencies organized under the Community Chest; 1930–1968, when the federal government took important initiatives; and since 1968, when the progress of the 'welfare state' has seemed to stop if not turn back." (Lieby, 1987, p. 765). While Lieby made this observation several years ago, further developments fit his description. The welfare State's trend toward turning back was highlighted in 1996 by the passage of the Personal Responsibility and Work Opportunity Act (PRWOA), which will be discussed further on. See the time line in Exhibit 4.

91

CHAPTER 3
Social Welfare
Policies and the
Birth of the
Profession:
Historical
Highlights

Time Line: Major Historical Events in Social Welfare and Social Work

EXHIBIT 4

1348	Black death. Feudal system begins to break down.
1349	Statute of Laborers (England).
1500s	Accelerated breakdown of feudal system (Commercial Revolution)
1601	Elizabethan Poor Law (England)
1642	Plymouth Colony enacts first colonial poor law, based on English Poor Law
1662	Settlement Act (England; idea migrates to colonies)
1795	Speenhamland Act (England)
1834	New Poor Law (England)
1865	Freedmen's Bureau (USA—ends in 1872)
1869	First Charity Organization Society (COS), London, England
1877	First COS in United States, Buffalo, NY
1884	First settlement house (Toynbee Hall, London)
1886	First settlement house in USA (Neighborhood Guild, NYC)
1889	Hull House, Chicago
1898	First formal social work education program (summer training by COS in NYC; evolves into New York School of Philanthropy, later Columbia School of Social Work)
1915	Flexner's report concluding social work is not a full profession
1917	First organization for social workers, National Workers Exchange
1919	American Association of Schools of Social Work formed (AASSW)
1921	American Association of Social Workers formed (from National Social Workers Exchange)
1928	Milford Conference. Determines social work is a single profession
1929	Stock market crash leads to Great Depression
	International Council on Social Welfare (ICSW) founded in Paris
1933	President Franklin D. Roosevelt launches "New Deal" program
1935	Social Security Act signed into law
1936	National Association of Schools of Social Administration (NASSA) established

(Continued)

1952	Council on Social Work Education (CSWE) forms, merging AASSW and NASSA; accredits MSW programs
1955	National Association of Social Workers (NASW) forms, merging seven separate social work organizations; accepts MSWs only
1956	International Federation of Social Workers (IFSW) established; membership consists of national social work organizations
1957	Greenwood article declares social work a full profession
1964	President Lyndon Johnson launches the War on Poverty
1967	The Work Incentive Program (WIN) established under the Social Security Act
1970	NASW admits baccalaureate social workers as members
1974	CSWE begins accreditation of baccalaureate social work education programs; Supplementary Security Income program established under the Social Security Act for aged, blind, and disabled; category of poor children omitted
1981	WIN program eliminated under the Reagan administration
1988	Family Support Act; parents receiving aid for dependent children under the Social Security Act must work when child is three
1996	Personal Responsibility and Work Opportunity Act signed into law by President Bill Clinton; eliminates right of poor children and parents to aid under Social Security Act; establishes Temporary Assistance to Needy Families (TANF) program
2000	Push by President George W. Bush to privatize formerly public assistance programs and provide federal funding to "faith-based" programs

The Progressive Years, 1900–1930

The early 1900s were a time of reform in the United States. Later, World War I slowed down reform efforts but did not entirely eliminate them. Women, for example, first gained the vote after the war, in 1920. Activists such as those involved in the settlement movement advocated and in many cases secured laws for the protection of women and dependent children, for better sanitation, and for better safety conditions in the factories. By 1920, 43 states had passed workers' compensation laws. Federal guidelines were soon established; today all states have workers' compensation laws that meet federal guidelines. National leadership in protective legislation for children was provided by the Children's Bureau, established in 1909 as part of the Department of Labor.

Voluntary organizations also expanded during this period. Examples include the establishment or significant growth of the Boy Scouts and the Girl Scouts, the American Cancer Society, the National Association for the Advancement of Colored People, The National Urban League, and the Red Cross.

Federal Initiatives, 1930–1968

93

CHAPTER 3
*Social Welfare
Policies and the
Birth of the
Profession:
Historical
Highlights*

A great economic depression followed the stock market crash of 1929. Voluntary organizations and state and local governments did what they could to meet what seemed like unending financial need. But soon local treasuries were empty, including both private charities and relief-giving units of local government. People turned to the federal government for help. President Herbert Hoover was a proponent of laissez-faire economic theory and a political conservative. He believed that the federal government should not interfere with the economic market. Desperate Americans, however, began to perceive the widespread and rapidly increasing poverty as a **public issue** (an issue affecting so many people that it is considered beyond the "fault" of each affected individual) rather than a **private trouble.** Franklin D. Roosevelt was elected president in 1932 because he promised to involve the federal government in solving the crisis.

Roosevelt ushered in a series of emergency programs on the federal level to meet immediate needs for **income maintenance** and employment. His overall program was known as the New Deal. The New Deal offered temporary cash assistance and work-relief programs to needy people regardless of race. Roosevelt's major long-term proposal was the Social Security Act, passed by Congress in 1935. Since 1935, almost all additional federal social welfare policy has been adopted as part of this act (Segal and Brzuzy, 1998).

The Social Security Act is a complex piece of legislation that has been amended many times. The 1935 law established three types of federal provisions: (1) **social insurance,** (2) **public assistance,** and (3) health and welfare services.

Social insurance and public assistance are quite different. Insurance programs require the payment of taxes (in this case, the social security, or FICA, tax) earmarked for a special fund available only to the insured. Following rules relating to the amount of money contributed, benefits cover the "expected" problems of a modern industrial society, such as the death of a breadwinner.

Public assistance programs, on the other hand, are funded out of general tax revenues, usually income tax revenues, and people may receive benefits even if they have never paid taxes themselves. One qualifies according to whether one fits a specified category (for example, elderly person) and in addition meets a **means test,** or has an income below a certain level specified by law. A stigma is often attached to public assistance benefits, because they are considered unearned.

The social insurance provisions of the original Social Security Act were (1) Old Age and Survivors Insurance (OASI) and (2) unemployment insurance. OASI was intended to provide income for retired workers, widows, and minor children of deceased workers. Later, in 1957, coverage was extended to include disabled persons. In 1965, Title XVIII, Medicare, was added to the act. (Medicare and Medicaid, Title XIX, will be examined in detail in Chapter 7.)

Three categories of people were originally eligible for aid under public assistance: (1) the blind, (2) the aged, and (3) dependent children. Later, Aid to Dependent Children was expanded to include the mother and in some cases the father; the program became known as **Aid to Families with Dependent Children (AFDC).** A fourth category of people eligible for aid, the permanently and totally disabled, was added in 1950 (McSteen, 1989). In 1965, Title XIX, Medicaid, was added to the act.

In 1974, to equalize benefits nationwide and to help remove stigma, public assistance income-maintenance programs for the blind, the aged, and the disabled were combined into one program known as Supplemental Security Income (SSI). SSI is funded and administered by the federal government, and people apply for benefits through federal Social Security offices, not local welfare offices.

AFDC was not included in the SSI program. Why? The answer seems to be that some categories of poor people are still considered undeserving of aid. Political passion can be inflamed by criticizing poor mothers without husbands, or men who for whatever reason fail to provide. Their children suffer accordingly. AFDC remained a poor relation of SSI, with benefits that varied from state to state but, on the average, maintained recipients well below the poverty line, until 1996. In August of that year, the Personal Responsibility and Work Opportunity Act (PRWOA) ended the AFDC program entirely. The PRWOA will be discussed more fully later in this chapter.

General Assistance   One category of people has never been eligible for assistance under the Social Security Act, able-bodied adults between the ages of 18 and 65 (age 60 for widows) who have no minor children. Sometimes able-bodied adults in need can receive help from local programs known as general assistance, or poor relief. These programs vary widely across localities. In many places they simply do not exist. Even as need increases, relief programs are frequently cut because funding bodies focus on saving tax revenues rather than helping the poor.

General assistance programs are residual in approach. Aid is offered on a temporary, emergency basis. People who apply experience a stigma. There are often requirements to pay the money back or to work a certain number of hours per week in a public works project. Some applicants may experience discrimination, such as denial of aid according to prejudices of an administrator. Aid may be cut off at any time. Levels of monetary assistance are very low.

Food Stamps and Other Federal Voucher Programs   The food stamp program was established by Congress in 1964. The program is administered by the United States Department of Agriculture, but state and local welfare departments process the applicants and provide the stamps. The program is means-tested, and allotments are based on family size and income. Food stamps are **vouchers,** or coupons, that may be used to buy most food items available at the supermarket.

Originally, many poor adults who qualified for no other aid could receive assistance in the form of food stamps. But in 1996, the Personal Responsibility and Work Opportunity Act (PRWOA) enacted large cuts in food stamp availability, cutting the program's funding by nearly $28 million over the six-year period to follow. Most legal immigrants were cut off by the new law, and benefits were authorized for only three months in any three-year period to unemployed adults without children. In 1998, food stamp benefits were restored to about 250,000 of the 935,000 immigrants who had previously been eligible, mostly those who were disabled or elderly, or immigrants seeking political asylum (Bills tackle welfare, patients' rights, 1998).

From a high of 27.5 million in 1994, food stamp rolls fell to 18.2 million in 1999 (Belsie, 2000). Yet more than 10 percent of U.S. households in 1999 were considered "food insecure" by the U.S. Department of Agriculture, meaning that they were not certain of access to adequate food to meet basic needs. Many who were still eligible for foods stamps were discouraged from applying by complicated application procedures (Katz, 2001).

In addition to food stamps, the federal government offers other voucher programs, such as fuel assistance, rent subsidies, and infant nutritional supplements. The Women, Infants, and Children program, known as WIC, is one of the best known of the latter. It provides supplemental foods to pregnant and breast-feeding women and their children up to age five. The program is means-tested; applicants with incomes up to 185 percent of the poverty line are eligible. Coupons or vouchers for specific food items are provided for purchases at grocery stores (Karger & Stoesz, 1998).

Post-Depression Trends   The Great Depression came to an end in the 1940s, when World War II provided full employment. The nation began to look at poor people as unworthy again. The 1950s set the stage for the social activism of the 1960s, however. Women who had worked full-time in paying jobs during World War II were sent back home to make room in the job market for returning veterans. Although returning to the home was more a philosophical idea than a reality for many women (especially for the poor and those from ethnic minorities, who often had no choice but to work outside the home), the 1950s gave rise to feminist activism based on women's loss of status and access to employment equality. The decade also harbored the beginning of the civil rights movement, sparked by Rosa Parks's refusal to give up her seat to a white man on a bus in Montgomery, Alabama, in 1955.

Then in the 1960s came the War on Poverty, under the leadership of presidents Kennedy and Johnson. This movement was stimulated by Michael Harrington's book *The Other America,* originally published in 1962, which exploded the myth that people in poverty deserve their own misery. Much liberal legislation was initiated in the 1960s, furthered by the civil rights movement as well as by renewed understanding of societal causes of poverty. The AFDC-UP (Unemployed Parent) program, the Food Stamp Program, WIC, the Head Start program, educational opportunity programs, college work-study programs, job training programs, Peace Corps, Vista (Volunteers in Service to America), Medicare, and Medicaid all were instigated during this period (Champagne & Harpham, 1984; Karger & Stoesz, 1998).

Increasing welfare rolls led to new public outcry, which led to the passage of the Work Incentive Program (WIN) in 1967. WIN was designed to encourage welfare recipients to take paid employment. Those who could find jobs were allowed to keep part of their welfare grant up to a certain earnings level. The program was unable to reduce welfare costs, however, as not enough jobs were available, and funds were lacking to provide adequate job training. In addition, day care facilities and inexpensive transportation were lacking (Champagne & Harpham, 1984).

Cutting Back the Welfare State, 1968 to the Present

Earned Income Tax Credit   Major efforts to reform the welfare system were made by Nixon's Republican administration from 1969 to his resignation in 1974 and by the Democratic Carter administration from 1977 to 1981, but their plans were not accepted by Congress. However, President Gerald Ford (Republican, 1974 to 1977) did sign into law an important provision of the tax code, the Earned Income Tax Credit (EITC), geared toward helping poor working families. This credit is based on the number of children in a given family and that family's income. If the income of working family members falls below a certain amount, the family may qualify for an income tax credit, depending on family size (Segal & Brzuzy, 1998). This law has become increasingly important today given the passage of the Personal Responsibility and Work Opportunity Act described below.

Welfare Reform   The president who was able to get major welfare reform proposals accepted was Ronald Reagan (Republican, 1981 to 1989). President Reagan was elected in 1980 with an apparent public mandate to lower taxes and inflation and to repair the budget deficit. Elected with massive financial support from right-wing conservatives, he and his administration were politically committed to investing in the military. Cutting taxes while building up the military obliged President Reagan to drastically reduce federal expenditures for income maintenance programs. He did so. The savings thus incurred were very small compared with the massive amounts of new money being poured into the military. The budget deficit became astronomical during Reagan's two terms of office. (President Reagan did not accomplish these deeds alone, but with the sanction of a Democratic Congress.)

The political agenda of the 1980s involved forcing able-bodied people, including the working poor, off welfare. The concept of aid returned to the old residual idea to assist helpless children on a temporary, emergency basis, and only as a last resort (an approach popularly called the safety net). The result was the 1981 Omnibus Budget Reconciliation Act. The financial incentive built into the WIN program (described above) was eliminated. Most of the working poor opted to keep their jobs despite loss of welfare benefits, but their financial circumstances were severely hurt, especially as many lost eligibility for Medicaid as well.

President Reagan signed another major welfare bill in 1988, The Family Support Act, just before he left office. This one was designed to force mothers who had remained on AFDC into the job market. All parents with children over three years old (one year at states' option) were required to work or enter job training programs (if available) under this bill.

However, it wasn't until 1996 that poor mothers and children lost all entitlement to aid under the provisions of the Social Security Act. The Personal Responsibility and Work Opportunity Act was signed into law by President Clinton in August of that year, ending six decades of guaranteed government aid for economically deprived children and families. The former AFDC program was eliminated by this bill. In its place, a new program called Temporary Assistance for Needy Families was established. TANF was to be funded by federal block grants to the states, and recipients were to be limited to 60 months of benefits over a lifetime (Balzakas, 1998).

Under TANF, no family or child is entitled to assistance. Each state is free to determine who can receive assistance and under what circumstances. If a state runs out of money in a given year, it can simply stop providing aid, and poor fami-

97

CHAPTER 3
*Social Welfare
Policies and the
Birth of the
Profession:
Historical
Highlights*

lies will have to wait until the following year for assistance (Segal & Brzuzy, 1998). Besides the fact that assisting needy families is optional for states, regulations are complex and confusing. Some of the most significant requirements are that states are not allowed to assist anyone for longer than five years. They must require parents to work after 24 months of assistance. When parents work, the state may, but is not required to, provide child care assistance. Minor parents may not be assisted unless living at home and attending school. Assistance must be eliminated or reduced if the family is uncooperative with respect to child support–related requirements (e.g., if the mother does not name the father). Assistance may be denied to children born into families already receiving public assistance (Karger & Stoesz, 1998).

While this law was touted as a way of ending welfare dependency, no national programs were created to help address the many external factors keeping poor people on the welfare rolls (e.g., lack of affordable day care, lack of a family-supporting minimum wage, lack of adequate job training programs, lack of jobs in the skill range of many recipients or in the geographic areas where they live, lack of educational opportunity, and lack of cheap transportation to places where jobs are available.)

Fortunately, Medicaid was not included in the TANF block grant, and poor families who meet the previous income guidelines continue to be eligible for coverage.

SOCIAL WELFARE POLICY IN THE TWENTY-FIRST CENTURY

The major trends that seem apparent at the beginning of the twenty-first century began, of course, in the twentieth. Requiring or encouraging poor single parents to work outside the home began early in a number of different government programs. The earned income tax credit, the major federal program left at the beginning of the twenty-first century that assists poor families, benefits only those with paid jobs. Another major trend, shifting responsibility for helping poor people to religious organizations, was first enacted into law in 1996, as part of the Personal Responsibility and Work Opportunity Act. Privatization of social services, including services run by religious organizations, received major emphasis by President George W. Bush when his administration took over in 2000.

The Working Poor and the Earned Income Tax Credit

Making work pay was the intent of the earned income tax credit, or EITC. Americans have always believed that the way out of poverty is by hard work, but today a worker with only a single dependent, toiling full-time at the minimum wage, cannot lift even such a tiny family out of poverty. The minimum wage is kept very low because of political philosophy as explained in Chapter 2. The conservative perspective opposes any interference with the economic market other than to assist business to increase investment.

As discussed by Katz (2001), one way to make work pay is to increase the minimum wage. But most employers are unwilling to do so, and they usually have enough power in Congress to make their wishes prevail. The EITC is a compromise between conservative and liberal perspectives. It is basically a tax reduction and wage supplement program for low- and moderate-income working families. It is intended to provide an incentive to work, and it spreads the cost of raising worker income among all taxpayers. That helps employers keep labor costs low, thus increasing their profits. It is delivered impersonally through the income tax system, so that it lacks the stigma of "welfare." Today, the federal government and 15 states provide earned income tax credit programs (Johnson, 2000).

The EITC lifts more children out of poverty today than any other federal program. About 4.7 million people, including 2.6 million children, gained an income above the poverty line as a result of the EITC in 1999 (Johnson, N., 2000). Kim (2001) notes that this translates into a modest reduction in child poverty of about 15% overall. Considering recipient families alone, the impact is greater: a 10 percent rise in disposable income and a 27 percent reduction in poverty. Kim notes an important problem, however: children whose caretakers do not work do not benefit, so that the very poorest are not assisted at all. As noted by Greenstein, Primus, and Kayatin (2000), while the 1999 census data showed a drop in the overall child poverty rate, the poorest children grew poorer. In 1999, the average poor child fell farther below the poverty line than in any other year since 1979, the first year the data were collected. (See Exhibit 5.)

Issues with EITC

EXHIBIT 5

The EITC can be considered a guaranteed income support for poor working families with children. In contrast, there is no longer a federal guarantee for those outside the labor market, since Congress eliminated the entitlement of impoverished children to AFDC in 1996. One critical issue concerning the U.S. family policy is the absence of a major public safety net for the most impoverished group of children whose parents are not attached to the labor force. In addition, this group excluded from the public safety net is more likely the children of unmarried/never married parents. Through welfare reform and the EITC expansion, the nation has created two subclasses of children within the low-income class—one with and the other without a public safety net, based solely on the parents' employment and marital status. The assumption underlying this discriminatory treatment is that children of the nonworking and/or unmarried are unworthy and undeserving of public support. That is, the public value of children is determined by their parents' employment status and lifestyles. The nation appears to believe that the children of this "underclass" have no vested value for America's future.

Source: Quoted from Kim, R. (2001). The effects of the earned income tax credit on children's income and poverty: Who fares better? *Journal of Poverty, 5* (1), 21.

Privatization

99

CHAPTER 3
*Social Welfare
Policies and the
Birth of the
Profession:
Historical
Highlights*

Privatization involves shifting the provision of social services and financial benefits from publicly operated government programs to private organizations, either nonprofit or for-profit. For example, many states now contract with private agencies and organizations to operate the Temporary Assistance to Needy Families (TANF) programs authorized under the 1996 Personal Responsibility and Work Opportunity Act (PRWOA).

The political philosophy behind privatization is conservative, that government should have a minimal role in promoting the public welfare especially when it involves provision of economic assistance to the poor, as this might interfere with the economic market. (Workers might be unwilling to labor long hours for low wages if given an alternative.) This philosophy promotes competition among private businesses as the most economical way to provide services and benefits at the lowest prices.

While many services and benefits have always been provided through the private sector in this country (private pensions, health insurance, private charities, etc.), public funds have rarely been used to purchase services from the private sector on such a massive scale as that set in motion by welfare reform efforts.

Early indications suggest that transfer of services to the private sector is no panacea for improvement. In Wisconsin, for example, two of the five private firms that contracted to manage TANF programs for Milwaukee County were found to spend large sums of public money on exorbitant salaries for top executives, large bonuses for staff, expensive restaurant meals, and even advertising their services in other states. At the same time, local TANF participants were

Community church conducts food drive for poor.

denied information on potential benefits such as child care, food stamps, and Medicaid; many were terminated because of absences due to child care needs. It appears that information and services were limited to maximize profits (Schultze, 2000; Murphy, 2000).

The Faith-Based Trend

Since the election of President George W. Bush, the term "faith-based initiative" has become part of the common parlance. This administration strongly promotes transferring the provision of formerly public social services and programs to private, religious organizations.

"Charitable choice" language first appeared in the 1996 PRWOA. This legislation permits public funds to be used for religiously oriented social service programs. While denominationally sponsored social service programs have been eligible for public funds for many years, these earlier faith-based programs have separated their social services from religious proselytizing. By contrast, charitable choice language in the PRWOA broadened eligibility to allow public funding for church-sponsored programs that incorporate pervasive religious content (FCNL, 2001, February).

Interestingly enough, faith-based groups have not rushed to take advantage of their new opportunities under PRWOA. As McLaughlin (2001) notes, the average American congregation spends only about 3 percent of its budget on activities beyond its walls. Just recruiting members and conducting services is time-consuming enough for many religious groups.

American citizens seem mixed in their response to faith based service. Lampman (2001), summarizing a recent study by the Pew Forum on Religion and Public life, writes:

> Americans believe religious groups can't do the social service job alone, and are selective about which services they would do best. They would pick them over other non-profits or the government to feed the homeless and to counsel prisoners. But, by a wide margin, they would prefer that government agencies handle literacy, healthcare, and job-training programs. Any nonprofit group could do a good job on mentoring or teen pregnancy, they say.

Promoting the provision of social services by faith-based groups comes at a risk. Religious organizations, for example, are exempt from employment non-discrimination laws. And beneficiaries in great need may find themselves required to espouse certain religious beliefs before they can receive food or shelter. Concerned that churches could hire social workers based on religion and deny employment to homosexuals, the U.S. Senate, in early 2002, refused to endorse this part of a Republican-sponsored faith-based bill that had already passed the House. A compromise was reached deleting that option but allocating new funds to block grants for which religious organizations could apply. Additional funds were provided to assist faith-based organizations to negotiate the federal grant process (Keifer, 2002). President Bush was expected to sign the compromise legislation as this text goes to press.

An important concern remains: the provision of social services by faith-based groups can allow the federal government to bow out of any responsibility to care for its poorest and most vulnerable citizens, and divert its tax revenue instead to huge increases in military spending. Such a massive transfer of resources is distinctly possible in the wake of the terrorist attacks of 2001, given a frightened population increasingly concerned about national security. The federal budget proposed by President George W. Bush in early 2002 included enormous increases in military spending with proposed cuts in many social service programs.

101

CHAPTER 3
*Social Welfare
Policies and the
Birth of the
Profession:
Historical
Highlights*

ISSUES AND CONCERNS IN INCOME MAINTENANCE

Poverty Programs That Maintain Poverty

Income maintenance programs, or programs designed to prevent or alleviate poverty by contributions to individual or family income, are commonly under attack in this country. Some people believe, like the social Darwinists, that poor people should not be helped at all or, like the laissez-faire economists, that taxation of the more fortunate to help the poor is unfair.

On the opposite side of the fence, some people believe that the help currently offered to poor people in this country is too limited. Most social workers probably take this position. The United States is one of very few modern industrialized nations that does not provide free medical care for everyone, for example. It is also among the very few modern industrial nations that does not provide ongoing monetary support to able-bodied adults who cannot find employment.

Most of our nation's income maintenance programs leave beneficiaries far below the poverty level. The less eligibility factor is probably involved, although it no longer is stated explicitly in the law. For example, in our chapter's case example, Tomas and Tomacita's mother was attempting to support her family on income she earned through participating in her state's TANF job training program. Her stipend was just over $650 per month, or $7,800 per year. Her budget looked roughly like this:

Income:	$650	Income from TANF
	175	Food stamps
	825	

Expenses:	$400	Rent (heat included)
	235	Food for three
	40	Electricity
	35	Laundry
	45	Transportation to TANF program
	55	Clothes (including diapers)
	20	Telephone
	825	

By comparison, the poverty line for a family of three in 2000 was $13,874. No wonder this mother couldn't afford a babysitter. No wonder she and many other TANF participants in her neighborhood frequently relied on Urban Neighborhood Center's food pantry to help keep body and soul together. Note that there was no room in this budget for child care, miscellaneous items, emergencies, or recreation. It seems as if we like to punish the poor just for being poor, as if they have no right to enjoyment or security of any kind.

The **poverty line** itself has not been revised or updated for many years, except for inflation. When developed in the 1960s, it was based on the price of food. The Department of Agriculture's least expensive food plan was multiplied by three, because an earlier study showed that the average family at that time spent about one-third of its income on food (Fisher, 1998). Today, however, housing and child care costs make up a much higher proportion of the average family's budget. A new analysis would clearly raise the poverty line, revealing a significantly larger number of families that actually experience poverty in the United States today.

Many American families currently try to survive on budgets too low for dignity, health, or hope. Grants for recipients of AFDC were always low, and they fell precipitously in real dollar value beginning in the early 1970s. Now, under PRWOA and TANF, there is no longer any federal mandate to assist children and families at all.

Poverty and the Minimum Wage

U.S. social policy seems based on the idea that anyone can find a job and that, by working, people can pull themselves and their families out of poverty. The problem is that this idea does not represent reality for large numbers of Americans today. Many people simply do not possess the educational qualifications or the technical skills required to get the jobs that are available.

In addition, many people who do get jobs remain in poverty even when they work full-time. This problem is rooted in government policy. The federal minimum wage in 1968 was set so that a worker employed full-time at that wage could maintain a family of three (husband, wife, and child) at 120 percent of the poverty line. Now, because the minimum wage has not been indexed to inflation (it was $5.15 per hour in early 2002), a full-time employee working at minimum wage earns only about 77 percent of a poverty-level income for a family of three.

The low minimum wage has devastating effects on children. Over 7 million of them live in homes where a working family member brings home an income below the poverty line (Johnson, 2000).

Goldberg, writing in the *Newsletter of the National Jobs for All Coalition* (Fall/Winter 2000), notes that:

> As would be expected in a tighter labor market, real hourly and weekly earnings are both up since 1995. However—real wages have *not* recovered the ground lost since 1973 and remain below 1979 levels as well. Nor in the past five years have they kept up with productivity gains.
>
> One-fourth of all workers earn poverty wages (less than the three-person poverty level in 1999), higher than the proportion of poverty-level workers in 1973. Over one-third of blacks (35.6%) and 45 percent of Hispanics earn poverty wages. Of special relevance for the consequences of welfare "reform" is the fact that two-fifths of black women and one-half of Hispanic women fall into this group of disadvantaged workers. In other words, many who have jobs are underemployed.

103

CHAPTER 3
*Social Welfare
Policies and the
Birth of the
Profession:
Historical
Highlights*

Mother stretching financial resources to
provide for her children.

The Feminization/Juvenilization of Poverty

Another issue concerning income maintenance is the feminization of poverty. Actually, this is not a new issue. Women on their own, or women heads of families, have always been particularly vulnerable to poverty because they generally are paid lower wages, no matter what the job, and they experience limited access to higher-paying positions. Paradoxically, they are also the ones who usually must pay to raise the children in single-parent households. Only slightly more than half of all single-parent families have a court order in place for child support, and of those, only about half receive full payment (Karger & Stoesz, 1998).

Strongly related to the feminization of poverty is the juvenilization of poverty. Although many two-parent families today are poor, single-parent households run a greater risk of poverty, as it is very difficult for many single wage-earners to lift a family above the poverty line. If that single wage-earner is a woman, the risk of poverty is especially great, and the children, of course, suffer the risk right along with their mother. One in every two children under the age of six living in a female-headed family lived below the poverty line in 1999 (Greenstein, Primus, & Kayatin, 2000).

Family Policy and Poverty

Sadly, family policy in the United States does little to combat poverty today. The same was true even when the AFDC program was mandated under the Social Security Act. States were allowed to set their own standards of assistance, and for the most part, the aid they provided through AFDC was well below the poverty line. Throughout most of the years of the program's existence, only dependent children in single-parent families were eligible, so that unemployed fathers had to leave home if their children were to receive help. A mother receiving aid from AFDC who tried to help her family by working found that her AFDC grant was reduced dollar for dollar (except for WIN program participants, 1967–1981) according to her earnings until it ended entirely, terminating her eligibility for medical assistance under Medicaid at the same time.

The PRWOA was passed under the apparent assumption that single nonworking parents on AFDC did not work due to psychological dependency on the program. In fact, AFDC policy discouraged work by subtracting from the grant every dollar earned and by terminating medical insurance once a mother's salary from employment equaled the AFDC grant to which she would otherwise have been entitled.

Unfortunately, the TANF programs established by PRWOA remove a mother's entitlement to any aid at all while doing nothing to assure that she can get a decent job and earn a wage that can support her children even at the poverty line.

Residual versus Institutional Concepts in Modern Society

Residual aspects of our welfare system (providing aid only after the family has "failed"—that is, after it has broken down under stress or otherwise been unable to provide) do not respond to realities of modern industrial society. The legislators who shaped the Social Security Act assumed that "needy families" would be those with a dead or disabled father. Today, however, many needy families have an able-bodied father (and/or mother) who cannot find a job or can only find one that pays an inadequate wage. Plants close or move to Third World countries where wages are lower, and so people lose employment through no fault of their own.

Unemployment, when viewed from the perspective of industrial society as a whole, is not really an "emergency" but a predictable situation related to changing technological needs. At any given time, some percentage of people are always out of work through no fault of their own (see Exhibit 6).

Given the modern situation with limited jobs and limited wages, the unemployment insurance provision of the Social Security Act provides an excellent example of a program based on an institutional view of social welfare. Unemployment benefits reflect society's understanding that people lose employment constantly as a result of economic and technological changes. Unemployment benefits are provided without stigma to almost anyone who loses a job. Still, they normally end after six months, whether the worker has found new employment or not. If the unemployed worker has dependent children, he or she may then apply for TANF, if such a program is available in his or her community. If aid from that source is unavailable, local general assistance is the only source of help other than family and friends. In many places even general assistance is nonexistent.

Administrative Barriers to Aid

A different type of concern is that our welfare system often discourages even eligible categories of people from applying for aid (see Exhibit 7). Forms are lengthy and complicated; they are especially confusing to people with limited education or whose first language is other than English. Work requirements under new TANF programs can be confusing and discouraging to people who lack child care provisions, adequate clothing for work, or transportation. Even if needy people decide

105

CHAPTER 3
*Social Welfare
Policies and the
Birth of the
Profession:
Historical
Highlights*

Work for Everyone?

EXHIBIT 6

At least two components have been left out of the welfare reform agenda. First, how can we ensure that everyone in America who can work has a job? Second, how can we improve the ability of Americans to compete in the global economy, that is, what are the most important educational and training efforts we can make to invest in human capital? The welfare reform debate drowned out these issues. Since one of the primary goals of welfare reform is employment, jobs need to be available. But welfare is not part of a strong public commitment to full employment, to ensuring that everyone who can work has the opportunity to do so. Without that commitment, welfare reform is doomed. All of the key reforms—job training, time limits, transition support, and so on—assume that jobs are available and that most recipients will be hired. But where local economies are depressed, that will not happen.

Source: Quoted from Bryner, G. (1998). *The great American welfare reform debate, politics and public morality.* New York: W. W. Norton, p. 319

to apply anyway, they may end up languishing on waiting lists, like Tomas and Tomacita's mother who was still waiting for child care assistance in this chapter's case example. Such complications are known as administrative barriers to aid.

Social Work Roles in Income Maintenance

Social workers have had a long history of involvement in income maintenance. For example, among the functions of the Charity Organization Society volunteers was the investigation of applicants to determine eligibility for financial and material aids. Settlement house volunteers lobbied in the political arena for mothers' pensions and other reforms related to income maintenance. Social workers were active in the development and administration of the Social Security Act (Wyers, 1987). For example, Harry Hopkins, a social worker, was a very influential leader in Roosevelt's New Deal administration.

Public and private social welfare agencies have historically been staffed by people who, although called social workers, usually lacked professional training. In 1962 an amendment to the Social Security Act required AFDC recipients to be offered social services in addition to monetary assistance, with the goal of eliminating their need for economic assistance (Wyers, 1987). However, such a goal was not achieved, and in 1972 social service provisions were formally separated from income maintenance in public departments of social welfare.

Large numbers of social workers have continued to be employed in the public welfare system since 1972. However, those with professional training usually assume social service or administrative roles rather than income maintenance roles. Social workers provide such social services in welfare departments as protective

---

An Anonymous Poem

EXHIBIT 7

When
fathers lack the strength
to carry on
and have to leave
why
do mothers suddenly
lose their universality?
with
a "TANF" or
an "unwed" or
a "welfare"
to prefix
their title,
must
they alter
what all mothers do
and begin being
screwtinized through
that bureaucratic
microscope?

---

services for children and the elderly, counseling for single parents (especially pregnant teenagers), foster care, and special-needs adoptions (for example, older children or children with disabilities).

MYTH AND REALITY ABOUT PUBLIC WELFARE: RESEARCH REVEALS THE TRUTH

An important function of research is to find out whether certain popularly held beliefs are true or not. In the case of the former welfare program known as AFDC, research found many myths false. Even so, Congress was able to abolish the program on the very strength of the common mythology. Here are a few of the myths, contrasted with facts as determined by research.

One myth was that families stayed on AFDC for generations. In fact, the vast majority (70%) left within two years. Another myth was that most people on welfare were able-bodied loafers. In fact, more than half were children, and of the adults, more than half were providing care for children under five years old. Many people believed that "welfare mothers" had vast numbers of children. Instead, AFDC families averaged about 1.9 children each, the same as the national average (NASW, 1994).

107

CHAPTER 3
*Social Welfare
Policies and the
Birth of the
Profession:
Historical
Highlights*

Up for Debate
*Proposition: Should the federal government become involved in the
workings of the market economy to better conditions for poor people?*

Yes	**No**
1. The minimum wage has been falling relative to inflation. A full-time minimum wage earner cannot support an average-size family above the poverty line. Government legislation should raise the minimum wage.	1. Market forces of supply and demand should determine wage levels.
2. The gap between rich and poor has been increasing over the past three decades. The government should use the tax system to redistribute wealth more equally.	2. People should be allowed to keep all wealth legally acquired.
3. People should be paid a living wage, one that can support a family above the poverty line.	3. People should be paid according to their productivity levels and/or market forces of supply and demand.
4. The government should provide jobs or job training for people who are unemployed and cannot find work.	4. The government should not interfere with the natural workings of the economic market.

Another myth was that welfare benefits were so high that people chose to live off the "fat of the land" rather than to work. In fact, only three states offered benefits as high as 75 percent of the poverty line, and 45 of the states offered benefits below 50 percent of the poverty line (Karger & Stoesz, 1998). The program was not expensive for the nation, but constituted only about 1 percent of the federal budget (Katz, 2001).

Many people believed that few women on welfare were white. The facts showed that toward the end of the program's existence about 39 percent of all AFDC mothers were African American, 38 percent were white, 16 percent were Latina, 2.8 percent were Asian, 1.3 percent were Native American, and 1.6 percent were of unknown race. While the number of white women on welfare almost equaled the number of blacks, minorities in general were over-represented because they were poorer (Karger & Stoesz, 1998).

A final myth was that people who received welfare were usually "cheats." But research consistently demonstrated that fraud in the AFDC program was very, very low. Many of the errors in eligibility were made inadvertently by program staff, given the complexity of regulations and procedures designed to prevent fraud. A careful analysis of quality control data for the AFDC program based on a 1987 survey placed the upper limit at 5.8 percent for payments in error because of misinformation from the client (Gibbs, 1991).

Such research challenging common myths can provide social work as a profession with needed facts to persuade local, state, and federal governments to upgrade social welfare programs so they can meet the real needs of real people, especially of children and the mothers who care for them. Whether the research is heeded is, of course, another matter entirely. (See the "Up for Debate" box.)

What will happen to our nation now that we no longer have a commitment to poor children and their parents? As Gary Bryner (1998, p. 315) writes:

> The symbolic loss of welfare as a national entitlement is not insignificant. The national commitment to an entitlement program for poor families was a small but visible component of a national ethic of fairness, justice, and common concern. Although welfare could and did promote pathological dependence in some recipients, it also could and did provide a bridge for families torn apart by death or divorce until they could become self-sufficient. It provided the opportunity for countless women to gain basic education, job training, and employment. It ensured an income for millions of children who might not have had other means of support. Rights and entitlements can be viewed as manifestations of our common concerns, our commitments to each other. In an era when many decry the collapse of collective values and ideals, we take a risk when we reject one example of collective commitment.

Currently, our national government seems committed to transferring welfare programs to private agencies and religious organizations. This is a path trodden centuries ago that has proved unable to handle the task in the past, especially during times of economic depression. Is this the right direction for our nation in the twenty-first century? And if not, how can it be changed?

The budget promoted by President Bush in the early months of his administration resulted in a tax cut strongly favoring wealthy people. While people of all tax brackets would keep a slightly larger percentage of their incomes, by far the largest number of dollars would go to people already very rich. The president also requested a substantial increase in military spending, when *current* spending was already more than twice that of all potential adversaries combined (FCNL, 2001, March).

Then came the terrorist attacks of September 2001, at a time when the nation was hovering on the brink of an economic recession (or was already in one, depending on the economist consulted). Suddenly most Americans became preoccupied with national security. The economic downturn worsened at the same time, partly due to disruption of economic institutions and activities in New York City. The nation declared war on Afghanistan, in an all-out effort to eliminate the terrorists thought to be harbored there. With an active war to finance, military spending increased. At the same time, conservatives who controlled the majority in the House of Representatives introduced further tax cuts favoring big business, with the intent of stimulating investment. This tax cut was defeated in the Democrat-controlled Senate, but President Bush proposed a national budget in 2002 that included enormous increases in military spending with large cuts in social services.

With fewer tax dollars coming in—and more going out in military spending—what does that mean for the ordinary citizen? Certainly there will be fewer resources to help people who are in need (except those directly involved in a national disaster, who will receive temporary relief funds). "Guns or butter" is an old saying in our nation's common folk wisdom. Can the United States really be secure when millions of its citizens, especially children, still lack access to basic necessities? Are guns a better collective investment than food, shelter, education, and health care for all American citizens? That is perhaps the most crucial question for the future (see Exhibit 8).

Where Your Income Tax Money Really Goes
The United States Federal Budget for Fiscal Year 2002
Total Federal Funds (Outlays): $1,438 Billion

EXHIBIT 8

Current Military, $334B;
Military Personel $78B, Operation and Maintenance $107B, Family Housing $4B, Procurement $54B, Research and Development $37B, Construction $5B, $1B Misc., Retired Pay $17B, DoE Nuclear Weapons $13B, NASA 50% $7B, Coast Guard $4B, International Security $7B

Past Military, $338B:
Veterans' Benefits $49B; Interest on National Debt (80% estimated to be created by military spending) $289B

Human Resources, $488B:
Education, Health/Human Services, HUD housing subsidies, Food Stamps, Labor Department, Social Security Administration

General Government, $206B:
Legislative, Justice Dept., State Dept., International Affairs, Treasury, Government Personnel, 20% interest on national debt, 50% of NASA

Physical Resources, $72B:
Agriculture, Commerce, Energy, HUD administration/ development, Interior Dept., Transportation, Environmental Protection, Army Corps Engineers, FCC

Total Federal Funds (Outlays): $1,438 Billion

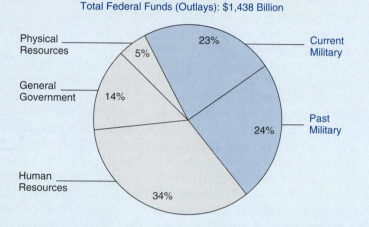

Physical Resources — 5%
Current Military — 23%
Past Military — 24%
Human Resources — 34%
General Government — 14%

HOW THESE FIGURES WERE DETERMINED

War Resisters League creates this leaflet each year after the President releases a proposed budget. However, with a new administration, the budget is revealed too late for our purposes. The figures here are from a line-by-line analysis of projected figures for 2002 in the "Analytical Perspectives" book of the Budget of the United States Government, Fiscal Year 2001. The percentages are federal funds, which do not include trust funds such as Social Security that are raised and spent separately from income taxes. What you pay (or don't pay) by April 16, 2001, goes only to the federal funds portion of the budget. The government practice of combining trust and federal funds (the so-called "Unified Budget") began in the 1960s during the Vietnam War. The government presentation makes the human needs portion of the budget seem larger and the military portion smaller.

"Current military" spending adds together money allocated for the Dept. of Defense ($286 billion) plus the military portion from other parts of the budget. Spending on nuclear weapons (without their delivery systems) amounts to about 1% of the total budget. "Past military" represents veterans' benefits plus 80% of the interest on the debt. Analysts differ on how much of the debt stems from the military; other groups estimate 50% to 60%. We use 80% because we believe if there had been no military spending most (if not all) of the national debt would have been eliminated. The government willingly borrows for war, but finds nothing extra for crises in human needs.

THE GOVERNMENT DECEPTION

Social Security & Medicare — 35%
Military, Veterans, Foreign Affairs — 18%
Interest on the National Debt — 12%
Physical & Community Development — 9%
Social Programs — 17%
Law Enforcement & General Government — 2%
Surplus Reserved for Debt Reduction — 7%

The pie chart to the left is the government view of the budget. This is a distortion of how our income tax dollars are spent because it includes Trust Funds (e.g., Social Security), and the expenses of past military spending are not distinguished from nonmilitary spending. For a more accurate representation of how your Federal income tax dollar is really spent, see the chart above.

Source: War Resisters League (www.warresister.org/piechart.htm), 339 Lafayette Street, New York, NY 10012.

An International Perspective

Comparative studies of poverty show that children in the United States do not do well compared with those in the rest of the industrialized world. Today, for example, the overall child poverty rate remains higher than that in most European countries and Canada (Greenstein, Primus, & Kayatin, 2000). Bradsher (1995) found that children in the United States were worst off in comparison with those of 18 modern industrialized nations, except for Israel and Ireland. The United States had the widest gap between rich and poor and the least generous social welfare programs of all 18 nations (and that was *before* the passage of the PRWOA).

Child poverty in the United States is to a large extent the result of political choices that determine social policy. In contrast, poverty has been eradicated in other countries that have chosen alternative policies. Norway is perhaps the best example, and its approach to poverty merits a close look.

Norway subscribes to what Katherine van Wormer (1994) describes as a "universalism" philosophy: Those in need are viewed as no different from anyone else. No one goes homeless or hungry. Homelessness is not a problem, because the government subsidizes low-cost housing in adequate supply for everyone. Buildings are well maintained and cheerfully decorated. A tax-free child care allowance is provided for every child, and single parents receive a double allowance. Paid, extended work leave is granted to all parents. Workers are given automatic sick leave when they ask for it, with full pay (the first two weeks' pay come from the employer, and subsequent pay comes from the government). Hospital care is provided free, and primary health care and medicines are low in cost. Income is equalized so that no occupational group earns more than twice the average earnings of another. Elderly people receive a basic pension from the government. No one is fantastically rich or terribly poor.

The cost of security like this for the citizens of Norway is a tax rate that is among the highest in the world. People with higher incomes pay progressively higher taxes. Food and services are expensive because of a sales tax of 20% on virtually everything. Norway has three dominant cultural orientations, however, that undergird humane social policies despite the cost: egalitarianism, trust in the social system, and kindness toward the weak and vulnerable.

Katherine van Wormer points out that these humane provisions for all Norwegian people are part of the larger social system, which manifests a helping ethic rather than a work ethic. Cooperation instead of competition is valued and carefully modeled even in the public schools, where children do not receive grades until they are 13, and then only rarely. Other important social values in Norway include caring for others and personal security (see Exhibit 9).

NASW Welfare Reform Principles

As part of its efforts to help achieve humane social policy, the NASW has developed several principles for welfare reform in the United States. These principles, released in 1994, are outlined in Exhibit 10. While few, if any, of these principles appear on the national agenda at the beginning of the twenty-first century, they remain important to consider and understand.

111

CHAPTER 3
*Social Welfare
Policies and the
Birth of the
Profession:
Historical
Highlights*

Value Change Needed?

EXHIBIT 9

Katherine van Wormer believes that only if the United States adopts values such as Norway's can it begin to develop similar social policies. She writes:

The consensus of social workers seems to be that they must work toward policy change. They must also work toward achieving value change. But whether these diverse "voices in the wilderness" will lead to institutionalization of the efforts will depend on the national sense of urgency and the belief that something can be done.

Norway is an example of the possible. . . . Norway has found another way and, in my opinion, a far better way.

Source: Quoted from Katherine van Wormer. (1994, May). A society without poverty: The Norwegian experience, *Social Work, 39*(3), p. 327.

NASW Welfare Reform Principles

EXHIBIT 10

1. The goal of reform should be to prevent and reduce poverty, not just reduce the use of public assistance.
2. Investing in human capital through universal opportunities, supports, and services is the best strategy for preventing poverty.
3. Under no circumstances should reform efforts jeopardize the well-being of children whom our welfare system is designed to serve.
4. No one should be penalized for the inability to secure employment due to depressed labor market conditions. A range of contributions, be they social or economic, should be recognized and rewarded.
5. Qualified, properly trained staff and manageable workloads are a necessary part of improving the welfare system.
6. All families are entitled to an adequate standard of living, regardless of work force attachment.
7. The heterogeneity of the welfare population requires that services provided and expectations for self-support reflect each family's unique strengths, needs, and circumstances.
8. The obligations imposed upon welfare recipients should be no greater and no less than those applied to the rest of the population.
9. As consumers of services, welfare recipients should be involved in all decision-making related to reform efforts, and their rights should be scrupulously protected.
10. Recipients of public assistance should not be stigmatized.

Source: Quoted from NASW Office of Governmental Relations (1994, March), *Welfare reform principles.* Washington, DC: National Association of Social Workers.

INTERNET SITES

http://www.statepolicy.org	Influencing State Policy
http://ist-socrates.berkeley.edu:3333/budget/budget.html	The National Budget Simulation
http://qsilver.queensu.ca/~appamwww/	Association for Public Policy Analysis and Management
http://www.publicwelfare.org/	Public Welfare Foundation
http://www.aphsa.org/	American Public Human Services Association
http://www.cbpp.org	Center on Budget and Policy Priorities
http://www.voiceinternational.org/fd/public.htm	Public Welfare Foundation
http://www.social-policy.org	The Social Policy Virtual Library
http://www.fcnl.org	Friends Committee on National Legislation
http://www.dundee.ac.uk/politics/socialpolicy	An Introduction to Social Policy
http://www.urban.org/news/focus/focus_welfare.html	Issue Focus: Welfare Reform
http://www.welfare-reform-academy.org	Welfare Reform Academy

SUMMARY

The cases of Tomas and Tomacita, and of Carla and Maria Romero dramatize the predicament of people who are dependent on a variety of income maintenance and social service programs in this country. The recent introduction of programs such as Temporary Assistance for Needy Families, replacing AFDC, along with cuts in funding for other public programs such as public health, impacts powerfully on the lives of poor children and families.

To understand why our income maintenance programs operate as they do, generally keeping recipients well below the poverty level, we must begin with the Old World background of the contemporary social welfare system in the United States. The Elizabethan Poor Law of 1601 was the law that English settlers brought to the colonies in America. The U.S. system has gradually evolved under the influence of values, politics, issues, and concerns stemming out of the American experience. A history of social welfare movements and income maintenance programs in the United States reveals a shifting political impact of two ways of thinking about our nation's social welfare system: the residual and the institutional. Residual services dominated the colonies and the nation as a whole up until the Great Depression (1929). Experiences during the Great Depression brought about the temporary dominance of the institutional approach to social welfare, and national programs such as Social Security were developed that lifted many people out of poverty. The trend of the 1980s and 1990s toward the residual view, that continues in the beginning years of the twenty-first century, has meant less aid for poor people and fewer resources to sustain the social worker's referral system of financial and material aid.

Issues for the future involve a rethinking of the nation's institution of social welfare. A contemporary, contrasting model from Norway was described, and welfare reform principles developed by the NASW were presented. The United States needs to determine how much interference with the free market is appropriate to alleviate poverty, which is deepening today among the poorer women and children. New social welfare planning needs to be based firmly on research, not on political rhetoric or myth.

113

CHAPTER 3
*Social Welfare
Policies and the
Birth of the
Profession:
Historical
Highlights*

KEY TERMS

Aid to Families with Dependent Children
   (AFDC)
almshouse
income maintenance
indoor relief
less eligibility
means test
mutual aid
outdoor relief
poverty line
private trouble

privatization
public assistance
public issue
social insurance
social welfare
Temporary Assistance for Needy Families
   (TANF)
vagrants
voucher
workhouse

DISCUSSION QUESTIONS

1. What is the relationship between social work and social welfare?
2. Compare and contrast the residual and institutional approaches to social welfare. Which approach do you think better meets the needs of modern industrial society? Why?
3. What major social values affect the American welfare system? Do these values complement one another or create conflict? How do they affect social welfare legislation?
4. What country in the Old World provided the model for early American social welfare programs? What law was particularly influential? Why?
5. What were the four major provisions of the Elizabethan Poor Law of 1601? What categories of poor were established? What assistance was offered to each category?
6. How did the concept of "deserving" or "worthy" poor affect poor relief in the Old World? Does this concept affect the American social welfare system today? How do you know?
7. What were the major innovations of the Speenhamland Act of 1795? What happened to this law and why? Are there parallel occurrences in this country today?
8. Describe the concept of less eligibility. What do you think of this approach to aiding poor people? Why?
9. Compare and contrast the Charity Organization Society and the settlement house movement in the United States. Comment on their purposes, goals, types of aid offered, and levels of intervention or methods used.
10. What were some major social accomplishments of the progressive years?
11. How did the federal government respond to the Great Depression with respect to relief of the poor? Which president ushered in the New Deal?

12. What were the major provisions of the Social Security Act of 1935? Which categories of persons obtained assistance? Which category did not?
13. What are some major myths about people who used to be assisted by the program known as AFDC? What facts correcting these myths have been determined through research?
14. Was the Personal Responsibility and Work Opportunity Act signed into law by President Clinton in 1996 a shift of the American welfare system toward the institutional or the residual? Do you think this legislation was based on findings from careful research? Why or why not?
15. Has the George W. Bush administration pushed the American social welfare system more toward the residual or the institutional?
16. Which political philosophy, liberal or conservative, tends to support a residual approach to social welfare? Which a more institutional?

CLASSROOM EXERCISES

While not required, it is suggested that students break into small groups of three or four to discuss these exercises. It may be helpful to choose a scribe to record and report major points to the class after the group discussion.

1. Imagine that you are a single parent with custody of a two-year-old toddler. Would you prefer to care for your child at home or work at a paid job outside the home and purchase child care? Why? Which arrangement do you think would be better for your child? Why?
2. Work out a budget sufficient to meet the needs of a single parent and a two-year-old child to the best of your ability. Then determine the wage that this parent would need to earn to make ends meet.
3. Given that American children have already suffered more poverty than those of most major western industrialized nations, why do you believe a Republican Congress enacted and a Democratic president (Clinton) signed the Personal Responsibility and Work Opportunity Act of 1996?
4. What do you think about the fact that poor children whose parents earn wages receive an income supplement through the Earned Income Tax Credit, but poor children whose parents do not earn wages receive no income assistance from the federal government?
5. The Speenhamland Act was passed in England in 1795 to help poor working families. In what ways was this wage supplement legislation similar to today's EITC? In what ways was it different? Do you think the same issues that led to the downfall of the Speenhamland Act may endanger the EITC? Why or why not?

RESEARCH ACTIVITIES

1. Since the passage of the Personal Responsibility and Work Opportunity Act of 1996, every state has developed its own program or set of programs to aid poor families. Many of these programs are called Temporary Assistance to Needy Families (TANF). Use your college library and the Internet to find out about the program your state has developed.
2. Interview social workers and other staff who work at one of your state's TANF offices. Find out what these workers see as the strengths of the current program. What problems have they observed? Or, simply go and observe how applicants are treated.
3. Use your library and the Internet to find out about what a nearby state is doing to aid needy families under the TANF program. Compare and contrast your own state's efforts with those of the nearby state.

115

CHAPTER 3
*Social Welfare
Policies and the
Birth of the
Profession:
Historical
Highlights*

INTERNET RESEARCH EXERCISES

1. The Internal Revenue Service has a website with information about the Earned Income Tax Credit (http://irs.ustreas.gov/prod/ind_info/eitc4.html).
   a. What change, beginning in the tax year 2000, was made in the IRS definition of "foster child" for tax purposes?
   b. In the overview page (click EITC Overview), does the application of the EITC always result in a refund?
   c. Can the EITC be taken as an advance through your payroll in some cases?
2. The issue of privatization of public social services continues to be important and controversial. The Urban Institute has a very thorough paper on the subject (http://urban.org/pubman/privitiz.html).
   a. Does the federal One-Stop Career Center initiative open the door to privatization?
   b. How does Wisconsin's W-2 (initiated under Gov. Tommy Thompson) fit into the privitization issue?
   c. What two arguments in support and what two arguments against, as listed in the paper, do you feel have the most merit? Why?
3. Settlement houses are certainly not a thing of the past. Examples of two settlement houses that are very much alive are Toberman Settlement House Inc. (http://www.toberman.org/home.htm) and East Side House Settlement (http://www.eastsidehouse.org).
   a. Has the purpose (or mission) of these settlement houses changed over the years since their founding? If so, how?
   b. What are the sources of funding for these agencies?
   c. If a student social worker served his/her field practicum in one of these houses, what activities would you expect him/her to perform?

REFERENCES

Balzakas, J. (Ed.). (1998, Spring). Welfare dynamics: Caseloads and time limits. *Poverty Research News, 2* (2).

Barker, R. L. (1987). *Social work dictionary.* Silver Spring, MD: NASW Press, 154.

Belsie, L. (2000, July 14). Americans turn away from food stamps. *The Christian Science Monitor,* 8, 9.

Bills tackle welfare, patient's rights. (1998, September). *NASW News,* 7.

Bradsher, K. (1995, August 14). Low ranking for poor American children. U.S. youth among worst off in study of 18 industrialized nations. *The New York Times,* p. A1.

Brieland, D. (1995). Social work practice: History and evolution. In R. L. Edwards (Ed.), *Encyclopedia of social work* (19th ed., Vol. 3, pp. 2250–2255). Silver Spring, MD: NASW Press.

Bryner, G. (1998). *The great American welfare reform debate, politics and public morality.* New York: W. W. Norton.

Champagne, A., & Harpham, E. (1984). *The attack on the welfare state.* Prospect Heights, IL: Waveland, 97–105.

Federico, R. (1984). *The social welfare institution* (4th ed). Lexington, MA: Heath, 94.

Fisher, G. M. (1998, Spring). Setting American standards of poverty: A look back. *Focus, 19* (2), 47–51.

Friends Committee on National Legislation (2001, February). *Washington Newsletter, 651,* 4–6.

Friends Committee on National Legislation. (2001, March). *Washington Newsletter, 652,* 6–8.

Gibbs, L. (1991). *Scientific reasoning for social workers.* New York: Macmillan, 250–252.

Goldberg, G. (2000, Fall/Winter). How many cheers for lower unemployment? *Good Jobs for All, Newsletter of the National Jobs for All Coalition, 6* (1), 2, 10.

Greenstein, R., Primus, W., & Kayatin, T. (2000, October 10). *Poverty rate hits lowest level since 1979 as unemployment reaches a 30 year low.* Center on Budget and Policy Priorities (online). Available: http.//www.cbpp.org/9-26-00/pov.htm.

Greenwood, E. (1957). Attributes of a profession. In P. E. Weinberger (Ed.), *Perspectives on social welfare* (1974 ed., pp. 426–439). New York: Macmillan.

Johnson, H. W. (1995). *The social services, an introduction* (3rd ed). Itasca IL: F. E. Peacock, 3–10.

Johnson, N. (2000, November 2). *A hand up, how state earned income tax credits help working families escape poverty in 2000: An overview.* Center on Budget and Policy Priorities (online). Available: http://www.cbpp.org/11-2-00sfp.htm.

Karger, K. J., & Stoesz, D. (1998). *American social welfare policy, a pluralist approach* (3rd ed.). New York: Longman.

Katz, M. B. (2001). *The price of citizenship.* New York: Metropolitan Books.

Kiefer, F. (2002, February 14). How new faith-based bill world affect local churches. *The Christian Science Monitor, 2,3.*

Kim, R. Y. (2001). The effects of the earned income tax credit on children's income and poverty: Who fares better? *Journal of Poverty, 5* (1), 1–22.

Lampman, J. (2001, April 11). Public wary of funding faith-based social services. *The Christian Science Monitor, 3.*

Lieby, J. (1987). History of social welfare. In R. L. Edwards (Ed.), *Encyclopedia of social work* (18th ed., Vol. 1, pp. 761–765). Silver Spring, MD: NASW Press.

McLaughlin, A. (2001, June 21). Few recruits for the "armies of compassion." *The Christian Science Monitor, 2.*

McSteen, M. (1989). Fifty years of social security. In I. Colby (Ed.) *Social welfare policy: Perspectives, patterns, insights* (pp. 172–174). Chicago: Dorsey.

Murphy, B. (2000, April). Why it failed; despite all of the hoopla, W-2 has failed to deliver on its promises. *Milwaukee Magazine,* 156.

NASW Office of Governmental Relations (1994, March). *Welfare reform principles.* Washington DC: National Association of Social Workers.

NASW Office of Governmental Relations. (1994, May 6). *Welfare reform: Myth busters.* Washington DC: NASW Press.

Popple, P. R. (1995). Social work profession: History. In R. L. Edwards (Ed.), *Encyclopedia of social work* (19th ed., Vol. 3, pp. 2250–2255). Silver Spring, MD: NASW Press.

Quadagno, J. (1982). *Aging in early industrial society: Work, family and social policy in 19th century England.* New York: Academic Press, 95.

Schultze, S. (2000, September 14). New W-2 director talking tough. *Milwaukee Journal Sentinal* (online). Available: http://www.Jsonline.com/w2/welfare/99/.

Segal, E., & Brzuzy, S. (1998). *Social welfare policies, programs, and practice.* Itasca, IL: Peacock Publishers.

Tropman, J. (1989). *American values and social welfare.* Englewood Cliffs, NJ: Prentice Hall, 134–135.

U.S. Bureau of the Census. (2001). *Poverty Thresholds in 2000* (online). Available: www.census.gov.

Van Wormer, K. (1994, May). A society without poverty: The Norwegian experience. *Social Work, 39* (3), 324–327.

War Resisters League. (2001, December 27). *Where your income tax money really goes* (online). Availabe: http://www.warresisters.org/piechart.htm.

Whitaker, W., & Federico, R. (1997). *Social welfare in today's world* (2nd ed). New York: McGraw-Hill.

Wilensky, H., & Lebeaux, C. (1965). *Industrial society and social welfare.* New York: Free Press, 138–139.

Wyers, N. (1987). Income maintenance system. In R. Edwards (Ed.), *Encyclopedia of Social work* (18th ed). Silver Spring, MD: NASW Press, p. 888.

117

CHAPTER 3
*Social Welfare
Policies and the
Birth of the
Profession:
Historical
Highlights*

FOR FURTHER READING

Bryner, G. (1998). *The great American welfare reform debate, politics and public morality.* New York: W. W. Norton.

    This text thoroughly examines the politics of social welfare reform and identifies several major areas that were not addressed, such as income provision for poor children without working parents, domestic abuse issues, provision of realistic employment opportunities, and the like. It discusses the importance of addressing the American position in the global economy, which will involve investment in a workforce that has skills sufficient to meet the needs of the twenty-first century.

Katz, M. (2001). *The price of citizenship.* New York: Metropolitan Books.

    Impressive and comprehensive, this contemporary text examines the American welfare state from its inception in the Social Security Act of 1935 through its apparent demise in 1996. It compares conceptions of public and private welfare systems in a variety of contexts.

Piven, F., & Cloward, R. (1971). *Regulating the poor: The functions of public welfare.* New York: Vintage Books.

    A classic work, this book examines the relationship between public relief policy, poverty, and civil disorder. In the context of extensive historical documentation, Piven and Cloward effectively argue that the function of public welfare is to maintain a low wage base within the parameter of avoiding civil disorder.

Segal, E. A., & Brzuzy, S. (1998). *Social welfare policy, programs, and practice.* Itasca, IL: F. E. Peacock Publishers.

    This contemporary text on social welfare policy and practice is well written and easy to read even for introductory students, yet it contains a wealth of information for the advanced reader. It begins by describing the foundations of social welfare policy, including historical origins. It then provides key content areas of contemporary social welfare policy. A particularly timely section discusses various aspects of social welfare policy practice.

Wilensky, H., & Lebeaux, C. (1965). *Industrial society and social welfare.* New York: Free Press.

    Another classic, this book provides a thorough examination of the ways in which industrialization has affected social welfare. Part one of the book examines the development of urban-industrial society and the emergence of related social problems; part two discusses social problems and the supply of welfare services; and part three describes the organization of welfare services in the United States.

CHAPTER 4

Poverty and Populations-at-Risk

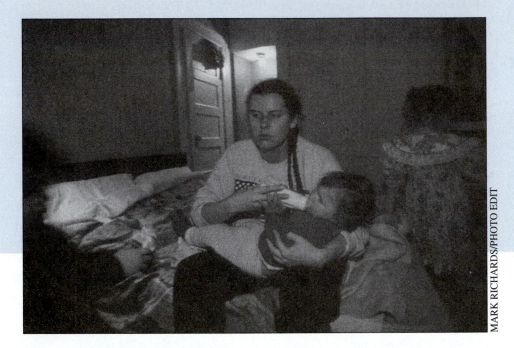

MARK RICHARDS/PHOTO EDIT

JUAN ATTENCIO

George Allen, BSW, picked up his ringing telephone. The secretary announced the arrival of a new client, Juan Attencio. George left his businesslike office and headed to the agency waiting room. There sat a powerfully built, middle-aged man clad in jeans and a T-shirt. He wore his black hair long, pulled back into a ponytail. The eyes were dark, vigilant. The man's skin was tan and his facial features, while regular and pleasing, didn't come from a standard mold. After introductions, George invited Juan to his office. The man seated himself on the far side facing the door, looking uneasily all around him.

George eased the tension, so common in initial sessions, with a cup of coffee and some small talk. He then explained that he was a social worker hired by Juan's employee assistance program to work with people experiencing difficulties. Juan nodded. "I know. I found your service listed in my employee benefits manual."

"That's good," said George. "Tell me, then, what brings you here today?"

"First," Juan said, "I need to ask you something. My manual said your organization sees people for up to four sessions. That hardly seems enough to begin. What can you do in four sessions?"

"That depends on the situation," George responded. "My role is to find out what you want to accomplish. Then, together, we develop a plan of action. That may be enough. If not, I can usually find additional resources for you."

Juan reflected a moment. Then he said abruptly, "Well, I have to do something." He leaned forward, his big hands on his knees. George noticed that the skin on Juan's hands was cracked with many oozing scabs.

"Just begin with whatever's on your mind," George said quietly.

Juan's face assumed a forced smile. "I'm the kind of man who likes to take care of other people," he began. "I even recently brought a friend home who's been living on the street, a Vietnam vet. But I've hurt the person who matters most to me. My wife, Yuri."

"Hurt her in what way, Juan? Mentally? Physically?"

"Both."

"Can you tell me what happened?"

"That's part of the problem. I don't know for sure. I was drunk."

Juan then told George a complicated story about taking his wife, Yuri, to a party the previous Saturday night. He and Yuri had agreed before they went that Yuri would drive home, as Juan planned to let off steam by getting drunk. But when the time came, Juan grabbed Yuri's arm and yanked her out of the car. Then he hit her hard enough to break her collar bone. Somebody called the police. In an alcoholic haze, Juan fought and was taken to jail. He was charged with battering his wife, resisting arrest, and assaulting an officer. Yuri bailed him out and allowed him to come home, but threatened to leave for good "if he didn't change." She also threatened to take their 18–month-old twin sons with her.

"Now . . . do you think you can help me?" Juan's request was delivered almost as a challenge.

George sat throughtfully for a moment. Where should he begin? He knew that crises often arise out of deeper, underlying problems, but the immediate issue was so serious he decided to start right there.

"Juan, have you ever hurt Yuri physically before?" he inquired.

"Never," Juan replied, *"I feel terrible about what I did. That's one of the reasons I'm here."*

"I am glad you realize that hitting your wife is a serious problem," said George, *"and I am relieved to hear it is the first time. We will make plans to deal with that before you leave today."*

He decided to probe further. *"You said you were drunk when you hurt Yuri, and that you had planned to get drunk. What was going on in your life for you to want to do that?"*

Juan answered thoughtfully. *"Part of the problem is that I was married before, and have a son and daughter living with my first wife. I have the Japanese sense of honor. I will not miss a child support payment."*

George was curious about Juan's reference to Japanese honor, but he decided to pursue the more immediate issue. *"Money is a problem for you, then?"*

"Always," said Juan.

"But you are employed? Otherwise you wouldn't be part of the employee assistance program. . . ."

"Yes, I've worked all my life, beginning with the army in Vietnam. But I have four children and a wife to support . . . and now my friend."

"For how long has money been a problem, Juan?"

"Ever since my second child was born. I had a good job as an auto mechanic. But. . ." (Juan looked down at his hands) *"my hands began to bother me. Cracks came. When grease got into the cracks, I could hardly work because of the pain. Wearing rubber gloves gave me a rash. In Vietnam, I was exposed to Agent Orange, and I think that's the cause of the problem. But my hands didn't begin cracking until a couple of years after I got home, so the Veterans Administration wouldn't help. I eventually switched to a different job at the garage—I pumped gas, collected money. But that meant a cut in pay. The rent took half my check—you know how rents are here in this part of California."*

George nodded. *"Tell me more,"* he said.

"Bills started to pile up. My wife, Betty, and I began to argue all the time about money. Finally, she decided she had to go back to work. Day care for the kids cost almost everything Betty earned, though, so we still couldn't manage. Finally, she went home to her parents. We were divorced a year later."

"Money is a problem in your new marriage too?" George asked.

"Yes. After Betty and I separated, I went to a technical school to get an associate's degree in electronics. I knew I could earn more money that way, and the work would be easier on my hands. I worked part-time to pay tuition, but I took out a loan to keep up my child support payments."

"Did you complete your degree?"

"Yes, and I also met Yuri at school. She's Japanese, and I'm half-Japanese. We understand each other. She's my best friend, and I don't want to lose her."

"You're half-Japanese, Juan? Are you partly Hispanic too?"

"Yes, my father's Mexican—Mexican American, that is—born in southern California. He's a career army man. He met my mother in Japan after World War II, during the occupation. I grew up in a military home, so that when the

Vietnam War came along, I was just expected to enlist. When I left the army after the war, I settled in California, where my parents have lived since my father retired."

"Do Yuri's parents live in California too?"

"Yes. They help us when they can, but her grandparents lost everything during World War II, when the federal government put Japanese Americans in internment camps and confiscated their property. They're elderly now and ill. Yuri's parents care for the grandparents, so we don't ask for much ourselves."

"How long have you and Yuri been having trouble with finances?"

"For our entire marriage. I warned Yuri that I was in debt, and we planned to hold off having a family of our own. But she got pregnant, and we had twins. Yuri kept her job as a nurse's aide for awhile, but day care for the twins cost nearly everything she earned, so she quit. We're always broke."

"You said you needed to let off steam last Saturday night, Juan. How much of that involved being stressed out over money, do you think?"

"Just about all of it. It feels rotten to be in my late 40s, to have worked hard my whole life, and to have nothing to show for it. My credit cards are maxed out. I'm two months behind in rent. Now I may go to jail, and my wife may leave me."

"You are clearly in a tough spot, Juan," George reflected. "Your money problems sound major. You face criminal charges. However, the abuse issue with your wife must be addressed first, right?"

"Yes. If Yuri leaves me, I lose my best friend and my family again."

"As I said earlier," George continued, "I will give you the name of an agency that specializes in counseling families that have experienced domestic abuse. There is a social worker there who is excellent with couples, and her partner runs groups for men who have trouble managing anger. I believe they can help you. I can authorize several sessions. Will you follow through and make an appointment right away?"

"Of course," said Juan.

"And I will call Yuri later today to make sure she has the telephone number of our local women's shelter," George said firmly.

"That's fine," said Juan, "only she won't need it," he muttered.

"I hope you are right, Juan. Now let's make another appointment for ourselves. I want to hear how things are going, and also to talk with you about some of your other issues—finances and what's going on in the legal realm." They agreed to meet together again in two weeks.

Juan had a flair for the dramatic. As he entered George's office for his next appointment, he handed him an official-looking document with a bow and a flourish. "Read this," he said. It was a notice to pay or vacate his apartment.

"Can you pay your back rent?" asked George.

"No way," said Juan.

The second session thus focused on money. With Juan's consent, George asked directly about his income and expenses. Juan's take-home pay appeared more than adequate, a little over $1,800 per month. However, of that amount, child support payments required $600. Rent, a bargain for his area, consumed $600 more. The school loan took another $150. Utilities cost approximately

$100, including electricity, gas, and telephone. That left $350 per month to make minimum credit card payments, buy gas to get to work, and feed and clothe Juan, Yuri, twin sons, and the veteran friend.

George reflected on how the official federal poverty statistics overlook many people who experience poverty. As a trained electronics technician, Juan's annual salary was well above the federally established poverty line. Nevertheless, he and his family experienced ongoing deprivation and financial need.

This time, George referred Juan to a budget counseling service that not only assisted clients to lower their ongoing expenses but intervened directly with landlords and other creditors to work out partial payments over time.

George then asked Juan about his session with the family counselor. He replied that it had been very helpful. Early in the session, the social worker had checked with Yuri to be sure she had the number of the local women's shelter. She had referred Juan to the batterers intervention program run by her partner. In addition, after listening to a description of Juan's behavior at home from Yuri, the worker had suggested that Juan might be suffering from posttraumatic stress disorder (PTSD) from his service in Vietnam. Yuri described him as moody and easily upset. He frequently woke up at night screaming, and slept with a loaded gun under his pillow, which terrified Yuri.

"And you see where I'm sitting now, George? I always want to sit with my back to the wall to make sure nobody sneaks up behind me. I guess that's a symptom too. The counselor thinks PTSD may have something to do with my attacking Yuri, especially combined with money pressures, raising twins, and too much alcohol."

George recognized the behaviors Juan described as possible symptoms of PTSD. Many veterans were far worse off, like Juan's homeless friend.

"Do you want to stay in counseling for a while, Juan? I certainly recommend it, and I will authorize several more sessions," said George.

"Yes," Juan said. "Yuri has promised to stay with me if I do."

"Fine," George said. "I'll authorize six sessions to begin with, and I'll consult with your therapist if you request more. Now, Juan, what about that gun? I'm very concerned about your sleeping with a loaded gun under your pillow."

"Yuri said the same thing, and so did the other social worker, our family counselor. So I gave it to my father for safekeeping."

"Good!" said George heartily. "I must admit I got very nervous when I heard about that gun." He paused and blew out a long breath between pursed lips. Then, changing the subject, "What's happening for you legally?"

"My father has sent me to his attorney, and is loaning me the money for now. But I don't know how I'm ever going to pay him back."

"That's something else to talk about with the budget counselor," said George. "This won't be an easy time for you, Juan. You may have to consider making some major changes in your life to bring your finances in line."

Juan left George's office with the name and telephone number of the budget counseling agency and a follow-up appointment with George for one month later.

At their next meeting, George learned that Juan and his family had moved to a small studio apartment at the suggestion of the budget counseling service. His veteran comrade had moved to a temporary city shelter. The budget service had nego-

tiated small payments over time with his creditors, and worked out a tight budget for other necessities such as food and clothing. Yuri was looking for a job where she might take the children. Juan's father continued to pay the legal expenses; the case was scheduled to come up in court shortly. Juan agreed to call after the court date to let George know the results.

When Juan called George again, the news was bad. Despite the fact that he had never been arrested before and had pleaded "no contest" to the charges against him, he received a sentence of 60 days in jail. Juan was worried that he might lose his job. He wondered whether George could help him in that area. Also, he wondered how Yuri and his children could survive without an income. She hadn't yet found work to which she could bring the children, and the jobs she could get paid wages too low to cover child care for twins.

George was able to assist one more time. He talked with Juan's employers, and they granted him a two-month leave of absence. He referred the family to the county's Temporary Assistance for Needy Families program. He expected that Yuri would be required to go back to work, but the program might pay for part of the child care costs. He made an appointment to see Juan the week after he was to be released from jail, wanting to provide support and encouragement. George felt Juan would need it badly again by then.

SOCIAL AND ECONOMIC JUSTICE

Juan Attencio belonged to a population-at-risk in the United States. Specifically, he was a member of an ethnic minority. **Prejudice** against ethnic minorities may possibly have influenced his harsh jail sentence, which was unusually severe for a first offense. (Although all case examples used in this text are composite stories to protect identities, this is the actual sentence given in the case that provided the major material for this vignette.) **Poverty** is another issue of **social and economic justice.** It may be defined broadly as the lack of resources to achieve a reasonably comfortable standard of living. Although Juan wasn't raised in poverty, he experienced it as an adult.

As mentioned in Chapter 1, social and economic justice and populations-at-risk constitute a curriculum area required of all baccalaureate degree programs by the Council on Social Work Education. They are intertwined in the real world.

Is There Social and Economic Justice?

Let us begin with the concept of social and economic justice. Do we have social and economic justice in the world today? What criteria could we use to make such a judgment? Justice involves fairness, and social justice concerns fairness among people.

At a very basic level, one may suppose that if social justice were realized in the world today, every baby born should have an equal chance to survive the first year of life. Every infant, after all, is helpless and dependent. Unfortunately, to borrow a famous quote from former President Carter, "The world isn't fair." Not, at least, if infant mortality rates are any indication.

According to the NASW's *Introducing International Development Content in Social Work Curriculum* (Healy, 1992):

> Each year, 14 million children die before reaching their first birthday. Many of these deaths are "unnecessary," meaning that they are caused by preventable factors: poverty, poor sanitation, malnutrition, and failure to immunize children against disease. The low status of women, teen pregnancies, and discrimination against racial or ethnic groups contribute to infant mortality in the United States and other countries.
>
> Rates of infant mortality (deaths of infants prior to their first birthday per 1,000 live births) vary greatly. The world rate of infant mortality averages about 71, but this figure hides a wide range of rates. Rates for individual countries ranged in 1989 from a low of 4 in Japan to a high of 173 in Mozambique. While Africa has the highest rates of child and infant mortality, greater numbers of children die in Asia. The United States now ranks 22nd among nations, and these rates have shown little recent improvement. . . . The national rate of 10.0 hides rates two to three times this high in inner city areas. Poverty and racism are factors in the domestic rates.

Thus we see that social justice has not been realized in the area of infant mortality. More recent data provides similar findings. The United States was still only 20th among nations in infant mortality by the year 2000 (see Chapter 7). The preceding quotation identifies important reasons: discrimination against racial and ethnic minority groups and women, otherwise known as populations-at-risk, a concept that will be discussed shortly.

What about economic justice? How can we know whether economic justice has been achieved in the world today? One way might be to find out whether most people have roughly the same resources, so that all can maintain a reasonably equitable standard of living.

We find, unfortunately, that economic justice is not manifest in the world either. According to Karger and Stoesz (1998), the richest 358 people in the world have a net worth equal to that of the 2.3 billion people who comprise the poorest 45 percent of the world's population.

Alarmingly, the gap between rich and poor has increased in recent years. In the United States, for example, according to the Friends Committee on National Legislation's *Washington Newsletter* (1998, April):

> The economic divide within the U.S. is growing. U.S. Census Bureau figures released last fall revealed that, in 1996, households in the top 5% of the income scale collected 21.4% of the national income. This level is the highest ever recorded by the Census Bureau in 30 years of collecting such data.
>
> The top 20% of all households (by income) earned nearly as much as the bottom 80% of households (49% vs. 51% of national income, respectively). These figures are also, essentially, all-time highs.
>
> Income inequality in the U.S. exceeds that of 14 other industrialized nations, including Japan, Germany, and the United Kingdom.

Data from the 1999 census indicate that the income gap in the United States has continued to increase in recent years. Households with earnings in the top 20 percent in 1999 collected 49.4 percent of all income. The bottom 20 percent received only 3.6 percent. The top 5 percent alone amassed 21.5 percent (Spending the surplus, 2001).

The Impact of Poverty

What is the matter with being poor? After all, some believe that poverty is beneficial, motivating family members to work hard, pull together, and practice frugality. Indeed, self-help efforts have assisted many poor people to survive. However, poverty is almost always harmful, because it substantially limits people's choices. Where it is severe, the means for securing necessities such as food and shelter are lacking, so that poverty can literally steal people's lives. Basic human needs include adequate food, shelter, clothing, access to health care, and child care when young children are present.

According to Sherman (1997, p. 5), America's poor children "walk a gauntlet of troubles that start at birth" (see Exhibit 1). Beyond severe health problems, poor children are more likely to suffer neglect and abuse, to land in foster care, to drop out of school, to experience unemployment or underemployment, and to end up dead or in jail (Bryner, 1998).

Poverty robs people of their hopes, dreams, and God-given potential. The pain and frustration of dreams deferred can lead to "self-medication" through alcohol and other drugs. Involvement in gangs can be seen as a way of achieving some kind of importance and belonging. Early pregnancy can be seen as a way of bringing love into an otherwise empty life, introducing another helpless and innocent being into this same environment.

Poverty, and how others treat people in poverty, can also result in a massive assault on one's self-esteem. The following story about a woman named Clarenine Williams illustrates this issue (Thousands off nation's welfare rolls, 2000, A9). Williams was participating in a "welfare to work" transition program in Florida.

> Williams, with an 11th grade education, has three children ages 7 to 10. Her husband, Jean, disabled for 20 years, is blind in one eye, has heart problems and artificial kneecaps. Her 10-year-old son takes medication for attention deficit disorder. She has medical problems and is getting ready to appeal a judge's ruling denying her disability benefits.

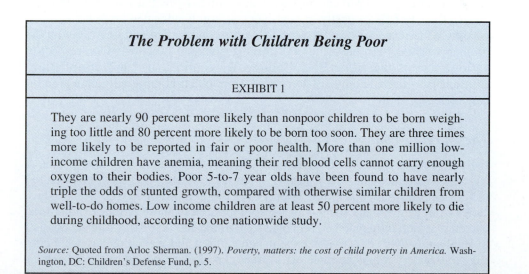

The Problem with Children Being Poor

EXHIBIT 1

They are nearly 90 percent more likely than nonpoor children to be born weighing too little and 80 percent more likely to be born too soon. They are three times more likely to be reported in fair or poor health. More than one million low-income children have anemia, meaning their red blood cells cannot carry enough oxygen to their bodies. Poor 5-to-7 year olds have been found to have nearly triple the odds of stunted growth, compared with otherwise similar children from well-to-do homes. Low income children are at least 50 percent more likely to die during childhood, according to one nationwide study.

Source: Quoted from Arloc Sherman. (1997). *Poverty, matters: the cost of child poverty in America.* Washington, DC: Children's Defense Fund, p. 5.

Williams started a $5.15 an-hour, part-time clerk's job on May 30. Two days later, the state sent a letter saying food stamps for her family were being cut from $147 a month to $62.00 a month.

The reason: "receipt of earned income." Her take home pay was $118.90 a week.

"We might as well be garbage under somebody's feet for all anyone cares," said Williams, 38.

The same article reported that only 40 percent of those in Williams' "transitional" program left because they were able to find a job. Most were "booted off the rolls" because they had exceeded time limits or failed to meet some other regulation. Lack of transportation and child care were problems for many, but they were cut off aid nevertheless.

SOCIAL POLICY AND SOCIAL JUSTICE

Increasing social inequities such as widening income gaps among American families do not happen according to accident or merit alone. They are strongly influenced by social policy. An important example is the minimum wage law and its effect on poverty. The minimum wage ($5.15 per hour in 2002) in no way guarantees that full-time work will bring a decent standard of living to a worker and family. That wage yields an annual income of $10,712, fully $1,157 less than the 2000 poverty line for a single parent and child, and considerably less than the poverty line for a family of three ($13,874) or a single parent with two children (U.S. Bureau of the Census, 2000).

The minimum wage, when adjusted for inflation, has not regained the value it lost during the 80s. Those who must live in poverty due to its diminishing value include 10 percent of the workforce—12 million people. They include restaurant and hotel staff, child care workers, home health care providers, and teachers aides (Raising the minimum wage, 1998).

By contrast, 11.8 percent of American families earned at least $100,000 per year in the late 1990s, mostly in dual-income, highly educated households. Such wealthy Americans may find it very difficult to understand and identify with the problems of the poor, providing a disturbing potential prognosis with respect to voting patterns that affect social policy. By contrast, in 1967, in inflation-adjusted 1997 dollars, only 3.2 percent of the population reported such a high income (Belsie, 1998).

The Working Poor

Forty percent of American families today living below the poverty line include at least one working adult. Many, unable to make ends meet, find themselves forced to seek help from food pantries. Twenty-six million families sought meals or groceries from pantries and shelters in 1997; 39 percent of these families had at least one employed family member. As noted by Pommereau (1998), "From economists to legal aid lawyers to activists, experts agree that while the nation has spent considerable energy moving people off welfare, the effort is bound to fail as long as the issue of adequate wages isn't addressed." In other words, moving people off welfare is not the same thing as addressing poverty. Unless work pays a living wage, ending welfare only further increases poverty.

Barbara Ehrenreich (2001), a journalist and author with a PhD who labored as a low-wage worker for a few very hard months as an experiment, learned that she literally could not make ends meet. This was true even though she had no dependents at the time and moved into the least expensive accommodations she could find. She worked as a waitress, a nursing home worker, a cleaner of private homes, and a floor worker at Wal-Mart, sometimes holding two jobs at once. Even working seven days a week, she was forced to find sources of free food to keep body and soul together.

Ehrenreich reported in her fascinating book, *Nickeled and Dimed: On (Not) Getting by in America,* that the Economic Policy Institute, after compiling data from dozens of studies, recently determined that $14.00 an hour, or approximately $30,000 per year, would be a fair living wage for a family of one adult with two children. This budget was not rock bottom: it would allow a telephone, child care at a licensed center, and health insurance. However, it was not sufficient to allow any restaurant meals, Internet access, video rental, alchohol, or cigarettes (see Exhibit 2).

Clearly, minimum wage workers in America today earn nothing close to a fair or "living" wage.

Fair Wages?

EXHIBIT 2

In fact, wages *have* risen, or did rise, anyway, between 1996 and 1999. When I called around to various economists in the summer of 2000 and complained about the inadequacy of the wages available to entry-level workers, this was their first response: "but wages are going up!" According to the Economic Policy Institute, the poorest 10 percent of American workers saw their wages rise from 5.49 an hour (in 1999 dollars) in 1996 to $6.05 in 1999. Moving up the socioeconomic ladder, the next 10 percent-sized slice of Americans—which is roughly where I found myself as a low-wage worker—went from $6.80 an hour in 1996 to $7.35 in 1999.

Obviously, we have one of those debates over whether the glass is half empty or half full; the increases that seem to have mollified many economists do not seem so impressive to me. To put the wage gains of the past four years in somewhat dismal perspective: they have not been sufficient to bring low wage workers up to the amounts they were earning twenty seven years ago in 1973. In the first quarter of 2000, the poorest 10 percent of workers were earning only 91 percent of what they earned in the distant era of Watergate and disco music. Furthermore, of all workers, the poorest have made the least progress back to their 1973 wages.

Source: Quoted from Barbara Ehrenreich. (2001). *Nickeled and dimed: On (not) getting by in America.* New York: Metropolitan Books, p. 202.

Homelessness

It is difficult to measure the full extent of homelessness, because many homeless people are not counted in the census due to lacking an address (Wright, Rubin, & Devine, 1998). Nevertheless, approximately 750,000 people are homeless in the United States on any given night, and between 1.3 and 2.0 million people will experience homelessness during any given year. Among the fastest-growing groups here are families with children, which constituted fully 40 percent of the homeless in 1995. Children under 18 constituted 27 percent of the urban homeless population in 1996 (Homelessness, 1998).

It is believed that many factors contribute to homelessness, but first and foremost, poverty is the major culprit. In many places, a full-time worker at minimum wage cannot afford an apartment given ever-escalating costs. Housing costs have risen due to urban renewal, gentrification (conversion of low-income neighborhoods to residential areas for the affluent), and condominium and cooperative conversion at the same time that low-income people have lost ground. Federal housing assistance policies have failed to provide adequate low-income housing, so that only 26 percent of those eligible for housing assistance actually receive it (Homelessness, 1998).

This difficult problem has been increasing since the passage of the Personal Responsibility and Work Opportunity Act. For example, the Catholic Church recently had to turn people away from its homeless shelter in San Diego because it was already operating at twice normal capacity (Ehrenreich, 2001). Homeless shelters in Milwaukee, Wisconsin, admitted 7,063 children in 2000, an increase of 47 percent over 1998, the first year data were compiled. Shelter workers stated that they believed welfare reform primarily caused the increase (Kissenger, 2001).

Already on the rise, homelessness increased even further in 2001 because of an economic recession that was exacerbated by the terrorist attacks in New York City and Washington, D.C. In New York, half of the more than 80,000 residents who lost their jobs were low-wage service workers. They had little or no economic margin of safety; record numbers swelled New York shelters after the attacks, with families constituting the largest share of the increase (Marks, 2001).

Homelessness increased in other parts of the nation in 2001 as well. In Chicago, for example, all shelters were filled to capacity. Many homeless families include one or more low-wage workers. A study by the National Low Income Housing Coalition in Washington, D.C., found that a minimum-wage worker could afford a typical two-bedroom apartment exactly nowhere in the entire nation, and a one-bedroom apartment in only 10 jurisdictions. Shiela Crowly, the coalition's president, stated: "There's an extraordinary mismatch between what rental housing costs and what low-wage workers earn" (Marks, 2001, p. 8). The result is increasing homelessness across the country.

Hunger

Besides homelessness, poverty leads to hunger. Hunger has also been increasing across the nation in recent years. The terrorist attacks made the situation more urgent in many places. According to recent estimates by the U.S. Department of Agriculture, about 31 million Americans are "food insecure," meaning that they

MICHAEL NEWMAN/PHOTO EDIT

Homeless families are increasing across the nation.

cannot be sure they will be able to put food on the table. After the terrorist attacks, a Washington-based hunger-relief organization, Share Our Strength, conducted a "flash survey" of food pantries across the United States. Many reported significant increases in demand for food but losses in needed donations. Second Harvest, another food relief organization, experienced similar issues: increased demand with losses in revenue. It is believed that donations that would normally have gone to local food pantries were diverted to New York instead (Gardner, 2001).

POPULATIONS-AT-RISK

Everyone in the world is, to some degree, "at risk." But not everyone faces the same degree of risk. What kinds of people are most at risk of poverty in the United States? Are they those who have bad luck, or those who are just too lazy to work hard? Research indicates that these commonly believed explanations for poverty are false. Certain categories of people are statistically more likely to be poor than others, for reasons beyond their own control but not reflecting chance or laziness. Those people who fall into the categories that research has found most likely to experience poverty are known as **populations-at-risk.**

As noted earlier, the concept of populations-at-risk is now a curriculum area required in baccalaureate social work education. Members of these populations make up the clientele with whom social workers do most of their work. Juan Attencio in this chapter's case example was a person at risk because he was half Hispanic and half Japanese, a member of two different ethnic minorities. Susan and Martha Dunn of Chapter 1 were at risk because they were female. Martha and Todd Dunn were at risk because they were children. Members of two or more categories of risk, such as children who are female or members of ethnic minorities, suffer increased risk.

During the 1980s, growth in child poverty rates led to the coining of the term **juvenilization of poverty.** Today, children constitute almost 40 percent of all poor persons. Poverty rates for children continued to grow into the 1990s, so that by 1994, almost 22 percent of all children, or more than 15 million, were poor (Segal & Brzuzy, 1998). Census data showed a drop in child poverty by 1999, to 16.9 percent, but the unrealistic formula for determining the poverty line (as discussed in Chapter 3) makes this figure extremely misleading in terms of children's actual experience.

Sherman (1997) points out that one in three American children spends at least one year in poverty. He notes that, in addition, while the official poverty thresholds are very low, most poor children live in families with incomes far below the official poverty level. Nearly half of poor children live in families with incomes below one-half of the poverty line. Only 28 percent of poor children suffered such abject poverty two decades before. He notes that children born to families as poor as these must often do without basics such as food, housing, or quality child care.

The risk of poverty for poor children of ethnic minority status is much greater. Often, it is not just their families that are poor but the entire wider environment in which they live. An interview with a Hispanic teen in Harlem illustrates how children raised in deprived urban environments feel about how they are valued in this society (Kozol, 1996, p. 57):

> "Think of it this way," says a 16 year old named Maria———. "If people in New York woke up one day and learned that we were gone, that we had simply died or left for somewhere else, how would they feel?"
>
> "How do you think they'd feel?" I ask.
>
> "I think they'd feel relieved. I think it would lift a burden from their minds. I think the owners of the downtown stores would be ecstatic. They'd know they'd never need to see us coming in their doors, and taxi drivers would be happy because they would never need to come here anymore. People in Manhattan could go on and lead their lives and not feel worried about being robbed and not feel guilty and not need to pay for welfare babies.
>
> "It's not like, 'Well, these babies just aren't dying fast enough,'" Maria says. "'Let's figure out a way to kill some more.' It's not like that at all. It's like—I don't know how to say this—." She holds a styrofoam cup in her hands and turns it slowly for a moment. "If you weave enough bad things into the fibers of a person's life—sickness and filth, old mattresses and other junk thrown in the streets and other ugly ruined things, and ruined people, a prison here, sewage there, drug dealers here, the homeless people over there, then give us the very worst schools anyone could think of, hospitals that keep you waiting for 10 hours, police that don't show up when someone's dying, take the train that's underneath the street in good neighborhoods and put it above where it shuts out the sun, you can guess that life will not be very nice and children will not have much sense of being glad of who they are. Sometimes it feels like we've been buried six feet under their perceptions. This is what I feel they've accomplished."

Clearly, in America we do not enjoy the situation often piously described as "women and children first." Children especially often come last, and if the interview quoted above is evidence, they apparently know it. Children often feel unappreciated and unloved as well as poor and deprived. However, the situation is not necessary or inevitable, but the result of choices our elected representatives have made in major social policy decisions (see Exhibit 3).

Social Policy and Child Poverty

EXHIBIT 3

Child poverty can and must be eliminated in this rich nation. America's extraordinarily high rate of child poverty is higher than for any other age group, higher now than in any year from 1966 to 1991, and higher than in any other Western industrialized nation. Other nations make other choices and have child poverty rates a fraction as large as ours.

A child in the United States is 60% more likely than a Canadian child, two times more likely than a British child, and three times more likely than a French or German child to live in poverty. Research has shown that the chief reason for these wide differences is that other nations have strong policies for boosting family income. These policies include making quality child care affordable for every family; generous parental leave for working parents; cash, food, and housing assistance for all needy families; and child allowances and guaranteed child support for all families regardless of income. These policies add up to help families hold family-supporting jobs and lift their children out of poverty.

To our shame, America lacks a prowork, profamily policy to stop poverty. The changes wrought by the 1996 federal welfare law eliminated the federal role in ensuring cash assistance and cut food aid and disability assistance to millions of families. But it failed to fund or encourage training, education, or job creation, and even fueled the shortage of funding for child care assistance by imposing underfunded work requirements for welfare families. The law did virtually nothing to help families get and keep jobs at family-supporting wages.

Although Congress and the President created a $3 billion fund for welfare-to-work services in 1997, the new money pales besides the tens of billions cut by the 1996 welfare law. The vacuum left by the repeal of the former welfare system remains largely unfilled, and the number of working poor families with children has swelled to record levels. Sixty-nine percent of poor children in 1996 lived in a family where someone worked.

Source: Quoted from Arloc Sherman. (1997). *Poverty matters: The cost of child poverty in America.* Washington, DC: Children's Defense Fund, p. 33.

Women

Women compose another population-at-risk. Although progress has been made over the past two decades, that progress, unfortunately, may be less than most people believe. Part of the problem is access to high-paying professions.

Women's limited ability to earn is shown by the disparity in average earnings between female and male full-time workers in the United States. By 2001, women earned only about 72 percent of what men did. While many have branched out into nontraditional professions (women increased their representation since 1989 in 106 of 497 occupations tracked by the U.S. Labor Department), most remained clustered in lower paying jobs such as sales workers, secretaries, cashiers, nurses, elementary school teachers, hairdressers, receptionists, and so on (Francis, 2001; see Exhibit 4). Moreover, women do the bulk of the caregiving in this society. They provide most of the care for children, elders, and other dependent persons both within their own

Progress for Women?

EXHIBIT 4

Barbara Reskin, a Harvard University sociologist, believes the 1990's have been less a period of dramatic progress than a "solidification" of the "big leap" women made in the previous two decades in shrinking their occupational segregation. . . . Just 20 occupations are home to almost half of all working women: nearly 30 million out of the total 63 million women in the labor force, according to the labor department. They account for 97 percent or more of all secretaries, receptionists, and registered nurses, for example.

Source: Quoted from D. Francis. (2001, June 6). Women demolish more career barriers. *The Christian Science Monitor*, p. 10.

homes and out in the paid workforce. However, our economic system undervalues caregiving work. It overlooks the fact that caregiving *is* work when provided in the home. For example, since wages are not involved, caregiving work at home does not qualify a woman for her own Social Security benefits, or for unemployment insurance if she is "fired" by her husband. It no longer entitles her for public assistance under the Social Security Act when she has dependent children. Outside the home, caregiving is poorly paid, exposing many female wage earners to poverty.

Part of the problem for women is that, although they continue to swell the ranks of people employed outside the home, they remain in lower positions. Francis (2001), for example, reports that women today head only two of the Fortune 500 companies. And while there are signs of improvement in representation of women in middle management levels, they are modest. Only about one-tenth of the Fortune 500 companies have women filling as many as one-quarter of the corporate officer positions (Francis, 2001) today. This situation persists despite the fact that women demonstrated greater leadership skills than men in a recent five-year corporate study; women managers outperformed men in 17 of 20 leadership skills studied, including planning, coaching, communication, empowerment of employees, and resourcefulness (Sappenfield & Day, 2001).

Women are usually the ones who shoulder the burden of child rearing in cases of divorce or birth out of wedlock. Yet child support payments tend to be undependable and/or too low to cover costs. Alimony, or support for a former spouse, is exceedingly rare today. Given women's restricted earning capacity, women-headed families suffer high rates of poverty in the United States, 27.8 percent in 1999 (Greenstein, Primus, & Kayatin, 2000).

The substantial poverty of women has led to the coining of the term **feminization of poverty.** Katherine van Wormer (1997, p. 258) illustrates how women suffer deprivations worldwide:

- Of the 1.3 billion people in poverty, 70% are women.
- In illiteracy, women outnumber men 2 to 1.
- Worldwide, women make up half of the electorates but hold just 10% of legislative seats and 6% of cabinet posts.

- In all regions, women outnumber men among the unemployed.
- The average wage paid to females was three-fourths males' average wage in nonagricultural jobs.

Older Adults

Older adults compose another population-at-risk. There is good news, however, for this group. Social Security amendments passed in the 1960s and 1970s (primarily Medicare and SSI) helped reduce poverty for people over age 65 from more than a third to about 10.5 percent in 1999, slightly less than the nation's overall poverty rate (Katz, 2001).

If older adults now enjoy a poverty rate lower than that for the population as a whole, how can they be considered at risk? The fact is that the overall figures hide wide discrepancies among older people. Older women have double the risk of poverty (14.9%) as compared to men (7.2%). Fully 60 percent of African American older women who live alone live in poverty (Segal & Brzuzy, 1998).

Elderly people frequently face discrimination in the workplace, and elderly women and members of ethnic minority groups are even more likely to face it. For those fortunate enough to receive a pension upon retirement, the pensions are almost always less than wages earned previously. Many people do not receive pensions at all. Companies are not legally required to offer pension plans, and those that do may go bankrupt and may be unable to honor their commitments. Today, many pension plans have been replaced by tax sheltered annuity options, which involve substantial employee contributions and financial risk.

Besides loss of pensions resulting from a company's bankruptcy, other older adults lose their pensions because they are laid off just before reaching retirement age. This is not an uncommon move for nonunionized businesses trying to cut down on expenses. Once laid off, it is very difficult for most older people to find jobs, since most firms look toward younger people for new hiring, despite laws intended to protect the elderly.

According to Katz (2001), approximately half of the American elderly today rely entirely on Social Security, a program never intended to be a sole support for retirement. The next 30 percent receive 90 percent of their income from the program.

The percentage of older adults who are considered to live in poverty would rise significantly if the standard for measuring poverty were updated, critics believe. The poverty line used as today's standard was established in the early 1960s. It resulted from surveys taken from 1955 through 1961 that indicated that the ratio of food consumption to all other household expenditures was 1:3. A basic food budget was then generated by the Department of Agriculture and was multiplied by 3 to determine the poverty line.

The food budget developed for the elderly was lower than that for younger people, so the official poverty line for the elderly was correspondingly lower as well. The percentage of older adults who are recognized to be poor today would go up considerably if the poverty line used were the same as that for younger people. The standard has increased since the 1960s only to account for inflation. More recent surveys have indicated that the current ratio of food costs to other necessary household expenditures is more nearly 1:5. If the newer ratio were used, a far greater percentage of older people would fall below the poverty line (Kart, 1994, p. 275).

Racial and **ethnic minority groups,** those with distinct biological or cultural characteristics different from the majority, are other major populations-at-risk. Groups that are considered minorities differ from country to country and from region to region. For example, although Hispanics are a minority group in the United States, that is not the case in Mexico or Latin America. The term "race" usually refers to physical or biological characteristics. In the United States, four racial **minority groups** are usually distinguished: Native Americans, African Americans, Hispanics, and Asian Americans. This can be confusing, since not all members of these groups are people of color. Persons who consider themselves Hispanic, for example, include both whites and nonwhites. Thus "Hispanics" can more accurately be considered an ethnic group rather than a race.

Ethnic groups share certain cultural characteristics that distinguish them from others, such as customs, values, language, and a common history. An ethnic group may contain members of different races, as in the example of Hispanics above, or it may differ culturally from the race it most resembles physically.

Racial and ethnic minority groups, earlier in this country's history, were expected to become part of a national "melting pot." Minority groups were thus pressured toward giving up cherished aspects of their cultural identities. Today, however, a new paradigm, or model for understanding, is emerging: **cultural pluralism** and ethnic diversity, in which difference is expected, acknowledged, and tolerated. This paradigm is increasingly embraced by social workers, and **cultural competency,** or the skill of communicating competently with people of contrasting cultures, is becoming an increasingly important expertise in social work practice (Lum, 1999).

KENT MEIREIS/THE IMAGE WORKS

Many older adults, especially racial minorities, suffer from poverty and neglect.

What minority groups have in common in the United States is that they have less power than the majority group. Lack of power renders minority group members vulnerable to discrimination and devaluation. (In this sense females are considered a minority group, even though they constitute a numerical majority.) Discrimination in the United States influences the amount minorities are likely to earn. For example, in 1995 the poverty rate for Hispanics was 30.3 percent, which was higher than that for African Americans for the first time, who suffered a rate of 29 percent. The poverty rate for Native Americans in 1995 was 30 percent, and for Asians 14.6 percent. These figures should be compared with a poverty rate of 11.2 percent for white Americans (Karger & Stoesz, 1998, pp. 86–88 and 125). By 1999 some rates had improved slightly: blacks 23.6 percent, Hispanics 22.8 percent as compared with 9.8 percent for whites (Greenstein, Primus, & Kayatin, 2000).

Sometimes one's racial or ethnic heritage affects where one can live more directly than income alone impacts it. Those who succeed financially despite discrimination, for example, may find themselves unwelcome and may be actively harassed in areas predominantly inhabited by persons of European background. (Fortunately, as a result of civil rights activism and legislation in the 1960s, such harassment is no longer legal. See Exhibit 5.)

In some cases, the cultural heritage of a minority group has been actively suppressed, not only in historical times but also in the present. Native American ways of life continue to be threatened in the United States, for example. In 1990, the U.S. Supreme Court upheld a decision suppressing the right of Native Americans to worship in traditional ways (*Smith v. Oregon Employment Division*, April 1990). In this case, two state employees were denied the right to participate in a traditional Native American religious ceremony involving use of peyote, a mild hallucinogen. Such decisions threaten religious freedom for all. In response to this perceived threat, Congress passed the American Indian Religious Freedom Act in 1993, but the Supreme Court declared that legislation

---

Segregation for African Americans

EXHIBIT 5

The segregation of African Americans survives at extraordinary levels throughout the nation, although it is generally a little worse in the North and in larger, more modern cities. It is much higher now than in 1860 or 1910. In 1930, in northern cities, except for Chicago and Cleveland, the average African American lived in a neighborhood dominated by whites; by 1970, this was totally reversed, and blacks in all northern cities lived far more often with other African Americans than whites. The average African American in major northern cities lived in a neighborhood that rocketed from 31.7 % black in 1930 to 73.5% in 1970.

Although it is often equated with poverty, racial segregation afflicts affluent as well as poor African Americans. Indexes of segregation remain about as high for them as for poor blacks.

Source: Quoted in Michael B. Katz. (2001). *The price of citizenship.* New York, Metropolitan Books, p. 48.

unconstitutional in 1997. Other recent Supreme Court decisions have exposed sacred Native American lands, even those on established reservations, to mineral exploitation.

In the worst-case scenario, sometimes members of majority ethnic groups try to exterminate others entirely. The example of the Holocaust against Jewish and Gypsy people, among others, under Germany's Nazi regime during World War II is a case in point. In the United States, hundreds of thousands of Native Americans were exterminated during the migration of white people across the continent. Millions of people of Tibet were massacred by the Chinese in the 1960s and 1970s. The recent ethnic cleansing in Bosnia, Rwanda, Kosovo, and other areas of the world provides chilling evidence that human beings still haven't learned that the example we set today plants seeds for the future.

Since the terrorist attacks in New York City and Washington, D.C., in the fall of 2001, the United States has had to deal with a powerful new challenge relating to minority ethnic groups. Since the men who hijacked the planes crashing into the World Trade Towers and the Pentagon were of Middle Eastern origin, people of that ethnic group immediately became suspect in this country. In an understandable effort to ward off possible further attacks, over 1,000 men of Middle Eastern origin were arrested; 500 are still in jail as this chapter is being written. Many are students. The policy currently enjoys a 70 percent to 80 percent approval rating by American citizens whose sense of security has been profoundly shaken (Grier, 2001).

In October 2001, the Justice Department under Attorney General John Ashcroft published a rule allowing investigators to listen in on conversations between detainees and their attorneys. Also in October, Congress passed "USA Patriot" legislation allowing student records to be subpoenaed if a judge agreed they might obtain information pertinent to terrorist investigations. At least 200 colleges immediately responded to such requests, which primarily but not exclusively sought foreign student records. As part of the same legislation, suspects' residences may be searched without their knowledge.

President George W. Bush declared the right to try people considered terrorists in military tribunals, where they would have no right of appeal, and requested that 5,000 Middle Eastern men submit "voluntarily" to FBI interviews. These actions represent a major infringement of the civil rights of Arab Americans and also chip away at the Bill of Rights protecting all American citizens. As acknowledged by Grier (2001, p. 8):

> Once bullets begin to fly, government officials must judge how much danger the nation is in, where those dangers lie, and whether the defense against them requires some abridgement of much-cherished individual rights—all under the pressure of onrushing time.
>
> History shows that they don't always get it right. The World War II internment of those of Japanese ancestry is today widely seen as a blot on the nation's honor.

Helen Thomas, a well-known newspaper columnist, reflects with great concern (2001, p. A4):

> We all know America is admired by people around the world because of our freedoms, especially those under the Bill of Rights, which protects citizens and even non-citizens. We are a nation that has been governed by laws that have endured for more than 200 years. If we lose our title of "land of the free," what have we got?

See Exhibit 6.

EXHIBIT 6

" I THINK ASHCROFT'S GETTING CARRIED AWAY WITH THIS ETHNIC PROFILING OF MIDDLE EASTERNERS..."

Source: Bill Shorr/United Features, *The Christian Science Monitor*, December 3, 2001, p. 10.

People with Disabilities

People with disabilities are another population-at-risk, since people who do not have disabilities may hold negative attitudes toward those who do. An extreme example of the inhumane treatment that may result took place in Nazi Germany, where many were sent to concentration camps and exterminated. In the United States, historically, many people with disabilities were sent to public institutions and sterilized so they would not reproduce. Today, persons with disabilities may find themselves subject to social ostracism, ridicule, job discrimination, and the like. The civil rights movement in the United States in the 1950s and 60s helped develop an awareness of social justice issues for the disabled, and they and their families began to advocate for legal rights and protections. Legislation important to disabled persons in the United States will be discussed in Chapter 13.

Societal definitions of disability differ with time and are hotly debated; the consequences are serious since certain protected populations can benefit from legislation from which others are excluded. For example, tens of thousands of poor children lost their federal disability benefits as part of 1996 welfare "reform" legislation simply because of changes in the legal definition of disability (Feldman, 1997).

Persons with disabilities experience many barriers, both social and economic, to full participation in today's world. Nearly two-thirds suffer unemployment, and of those who can find work, approximately half earn less than $15,000 per year. Employment for people with disabilities actually decreased 4 percent between 1970 and 1990, a period in which labor force participation among the general population increased by 10 percent (Segal & Brzuzy, 1998). The Americans With Disabilities Act of 1990 was designed to help alleviate this problem. It will be discussed in more detail in Chapter 13.

Gay and Lesbian Persons

Discrimination is a fact of life for most gay and lesbian persons, and unlike other groups who suffer this problem, federal civil rights protections have not yet been extended to include them. The reason seems to be that many people, because of their personal or religious values, do not accept those whose sexual orientation is toward persons of the same gender. While people have the right to choose their own values, discrimination against gays and lesbians is nevertheless discrimination against members of a significant minority group.

Without civil rights protections, people who are gay and lesbian can be fired from their jobs, denied home mortgages, refused apartment rentals, and so on, without legal recourse. To protest these and other discriminatory practices, hundreds of thousands of gays, lesbians, and other civil rights activists marched on Washington in 1993 seeking to obtain civil rights protection under the law. The efforts failed to obtain their immediate objective, but gay rights did gain recognition as a national issue.

In 1994, a Republican Congress was elected, making progress toward federal protection for gays very unlikely. Instead, concerned that the state of Hawaii was about to legalize gay marriages, Congress responded by passing the Defense of Marriage Act of 1996. This act permitted states not to accept as legal gay marriages performed in any other state.

Finding the federal government unresponsive to their cause, civil rights activists in the gay community turned to local grass roots organizing. When the state of Colorado passed a ban against antidiscrimination protection laws for gays and lesbians, these activists scored a victory when they appealed the ban to the Supreme Court. In the 1996 case of *Romer v. Evans,* the Supreme Court ruled that Colorado's prohibition was unconstitutional (Segal & Brzuzy, 1998).

In the year 2000, gays and lesbians won a joyful victory in Vermont, when the state legislature approved civil unions for same-sex couples, legally equivalent to marriage (Marks, 2000, April 27). Still, such victories for gays and lesbians today are few, and they remain a population of people who, in most states, may be discriminated against without legal recourse. For this reason, many still choose to keep their sexual orientation secret, causing untold hardships for unknown numbers of people.

RACIAL AND ETHNIC DIVERSITY IN THE UNITED STATES

The population of the United States is becoming increasingly diverse. Part of the growth in diversity stems from the natural increase of racial and ethnic minorities who have lived in the United States for generations, which tends to be higher than that of whites. Another aspect relates directly to war. For example,

139

CHAPTER 4
*Poverty and
Populations-at-Risk*

thousands of Vietnamese and Hmong people who fought in the Vietnam War as U.S. allies were forced to flee when the United States was defeated. Refugees continue to come to this country to escape dangerous political circumstances that relate back to that time. Other refugees flee war or economic distress in other parts of the world—for example, Cuba, Haiti, eastern Europe, Latin America, and Mexico.

Given the growing diversity of the U.S. population, and the fact that many ethnic groups desire to retain their unique cultural heritage, increasing numbers of social workers have embraced human diversity and cultural pluralism as paradigms to replace the older model of the melting pot. Embracing diversity is a process undertaken by many social workers not to increase divisiveness among diverse groups but to increase understanding and tolerance. Hopefully, understanding difference is a process that can lead to greater acceptance among people of diverse backgrounds. Greater honoring of minority rights in a democracy governed by majority rule can be another desirable outcome. Learning about difference, and teaching respect for all persons regardless of racial or ethnic background, can help social workers participate in the development of a more just Society.

Native Americans

Native Americans were the first Americans. Scientists believe that they originally migrated across the Bering Strait from Asia. By the time the first Europeans arrived, there were approximately 1.5 million native peoples thriving in North America, representing a wide variety of tribal groups, customs, and languages (Lum, 1992).

For Native Americans the coming of the Europeans was a catastrophe. Europeans immigrated in massive numbers, bringing new diseases that decimated many Indian populations and dangerously armed with the power of the gun. They drove the Indians from their lands and frequently massacred those who resisted. White Americans glamorize the western frontier, but what actually happened there and elsewhere in what is now the United States was systematic genocide. The "Trail of Tears" is an example. Under the Indian Removal Act of 1830, the U.S. government rounded up more than 100,000 Indians from five tribes (Cherokee, Choctaw, Chickasaw, Seminole, and Creek) in southern states and herded them into a forced march to the Oklahoma Territory. Thousands of people died along the way.

The native peoples resisted, but eventually the tribes were defeated. After the Civil War, Congress decreed that all Indians were wards of the government; no tribal sovereignty would be honored, regardless of previous treaties. Native Americans were then confined to reservations. In 1887 the Dawes Act divided reservation land into parcels, 160 acres for each adult and 80 acres for each child. On the surface, such division might appear reasonable. But most of the land set aside for Indians on reservations was extremely arid and thus unsuitable for agriculture. Whites had killed off most of the wildlife, including the buffalo. The Indians were destitute. Their way of economic sustenance had been destroyed forever, and they were dislocated from their ancestral lands. The result was that many had to sell their allotments for short-term survival, and that opened up the reservation areas to further exploitation by white people (Lum, 1992).

Beginning in the early 1900s additional efforts were made to destroy Native American culture. Children were forced to attend white boarding schools far from their reservations. They were forbidden to speak their own languages or to honor their own religious traditions. This practice continued into very recent times. Native Americans were granted full citizenship as late as 1924. In 1934 the Indian Reorganization Act indicated the beginning of change in federal policy toward recognition of cultural integrity. Tribes were allowed to establish tribal councils and to develop limited self-government. Loan funds were created, and purchase of new land by Native Americans was permitted.

Court cases have begun to establish the right of Native Americans to recover some of what was stolen from them. For example, in 1985 the U.S. Supreme Court in *Oneida Nation of Wisconsin v. State of New York* ruled that tribes have a right under common law to recover land wrongfully taken from them after the passage of the U.S. Constitution. Similar cases will undoubtedly be tested in the courts of the future (Lum, 1992).

Today the United States Department of Interior's Bureau of Indian Affairs and the U.S. Public Health Service assist Native Americans to maintain their distinctive way of life. However, many tribes would prefer to operate more independently from the federal government. Clearly, something different or additional is needed. Approximately 31.6 percent of Native Americans live below the poverty level and unemployment averages 56 percent (Federal trust responsibilities shirked, 1998). Tuberculosis, chronic liver disease, diabetes, pneumonia, and alcoholism are major health problems; suicide rates are double the national average (Karger & Stoesz, 1998).

There are currently more than 2 million Native Americans who belong to more than 500 tribes and live on over 300 different reservations in the United States including Alaska (Karger & Stoesz, 1998). They constitute approximately 1 percent of the total population (Belsie, 2001). To be effective in working with native peoples, social workers need to learn about their various cultures and family structures. Indian families that have maintained traditional lifestyles, for example, have different needs than those that are bicultural or more fully assimilated. Today, about a third live in urban areas, about a third on reservations, and about a third move back and forth (Van Wormer, 1997).

African Americans

The first African Americans came to this country in 1619 not as slaves but as indentured servants. The institution of slavery did not take firm hold in this country until the late 1600s, when the South developed an agricultural economy dependent on slave labor (Lum, 1992).

The legacy of slavery is profound and reaches to the present day. Africans were different from other immigrant groups because the vast majority, including most of the indentured servants, were brought to this country as captives against their will. Unlike other immigrant groups, they had no stable community of free kinsmen or countrymen to turn to for assistance upon arrival. Instead, slave traders systematically separated families and tribal members and sold them apart from one another to reduce chances of coalition and revolt. Native languages and religious traditions were forbidden. Every attempt was made to suppress the spirit of the slaves. Laws denied them the right to marry, to maintain families, to assemble in groups, to learn to read and write, or to sue for redress of grievances. Slaves were considered not persons but property.

Slavery existed at first in both northern and southern states and territories. Rhode Island was the first state to free its slaves, in 1784, a few years after the American Revolution (Quarles, 1987). By the time of the Civil War there were approximately half a million free blacks in the nation (Logan, Freeman, & McRoy, 1990). They were strictly regulated, however. All had to carry special papers certifying their free status, and they could be sold back into slavery if their papers were lost or stolen. In most states they were denied the right to vote, hold public office, or testify in court.

The Civil War from 1860 to 1865 freed the slaves but at great cost. One in four died from disease and deprivation related to the terrible conflict (Logan, Freeman, & McRoy, 1990). The first federal social welfare agency, the Bureau of Refugees, Freedmen, and Abandoned Lands, known as the Freedman's Bureau, was established two months before the end of the war, in anticipation of the enormous human need that would follow. The Freedman's Bureau distributed food, clothing, and medical supplies to starving blacks and whites alike. It also established 46 hospitals, several orphan asylums, and over 4,000 schools for African American children. It established institutions of higher learning for African Americans, including Howard, Atlanta, and Fisk Universities (Axinn & Levin, 1992). Unfortunately, the Freedman's Bureau was terminated in 1872. Had it been allowed to continue, the conditions for African Americans as a whole today would probably be much improved.

After slavery, all former states of the Confederacy except Tennessee passed "Black Codes" that limited the property rights of African Americans and forbade them to hold skilled jobs such as craftsman or mechanic. In Georgia, unemployed African Americans could be rounded up and put on chain gangs as criminals. State and local welfare programs for blacks were inferior to those for white people. Orphaned black children in Mississippi, for example, were apprenticed, and their former "masters" were given preference. No guarantees for adequate food, clothing, or education were written into the terms of indenture, as were included for white children (Axinn & Levin, 1992).

Under such difficult conditions, mutual aid and self-help were crucial for the survival of African Americans. The extended family rescued thousands of orphaned children, and churches organized orphanages, day care centers, and kindergartens. Churches also helped care for sick and elderly members and arranged for the adoption of children. African American lodges like the Masons and the Odd Fellows raised funds and provided needed services, as did various women's organizations (Logan, Freeman, & McRoy, 1990).

African Americans now make up over 12 percent of the U.S. population, more than 31 million people (Appleby, Colon, & Hamilton, 2001). Today they constitute the second largest minority group, after Hispanics. Among the many strengths of

African American people is the fact that mutual aid extends beyond nuclear family boundaries. Aid is routinely offered to extended family members, friends, and neighbors, permitting survival of many in need.

It is important for social workers to remember that there is no single African American family structure. African American families may be nuclear (including two biological parents or blended in a variety of ways) or single-parent; they may be wealthy, middle-income, or poor. However, because of the realities of discrimination and limited opportunity, a disproportionate number are poor, increasing the chances of involvement with the social service system.

Hispanics or Latinos

Latinos are classified as Hispanics by the U.S. Bureau of the Census, but "Latino" was the term coined by the people it was meant to identify (Colon, 2001). Including people from 26 countries, Latinos form a rapidly growing, diverse minority group that constitutes 13 percent of the population, according to the 2000 census, or about 35 million people (Blase, 2001). They recently overtook African Americans and became the nation's largest minority group (Wood, 2001). Approximately 68.9 percent are of Mexican origin, 11.3 percent Puerto Rican, 5.2 percent Cuban, and 14.6 percent Central and South American (Zuniga, 2001).

Texas, New Mexico, Arizona, and California originally belonged to Mexico. There were border disputes in Texas and California between white settlers and Mexicans, however. Texas declared its independence from Mexico in 1836, and the United States admitted it as a state in 1845. President Polk accepted the boundary claimed by Texas rather than that claimed by Mexico, and ordered General Zachary Taylor to enter the eastern bank of the Rio Grande to defend the disputed territories, thus precipitating the Mexican–American War. Mexico City was captured in 1848, resulting in the Treaty of Guadalupe Hidalgo. Under this treaty, the United States took ownership of the territories (Mexican War, 1995).

Mexicans who lived in the formerly disputed territories (lands that became Texas, New Mexico, Arizona and California) were allowed to stay, with American citizenship, or to leave for what remained of Mexico. Those who chose to stay in the United States were supposed to keep ownership of the lands they held before the war. However, the burden of proof of ownership was placed on the Mexicans, and many legal records were destroyed during and after the war. Gradually, people who stayed lost their land, becoming second-class citizens (Lum, 1992).

After losing their land, Mexican Americans resorted to work as laborers, primarily in agriculture. And because economic conditions in Mexico were poor, other Mexicans crossed the border to seek work in the United States. These immigrants, legal and illegal, formed the backbone of the migrant laborers who traveled the nation to harvest crops according to the season. Low wages, poor housing, and lack of sanitation and health care greeted them in many places. As a result, strong efforts were made to win the right for farm workers to form unions and engage in collective bargaining. This challenge continues today. In the late 1980s, work of self-advocacy organizations such as La Raza resulted in amnesty being offered to many illegal aliens who had lived in the United States for a significant period of time.

Puerto Ricans form another major group of Hispanic or Latino people in the United States. Puerto Rico became part of a commonwealth of the United States in 1917. Many Puerto Ricans later migrated to the mainland to pursue economic opportunity, usually settling in New York City. Today most still live in the northeastern region of the country. Unfortunately, many subsist in inner-city neighborhoods and suffer high rates of unemployment. Drug use and crime are common (Lum, 1992).

Cubans migrated to this country in large numbers in the early 1960s to escape the Castro government. They settled primarily in Florida. Early immigrants from Cuba were usually professionals and businesspeople who were economically advantaged. Later, however, many of the immigrants arrived destitute and required numerous services for basic survival. Latino immigrants from Central America have also come primarily as refugees. In particular, wars in Nicaragua and El Salvador have forced many to seek asylum. Numerous people have been denied entry and have been returned forcibly to dangerous situations. The needs of those who have been allowed to stay have deeply taxed the resources of agencies and programs designed to assist (Lum, 1992). There has been widespread pressure in the United States in recent years to modify immigration policy and for the federal government to assume social welfare costs (education, housing, financial aid, health services) that ordinarily have been borne by states and municipalities.

Given such multiple origins, it is easy to understand that Hispanic peoples are racially as well as ethnically diverse. When asked to describe their cultural heritage, most Hispanics refer to their national identity (for example, Mexican or Brazilian). Not all speak Spanish, nor do all have surnames that appear Spanish in origin (Castex, 1994).

Like other minority groups, Latino Americans face discrimination and limited economic opportunity in the United States. Although most Latinos live in urban inner-city neighborhoods, those who live in rural areas suffer poverty as well. Mexican Americans make up the largest group in the migrant labor force, for example. To make ends meet, migrant children often work with their parents in the fields from a very early age, interrupting their schooling.

Asian Americans

Asian Americans make up nearly 4 percent (Belsie, 2001) of the U.S. population. They derive from over 20 countries, including Japan, China, Korea, India, Vietnam, Cambodia, Laos, Thailand, the Philippines, and Samoa. Nearly 40 percent live in California alone, and 11 percent live in Hawaii. Others have settled in eastern coastal regions and parts of the northern Midwest. Asian peoples are heterogeneous in language and culture (Dubois & Miley, 1999).

The Chinese were the first Asian people to come to America in large numbers. They arrived in relatively recent times, toward the middle of the nineteenth century, attracted by economic opportunity. In Hawaii the Chinese worked as sugar plantation laborers, and in California they took part in the Gold Rush of 1849. Many became construction workers for the Southern Pacific Railroad. Their success led to fear of competition, which culminated in the

Chinese Exclusion Act of 1882, barring further immigration. People of Chinese descent were denied citizenship and the right to intermarry (Lum, 1992).

Large numbers of Japanese emigrated during the early twentieth century, in response to a need for farm workers in California. The Immigration Act of 1924 closed the door to immigration of Asians after that time, however. This law set low immigration quotas for dark-skinned people of all nationalities and excluded Asians entirely. Then, after the bombing of Pearl Harbor in 1941, Japanese Americans were forcibly interned in camps for the duration of World War II. Their property was liquidated, as mentioned in this chapter's case example. Although the U.S. Supreme Court in 1944 declared this treatment of Japanese people unconstitutional, not until 1988 were petitions for redress of grievance accepted by Congress. The settlement even then was token: $20,000 for each living survivor.

The 1965 Immigration Act changed U.S. policy to make it more equitable to people of diverse racial and ethnic heritages. Political refugees from the Philippines and Korea included many educated Asian professionals at that time. Then the Vietnam War brought waves of refugees from Vietnam, Laos, and Cambodia, particularly after the fall of Saigon in 1975. The early refugees were highly educated people who had been allies of the Americans. Later refugees included less privileged people, who have experienced much more difficulty adjusting to life in the United States and greater economic hardship. Although American churches have assisted these refugees through sponsorship of Church World Services, many Americans have expressed resentment toward them because of perceived competition for scarce jobs and other resources (Lum, 1992).

Important for social workers to understand is that many refugees suffer from posttraumatic stress disorder (PTSD), the disorder experienced by Juan Attencio in this chapter's case study. The disorder involves a characteristic set of responses to a traumatic event or events. Symptoms include difficulty sleeping and concentrating, irritability, outbursts of anger, hypervigilance, and an exaggerated startle response. Sufferers rarely seek help, however, because of language and cultural barriers. A study of Cambodian immigrants, for example, found that 86% suffered from PTSD more than a decade after leaving their homelands, having endured the deaths of family and friends and long periods of starvation. Yet only one had sought mental health treatment (Carlson & Rosser-Hogan, 1994).

Traditional values strongly affect Asian family life today. These values include unquestioning deference to parental authority; compliance of children even to the point of sacrificing personal ambition (reinforced by use of shame and threat of losing face); self-control and modesty of behavior; subordination of self to the group; internalization of problems (not talking about them); and detached resignation or acceptance of fate (Dubois & Miley, 1999). Families may experience stress when children encounter other values and begin to question differences. Yet, by internalizing problems and avoiding shame, families tend not to seek help. Social workers need to carefully assess individual families who do seek help to find out where they fall on the continuum between traditional and wider American cultural values.

POTENT FORMS OF DISCRIMINATION IN THE UNITED STATES

Although Americans proclaim an overall belief in equal justice for all, and although various social movements have produced important legislation to protect the rights of minority groups, a marked discrepancy still exists between principle and practice today. Certain potent societal "isms" are clearly still in evidence.

Isms are prejudices common to large segments of society that relegate people who are perceived as different to a lower social status. Isms in the United States stem from cultural teachings such as white is better, male is better, young is better, and heterosexual is better. Isms have many consequences, varying from attempted extermination of the devalued population to milder forms of social discrimination such as lack of access to certain jobs and lower pay. Sadly, people who suffer discrimination often take their poor treatment to heart so that they suffer loss of self-esteem as well.

Racism

Racism is the belief that one race is superior to others, a belief that tends to justify exploiting members of other races. In the United States, the majority race includes a variety of white-skinned ethnic groups of European origin, who tend to consider themselves superior to people of racial groups with darker skin. Racism leads to discrimination against people of color perpetrated by both individuals and social institutions such as governmental bodies and private organizations. Institutional racism, or patterns of racial discrimination entrenched in law and custom, lives on in many subtle forms today. It was far more blatant, of course, before the civil rights movement of the 1960s and early 1970s. The civil rights movement was sparked in 1955 by Mrs. Rosa Parks's courageous refusal to obey a white man's demand that she give up her seat on a Montgomery, Alabama, bus as required by racist laws.

Today, overtly racist laws have been ruled unconstitutional, but subtler institutional racism and personal affronts continue. Subtler racism tends to maintain people of color in inferior schools, segregated neighborhoods, and lower paying jobs. Personal affronts include incidents such as that experienced by Mr. Talmadge Branch, who stopped at a tavern in Perry, Florida, on his way to Tallahassee in spring 2001. Branch, a state legislator from Maryland, happens to be African American, and the bartender directed him out of the main customer area to a back room. The incident is now in court as a discrimination case (Waddel, 2001, March 9). It is also common for law-abiding black motorists to be stopped by police simply for driving through white neighborhoods, or to be questioned if standing with a small group on a street corner, even in a predominantly African American neighborhood.

Sexism

Sexism is the belief that one sex is superior to the other, usually that males are superior to females. This belief tends to justify exploiting females economically and sexually. Sexism is undergirded, unfortunately, by various organized religions that cite ancient texts alleging the superiority of the male. However, modern scholars have found substantial evidence indicating that these texts were selectively edited over time to conceal the value of female roles and to stifle women's leadership potential. Whole books have been written about this fascinating subject, including *The Gnostic Gospels* by Elaine Pagels (1979) and *The Chalice and the Blade* by Riane Eisler (1987).

Although numerous laws have been adopted in recent times to help create equal opportunity for females, a constitutional amendment, stating simply, "Equal rights under law shall not be denied or abridged by the United States or by any State on account of sex," was never ratified. Many women helped fight to maintain gender inequality, fearing loss of certain legal protections such as exemption from military draft. However, it is unlikely that the draft, if reinstated in the future, would exclude women anyway. Women's contributions to the paid labor force are simply too important to ignore today.

Discrimination against females has important effects. Girls and young women tend to limit their aspirations to the types of positions they perceive they can get. Unskilled women, for example, tend to fill service positions, while educated women disproportionately select service professions like nursing, teaching, and social work. Women are characteristically paid less than men even with the same education, the same job position, and the same number of years of paid work experience. This injustice forces many women to remain economically dependent on men.

Ageism

Ageism is the belief that youth is superior to age, that old people have outlived their usefulness and therefore are of little value. Ageism involves such stereotypes as that the majority of old people are senile, old-fashioned, and "different." These stereotypes tend to justify discrimination against the elderly.

Recently, a "new ageism" has taken shape, emanating from a perception that the elderly have made significant economic gains as a result of Social Security benefits. Robert Butler (1994), the social scientist who originally coined the term *ageism,* describes this phenomenon as "a dangerous viewpoint that envies the elderly for their economic progress and, at the same time, resents the poor elderly for being tax burdens and the nonpoor elderly for making Social Security so costly." He notes that many older adults are, in fact, still very poor.

Butler points out a peculiar irony. Most people dream of a long life, and in general this hope is being realized. However, instead of celebrating, younger people view the elderly as potential economic burdens. They fear that the Social Security system will be bankrupt by the time they become old. Butler points out that this fear is greatly exaggerated and that, because of the falling birthrate, the total dependency-support ratio (ratio including dependents both below 18 and over 64) has been steadily declining since 1900. It will continue to do so until 2050.

Myths that most older adults are senile and physically debilitated are simply that: myths. Most elderly describe their health as being reasonably good. Memory loss is associated more with stress than with age, and it is usually reversible. The exception is memory loss caused by medical factors, such as Alzheimer's disease (see Chapter 11). Younger people, however, can be victims of this disease as well. Various studies have shown that what appear to be characteristics of aging, such as decreased mobility and memory loss, can also afflict younger people. The difficulties can often be reversed even among the very old with proper health and mental health care.

Heterosexism and Homophobia

Heterosexim is the belief that heterosexuals are superior to homosexuals. **Homophobia** is the fear, dread, or hatred of people who are homosexual. Both lead to social and economic discrimination against people who are gay or lesbian. There was a time when homosexuality was viewed as a mental disorder. However, research has led to the knowledge that sexual orientation has nothing to do with one's mental health (except, of course, that discrimination can result in fear and depression). For this reason, homosexuality is no longer listed as a pathology in the *Diagnostic and Statistical Manual of Mental Disorders* used by most mental health professionals. Gays and lesbians are similar to other people in every way except their sexual orientation. No one understands the causes of homosexuality, but it generally is not considered a personal choice; hence, most gays and lesbians prefer to speak of **sexual orientation** rather than "sexual preference."

Some fundamentalist religious groups view the terrible AIDS epidemic as punishment for a homosexual lifestyle, probably because the disease seems to have spread originally in the United States through sexual contact between gay males. However, this point of view does not survive wider analysis. In other parts of the world where the disease began, it was primarily spread through heterosexual contact. Moreover, lesbians have a very low incidence of the disease. In the United States today, people are increasingly contracting AIDS through heterosexual contact. AIDS today is commonly spread through contaminated needles, so that people who take drugs intravenously are at high risk.

People who are gay and lesbian suffer ongoing legal and economic discrimination in the United States today. For example, while heterosexual couples can marry, enjoying specific legal advantages such as shared health insurance benefits, inheritance rights, "next of kin" hospital visitation privileges, and lower automobile insurance premiums, committed gay and lesbian couples generally enjoy no such benefits. Instead, their love is frequently denigrated as "abnormal," and marriage and its legal rights are forbidden.

Fortunately, positive changes are slowly coming about through the efforts of human rights activists, including many gays and lesbians. For example, the gay rights movement in San Francisco won the right for homosexual couples to register as domestic partners, an arrangement conferring certain legal benefits. Other municipalities and businesses have instituted employee benefit plans that include partners in committed relationships (nonlegally married couples, no matter what their sexual orientation). The state of Vermont approved civil unions of same-sex couples in 2000. Some religious organizations such as the Quakers provide marriage ceremonies for gay and lesbian couples who are members. These marriages do not yet carry legal rights, but they provide social recognition and support.

Unfortunately, however, these hard-won victories are continually jeopardized by backlash legislation, such as the Defense of Marriage Act passed by Congress in 1996 when it was concerned that Hawaii might legalize gay and lesbian marriages. This law, as described earlier, allows states to ignore marriages of gays and lesbians performed in other states.

AFFIRMATIVE ACTION POLICY: UNDER ATTACK

Due to discrimination, prejudice, and the "isms" discussed above, populations at risk suffer economic hardships in this country through no fault of their own. There are two main approaches in the United States today to addressing such injustice: **nondiscrimination** and **affirmative action.** Nondiscrimination laws or practices simply ban discrimination. In 1941, for example, President Franklin Roosevelt issued an executive order barring discrimination against African American contractors in the war effort. There was no way for him to enforce his order, however, so it was ignored. The Civil Rights Act of 1964 was the first powerful national legislation to bar discrimination, carrying with it the power of the courts. Title VII of this act, as amended in 1972, prohibits employment discrimination against people on the basis of race, color, religion, sex, or national origin. (Age and disability are now protected categories as well.)

Despite the 1964 law, discrimination persisted vigorously. By the early 1970s, to carry out the law's intent, courts began requiring companies and universities that lost discrimination cases to engage in "affirmative action" efforts to improve compliance. Affirmative action required targeted outreach toward minorities. This meant that in some cases, a member of a minority might be recruited or hired ahead of a member of a nonprotected category.

This approach has always been controversial. The first major legal challenge took place in 1978, when Allen Bakke, a white male denied admission to medical school at the University of California, sued the university. He argued that he was better qualified than some of the minority applicants who were accepted. He won his case, and as part of the ruling, specific quotas for minority admissions at colleges and universities were prohibited.

Court decisions since 1978 have been inconsistent, sometimes upholding affirmative action efforts and sometimes not. However, given conservative political trends over the past three decades, affirmative action has largely been under attack. Conservatives argue that it discriminates against members of the majority group. They insist that Title VII of the Civil Rights Act should be interpreted narrowly and applied only to specific individuals suffering specific instances of discrimination, not to categories of people (women, ethnic minorities, etc.) who demonstrably suffer discrimination as a group.

As a powerful example of the conservative trend, Proposition 209 was passed in California in 1996 and upheld in state court. It prohibits racial and gender preferences in employment, public education, and state contracts. As another example, a federal judge in Detroit in 2001 ruled against the University of Michigan's use of racial distinctions in law school admissions (Grier, Chinni, & Clayton, 2001)

It is interesting to note, however, that with respect to the Michigan case, 20 leading corporations (including Intel, Microsoft, Kellogg, Texaco, Kodak, and Dow Chemical) went on record supporting the university (Knickerbocker, 2000). The reasons? These businesses believed that a more diverse student body would improve their own competitive stance in a global market (see Exhibit 7).

In addition, the Regents of the University of California voted unanimously in 2001 to end their ban on affirmative action in admission and hiring, challenging the 1996 state law. The reason was an alarming drop in diversity on campus (The University of California, 2001). Beginning in fall 2001, factors beyond grade point average and test scores (such as hardship and special talents) were explicitly to be considered (Sappenfield, 2001).

The United States Equal Opportunity Employment Commission states:

> Affirmative action is one part of an effort to remedy past and present discrimination and is considered essential to assuring that jobs are "genuinely and equally accessible to qualified persons, without regard to their sex, racial or ethnic characteristics." (Quoted in Frappier, 1995, p. 5)

Are jobs genuinely and equally accessible to all qualified persons today, so that affirmative action efforts are really unnecessary, as espoused by people of a conservative political orientation? Evidence is to the contrary. For example, women are still clustered in a few occupations and are paid less than men even in the same positions, as discussed previously. The presidential Glass Ceiling Commission found that people of color and women were not able to progress as far as their qualifications and abilities would otherwise carry them if they were white and male (Efforts to end affirmative action continue, 1997). Men hold 95% of senior management positions in the top Fortune 1000 industrial companies and the top Fortune 500 service companies, and 97% of them are white (Popple & Leighninger, 1999).

Business for Affirmative Action

EXHIBIT 7

"Diversity is . . . a fundamental business strategy," says A. G. Lafley, CEO of Procter & Gamble, one of the companies supporting the University (of Michigan). "Our success depends entirely on our ability to understand these diverse consumers' needs and to work effectively with customers and suppliers around the world.

"All the data I've seen in 30 years of being in business—and all of my personal experience at Procter and Gamble over the last 23 years—convince me that a diverse organization will out-think, out-innovate, and out-perform a homogeneous organization every single time."

Source: Quoted from Brad Knickerbocker. (2000, October 25). Affirmative action's unlikely ally, *The Christian Science Monitor*, 1,5.

EXHIBIT 8

Source: Bennett, *The Christian Science Monitor*. Reprinted with permission.

Due to such powerful statistical evidence of continuing discrimination, supporters of affirmative action policies believe it is important to go beyond conservative interpretations of the civil rights law and create systematic remedies for past and present discrimination against minorities (see Exhibit 8). Such efforts, however, seem unlikely to prevail at the beginning of the twenty-first century. The president, the House of Representatives, and the Supreme Court all profess conservative positions at this time. See the "Up for Debate" box.

THE INTERNATIONAL CODE OF ETHICS

Few people indeed are free of prejudice (ideas and feelings conceived before important facts are known). Prejudice is taught, directly or indirectly, almost everywhere. The challenge is to acknowledge and explore the prejudices we have learned, to reeducate ourselves about people who are different, and to take care not to confuse difference with inequality in value. We can teach ourselves to treat everyone with dignity and respect, even when unresolved feelings of prejudice persist. Social work values and ethics insist that we do no less. The International Code of Ethics is especially pertinent (see Exhibit 9). This code illustrates that, as long ago as 1976, the International Federation of Social Workers recognized that human beings are diverse and that each and every person has unique value and the

Up for Debate

*Proposition: Affirmative action programs should be maintained
to assist in provision of equal opportunity for all.*

Yes	No
Affirmative action programs help correct past discriminatory hiring practices by seeking qualified applicants of color and women.	Affirmative action programs may discriminate against people who are white, especially white males.
Affirmative action programs help assure that jobs are genuinely and equally accessible to qualified persons without regard to sex, racial, or ethnic characteristics.	Affirmative action programs may tend to hire women and people of color rather than others who are equally or sometimes more qualified.
Affirmative action programs help assure that qualified persons of merit gain employment, even if minority or female, rather than applicants who simply happen to be white and male.	Affirmative action programs may help qualified minorities and females gain employment rather than white males who may be equally and sometimes more qualified.
In a democratic, multiracial society, integrated institutions can provide higher levels of service than agencies run entirely by one sex and race.	The most qualified applicants should always be hired, even if they all happen to be white and male.

The International Code of Ethics

EXHIBIT 9

The following ethical principles are quoted from the International Code of Ethics for Professional Social Workers, as adopted by the International Federation of Social Workers in 1976:

1. Every human being has a unique value irrespective of origin, ethnicity, sex, age, beliefs, social and economic status or contribution to society.
2. Each individual has the right of self-fulfillment to the degree that it does not encroach upon the same right of others.
3. Each society, regardless of its form, should function to provide maximum benefits to its members.
4. The professional social worker has the responsibility to devote objective and disciplined knowledge and skill to aid individuals, groups, communities and societies in their development and in the resolution of personal-societal conflicts and their consequences.
5. The professional social worker has a primary obligation to the objective of service, which must take precedence over self-interest, personal aims or views.

right to self-fulfillment. The professional social worker, regardless of "self-interest, personal aims or views," has a primary obligation to provide professional service. This involves devoting "objective and disciplined knowledge and skill to aid individuals, groups, communities and societies in their development and in the resolution of personal-societal conflicts and their consequences."

INTERNET SITES

http://www.clasp.org/	Center for Law and Social Policy
http://www.disrights.org/	The Disability Rights Activist
http://www.ngltf.org/	National Gay and Lesbian Task Force
http://cpmcnet.columbia.edu/dept/nccp/	National Center for Children in Poverty
http://www.wlo.org/	Women Leaders Online
http://www.chd-prevention.org/ empowerment/	The Empowerment Project
http://www.libertynet.org/edcivic/ welref.html	About Welfare Reform
http://www.cbpp.org	Center on Policy and Budget Priorities
http://www.eeoc.gov/facts/fs-preg.html	Facts About Pregnancy Discrimination
http://www.affirmativeaction.org/	The American Association for Affirmative Action
http://www.ncpa.org/~ncpa/pd/affirm/ affirm.html	National Center for Policy Analysis
http://www.cde.ca.gov/iasa/ diversity.html	Diversity: Issues and Responses
http://www.ed.gov/pubs/ EdReformStudies/SysReforms/ tharp1.html	Research Knowledge and Policy Issues in Cultural Diversity and Education

SUMMARY

This chapter begins with the story of Juan Attencio, whose father is Hispanic and whose mother is Japanese. Despite Juan's education as an electronics technician and a full-time job, his daily experience has been one of destructive poverty. He is attempting to support his current nuclear family of four as well as two children from a prior marriage and a friend who has a disability. Juan's poverty, combined with post-traumatic stress disorder, contributed to substance abuse, to abuse of his wife, and to criminal charges leading to a jail sentence. The severity of Juan's sentence for a first offense may have been related to his ethnic minority status. The chapter proceeds to explore the concepts of social justice and populations-at-risk. Evidence from countries around the world, including the United States, is cited indicating that social justice is not yet evident in the world today. Groups of people most likely to suffer poverty and discrimination are identified as populations-at-risk. Major populations-at-risk in the United States include children, women, older adults, members of racial and ethnic minority groups, people with disabilities, and gays and lesbians.

Racial and ethnic diversity in the United States is discussed, and brief historical backgrounds are provided for Native Americans, African Americans, Hispanics, and Asian Americans. The older concept of a melting pot is contrasted with the more current concepts of pluralism and cultural diversity.

The chapter continues with a discussion of various kinds of prejudice and discrimination: racism, sexism, ageism, heterosexism, and homophobia. It concludes with a discussion of affirmative action policy and with quotations from the International Code of Ethics for Professional Social Workers.

KEY TERMS

affirmative action
ageism
cultural competency
cultural pluralism
ethnic group
feminization of poverty
heterosexism
homophobia
isms
juvenilization of poverty

minority group
nondiscrimination
populations-at-risk
poverty
prejudice
racial group
racism
sexism
sexual orientation
social and economic justice

DISCUSSION QUESTIONS

1. What groups are the major populations-at-risk in the United States today?
2. What are the major risks faced by populations-at-risk? Why are they at risk?
3. Identify the major racial groups in the United States. Which ones are minority groups? What obstacles do members of minority groups face in the majority American culture?
4. Compare and contrast the concepts of ethnicity and race.
5. Females constitute a numerical majority in the United States. In what sense, then, are they considered a minority group?
6. Define prejudice. What major types of prejudice are common in the United States today?
7. According to the text, what can each person do to help increase harmony among diverse groups in this country today?
8. How must an ethical social worker treat all persons, regardless of prejudices she or he may harbor?
9. Compare and contrast the concept of the melting pot with the concepts of cultural pluralism and ethnic diversity. Which paradigm do you prefer, and why?
10. What are major arguments in favor of affirmative action policies in this country today? What are arguments against such policies? What do you personally think about affirmative action policies? Why?

CLASSROOM EXERCISES

While not required, it is suggested that students break into small groups of three or four to discuss these exercises. It may be helpful to choose a scribe to record and report interesting points to the class after the group discussion.

1. Describe and discuss the population characteristics of the place where you grew up (if you moved frequently, choose the place you lived in the longest, or lived in most recently). What populations-at-risk can you identify?
2. What social justice issues did you identify then, or can you identify now, that relate to the populations-at-risk you encountered growing up?
3. Many people today do not understand the reasons for affirmative action, especially members of the majority group. Identify those cited in this text supporting affirmative action and think of at least three more from your own experience.
4. Compare and contrast the concepts of nondiscrimination and affirmative action. Which approach do you think best meets the needs of the United States today as part of a developing family of nations? Why?

RESEARCH ACTIVITIES

1. Select one of the major populations-at-risk discussed in this chapter and do a research project to gather the most current information regarding the percentage of the current population that its members represent, the percentage of its members experiencing poverty, the percentage suffering unemployment, and so on.
2. Examine the laws of your state to find out whether legal protections are offered to gays and lesbians with respect to employment and child custody issues. Are gays and lesbians allowed to adopt in your state? What is your opinion regarding legal protections for people who are gay or lesbian? Give your reasons.
3. Examine the buildings on your campus to find out whether they are accessible to people with disabilities. If not, what major barriers did you find? Conduct interviews with campus administrators to find out if they are aware of accessibility problems and whether plans are being developed to improve accessibility.

INTERNET RESEARCH EXERCISES

1. An interesting point of view is presented in an article appearing on the website of FAIR, the national media watch group (http://fair.org/extra/best-of-extra/geezer-bashing.html).
   a. What are some of the "solutions" to budget problems reported in this article?
   b. What was Senator Patrick Moynihan's word for the reported insolvency of the Social Security reserve?
   c. What is the greatest threat of ageism that you see having read this article?
2. The Administration on Aging, an agency of the federal government, has an interesting "Profile of Older Americans: 2000" (http://www.aoa.gov/aoa/STATS/profile/default.htm).
   a. According to the report, what percentage of the population did people 65 and older represent in 1999? What is the percentage projected to be in 2030?
   b. What was the primary source of income for people 65 and older in 1998?
   c. What were the five top chronic conditions reported by older persons in 1996?

3. The United Nations presented a five-year follow-up report on the 1995 Fourth World Conference on Women. The Feminization of Poverty is one subject reported (http://www.un.org/womanwatch/daw/follow-up/session/presskit/fsl.htm).

    a. The paper speaks of a wider definition of poverty. What does this wider definition mean?

    b. The paper states that the negative impact of the globalization of the world economy is borne disproportionately by women. How do they arrive at this conclusion?

    c. What is a critical factor, according to the paper, for the freeing of all people caught in the cycle of poverty and hunger?

REFERENCES

Appleby, G., Colon, E., & Hamilton, J. (2001). *Diversity, oppression, and social functioning.* Boston: Allyn and Bacon.

Axinn, J., & Levin, H. (1992). *Social welfare: A history of the American response to need* (3rd ed.). New York: Longman.

Belsie, L. (1998, October 13). New clout for the comfortable. *The Christian Science Monitor, 1,* 18.

Belsie, S. (2001, March 14). Ethnic diversity grows, but not integration. *The Christian Science Monitor,* 1, 4.

Blase, J. (2001, June 21). Defining "Hispanic" and "Latino." *The Christian Science Monitor,* 13.

Butler, R. (1994). Dispelling agism: The cross-cutting intervention. In R. D. Enright, Jr. (Ed.), *Perspectives in social gerontology* (p. 5). Boston: Allyn and Bacon.

Bryner, G. (1998). *Politics and the public morality.* New York: W. W. Norton & Company.

Carlson, E. B., & Rosser-Hogan, R. (1994, January). Refugee's stress rate reveals lasting war effects. *Brain Mind Bulletin,* 19 (4), 1.

Castex, G. M. (1994, May). Providing services to Hispanic/Latino populations: Profiles in diversity. *Social Work,* 39 (3), 290.

Colon, E. (2001). A multidiversity perspective on Latinos. In G. A. Appleby, E. Colon, & J. Hamilton, *Diversity, oppression and social functioning* (pp. 92–107). Boston: Allyn and Bacon.

Colon, E., Appleby, G., & Hamilton, J. (2001). Affirmative practice with people who are culturally diverse and oppressed. In G. A. Appleby, E. Colon, & J. Hamilton, *Diversity, oppression and social functioning* (pp. 241–252). Boston: Allyn and Bacon.

Dubois, B., & Miley, K. K. (1999). *Social work, an empowering profession* (3rd ed.). Boston: Allyn and Bacon.

Efforts to end affirmative action continue. (1997, August/September). *Friends Committee on National Legislation Washington Newsletter,* 3.

Ehrenreich, B. (2001). *Nickeled and dimed: On (not) getting by in America.* New York: Metropolitan Books.

Eisler, R. (1987). *The chalice and the blade.* San Francisco: Harper.

Federal trust responsibilities shirked. (1998, Summer). *Friends Committee on National Legislation Indian Report,* 2.

Feldman, L. (1997, October 24). Fraud busters cut benefits for disabled children. *The Christian Science Monitor,* 4.

Francis, D. R. (2001, June 6). Women demolish more career barriers. *The Christian Science Monitor,* 1,10.

Frappier, N. S. (1995). Affirmative action in the persistence of racism. *Race, Rights, and Resistance, a Special Issue of Social Work Perspectives,* 5 (2), 5–10.

Gardner, M. (2001, October 24). The invisible hungry—their numbers grow. *The Christian Science Monitor,* 17.

Greenstein, R., Primus, W., & Kayatin, T. (2000, October 10). Poverty rate hits lowest level since 1979 as unemployment reaches a 30 year low. *Center on Budget and Policy Priorities* (Online). Available: http://www.cbpp.org/9-26-00pov.htm.

Grier, P. (2001, December 13). Fragile freedoms, which civil liberties, and whose, can be abridged to create a safer America? *The Christian Science Monitor,* 1, 8, 9.

Grier, P., Chinni, D., & Clayton, M. (2001, March 19). Affirmative action in jeopardy. *The Christian Science Monitor,* 1, 4.

Growing economic inequality within a growing economy. (1998, April). *Friends Committee on National Legislation Washington Newsletter,* 1.

Healy, L. M. (1992). *Introducing international development content in the social work curriculum.* Silver Spring, MD: NASW Press.

Homelessness (1998, April). *Friends Committee on National Legislation Washington Newsletter,* 3.

Karger, H. J., & Stoesz, D. (1998). *American social welfare policy, a pluralist approach.* New York: Longman.

Kart, C. S. (1994). *The realities of aging: An introduction to gerontology* (4th ed). Boston: Allyn and Bacon

Katz, M. B. (2001). *The price of citizenship.* New York: Metropolitan Books.

Kissenger, M. (2001, May 20). Home is just a dream. *The Milwaukee Journal Sentinel,* p. 2.

Knickerbocker, B. (2000, October 25). Affirmative action's unlikely ally. *The Christian Science Monitor,* 1, 5.

Kozol, J. (1996). Amazing voices. *The Family Therapy Networker,* 52–59.

Logan, S. M. L., Freeman, E. M. & McRoy, R. G. (1990). *Social work perspective with black families: A culturally specific perspective.* New York: Longman.

Lum, D. (1992). *Social work with people of color: A process-stage approach* (2nd ed.). Pacific Grove, CA: Brooks/Cole.

Lum, D. (1999). *Culturally competent practice, a framework for growth and action.* Pacific Grove: CA: Brooks/Cole.

Marks, A. (2000, April 27). Vermont hunches revolution by allowing same-sex unions. *The Christian Science Monitor,* 2.

Marks, A. (2001, November 29). U.S. shelters swell—with families. *The Christian Science Monitor,* 1, 8.

Mexican War. (1995). *The encyclopedia Americana, international edition* (Vol. 18). Danbury, CT: Grolier.

Pagels, E. (1979). *The gnostic gospels.* New York: Random House.

Pommereau, I. (1998, June 2). Is the economic boom leaving too many people behind? *The Christian Science Monitor,* 3–4.

Popple, P. R., & Leighninger, L. (1999). *Social work, social welfare, and American society* (4th ed.). Boston: Allyn and Bacon.

Quarles, B. (1987). *The Negro in the making of America* (3rd ed.). New York: Macmillan.

Raising the minimum wage. (1998, April). *FCNL Washington Newsletter,* 5.

Sappenfield, M., and Day J. (2001, January 16). Women, it seems, are better bosses. *The Christian Science Monitor,* 1, 3.

Sappentield, M. (2001, November 19). New scale to weigh college applicants. *The Christian Science Monitor,* 1, 5.

Segal, E., & Brzuzy, S. (1998). *Social welfare policy, programs, and practice.* Itasca, IL: F. E. Peacock Publishers.

Sherman, A. (1997). *Poverty matters, the cost of child poverty in America.* Washington, DC: Children's Defense Fund.

Spending the surplus. (2001, March). *Friends Committee on National Legislation Washington Newsletter,* 1.

Thomas, H. (2001, December 14). We Need to Stand Up for Our Rights. *The Daily News,* West Bend, WI, A4.

Thousands off nation's welfare rolls, but some say they're worse off. (2000, July 3). *The Daily News,* A9.

The University of California rescinded its ban on affirmative action admission. (2001, May 18). *The Christian Science Monitor,* 24.

U.S. Bureau of the Census, (2001). Poverty thresholds in 2000 (online). Available: www.census.gov.

Van Wormer, K. (1997). *Social welfare: A world view.* Chicago, Nelson-Hall.

Waddell, Lynn. (2001, March 9). The customer who wouldn't drink out back. *The Christian Science Monitor,* 1.

Wood, D. B. (2001, July 16). Latinos redefine what it means to be manly. *The Christian Science Monitor,* 1, 3.

Wright, J. D., Rubin B. A., & Devine, J. A. (1998). *Beside the golden door: Policy, politics and the homeless.* New York: Aldine de Gruyter.

Zuniga, M. E. (2001). Latinos: Cultural competence and ethics. In R. Fong & S. Furuto (Eds.), *Culturally competent practice* (pp. 47–59). Boston: Allyn and Bacon.

FOR FURTHER READING

Appleby, G., Colon, E., & Hamilton, J. (2001). *Diversity, oppression and social functioning: Person-in-environment assessment and intervention.* Boston: Allyn and Bacon.

These authors offer an ecological framework for working with diverse clients who have experienced discrimination and oppression. Populations addressed include people of color, women, lesbians and gays, people with disabilities (physical, cognitive, and emotional), and people of all colors and abilities who have experienced class-based discrimination.

Fong, R., & Furuto, S. (2001). *Culturally competent practice: Skills, interventions and evaluations.* Boston: Allyn and Bacon.

This book is designed to assist social work practitioners to become more culturally competent in working with people of color. It presents the knowledge, values, and skills required to work with the four major ethnic groups present in America today: African Americans, Latino/Hispanic Americans, First Nations Peoples, and Asians and Pacific Islanders. A particular focus is empowerment on micro, mezzo, and macro levels of practice.

Healy, L. M. in collaboration with the International Committee, Council on Social Work Education. (1992). *Introducing international development content in social work curriculum.* Silver Spring, MD: National Association of Social Workers.

A wealth of information, this volume is intended to assist BSW and MSW programs to integrate international content into the curriculum. It introduces curriculum modules that provide outlines for content and suggests resource materials for examining global poverty, the rights of children, and international social work practice. The need for international content in contemporary social work education is examined, and the concept of the developing nation is explored.

Karger, H. J., & Stoesz, D. (1998). *American social welfare policy: A pluralist approach.* New York: Addison Wesley Longman.

This volume explores social welfare policy from a variety of perspectives. Part One examines American social welfare policy and provides an in-depth analysis of poverty in America today. Part Two explores the voluntary and for-profit social welfare sector. Part Three examines the government sector, including social insurance programs, public assistance, and health care policy. Part Four examines the American welfare state in perspective, including the international context.

Sherman, A. (1997). *Poverty matters: The cost of child poverty in America.* Washington, DC: Children's Defense Fund.

This impressive monograph presents many-faceted findings regarding the high cost of child poverty in America, not only to the children themselves but to the nation. It describes in detail exactly why poverty hurts children and examines the high economic costs of poverty. The book includes a thoughtful plan regarding how to eliminate child poverty.

Professional Practice Settings

Part Two is the heart of this text. Part One provided background information defining social work, explaining the role of the generalist social worker, and discussing the choice of social work as a career. It introduced theoretical perspectives important to social workers, including those that affect practice activities and those that influence political processes impacting social policy development. In addition, Part One explored issues of social and economic justice, poverty, populations-at-risk, and major social welfare programs designed to assist people in need. In this section the focus on generalist social work practice is sustained as the details of what social workers do are examined.

Regardless of where they practice, regardless of the socioeconomic population or problem situation they work with, all social workers need an understanding of current social welfare programs in order to serve clients effectively. It is not possible to understand social work in health care, for example, without some understanding of the Medicare and Medicaid programs, HMOs, and the politics of health care, all of which are described in detail in Chapter 7.

Nine different settings were selected from the numerous areas in which social workers practice: family and children's services, mental health, health care, the workplace, schools, chemical dependency programs, services for older adults, criminal justice settings, and programs for people with disabilities. Each chapter focuses on one specific field of practice and reviews the history of the profession of social work in that area. Each explores the knowledge and skills needed by professionals in that field, and each examines the ethical and value issues that the social workers encounter. The populations that are served, especially those at greatest risk, are introduced. Legislation and public social policy are explored, and research that both evaluates and guides social work practice is described. Finally, each chapter features an extensive case study that examines clients representing diverse ethnic, racial, age, and socioeconomic groups.

Through our discussions we explore the richness and variety of social workers' day-to-day work, the social problems encountered in contemporary society, and the challenges facing professional social workers.

CHAPTER 5

Family and Children's Services

BOHDHAN HRYNEWYCH/STOCK BOSTON

OUTLINE

LaTanya Tracy's great-grandmother, Ruby Bell Lowe, called Protective Services in a panic early one morning. Ruby had become exhausted from trying to care for LaTanya, an infant of only nine months. The baby had been crying all night, and Ruby had gotten little sleep. In her mid-80s, the elderly woman had been caring for LaTanya single-handedly for the past three weeks, ever since Natasha Tracy (Ruby's granddaughter and LaTanya's mother) had asked her to babysit late one evening. Ruby had felt uneasy accepting at that hour, suspecting that Natasha planned to go out drinking, but she had agreed for the baby's sake.

Natasha had not returned the following morning as promised, and LaTanya was keeping Ruby awake night after night. Exhausted and angry, Ruby had remembered that a social worker from the County Department of Protective Services had been helpful a few years before when Natasha neglected her parental responsibilities to her son, Martin, because of a drinking habit.

*The intake worker with whom Ruby spoke at Protective Services checked the computer files, and found that Natasha Tracy, 24 years old, had indeed been referred to the department previously. At that time, Natasha's young son, Martin, had been placed temporarily in foster care due to **neglect,** or failure to provide appropriate care, brought on by Natasha's drinking. The boy had been returned to his mother, however, after only eight months, and the case had been closed. That was because Natasha had entered an alcohol treatment program and had followed all court orders carefully. There had been no further referrals for child neglect until Ruby's anxious telephone call. The intake worker at Protective Services, on consultation with her supervisor, accepted the case for investigation and referred it to the social worker who had worked with Natasha previously, an experienced professional named Lauren White.*

Lauren White, BSW, like Natasha, was a woman of African American descent. She knew from personal as well as professional experience that black families have many strengths. In times of difficulty, for example, extended family members such as Ruby frequently pitch in to help care for needy infants and children. Grandparents, great-grandparents, aunts, uncles, older siblings, even neighbors frequently help out when needed. Lauren checked her files to assist in recalling the facts of the former case. Four years before, the paternal grandmother had called to report neglect of Natasha's then infant son, Martin. At that time Natasha was abusing alcohol, marijuana, and cocaine. A single parent, she was trying to cope with a baby with no assistance from that baby's father.

The case with Martin had a satisfactory ending, at least at the time. Once the little boy had been placed in foster care, Natasha had been willing to work hard to meet the conditions required by the court to get him back: regular participation in an alcohol and drug abuse treatment program and in a parenting class. Once court conditions had been met, Martin had been returned home, and the case had been closed shortly thereafter.

Lauren White's first step was to call Ruby Bell Lowe. She remembered the great-grandmother from her previous work with Natasha. Besides, no current telephone number had been given for Natasha and the number on file was no longer working. From Ruby, Lauren learned that Natasha's telephone had been disconnected, and that Ruby could not take the bus to Natasha's apartment to talk with her as she was too frail to climb the steps into the vehicle, especially with an infant in her arms. Ruby told Lauren that she didn't think she could keep LaTanya much longer. The baby had severe asthma attacks that frightened the elderly woman. Ruby gave Lauren Natasha's address. She explained that she believed her granddaughter was abusing alcohol and possibly other drugs again. When Lauren asked where Natasha's son, Martin, was currently staying, Ruby didn't know.

Natasha Tracy opened the door of her apartment hesitantly at Lauren's knock, wearing an old bathrobe and smelling of alcohol although it was early in the afternoon. She recognized her former worker and invited her in with an embarrassed smile. She offered Lauren a seat on an ancient sofa and sank into a nearby chair with a sigh. "I know," she said, "I'll bet my grandmother called you."

Lauren replied that the elderly woman had done just that. "Ruby is very worried about you, Natasha," the worker continued, "and LaTanya is hard for her to care for, as you can imagine. What has happened that you felt you had to leave LaTanya with your grandmother?"

Thus began a long, hesitant conversation in which Natasha seemed almost grateful to have someone to talk with, even if that someone was a social worker from Protective Services with the power to take away her children. Natasha explained that things had gone well enough for a couple of years after her son, Martin, had come home. She had been able to care for the little boy herself because she had received a small stipend from AFDC (Aid to Families with Dependent Children). But then she had become involved with an abusive boy friend, LaTanya's father. This man frequently struck her when he was angry, and ridiculed her when she cried. Before LaTanya was born, he was arrested for armed robbery. He was now serving a long prison sentence. That solved the **abuse** *problem, but left Natasha alone with a young son and an infant with severe asthma.*

After LaTanya was born, it happened that the AFDC program was repealed, replaced by Temporary Assistance to Needy Families (TANF; see Chapter 3). Under her state's program, TANF required Natasha to find a job when LaTanya was 12 weeks old. The young mother had complied but soon felt exhausted most of the time, and the child care promised by TANF had not come through. Female relatives and friends who might have assisted regularly before AFDC was repealed were now working outside their homes themselves, so that they could only help from time to time. Natasha soon lost her new job because she was absent caring for LaTanya too often. Discouraged, the young mother began to drink again. Eventually, realizing she was unable to care for her children properly, she took LaTanya to her grandmother's house and Martin to the home of his paternal grandmother. That was three weeks ago. Now, Natasha's drinking was completely out of control, and she was in debt to her landlord for her rent, facing eviction.

Lauren White realized that here was a young woman with multiple problems, but that she and her extended family had many strengths. First, there were two elderly grandmothers willing to help as long as possible. Probably other relatives could be found to help from time to time as well. Second, Lauren knew from past experience that Natasha was a good mother when she was not drinking. She had even been responsible enough to find other caretakers for her children when she realized her drinking was out of control. Third, Natasha was willing to admit that she had a substance abuse problem, and was eager to enter treatment if a program could be found that accepted Medicaid (see Chapter 10), a government health insurance program for certain categories of poor people.

Lauren had her work cut out for her to find resources to help Natasha. But she was successful. An aunt was able to help Ruby care for LaTanya until Natasha felt ready to take the baby home again. Family members also loaned the young woman money to pay back rent. Lauren was able to arrange counseling for Natasha at the Islamic Family Center. While Natasha was not a Black Muslim, the Islamic Family Center was willing to accept her as a client even with Medicaid's low payment schedule. Natasha's counselor there connected her with an Alcoholics Anonymous group that met in her neighborhood. Partly motivated by the provisions of the court order that Lauren White secured, and partly motivated by the encouragement and support she now received in counseling, Natasha attended her AA group faithfully and regained control of her drinking habit.

Within a few weeks, Natasha stopped drinking entirely. After that, she was able to bring her children home under Lauren White's supervision. She found another job, and was able to work regularly enough to keep it. Part of the reason she was able to work regularly this time was that as a Protective Services client, child care services were provided. Natasha continued counseling regularly at the Islamic Family Center and attending her AA group.

After a few more months had passed, Lauren knew that Natasha was ready for release from supervision from Protective Services. She worried, however, because once Natasha ceased to be a Protective Services client, funding for child care through the agency would stop. Lauren realized that she would need to become involved in advocacy for Natasha with the TANF program to assist her in being readmitted and to help ensure continuity in child care. Without that, Natasha would be right back in the situation that precipitated her previous substance abuse. Lauren knew that her task would not be easy, but she was willing to go beyond the call of duty to do what she could to ensure a decent future for LaTanya, Martin, and Natasha Tracy.

HISTORICAL PERSPECTIVES ON FAMILY AND CHILDREN'S SERVICES

Children and families in need have been helped by family members and other members of their villages or tribes since well before written history. Otherwise, we could not have survived as a species. Human infants are born almost totally helpless. For this reason it is cooperation among various members of humankind, not competition, that truly has enabled humanity to survive. Early human beings foraged for food and shelter at the mercy of an unpredictable environment. Survival itself was precarious, as it still is today in many areas of the world.

Formal services to help those in need are a relatively recent invention. In earlier times, infanticide and abandonment were the primary means available to families to deal with infants they couldn't care for. In the ancient Greek city of Athens, a child's birth was recognized socially only five days after the biological event. Before that, he or she could be disposed of. In situations of great poverty today, families still occasionally resort to infanticide or abandonment.

As recently as the middle of the eighteenth century, nearly half the children born in London died of disease or hunger before they were two years old. In eighteenth-century France, two-thirds of all children died before they reached age 20 (Kadushin & Martin, 1988). A high death rate is probably a major reason rates of childbirth have been very high in the past, and they remain high in poorer countries even today; adults have multiple offspring in the hope that one or two will survive.

Both Jewish law from the Old Testament and early Christian teachings stressed the importance of caring for needy children and families. The Catholic Church, in particular, exhorted the sanctity of all human life and taught (as it still does) that not only infanticide but also birth control and abortion were unacceptable. By preaching against all methods of regulating family size, the church obligated itself to help needy parents care for mouths they otherwise could not feed. A portion of church revenues was set aside for this purpose as early as the second or third century. Infants were often abandoned at church gates (Kadushin & Martin, 1988).

Under secular law, in early Europe there was no recognition of the rights of the child; the father had absolute control and no obligation to protect or maintain a child. Many babies were abandoned. The first known asylum for abandoned infants was founded in Milan in the year 787. After that, many other orphanages were established, among them the London Foundling Hospital, founded in 1741, "to prevent the murders of poor miserable children at birth and to suppress the inhuman custom of exposing newborn infants to perils in the streets, and to take in children dropped in churchyards or in the streets or left at night at the doors of church wardens or overseers of the poor" (Kadushin & Martin, 1988, p. 43).

Other mutual aid groups that helped children and families were the guilds (small groups of merchants and craftsmen that generated basic income to meet family economic needs of their members). However, with changes in technology, guilds ceded their function to factories, which were large, impersonal places of work with no sense of obligation to those who labored. Secular law began to provide some assistance to replace or supplement informal charity by church or guild. Life was still very hard, since assistance was extremely limited in kind and form. By the mid-1500s the average human life span was only about 30 years, and children were earning their own living by age seven or eight. An English statute of 1535 reads, "Children under 14 years of age and above 5 that live in idleness and be taken by begging may be put to service by the government of cities, towns, etc., to husbandry or other crafts of labor" (Kadushin & Martin, 1988, p. 47).

The English Poor Law of 1601 codified many previous laws dealing with the needy. As described in Chapter 3, aid was usually offered only in almshouses or workhouses. The death rate in these institutions was extremely high because the sick and insane were usually housed with everyone else. Destitute families were separated, as children were apprenticed out to whoever offered to take them for the least cost to the parish.

English poor laws were brought to the New World in the 1600s, so that help for needy children and families in America through the mid-1800s remained roughly the same: the almshouse for most destitute people, with children being apprenticed out as soon as possible. Death rates and sheer human misery were high. Some towns did offer temporary "outdoor relief" (assistance in one's own home), but this practice was rare.

In 1853 Reverend Charles Loring Brace took an innovative approach to helping poor children with the founding of the New York Children's Aid Society. Brace developed training schools, workshops, and living quarters for the city's destitute children, but the magnitude of their needs and the growing problem of juvenile delinquency alarmed him. He responded by devising a plan to ship the children out of the city to farmers in the West who could use their labor. He viewed this as a way of finding foster homes for the children and also to "drain the city" of a serious problem. Beginning in 1854, more than 50,000 children were sent west on Brace's "orphan trains." They were generally turned over to anyone who would take them. Many people opposed the plan, of course, including parents who hated to see their children go but were too poor to support them. Charity workers sometimes called the program "the wolf of indentured labor in the sheep's clothing of Christian charity." The westward transport continued, however, for over 25 years (Trattner, 1999, p. 118). A positive legacy was a growing public interest in foster care for needy children.

In the late 1800s, laws began to be passed in the United States against the use of "mixed almshouses." One result was that more orphanages began to be established. Most excluded African American children, so that black people were forced to continue to rely on a strong network of extended family and friends for basic survival. African American fellowship lodges such as the Odd Fellows, the Masons, and the Knights of Pythias and women's clubs such as the National Association for Colored Women were also instrumental in helping meet the needs of African American children and families (Prater, 1992).

Chapter 3 describes a federal program that assisted African American families for a brief period after the Civil War, the Freedmen's Bureau. This federally funded organization, almost revolutionary in concept, provided education, work, land, and relief directly to black families in the home setting. Had it continued, it is probable that circumstances for African American people in the United States would be very much improved today.

Also in the late 1800s the first major organization that was committed to helping families stay together in times of need, the Charity Organization Society, took shape, first in England and then in the United States. "Friendly visitors" were sent into poor people's homes to counsel parents toward better ways of living. The distribution of material aid to people's homes was centrally coordinated. Early friendly visitors believed poverty could be relieved by "moral uplift" of the poor. Later on, as workers became more knowledgeable about causes of poverty (such as low wages and poor health), they began to advocate for social reform as well. Also established were settlement houses to aid neighborhood development, particularly in immigrant communities. Through self-help programs and social group work, settlement house workers provided support and assistance to many needy children and families. (The Charity Organization Society, the forerunner of today's family service agencies, and the settlement house movement are discussed in Chapter 3.)

The Child Welfare Movement and Protective Services Programs

The child welfare movement was a major contributor to the birth of the social work profession. Its roots can probably be traced to Brace's founding of the New York Children's Aid Society in 1853. While the practice of shipping children west became controversial, as it divided families and subjected children to serious trauma, Brace's efforts publicized the plight of poor children and orphans. Many Children's Aid Societies were founded in other cities. By the 1870s, some of these societies began to board impoverished children in family homes instead of sending them west, the beginning of foster care and adoption programs in this country (Karger & Stoesz, 1998).

Public debate arose around the use of orphanages versus foster homes for needy children. This question was resolved, at least in theory, with the 1909 White House Conference on Children. The conference was attended by Jane Addams, famous leader of the settlement house movement. It recognized the importance of families and unequivocally recommended foster rather than institutional care. Though many children continued to be placed in large institutions due to funding considerations and lack of available homes, the 1909 conference focused national attention on the plight of poor children. It was so successful that the conference has reconvened every 10 years except during the Reagan administration.

The need for protective services, the type of social services mobilized in the LaTanya Tracy case described in this chapter, formally came into recognition around 1875. The catalyst for protective services was a 10-year-old girl named Mary Ellen Wilson (see Exhibit 1).

Because of increased public awareness of abuse to children as a result of the Mary Ellen case, many Societies for the Prevention of Cruelty to Children were created throughout the country in the late 1800s. These were private, voluntary agencies. In some parts of the nation they still exist; in other parts they have merged with various other social agencies serving children.

Formalized public services to protect children were not mandated by law in the United States until passage of the Child Abuse Prevention and Treatment Act of 1974. Federal funds were provided to the states for this purpose, and a national Center on Child Abuse was established. Title XX of the Social Security Act was also passed in 1974 and provided block grants to the states, which helped finance child abuse programs (Segal & Brzuzy, 1998). Some states had provided these services on their own initiative for a number of years, but all states created protective services programs by 1978.

Establishment of protective services programs was accompanied by new laws requiring certain categories of professionals, such as doctors and social workers, to report suspected child abuse to designated authorities. Unfortunately, most protective services programs are seriously underfunded and understaffed in terms of the number of referrals received, so that workers can provide service only in situations of crisis proportions. Reports of abuse and neglect continue to rise today; the situation is considered extremely serious by child welfare experts. But the number of cases actually investigated has been steadily falling (Karger & Stoesz, 1998).

The Case of Mary Ellen

EXHIBIT 1

Mary Ellen Wilson was badly abused by a woman to whom she had been indentured at 18 months of age. The woman later admitted in court that Mary Ellen was the illegitimate daughter of her deceased first husband. Neighbors tried to help the girl because she was beaten regularly and kept as a virtual prisoner in her home. In 1874, they enlisted the help of a visitor to the poor, who appealed for assistance to the police and various charitable societies. As no assistance was forthcoming, the visitor then appealed to the president of the New York Society for the Prevention of Cruelty to Animals (SPCA), who sent an investigator. Due to conditions documented by the SPCA, a court order was obtained to temporarily remove the child from the home. The president of the SPCA then took Mary Ellen's case to court as a private citizen. He called it to the attention of the *New York Times,* however, as a means of publicizing the problem of cruelty to children. The newspaper story succeeded in arousing widespread public concern. Mary Ellen was removed from the abusive home permanently, and her foster mother was sentenced to a year in prison.

Source: Based on Sallie A. Watkins. (1990, November). The Mary Ellen myth: Correcting child welfare history, *Social Work 35*(6), pp. 501–503.

Families who are reported to protective services units are often referred for more intensive counseling to private family service agencies, those connected historically with the Charity Organization Society. These agencies provide remedial services such as counseling to help improve conditions for neglected or abused children. They also usually provide preventive and educational programs. For example, member agencies of Family Service of America all provide family counseling, family life education programs, and family advocacy services.

The Family Preservation and Support Services Act was passed as part of the Omnibus Budget Reconciliation Act of 1993. This law aims to strengthen families by providing funds to states to develop new family support and preservation services. Responsibility for developing plans for specific programs rests with the states, which must target services in areas of greatest need and must utilize community-based strategies that involve community groups, residents, and parents in the planning process (Allen, Kakavas, & Zalenski, 1994).

Children's Rights as International Law

The idea that children have rights is quite new. The United Nations, in November 1954, proclaimed through the General Assembly's Declaration of the Rights of the Child that children all over the world have certain rights (see Exhibit 2). These rights became international law in 1990 as the Convention on the Rights of the

United Nations Declaration on the Rights of the Child	
EXHIBIT 2	

Every child in the world has rights.

Every child has the right to have a name and a country.

Every child has the right to have enough food to eat, a place to live, and a doctor's care.

Every child who is handicapped has the right to special treatment and care.

Every child has the right to grow up in a family feeling safe, loved, and understood.

Every child has the right to go to school and to play.

Every child has the right to be watched over and taken care of in times of danger.

Every child has the right to be protected from cruelty or unfair treatment.

Every child has the right to grow up without fear and hatred and with love, peace and friendship all around.

Source: From the Convention on the Rights of the Child, 1990. Reprinted by permission of the Secretary of the Publications Board, United Nations. Quoted in C.S. Ramanathan and N. J. Link. (1999). *All our futures, principles, and resources for social work practice in a global era.* Belmont, CA: Brooks/Cole, p. 107.

Child. Ninety-six percent of the world's children now live in countries that have ratified the convention, but unfortunately the children of the United States are not among them (Ramanathan & Link, 1999).

Underscoring the importance of children's rights, the International Federation of Social Workers has developed an international policy supporting the Convention on the Rights of the Child.

SERVICES AND THEIR PROVIDERS

A significant percentage of child and family services are offered by professional social workers. The 1980 Adoption Assistance and Child Welfare Act recommends a minimum of the baccalaureate-level degree in social work but does not require it. While this important work is often performed by people without appropriate training or experience, the social work degree remains the best professional education for entry into the field. The worker with this background can be instrumental in improving the quality of service.

Services to children and families can be classified in several ways, but one of the simplest is to divide them into two major categories: in-home and out-of-home. (Be careful not to confuse these contemporary service categories with *indoor and outdoor relief* as offered under historic English poor laws.)

Major Categories of In-Home Services
EXHIBIT 3

• Financial aid	• Day care
• Family-based services	• Homemaker services
• Protective services	• Family life education
• Family therapy	

In-Home Services

In-home services (see Exhibit 3) are provided to a family in order to help members live together more safely, more comfortably, or more harmoniously in their own homes. They are preventive in orientation. Paradoxically, some (like day care) may be offered outside the home, but the goal is to assist families to stay together. In-home services are described in the following section. A discussion of out-of-home services appears later in this chapter.

Financial Aid Many families require financial aid to survive. The major programs available were described in Chapter 3 and will be reviewed briefly here. The federally administered Social Security program provides income to families in which a breadwinner who has paid sufficient Social Security taxes has died, become disabled, or retired.

States may provide financial aid to poor families for no more than five years in a given parent's lifetime under the Temporary Assistance to Needy Families program. This is an optional program authorized by the federal Personal Responsibility and Work Opportunity Act of 1996. TANF replaced AFDC, or Aid to Families with Dependent Children, a program that had previously entitled poor children to aid under the provisions of the Social Security Act.

Medicare and Medicaid programs provide funding for medical care for many families in need. They are authorized by amendments to the Social Security Act. Medicare primarily provides funds for elderly and disabled people. Medicaid is available to certain categories of poor people who pass a means test. Most people who qualify for TANF also qualify for Medicaid.

Food stamps provide financial assistance to families in voucher form. The amount of aid given depends on the number of people in a household and on the combined household income. Eligibility for food stamps has become more restrictive in recent years, as described in Chapter 3.

Other forms of financial aid include subsidized school lunch programs, surplus food distributions, and rent assistance provided by the United States Department of Housing and Urban Development. Availability of these and other aid programs varies according to the year, the state, and the locality.

Family-Based Services Family-based services were prompted by the Federal Adoption Assistance and Child Welfare Act of 1980, which required states to maintain children in the least restrictive environment possible (Smith, 1998). They include both family preservation and family support services, for the purpose of keeping families together, healthy, and safe. Toward this end, families may utilize all the other services described in this section.

Family preservation services are designed specifically to help families that have been reported to public authorities for problems of neglect and abuse, when the children are at immediate risk of placement outside the home. Crisis workers or teams of workers may spend as much as 8 to 10 hours per week or more in the family home, for approximately three weeks to three months. Emergency services are available 24 hours a day. If the children must be placed temporarily outside the home, intensive follow-up services are provided after they return. Respite care is offered to provide temporary relief for parents or other caregivers. Services focus strongly on parenting skills. An example of a family preservation effort is provided at the beginning of Chapter 13.

Family support services are designed to increase the strength and stability of all families—biological families, in particular, but also adoptive, foster, and extended families. Services are long-term and include home visits, generalist family casework to help prevent or resolve a variety of problems, parent support groups, and parenting skills training. Respite care for temporary relief of parents and other caregivers is provided. Family support centers are a frequent locus of service delivery. These centers provide information and support on a drop-in basis, and they may also provide structured activities to help parents and children strengthen their relationship. The centers frequently offer screening programs to determine whether young children have any special needs (Allen, Kakavas, & Zalenski, 1994). Family support services may also be offered at a variety of more traditional agencies, both public and private.

Protective Services   **Protective services** are designed to shield children from maltreatment, including both abuse and neglect. Lauren White of the LaTanya Tracy case was a protective services worker. The Child Abuse Prevention, Adoption and Family Services Act of 1988 provides a general federal definition of maltreatment (quoted in Gustavsson & Segal, 1994, p. 75):

> The physical or mental injury, sexual abuse, or exploitation, negligent treatment or maltreatment of a child by a person who is responsible for the child's welfare, under circumstances which indicate that the child's health or welfare is harmed or threatened thereby, as determined in accordance with regulations prescribed by the Secretary of the Department of Health and Human Services.

While each state has its own definition of child maltreatment, the preceding federal definition specifies that it may be physical, mental (including emotional), or sexual, and it may involve active abuse or negligence.

Protective services workers usually begin by investigating and monitoring a referred child's own home. They counsel both children and parents, inform parents of legal requirements, and use as motivation for positive change both skillful professional relationships and **sanctions,** or penalties for noncompliance, provided by the court. In situations of extreme risk (and when such resources exist), protective services workers may mobilize family preservation teams for intensive in-home intervention as described above. Where safety issues remain serious, children may be placed in foster care, ideally in the homes of relatives whom they already know.

S. RUBINS/THE IMAGE WORKS

Family struggling in the wake of TANF sanction.

Protective services workers provide families with information about other in-home services potentially available to them. Workers make referrals and urge families to use all resources available. Sometimes workers obtain court orders to require families to utilize particular resources. Natasha Tracy, for example, was ordered by the court to participate in counseling because of her substance abuse and child neglect.

The primary goal of protective services programs under the Adoption Assistance and Child Welfare Act of 1980 was to preserve families while providing safe environments for children at risk. This law emphasized rehabilitation of parents so that children could leave the limbo of foster care and return to their own homes (McKenzie & Lewis, 1998). However, despite the good intention of this law, many children then remained in the limbo of foster care awaiting parental rehabilitation, in situations where the parents indicated little or no interest in change. The Adoption and Safe Families Act, signed into law by President Clinton in November 1997, acknowledges the importance of family preservation and support services but also encourages more timely **permanency placement,** recognizing children's developmental need to have a permanent home. The bill authorizes bonuses to states to increase adoptions of children and also speeds up timelines for holding hearings initiating proceedings to terminate parental rights (Adoption and safe families act, 1998).

In recent years, child maltreatment reports have been increasing. Between 1986 and 1996, for example, reports increased nationwide by 49 percent. In 1995 alone, 3,100,000 children were reported as suspected abused to child protective services agencies, and 996,000 of these reports were confirmed (Wilhelmus, 1998).

Family Therapy   Family therapy is a service available to families experiencing many different kinds of distress. Although it usually is conducted in professional offices, it is considered an in-home service because it assists family members to live together more safely and harmoniously.

Family therapy is a practice concentration within the social work profession, and it requires a master's degree. Postgraduate training is also recommended. Family therapy may be provided by members of related professions as well, such as psychologists or psychiatrists. Sometimes family therapists work in teams in which a psychologist administers psychological tests, a psychiatrist administers medication, and both serve as consultants to the social worker, who usually does the ongoing counseling. As we saw in Chapter 1, assisting individuals and families is frequently an interdisciplinary, collaborative effort.

Day Care   Day care is considered an in-home social service, even though it is often provided outside the home. This service permits a working parent who has no partner, or two working parents, to maintain their young children as part of the household.

Too common are "latchkey children," who spend part of their day in school and part at home alone, having let themselves in. Even this arrangement, however, is not feasible for families with infants and toddlers; without day care, these very young children would require foster care. For this reason, many states and counties have established programs by which day care is publicly subsidized, and a sliding fee is charged according to the income of the parent(s). The replacement of AFDC by TANF makes subsidized day care programs particularly imperative today since most poor mothers have to work outside the home. Yet there is still no national mandate for such a service.

Day care centers only occasionally include social workers. Child care workers usually complete educational requirements in early childhood education. But even when not actually employed by day care centers, social workers need to know about them in order to make appropriate referrals.

Day care centers that serve special populations of children are probably most likely to have social workers on staff. For example, some centers offer care for children with developmental disabilities or for those adjudicated by the courts as **children-at-risk.** At-risk children usually come through the recommendation of protective services social workers, who have determined that these children would be reasonably safe at home if their parents were relieved of child care responsibilities during all or part of the day. Many parents who are referred to protective services because of abuse or neglect of their children are capable of providing reasonable child care if relieved of the stress of 24-hour ongoing responsibility, especially if the day care center provides a social worker to assist the parents in working on their own problems.

Homemaker Services   Homemaker services may be provided to families in which one member is too ill, too old, or too emotionally unstable to carry out normal household tasks. Such services may also be provided on a short-term basis to care for children when a parent is temporarily absent because of physical illness or mental breakdown. Sometimes a homemaker is assigned to a family that has been reported to protective services for neglect, as a temporary corrective measure. In these cases, homemakers assume a teaching or modeling role.

The provision of homemaker services can allow families to stay together in their own homes under circumstances that might otherwise break them up, sending children to foster homes or the elderly to nursing homes. Services may include cleaning, shopping, cooking, and laundry. They are offered at low cost to eligible families through public or private social service agencies and, in most cases, are provided by aides rather than social workers. Homemaker services are a major resource for social workers trying to keep families together during crises.

Family Life Education Family life education is an in-home social service intended to prevent as well as to help solve family problems. This type of educational program is often offered at traditional family service agencies and also at family support centers that are being developed in some areas of the country. Usually family life education classes are held at the sponsoring agencies, but sometimes workers go out into the home setting. Topics covered vary with the setting, but typically they include information about the developmental stages of childhood, weaning and toilet-training issues, building self-esteem in both children and parents, parenting skills, communication skills, and constructive methods of discipline.

Out-of-Home Services

Sometimes, regardless of the amount of effort invested in high-risk families by protective and other supportive services, family circumstances still remain unsuitable for the upbringing of a child. In these cases, **out-of-home services** must be substituted (see Exhibit 4). If adult family members should be incapacitated by accident or illness, casework counseling will be available in the hospital, rehabilitation center, or other appropriate agency setting. For their children, substitute services will be needed. In situations of short-term disability, a homemaker may be the best answer, enabling children to remain in their own homes. For longer-term needs, out-of-home substitute services may be considered.

Foster Care The type of foster care available to LaTanya and Martin Tracy was perhaps the very earliest form of substitute care: care in a relative's home. Placement may be informal, purely a family matter. However, placement by a government agency such as a department of child welfare involves the licensing of foster homes. Requirements for licensing include such factors as the amount of space in a house compared with the number of people living there, the number of bedrooms, and compliance with building codes and fire safety regulations. In addition, prospective foster parents must be investigated with respect to character, reliability, and parenting skills. Usually, social workers are the professionals who conduct foster home studies and recommend acceptance or rejection.

Major Out-of-Home Services
EXHIBIT 4
• Foster care   • Institutional care • Adoption   • The judicial system • Group homes

Once a foster home is accepted, social workers supervise the home. They visit on a regular schedule and talk with both foster parents and children, to make sure that a constructive relationship is developing. When there is a problem, social workers become involved in solving it. Often, a visitation by the natural parent will create difficulty in a foster care situation (Wilhelmus, 1998). Sometimes natural and foster parents get along well and work cooperatively. A good worker can help facilitate this ideal situation. However, it is not unusual for the natural parents to feel antagonistic toward the foster parents; then the worker must become actively involved in preventing or mediating disputes. Sometimes the natural parent never visits, and the child becomes depressed or withdrawn emotionally, or perhaps acts out unhappy feelings by misbehaving. Then the foster parents may need help coping with the child's behavior. An endless number of normal and not-so-normal crises in child rearing can occur in a foster home, and the social worker's role is to do whatever is needed to ensure the best possible care for the child.

Some foster homes are specialized; they are licensed to care for children who have unusual needs, such as physical or mental disabilities, behavioral disturbances, or emotional illness. Overall, the demand for qualified foster homes greatly outstrips the supply, and the number available has declined 30% since 1984 (Wilhemus, 1998). Special-needs homes are particularly hard to find.

Normally, while a child is in foster care, the social worker works with the biological as well as the foster parents. The purpose of this work is to enable the natural parents to prepare for the successful return of their child, wherever possible.

Adoption   Sometimes out-of-home substitute care goes beyond the temporary and becomes permanent by adoption. Adoption benefits needy children by providing a permanent plan of care. It provides children and their adoptive parents the same legal rights and responsibilities with respect to one another as are available to biological parents and their children. Children become available for adoption only when the rights of both natural parents have been terminated. Occasionally parental rights are terminated involuntarily by court order—for example, in circumstances of extreme, documented battery to the child. More often biological parents themselves decide that they are not in a position to provide the kind of parenting they wish for their child.

The Adoption and Safe Families Act of 1997, as discussed above, encourages increased recognition of children's need for permanent homes. To this end, incentives are offered to speed up adoption procedures in situations where evidence is persuasive that the biological parents will be unable to provide safe and suitable homes in the foreseeable future.

Social workers often provide counseling for people trying to reach the difficult decision of whether or not to place a child for adoption or even, in recent times, whether or not to continue a problem pregnancy. This decision is now more complicated for a young mother than it was only a few years ago. Termination of pregnancy is potentially an option in many circumstances, but the U.S. Supreme Court's 1989 *Webster* decision provided states with more regulating power. In recent years more and more states have used this power to enact restrictive laws. Moreover, in the recent past a single mother could decide by herself to terminate parental rights and could allow a child born out of wedlock to be placed for adoption. Today, however, the biological father of the child, if known, must agree in writing. Sometimes biological fathers sue for custody and gain it against the mother's will.

Usually, married couples have the best chance to adopt, but single adults also are considered. People who want to adopt a child typically apply at an agency, either public or private (secular or church-related), that provides this service. Before being accepted as appropriate parents, applicants must undergo a careful adoption study, which usually is conducted by a social worker. Waiting lists are very long, however, for healthy babies. Because of the waiting lists, many people today try to adopt privately through an attorney; they still must undergo a satisfactory home study, however.

Children who have special characteristics or needs (such as those who are older, part of a sibling group, of mixed race, or disabled in some way) are harder to place and may spend their lives in foster homes. These are the children that single people or older couples are usually encouraged to adopt. An important task for social service agencies is the recruitment of good adoptive homes for children who might otherwise never find permanent homes.

States are authorized under the Adoption Assistance and Child Welfare Act of 1980 to provide adoption subsidies for hard-to-place children. The medical costs of raising physically fragile children, for example, can be exorbitant. Subsidies make adoption a more realistic choice for many families. Adoption subsidies cannot exceed foster care rates (Gustavsson & Segal, 1994).

Adopted children may want to try to find their biological parents at some point in their lives. In recent years the law has been changed in many states to allow adopted persons (when they become adults) to have access to some of their social service agency records. Parents who terminate their rights and place a child for adoption today may opt, in some states, to note in the records that they would be willing for the adult child to contact them.

Group Homes Group homes may be run by public agencies or by private organizations. Among the various types are homes that serve people with mental retardation, physical disabilities, or mental illness. Group homes usually are licensed to house eight people, a number large enough so that residents can have a variety of others to meet and talk with but small enough so that they can receive individual attention. Homes for children usually have a stable staff of youth care workers, often BSWs, supplemented by a housekeeping staff and child care aides. The aim is to make the setting as familylike as possible.

This type of out-of-home service meets several needs. First of all, given the shortage of licensed foster homes, group homes can provide shelter when regular foster homes are not available. In some cases, group home care may meet a particular child's needs better than a foster home can. For example, some teenagers cannot make the emotional investment necessary to develop close relationships with foster parents. They may be much more willing to relate to peers in a group home.

Shelters for runaways have emerged in many cities over the past two decades. Originally founded by volunteers, many shelters have become licensed as foster group homes. Runaway shelters usually provide bed, board, and crisis counseling, and their ultimate goal is to reunite families under conditions that are safe for the children.

One drawback of runaway shelters from the point of view of the children involved is that their families must provide consent in order for them to stay, because of laws relating to kidnapping and to the children's status as legal minors.

However, if a family refuses to give consent and if the staff of the shelter believes the runaway child is in danger, a protective services worker will be contacted. This worker will also assess the situation and can obtain a temporary court order allowing the child to remain in the shelter until the case can be heard in court.

Shelters for battered women and their children, which were introduced in Chapter 1, can be thought of as another type of group home for family members who are "running away from home." These shelters provide short-term bed and board. In addition, most provide information and referral services and crisis counseling. Usually, shelters are more widely available for battered women than for battered men. This is because women, unfortunately, are most often the victims of battery and because women activists (including social workers) usually were the driving force behind the creation of the shelters. Battered men can sometimes obtain counseling at shelters originally organized to serve only women. A service increasingly provided by both types of shelters is counseling for children who have experienced violence in their homes.

Institutional Care Institutional placement is another out-of-home option for the care of minor children. Generally, this option is viewed as the choice of last resort, because it provides the least "normal" environment for the upbringing of children. Historically, children who lost their parents in some way were placed in large institutions known as orphanages, where they spent the remainder of their childhood. In the past two or three decades, however, most such facilities have been closed and have been replaced by foster homes and small group homes. When large child care institutions still exist, it is usually because they provide specialized treatment or short-term emergency shelter for children awaiting placement in more nearly normal environments such as foster homes or small group homes.

Some children are placed for a year or more at a type of institution known as a residential treatment center. These children usually have been determined by professional evaluation to be seriously emotionally disturbed, and they often are referred by courts in an effort to control delinquent behavior as well as to provide counseling and therapy. The residential treatment center provides a comprehensive range of services that typically involves behavior modification programs to control delinquent behavior (an approach sometimes called milieu therapy), individual counseling, family therapy, and instruction by teachers skilled in working with the emotionally and behaviorally disturbed.

The children who are placed in residential treatment facilities usually have been referred first to special education services in their respective community schools. Federally mandated special education policy requires treating children in the least restrictive environment possible, so a given child will initially be placed part-time and then full-time, if necessary, in a local special education classroom. Only if these interventions fail completely will a child be referred to a residential treatment center, which provides a highly restrictive, structured environment. Treatment in a residential care facility is very expensive; most families cannot afford the cost, and many communities are unwilling to underwrite it. Therefore, many children who are out of control and who might benefit from total milieu therapy simply do not receive it.

The Judicial System   The final major out-of-home service for children that we will examine is the judicial system. If a child has committed frequent and/or severe-enough crimes, he or she may be sentenced by the court to what amounts to a jail for minors. Pending a court hearing for an alleged offense, a child may be held temporarily in a detention center. This step is truly a last resort, and it usually represents the failure of other services. This is what is likely to happen when a child needed residential or other treatment early in life but the care was not provided because of its cost. Attention to short-term budgetary concerns without consideration of long-term costs, both human and monetary, has been tragically characteristic of social planning in the United States for more than two decades (see Exhibit 5).

Child Welfare in the United States Milestones

EXHIBIT 5

1642	Plymouth Colony enacts poor law similar to Elizabethan Poor Law of 1601.
	Destitute children and orphans are apprenticed.
1790	First publicly funded orphanage in U.S.A., Charleston, South Carolina.
1853	Reverend Charles Loring Brace founds Children's Aid Society, New York City.
1865	Freedmen's Bureau founded, first federal welfare agency; in action until 1872.
1877	Society for Prevention of Cruelty to Children founded in New York City.
	First Charity Organization Society in U.S.A. founded in Buffalo, New York.
1886	First Settlement House in U.S.A. founded in New York City.
1889	Hull House founded in Chicago by Jane Addams.
1909	White House Conference on Children.
1912	U.S. Children's Bureau funded.
1935	Social Security Act: dependent children who are poor receive entitlement to aid.
1974	Child Abuse Prevention and Treatment Act.
1993	Family Preservation and Support Services Act.
	Family and Medical Leave Act.
1996	Personal Responsibility and Work Opportunity Act ends entitlement of poor children to aid under Social Security Act.
1997	Adoption and Safe Families Act.

CLIENT SELF-DETERMINATION AND PROFESSIONAL DECISION MAKING

The social work profession holds as an important principle the right of clients to make their own decisions. A major principle of the social work code of ethics, 1.01, deals specifically with **self-determination** (see Appendix). It states:

> Social workers respect and promote the right of clients to self-determination and assist clients in their efforts to identify and clarify their goals. Social workers may limit client's right to self-determination when, in the social worker's professional judgement, clients' actions or potential actions pose a serious, foreseeable, and imminent risk to themselves or others.

The LaTanya Tracy case is a good example of a situation in which a social worker, Lauren White, in her professional role as a protective services worker, determined that Natasha Tracy's actions were posing a serious risk to herself and her children. Thus, while the principle of self-determination would normally guide a social worker to honor a client's own decisions, Natasha's substance abuse presented a substantial enough risk to justify Lauren's intervention ethically as well as legally. However, Lauren maximized her profession's ethical principle of self-determination to the greatest extent possible under the circumstances. She listened respectfully to Natasha, helped her client identify the many problems in her life that needed addressing, helped the young mother remember the importance of caring for her children, and assisted in developing a plan of action that would solve many of her problems and eventually permit the children to return home.

WOMEN, CHILDREN, AND ETHNIC MINORITIES: POPULATIONS-AT-RISK

Is raising children a task that is of value to our nation as a whole, not just a particular family? If, say, every parent vanished, leaving their children behind, would it be worthwhile for the adults who were left to raise those children—not due to compassion but self-interest?

In this country, we are so accustomed to thinking of child rearing as a family responsibility that we forget that the nation as a whole benefits. Besides what children add to the tapestry of human experience, their survival is essential to carrying on all the fundamental tasks of the economic market. Today's productive adults will grow old and die tomorrow; they will need replacement. Thus, despite appearances, it is in the national interest to provide for children so that they can grow up emotionally stable, well educated, and capable of contributing to the common good.

Because we don't seem able to recognize the value of raising children in America, however—to recognize child rearing as valid work—we do not consider the task worth paying for. The PRWOA rescinded any national responsibility to assist poor parents in their child rearing job. Thus, as described in our chapter's case example, when the men in Natasha Tracy's life abandoned her to raise her two children alone, so did the nation. She then faced an impossible dilemma.

Natasha needed to hold a paying job to feed herself and her two children, but her paycheck wasn't large enough to purchase child care. She needed to purchase child care to keep her job. This dilemma is experienced by millions of poor women today.

Clearly, the members of the United States Congress (the vast majority being men) did not consider child care as work when they voted for the PRWOA. Their intent was to force poor mothers into the "workforce," by which they meant the paid labor force. Poor mothers who stayed at home to care for their children were seen as lazy and dependent. However, many people have a very different point of view (Mink, 1998; see Exhibit 6).

Child care is work indeed. When purchased in the economic market it costs far more than the stipend that was offered to mothers under the former AFDC program to care for their own children. In Wisconsin, for example, a poor mother with one child received approximately $450 per month under AFDC. Under TANF, she must take a job when her baby is three months old. Infant care in a licensed day care center in Milwaukee County, Wisconsin, averages $758 per month (Pierce, 2000). Across the nation, day care costs averaged $5,750 per year for toddlers in two-thirds of cities surveyed in 2000, and between $4,000 and $6,000 per year for four-year-olds. Day care costs exceeded college tuition in many areas (Hartill, 2001, June 20).

Yet poor mothers who were forced off AFDC and found paying jobs earned wages averaging only between $6 and $7 per hour (Weinstein, 2000), or about $12,000 to $14,000 annually for full-time work. That income pulls a mother with

---

Should Single Mothers Be Forced to Work outside the Home?

EXHIBIT 6

Poor single mothers already shoulder a double burden in parenting; should social policy require them to perform yet another job? The issue is not whether women with care-giving responsibilities should enjoy full opportunity and equality in the labor market. Of course they should. The issue is coercion. Why should poor single mothers—and *only* poor single mothers—be forced by law to work outside the home?

Care-giving, especially for young children—and 63 percent of mothers on welfare have children under age five—involves more than baby-sitting. It includes managing a household, doing housework, and most important, nurturing, loving, and comforting. Meeting the basic challenges of family work—nutritious meals with very little money, schlepping to the laundromat without a car, attending to a child's schedule of needs, cleaning, mending, caring—takes time, effort, energy, and responsibility (the very skills and sacrifices assigned economic value in the outside labor market). For a solo care-giver who is poor, it can be a labor-intensive, full-time job.

Source: Quoted from Gwendolyn Mink. (1998). *Welfare's end.* Ithaca, NY: Cornell University Press.

one child just above the official poverty line ($11,869 for a family of two in 2000), so the nation hailed a drop in the official poverty rate after the "end of welfare." Low-wage families remained destitute, nevertheless. A large percentage of the mother's wages is required to pay for day care. TANF programs vary in the amount of day care assistance they offer, but nationally, only 10 percent of the 14.7 million children whose families qualified for federal subsidies in 1999 actually received them (Telcher, 2000).

In the years since the passage of the PRWOA, welfare caseloads have dropped by about half (Sappenfeld, 2001). The official poverty rate, although not the actual experience of poverty, has dropped as well, as discussed previously. But poverty has deepened among the 16.9 percent of children who remained below the official line according to 1999 census data. Mothers who had employment barriers such as lack of transportation, limited education, health problems, and limited skills often could not find work (Weinstein, 2000). Yet many were forced out of TANF programs anyway, due to sanctions for missing training or work in transitional programs, often due to child care issues. These families are extremely vulnerable to abuse, as they now must accept help whatever the source. Ethnic minority families have probably suffered the most, since discrimination is another employment barrier. While overall, 16.9 percent of children fell below the poverty line nationally in 1999, of those, only 9.4 percent were white, non-Hispanic. Fully 30.3 percent of Hispanic children fell below the line and 33.1 percent of black children (Greenstein, Primus, & Kayatin, 2000).

Other disturbing data document that approximately half the states now deny benefits to children born into families already receiving welfare, a practice permitted under TANF. Thus, many thousands of innocent infants have no source of support outside of their families, which are already destitute (Bills tackle welfare, patients' rights, 1998).

Poor parents trying to better themselves through education are penalized by most TANF programs, which do not consider education the equivalent of "work." For example, "architects of Wisconsin's W2 welfare reform plan were so bent on moving people off the dole that they locked participants out of meaningful training. The reforms kicked some 10,000 people—virtually all women—out of training programs at places like Milwaukee Area Technical College. Instead of being allowed to complete course work that could lift them out of poverty, they were shoved into jobs paying little more than minimum wage and without much chance for advancement" (Gunn, 1998, November).

A further concern is that lack of a safety net makes it much more difficult for women who are battered to leave their abusive husbands or partners. Studies document that in the United States, a woman is beaten every 18 minutes, and four or five are killed by their husbands every day (Van Wormer, 1997). TANF programs usually allow exceptions from the work requirement for women who are abused, but exceptions involve complicated application processes that many poor women are unable to navigate, especially under severe stress.

One result of increased poverty is increased homelessness. Studies vary in their findings, but women constitute from one-quarter to one-third of the homeless today, and children under 16 make up approximately another tenth; together, women and children constitute approximately 36 percent of the homeless population. This group is thought to be the fastest-growing nationwide, although documentation is sketchy (Wright, Rubin, & Devine, 1998; Nifong, 1997). Ironically, a typical response to homelessness nationally is to criminalize it, rather than to find solutions. For example, sleeping or dozing in public places is a crime in Dallas, Texas. In Tucson, it is a crime to sit or lie on public sidewalks. In New York, homeless people are routinely arrested (Foscarinis, 1999).

In summary, from the perspective of many in the social work profession, welfare reform has abandoned America's most vulnerable populations, especially its children but also women and ethnic minorities. While some of the states have developed TANF programs that help alleviate poverty, the nation itself seems to have turned its back on poor families. The primary effort has been to force poor parents, most of them women, into low-wage employment outside the home.

Reproductive Rights and Single Parenting

Ironically, at a time when the nation is abandoning poor children, it continues to deny poor mothers the means to terminate unwanted pregnancies. In 1973, the Supreme Court ruled that women have a constitutional right to safe and legal abortions *(Roe v. Wade),* but the "Hyde amendment" of 1976 denied Medicaid funding for abortions to poor women. That amendment remains in force today. Since the 1973 ruling, all women have found it increasingly difficult to get an abortion, poor or not. Many states have passed restrictions such as parental notification for minors and mandatory waiting periods. Over a hundred clinics have been shut down by disruptive demonstrations and threats on people's lives. Since 1992, seven abortion providers have been killed by those who paradoxically profess a "right to life."

> "We've lost a lot of ground on the state and local levels—since Republicans took over Congress in 1994," says Kate Michelman, president of the National Abortion and Reproduction Rights Action League. "Over the last six years, there were more than 130 votes on reproductive rights or health policy, and we lost all but 25 of them." (Marks, 2001).

No one knows for certain what the future will bring with respect to reproductive rights in the United States, but a conservative president is in office at the turn of the century, and more than one Supreme Court justice is likely to retire soon. President George W. Bush will select any replacements. Although the Senate must ratify his choices, women's reproductive choice is clearly in jeopardy.

Hostility of lawmakers toward women who become pregnant out of wedlock may help explain the federal government's paradoxical refusal both to fund abortions for poor women and to help them finance raising their children. After all, lawmakers in this country are overwhelmingly male. Mimi Abramovitz, a social critic, believes that welfare "reform" was driven partly by political expediency and also a desire to punish women who do not conform to a two-parent family ethic (see Exhibit 7).

Despite the fact that the PRWOA seems intended to penalize single-parent families, more than half of all children in the United States today will spend time in one during their developmental years (Karger & Stoesz, 1998). Approximately 85% of single-parent families are female headed, and thus at high risk of poverty. Hence many, many children will suffer under the new law.

Welfare Reform to Punish Nontraditional Families?

EXHIBIT 7

The drive to reform welfare that began in the early 1980's and culminated with the PRWOA in 1996 was never about welfare alone. In fact, the attack on welfare helped to fulfill other political agendas. Liberal politicians bashed welfare and the poor to establish their conservative credentials. Business and industry turned against welfare arguing that it undercut their profits. The social conservatives used welfare reform to promote their own version of family values that ruled out all but the two-parent, heterosexual household.

Source: Quoted from Mimi Abramovitz. (2000). *Under attack, fighting back, women and welfare in the United States.* New York, Monthly Review Press, 17.

Single teens have been especially vilified for bearing children out of wedlock, and aid has been explicitly denied them under PRWOA, apparently as a deterrent. Interestingly enough, however, teen birth rates began to decrease in 1991, well before the PRWOA was passed, and the downward trend has continued to a record low (Teen pregnancy rate falls, 2001). Moreover, research indicates that approximately two-thirds of teen mothers have been sexually abused. As reported by Van Wormer (1997, p. 329):

> A growing body of research, including a recent study by the Alan Guttmacher Institute, indicates that childhood sexual abuse is a potent factor in teenage childbearing (reported in *NASW News,* 1995). Up to two-thirds of teen mothers say that they had sex forced on them by older men; an earlier study of almost 200,000 births by teenage mothers revealed that 70% were fathered by adults. These findings put a different angle on the early pregnancy phenomenon that is so persistent in the United States.

If the above data are true, denying aid to poor babies of teen mothers will have little affect on the teen birth rate, yet sadly, both the teens and their babies will continue to suffer abuse, this time via abandonment to poverty by the wider society in which they live. Social workers will have their work cut out for them trying to help these young women and their families now that entitlement to public aid has become a thing of the past. (See the "Up for Debate" box.)

Gay and Lesbian Families

According to Benkov (1994, p. 323), "It is no accident that the rise of lesbian parenting has coincided with the burgeoning of single heterosexual women choosing to have children. The idea that women could shape their intimate lives according to their own standards and values rather than conform to constricting social norms was powerful in its own right."

Up for Debate
Proposition: Poor children should be entitled to public assistance

Yes	No
Children, especially young children, need a parent to care for them at home for consistent parental bonding, supervision, and a sense of security.	Even in many intact, middle-class families today, both parents have to work to make ends meet.
Day care services affordable to poor parents who have to work outside the home are likely to be unregulated and of poor quality, putting poor children at increased disadvantage.	Day care services may be available in centers offering a sliding fee. Besides, babysitting for other people's children can provide welfare mothers a means of earning an income.
Poor parents usually have been disadvantaged with respect to education; they often must accept jobs at or near minimum wage, which is too low to raise their families out of poverty.	If public assistance is offered to poor children, their parents may opt not to work outside the home, thus depriving potential employers of low-wage workers.
Many studies, both national and international, have shown that good welfare programs do not increase birth rates in single-parent families. Besides, regardless of the circumstances of their birth, all children deserve a minimum standard of living even if their biological parents cannot provide.	Assisting poor children may encourage poor, single mothers to have more children whom society does not want.

How to become parents presents practical problems for both **lesbian** women and **gay** men, because their sexual orientation is toward members of the same gender. Adoption is a possibility for some, although many programs discriminate against people of same-sex orientation. Those who want to become biological parents face a different challenge. Some women may ask male friends to consider becoming sperm donors, while others may turn to sperm banks. Use of medically administered sperm banks eliminates the potential danger of later court battles for parental rights (donors in medically controlled donor insemination programs waive parental rights and responsibilities) so that many women prefer this option. Gay men, on the other hand, unless they or their partners have custody of children from prior heterosexual relationships, must find surrogate mothers. For them the risk that a surrogate may later sue to gain custody is an ever-present concern.

Sperm banks have been available for decades, but people have become more aware of them in recent years, so that some interesting questions have arisen. For example, are multiple women inseminated by the same man? Is it likely their children might meet in the future? Do children conceived in this way want to locate their fathers?

Gay couple cares for adopted daughter.

According to Engber and Klungness (2000), most sperm banks have developed policies to limit the likelihood of encounter with half siblings. Sperm from a given donor may not be used for more than 10 pregnancies, for example, and sperm is shipped all over the nation, not just to a local area. Thus, the likelihood of a child later entering a relationship with a half sibling is extremely small.

When the practice of artificial insemination was first begun, secrecy was practiced. Donor records were destroyed to protect the privacy of the adults involved. However, similar to adoptive children, some children conceived through artificial insemination wish to meet their biological father. Many sperm banks today provide an option for donors to be contacted by children once they have turned 18. Some of them require potential donors to grant grown children that right.

Many gays and lesbians share parental responsibilities with committed partners who may try legally to adopt the biological children of their mate. Such adoptions have been difficult to obtain in court, although spouses in heterosexual marriages where children have been conceived through alternative means are automatically considered the legal parents of these offspring. Some gay and lesbian couples who have intentionally conceived children together form extended families and share both parenting and financial responsibilities.

According to Savin-Williams and Esterberg (2000), research indicates that children who are raised by lesbian or gay parents show no difference from those raised by heterosexuals with respect to gender identity, sex-role behavior, self-concept, intelligence, personality characteristics, or behavioral problems. They are also no more likely to suffer any kind of sexual abuse.

Regarding gay and lesbian families, Benkov (1994, pp. 344–345) writes:

> Lesbian and gay parents essentially reinvent the family as a pluralistic phenomenon. They self-consciously build from the ground up a variety of family types that don't conform to the traditional structure. In doing so, they encourage society to ask, "What is a family?". . . "What is a mother, a father, a parent, a sibling? Can a child have two or more mothers or fathers? Is one more 'real' by virtue of biological or legal parent status? How does society's recognition (or its absence) foster or impede parent-child relationships? To what extent does the state shape family life? To what extent can nontraditional families alter the state's definition of family?"

Gay parents find that the act of raising children can make the "coming out" process a daily reality, not just a "one shot deal" during a person's youth. How much privacy should be maintained about one's sexual orientation? How, for example, does one respond when a lady in the grocery store exclaims loudly: "What a lovely child; does your husband have red hair too?" Or when the checkout clerk coos something similar, and one's child responds proudly: "I don't have a daddy, I have two moms!" What about when one's child is teased at school for not having a daddy? One's own internalized homophobia may need to be confronted at times like this. Gay and lesbian communities are stretched by the presence of children as well. For example, should child care be provided at gay pride events? Should events appropriate for children be scheduled (Greenler, 2001)? Redefining family in community context is a challenge experienced by all in our changing times.

Multiracial Families

Multiracial families are now a part of the American scene, though as yet a fairly small part. For the first time in 2000, the United States census permitted people to classify themselves in more than one racial category. Approximately 2 percent took advantage of the opportunity (Belsie, 2001). Interracial marriage is one way to form a multiracial family; another is to adopt a child of a different race. Each process presents its own opportunities and challenges.

According to Diller (1999), children raised in multiracial families are quite capable of developing healthy ethnic identities. They can integrate different cultural backgrounds into a single sense of self, and they tend to welcome the opportunity to discuss who they are ethnically with other people. Children may meet special challenges in school, where the question "what are you" requires a skillful response. Teens especially may be pushed by peers to adopt part of their racial identity and reject another; their single-race parents may have difficulty understanding the pressures involved. Still, supportive parents can make an important difference in helping interracial children cope with a complex and sometimes hostile world.

Interracial couples face special challenges; it is common for at least one set of in-laws to reject the chosen partner, for example. Interracial couples may find themselves socially isolated not only from families of origin but from former friends. In response, many associate mostly with other interracial couples. Moreover, each partner brings different cultural expectations to the marriage, so that role expectations may require skillful negotiation. Many couples meet these challenges successfully, however.

Intercultural adoptions involve a different set of challenges. They are usually opposed by people of color, especially African Americans and Native Americans, who believe that white parents cannot provide minority children appropriate exposure to their cultural heritage or teach them how to cope with discrimination in the wider society. Many children of color adopted by white parents in the United Staes today come from overseas. Special efforts must be made to help these children learn about their cultural heritage.

DIVERSE FAMILY STRUCTURES AND SOCIAL WORK'S ETHIC OF CULTURAL COMPETENCE AND SOCIAL DIVERSITY

Social workers today frequently work with families to help strengthen the relationships among members, to foster nonviolent parenting skills, to assist in finding financial and material resources, to help protect abused and neglected children, to help arrange foster care, to provide home studies for adoption, and the like. For this reason, it is very important that workers recognize, understand, and respect family diversity, whether ethnic, cultural, lifestyle, socioeconomic, or whatever.

The social work code of ethics, 1.05 (c) states:

> Social workers should obtain education about and seek to understand the nature of social diversity and oppression with respect to race, ethnicity, national origin, color, sex, sexual orientation, age, marital status, political belief, religion, or mental or physical disability.

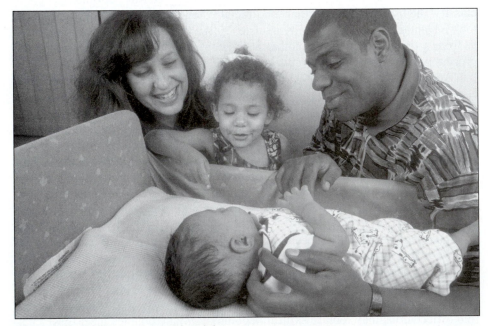

The modern family may be multi-racial.

Social workers who work with families today need to recognize and respect the increasingly diverse forms. They may need to seek new information and gain new skills to provide the most effective service. Hence, the importance of the above provision of the professional social work code of ethics.

FAMILY POLICY, DOMESTIC AND INTERNATIONAL: RESEARCH RAISES QUESTIONS

Is there something wrong with social policies impacting families in the United States today? While lip service is given to family values, few governmental supports to help families survive in today's world are provided. A basic symptom of major problems: Research data demonstrate that 23 other nations have lower infant mortality rates than the United States. Moreover, twice as many black children die in their first year as white children (Van Wormer, 1997). Clearly, poor women do not have sufficient access to prenatal care, among other concerns.

Moreover, many American families today are very poor, and instead of reaching out to help them more, Congress in 1996 repealed entitlement to any aid at all, as discussed in detail previously. Loeb (1999) writes that poverty among children in the United States is extremely high compared to that of other industrialized countries, real wages have stagnated, and the gap between rich and poor is growing (see Exhibit 8).

How do other nations help keep their children out of poverty? Many different approaches are taken, but most western industrialized nations provide universal health care. Many nations also provide universal, non-means-tested children's

---

A "Soft Apocalypse"

EXHIBIT 8

Sociologist Todd Gittlin calls the [increasing economic uncertainty in America] the "soft apocalypse." The gap between rich and poor is greater today than at any point since the Great Depression—companies have downsized, and real wages have stagnated—so that the average American manufacturing worker now makes less than those in eleven other countries, including Germany, Austria, Sweden, France, and Japan. The wealthiest one percent of Americans now control more of the nation's wealth than the bottom 95%. The United States has the industrialized world's highest rate of infant mortality, homelessness, and child poverty. We also lead in the rates of murder, rape, and other violent crimes, and in no country in the world is a higher percentage of the population in prison. We have the most billionaires, the highest executive salaries, the greatest inequality in wealth, the biggest military budget, including the most military aid to developing countries, and a commanding lead as the world's largest arms trader.

Source: Quoted from Paul Rogat Loeb. (1999). *Soul of a citizen, living with conviction in a cynical time.* New York, St. Martin's Griffin, 86–87.

allowances to help keep families out of poverty in the first place, recognizing that children bring additional expenses to every family. Some countries provide an additional stipend if a noncustodial parent fails to keep up with child support payments. Many nations provide universal day care, either free or on a sliding scale. Others provide paid maternity and/or paternity leaves for as long as a full year, with the guarantee that one has a job when one is ready to return to work. Unfortunately, however, all these benefits are in jeopardy today because of intense international competition from global corporations and trends in privatization of social services (Van Wormer, 1997).

The good news is that government programs *can* make a difference to children and *can* help strengthen families. The low point in U.S. child poverty rates in 1969 quoted by Van Wormer was not an accident, but the result of the combined effects of many important programs in the War on Poverty at that time. The War on Poverty was not lost because it could not be won, but rather because the money was diverted to the military budget and the conflict in Vietnam.

The bad news is that now our nation is at war again, in what may prove to be extended combat on many fronts with an elusive enemy. The long-standing debate of "guns versus butter" tends to get lost in wartime, as the cry for guns overshadows everything else. Yet since the terrorist attacks, homelessness has grown in the United States. Nearly 30,000 reside in New York shelters alone, an all-time high. Part of the problem, of course, is that more than 80,000 people lost their jobs in the city due to the terrorist attack.

Many New Yorkers, however, will benefit from the relief funds temporarily pouring into the city. Other areas of the country are suffering also, but donations are harder to come by. Reverend Donald Health, a Catholic priest who works at a food pantry in Attleboro, Massachusetts, describes what he calls the "heat or eat" syndrome that he experiences in his own area. "You either heat your home or you eat, and the statistics are horrible for the number of people who go without meals—Lately, I've been beating my head against the wall." When he asks for donations, people respond, "I gave to New York" (Paulson, 2001).

Research conducted by America's Second Harvest found a 90 percent increase in the number of people served by its network of food banks from 1997 to 2001. Says Martha Picket, chief operating officer, "When you look at having conducted these interviews when the economic expansion was still going full-out, and we still had more people turning to hunger relief charities than four years earlier—that's very concerning." Demand, not surprisingly, significantly increased after September 11, 2001. Kathy Murphy, of the Second Harvest Food Bank of Central Florida, reports that "one in 10 of our neighbors requires food assistance on a normal day in central Florida. When you couple that with 88,000 people affected [since September 11 by layoffs or shortened work hours] I'm not sure where that's going to leave us" (Paulson, 2001).

Research thus indicates a growing need for basics such as food and shelter for poor citizens in the United States, at a time when tax revenues are decreasing due to both an economic recession and tax cuts, and military spending is increasing. Government, therefore, is not likely to increase aid to needy families in the near future. And current trends indicate that private charitable giving may be down as well, or diverted to New York. Eugene Tempel, director of the Center on Philanthropy at the University of Indiana, states:

> When you analyze what happens in times of crisis, there may be a kind of pulling together where Americans give more generously. But individuals' increased generosity can't make up for the fact that corporations and foundations, often responsible for the largest donations, typically give a fixed percentage of their profits. This year, those have plummeted. In addition, many corporations focused their giving on New York. The tragedy in New York has been given so much attention that it's distracted people from local needs. (Paulson, 2001)

Americans may well be on their own in trying to feed and care for their families in increasingly hard times ahead. Will they be able to meet their needs in the workplace?

HOW FAMILY-FRIENDLY IS THE AMERICAN WORKPLACE?

Given that the shrinking of government programs is forcing more and more parents to work outside the home, the question of whether the workplace is family-friendly becomes increasingly important. Studies show, unfortunately, that the workplace in the United States has a long way to go in this area. For example, while a recent study by the Families and Work Institute reported some flexibility in work hours to help families (nearly 90 percent of the 1,000 companies surveyed allowed workers to take time off to attend their children's school events, more than two-thirds allowed flex-time, and half let workers stay home with ill children without using vacation or sick days), there were still large unmet needs. For example, only 9 percent of the companies surveyed offered child care at or near the workplace, only 33 percent offered maternity leaves of more than 13 weeks, and only 23 percent offered elder care resource and referral services (Report: Companies far from being truly family-friendly, 1998).

Other recent studies have found that two adults must work four different jobs in 6 million American homes to keep their families afloat. The average American family has added more than four weeks of work in the past two decades to make ends meet (Francis, 2001). Ninety percent of the parents interviewed in one poll stated that a time crunch was the worst problem in their lives. Wage and tax squeezes were cited as the next most difficult problems. Sylvia Hewlett (quoted in Gardner, 1998), believes that managerial greed leaves employees overworked, underpaid, and lacking enough time with their children. Moreover, she states that government policies are hostile to families—that tax policies, for example, allow more deductions for expenses incurred in raising horses than for expenses incurred in raising children. Hewlett believes that these inequities place terrible burdens on today's parents.

CURRENT TRENDS IN THE UNITED STATES

William Clinton came into office in 1993 with an apparent agenda to improve family well-being in the United States. His administration provided support for families when it first took office by initiating passage of both the Family and

Medical Leave Act of 1993 and the Family Preservation and Support Services Act of 1993. The Family and Medical Leave Act permits 12 weeks of unpaid leave for people working for businesses with 50 or more employees. Leave can be taken when a child is born, adopted, or taken into foster care; or for medical reasons to provide health care for a relative or for oneself. The leave is unpaid, however, so that many people cannot afford to take it. The Family Preservation and Support Services Act was intended to provide services to all families, not only families at risk. Its implementation is a collaborative effort between the states and the federal government.

As is well known, however, the Clinton administration was unable to pass legislation to provide universal health care, so that poor Americans still find access to such care extremely limited. And as discussed previously, the program that President Clinton actually signed into law that most affected poor families in this country eliminated their entitlement to government aid under the Social Security Act. The PRWOA of 1996 permitted, but did not require, states to develop their own programs of assistance to poor families within certain federal guidelines, and limited any such aid offered to five years in a given parents's lifetime.

George W. Bush took office as president in 2001 without a popular mandate. He was not elected by a majority of Americans. He might even have lost the deciding electoral votes in Florida if a conservative Supreme Court had allowed a recount, as many legal scholars insist was required by law. (Later tallies indicate that Bush probably would have won an official recount, but only if ballots cast for his opponent, clearly yet improperly marked due to faulty ballot design, were disqualified.)

Bush took office with major political obligations—to wealthy businessmen, the religious right, and the National Rifle Association, among other conservative constituencies that had financed his campaign. Hence, it is not surprising that in his early days in office he proposed and was able to pass a substantial tax cut favoring the wealthiest of Americans. He included an increase in the tax credit for minor children, from $500 per child to $1,000, but that credit only benefits wealthier families who have enough tax liability to claim it. At the same time, Bush proposed a $200 million cut in child care subsidies for low-income families (Gardner, 2001). He reinstated the "gag rule" so that federally funded family service agencies could not inform pregnant women of their option for abortion. He pledged to privatize social service programs and proposed public funding for faith-based organizations (see discussion in Chapter 3). Even more telling, he proposed a substantial buildup in military spending, a major benefit for big business, well before the events of September 11. These trends continue as this chapter is being written, exacerbated, of course, by the military operations in Afghanistan and in other areas of the world and the hunt for terrorists. The Republican administration's preference regarding "guns or butter" is rather clear and enjoys much greater public support since the terrorist attacks, due to a nervous citizenry.

Today, the national trend is away from government assistance to families, particularly away from federal assistance. More and more parents have thus been forced to work outside the home to make ends meet, so that children are increasingly left without adequate parenting or supervision. Most parents want to do a good job with their children, but they are often too overwhelmed with work outside the home to manage the parenting job as well as they would like.

The "tough" part of welfare reform is now upon us (Sappenfeld, 2001). The five-year deadline for state TANF programs to move welfare recipients into paying jobs under the 1996 PRWOA expired in fall of 2001. Those with enough education, transportation, child care, and good luck found jobs, but others were not so fortunate. Under the welfare reform law, states can provide exceptions to 20 percent of their TANF clientele and still receive federal funds, but in many areas the need is greater. An economic downturn occurred at the turn of the century; the economy in early 2001 was losing jobs at the fastest rate since the recession a decade before. Many newly hired, former welfare recipients began experiencing the "last hired, first fired" phenomenon (Francis, 2001, May 7). Then, the economic downturn worsened after the terrorist attacks in New York City and Washington D.C.

For poor families, employed or not, life has become harder. For example, while 42 percent of children in families headed by women remained poor in 1999, many lost access to food stamps due to tougher eligibility standards (or lack of information about eligibility). Specifically, only 72 of every 100 poor children received food stamps in 1999, down from 88 in 1995 (Weinstein, 2000). In a like manner, many poor families lost health care under Medicaid. Enrollment declined 27 percent between 1995 and 1999 (Gullo, 2000), a loss of nearly 1 million people.

Meantime, recent research has tagged the price of raising a child born at the turn of the century (birth to age 17) at about $165,000. Low-income families will spend about $121,230, and upper-income families as much as $244,770 (Hartill, 2001). Poor families struggle to meet the costs. Their children often miss out on the intellectually stimulating care they might receive at certified day care centers, because, although they might benefit the most from these services, the parents cannot afford the fees. Instead, poor children are frequently cared for by siblings or relatives. One study found that about half of lower-income families depend on relatives, including youngsters or teens, for child care. Another revealed that more than 15 percent of low-income parents leave their four- to seven-year-old children alone regularly or in the care of siblings under 12 years of age (Telcher, 2000).

Current trends for American families look rather bleak. Federal aid continues to decrease. But with shrinking federal involvement in services to families, and very limited family-friendly policies available in the work setting, smaller units of government are beginning to develop programs to help fill the gap in some places. For example, former Massachusetts Governor William Weld included in his final budget allocation $5 million to provide home visits to all first-time teenage mothers in the state. The Massachusetts plan is based on a Hawaiian Healthy Start initiative in which new mothers are assessed for risk while in the hospital for delivery. Those considered "at risk," with their approval, are assigned a home visitor who provides hands-on help for five years. The purpose of Hawaii's program is prevention of child abuse, and it has achieved documented success (Hands-on help for mothers, 1997).

In the foreseeable future, efforts to strengthen families are likely to come from state and local governments and volunteer groups, such as the examples described above. The good news is that small programs can be tailored to meet specific needs of specific communities. The bad news is that such efforts are fragmented, without dependable funding, and not available to all who need them.

INTERNET SITES

http://www.aamft.org/	American Academy for Marriage and Family Therapy
http://www.acf.dhhs.gov/	The Administration for Children and Families
http://fostercare.org/	The Foster Parent Home Page
http://www.nafbs.org/	National Association of Family Based Services
http://homepage.dtn.ntl.com/terence.p/barefoot/reading.htm	Recommended Reading on Radical Social Workers
http://childrensdefense.org	The Children's Defense Fund
http://www.yfc-libertyville.com/	Youth and Family Counseling
http://web.lemoyne.edu/~bucko/indian.html	Native American Research Page
http://www.fcnl.org/issues/nat/sup/indians_welfare_act.htm	The Indian Child Welfare Act
http://www.mdarchives.state.md.us/msa/refserv/html/afro.html	Maryland State Archives African American Resources
http://www.census.gov/Press-Release/www/1999/cb99-37.html	Two-Thirds of African American Families Have Children, Census Bureau Reports

SUMMARY

This chapter's case study describes the case of LaTanya Tracy, an infant who has been left in the care of her great-grandmother. Unable to cope, the great-grandmother calls for help from her local protective services program. The case study illustrates how the problem was successfully resolved through the skilled intervention of a baccalaureate social worker, Lauren White.

A historical context is provided for family and children's services. Mutual aid among family members came first, supplemented later on an emergency basis by churches. Secular law eventually provided certain kinds of assistance, such as the categorical aids under the Elizabethan Poor Law of 1601. Formal assistance to families beyond the financial and material came even later. For example, the first protective services case was not taken to court until 1875, and then it was brought by the president of the SPCA, a private organization to help animals. Not until the 1970s did the federal government, through Title XX of the Social Security Act, require all states to provide protective services for children. Legislation requiring protective services did not mandate adequate funding, however, so that many neglect and abuse cases reported today are never investigated.

Various in-home supportive services available to meet special needs of children and families include financial aid, family-based services, protective services, family therapy, day care, homemaker services, and family life education. Among out-of-home substitute services are foster care, adoption, group homes, institutional care, and the judicial system.

The social work value of self-determination guides and challenges Lauren White. Here is a situation where her primary client is a tiny infant whose mother has become neglectful due to substance abuse. How can the value of self-determination be applied in a situation like this?

Research findings that reveal persisting poverty in the United States and decreasing public assistance to impoverished families are explored. The possible relationship of modern family diversity to the curtailment of public assistance is considered. Data indicating various negative impacts of welfare reform are discussed. Social policies and services that assist families in other industrialized countries are compared with those in the United States.

Finally, trends in U.S. family policy at the beginning of the Bush administration are identified, especially the trend toward decreased financial and material assistance from the federal government and increasing reliance on state, local, and voluntary efforts.

KEY TERMS

abuse	out-of-home services
children-at-risk	permanency placement
gay	protective services
in-home services	sanctions
lesbian	self-determination
neglect	

DISCUSSION QUESTIONS

1. In child protective services, why are major attempts made to keep children in their own homes whenever possible and, if that is not possible, to place children in the homes of relatives?

2. Which do you think is more important, if a choice must be made: guaranteeing a child's safety by providing permanence in an adoptive home, or making every effort to reunite a child with his or her biological parents? Why?

3. What types of in-home services are provided to children and families under the social welfare system? Describe each briefly.

4. What types of out-of-home services are available under the American social welfare system? Describe each briefly.

5. What is the social work principle of self-determination? Where specifically is it identified as an ethical principle for social workers? How did Lauren White exercise this principle, given that her primary client was a legal minor?

6. In what year were formal public services to protect children established by federal law in the United States? By what year did all states actually provide these services? Are the services provided adequate today?

7. For how long have social workers been working with families in this country? Compare and contrast the approaches taken by the Children's Aid Society of Charles Loring Brace, Societies for the Prevention of Cruelty to Children, Charity Organization Societies, settlement houses, and so forth.

8. What factors seem to be involved in the substantial amounts of poverty found in American families today?

9. What do you think about the idea that government aid to families may have been cut to punish female heads of households and nontraditional families? Do you think this is a realistic theory? Do you think curtailing such aid in order to encourage traditional families is a good idea? Why or why not?

10. What family policies in other countries help prevent child and family poverty? What do you think of these policies? Why?

11. What major pieces of legislation were passed early in the Clinton administration that can help strengthen American families? What major legislation failed to pass Congress?

12. What are the major provisions of the Personal Responsibility and Work Opportunity Act? What have been some early results? Do you think this legislation will strengthen American families? Why or why not?

CLASSROOM EXERCISES

While not required, it is suggested that students break into small groups of three of four to discuss these exercises. It may be helpful to choose a scribe to record and report interesting points to the class after the group discussion.

1. Think about all the families you know. About what percentage are "traditional," meaning that they include both biological parents and their children? Then think about the nontraditional families you know. What types can you identify (single parent, separated, widowed, or divorced; single parent, never married; heterosexual unmarried couple with children; gay or lesbian couple with children; blended families with stepparents; etc.)?

2. We have long had a dialogue in our nation concerning whether mothers should remain at home to care for their children. The 1996 PRWOA no longer allows poor mothers to do so. What do you think about the wisdom of this policy? What factors make it more difficult for a single mother to work outside the home as compared with a mother who has a partner? What types of supports do other western industrialized nations provide to working single-parent families to help avoid destitution?

3. If you could improve the 1993 Family and Medical Leave Act to make it more available to all American families, what would you do?

4. What is the cost to American families of the high military budget? Which do you believe leads to a more secure nation, "guns or butter"? Why?

RESEARCH ACTIVITIES

1. Pay a personal visit to a family service agency in your city or county. Is the agency public or private (government-run or run by a voluntary organization)? If private, is it a for-profit or nonprofit agency? Find out what kind of services are offered. What do the various services cost? Are sliding fees available?

2. Interview a social worker employed by the protective services program in your area. Find out about the worker's educational background and how helpful the worker believes it was. Find out what the worker finds most challenging about his or her job. What does the worker find rewarding about the work?

3. Interview four friends to learn about their family structures, both currently and in the past. How much diversity do you encounter?

4. Visit a local Head Start program where many of the children come from disadvantaged backgrounds. If you can, interview teachers, social workers, and parents. In what ways do these different sets of people believe the program enriches the children's lives? Do you find any similarities in perspective? Any differences? What social justice issues can you identify as a result of your interviews?

INTERNET RESEARCH EXERCISES

1. In the archives of the website of the *Boston Globe* can be found an interesting article on the changes taking place in society's approach to foster children (http://search/boston.com/slobe/metro/packages/adoption/permanency.htm).
   a. According to the article, what is happening to the philosophy of family unification?
   b. What is cited as being a problem with family unification?
   c. What are some of the provisions of the Adoptions and Safe Family Act?
2. A county prosecutor in Indiana demonstrates a proactive approach to elder abuse (http://www.charkprosecuter.org/html/aps/aps.htm).
   a. What is the estimated ratio of those who actually report the abuse to those who don't report it, according to this report?
   b. Is it usual for a person outside the family to be the abuser?
   c. What does the paper suggest that everyone can do to prevent this problem from worsening?
3. An interesting organization formed in 1985 whose mission is to promote and ensure fair, accurate, and inclusive representation of individuals and events in all media as a means of eliminating homophobia and discrimination based on gender identity and sexual orientation. The Gay and Lesbian Alliance Against Defamation (GLAAD) has a website to help achieve these goals (http://glaad.org).
   a. After reading the section "About GLAAD," what methods does this group use to achieve its goals?
   b. What is a media resource center? Has GLAAD's media resource center been used by the media?
   c. Do you feel that this group has made progress toward achieving its stated goals?

REFERENCES

Abramovitz, Mimi. (2000). *Under attack, fighting back: Women and welfare in the United States.* New York: Monthly Review Press.

Adoption and safe families act clarifies child welfare commitments. (1998, February). *Partnerships for Child Welfare,* 5(5), 3.

Allen, M., Kakavas, A., & Zalenski, J. (1994, Spring). Family preservation and support services. *The Prevention Report.* Iowa City: National Resource Center on Family Based Services, University of Iowa School of Social Work, 2.

Belsie, L. (2001, March 14). Ethnic diversity grows, but not integration. *The Christian Science Monitor,* 1, 4.

Benkov, L. (1994). Reinventing the family. In A. S. Skolnick and J. H. Skolnick (Eds.), *Families in transition* (10th ed.). New York: Longman.

Bills tackle welfare, patients' rights. (1998, September). *NASW News,* 7.

Children's Defense Fund. (1998, May 2). *New studies look at status of former welfare recipients* (online). Available: http://childrensdefense.org/fairstart_status.html.

De La Cruz, Donna. (2001, November 19). *Homeless population climbs in some of the nation's largest cities, experts say* (online). Available: http://www.nandotimes.com/nation/story/174004p-168641c.ntml.

Diller, J. V. (1999). *Cultural diversity: A primer for the human services.* Pacific Grove, CA: Brooks/Cole.

Eighty-one years of paving the way, a history of family planning in America. (1997, Fall/Winter). *Planned Parenthood Today,* 4, 5.

Engbur, A., and Klungness, L. (2000) *The complete single mother.* Holbrook: MA: Adams Media Corporation.

Foscarinis, M. (1999, December 9). Stop punishing the homeless. *The Christian Science Monitor,* 11.

Francis, D. R. (2001, May 7). Job gains for poor now at risk. *The Christian Science Monitor,* 1, 2.

Francis, D. R. (2001, June 27). The dollars and cents of America's work ethic. *The Christian Science Monitor,* 1, 4.

Gardner, M. (2001, April 18). What the Bush budget does for children. *The Christian Science Monitor,* 3.

Gardner, M. (1998, May 27). Parents face "hostile" policies in raising children. *The Christian Science Monitor,* 13.

Greenler, K. (2001, July). Personal communication.

Greenstein, R., Primus, W., & Kayatin, T. (2000, October 10). *Poverty rate hits lowest level since 1979 as unemployment reaches a 30 year low.* Center on Budget and Policy Priorities (online). Available: http://www.cbpp.org/9-26-00pov.htm.

Gullo, K. (2000, June 19). *Nearly one million lost Medicaid.* Associated Press (online).

Gunn, E. (1998, November). Lock out, the state's neediest workers are deprived of what will help them most. *Milwaukee Magazine,* 108.

Gustavsson, N. S., & Segal, E. A. (1994). *Critical issues in child welfare.* Thousand Oaks, CA: Sage Publications.

Hands-on help for mothers (1997, August 18). *The Christian Science Monitor,* 1.

Hartill, L. (2001, June 20). Thank your parents, kids. You've already cost them $165,000. *The Christian Science Monitor,* 14.

Kadushin, A., & Martin, J. (1988). *Child welfare services* (4th ed.). New York: Macmillan.

Karger, J., & Stoesz, D. (1998). *American social welfare policy, a pluralist approach* (3rd ed.). New York: Addison Wesley Longman.

Kissinger, M. (2001, May 20). Home is just a dream. *The Milwaukee Journal Sentinel,* 2.

Loeb, P. R. (1999). *Soul of a citizen, living with conviction in a cynical time.* New York: St. Martin's Griffin.

Marks, A. (2001, July 16). In abortion fight, lines have shifted. *The Christian Science Monitor,* 1, 4.

McKenzie, J. K., & Lewis, R. (1998). Keeping the promise of adoption and safe families act. *The Roundtable,* 12 (1), 1–9.

Meyers, M., Han, W., Waldfogel, J., & Garfinkel, I. (2001, March). Child care in the wake of welfare reform: The impact of government subsidies on the economic well-being of single-mother families. *Social Service Review, 75* (1), 30–59.

Mink, G. (1998). *Welfare's end.* Ithaca, NY: Cornell University Press.

Nifong, C. (1997, December 15). Ranks of homeless include more families. *The Christian Science Monitor,* 14.

Paulson, A. (2001, November 20). More need help putting food on table. *The Christian Science Monitor,* 1, 4.

Pierce, D., with Brooks, J. (2000, Winter). *The self-sufficiency standard for Wisconsin.* Madison, WI: Education Fund of the Wisconsin Women's Network.

Prater, G. S. (1992). Child welfare and African-American families. In N. A. Cohen (Ed.), *Child welfare: A multicultural focus.* Boston: Allyn and Bacon.

Ramanathan, C. S., & Link, R. J. (1999). *All our futures: Principles and resources for social work practice in a global era.* Belmont, CA: Science and Behavior Books.

Report: Companies far from being truly family friendly. (1998, July 14). *The Daily News,* West Bend, WI, A10.

Sappenfeld, M. (2001, May 8). Now, the tough part of welfare reform. *The Christian Science Monitor,* 2.

Savin-Williams, R., & Esterberg, K. G. (2000). Lesbian, gay, and bisexual families. In D. Demo, K. Allen, & M. A. Fine, *Handbook of family diversity* (pp. 197–215). New York: Oxford University Press.

Segal, E., & Brzuzy, S. (1998). *Social welfare policy, programs, and practice.* Itasca, IL: F. E. Peacock Publishers, Inc.

Smith, M. K. (1998, January). Utilization-focused evaluation of a family preservation program. *Families in Society: The Journal of Contemporary Human Services,* 1–19.

Teen pregnancy rate falls to record low. (2001, June 13). *The Daily News,* West Bend, WI, A11.

Telcher, S. A. (2000, January 3). When children are caregivers for children. *The Christian Science Monitor,* 3.

Trattner, W. I. (1999). *From poor law to welfare state: A history of social welfare in America* (6th ed.). New York: The Free Press.

Van Wormer, K. (1997). *Social welfare: A world view.* Chicago: Nelson Hall Publishers.

Watkins, S. A. (1990, November). The Mary Ellen myth: Correcting child welfare history. *Social Work, 35* (6), 501–503.

Weinstein, D. (2000, April). *Welfare to what?* The Children's Defense Fund (online). Available: http://www.childrensdefense.org/fair-start-welfaretowhat_2000.htm.

Wilhelmust, M. (1998, March). Mediation in kinship care: Another step in the provision of culturally relevant child welfare services. *Social Work,* 43 (2), 117–126.

Wright, J., Rubin, B., & Devine, J. (1998). *Beside the golden door: Policy, politics, and the homeless.* New York: Aldine de Gruyter.

FOR FURTHER READING

Cohen, N.A. (Ed.). (1992). *Child welfare: A multicultural focus.* Boston: Allyn & Bacon.

Although this book examines child welfare from a generalist perspective and includes substantial material on the history of the field, its major contribution centers on extensive historical and contemporary information regarding child welfare and African American families, Asian and Pacific Islander families, and Hispanic families. Special issues of child welfare in rural areas are also examined.

Demo, D. H., Allen, D. R., and Fine, M. (Eds.) (2000). *Handbook of family diversity.* New York: Oxford University Press.

This edited volume provides a wealth of information about diversity in American families today. The first section provides historical perspectives on family diversity. Subsequent sections discuss gender dynamics, family structure issues, racial and cultural diversity, class diversity, and applications to family social work.

Gustavsson, N. S., & Segal, E. A. (1994), *Critical issues in child welfare.* Thousands Oaks, CA: Sage Publications.

Gustavsson and Segal's book examines several salient issues in child welfare, including children's rights, health needs, and the challenges of public education. Part Two examines the residual nature of child welfare services and identifies major effects such as the juvenilization of poverty and child abuse and neglect. New threats to children such as HIV and homelessness are explored in Part Three. Part Four proposes several areas for further research.

Loeb, Paul R. (1999). *Soul of a citizen: Living with conviction in a cynical time.* New York: St. Martin's Griffin.

This book should be read by every student and practitioner of social activism. Painfully aware of the social ills that plague this nation today, Loeb nevertheless remains able to transcend cynicism and eloquently describes the ways and the reasons he is able to do it. He debunks the myth that the activists of the 60s all turned yuppie and tells the story of myriad ordinary people who have invested their lives in making a positive difference.

National Research Council. (1993). *Understanding child abuse and neglect.* Washington, DC: National Academy Press.

This book records the findings of a panel of 16 professionals representing a variety of disciplines, including psychology, psychiatry, social work, sociology, and anthropology. It recognizes the complex interplay of factors that influence child maltreatment. Various chapters discuss the scope of the problem, interrelated causes and consequences, prevention, interventions, and treatment. Ethical and legal issues in maltreatment research are also addressed.

Seccombe, K. (1999). *So you think I drive a Cadillac?* Boston: Allyn and Bacon.

This unusual book provides the perspective of welfare recipients regarding welfare programs and welfare reform. It puts a human face on welfare, and examines effects of stigma and discrimination on the people who receive it. The book explores how people survive on severely inadequate budgets and how they juggle their day-to-day decisions regarding whether to buy clothes for the children or pay the telephone bill. The book also describes how social and economic reality such as lack of well-paying jobs traps people in the system.

Wright, J. D., Rubin, B. A., & Devine, J. (1998). *Beside the golden door.* New York: Aldine de Gryter.

This book presents an enormous amount of information on homeless people and families in the United States today, and examines various reasons this population is undercounted. The book presents various theories of homelessness and the relationship of homelessness to social policy in international perspective. Mental illness and substance abuse are explored and discounted as primary underlying reasons for the expansion of homelessness.

CHAPTER 6

Social Work in Mental Health

DAVID DEERINWATER

Roberta Sholes, a BSW with several years of experience at the Oklahoma State Mental Health Center, had just returned from vacation in the eastern part of the state, where she had visited Oklahoma Indian country. Now she would be working with a newly admitted Cherokee man who was from that area. Psychiatric **staffings** *(multidisciplinary patient care meetings) always excited Roberta's interest but today she was especially eager to meet Mr. Deerinwater, her new client.*

Sadly, the first of the five persons discussed by the team was a young woman who was critically ill following an aspirin overdose. Next was a 55-year-old attorney who had been readmitted following an episode of frenetic behavior; he had discontinued taking the medication prescribed for his bipolar disorder. Following him were two elderly women who had been admitted with severe depression. Then the psychiatric resident who had admitted Mr. Deerinwater began by sharing what he knew about his case.

David Deerinwater had come to Tulsa from a ranch in the Goingsnake District of Oklahoma about 10 years ago, in search of employment. Living in a series of one-room, inner-city apartments, he sustained himself with odd jobs and some janitorial service work; he had few social contacts although he seemed to identify strongly with his tribal people. Mr. Deerinwater had been living on the streets for at least six months and seemed to have no possessions and no family or friends in the city. Increasingly isolated, his energy seemed to decline, and he lost weight. On admission, speech was of a muttering, incoherent quality and his gestures suggested that he might be hearing voices. Mr. Deerinwater voluntarily admitted himself to the hospital through the assistance of a social worker from the hot meal site where he had obtained food for the past six months. The admitting diagnosis was **schizophrenia,** *undifferentiated type, a severe form of mental illness.*

As Mr. Deerinwater was being wheeled into the staff meeting, Roberta was startled to see the cold, distant expression in his dark eyes. He stared straight ahead, completely unresponsive to the questions that were asked, and yet Roberta sensed that he had some awareness of what was happening around him. After he left, it was confirmed that Roberta would be the social worker for Mr. Deerinwater.

When Roberta went to see Mr. Deerinwater later in the day, she found him in his wheelchair on a sun porch, staring at the trees and park area beyond the window. She was pleased when he motioned her to sit down. Remembering the quiet pride of the Cherokee men she had seen, Roberta sat beside him for a time, not speaking. After a while and without turning to her, he asked, "Well, what do you want?" It was a good sign that he acknowledged her presence, and Roberta was pleased. She explained simply that she wanted to help. He replied, "That is not possible." Roberta then introduced herself slowly and said again that she wanted to help. Several minutes passed before he replied, "Then you will help me to get out of here." Roberta told Mr. Deerinwater that she would need his help for that, and that she would work with him to accomplish it. She wasn't sure he heard her. He no longer seemed aware of her as he stared into the distance.

The next morning David Deerinwater greeted Roberta with an almost imperceptible wave of his hand. She again sat quietly beside him. Then, because it was a beautiful, warm day, Roberta asked Mr. Deerinwater if he would like to go outdoors with her for a few minutes. For a moment his expression appeared to be one of startled disbelief. Then a somber, closed expression again came over his face, but he nodded assent. Roberta wheeled his chair outdoors and across the carefully tended lawn to the shade of the ancient catalpa trees. David Deerinwater inhaled deeply. He was silent, perhaps more peaceful than she had seen him previously. Roberta began telling him about the hospital, its location, its purpose (to help people get well and return to their homes), and the staff and how they worked together. Again, Roberta stressed that she would need his help, adding that she needed to understand about his life, his growing up years, his family. Again Mr. Deerinwater nodded his head, acknowledging that he understood, but he added, "I am very tired now."

The next morning Roberta was surprised to find David Deerinwater waiting for her at the nurse's station. He was no longer using a wheelchair, she noted. She took him to the sun porch. Once there, he spoke: "You said that you could help me to get out of here." She replied that was just what she aimed to do, but that she wanted to be sure that he was feeling better and that he would have a place to go. He replied, haltingly, that he was eating and sleeping much better now, but he was feeling cooped up and didn't think he could stay much longer. Although Mr. Deerinwater was not an easy person to interview, Roberta appreciated the quiet dignity beneath his cool, distant gaze. She tried not to hurry him as she gently asked about his family and his experiences as a child.

Slowly and somewhat hesitatingly, over the next half hour, David Deerinwater gave Roberta a picture of his youth in the Goingsnake District, including memories of stomp dances (social events centering on spiritual dances), green corn feasts in the fall, and much hard work on the ranch. He spoke, too, of having been sent to boarding school with other Indian children, and of the pain he felt when teachers spoke degradingly of Cherokee Indian life and reprimanded the children for speaking in their Cherokee language. He recounted serene times with family as well as hardship and poverty. David's father had been chronically ill with diabetes and had died when David was 16. Joe, three years older than David, had taken on major responsibilities for his mother, David, and three younger girls. The family had relied on help from friends and neighbors and had worked their small ranch and summer garden; that was how they had survived. Roberta realized that Mr. Deerinwater was beginning to develop some trust in her when he willingly signed a form giving Roberta permission to share information about him with his family and with the Health and Social Services Department of the Cherokee Nation.

Roberta had not worked with a Cherokee Indian before, and she realized that she would need to acquire a better understanding of this ethnic group before she could adequately assess Mr. Deerinwater's situation and begin to develop a plan with him for life beyond the hospital. She placed a long-distance telephone call to the Health and Social Services Department of the Cherokee Nation and found that Dorothy White, one of the social workers in the office, knew the Deerinwater family. Ms. White offered to drive to their small ranch and ask David Deerinwater's mother to telephone Roberta the next day from the Cherokee Nation office, since the family had no phone. She also volunteered to send Roberta information about the Cherokee Nation's services. She suggested it might be important to the patient's potential recovery, both physically and mentally, that he return to his home.

She said she suspected that he really needed to be back with his people, where he would be understood and cared for by his family. Through the Cherokee Nation clinic, he could receive medical, rehabilitative, and mental health services that incorporated the beliefs and values of the Cherokees. She explained that the clinic offered group services, for example, that helped people come together to achieve harmony with each other, the community, and the natural world.

Ms. White proved to be extremely helpful. When she called Roberta the next day, she had both Mrs. Deerinwater and Joe (David's brother) in her office. Mrs. Deerinwater was very eager for news about her son. She was especially concerned about her son's weakness and nutritional state, and she concluded by saying, "We will bring him home." Roberta explained that David was not yet well enough to leave the hospital and that he would have to determine for himself whether he wished to return home or remain in Tulsa. For now, however, he needed to gain strength and to continue taking his medication. Mrs. Deerinwater replied that she knew what he would eat; she would cook for him. Then Joe Deerinwater came to the phone and said that he and his wife would drive to the city the next day. They would stay with friends and could visit David daily. They would bring food prepared by his mother. Roberta replied that she would be eager to see them.

*In the days that followed, David Deerinwater benefited greatly from the visits of family members and his nutritional status improved considerably. He also seemed to be responding well to his **psychotropic medication** (drugs prescribed by doctors to influence mental functioning, mood, or behavior). Although increasingly coherent, he remained isolated, interacting minimally with other patients. Roberta explained to the staff that David, like most Native Americans, did not engage readily in frivolous social conversation and would be unlikely to socialize unless he had a reason to do so. He also was probably quite frightened of the institution. Roberta had learned to adjust her own sense of time when speaking with Mr. Deerinwater and she had learned to respect periods of silence. She helped other staff to communicate more effectively with him, too.*

In the final staffing before discharge, the psychiatric resident described Mr. Deerinwater's response to medication as being very good. The psychologist's summary of the psychological testing he had completed supported the early diagnosis of schizophrenia. The staff was very interested in Roberta's assessment, which included a history of David Deerinwater within the context of his family and his ethnic community, and his sense of unity with nature. Roberta was not as convinced as the other team members that David Deerinwater's mental illness was as serious as the diagnostic label, schizophrenia, suggested. He was much more oriented to reality than was usual for schizophrenic patients. She explained the perspective of the Cherokee Nation health center that often behaviors that are appropriate in one culture (such as an Indian's seeing signs in birds or the sky) are considered to be very inappropriate, sometimes even to be indicators of mental illness, in another culture and that research reports suggested that the actual incidence of schizophrenia among Native Americans appeared to be very low (La Fromboise, 1988; Snowden & Cheung, 1990; Bates & Van Dam, 1984).[1]

Fourteen days after admission, David Deerinwater was released. His discharge diagnosis remained schizophrenia, undifferentiated. David Deerinwater had decided to return home to live with his mother but would be receiving follow-up care from the Cherokee Nation health center, which provided a full range of mental health services, including access to tribal medicine men and spiritual healers. He could also see the vocational rehabilitation counselor at the Cherokee Nation about future employment and career options. Roberta was satisfied that David would receive social work services and health care that respected his cultural heritage.

As she said farewell to David, Roberta thought about the Cherokee people and the Deerinwater family. She realized how much she had learned from this person, his family, and community and how much they had enriched her life.[2]

KNOWLEDGE, VALUES, AND SKILLS FOR MENTAL HEALTH WORK

Areas of Responsibility: Knowledge and Skill

Roberta Sholes is a good example of a competent generalist BSW social worker. Take, for instance, the interviewing skills she demonstrated. She spoke quietly, gently, and slowly to David Deerinwater, helping him to focus on her words. She reassured him yet confronted him with reality. Roberta's respect for the culture of the Cherokee people and the value of Cherokee family life was clearly present in her interviews with the Deerinwater family and the action she took to involve the Cherokee community in David Deerinwater's mental health care. Would this have been the approach used by David Deerinwater's psychiatrist, nurse, or other mental health professionals? Probably not, but it is uniquely consistent with social work intervention in mental health.

To prepare for a career in mental health, Roberta Sholes might have had a field placement in a mental health setting, although even if she did not, there is a good likelihood that any field placement would present opportunities to work with people who are experiencing mental or emotional problems. The courses Roberta completed for her social work major probably didn't have titles such as "therapy" or "counseling" but, as can be seen from Roberta's competence, the social work courses prepare students well for work in the mental health field. Roberta might also have taken elective courses such as abnormal psychology if she planned to seek employment in the mental health field.

BSW social workers are not expected to take responsibility for complex psychotherapy. That is the role of MSWs, and if Roberta decided that she would like to become a therapist, she would need to pursue a master's degree. The MSW curriculum, or course, has a generalist practice base, but most MSW programs provide an opportunity to complete a concentration in mental health or clinical social work. With additional experience, MSWs can be licensed to practice psychotherapy. In some parts of the United States where MSWs are in short supply; BSWs assist and sometimes even assume major responsibilities for therapeutic work, especially in state hospitals and with persons who have persistent and major mental disorders. BSWs, however, do not claim to be psychotherapists, and they are alert to situations that require assistance from or referral to someone with advanced expertise. Mental health crises or emergencies are not uncommon in generalist social work practice across all possible settings; therefore, BSWs do need to have confidence in their ability to work with people with a wide range of problems. BSWs in mental health settings such as hospitals often provide crisis intervention, work with the families of patients, and counsel persons individually and in groups. They serve as the hospital's link to the community, teaching its staff about the population while at the same time offering preventive mental health education within the community.

In many community-based programs, BSWs carry important responsibilities for people who are chronically mentally ill. Dorothy White, the social worker in the Cherokee Nation's Health and Social Services Department, was also a BSW who provided advocacy, counseling, and case management services to Cherokee families. After David Deerinwater's discharge from the hospital, Dorothy or another social worker in the department would serve as his **case manager.** A case manager coordinates and ensures that all the services needed by a client (medical, financial, legal, and so on) are, in fact, provided. The case management function requires that the social worker be skilled both in working within the community and in working individually with lonely, isolated, and sometimes resistant persons. The generalist preparation of BSWs—especially their courses in practice methods and field experience—prepares them with the knowledge and skills they need for the diverse and challenging practice responsibilities they can expect to have in the mental health field.

Psychotherapy is the realm of the MSW. In the past, a social worker who was qualified to engage in psychotherapy was called a psychiatric social worker. Today the term used most often is **clinical social worker.** The NASW expects social workers who engage in private practice of psychotherapy to hold the ACSW at a minimum. As Chapter 1 noted, the NASW also recognizes with QCSW (qualified clinical social worker) certification persons who have achieved certain standards, including 3,000 hours of clinical experience. The DCSW (diplomate in clinical social work) is reserved for advanced clinical social workers with five years of post-MSW clinical experience (NASW, Online, 2001). Many states also license clinical social workers.

All social workers in mental health settings, whether BSWs or MSWs, are responsible for collecting and assessing data that contribute to the mental health team's diagnosis and understanding of individual people in relation to mental health. These social workers are responsible, too, for creating intervention plans in collaboration with people, for implementing the intervention, for monitoring and evaluating the outcomes, and for terminating relationships with clients. Knowledge of the community and its resources is one of social work's unique contributions to the mental health team. The social worker also brings to the team an understanding of social policy and its impact on programs that exist and programs still needed to prevent and treat mental illness. An understanding and sensitivity to the culture or lifestyle of diverse groups is another contribution made by social workers in mental health settings. When Roberta Sholes provided information about the Cherokee Indian culture and cautioned members of the mental health team not to assume psychosis in David Deerinwater, she was making this kind of contribution. In sharing knowledge about cultural practices, social policy issues, or even community resources, social workers continually educate others.

Values and Integrity

Knowledge and skills alone, however, do not make a good social worker. A third dimension is essential: values. Social workers demonstrate integrity when their personal values and actions are compatible with those of the profession. Professional social work values compel attention to and respect for the uniqueness and intrinsic worth of each person. Social workers empower clients and encourage them to be as self-directing as possible. They are very careful to respect privacy and confidentiality. Their professional values compel social workers to go even further. They urge social workers to work to make social institutions more humane and more responsive to people's needs. In mental health settings, these values take on special meaning. Our society tends not to respect the mentally ill, especially those who are chronically ill. Thus, social workers often have to advocate on behalf of the mentally ill. Within their communities and especially within the health care institutions that employ them, social workers attempt to create an environment that deals humanely with persons who are mentally or emotionally ill.

In this chapter's case study Roberta Sholes demonstrated much sensitivity for David Deerinwater as a client. Her respect for his uniqueness and worth led her to learn more about Native American ethnicity. Even if she believed that returning to his home community was in David Deerinfield's best interests, she did not force this plan on him. Instead, she engaged him in making decisions about his own posthospital care. Because of Roberta's respect for confidentiality, she obtained written permission before sharing information with his family or other agencies.

Few professions stress values in the way that social work does. This is especially apparent when a social worker practices in a **secondary setting** (one in which social work is not the primary function), such as mental health. Schools and courts are other examples of secondary settings. Not only do social workers in secondary settings need conviction about their values, but they also need to acquire an understanding of the primary function of the setting that they are in. In field practicum courses and on the job, social workers learn about the organizational context in which they work.

Specific Knowledge Base for Mental Health

The settings in which social workers are employed almost always require an additional layer of knowledge and skills. Because social workers are flexible and tend to move from one area to another during their professional careers, this gives them a splendid opportunity to acquire a rich array of specialized knowledge. When they become field placement students or are employed with organizations that serve people with HIV/AIDS or in domestic abuse settings, social workers quickly begin to learn about those specific problem areas. In secondary settings, such as school social work and health care, skills must be developed in interdisciplinary teamwork relationships.

Teamwork Relationships   The ability to work as a part of an interdisciplinary team is an important skill in the mental health field. Teamwork skills are key among the credentials sought by employers. The traditional mental health team consists of a psychiatrist, a psychologist, a psychiatric nurse, and one or more social workers. Roles overlap considerably in mental health. All team members provide psychotherapy, often as co-therapists in family and group therapy. Each team member also performs a unique function (see Exhibit 1). This traditional team may be supplemented by speech, recreational, art, and occupational therapists. Teachers are an added component in children's mental health programs.

In addition to direct work with the consumers of mental health services, the roles for social workers in mental health have expanded considerably to include administration of mental health programs, teaching of psychiatric residents as well as nursing and social work students, community mental health education, proposal writing and lobbying for funding, advocacy, crisis intervention, discharge planning, and, of course, therapy for individuals, families, and groups. It is not surprising, then, that mental health teams often comprise several social workers but just one psychiatrist, one psychologist, and one or two nurses.

In our case study, the psychiatric facility's mental health team consisted of:

1. The chief psychiatrist, who served as team leader, conducted staffings, supervised residents, wrote prescriptions, and did some individual therapy.
2. Three psychiatric residents, who were assigned for a six-month period. (Because they were students, they carried a limited number of cases and were under the supervision of the chief psychiatrist.)
3. Two psychiatric nurses, who administered all nursing and bedside care of patients, participated as cotherapists in group therapy, and supervised student nurses.

The Traditional Mental Health Professional Team

EXHIBIT 1

- *Psychiatrists* prescribe medication. They hold the MD (doctor of medicine) degree and have additional training in psychiatry.
- *Psychologists* administer and interpret psychological tests. They generally hold the PhD degree in clinical psychology, although in some areas persons with a master's degree in psychology may serve on the professional team.
- *Psychiatric nurses* have training in nursing, which enables them to administer prescription medications, give injections, and assist in various other medical procedures. They generally hold a master's degree in nursing; again, however, in some regions of the country, nurses with a baccalaureate degree in nursing (BSN) serve on mental health teams.
- *Social workers* have specialized knowledge about a community's resources. They generally obtain the social history of a patient (a chronology of the individual's life events), which assists the team in arriving at a diagnosis and a treatment plan. Both BSWs and MSWs function as members of the mental health team; MSWs carry primary responsibility for psychotherapy

4. Two MSWs and one BSW, who provided individual, family, and group therapy; obtained social histories; and linked the hospital with the community.
5. One clinical psychologist, who administered and analyzed psychological tests and engaged in individual, family, and group therapy.

The mental health team in the case study was fairly typical of the teams in teaching hospitals. In hospitals that are not connected with a university medical school, the mental health team generally has no medical or nursing students and hence is much smaller. Considerable effort is required to keep a team in any setting functioning smoothly, for friction is inevitable when professional roles overlap. Team members learn quickly that they need to understand the perspectives of other professionals who make up the mental health team.

Classification and Treatment of Mental Disorders   Social workers in mental health settings clearly need an understanding of mental illness. They need to be able to use the terminology of the current psychiatric mental illness classification system. Social work students at the baccalaureate level and in master's programs are generally introduced to the classification system as part of their coursework. Becoming truly adept at its use usually occurs with employment in a mental health setting (or in substance abuse or any other settings that use the same system of classifying mental disorders). The system widely used in the United States was created by the American Psychiatric Association and is known among mental health professionals as the **Diagnostic and Statistical Manual of Mental Disorders (DSM).** The 2000 version of the manual, which is currently in use, is known as the *DSM-IV-TR*. It comprises five major sections called axes. The axes incorporate a numerical coding system that is used on hospital and insurance forms in place of lengthy descriptive terms. Hundreds of specific diagnostic categories are listed under the five *DSM-IV-TR* axes. Exhibit 2 provides a very abbreviated overview of the diagnostic system (American Psychiatric Association, 2000).

The current *DSM* explains that definitions of **mental disorder** are not precise. Instead, they reflect behavioral patterns that occur in individuals and that cause suffering, pain, or some level of disability. An understandable and culturally sanctioned behavioral response to an event (a grief response to death, for example) is not considered a mental disorder. Behaviors considered deviant by society (religious, political, or sexual behaviors), or conflicts between individuals, are also not mental disorders unless there are symptoms of dysfunction. The *DSM* states clearly that it isn't people who are diagnosed; their disorders are. So it is not correct to speak of a "schizophrenic," but it is appropriate to refer to a "person with schizophrenia" (American Psychiatric Association, 2000).

For many years, the two major forms of mental illness where known as psychoses and neuroses. Psychoses were understood to be the most serious form of mental illness. They were usually though to include "loss of contact with reality. Not knowing the current day, month, or year; hearing voices that aren't there; or believing oneself to be Napoleon or Christ" (Ray & Ksir, 1993, pp. 157–158), for example.

***Overview of* DSM-IV-TR *Classification System
Using a Fictitious Case***

EXHIBIT 2

Axis I   CLINICAL DISORDERS

Example: 296.23, Major Depressive Disorder, Single Episode, Severe, Without Psychotic Features

Axis II   PERSONALITY DISORDERS and MENTAL RETARDATION

Example: 301.6, Dependent Personality Disorder

Axis III   GENERAL MEDICAL CONDITIONS

Example: Overdose of Aspirin

[*Note:* The numerical code for general medical conditions comes from a source other than *DSM-IV-TR.*]

Axis IV   PSYCHOSOCIAL AND ENVIRONMENTAL PROBLEMS

Example: V61.1, Divorce

Axis V   GLOBAL ASSESSMENT OF FUNCTIONING

Example: GAF52, Some danger of hurting self or others

[*Note:* The GAF number comes from the patient's score on the Global Assessment of Functioning scale.]

Source: American Psychiatric Association. (2000). Examples of how to record results of a *DSM-IV-TR* multiaxial evaluation. In *Diagnostic and statistical manual of mental disorders: DSM-IV-TR* (4th ed., rev.). Washington, DC: American Psychiatric Association, p. 35.

Today the American Psychiatric Association believes that our understanding of **psychosis** is still evolving. The *DSM* published in 2000 suggests several slightly different ways of looking at psychosis. Its narrowest definition requires the presence of **hallucinations** or **delusions.** Delusions are disorders of thinking in which a person holds a strong but inaccurate belief about reality, often believing herself or himself to be persecuted. Hallucinations are also misperceptions of reality, often accompanied by responses to voices the person believes that she or he hears. In both cases the person's behavior may be very inappropriate. The broadest definition requires neither hallucinations nor delusions but the presence of symptoms such as disorganized speech or catatonic behaviors (immobility or peculiar movements of the limbs, for example).

The current *DSM-IV-TR* lists eight psychoses, some stemming from such clear physical causes as brain tumors or chronic alcohol use, and others that have no clearly known cause. As the case study at the beginning of the chapter noted, schizophrenia is one of the psychoses. There are many misconceptions about this mental disorder—most commonly, that it entails one personality that has split into two, or that multiple personalities have emerged out of a single personality. Although such symptoms can occur, they are not usual or necessary in order for a diagnosis of schizophrenia to be made. In fact, the characteristic symptoms of schizophrenia include:

- Delusions
- Hallucinations
- Incoherent and very disorganized speech
- Grossly disorganized or catatonic behavior (American Psychiatric Association, 2000, pp. 297–298).

Schizophrenia is a likely diagnosis if hallucinations or delusions have been present for the greater part of one month and with some level of symptoms apparent in the previous six months.

Neurosis is a term that is not used in the *DSM-IV-TR*. In the past it referred to a mental disorder that was less serious than a psychosis, such as a thinking or emotional disorder involving anxiety, phobias (irrational fears), or psychosomatic complaints. The *DSM-IV-TR* instead classifies a large number of anxiety-related states under the heading anxiety disorder. Panic attack and posttraumatic stress conditions are considered anxiety disorders.

Mood disorder, as the name implies, is a category that focuses on disturbances of mood. This is a relatively new diagnostic category, one that contains very serious as well as more minimal dysfunctions of mood. Depressive (low mood) and manic (abnormally high mood) states are represented, as well as bipolar states in which periods of both depression and mania occur. Psychosis, anxiety disorder, and mood disorder are three of the most commonly cited categories of mental disorders, but each contains multiple subdivisions, and numerous other categories also appear in *DSM-IV-TR*.

Social workers have developed a fair amount of skepticism about diagnostic labels such as those used in the *DSM-IV-TR*. To label someone as schizophrenic, for example, can be very damaging; a person so labeled is expected to perform (or not to perform) in a specific, predetermined manner. When this label is known to hospital or clinic staff, schools, correctional facilities, employers, or other organizations, other people are likely to assume or to anticipate the expected behaviors. One's political career or administrative promotion can be jeopardized if that person was ever labeled, correctly or incorrectly, with a psychiatric diagnosis. Diagnostic labels can follow a person for life. Although medical information is supposedly confidential, private, and protected by law, in reality it is remarkably available to a large number of persons that the client has never even seen. A child's school record, for example, is passed from one teacher to another, complete with psychological evaluations. Medical records are handled not only by doctors, nurses, and therapists of many kinds, but also by clerks, aides, medical records personnel, and insurance staff.

Persons with psychiatric labels may be stereotyped or subjected to bias by others, but they may also begin to define themselves by the label they have been given. Even if clients do not know their specific diagnosis, they do understand that they are considered to have a mental problem. This knowledge hardly creates positive self-regard, nor does it arouse eagerness to tackle even the routine problems and activities of daily living.

Social workers Herb Kutchins and Stuart Kirk have been studying the *Diagnostic and Statistical Manual* over many years and through several of its revisions (Anello, Kirk, & Kutchins, 1992; Kirk & Kutchins, 1992; Kutchins & Kirk, 1989). Their 1997 book, *Making Us Crazy: DSM—The Psychiatric Bible and the Creation of Mental Disorders,* attracted national attention with its critique of the *DSM-IV.* In this book Kutchins and Kirk severely criticize the ever-lengthening list of mental disorders that may be used to label human behavior. They report that this growing list serves the insurance industry but stigmatizes people whose problems are those of daily living, of coping with the stresses of life, not true medical situations. Moreover, the social context of the labeled behavior is not assessed. Another consideration, now that more diagnostic categories are available, is the therapist's awareness that insurance reimbursement is greater for some categories than for others.

This chapter's debate box reflects just a few of the arguments in support of and in opposition to social workers' use of the *Diagnostic and Statistical Manual of Mental Disorders.* Although the issue remains unresolved in the social work profession, social workers often do work in health care systems that use diagnostic labels extensively. This was true for the social worker in the case study at the beginning of this chapter. When Roberta Sholes first began her employment at Oklahoma State Mental Hospital, she was required to learn to use the *DSM-IV-TR* classification system. The hospital routinely used it for processing insurance reimbursement forms, and the staff used it to formulate diagnoses for medical records. Although Roberta found the use of this or any labeling system frustrating, she also found that the *DSM-IV-TR* did help her to learn more about the nature of mental illness and the way it was viewed by other members of the mental health team. Although she had not taken a course on *DSM-IV-TR,* her college course work had provided the basis on which, after graduation, she was able to acquire this and other knowledge specific to her practice setting. She learned to differentiate between the most serious mental disorders, the psychoses, and less serious forms of mental disorder, such as milder forms of depression, of which she had already seen a number of cases. She also learned that social workers, like all other members of the mental health team, work with people who experience the entire range of mental disorders. Social workers, however, have the unique responsibility to advocate for clients. (See the "Up for Debate" box.)

Learning about some of the psychotropic medications used in treating mental illness also became a reality of Roberta's job. She found that although psychiatrists are no longer the only members of the mental health team who have the sole authority to prescribe medication, at her institution they did retain primary responsibility for writing prescriptions. All of the other team members, including social workers, also needed to develop some familiarity with these medications, their uses, and their side effects so that they could be alert to possible complications. Almost all medications, Roberta found, do have some potential side effects, and some side effects are more extreme than others.

Some of the drugs that typically produce remarkably positive results in the treatment of psychosis can have negative side effects: loss of sense of balance, trouble walking, even severe emotional reactions. Sometimes the side effects are so serious that people have to be hospitalized in order for their medications to be changed or for additional drugs to be prescribed to suppress negative side effects. When unpleasant side effects occur, people are likely to discontinue taking their prescribed medication, and this may result in reoccurrence of behaviors symptomatic of the

Up for Debate
Proposition: Baccalaureate social workers should be required to take a course on DSM-IV-TR

Yes	No
1. A very wide range of health and human service agencies use *DSM-IV-TR* in their routine assessments.	1. Not all social workers work in settings that require or incorporate use of *DSM-IV-TR* diagnostic categories.
2. The *DSM-IV-TR* helps social workers to understand client behaviors.	2. Social workers should learn to understand the social contexts of human behavior.
3. It is necessary for social workers to be able to communicate effectively with team members whose language is strongly influenced by the diagnostic categories of *DSM-IV-TR*.	3. Social workers will be more effective in their interventions and less dependent on a medical model if they focus on client strengths.
4. Insurance companies will not reimburse for services provided if the social worker does not utilize recognized diagnostic categories.	4. Social workers should avoid using stigmatizing labels.

mental illness (Blair & Ramones, 1998). The newer medications that have come on the market in recent years have fewer side effects than drugs previously used to treat mental disorders. They have been of significant benefit to large numbers of people. With the newer drugs, though, some people feel so well that they discontinue taking their medications without the advice of the physician. They are then at high risk of relapse. Other people are unable to afford the extraordinarily high cost of some of the newer psychotropic drugs, since costs may be as much as $6,000 per month!

Tranquilizers can be dangerous, even life threatening, if taken with alcohol. They can also create lethargy and such overwhelming sleepiness that the person has considerable difficulty holding a job or studying. The opposite effect, hyperactivity, can occur with drugs prescribed for depression.

Social workers, however, are taking increasing responsibility for monitoring medication use by their clients. Monitoring includes education regarding use of medications for both the client and family members, who may not be well informed. Ongoing communication with the physician who has written the client's prescriptions is also a monitoring function (Landers, 1998).

Some of the psychotropic drugs currently used in the medical management of mental disorder are listed in Exhibit 3. A list such as this cannot remain up to date for long, since breakthroughs in pharmaceutical research may result in new medications being added and older drugs dropped in just a short time. Many

A Sample of Major Psychotropic Medications

EXHIBIT 3

Drug Type	Examples of Disorder Treated	Generic Name	Brand Name	Usual Daily Dosage
Antipsychotic	Schizophrenia, bipolar disorders, major depressions, organic mental disorders	Chlorpromazine	Thorazine	300–800 mg
		Chlozapine	Clozaril	400–600 mg
		Fluphenazine	Prolixin	1–20 mg
		Haloperidol	Haldol	6–20 mg
		Olanzapine	Zyprexa	10–20 mg
		Risperidone	Risperdal	4–6 mg
		Thioridazine	Mellaril	200–700 mg
Antidepressant	Major depressions, dysthymia (persistent minor depression), adjustment disorders	Phenylzine	Nardil	10–30 mg
		Tranlaypromine	Parnate	10–30 mg
		Amitriptyline	Elavil, Endip	100–200 mg
		Amoxapine	Asendine	200–300 mg
		Imipramine	Tofranil	100–200 mg
		Fluoxetine	Prozac	20–40 mg
		Paroxetine	Paxil	20–50 mg
		Sertraline	Zoloft	50–200 mg
Mood Stabilizer	Bipolar disorder	Lithium	Eskalith	900–2100 mg
			Lithobid	900–2100 mg
		Valproic Acid	Depakene	1200–1500 mg
			Depakote	1200–1500 mg
		Carbamazepine	Tegretol	400–1600 mg
Antianxiety	Anxiety disorders (including panic disorders, phobias, obsessive-compulsive disorder, posttraumatic stress disorder)	Diazepan	Valium	2–60 mg
		Alprazolam	Xanax	0.5–6 mg
		Chlordiazepoxide	Librium	15–100 mg
		Triazolam	Halcion	0.125–0.25 mg
		Buspirone	Buspar	5–15 mg
		Oxazepam	Serax	30–120 mg
Psychostimulant	Attention deficit hyperactivity disorder	Amphetamine	Adderall	20–40 mg
		Dextroamphetamine	Dexedrine	20–40 mg
		Methamphetamine	Desoxyn	20–40 mg
		Methylphenidate	Ritalin	20–40 mg

Source: K. J. Bentley & J. F. Walsh. (2001). *The social worker and psychotropic medication: Toward effective collaboration with mental health clients, families, and providers* (2nd ed.). Belmont, CA: Brooks/Cole, 75–139.

people today, however, are very reluctant to take prescribed medication; recently there has been renewed interest in use of vitamins and herbs as an alternative in treating mental disorders.

Social workers also have ethical questions related to use of psychotropic medications, especially when they are prescribed for children. Concerns relate to the appropriateness of drugs (use of amphetamines for children, for example), possibility for negative side effects, and the potential development of psychological dependence on drugs. There is concern that children could learn to cope with normal stresses by taking medication rather than learning healthy adaptive behaviors. When children are in foster and institutional care and in the custody of the state, there are times when social workers must make decisions on the child's behalf about medical care. These are not easy decisions. Social workers are often in the unique position of being able to make clear to the physician the preferences and circumstances of the client and to help the client understand the medical situation and available options. The social worker is the professional who "spends more time with the client and family than others on the treatment team; he or she may be best informed about their perspectives regarding medication and other interventions" (Bentley & Walsh, 2001, p. 131).

Today treatment of mental disorders often consists of a combination of medication, monitoring, various forms of psychotherapy, and patient education. The treatment programs that deliver these services have come to be known as **behavioral health care.** According to the Joint Commission on Accreditation of Healthcare Organizations, behavioral health care services cover a very broad area, including mental health, mental retardation, developmental disabilities, and cognitive rehabilitation services. These may be provided during hospitalization or on an outpatient basis (Joint Commission, 1998). Hospitalization, when needed, tends to be much briefer than in the past, in part due to psychotropic medications but also to curtailed length of stay dictated by insurance or managed care corporations. Now many patients (like David Deerinwater) remain hospitalized only a matter of days, followed by outpatient treatment to continue psychotherapy and to monitor the medication. Monitoring is necessary because sometimes people are still too heavily medicated when they leave the hospital. Then either they cannot function properly or they become discouraged and discontinue medication.

Hospitalization and, for that matter, even medication are not necessary for all persons who are experiencing mental health problems. Social workers are among the professionals who provide counseling and psychotherapy for individuals, families, and groups with the objective of preventing and treating mental and emotional disorders.

GENERALIST PRACTICE WITH GROUPS AND COMMUNITIES

The David Deerinwater case study is an example of generalist social work intervention occurring simultaneously at several different systems levels: the individual client, the family, the mental health team, and the community. The primary focus of Roberta Sholes's social work service, however, was the individual client, David Deerinwater. We will now examine social work in other types of mental health settings and in practice situations in which the target for intervention is not an individual but a group or a community.

The next example comes from Gitterman and Shulman's book, *Mutual Aid Groups* (Vastola, Nierenberg, & Graham, 1994). The children in this group were referred to the mental health clinic for emotional problems that they experienced after the death of a parent or someone of significance to them. Each of the five children in the group was first seen in an individual pregroup session in which the group was described; all the children expressed a desire to participate.

In the first group session, the social worker asked the children to introduce themselves. She asked if anyone knew why the group was meeting; the children readily responded that it was a group for children whose parents had died. She explained in more detail how the group was planned to help kids to help each other through this difficult time. She asked the group, "What do you think about being here?" Several children said that the group was a good idea. Then, spontaneously, they began to tell their own stories, identifying who had died and how it had happened. In the next weeks the children continued to work out their grief. There were several episodes of angry outbursts. In one a child cried out, "I don't want anyone talking about my grandfather. . . . I just don't want anybody saying that he died!" Other group members agreed: "Nobody really wants to talk about a person's dying, it's too hard" (Vastola, Nierenberg, & Graham, 1994, p. 87).

But they did talk. They also shared personal experiences, such as nightmares, that they could not discuss with anyone else. The social worker encouraged group members to bring in pictures or personal mementos. In one touching episode a boy removed from his jeans pocket a tattered, frayed picture of a beautiful young woman—his mother when she was a teenager. The social worker was able to tell this child how he could have the picture laminated so that he could retain this treasured object. The children also had curiosity and many unanswered questions

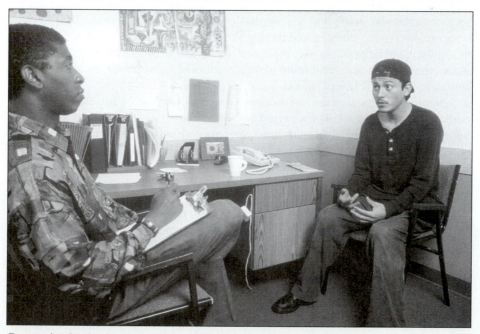

Contracting begins in a pregroup session with a potential group member.

about funeral homes, autopsies, and the decomposition of human bodies. Their questions were respected, and factual information was provided. They needed to be reassured that, if their present caretaker died (one child had lost both parents and was living with an aunt), there would be someone who would care for them.

Although the children found it difficult to terminate the group at the end of 12 weeks, the social worker encouraged the children to verbalize their painful feelings about ending the group. She also helped them to review what they had gained from the group and to think about how they might be able to apply their newly acquired skills in the future. These children had named their group "The Lost and Found Group."

Community Practice

In addition to practice with individuals and groups, social workers seek to assist communities, at-risk populations, or organizations to promote mental health or to design programs for people with mental health problems. Examples of community practice often appear in *NASW News,* the monthly publication of the National Association of Social Workers.

Sally Erickson, a Hawaiian social worker, was featured in one article. Erickson helped to write a grant proposal that resulted in funding from the U.S. Department of Housing and Urban Development (HUD) for a program that serves persons with severe mental illness. She subsequently became the director of the new program, Pu'uhonua Safe Haven, which offers food, shelter, and mental health services to severely and chronically ill persons, some of whom have lived on Honolulu's streets for 15 or more years (Safe havens, 1997).

"Practitioner Leads Life in Spotlight" was the *NASW News* headline that introduced Doris Wild Helmering's very public efforts to assist families. She shifted from a career focusing on agency-based family and group therapy to author for the *St. Louis Post-Dispatch* and has written over 900 weekly columns dealing with topics related to relationship and family issues. The newspaper column led to radio talk show guest appearances (over 250 of them) and to appearances on *Oprah* and other television shows. Helmering has also authored eight books, including one on cognitive therapy (O'Neill, 1999).

Social workers also use political processes as they work for change in communities and the nation. The growing consumer movement in mental health, composed primarily of persons who have experienced poor treatment by the mental health system, is being assisted by social workers. In some communities, social workers join attorneys in advocacy for patients whose legal rights have been violated by illegal detainment in mental hospitals, by improper use of restraints and medication, or by inappropriate discharge planning.

The National Association of Social Workers, representing all social workers in the United States, seeks to influence our government's policies in ways that will benefit vulnerable people, including people at risk of mental health problems. NASW staff member Nancy Bateman was a member of the team that developed a national strategy to prevent suicide. The report, issued by the Office of the U.S. Surgeon General, calls for increased attention to suicide screening in primary health care and the development of community-based suicide prevention as well as comprehensive support programs that strengthen support networks of at-risk persons (National suicide prevention strategy issued, 2001). The national suicide prevention report reflects NASW's concern about inadequate availability of mental health sevices. Many of the other concerns addressed in the NASW Policy Statement on Mental Health also appear in the surgeon general's national suicide prevention policy. An overview of the NASW statement appears in Exhibit 4.

NASW Policy Statement on Mental Health

EXHIBIT 4

To further improvements that have been made in the prevention, diagnosis, assessment, and treatment of mental illness, it is the position of NASW that:

- All people residing in the United States be entitled to receive mental health care, both for severe and persistent mental illness and for acute mental health problems that impair the individual's functioning.
- Mental health treatment be provided in parity with treatment for other types of illnesses in all health care plans.
- A full range of the most efficacious pharmacological and psychosocial services be available to all mental health consumers to ensure that consumers achieve optimal functioning in all areas of their lives. Within this range of services, consumers should be given choices among service options that meet their needs and individual preferences.
- Social workers, in collaboration with the consumer, should involve family members and significant others in assessment and treatment planning.
- Incarceration of people with mental illness should not be used as an alternative to appropriate psychiatric treatment, but when it cannot be avoided, individuals should have access to mental health services to include assessment and screening, medication, counseling, and discharge planning and referral.
- A more integrated system of care be developed to facilitate access to services. Integration is of particular concern to consumers with severe mental illness and/or dual diagnoses who must negotiate more than one system to obtain care.
- Social insurance (such as SSDI) and public assistance payments be increased to a level that provides a decent standard of living to those with mental disorders. The efforts of people with mental illness to work should be encouraged and should not result in negative sanctions from social insurance, public assistance, or other programs.
- Social workers consider consumers' wishes and civil rights and family wishes when consumers pose a danger to themselves or others. In light of the trend toward "involuntary outpatient commitment" (including forcing administration of medication) careful evaluation must be done to assure protection of consumers' right to self-determination and to assure the people's right to a safe community.
- Treatment in the most therapeutic and least restrictive environment, including use of consumer's native language, should guide the work of social workers. Social workers should take the lead in advocating for a viable array of community-based mental health services, based on the need for these services, as opposed to cost containment.
- Social workers support the self-help, consumer empowerment, and advocacy efforts of people with mental illness and their family members.

Source: R. W. Mayden & J. Nieves. (2000). Mental health. Policy Statement approved by the NASW Delegate Assembly, August 1999. *Social work speaks: National Association of Social Workers policy statements 2000–2003.* Washington, DC: NASW Press, 226–227.

Clearly, social work practice in mental health is not limited to counseling and psychotherapy. Instead, mental health social workers influence the lives of many persons as they create change in the broader community. Their social change efforts combined with the efforts of social workers who focus on intervention with groups, families, and individuals demonstrate how social work practice contributes to the prevention and treatment of mental illness.

SOCIAL WORKERS RESPOND TO DISASTER: DEALING WITH PSYCHOLOGICAL TRAUMA

According to Ken Lee, social workers may be the best equipped of all mental health professionals to respond to disasters. Lee, a social worker from Hawaii and member of the American Red Cross Air Incident Response Team, is also a mental health trainer for the Red Cross. He was one of countless mental health professionals who assisted at the "Ground Zero" site following the terrorist attack on the World Trade Center in New York in 2001.

In an *NASW News* story (Social work in the public eye, 2002), following September 11, 2001, Lee identified three intervention strategies used by social workers at the time of a disaster. The first, crisis intervention, has already been discussed in this chapter. In community disasters, providing basic needs such as food and water to victims, family members, or rescue workers is the critical first step in intervention. This creates a bridge that enables the social worker to touch and care for raw emotional needs. Helping people to tell their story, offering affirmation, support, and encouragement, is the core of crisis intervention. Defusing, a related strategy enabling people to ventilate—to talk, cry, scream, express rage—takes "the fuse out of a potentially explosive situation" (p. 15), according to Lee. Defusing often frees people to engage with the social worker or family members in the immediate problem solving that must be done in the wake of the disaster. Debriefing, the third strategy, is used with and on behalf of the social workers and other professional disaster relief staff or volunteers. Debriefing usually takes place in a formal group setting. People share their experiences and their reactions to them. They are supportive of each other. Information related to the cause and extent of the disaster is provided along with updates about additional assistance that will be available in the next days.

Acute Traumatic Stress

During and immediately following disasters, people may be subjected to overwhelming physical and psychological distress. Normal reactions cover a wide spectrum of behaviors. Emotionally, people may experience shock, feeling as though they are in a fog, an unreal world. They may feel numbness and have no physical pain even in the presence of profound injuries. Or they may react with terror, panic, anger and hostility, grief, or a marked sense of isolation. They may be confused and disoriented, have difficulty making decisions, experience "racing" thoughts, or replay the experience over and over again in their minds. Lee, in the fatigue, and black stares" (p. 15). Withdrawal and difficulty communicating is a common behavioral response to traumatic exposure. So is pacing, aimless walking, or an exaggerated startle response. Physical symptoms may include rapid heartbeat, dizziness, stomach upset, headache, and difficulty breathing. Physical symptoms need prompt medical evaluation, of course (Lerner & Shelton, "How do people respond," 2001). The 10 stages of acute traumatic stress management are shown in Exhibit 5.

Posttraumatic Stress Disorder (PTSD)

Social workers and other mental health professionals know that immediate mental health intervention at the time of the disaster or traumatic experience may prevent or minimize the development of an enduring stress disorder. That is why the kind of crisis intervention provided by persons trained in disaster work, like Hawaiian social worker Ken Lee, is so critical in the first hours following a disaster. When the symptoms listed above last beyond a month, however, or depression, alcohol abuse, or intense anxiety emerge and persist, the person should be evaluated for possible posttraumatic stress disorder. According to the National Institute of Mental Health, "most people with PTSD try to avoid any reminders or thoughts of the order" that they experienced (NIMH, 2001, p. 1). Unless it is treated, PTSD may impair children as well as adults, making it nearly impossible for them to study, work, sustain parenting responsibilities, or even maintain self-care.

People recover from trauma in their own time and using their own strengths and with the support of their family, friends, and community. Life may never be the same again, especially if there has been a death or permanent disability. Many people, however, do survive disasters, and there are even people who actually grow and thrive as a result of their experience. In the weeks that follow the traumatic experience, there is first a period of disorganization with depression and anger, and then a period of reorganization when new patterns for functioning evolve and new relationships are built (Lerner & Shelton, 2001).

Posttraumatic stress disorder, if it occurs, can be treated through individual or family counseling, or with group therapy. Some therapeutic models focus on helping the person cognitively, by increasing their intellectual comprehension of the experience and their reaction to it. Behavioral methods seek to change ineffective responses to behaviors that strengthen the person's ability to cope. Medication is sometimes used in conjunction with counseling (NIMH, 2001). Social workers often use a holistic approach that identifies strengths in the person and connects people with others who can help: family members, friends, and coworkers. Spiritual beliefs are another source of support that is valued. Referrals are made to community resources if appropriate.

Mental health treatment for posttraumatic stress disorder or for any other mental health problem is much like treatment for a physical ailment. It can be taken care of very quickly in some cases, or it may require ongoing care and monitoring. Financing mental health care is the next topic we will explore.

EXHIBIT 5

Trauma Response®

Infosheet™

PRODUCED AS A PUBLIC SERVICE OF
THE AMERICAN ACADEMY OF EXPERTS IN TRAUMATIC STRESS, INC.
368 VETERANS MEMORIAL HIGHWAY, COMMACK, NEW YORK 11725
TEL. (631) 543-2217 • FAX (631) 543-6977
WWW.ATSM.ORG • WWW.TRAUMATIC-STRESS.ORG • WWW.AAETS.ORG

How Do People Respond *During* Traumatic Exposure?

Reprinted from *Acute Traumatic Stress Management*™
by Mark D. Lerner, Ph.D. and Raymond D. Shelton, Ph.D.
© 2001 by The American Academy of Experts in Traumatic Stress, Inc.

The following emotional, cognitive, behavioral and physiological reactions are often experienced by people *during* a traumatic event. It is important to recognize that these reactions do not necessarily represent an unhealthy or maladaptive response. Rather, they may be viewed as *normal* responses to an *abnormal* event. When these reactions are experienced in the future (i.e., weeks, months or even years after the event), are joined by other symptoms (e.g., recurrent distressing dreams, "flashbacks," avoidance behaviors, etc.), and interfere with social, occupational or other important areas of functioning, a psychiatric disorder may be in evidence. These individuals should pursue help with a mental health professional.

Emotional Responses during a traumatic event may include *shock*, in which the individual may present a highly anxious, active response or perhaps a seemingly stunned, emotionally-numb response. He may describe feeling as though he is "in a fog." He may exhibit *denial*, in which there is an inability to acknowledge the impact of the situation or perhaps, that the situation has occurred. He may evidence *dissociation*, in which he may seem dazed and apathetic, and he may express feelings of unreality. Other frequently observed acute emotional responses may include panic, fear, intense feelings of aloneness, hopelessness, helplessness, emptiness, uncertainty, horror, terror, anger, hostility, irritability, depression, grief and feelings of guilt.

Cognitive Responses to traumatic exposure are often reflected in impaired concentration, confusion, disorientation, difficulty in making a decision, a short attention span, suggestibility, vulnerability, forgetfulness, self-blame, blaming others, lowered self-efficacy, thoughts of losing control, hypervigilance, and perseverative thoughts of the traumatic event. For example, upon extrication of a survivor from an automobile accident, he may cognitively still "be in" the automobile "playing the tape" of the accident over and over in his mind.

Behavioral Responses in the face of a traumatic event may include withdrawal, "spacing-out," non-communication, changes in speech patterns, regressive behaviors, erratic movements, impulsivity, a reluctance to abandon property, seemingly aimless walking, pacing, an inability to sit still, an exaggerated startle response and antisocial behaviors.

Physiological Responses may include rapid heart beat, elevated blood pressure, difficulty breathing*, shock symptoms*, chest pains*, cardiac palpitations*, muscle tension and pains, fatigue, fainting, flushed face, pale appearance, chills, cold clammy skin, increased sweating, thirst, dizziness, vertigo, hyperventilation, headaches, grinding of teeth, twitches and gastrointestinal upset.

**Require immediate medical evaluation*

Source: M. D. Lerner & R. D. Shelton (2001). *Acute traumatic stress management.* The American Academy of Experts in Traumatic Stress, Inc. Reprinted at http://www.aaets.org and retrieved September 29, 2001.

SERVING MENTALLY ILL PERSONS: FROM COST CONTAINMENT TO CASE MANAGEMENT

Mental health care—in fact, all of health care—is changing rapidly in the United States, with social workers and their clients squarely in the middle of this revolution. Cost containment efforts, called **managed care,** that attempt to avoid expensive services such as hospitalization are fueling this revolution. Essentially managed care refers to a variety of administrative structures and processes used to oversee the delivery of health care with the intent of providing adequate and necessary services. However, according to a U.S. government report: "The primary motive is to reduce expenditures by withholding services that are deemed unnecessary, and by substituting less expensive alternatives for more expensive treatments, such as inpatient care" (Center for Mental Health Services, 1996, p. 3). The impact of managed care on mental health services has been dramatic on the range of services that comprise the field of mental health.

Hospitalization is the most expensive, most restrictive, and often the least desired service from the perspective of the client. But when mental illness results in such severe functional impairment that the individual is in considerable distress, is unable to care for herself or himself, or is a threat to the safety of others, hospitalization may become necessary. David Deerinwater, the man in this chapter's case study, is an example of a person whose life may have been saved by hospitalization.

A remarkable shift in the use of hospitalization has occurred in mental health care. Before 1955 the number of patients in mental hospitals grew steadily. The large-scale implementation of psychotropic medication beginning in 1955 led to the hospital discharge of millions of chronically mentally ill persons in the 1960s, a policy change that acquired its own title, **deinstitutionalization.** Over the next decade as the effectiveness of psychotropic medication grew, the length of inpatient stay declined and the shift to outpatient services dramatically expanded.

The plan to provide deinstitutionalized persons with well-integrated, publicly funded community mental health services did not materialize. While some persons received needed care, many others did not. The numbers of homeless, chronically mentally ill persons increased dramatically, calling public attention to the inadequacies of the community mental health centers in meeting the needs of this population. In the 1970s, the National Institute of Mental Health (NIMH) sponsored programs to test new forms of service delivery, many of which incorporated case management. Case management had previously been mandated to ensure coordinated services to persons with developmental disabilities (the Developmental Disabilities Act of 1970) and for children with special needs (Education for All Handicapped Children Act of 1975). Although case management arose out of a desire to design alternatives to costly inpatient care, the emphasis initially was on advocacy, access to needed care, and coordination of services. By the 1980s there was a shift to use of case management for cost containment purposes. In 1987, Fisher defined case management as "a systematic approach to identifying high-cost patients, assessing potential opportunities to coordinate their care, developing treatment plans that improve quality and control costs, and managing patients' total care to ensure optimum outcomes" (cited in Vourlekis & Greene, 1992, p. 5).

In the 1980s private insurance corporations began to cover mental health services, though not at the same level as other health care. Private general hospitals expanded their inpatient and outpatient facilities. Gradually states began to turn over their mental health programs to private enterprise to administer. A system that had once been largely a governmental operation was gradually transformed to a nonprofit and then, increasingly, to a for-profit economy. Managed care's momentum and influence grew rapidly in the 1990s. Harvard researchers studying the impact of managed care and privatization in the state of Massachusetts found that the length of hospitalization had decreased most dramatically for children and adolescents. At the same time, emergency room visits increased and rapid readmissions to hospitals were occurring (Wieman & Dorwart, 1998). Of special concern was the potentially serious impact on persons with serious and persistent mental disorders.

By the 1990s, most Americans who had health care insurance found that their health care services were being monitored by a managed care organization. To counteract rising medical costs, managed care corporations implemented what they called case management. This form of case management utilized trained staff, mostly nurses but also some social workers, as gatekeepers who were responsible for limiting access to hospitalization and other costly health care services. Behavioral health care (mental health and substance abuse services) was closely monitored by most systems. Even referral for outpatient assessment and treatment services required prior approval by the primary care physician. Over time, managed care corporations began to see that mental health care had special characteristics that differed from other forms of health care. Diagnoses were less precise; treatment might require a larger array of professional disciplines and might require such nonmedical procedures as building social support networks for clients.

Some managed care organizations now differentiate those strictly gatekeeping functions related to behavioral health from case management. **Utilization review** is the term used to refer to decisions that relate strictly to access to medical care: no further knowledge of the social and psychological client issues is needed. Case managers (nurses, psychologists, social workers, and others) are used to provide much more intensive involvement with the client. This might include helping people to access the best level of care and to make efficient use of mental health services, monitoring to ensure ongoing involvement in care to prevent relapse, and ensuring that care obtained continues to be of high quality. A physician and respected writer of managed care texts explains:

> Comprehensive case management goes beyond determination of medical necessity and seeks to promote enhancement of the quality, efficacy, and continuity of care. As such, it is a more demanding discipline than simple UR [utilization review]. It is practiced optimally by qualified front-line case management staff with a minimum of 5 to 10 years of relevant clinical experience who are thoroughly trained in case management techniques, backed up by readily available doctoral level advisors with relevant clinical experience. (Kongstvedt, 1997, p. 260).

This description of case management is remarkably similar to the kind of case management that social workers have been doing for decades. Unfortunately, however, not all managed care organizations have such an enlightened approach. Many continue to function primarily in a utilization review mode, but they continue to call it case management. This is very confusing to the public.

So, what would social work case management in mental health look like? To begin with, the same multiple phased change process is used that was described in Chapter 2 of this book. The process begins when the social worker reaches out and seeks to engage the client, establishing a sound working relationship. At the same time, information is gathered about the nature of the mental health problem, other issues in the client's life, and the strengths that the client brings to the situation. Then, with the collaboration of the client, a plan is developed and the case management intervention is implemented. Monitoring is done regularly by the social worker and client to ensure that the client's needs are being met. The case management relationship may be terminated because the client no longer needs this service, because the social worker leaves the agency and a new case manager is assigned, or because the client chooses to end the service.

Case management generally, although not always, involves long-term work with people who have multiple and complex problems. In mental health work, these may be persons with severe and persistent mental illness. Some clients may be resistant. Some may have been or currently are homeless. Case managers seek to connect clients with needed services. At times strong advocacy is needed to convince an organization or professional person to provide needed care. Finding a dentist who will see a 45-year-old man who has not had dental care in 25 years may not be easy. Helping the client to agree to accept the needed service and to keep follow-up appointments may be no easier, but accomplishing these challenges can be very rewarding.

Exhibit 6 provides an example of case management involving a 36-year-old Asian woman. The social worker writers of this case study point out that case management is a more comfortable fit with many Asian people than the traditional clinical service model of American outpatient mental health care. Asian people tend to view health and well-being holistically, with mental, physical, emotional, and spiritual elements inseparable. Family relationships are highly valued, and a person's self-concept is intrinsically related to her or his involvement with family. When refugees have endured war, separation from family, and political persecution before coming to the United States, they may transfer their sense of family obligation to others, especially people of their same culture but may be very guarded and reluctant to trust professional people or service providers. They may appreciate home visits, however, and may gradually accept help from a social worker who sustains contacts and demonstrates concretely his or her willingness to help (Eng & Balancio, 1997).

Social workers at many different educational levels are involved in case management. Doctoral-level social workers may provide consultation and expert backup for case managers. MSW social workers may supervise case management programs or may provide clinical case management themselves. BSW social workers provide extensive case management services. You may recall that Chapter 1 described the NASW certifications available to BSW and MSW social work case managers, the C-ASWCM (for MSWS) and the C-SWCM (for BSWs). Other professionals—such as nurses, psychologists, and professional counselors—also provide case management services. Some organizations use persons with no academic credentials beyond a high school degree to assist professional staff or to provide case management with special populations.

A Case Management Case Study: Sue Xiong

EXHIBIT 6

Sue Xiong (not the client's real last name), a 36-year-old single Cambodian woman, was referred to an outpatient mental health clinic following her third hospitalization within a year. She was unemployed, had no family, and had come to the United States three years previously. She was diagnosed with a bipolar disorder and had never kept the previous outpatient appointments given her on discharge from the hospital. She had also not taken any of the medications previously prescribed. She was said to be in denial about her psychiatric diagnosis but to have complaints about physical disorders.

The social work case manager who was assigned visited Sue Xiong at the hospital before discharge in order to begin the engagement, relationship-building process and to obtain information about her diagnosis and medical recommendations. It quickly became apparent to the social worker that the client believed her three hospitalizations resulted from problems associated with her menstrual cycle. She refused to accept appointments at the outpatient mental health clinic but did agree to regular home visits after the social worker volunteered to take her to a medical clinic to have her concerns about her menstrual irregularities assessed. She was also very relieved when the social worker agreed to help her apply for temporary financial assistance.

In the next two months the social worker met with Sue Xiong regularly and also accompanied her to the women's health clinic and the financial aid office. She often spoke to Sue about mental health and helped her to understand more about how mental health services are provided in this country. The client gradually became more comfortable and open to considering use of medication to treat the stressful mood-related symptoms she now acknowledged.

After two months Sue Xiong decided to come to the mental health clinic to meet with a psychiatrist. She accepted the medication that was prescribed and, with the social worker's encouragement and support, took the medication regularly. Two years after their first visit, Sue Xiong was employed, having also accepted assistance from the vocational rehabilitation service that the social worker connected her with.

Source: A. Eng & E. F. Balancio. (1997). Ch. 25, Clinical case management with Asian Americans. In E. Lee (Ed.), *Working with Asian Americans: A guide for clinicians* (pp. 400–407). New York: The Guilford Press, pp. 403–404.

PRACTICE WITH DIVERSE POPULATIONS

The Sue Xiong case study in Exhibit 6 illustrates the importance of understanding the cultural dimensions of practice. Take another look at this case study. Why was the social worker successful in helping Sue when previous efforts to help her accept the mental health care she needed were not successful? This social worker's understanding and appreciation for Sue Xiong's cultural heritage, values, and her culturally linked views of health care were intrinsically a part of the way the social worker chose to engage and work with the client.

Unfortunately, social workers and other mental health professionals do not have a good history of sensitivity to ethnic differences in the people they serve. Today, however, social work education is seeking to prepare students to work with an increasingly wide range of populations in ways that will empower individuals and their communities and will safeguard the integrity of family life, as it is defined by diverse populations. This concept, referred to as cultural competence, was introduced in Chapter 4 of this text, but it is a theme that is repeated throughout the book.

Cultural competence involves knowledge of the history and patterns of oppression experienced by cultural and ethnic groups, the traditions, and the values of those groups. It requires appreciation for differences in cultures. Doman Lum, a Hawaiian social work educator, explains cultural competence as "development of academic and professional expertise and skills in the area of working with culturally diverse populations" (1999, p. 3). He underscores the need for social workers to look carefully at their own "ethnic identity, cultural background, and contact with ethnic others" (p. 3). Because many of us as social workers come from backgrounds with mixes of culture, race, socioeconomic status, sprituality, and other forms of diversity, looking at our own ethnic identity is not easily done. Yet our appearance, the way we talk, and the way we present ourselves immediately convey messages more powerful than we know to clients of contrasting cultures and backgrounds. If we are to begin to develop skill in utilizing culturally appropriate interventions, we do need to build self-awareness and appreciate our own uniqueness as well as that of each individual client. Social work researchers such as John Red Horse provide guidelines that aid our understanding of the intensity and the differences in our own and our clients' identification with cultural roots.

John Red Horse classified Native American families along a spectrum from traditional to "panrenaissance." Family members in a *traditional* family, for example, use their native language in the home and community, practice the native religion, and sustain tribal beliefs regarding disease. These families rely on traditional rituals and ceremonies to rid them of mental and physical illness and to bring their mind and body back into harmony with the spiritual world and the universe. One step from traditional families is *neotraditional* families in which some members use the English language and have adopted new rituals and spiritual healers; most family members, however, retain traditional beliefs. The *transitional* family uses English in the community but speaks the native language at home. Traditional beliefs are retained, but family members often travel a considerable distance back to the homeland to participate in religious and ceremonial rituals; these family members gradually begin to use contemporary American health care. *Bicultural* families speak English and retain traditional beliefs in the Great Spirit but begin to adopt some non-Indian spiritual beliefs.

American health care systems are used, but family members prefer Native American health care services that are parallel to those in the larger community. *Acculturated* families have lost their native language, religion, and often even their extended kinskip system; they rely on American contemporary health care systems. Finally, *panrenaissance* families seek to renew their native language fluency and to revitalize some aspects of the traditional religion. Some members of these families are very critical of American health care systems and actively pursue the expansion of all-Indian parallel health care services that respect traditional beliefs and practices (1988).

Incorporating all of these understandings into interviews—along with warmth, empathy, and respect—takes time to learn but will become a part of every student's professional preparation for a career in social work. Classroom role plays of interviews plus actual experience in fieldwork are just the beginning of cultural competence, which is acquired over a professional lifetime. Exhibit 7 provides further information about some of the desirable characteristics of culturally competent social work interviewers.

Some Desirable Characteristics of Culturally Sensitive Interviewers

EXHIBIT 7

1. The culturally sensitive interviewer exerts maximum effort in the early part of the interview when the interviewee's mistrust and suspicion are highest, when the interviewer is apt to be perceived as a stereotype rather than an individual, and in terms of the interviewer's status as a representative of the mainstream culture rather than as a person.

2. Culturally sensitive interviewers are aware of the cultural factors in the interviewee's background that they need to recognize and accept as potential determinants of the interviewee's decision to come for help, the presentation and nature of the problem the client brings, and the choice of intervention.

3. The culturally sensitive interviewer is ready to acknowledge and undefensively and unapologetically raise for discussion cross-cultural factors affecting the interview.

4. Culturally sensitive interviewers are ready to acknowledge the limitations of their knowledge of an interviewee's cultural background and are ready to undefensively solicit help from the interviewee in learning what they need to know.

5. Culturally sensitive interviewers are aware of indigenous cultures' strengths, culturally based community resources that might be a source of help, and that some kinds of help may be culturally inappropriate.

6. Culturally sensitive interviewers are aware of the problem of disenfranchisement, discrimination, and stigmatization frequently associated with minority group status.

7. Although sensitive to cultural factors that might be related to clients' problems, the culturally sensitive interviewer is aware that such factors may be peripheral to the situation of a particular client, that personality factors may be of more significance than racial or ethnic cultural factors, and that culture does not adequately define the interviewee, who is unique.

Source: A. Kadushin & G. Kadushin. (1997). Box 12.2 Desirable characteristics of the culturally sensitive interviewer. *The social work interview: A guide for human service professionals* (4th ed.). New York: Columbia University Press, pp. 347–348.

In the David Deerinwater case at the beginning of this chapter, Roberta Sholes demonstrated sensitivity throughout her work with the client, his family, and the Cherokee community. The result was that Mr. Deerinwater was reunited with his family, and he gained access to a whole set of support networks that would perhaps otherwise not have been available to him. Roberta's newly gained knowledge of Cherokee beliefs, history, traditions, even food preferences helped other members of the hospital's mental health team to understand this client and others like him. Perhaps it also helped to humanize the institution on behalf of future Native American clients.

NATIVE AMERICAN HISTORY: THE CHEROKEE EXPERIENCE

Roberta Sholes's research led her to the discovery that one of the best recent historians for the Cherokee people was Wilma Mankiller, whose baccalaureate degree was in social work. Mankiller was also the first woman to hold the position of principal chief of the Cherokee Nation. According to Mankiller, Cherokee people had long been living in the Great Smoky Mountain region when European settlers arrived on the coast of the United States. The Cherokees developed remarkably advanced communities, attaining wealth through their farms and plantations as well as commercial trading contracts with merchants in European countries. The discovery of gold on Cherokee land in Georgia ultimately led to broken treaties with the U.S. government and to President Andrew Jackson's order for removal of the Cherokee people to western lands. In 1835, 7,000 federal soldiers arrived; they rounded up Cherokee families, held them in stockades, and then forced them westward at gunpoint for the historic Trail of Tears. It is believed that of the 18,000 persons forcibly removed, approximately 4,000 died. According to Wilma Mankiller:

> Old ones and small children were placed in wagons, but many of the Cherokees made that trek by foot or were herded onto boats. Some were in shackles. Thousands perished or were forever scarred in body, mind, and soul. It was not a

The former Cherokee Female Seminary, now home of Northeastern State University (Oklahoma) Social Work Program.

COURTESY OF DR. SARA BROWN

friendly removal. It was ugly and unwarranted. For too many Cherokees, it was deadly. The worse part of our holocaust was that it also meant the continued loss of tribal knowledge and traditions. (Mankiller & Wallis, 1993, p. 47)

The first winter in Oklahoma resulted in additional deaths from starvation and freezing. By 1839, however, homes were built and communities established. A new constitution was written, and Tahlequah was established as the Cherokee capital. Always respectful of education, the Cherokee Nation created a public school system by 1841, and in 1851 male and female seminaries were established for higher education. The strong work ethic and tribal pride of the Cherokees resulted in the rapid development of commerce, farms, government, and a judicial system. In 1862, during the Civil War, Cherokee land was invaded and taken by the Union Army. War destroyed ranches, homes, and the Cherokee economy. In the 1870s railroad expansion brought homesteaders from the East. Despite the protest of Indians, the federal government sold previously protected Indian Territory to white settlers.

The General Allotment Act (the Dawes Act) of 1887 dealt a severe blow to Indian territories across the United States. The act provided private ownership of parcels of land—allotments—to individual Indians, with the remaining lands reverting to the U.S. government for homesteading or other purposes. The next blow to Indian independence and self-rule came in 1898 with passage of the Curtis Act, which ended tribal courts as of that year and tribal government by 1906. Many Cherokees unknowingly sold their parcels of land for little or nothing and were left destitute. The Dawes Act dispossessed Indians in Oklahoma and across the country of nearly all their holdings.

In 1934, the Indian Reorganization Act, which provided for the reestablishment of tribal governments, was passed supported by John Collier, a former social worker and Franklin D. Roosevelt's appointee as head of the Bureau of Indian Affairs. Collier was a crusader for the welfare of Native Americans. The Cherokee and many other Indian tribes were able to regroup and rebuild their governmental structures and communities under the provisions of the Indian Reorganization Act.

The history of the Cherokee Nation reflects the history of Native American people generally. All shared common experiences of broken treaties and harsh treatment from the U.S. government. All tribes today continue to struggle with poverty; discrimination by the majority society persists. Weaver, in a 1998 article in *Social Work,* insists that effective service to Native American clients requires that social workers acquire knowledge of the historical trauma suffered by Indian people.

While Indian leaders such as Wilma Mankiller have engendered increasing self-respect and pride among native people, the historical tearing of family structures that resulted from the Trail of Tears and all other Indian removal programs is only now beginning to be addressed. Treatment programs—especially in Indian mental health and substance abuse programs—promote Native American intergenerational healing by focusing on both the strong survival skills and the unhealthy coping behaviors that people used when faced with a hostile environment. Although the history of broken treaties and oppression of Native American people goes back many years, it has links to our time. Almost all Indian families today include someone who was humiliated and traumatized by Indian boarding schools or who lost family members—generally children—taken by Indian agents or social workers, sometimes even given over by parents for adoption into non-Indian homes to avoid overwhelming poverty. Much healing remains to be done according to Linda Ketcher Goodrich, deputy director of the Cherokee Nation Health Services (personal interview, July 21, 1993).

SOCIAL WELFARE POLICY AND MENTAL HEALTH

As social workers today attempt to educate the community or to influence social policy in the area of mental health, they do so within the context of prior legislation and with an understanding of the history of human response, including the social work profession's response to mental illness. Attitudes toward mental illness today still reflect the mixture of repulsion, fear, and even amusement with which the mentally ill were regarded for centuries. But progress has been made both in our understanding of and attitudes toward mental illness and in our technologies for treating it.

Gradual Enlightenment

To understand the mental health system in the United States today, we must look back to its roots. The colonists who first came to the United States from European countries brought with them attitudes that were harsh and notions about caring for the mentally ill that stressed containment and coercion, whips, and chains. The first state hospital for the mentally ill in the United States was opened in Williamsburg, Virginia, in 1773. Before this, the mentally ill were cared for by their families or in poorhouses (almshouses) that also provided for poor people, for people with tuberculosis and other contagious diseases, and for mentally retarded and handicapped persons.

Almost simultaneously in the United States and Europe during the late 1700s and early 1800s, leaders emerged whose reform activities produced a shift in societal attitudes toward mentally ill persons. In Paris, Phillipe Pinel, a physician, attracted public attention in 1779 when he struck off the chains of the mentally ill men at Biscetre, a "lunatic asylum." A Quaker religious community in York, England, provided funds to William Tuke to develop an institution for the humane treatment of mentally ill persons (no chains were permitted). In the United States, Dr. Benjamin Rush, a physician and one of the signers of the Declaration of Independence, instituted many reforms at Pennsylvania Hospital; he also wrote the first American text on psychiatry.

A Courageous Researcher and Reformer: Dorothea Dix

The most famous reformer, however, was Dorothea Lynde Dix, an activist and reformer whose work in the mid-1800s attracted attention to the inhumane treatment of the mentally ill in the United States. A schoolteacher, Dix volunteered to teach a Sunday-school class at the East Cambridge women's jail near Boston in 1841. Here she discovered that it had become common practice to place mentally ill poor people in prisons. She was horrified by the inhumane conditions in which they were kept, and she felt compelled to do something about it. Dix's well-trained mind told her that only carefully conducted research to document the conditions of the mentally ill would elicit the attention of public officials. Accordingly, she set about visiting every jail, prison, and almshouse in Massachusetts. The following description of her visit to a Saugus, Massachusetts, poorhouse one Christmas Eve is characteristic of what she uncovered:

> They ascended a low flight of stairs into an entry, entered a room completely un-furnished, no chair, table, bed. It was cold, very cold. Her conductor threw open a window, a measure imperative for the digestive stability of a visitor. On the floor sat a woman, her limbs immovably contracted, knees brought upward to the chin, face concealed, head resting on folded arms, body clothed with what looked like fragments of many discarded garments. They gave little protection, for she was constantly shuddering.
>
> "Can she not change positions?" inquired Dorothea. No, the contraction of her limbs was caused by "neglect and exposure in former years," before, it was inferred, she came under the charge of her present guardians.
>
> "Her bed." As they left the room the man pointed to an object about three feet long and from a half to three-quarters of a yard wide, made of old ticking and containing perhaps a full handful of hay. "We throw some blankets over her at night." (Wilson, 1975, pp. 109–110)

Dix systematically recorded her findings: a woman kept in a cage; another fastened to a stone wall with chains; a man whose feet had been damaged by frost-bite who was kept in a box; many mentally ill persons kept in woodsheds without light, heat, or sanitation. The dates, places, and details of her investigations were all documented in a 30-page report that was presented to the Massachusetts legislature in January 1843. According to one biographer, on reading the report, the legislature "exploded like a bombshell. Years later a commentator would refer to it as 'the greatest sensation produced in the Massachusetts legislature since 1775.' Another would call her investigation 'the first piece of social research ever conducted in America' " (Wilson, p. 124). Legislation authorizing the building of hospitals to treat persons with mental illness was passed in Massachusetts as a result of Dix's investigations, but her work was not done.

Despite ill health, Dix traveled throughout the United States and Canada, continuing her research and reporting on inhumane treatment of people with mental illness. Through her efforts the Canadian government authorized construction of a new mental hospital for western Canada, and the Kentucky legislature approved construction of a new wing for an existing hospital in Lexington. Illinois, Tennessee and many other states appropriated funds for hospitals. Since many states were either unwilling or unable to finance hospitals for the mentally ill, Dorothea Dix decided to go to the federal government for help. Through her tireless efforts a bill was passed by Congress that would have permitted funds from the federal government's sale of western lands to be used to care for the mentally ill, but President Franklin Pierce vetoed the bill in 1854.

Unfortunately, the new state hospitals—founded on the principle of humane treatment—soon deteriorated, causing alarm for Dix and her followers. Mental hospitals became dumping grounds for society's problems. For example, hospital wards were filled with immigrants, and antiforeign sentiment defined institutional policy. The foreign-born were housed separately from nonimmigrants and often in inferior quarters. African American people—in those states that even admitted them to state hospitals—were also segregated. By 1900 conditions in state hospitals were investigated and were vividly described in news articles. Across the country, reformers, inspired by the earlier work of Dorothea Dix, demanded strict guidelines for the proper care of the mentally ill.

In 1905 Clifford Beers's book, *A Mind That Found Itself,* captured a more receptive public than might have been the case had it not been for the work of Dorothea Dix, Benjamin Rush, and others. The book told the author's personal story. Beers, a Yale University graduate, suffered a mental breakdown and endured years of inhumane treatment in both private and state facilities. He eloquently described what he saw and heard from attendants and others, even when he was severely ill and in a catatonic state. The book aroused the interest of the public as well as professional people. Beers subsequently founded the Connecticut Society for Mental Hygiene and assisted in the development of the national and international mental hygiene movement, which advocated for federal government intervention in the problem of mental illness.

The Twentieth Century

When the profession of social work emerged at the beginning of the twentieth century, social casework, emerging from the work of the Charity Organization Society, was the primary social work method in the mental health field. The pivotal work done by Mary Richmond, the founder of social casework, in her seminal texts, *Social Diagnosis* (1917) and *What Is Social Casework?* (1922), demonstrated the strong relationship between poverty and the mental health, personality development, and adjustment of social work clients.

While Richmond was working to conceptualize social casework, social work in health care was emerging. In 1907, Mary Antoinette Cannon was hired by Massachusetts General Hospital to work with mentally ill patients. She was the first social worker to enter this field of practice. Mary Jarrett was employed in 1913 as the first director of social services at the Boston Psychopathic Hospital, where she is said to have coined the term *psychiatric social worker.* Soon social workers began to be routinely hired by hospitals and clinics to provide therapy.

World War I, from 1914 to 1918, resulted in battle casualties that were psychological as well as physical. *Shell shock* was the term used to describe psychiatric problems created by war experiences. Mental health staff, including social workers, was needed. Recognizing the need for social workers trained to work with psychiatric disorders, Jarrett initiated a specialized psychiatric social work training program in 1918 at what is now the Smith College School for Social Work.

Sigmund Freud's writings had been introduced into the United States in the early 1900s, and by the 1920s, Freudian theory was well accepted as the most useful approach to the treatment of mental illness. Sigmund Freud taught that mental illness derived from unresolved conflicts and that patients could best be helped by remembering and discussing early events, even dreams, with a trained person. As Freudian theory was popularized, more and more middle-class and upper-income people began to avail themselves of the growing number of private and public mental health services. Child guidance clinics, established initially within juvenile court systems, focused on the needs of emotionally troubled children. The first such clinic, opened in St. Louis in 1922, set a precedent by being staffed by a psychiatrist, a psychologist, and a social worker. This soon became the traditional mental health team.

The mental health system in the United States, especially the public mental health sector, grew rapidly during the 1920s and 1930s. The demand for social workers to staff the clinics and hospitals spurred growth of the profession. The American Association of Psychiatric Social Workers, founded in 1926, became a strong force within the profession. In 1955 it merged with other specialized social work organizations to form the National Association of Social Work.

The first book on child psychotherapy, *The Dynamics of Therapy in a Controlled Relationship* (1933), written by Jessie Taft, was based on her experiences with a social work agency, the Children's Aid Society in Pennsylvania. Taft, a psychologist, was strongly influenced by the psychoanalytic work of Otto Rank, and she brought his theoretical base to her teaching at the Pennsylvania School of Social Work. Taft and Virginia Robinson, a social worker on the school's faculty, developed what came to be known as the functional school of social work. Use of time and time-limited casework was a major focus of functional theory, thus making the functional school a precursor of modern day brief therapy.

When World War II began in 1939, officer-level positions for psychiatric social workers were created by the army, and social workers functioned on military neuropsychiatric teams. During the war, approximately 1 million patients with neuropsychiatric disorders were admitted to U.S. Army hospitals (Callicutt, 1987). This resulted in an expansion of psychiatric social services, especially group work, for the military and their families. By the end of the war, in 1945, the military services and the Veterans Administration hospitals had become the largest employers of professional social workers (Leiby, 1987).

The first major piece of mental health legislation passed by the U.S. government was the National Mental Health Act of 1946. The act provided federal funding for research, training, and demonstration projects to help the states develop programs for the prevention and treatment of mental illness. The act set the stage for the creation of the National Institute of Mental Health (NIMH) in 1949. The leadership and authority of this federal organization came to be well recognized, and it had a major impact on the development of state mental health programs.

During the 1950s, social work continued its growth in the mental health field. Within the profession itself, social casework dominated practice from the 1940s through the 1960s. Prominent among the theorists and writers were Helen Harris Perlman, whose book, *Casework: A Problem-Solving Process* (1957), integrated the theories of the functional school (Taft and Robinson) and the diagnostic approach (Hamilton), and Florence Hollis, author of *Social Casework: A Psychosocial Therapy* (1964). Hollis's work has been described as the springboard for the clinical social work movement (Meyer, 1987).

The Community Mental Health Centers Construction Act of 1963 was the next major piece of legislation in mental health policy. With the strong support of President Kennedy, this act gave credibility to the leadership and commitment of the federal government in mental health. It provided grants for the construction of the community mental health facilities that were to provide care for the persons released from hospitals for the chronically mentally ill. It defined the continuum of care to be given and required that care be provided even to patients who could not afford to pay for it. Many historians believe that this legislation revolutionized the mental health system in the United States, for it resulted in large-scale development of community mental health programs as well as the deinstitutionalization of patients.

Decisions in the 1970s by the U.S. Supreme Court *(O'Connor v. Donaldson)* and the U.S. Court of Appeals for the Fifth Circuit *(Wyatt v. Stickney,* an Alabama case) set precedents in the areas of mental health and developmental disability. The rulings directed that mental patients who had been committed to a hospital had a right to release (assuming they were not dangerous to themselves or others) if they were not receiving treatment. Care for mentally ill or retarded persons was to be provided in the least restrictive (that is, the least confined and most home-like) setting possible.

A consumer movement emerged at this time and grew remarkably quickly. The National Alliance for the Mentally Ill (NAMI) was founded in 1979 of consumers (this term is preferred to *patients*), family members, and concerned professionals. Today NAMI continues to support research, education, and social policy and political activity that will enhance access to community-based services. The organization is supported by members and now has affiliate offices in all 50 states and a membership exceeding 220,000 (NAMI, 2001).

The Mental Health Systems Act of 1980 continued funding for community mental health centers and attempted to address the ramifications of deinstitutionalization. Across the country thousands of persons who had lived many years in state hospitals, receiving only custodial care, had been released. Some had been living on the streets for many years. In order to meet the basic needs of homeless mentally ill persons and others needing follow-up care, the act authorized the use of case management. Almost immediately many new programs for homeless persons and others with persistent and serious mental illness were put into place.

The Omnibus Budget Reconciliation Act of 1981, supported by President Ronald Reagan but opposed by many people in the mental health field, discontinued the federal government's leadership in the development of mental health services. (Previously, as governor of the state of California, Reagan had proposed closing all state mental health institutions.) This act effectively repealed the Mental Health Systems Act and shifted responsibility for funding and future development of mental health programs to the individual states in the form of block grants. Most states had already closed or substantially reduced their mental health facilities. With new responsibility for mental health care, many states developed contractual arrangements with counties and, more recently, with private organizations to provide community-based services to persons with more serious and chronic forms of mental illness.

The election of President Bill Clinton in 1992 signaled a readiness for new approaches to health care financing, and, indeed, many Americans supported some form of national health care. The Clinton administration's plan, however, disappointed many in the mental health field because of the strict limitations placed on outpatient mental health care and the sizable co-payment (50%) it required. In the years that followed the withdrawal of the Clinton health care plan, impetus for meaningful health care reform seemed to have been swept away. Managed health care programs expanded very rapidly and proved effective in containing rapidly rising health care costs, but managed care placed many restrictions on both inpatient and outpatient mental health care. Today concern persists regarding the possible negative ramifications for clients of managed care (Rose & Keigher, 1996; Wieman & Dorwart, 1998).

POLICY AND PRACTICE: FUTURE ISSUES

The mental health consumer movement begun in the later decades of the twentieth century gathered steam as it moved into the new millennium. As the public became increasingly informed about the limited access to mental health care and the abuses experienced by people in short-term care, reforms were sought. Media reports such as social worker Terrance Johnson's report of abuses of Charter Hospital's patients on the *60 Minutes* CBS television show resulted in calls for action. Johnson found children placed in restraints and sometimes hurt: one child died; uncredentialed and poorly trained staff ran group sessions and wrote assessments; psychiatrists wrote notes in the records of patients they hadn't even seen (O'Neill, 1999). Charter Hospital took quick action to correct the reported deficiencies, but soon the entire Charter Hospital system closed.

Access to care, especially care that does not discriminate against or stigmatize people because of their mental illness, has become central to the reform effort. Two specific policy thrusts have emerged: a "bill of rights" that specifies what consumers should be able to expect from mental health providers and access to mental health treatment that is equal to the access provided for physical illness—"parity."

When it was apparent that health and mental health reform would not be accomplished in the way that he had hoped, President Clinton spearheaded a **Mental Health Bill of Rights.** This set of principles seeks to ensure that basic consumer rights are met. The bill of rights was implemented in Federal Employee Health Benefit Plans in 1997 but was intended to provide guidance for state and private mental health service providers as well. The bill addresses eight areas. These include consumers' right to information about their health plans, the right to information about the professionals who deliver services, the right to a reasonable choice of providers, access to emergency services, the right to participate in treatment decisions, the right to receive respectful care, confidentiality, and the right to appeal decisions of the health care plan. The bill concludes with a statement about consumer's responsibilities (KEN Publications/Catalog, n.d.). In an unprecedented move, nine professional organizations representing over 500,000 mental health practitioners collaborated and jointly published a Mental Health Bill of Rights (shown in Exhibit 8). NASW was one of the nine sponsors. This initiative certainly reflects the level of professional practitioner support for patient's rights reform and an end to stigmatization and discrimination for persons who suffer from major or minor mental disorders.

Consumers of mental health services and their watchdog organizations, NAMI and the National Mental Health Association, have galvanized public support for meaningful mental health parity legislation. Years of reduced access to mental health care—from deinstitutionalization of the 1970s, to Reagan's Omnibus Budget Reconciliation Act of 1981, to managed care—led to public outcry in the

EXHIBIT 8

Our commitment is to provide quality mental health and substance abuse services to all individuals without regard to race, color, religion, national origin, gender, age, sexual orientation, or disabilities.

RIGHT TO KNOW

Benefits: Individuals have the right to be provided information from the purchasing entity (such as employer or union or public purchaser) and the insurance/third-party payer describing the nature and extent of their mental health and substance abuse treatment benefits. This information should include details on procedures to obtain access to services, on utilization management procedures, and on appeal rights. The information should be presented clearly in writing with language that the individual can understand.

Professional Expertise: Individuals have the right to receive full information from the potential treating professional about that professional's knowledge, skills, preparation, experience, and credentials. Individuals have the right to be informed about the options available for treatment interventions and the effectiveness of the recommended treatment.

Contractual Limitations: Individuals have the right to be informed by the treating professional of any arrangements, restrictions, and/or covenants established between third-party payer and the treating professional that could interfere with or influence treatment recommendations. Individuals have the right to be informed of the nature of information that may be disclosed for the purposes of paying benefits.

Appeals and Grievances: Individuals have the right to receive information about the methods they can use to submit complaints or grievances regarding provision of care by the treating professional to that profession's regulatory board and to the professional association. Individuals have the right to be provided information about the procedures they can use to appeal benefit utilization decisions to the third-party payer systems, to the employer or purchasing entity, and to external regulatory entities.

CONFIDENTIALITY

Individuals have the right to be guaranteed the protection of the confidentiality of their relationship with their mental health and substance abuse professional, except when laws or ethics

(Continued)

dictate otherwise. Any disclosure to another party will be time limited and made with the full written, informed consent of the individuals. Individuals shall not be required to disclose confidential, privileged or other information other than: diagnosis, prognosis, type of treatment, time and length of treatment, and cost.

Entities receiving information for the purposes of benefits determination, public agencies receiving information for health care planning, or any other organization with legitimate right to information will maintain clinical information in confidence with the same rigor and be subject to the same penalties for violation as is the direct provider of care.

Information technology will be used for transmission, storage, or data management only with methodologies that remove individual identifying information and assure the protection of the individual's privacy. Information should not be transferred, sold or otherwise utilized.

CHOICE
Individuals have the right to choose any duly licensed/certified professional for mental health and substance abuse services. Individuals have the right to receive full information regarding the education and training of professionals, treatment options (including risks and benefits), and cost implications to make an informed choice regarding the selection of care deemed appropriate by individual and professional.

DETERMINATION OF TREATMENT
Recommendations regarding mental health and substance abuse treatment shall be made only by a duly licensed/certified professional in conjunction with the individual and his or her family as appropriate. Treatment decisions should not be made by third-party payers. The individual has the right to make final decisions regarding treatment.

PARITY
Individuals have the right to receive benefits for mental health and substance abuse treatment on the same basis as they do for any other illnesses, with the same provisions, co-payments, lifetime benefits, and catastrophic coverage in both insurance and self-funded/self-insured health plans.

DISCRIMINATION
Individuals who use mental health and substance abuse benefits shall not be penalized when seeking other health insurance or disability, life or any other insurance benefit.

BENEFIT USAGE
The individual is entitled to the entire scope of the benefits within the benefit plan that will address his or her clinical needs.

BENEFIT DESIGN

Whenever both federal and state law and/or regulations are applicable, the professional and all players shall use whichever affords the individual the greatest level of protection and access.

TREATMENT REVIEW

To assure that treatment review processes are fair and valid, individuals have the right to be guaranteed that any review of their mental health and substance abuse treatment shall involve a professional having the training, credentials and licensure required to provide the treatment in the jurisdiction in which it will be provided. The reviewer should have no financial interest in the decision and is subject to the section on confidentiality.

ACCOUNTABILITY

Treating professionals may be held accountable and liable to individuals for any injury caused by gross incompetence on the part of the professional. The training professional has the obligation to advocate for and document necessity of care and to advise the individual of options if payment authorization is denied.

Payers, and other third parties may be held accountable and liable to individuals for any injury caused by gross incompetence or negligence or by their clinically unjustified decisions.

PARTICIPATING GROUPS

- American Association for Marriage and Family Therapy (membership: 25,000)
- American Counseling Association (membership: 56,000)
- American Family Therapy Academy (membership: 1,000)
- American Nurses Association (membership: 180,000)
- American Psychological Association (membership: 142,000)
- American Psychiatric Association (membership: 42,000)
- American Psychiatric Nurses Association (membership: 3,000)
- National Association of Social Workers (membership: 155,000)
- National Federation of Societies for Clinical Social Work (membership: 11,000)

Source: NASW On-Line. (1999, November 21). Mental Health Bill of Rights Project; Joint initiative of mental health professional organizations: Principles for the provision of mental health and substance abuse treatment services. Retrieved August 25, 2001, from http:www.naswdc.org/practice/mental.htm.

1990s. This forced an increasingly conservative U.S. Congress to pass the **Mental Health Parity Act of 1996** and many states to pass their own parity acts. "Parity," here, refers to efforts to equalize benefits for physical and mental health care. (Note the areas of parity specified in the Exhibit 8 Bill of Rights.) The 1996 act was breakthrough legislation and widely acclaimed, but it failed to meet expectations. Its limitations became apparent quite quickly: only employers of 50 or more were mandated to comply and only if they offered provisions for mental health care. Not surprisingly, some employers immediately discontinued any mental health care in their health insurance. The law also allowed insurance plans to limit the number of outpatient visits it will pay for, limit hospital stays, and permitted charging higher co-payments than people were asked to pay for their physical health care.

Social workers, including NASW lobbyists, sought passage of legislation that would rectify the limitations of the 1996 legislation. A number of bills were introduced between 1999 and 2001. None passed, including the Mental Health Equitable Treatment Act of 2001, a bill that had broad political sponsorship plus the enthusiastic support of NAMI and other organizations. This bill covered the full range of mental disorders, unlike the 1996 Act, and it prohibited unequal limits on mental health benefits. Just a handful of conservative members of the House of Representatives were responsible for defeat of mental health parity legislation in the final days of 2001. The older 1996 law was extended for one additional year (Wyffels, 2001). It does appear, however, that momentum is building now, and some form of meaningful mental health parity legislation seems closer than ever to accomplishment.

The masses of people who are not currently covered by health insurance may have little to gain by a parity law. A continuing issue compelling political action by social workers and other health care advocates is health care, including substance abuse and mental health care, for all citizens. Quality of health care will also remain an issue into the future. The evolution of cost containment health care policy in the United States, especially the advent of managed care, has had a major impact on the practice of social workers. The traditional, open-ended therapies used in the past by social work psychotherapists and the long-term involvement so characteristic of many BSW caseloads have given way to brief, highly focused approaches to practice. In many settings, intermittent services have replaced long-term case contact. Managed care has encouraged the use of groups, often with a psychoeducational focus instead of individualized psychosocial therapy, for inpatient as well as community-based practice. The use of standardized protocols, sometimes referred to by insurance companies as **preferred practices,** is a recent response to the demand for short-term, highly focused intervention. These protocols, or preferred practices, are directives that determine the practices to be followed for specific client problems (Mitchell, 1998).

Mental health social and economic policies will continue to influence social work practice and new forms of practice are likely to evolve. Short-term approaches may be increasingly demanded. Some that have emerged recently derive from more traditional practice. Cognitive behavioral therapy, for example, seeks to retrain clients whose difficulties result from the use of dysfunctional or negative thought patterns. Strategic or solution-oriented approaches help clients to focus narrowly on ineffective behaviors and reframe or obtain new perspectives that enable the achievement of goals. Time-limited family and group interventions, even single-session treatment approaches, are emerging (Fangor, 1995). Social workers are also becoming skilled in the use of computer groups, enabling caregivers of persons with Alzheimer's disease, for example, or chronically ill children to benefit from groups in privacy and without leaving their homes (Schopler, Abell, & Galinsky, 1998).

Not all mentally ill persons will benefit from brief interventions. One of the concerns of the National Alliance for the Mentally Ill is the need for ongoing service for persons with persistent, serious mental health problems. Case management, especially that which employs BSWs, has come into prominent use to ensure quality of life and freedom from hospitalization for persons with chronic illness. The Internet has also provided social workers with rapid access to updated information about mental disorders and their treatment as well as current legislation. The Internet has also provided opportunities for mental health professionals and concerned citizens to organize efforts to affect mental health policy. (See the Internet Sites for further information on mental health and also to find social and political action resources that support mental health legislation.)

Future trends in mental health social work practice will surely continue to be strongly influenced by the evolution of health care policy. Cost containment is likely to remain a pressing issue. With insurance companies imposing time limits, social workers and other mental health practitioners will work under considerable pressure to meet clients' needs more quickly. Social workers of the future will have opportunities to design new practice approaches that will meet client needs, they will retain leadership in creating and administering mental health programs, and they will need to become more active in political process and policy development. Clearly, compassion for clients, commitment to professional values, and strong advocacy skills will be necessary attributes of future mental health social workers.

INTERNET SITES

http://www.mentalhealth.org/	Center for Mental Health Services
http://www.nimh.nih.gov/	National Institute of Mental Health
http://www.nmha.org/	The National Mental Health Association
http://www.hms.harvard.edu/dsm/wmhp/	World Mental Health Project
http://www.nami.org/	The National Alliance for the Mentally Ill
http://www.cmha.ca/english/index.html	Canadian Mental Health Association
http://www.wfmh.com/	The World Federation for Mental Health
http://www.surgeongeneral.gov/library/mentalhealth/home.html	Mental Health: A Report of the Surgeon General
http://narmh.org/	National Association for Rural Mental Health
http://www.suicidology.org/index.html	American Association of Suicidology
http://www.clinicalsocialwork.com/	Pat McClendon's Clinical Social Work
http://cim.usuhs.mil/ps02001/childpsychopath.htm	Childhood Psychiatric Disorders (Walter Reed Army Medical Center)

SUMMARY

Roberta Sholes's work with David Deerinwater demonstrated the unique contribution that social work can make to the mental health team. Her sensitivity to the cultural dimensions of the case enriched her work with the client and enabled her to help other professional staff in their work, too. Most significantly, this BSW social worker helped David Deerinwater to achieve his goal and to reintegrate with his family and his people. As a generalist social worker, Roberta had the skills to work within a complex organizational structure, with families as well as individuals, and she was able to understand and use community systems.

Although they are not educated in a medical profession and they have serious concerns about the use of certain diagnostic labels, social workers whose careers are in mental health settings must learn the diagnostic terminology used by members of the mental health team. The chapter, therefore, introduced readers to the *Diagnostic and Statistical Manual of Mental Disorders* of the American Psychiatric Association. An introduction to the more commonly used psychotropic medications was also provided.

The chapter also traced the development of the U.S. response to mental illness from colonial times to the present. Key figures in reforms of the mental health system were Dorothea Lynde Dix, whose research and publications called the nation's attention to the inhumane treatment of the mentally ill, and Clifford Beers, whose book, *A Mind That Found Itself,* furthered public understanding of mental illness and helped promote an emerging mental hygiene movement. Mary Antoinette Cannon, Mary Jarrett, Jessie Taft, and Virginia Robinson were instrumental in the development of professional social services for the mentally ill and of training programs for social workers. Sigmund Freud's works resulted in improved approaches to treatment of mental illness, approaches that were quickly incorporated into the curricula of schools of social work as well as medicine, psychology, and nursing.

Social policy initiatives were described. These included federal legislation that created the National Institute of Mental Health and other laws such as the Community Mental Health Centers Construction Act of 1963 and the Mental Health Systems Act of 1980, all of which promoted programs for the mentally ill. This period of growth, however, ended in the early 1980s as federal budget deficits resulted in cutbacks of funding for programs. The Omnibus Reconciliation Act of 1981 shifted primary responsibility for leadership in the development of mental health services to the individual states. Concern about increasing health care costs and growing public reluctance to support health and human services marked the 1990s, signaling shifts in the way that social workers and all mental health professionals would provide care. Policies designed to curtail rising costs nourished the growth of managed care in the field of mental health. As access to mental health care declined, the organization known as NAMI, supported by social workers and other mental health professionals, promoted media attention to the growing problems in the mental health field. Nine professional mental health organizations, including the NASW, disseminated a joint Mental Health Bill of Rights. Discriminatory and abusive treatment of persons with mental disorders increasingly became an issue of concern to the public. Some states developed limited mental health parity laws in response, and several efforts to achieve federal legislation were attempted. None, however, ensured meaningful equality in physical and mental health care. A bill that might have accomplished this was defeated in the final days of 2001. Despite this, it is clear that momentum for mental health parity legislation is growing, and social workers will be among those actively engaged in seeking passage of this legislation. One of the most pressing needs in the United States is for health insurance that will cover all U.S. citizens so that the massive number of uninsured persons will have access to health care, including mental health care. This concern will be discussed further in the next chapter.

In the next chapter, too, readers will meet Linda Sanders, a student in her senior year field placement in a community general hospital. Social work roles that were introduced in Chapter 1 of this text will be apparent in Linda's fieldwork practice, especially the advocacy role. There will be other similarities with Chapter 6. The values and ethics that guide practice will be familiar. Also familiar will be interdisciplinary teamwork relationships that social workers engage in each day of their practice.

This chapter concludes with trust that the spirit of openness to new knowledge that has pervaded the social work profession since its inception will keep social workers in the future alert to new learning for their work in the field of mental health. Firm grounding in professional values will also guide social workers of the future as they continue to provide leadership and strong advocacy for vulnerable populations such as persons with mental and emotional disorders.

KEY TERMS

acute traumatic stress
behavioral health care
case manager
clinical social workers
deinstitutionalization
delusions
*Diagnostic and Statistical Manual
  of Mental Disorders (DSM)*
hallucinations
managed care
mental disorder
Mental Health Bill of Rights

Mental Health Parity Act of 1996
mood disorder
neurosis
posttraumatic stress disorder (PTSD)
preferred practices
psychosis
psychotropic medication
schizophrenia
secondary setting
staffing
utilization review

DISCUSSION QUESTIONS

1. Consider what might have happened to David Deerinwater if social workers at Oklahoma State Mental Hospital were not responsible for assisting with discharge planning. What might the outcome have been if a nurse or other staff member had been responsible for the discharge plan?
2. What social work values apply to practice in mental health? In what ways did Roberta Sholes demonstrate adherence to social work values?
3. Which professions make up the traditional mental health team? In what ways are these professions different? In what ways do they overlap?
4. Why are social workers skeptical about the use of classification systems like the *DSM-IV-TR?* Are there any advantages to using such a system to classify mental disorders?
5. Why is Dorothea Dix important in the history of mental health care?
6. Identify some of the pioneering social workers in the field of mental health, and describe their contributions.
7. What is meant by the statement that social workers overidentified with Freudian psychology?

8. What are the positive and negative implications of deinstitutionalization for the mentally ill? For their families? For the community?
9. What is acute traumatic stress? What are the behavioral reactions of people when they are in acute traumatic stress? Give examples of situations that might result in acute traumatic stress. How can social workers be helpful?

CLASSROOM EXERCISES

While not required, it is suggested that students break into small groups of three or four to discuss these exercises. It may be helpful to choose a scribe to record and report important points to the class after the group discussion.

1. Why do many hospitals that treat people with mental illness have policies requiring that social workers be part of their mental health team? What special expertise do social workers bring to a mental health team, as illustrated in the Deerinwater case?
2. How has the National Association of Social Workers been involved in influencing national social policy affecting people at risk of mental health problems?
3. From information provided in this chapter, do you think the primary purpose of case management is client service or cost containment? Explain your reasons.
4. What are two major thrusts of recent national social policy reform efforts attempting to assist people with mental illness? How are these thrusts illustrated in former President Clinton's Mental Health Bill of Rights? The Mental Health Parity Act of 1996? What were some major problems with the 1996 law?

RESEARCH ACTIVITIES

1. What specific concerns do consumers of mental health services and their families have? Contact a local unit of NAMI or your local or state Mental Health Association to learn about the needs and issues of people with mental disorders who live in your area. Your state NASW chapter may also be a good source of information. Consider volunteering with one of these organizations to assist with political acitivity in support of programs that serve persons with mental illness. Find out, too, how volunteers can be helpful in other ways.
2. Select a specific mental disorder as a research topic. Use both the Internet and your school's library to obtain information about this form of mental illness and its treatment.
3. Study the many types of mental health resources in your community. Select one that provides prevention services and one that focuses on treatment. Interview a social worker in each setting to obtain information about the nature of social work services provided.
4. Conduct a small, informal survey in your neighborhood to learn how people might react if a group home for the mentally ill was proposed.

INTERNET RESEARCH EXERCISES

1. The National Institute of Mental Health offers information on bipolar disorder on its website (http://nimh.nih.gov/publicat/manic.cfm).
   a. What percentage of the U.S. adult population suffers from bipolar disorder?
   b. What are the symptoms of (1) depression and (2) mania?
   c. What evidence is given to support the thesis that bipolar disorder has some sort of genetic basis?

2. An evaluation of the effects of the Mental Health Parity Act of 1996 may be found on the Internet (http://www.mentalhealth.org/cmhs/ManagedCare/Parity/ParityActimpct.asp).
   a. What was the primary provision of the act?
   b. To what extent did employers drop or restrict mental health coverage as a result of the act?
   c. According to this evaluation, were the effects of the MHPA positive or negative? Explain.
3. An article appeared in the *Wall Street Journal* regarding deinstitutionalization in August 1998. It may be read on the Web (http://www.psychlaws.org/GeneralResources/Article2.htm).
   a. What does the article cite as the reason the procedure has "gone awry"?
   b. Why are more persons with serious mental health disorders not helped with outpatient commitment?
   c. In the opinion stated in this article, are the states in any way responsible for the problem?

REFERENCES

American Psychiatric Association. (2000). *Diagnostic and statistical manual of mental disorders* (4th ed., text revision). Washington, DC: Author.

Anello, E., Kirk, S. A., & Kutchins, H. (1992). Should social workers use the DSM-III? In E. Gambrill & R. Pruger, *Controversial issues in social work* (pp. 139–156). Boston: Allyn & Bacon.

Bates, C. E., & Van Dam, C. H. (1984). Low incidence of schizophrenia in British Columbia coastal Indians. *Journal of Epidemiology and Community Health, 38* (2), 127–130.

Bentley, K. J., & Walsh, J. (2001). *The social worker and psychotropic medication: Toward effective collaboration with mental health clients, families, and providers* (2nd ed.). Belmont, CA: Brooks/Cole.

Blair, D. T., & Ramones, V. A. (1998). Utilization of psychotropic medication on an as needed (PRN) basis [Electronic version.] *Perspectives: A Mental Health Magazine.* Retrieved June 26, 1998, from http://www.cmhc.com/perspectives/articles/art06981.htm.

Callicutt, J. W. (1987). Mental health services. *Encyclopedia of social work* (18th ed., Vol. 2, pp. 125–135). Silver Spring, MD: National Association of Social Workers.

Center for Mental Health Services. (1996). *Mental health, United States, 1996.* Mandershield, R. W., & Sonnenschein, M. A., Eds. DHHS Pub. No. (SMA)96-3098. Washington, DC: Superintendent of Documents, U.S. Government Printing Office.

Eng, A., & Balancio, E. F. (1997). Clinical case management with Asian Americans. In E. Lee (Ed.), *Working with Asian Americans: A guide for clinicians* (pp. 400–407). New York: The Guilford Press.

Fangor, M. T. (1995). Brief therapies. *Encyclopedia of social work* (19th ed., Vol. 1, pp. 325–334). Washington, DC: National Association of Social Workers.

Joint Commission on Accreditation of Healthcare Organizations. (1998). *Lexikon* (2nd ed.). Oakbrook Terrace, IL: Author.

Kadushin, A., & Kadushin, G. (1997). Desirable characteristics of the culturally sensitive interviewer. *The social work interview: A guide for human service professionals* (4th ed.). New York: Columbia University Press, 347–348.

KEN Publications/Catalog. (n.d.). Final report, consumer bill of rights & responsibilities. Retrieved August 25, 2001, from http://www.mentalhealth.org/consumersurvivor/billofrights.htm.

Kirk, S. A., & Kutchins, H. (1992). *The selling of DSM: The rhetoric of science in psychiatry.* New York: Aldine de Gruyter.

Kongstvedt, P. R. (1997). *Essentials of managed health care* (2nd ed.). Gaithersburg, MD: Aspen Publishers, Inc.

Kutchins, H., & Kirk, S. A. (1989). Human errors, attractive nuisances, and toxic wastes: A reply to Anello. *Social Work, 34*(2), 187–188.

Kutchins, H., & Kirk, S. A. (1997). *Making us crazy: DSM—The psychiatric bible and the creation of mental disorders.* New York: The Free Press.

LaFromboise, T. D. (1988). American Indian mental health policy. *American Psychologist, 43*(5), 388–397.

Landers, S. (1998). Medication management playing larger, crucial role: Collaboration puts treatment plans together. *NASW News, 43*(6), 3.

Leiby, J. (1987). History of social welfare. *Encyclopedia of social work* (18th ed., Vol. 1, pp. 755–777). Silver Spring, MD: National Association of Social Workers.

Leigh, J. W. (1998). *Communicating for cultural competence.* Boston: Allyn & Bacon.

Lerner, M. D., & Shelton, R. D. (2001). How can emergency responders help grieving individuals? and How do people respond during traumatic exposure? *Trauma response infosheet.* Retrieved September 29, 2001, from the American Academy of Experts in Traumatic Stress Web site: http://www.aaets.org.

Lum, D. (1999). *Culturally competent practice: A framework for growth and action.* Pacific Grove, CA: Brooks/Cole.

Mankiller, W., & Wallis, M. (1993). *Mankiller: A chief and her people.* New York: St. Martin's Press.

Mayden, R. W., & Nieves, J. (2000). Mental health. Policy Statement approved by the NASW Delegate Assembly, August 1999. In *Social work speaks: National Association of Social Workers policy statement 2000–2003* (pp. 226–227). Washington, DC: NASW Press.

Meyer, C. (1987). Direct practice in social work: Overview. In *Encyclopedia of social work* (19th ed., Vol. 1, pp. 409–422). Silver Spring, MD: National Association of Social Workers.

Mitchell, C. G. (1998). Perceptions of empathy and client satisfaction with managed behavioral health care. *Social Work, 43*(5), 404–411.

NAMI (2001). NAMInet. Retrieved August 24, 2001, from http:www.nami.org/naminet_announcement.html.

NASW Online. (1999, August 9). Retrieved August 15, 2001, from http://www.naswdc.org/Default.htm. Available: for ACSW: http://www.naswdc.org/credentials/acsw.htm; for C-SWCM and C-ASWCM: http://www.naswdc.org/credentials/casemgmt.htm; for QCSW: http:www.naswdc.org/credentials/qcsw.htm; and for DCSW: http:www.naswdc.org/credentials/dcsw.htm.

National suicide prevention strategy issued. (2001). *NASW News, 46* (7), 10.

NIMH. (2001, January 1). *Reliving Trauma.* Retrieved September 29, 2001, from http://www.nimh.gov/publicat/reliving.cfm.

O'Neill, J. V. (1999). Advocacy takes a new tack. *NASW News, 44* (8), 4.

O'Neill, J. V. (2001). Practitioner leads life in spotlight. *NASW News, 46* (7), 13.

Ray, O., & Ksir, C. (1993). *Drugs, society, & human behavior* (6th ed.). St. Louis: Mosby.

Red Horse, J. (1988). Cultural evolution of American Indian families. In C. Jacobs & D. D. Bowles (Eds.) *Ethnicity and race: Critical concepts in social work* (pp. 86–102). Silver Spring, MD: National Association of Social Workers.

Rose, S. J., & Keigher, S. M. (1996). Managing mental health: Whose responsibility? *Health and Social Work, 21*(1), 76–80.

Safe havens from the streets. (1997, November). *NASW News, 42*(10), p. 15.

Schopler, J. H., Abell, M. D., & Galinsky, M. J. (1998). Technology-based groups: A review and conceptual framework for practice. *Social Work, 43*(3), 254–267.

Snowden, L. R., & Cheung, F. K. (1990, March). Use of inpatient mental health services by members of ethnic minority groups. *American Psychologist, 45*(3), 347–355.

Social work in the public eye. (2002). *NASW News, 47*(1), 15.

Vastola, J., Nierenberg, A., & Graham, E.H. (1994). The lost and found group: Group work with bereaved children. In A. Gitterman & L. Shulman (Eds.). *Mutual aid groups, vulnerable populations, and the life cycle* (2nd ed., pp. 81–96). New York: Columbia University Press.

Vourlekis, B. S., & Greene, R. R. (Eds.). (1992). *Social work case management.* New York: Aldine De Gruyter.

Weaver, H. N. (1998). Indigenous people in a multicultural society: Unique issues for human services. *Social Work, 43*(3), 203–211.

Wieman, D. A., & Dorwart, R. A. (1998). Evaluating state mental health care reform: The case of privatization of state mental services in Massachusetts. In M. Gibelman and H. W. Demone, Jr. (Eds.). *The privatization of human services* (Vol. 1, pp. 53–78). New York: Springer.

Wilson, D. C. (1975). *Stranger and traveler: The story of Dorothea Dix, American reformer.* Boston: Little, Brown & Co.

Wyffels, M. (2001, December 19). House-Senate Conference Committee votes down Domenici-Wellstone parity amendment. *NAMI: The nation's voice on mental illness, 02* (39). Retrieved January 1, 2002, from http://www.nami.org/update//20011219.htm.

FOR FURTHER READING

Anthony, W. A., Cohen, M., Farkas, M., & Cohen, B. (2000). The chronically mentally ill: Case management—More than a response to a dysfunctional system. *Community Mental Health Journal, 36* (1), 97–106.

Before deinstitutionalization, persons with chronic and severe mental illness were confined to state mental hospitals where their needs were met 24 hours a day. In these large custodial institutions, they had no control over their lives. After deinstitutionalization even the basic needs of a large portion of persons with severe mental disorders were not met. Case management sought to rectify that situation but, again, it was driven by the service system's goals. This article seeks to redesign case management, soliciting clients' goals and making intervention efforts focus on achievement of those goals. The authors see case management as the kind of program that should normally be made available to all persons who are disabled by serious mental illness, not merely an intervention emerging from the safety needs of the community or the service goals of community organizations. The following case management activities are described in the article: connecting with clients, planning, linking persons to services, and advocating for service improvements.

Bentley, K. J. (Ed.). (2002). *Social work practice in mental health: Contemporary roles, tasks, and techniques.* Pacific Grove, CA: Brooks/Cole.

Although this text is targeted for MSW as well as BSW readers, the focus on professional role makes the book highly useful for generalist social workers employed in the mental health field. Chapters emphasizing the following roles may be of special interest to

BSW students: crisis counselor, mediator, skills trainer, case manager, medication facilitator, consumer and family consultant, interagency and interdisciplinary teamwork, advocate and community organizer. Chapters are readable and practical. They consistently address relevant empirical research and theory base, social work tasks and responsibilities across systems levels, skills and techniques, model programs, and special challenges for social workers. Most chapters include a "case dilemma" that depicts the real-life challenges for social workers.

Bentley, K. J., & Walsh, J. (2001). *The social worker and psychotropic medication: Toward effective collaboration with mental health clients, families, and providers* (2nd ed.). Belmont, CA: Brooks/Cole.

Baccalaureate-level social workers in mental health settings are likely to become involved with clients' medication issues in ways that they probably never anticipated as college students. This text is a splendid aid in understanding psychotropic medications. The text explains how and why psychotropic medications are used and the many potential roles of social workers in medication management, educating clients and families, and the legal and ethical concerns related to client refusal to comply with prescribed medication regimens. The text demonstrates social workers' unique opportunities to assist clients with their medication-related concerns. The authors suggest ways for social workers to assist physicians and psychiatrists in understanding the cultural and socioeconomic factors that underpin clients' fears and concerns about psychotropic medications.

Kirsthardt, W. (1997). The strengths model of case management: Principles and helping functions. In D. Saleebey (Ed.). *The strengths perspective in social work practice* (2nd ed.). New York: Longman.

All of the goodness and joy of the strengths model, which nourishes the resilience and resources of people, is found in this chapter, which focuses on work with people who are struggling with persistent mental illness and, often, poverty. The author puts aside the concept of pathology and instead teaches helping strategies that engage abilities, capacities, and connections between people and their communities. Kirsthardt's guidelines for a strength assessment ask such questions as: Where are you living now? Where will you sleep tonight? Do you have friends? What are your interests? This article and this book are great antidotes for so-called burnout.

Kutchins, H., & Kirk, S. A. (1997). *Making us crazy: DSM—The psychiatric bible and the creation of mental disorders.* New York: The Free Press.

Written in an energetic, upbeat style, this critique of the American Psychiatric Association's manual of mental disorders captured the attention of the American public as well as mental health professionals. The authors' penetrating analysis of the political battles that are waged and the compromises that are made with each edition of the *DSM* may engender a bit of healthy disrespect for this so-called bible. The authors also expose the link between the power of the *DSM* and the income therapists receive from insurance companies that will not pay for treatment unless a *DSM* label is supplied. *Making Us Crazy* illustrates how clients become victims of *DSM* through this labeling process.

Williams, J. B. W., & Ell, K. (Eds.). (1998). *Advances in mental health research: Implications for practice.* Washington, DC: NASW Press.

This book is highly recommended for its scholarly review of research, especially research that has been conducted by or holds value to social workers in mental health practice. The critical analysis of its contributors reflects the growing proficiency of the profession's qualitative and quantitative research capacity. Research on psychopathology is the focus of Part One, which addresses the major mental health disorders: mood, anxiety, personality, stress-related and substance use disorders as well as schizophrenia. These disorders are carefully described, clinical implications are noted, and the most recent research findings from genetic linkages to psychosocial factors are identified. Mental health services and treatment, ranging from psychopharmacological to short-term and community-based, are addressed in Part Two.

NOTES

1. Reports about the incidence of schizophrenia among Native Americans vary widely. Beverly Patchell, RN, MS, program director of the Jack Brown Center in Tahlequah, Oklahoma, observed in a personal interview on July 7, 1993, that in her experience with Cherokee and other Indians, she found schizophrenia to occur very rarely, although she found that persons might appear schizophrenic while under great stress.

2. Contributions to this case study were made by Dr. Wanda Priddy, former practicum program coordinator, and Dr. Dolores Poole, Northeastern State University Social Work Department; by Delores Titchywy Sumner, Comanche tribe, assistant professor of library services, special collections librarian, John Vaughn Library/Learning Resources Center, Northeastern State University, Tahlequah, Oklahoma; Linda Ketcher Goodrich, ACSW, deputy director of the Cherokee Nation Health Service, and Beverly Patchell, RN, MS, program director, Jack Brown Center of the Cherokee Nation, Tahlequah, Oklahoma; and Isaac Christie, Malcolm Montgomery, and Jan Mowdy, Behavioral Health Unit, W.W. Hastings Hospital, Tahlequah, Oklahoma.

CHAPTER 7

Social Work in Health Care

MYRLEEN FERGUSON/PHOTO EDIT

OUTLINE

KATHERINE LEWANDOWSKI

As Linda Sanders walked down the corridor on the third floor of St. Anne's Hospital, she smiled at some of the nurses she passed. She was just beginning to know the staff, now that she was entering the second month of her senior-year social work field placement at this community general hospital. After all the years of classroom courses, it felt really good to finally be in a program that permitted her to do field work and apply what she had learned.

Linda was thinking now about the patient she was about to visit. Katherine Lewandowski was an 86-year-old widow who had been placed in a nursing home two months ago because she had suffered several minor fractures as a result of **osteoporosis,** *a bone-thinning disease most commonly found in women over 50. Because of her condition she could no longer live at home. Linda liked the silver-haired, frail woman who spoke both Polish and English. Katherine had a hearty sense of humor, but it was revealed infrequently during her hospitalization, for she was frightened of the medical setting and of staff in white uniforms. Fortunately, she had related well to Linda from the start.*

As she approached the patient's room, Linda recalled her two previous visits with Katherine. She had provided emotional support, which the elderly woman badly needed at the time of her arrival at St. Anne's. In the days that followed her admission to the hospital—necessitated by a fall at the nursing home, which had fractured her hip—Linda had tried to help Katherine understand and accept the recommended surgical procedure to repair the break. The surgery, performed three days ago, had gone well.

Linda tapped lightly on the door and entered the room. She glanced at Katherine and was startled by her appearance. Katherine's eyes were closed, but there were tears on her cheeks. Her color was poor. From her movements it was clear she was in pain. When Linda spoke a quiet, gentle greeting, Katherine opened her eyes. Linda delivered the message she had come with, that the doctors felt Katherine could return now to her nursing home; an ambulance would take her there in the morning. Linda had spoken with Katherine's daughter, Loretta, who had said that she would visit her mother at the nursing home the next evening. Katherine's response to this message was to turn her head toward the wall. Linda asked if Katherine had any questions, if there was anything she could do. Katherine closed her eyes; then, after a silence, she said, "No." Gently, Linda

249

*asked, "Katherine, are you okay? You seem to be upset. Can we talk about what-
ever is troubling you?" Katherine turned her face even more toward the wall.
When she said, "I am all right," her tone was one of dismissal.*

*Linda was troubled as she left the room. She wondered whether Katherine was
really ready to be discharged from the hospital. Katherine was in pain, and she
was weak and obviously distressed. Linda discussed her concerns with Katherine's nurse, but the nurse said that she had already been in the hospital over
5 days, and that most patients with hip fractures were able to leave in that period
of time. Linda then spoke with her field instructor, who advised her to contact
Katherine's doctor. The physician seemed somewhat annoyed with Linda's call
and indicated that Katherine had used all the days of hospital care allowed by
Medicare. She could recuperate just as readily in the nursing home.*

*Again Linda sought clarification from her field instructor, an experienced so-
cial worker whom Linda admired and respected. Marge O'Brien helped Linda to
review carefully what she had observed in Katherine's behavior. Then Marge explained that Medicare paid the hospital based on diagnosis, and this determined
length of stay. The Business Office had notified the doctor that Katherine was
reaching the end of her predetermined hospital stay. The doctor's discharge plan
for Katherine was final unless it was clearly inappropriate or threatened the patient's well-being. Linda had already alerted the doctor to her concerns, which
was a very important form of advocacy, since the doctor would continue to be responsible for Katherine in the nursing home. Marge was very sensitive to Linda's
concerns about Katherine. Premature hospital discharges were increasing, she
said, because of efforts to reduce the high cost of medical care. Hospital social
workers were increasingly alarmed about the risk to patients. Marge directed
Linda to report her concerns to Katherine's daughter immediately and also to the
social worker at the nursing home.*

*When Linda telephoned Katherine's daughter, Loretta said she was con-
cerned, too, but she felt the doctor must surely know what was best. Linda encouraged Loretta to remain in close contact with the doctor and to advise him of any
change in her mother's condition. Then, as she made ambulance arrangements
and gathered medical information for the nursing home, Linda was alert to any
additional data that she could use to seek a delay in Katherine's discharge. There
were none. Linda faxed the necessary forms and medical records to the nursing
home; then she telephoned the social worker there to report her observations and
her concerns about Katherine.*

*Two days later, when Linda returned to the hospital for her next field place-
ment day, she asked about Katherine. The nursing staff reported that Katherine
had been discharged and returned to the nursing home without incident. Linda
continued to think about Katherine, however, knowing that the discharge to the
nursing home—which was still not "home" for her—and the uncomfortable ambulance ride might have been quite difficult.*

*On Sunday evening Linda picked up the section of the Sunday paper that con-
tained the classified ads and the obituary column. She thought she would check
the advertised social work positions. Suddenly the obituary column caught her attention. There was Katherine! She had died three days after returning to the nursing home. Linda was stunned. She reviewed her telephone call with Katherine's*

daughter, her last conversation with Katherine, and her phone call to the doctor.
Could Katherine's death have been prevented? Had she given up too quickly?
What else could she have done? As she thought about it, Linda realized that it was
possible that Katherine might have had additional health complications after returning to the nursing home. She turned back to the newspaper. Then she recognized the name of another patient who had been discharged recently, and then she
saw another name she knew. Reading on, she counted five recently discharged elderly patients' obituaries. Feeling very troubled, Linda put the newspaper down.
She knew that she would have many more questions to ask her field instructor.

251

CHAPTER 7
*Social Work
in Health Care*

EDUCATIONAL PREPARATION FOR HEALTH CARE PRACTICE

Liberal Arts and the Generalist Professional Curriculum

The deaths of Katherine Lewandowski and other recently discharged patients
raised important questions regarding the hospital's discharge procedures for Linda.
She could sense her thinking shift from a focus on individual patients to a broader
concern about all the hospital's elderly ill patients and the procedures related to
their discharge. Reports of the rapidly changing health care system were frequently discussed in Linda's classes; changes throughout the system would surely
affect vulnerable patients like Katherine Lewandowski. Suddenly Linda began to
appreciate the relevance of the course in social welfare policy that she had taken as
part of her BSW program—and even of the courses in history and political science
that she had taken years earlier as part of the liberal arts requirements of her
school.

Linda's field instructor believed that the hospital's discharge planning needed
to be reevaluated. In fact, Marge O'Brien and the director of the Social Work Department were just about to implement a plan to engage key hospital personnel in
a review of the current discharge planning procedures. As a student in her first
field placement, Linda would participate in but not direct the social work action
that lay ahead. The hospital itself and its mechanisms for changing policies and
procedures would become the target for social work intervention. Data would be
collected to determine mortality rates after discharge. The social work staff would
attempt to engage hospital administrative staff and physicians in an analysis of discharge procedures.

An issue as sensitive as that which Linda and the hospital social workers
were raising could result in a number of heated committee meetings even before a plan to study the discharge mortality linkage might be fully developed.
The chief of medical staff and the administrator of the hospital would want to
protect the hospital from adverse publicity. Linda was aware, too, that policy
created at the federal level regarding Medicare payment to hospitals strongly
influenced the procedures related to discharge planning at St. Anne's, for hospitals depended on reimbursements from Medicare and Medicaid. The policies of
these federal programs would remain a strong consideration if hospital administration wished to develop new procedures related to the discharge of elderly
ill patients.

While Linda assisted the social workers from St. Anne's Hospital with the review of discharge-planning policies, she would assist and learn from them as they continued their regular professional responsibilities. This included seeing patients on a one-to-one basis to counsel, to intervene in crises, and to help families with discharge plans. Often, too, Linda and the social workers referred patients and their families to other community resources, such as nutrition or hot meal programs and substance abuse treatment. Generally, hospital social workers did not engage in long-term counseling with individual patients; therefore, patients who needed ongoing, intensive counseling were referred to local social service agencies or to private practitioners in social work, psychology, or psychiatry. Some hospital social work staff worked with groups of patients such as those newly diagnosed with cancer or who were dependent on alcohol or drugs. One social worker had developed a support group for people who had had strokes and for their friends and families. As a field placement student, Linda was able to acquire group work skills by assisting with the group. Linda's field placement gave her a strong sense of growing professional competence.

Births and deaths, accidents and injuries, acute illnesses and chronic diseases—these are the concerns in health care settings. Social workers must have a solid knowledge base if they are to further other health care team members' understanding of the emotional factors in illness. Coursework in the liberal arts provides a basic understanding of the biological sciences as well as the social, psychological, and cultural sciences. As we saw in Chapter 1, unlike the training of other health care providers, the social worker's professional education stresses the person within his or her environment. The generalist social worker is prepared to intervene with individual persons, like Katherine Lewandowski; with entire families

Poverty places families, especially children, at risk of malnutrition, disease, and accidents.

or with selected family members (Katherine's daughter, for example); with small groups; with organizations (like St. Anne's Hospital); and with large groups, neighborhoods, and communities.

Social work students begin their education with liberal arts courses in such areas as literature, writing, philosophy, sociology, and psychology. By the sophomore and junior years, the curriculum includes professional courses in practice methods, research, human behavior in the social environment, cultural diversity, and social policy. The liberal arts courses teach students to think critically, to question, and to analyze. They also provide knowledge about human beings, society, and different cultures that professional courses later build upon. This is especially true of the courses in human behavior and social policy. Coursework in practice methods provides the skill base and the knowledge of social work practice theory that leads to competent social work practice in health care or other settings. Beginning in the second semester of the junior year or in the senior year, baccalaureate students spend a minimum of 400 hours in field work. It is in field work that all the theory is applied and that students acquire the competence to practice social work when they graduate.

Hospitals like St. Anne's generally employ both BSW and MSW social workers. MSWs generally staff specialized services such as cardiac intensive care and neonatal nurseries because of their complex nature and immediacy of the services needed by patients and families. Especially fast-paced areas such as ER (emergency room) also require very skilled, experienced social workers; except in small hospitals and sometimes in rural areas, MSWs are given these responsibilities. The MSW curriculum is also based on liberal arts preparation and a generalist perspective, but advanced, specialized courses are also taken.

Values and Ethics

Hospitals and other health care settings work daily with frightened, hurting, vulnerable people. As organizational systems, hospitals often deliver services in ways that seem cruel and heartless to patients. Social workers in health care, guided by the values of the profession, can help to humanize the health care environment for people and teach staff how to individualize patients. Among the values that the profession holds are regard for individual worth and dignity, the right of people to participate in the helping process, and the right of clients to make decisions that will affect them.

These values and the code of ethics of the National Association of Social Workers were introduced in Chapter 1. The code of ethics, which is reprinted in the Appendix of this text and incorporated in social work students' coursework, provides guidelines that further support ethical social work practice. Health care is a field of practice that challenges social workers to sustain their commitment to professional values and ethics. The health care environment is itself sometimes contradictory to social work values. This is especially true when the policies of our country, our states, and even our employers' insurance companies eliminate or reduce access to health care for poor persons.

Linda Sanders, the student social worker in this chapter's case study, was shocked by Katherine Lewandowski's death and the deaths of several other patients. As a social worker, she valued Katherine and the others, even though she did not know them. She was startled by the serious questions of ethics and values in this case. Was Katherine discharged from the hospital prematurely? If so, why? Were there compelling circumstances related to her ability to pay for extended hospitalization? If so, what was the nature of the policies and procedures that resulted in her premature discharge? Were they created by the doctor, by the hospital, or by governmental regulations? Is it right that some patients may die because they are discharged from the hospital too soon? If the patient (or family)—encouraged by the social worker—challenged the order for discharge, would there be an economic threat to the patient, the doctor, and the hospital? Would there be a threat to the continuation of the social work student—or of the social work services department that initiated the challenge? Clearly these are questions of social and economic justice!

Biomedical ethics is not a concern for physicians alone. Social workers too, especially those in the health care field, encounter ethical and value-laden issues in daily practice. Often social workers assist patients and families with decisions about continued use of life-support systems for terminally ill persons or for profoundly disabled infants. Social workers frequently serve as the "conscience" of institutions as they challenge policies and procedures that have negative impacts on people. That, in fact, is the role assumed by Linda and the social work staff at St. Anne's Hospital after the death of Katherine Lewandowski. Students preparing for careers in social work develop an understanding of moral and ethical problems through liberal arts courses, such as philosophy and theology, and through content regarding ethics and values in their social work courses.

The Community and Populations-at-Risk

The health care social worker is the essential link between the patient, the health care facility (whether hospital, clinic, health department, or nursing home), and the community and its resources. The social worker's professional education includes the history and development of social policy and social welfare programs (privately sponsored as well as governmental). Social workers learn to analyze and critique policy and how to affect the creation of policies and programs.

Knowledge of the community means more than a mere listing of community resources, which would be available to any hospital employee. Truly understanding the community means understanding the diverse racial and ethnic groups that make up that community, their traditional beliefs about illness and health care, and any special "healers" that people might turn to. The faith and spiritual values of the community must be understood and respected by social workers. Often such values are the one vital, sustaining source of strength for a patient or a family. In health settings social work has traditionally been the professional discipline that interprets the ethnic, class, or cultural roots of beliefs and behaviors that have influenced patients' responses to illness. Armed with knowledge of cultural diversity and the community, social workers sometimes help families to design remarkably creative plans for posthospital care or as an alternative to nursing home placement.

There has been a long history of disparity of health services to lower-class and minority people in the United States. Of serious concern to social workers are the poor (especially members of racial and ethnic minority groups), people with disabilities, and suspected AIDS carriers. These are populations that are seriously at risk, since some health care professionals avoid or even refuse to treat them (Reamer, 1993). The number of underinsured poor and middle-class persons is increasing, too. It has become extremely difficult for social workers to locate health services for persons in poverty and those without adequate health insurance. Sometimes it is even difficult to sustain contact with culturally diverse patients whose needs are not met or whose health care has been delivered in an insensitive, disrespectful manner. As Devore and Schlesinger point out, "advocating for the poor, for those who do not speak English, and for those who have greater faith in the spirits than in modern medicine requires a high degree of self-awareness and comfort with the identity 'social worker' " (1987, p. 260).

For social work students, awareness and appreciation of human diversity and community norms is built gradually. This learning starts with the liberal arts courses taken in the freshman and sophomore years. Courses in literature, history, political science, and sociology help prepare social work students to understand the influences of class, gender, race, and ethnicity. Students begin to understand such concepts as social norms and roles, and to appreciate the rich contributions of many cultures to contemporary society. Social work courses taken in the junior and senior years further prepare students for practice within the community and with a variety of populations. The field practicum that concludes the baccalaureate-degree program enables students to demonstrate competent social work practice, not in a classroom but out in the community.

Continuing Professional Education

The nature of the health care setting—rural versus metropolitan, pediatric clinic versus HIV/AIDS program, Lutheran or Jewish hospital versus county hospital—calls for additional learning. The generalist social worker entering practice will learn both on the job and through any specialized courses, workshops, or seminars that might be available. The need to learn does not end here. The constant need to learn more is one of the challenges of health care social work, even for very experienced social workers.

Rapid changes in the U.S. health care system, evolution in health care delivery (outpatient surgeries, for example), and new social work practice theory and methods all demand ongoing educational development. The licensure or certification laws of many states also require that social workers provide proof that they have engaged in continuing education. In those states, all social workers will seek out appropriate learning opportunities. Health care social workers may look for conferences, workshops, seminars, or university courses specifically related to the client population they work with.

There are other, less formal ways too for social workers to continue their learning. Across the country, nursing home social workers have formed regional groups to keep up to date about changing regulations and to sponsor annual conferences for their own professional growth. The American Hospital Association has special programs for hospital social work directors. The National Association of Social Workers conducts an annual national conference and also provides an array of local and statewide seminars with valuable educational content for health care social workers.

Professional literature also provides essential ongoing learning, and the health care field has several excellent journals, among them *Health & Social Work,* published by the NASW, and *Social Work and Health Care,* published by Haworth Press. Journals are vital for career-long development of social workers. They offer cutting-edge research, new ideas, and clearly articulated professional viewpoints.

HEALTH CARE SERVICES

Linda Sanders's social work field placement was in a community general hospital, but hospitals are not the only health care settings that employ social workers. The U.S. health care system, fueled by a desire to sustain profitability while controlling rapid increases in health care costs, created a wide variety of new health care ventures in the 1990s. In metropolitan areas, many inner-city hospitals were abandoned or closed and public health services were cut back. Meanwhile, mergers and acquisitions of hospitals, nursing homes, subacute centers, HMOs, pharmacies, and diagnostic testing centers created giant, profitable, in some cases multinational health care corporations (Weiss, 1997). Users of health care and all of the health care professions have been impacted by these changes. Dramatic change in health care is likely to continue.

The result of ongoing change throughout the system is that social workers may now be found in a very wide variety of health care settings (see Exhibit 1 for a sampling of settings). As the list of settings suggests, social work is a viable profession in a growing number of health-related community organizations. Studies reported in Chapter 1 done by NASW and the Association of Baccalaureate Social Work Program Directors showed that many BSW and MSW social workers are employed in the health field (NASW Practice Research Network, 2000; Rogers et al., 1999).

Settings for Health Care Social Work

EXHIBIT 1

General hospitals	Women's health centers
Children's hospitals and other specialized hospitals	Health planning boards
Physicians' offices	Specialized health organizations (American Cancer Society, National Kidney Foundation)
Public health clinics	
Health maintenance organizations (HMOs)	Hospice programs
	Insurance companies
Rehabilitation services	Private social work practice
Nursing homes and subacute centers	Homeless shelter health clinics
Home health care organizations	Outpatient clinics

Acute Care

The majority of health care social workers today are employed in **acute care** (facilities that provide immediate, short-term care): hospitals, inpatient and outpatient clinics, rehabilitation centers, **hospice** programs (which care for terminally ill persons in environments that are less restrictive than hospitals), and **subacute centers.** Subacute centers provide intensive medical services for people who do not need to remain in the hospital but also may not need, or hopefully can avoid, long-term care. Subacute care—while lengthier and somewhat less expensive than hospitalization—is fast paced. Subacute care facilities are relatively new and not available in all communities. This is one of the areas in which evolution in the nation's health care systems has produced a new area for social work practice.

> Services provided by the acute care social worker are usually short-term, episodic, and intensive, because average length of stay in acute care is now less than two days. Service functions traditionally include social risk screening, discharge planning, psychosocial interventions, case consultation, collaboration, health education, information and referral, quality assurance, agency planning, program consultation, and community planning. (Poole, 1995, p. 1162)

Hospital social work is changing dramatically, as hospitals themselves are changing. Once there were hospital social work departments headed up by MSW social workers. Now social workers are employed by hospitals but they often work out of designated units such as cardiac intensive care, the spinal cord injury area, or the unit that cares for high-risk newborns (neonatal intensive care). Social work service to hospital emergency rooms is taking on increased importance. Twenty-four-hour social work staffing is now provided in many busy metropolitan hospitals. Nonetheless, as Keigher states, "hospitals no longer dominate the field [of health care]. Indeed, they have become remarkably limited, providing mainly specialty treatment and highly technological diagnostics" (Keigher, 2000, p. 7). The shift away from hospitals to outpatient, community-based, and in-home health services means that hospital social work is evolving into a broader concept: health care social work.

The National Association of Social Workers has developed a policy statement that addresses some of the political issues related to health care. The statement (see Exhibit 2) is based on social work values and principles. It clearly supports the right of all persons to a full range of health care services.

Long-Term Care

Although most people think of a nursing home when they think about long-term care, a growing number of services are, in fact, included within the purview of long-term care. In addition to nursing homes, some of the community-based services include "home health care, homemaker and chore services, transportation, home-delivered meals, adult day care, visitation, and telephone reassurance" (Garner, 1995, p. 1625). **Long-term care** consists of any combination of nursing, personal care, volunteer, and social services provided intermittently or on a sustained basis over a span of time to help persons with chronic illness or disability to maintain maximum quality of life.

NASW Policy Statement on Health Care

EXHIBIT 2

PROMOTING THE RIGHT TO HEALTH CARE

NASW supports a national health care policy that ensures the right to universal access to a continuum of health and mental health care to promote wellness, maintain optimal health, prevent illness and disability, treat health conditions, ameliorate the effects of unavoidable incapacities, and provide supportive long-term and end-of-life care. These policies are based on the principle of universality available to all people in the United States, regardless of financial status, race, ethnicity, disability, religion, age, gender, sexual orientation, or geographic location.

NASW supports:

- Efforts to enlarge health care coverage to uninsured and underinsured people until universal health and mental health coverage is achieved.
- Economic, social, occupational, and environmental policies that contribute to maintaining health, recognizing the relationship between these factors and quality and longevity of life.
- Giving all patients the opportunity to retain or regain their social roles and functional capacities within the limits of their mental, physical, sensory, and chronic condition.
- Giving all patients and their families necessary and appropriate care and benefits.
- A mandatory assessment and follow-up services by a social worker for any patients deemed high risk, including those experiencing a life-threatening disease or with a chronic and/or acute diagnosis.
- Mandating the provision of health and mental health care for all people regardless of employment status.
- Ensuring that payment systems are financially neutral, so that service providers neither lose nor make money based on whether they provide or withhold treatment.
- Ensuring that patients receive necessary and appropriate care, including social work services.

Source: R. W. Mayden & J. Nieves (2000). Health care. Policy statement approved by the NASW Delegate Assembly, August 1999. *Social work speaks: National Association of Social Workers policy statements 2000–2003.* Washington, DC: NASW Press, 153–154.

Not all users of long-term care are the elderly, but with the population of older persons increasing, a growing segment of long-term care consumers are likely to be older persons. **Cost containment** concerns—concerns about the need to control rising health care costs—have limited the funding available for home-based care from both Medicare and private insurance. These programs and Medicaid are more likely to provide for nursing home care. Social work researchers among others have pointed to the need to lower the eligibility requirements to accommodate larger numbers of persons in community-based care (Robert & Norgard, 1996; Slivinski, Fitch, & Wingerson, 1998).

Nursing homes are one of the most common forms of long-term care. In the United States a large portion of nursing homes are owned by proprietary (for-profit) corporations. There are also private, nonprofit homes (some operated by religious denominations) plus federal (Veterans Administration), state, and county public facilities. Nursing homes are licensed by the state. Nursing services are provided 24 hours per day, augmented by physical, occupational, and activity therapists, dieticians, and social workers, among others.

The newest development in long-term care is assisted living facilities for older adults who are fairly independent. Assisted living units are often attached to existing nursing homes, thus providing for a range of care, depending on need. Assisted living is an evolving area for social work practice and an interesting one. Residents of assisted living have intellectual, social, political, and spiritual interests and considerable capacity to enjoy them, thus making field trips, even travel, a possibility. Groups of many kinds can be used by creative social workers to meet the social, intellectual, and emotional needs of residents.

The NASW listing of clinical indicators for social work in nursing homes identifies the following as major functions and services that are provided by social workers:

1. Facilitating the admissions process.
2. Developing an individualized plan of care.
3. Facilitating the social and psychological well-being of residents and their families.
4. Involving the entire facility in meeting psychosocial needs of residents.
5. Planning discharges to ensure appropriateness and continuity of care for transfers within and discharges from the nursing home. (1993, pp. 4–5)

In thinking about the ways in which social workers implement the NASW clinical indicators policy statement, we can recall the case study from the beginning of this chapter. We might ask: What might the nursing home social worker have done at the time of Katherine Lewandowski's admission to the nursing home to help this elderly woman? If social history information had been obtained at the time of admission, the social worker would have learned that Katherine Lewandowski had a very strong sense of family, of identity with her Polish ethnicity, and of faith in the Catholic religion. The social worker would have understood the cultural origin of Katherine Lewandowski's sense of abandonment: the highly valued Polish custom of caring for elderly persons within the family, with nursing home placement used only as a final resort. The social worker would also have recognized that Katherine's despair was heightened by significant losses: the death of her husband five years ago, the death of a son from cancer 18 months ago, and the loss of control over her own body as she became increasingly frail and handicapped by osteoporosis.

Katherine Lewandowski could have benefited from encouragement and reassurance provided by the social worker during frequent visits to her room and also to the hospital when Katherine had surgery. The social worker could have helped other nursing home staff to understand Katherine and to be more sensitive to her needs. The activities staff, for example, could have been urged to engage Katherine in socialization activities with other Polish women in the nursing home, thereby helping her to reestablish her sense of identity and linkage to a familiar community. The Catholic chaplain or a priest from Katherine's parish might have been a significant resource, helping her to find comfort in her faith and thereby engage another source of strength. Too often the spiritual life of clients is ignored in hospitals and nursing homes.

Nursing home social work offers unique opportunities for long-term involvement with people during a phase in their lives when many crises may occur. This area of social work practice also offers opportunities to work with families and with groups, to provide education for resident care staff, and to be one of the decision makers that influences the organization's policies and procedures. Nursing home social workers have remarkable opportunities to become very strong advocates for their clients.

Home Health Care

Home health care is the provision of health care services, including social services, to people in their own homes. The resurgence of home health care in recent years has been generated by economic concerns, by the growing number of terminally ill elderly and AIDS patients, and by humanitarian interests that seek to provide care to loved ones within the comfort and security of their own homes.

Home health services are provided by large organizations such as the Visiting Nurse Association, by hospitals, by public health departments, and by proprietary corporations. Social workers are key members of the home care team today. They help family members, especially those in caregiver roles, to work through their feelings of frustration, anger, grief, and pain. Supporting the family and preventing personal and group breakdown during the caregiving time is an objective of the social workers. They also help the family to locate needed resources, such as financial aid and bedside nursing equipment. Others routinely on the team are physicians, who provide supervision, and nurses. Ancillary staff often include homemakers, physical therapists, and dieticians.

With their professional colleagues, home care social workers increasingly deal with ethical dilemmas related to questions about how much autonomy and self-determination to support with elderly persons who have physical or cognitive disabilities, or when family caregivers become overburdened (Healy, 1998). Home health hospice programs—which now serve children and adults of all ages with AIDS, cancer, and heart disease—raise similar ethical questions. Nonetheless, this is a growing field of service and one that offers considerable satisfaction as well as challenges.

Primary Care

Primary care, often referred to as "first contact care," is health care provided in the community by health care professionals trained to assess and treat routine health care needs. Today these professionals are primarily family care physicians, internists, pediatricians, and, to a limited degree, nurse practitioners and physician assistants. Care is normally provided by HMOs, in physicians' offices or clinics, in outpatient departments of hospitals, or in public community health programs.

Although most public community health programs and hospital outpatient departments employ social workers, growth in employment of social workers in physicians' offices has been limited by lack of insurance coverage for social work services. As cost containment policies continue to evolve, however, it is possible that the use of nurse practitioners and other allied health professionals such as social workers will grow (Oktay, 1995).

HMOs

The list of settings for social work in health care that was provided earlier in this chapter included **health maintenance organizations** (HMOs). Today much of our health care is delivered through HMOs' systems that contract with employers to provide a wide range of health care services for employees for a set monthly fee. The membership rolls of HMOs also include large numbers of Medicare and Medicaid patients. The physicians and other medical staff, including social workers, are employed by the organization, or they may be paid on a fee-for-service basis.

The social work services provided by the HMO staff are very similar to the kinds of services provided by social workers in hospital settings: evaluations, counseling (including crisis intervention and brief therapy), pre- and posthospital planning (in conjunction with the hospital's social worker), preliminary screening of patients referred for psychiatric treatment, and referral to community resources. Some of the specific problems that social workers in HMOs deal with include issues related to newly diagnosed or ongoing illness (cancer, HIV, kidney disease, and others), anxiety and depressive disorders, family problems, and substance abuse (Health Key Medical Group, 1986).

Insurance Corporations

Financing of the United States health care system today functions primarily through health insurance corporations. Because of buyouts and mergers in the 1990s these are increasingly large, often multinational corporations. Employers and private persons purchase insurance through these corporations, which assume responsibility for contracts with and payment to health care providers. Even the federal government Medicare and Medicaid programs use private insurance corporations as their carriers.

A very interesting new development in health care social work is the establishment of social work departments within insurance companies. Julie Litza, who has a BSW plus a master's degree in Health Administration, directs the Healthy Baby Project with UnitedHealth Group. With a staff of two BSWs and a field placement student, Julie provides preventive care for the insurance company's Medicaid subscribers immediately following the birth of a baby. Educational information is shared with the mother at the hospital prior to discharge or in followup telephone contacts; mailed information is a final resort. Mothers are assisted with names of primary care physicians for their babies, with the paperwork needed to obtain Medicaid care for the new baby, with information about lead screening, and with any other community service referrals needed. Julie designed the Healthy Baby Project as well as recently implemented prenatal care coordination and a child care coordination program that provide home visits and case management services from social workers. These programs are funded by the state Medicaid program. Now on the drawing board is another social service program for persons 15 years of age or older who have disabilities (personal interview, July 23, 2001).

HEALTH CARE IN RURAL AREAS

The nature of the community in which health care is provided is also significant in contemporary social work practice. Health care facilities in rural areas, for example, often require considerable community involvement from the social worker. In rural settings social workers call on all their generalist practice skills as they work with families and communities to provide care following hospitalization or to help people obtain health care. Long distances between health centers, isolated dwellings, poverty, and lack of transportation make it difficult for many rural people to obtain high-quality health care. Pregnant rural women, for example, are at increased risk because they often have inadequate access to prenatal care. Their generalist practice skills were enormously helpful to several Pennsylvania social workers when they organized rural community leaders and developed health and social services for pregnant women. Included were a mobile unit for prenatal care, an information and referral service, health education, and clinical care and follow-up services (Pistella, Bonati, & Mihalic, 1999).

Hospitals in rural areas or small towns generally have no more than 50 to 100 beds. Complex and expensive medical services such as **hemodialysis** (a procedure to cleanse the blood of persons with chronic kidney disease) are often not provided. The severe financial pressure experienced by small hospitals is apparent in the following statement:

> The existence of rural hospitals is financially tenuous due to the Prospective Payment system, which differentially reimburses rural facilities at lower rates than urban facilities. Physicians and hospital social workers provide services within these severely cost-conscious organizations to patients from communities, which are also aftercare resource poor. (Egan & Kadushin, 1997, p. 1)

Usually the hospital employs only one or two social workers. Generalist practice skills are vital. Social workers in small health care facilities have to be very knowledgeable about the local community and its resources. Often, when needed resources such as home health care are not available, the social worker helps to create them or calls on clergy, police, or neighbors for assistance. In small towns friends, neighbors, and coworkers sometimes provide exceptional help, as this single mother of a son with AIDS explains:

> And then when he was deteriorating so bad in December, I just decided that I needed to be at home with him. I was given an open-ended leave, and when my accumulated hours of pay were used up, they let people donate hours to me, and I never lost a paycheck. I work with a really super group of people . . . very caring, very giving. (McGinn, 1996, p. 276)

Rural communities sometimes lack information about medical conditions such as AIDS. This may exacerbate existing lack of tolerance for diversity. Sometimes negative responses to people who are HIV-positive stem from concerns about contagion and also from moral judgments that derive from very strong reli-

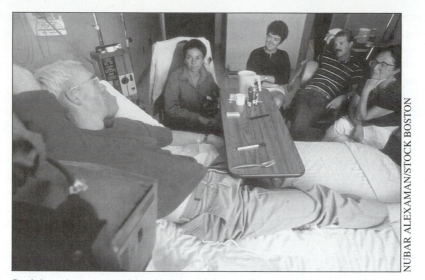

NUBAR ALEXAMAN/STOCK BOSTON

Social worker meets with spinal cord injury patient and his family.

gious values. Social work support for the patient and family then is needed to deal with the emotional burden, with social isolation, and also with the lack of resources in the community (McGinn, 1996).

The rural health care facility—a rehabilitation center, hospital, or nursing home—often serves people from a very large geographical area. The social worker must have a good understanding of several counties' welfare and human service resources. One county may have a Meals on Wheels program, for example, while another does not or can provide only general nutrition but no special diets (such as a diabetic diet). A large geographical area may also mean long-distance travel for the social worker when a home visit is needed.

Social workers in rural health care settings often work independently without the support of social work colleagues in similar settings in the area. Professional isolation is a problem. Even within the health facility the social worker must make decisions without the assistance of a social work supervisor, consultant, or another social worker. Continuing education programs of the NASW and the American Hospital Association provide important support. In many areas regional organizations have sprung up and are often the rural social worker's professional lifeline.

EMERGENCY ROOM: TRAUMA AND CRISIS AMIDST HUMAN DIVERSITY

Hospitals that operate large, active emergency care facilities employ social workers on all shifts, seven days a week. In smaller facilities, social workers staff emergency rooms during periods of high demand and they function on an on-call basis during less busy periods. Every television viewer knows well the life-and-death drama of the hospital emergency room. For the social worker, emergency room practice means fast-paced crisis intervention work and brief contact with clients. For example, the 17-year-old who took an overdose of aspirin when her boyfriend threatened to end their relationship needs someone to help her sort out her embarrassment and shame, after the aspirin has been removed from her stomach. The social worker makes a rapid assessment of the young woman's psychosocial situation and determines that referral for counseling is needed both for the young woman and for her family.

Consider another example: A five-year-old boy is treated for multiple fractures suffered in a car accident. He will be admitted to the hospital after receiving initial care in the emergency room. Every 15 minutes the social worker provides information to the parents—information obtained from the doctors and nurses who are with the boy. The parents, a young Puerto Rican couple, show their immense concern about their son very openly. The wife, who is pregnant, is extremely nervous and is breathing irregularly, and she appears to be about to have an *ataque* (an episode similar to a seizure; *ataques* are sometimes experienced during periods of severe emotional stress and are recognized in the Puerto Rican culture as a cry for help). The husband's anger with the hit-and-run driver who injured his son takes the form of angry threats, loudly voiced, and of demands that the hospital staff do something to save his son. The social worker provides emotional support to the parents and helps them to a room where they have more privacy and where additional family members can be with them as soon as the social worker is able to contact them.

Before the evening ends, the social worker will also have helped a 55-year-old white middle-class woman whose husband's life could not be saved following his third heart attack; an elderly Catholic nun who required admission to the hospital because of pneumonia; and a poor, inner-city African American mother and infant who were hungry and whose heat had been turned off by the landlord for nonpayment of rent. The emergency room social worker interpreted medical information to waiting families, offered psychological strength, demonstrated concern and caring, confronted inappropriate behavior, used crisis counseling techniques, and connected people with needed community resources. In addition, the social worker helped the doctors and caregivers to understand and appreciate the cultural dimensions that influenced patients' responses to pain and their families' responses to crisis.

When disaster strikes a community, as it did in Washington, D.C., and New York City in 2001, hospital emergency rooms receive injured and psychologically traumatized patients. All hospitals have disaster plans, so social workers and other staff know their roles in advance. Emergency care of medical needs must take priority, of course. Social workers are important members of the team. They assess and comfort children and adults whose injuries do not appear to require immediate care, if all medical staff are needed for more seriously injured persons. They provide emotional assistance to persons whose trauma is threatening their mental health status. In fact, they provide many of the psychosocial services for persons in acute traumatic or posttraumatic stress that were described in Chapter 6.

In Israel, where terrorist attacks and bombardment occur with some frequency, hospital social workers' responsibilities during disasters are likely to include:

- Psychosocial assessment and intervention for people arriving with problems primarily psychological in nature.
- Counseling and support to injured persons whose stress includes fear of dying, grief over the death of a coworker or family member, inability to lo-

cate family members or friends or to know their fate, behavioral outbursts reflecting their stress but impeding health care staff, fear of abandonment or of overwhelming terror.

- Preparation of family members for their encounters with medical staff and with the disaster victim.
- Liaison between family members and health care professionals.
- Collaboration with community resources to provide emergency shelter, food, and other needs (Shahar, 1993).

Social workers' well-developed interdisciplinary teamwork relationships are extremely valuable when serious emergencies strike. The experience and expertise hospital social workers develop in their day-to-day work with persons who are ill, injured, dying, or recovering from surgery and facing a bright new future—all of this serves the social worker, the health care team, and traumatized persons who are helped during times of disaster.

THE OUTPATIENT CLINIC: A SICKLE-CELL DISEASE GROUP

People with chronic diseases like some forms of sickle-cell anemia need comprehensive, continuing professional care. The fragmentation of the health care system today—along with the complex psychosocial ramifications of sickle-cell anemia—reduce the likelihood that patients will actually receive the consistency of care they need. **Sickle-cell anemia** is an inherited blood disorder. It occurs in all populations of the world, but in the United States it is most common among African Americans. When the disease is in an acute phase, moderate to severe pain occurs, sometimes with complications requiring blood transfusions and other intervention. The frequency of acute phases varies; some persons are able to function normally and manage to control pain with oral medication, while other people experience frequent, severe pain with major debilitating complications, including leg ulcers, kidney and bone disease, and strokes. There is no known cure for sickle-cell disease.

Dennis Butler, a social worker, and Lou Beltran, a physician, formed an education group for patients who—although dependent on an outpatient clinic for health care—were angry and dissatisfied; the resident family practice physicians who provided the medical care saw them as noncompliant, as exaggerating their pain, and as wanting drugs. Although the group was designed to educate the patients and family members about the disease, the family practice residents were invited to participate. Many did so, with quite beneficial results (1993).

The group was formatted as a five-session educational program and was offered twice in a two-year period. Attendance ranged from 8 to 24 persons; the groups met for 1 1/2 to 2 hours. Like most groups, there were complications. When educational materials that were used initially did not work well for the patients, a subgroup decided to review the handouts and recommend more appropriate materials. This was important because many of the patients had little understanding of sickle-cell anemia beyond what they had learned from other clinic patients. Common misconceptions were that sickle-cell disease was contagious and that even today most persons with the disease died in their twenties. The topics covered in this group are outlined in Exhibit 3.

Topics for an Education-Focused Group: Sickle-Cell Disease

EXHIBIT 3

SESSION 1: INTRODUCTION

Who gets sickle-cell disease and why?

Sickle-cell disease and sickle-cell trait

Sickle-cell myths

SESSION 2: MANIFESTATIONS

Pain crisis

Sepsis [pus-forming, or pathogenic, organisms in the blood]

Hemolytic disease [one in which the body destroys its own red blood cells]

Aplastic crisis [critical episode requiring immediate care]

Others

SESSION 3: TREATMENT AND PREVENTION

Acute medical care:

    Hydration [ensuring proper balance of body fluids]

    Pain medication

    Transfusions

    Relaxation techniques

Screening

SESSION 4: PSYCHOSOCIAL ASPECTS

Developmental delays

Impact on the family

Depression, anxiety

SESSION 5: COMMUNITY RESOURCES

Medical

Vocational

Disability

Counseling

Source: D. J. Butler & L. R. Beltran. (1993). Functions of an adult sickle-cell group: Education, task orientation, and support. *Health & Social Work, 18(1),* p. 51. Definitions in brackets are those of this text's authors.

Group interaction was strong. The members developed an informal telephone support network to keep each other informed when a group member was in crisis. Some group members had as many as 12 to 15 hospitalizations a year, and three young group members died unexpectedly when in acute pain crises. The group leaders, because they were on the staff of the medical facility, often advocated with other physicians, nurses, and staff on behalf of group members. The group, over time, resulted in improved physician–patient relationships. Patients learned to express their fears. Participating residents gained increased understanding of the patients and greater sensitivity to them.

SOCIAL WELFARE POLICY AND PROGRAMS IN HEALTH

Social work practice occurs within a political context and political systems profoundly influence health care. The health care system in the United States is not a uniform national program designed to dispense resources as widely as possible, as is the case in most other industrialized countries. Instead, the U.S. system is a conglomerate of large and small public and private programs, institutions, services, and payment plans. Reflecting the larger U.S. political, economic, and social systems, health care is primarily a for-profit system with governmental programs such as Medicare supporting and mixing with private enterprise. Rising costs and unequal access to care have made health care issues especially volatile in contemporary American politics. These contemporary concerns have deep roots in history.

Early History: Caring for the Poor and Sick

It is not clear when health care institutions were developed, but archaeologists have uncovered ruins of what may have been such facilities dating from the sixth century B.C. The tithing of the early Christians produced funds that churches could use for the care of the poor and the sick. Around the third century A.D., monks of the Roman Catholic Church began to provide rescue service and health care to avalanche victims in shelters known as hospices. The victims were mostly southern Europeans who were fleeing from famine and economic hardship and were trying to reach northern regions in search of a better life. They were unfamiliar with and unprepared for the harsh weather of the mountains. Gradually the term *hospice* came to be used for institutions that cared for ill persons. In western Europe hospices housed not only the sick but, until almshouses were organized, the poor as well. Gradually hospices developed into larger institutions that were run primarily by religious orders of priests or sisters. (Even today, in most of Europe, a nurse is called "sister.") In England during the mid-1500s, monasteries were confiscated by the Crown in the historic dispute between Henry VIII and Rome. With the seizure of religious holdings, the settings that cared for the sick were gradually converted into publicly held institutions.

Origins of Health Care Social Work

The English forerunners of today's health care social workers were the **lady almoners,** persons who provided food and donations to the poor. In 1895 a lady almoner was stationed at the Royal Free Hospital with the understanding that she was to interview patients to determine who would receive free, or partly free, medical service, "and to exclude those unsuitable for free care. But in serving this restricted purpose the worker was soon aware that many patients accepted for medical treatment were in sore social difficulties as well" (Cannon, 1952, p. 8). This early social worker, like many today, preferred to define the nature of her professional practice herself, rather than permitting hospital authorities, physicians, or others to govern how she understood and carried out her professional responsibilities. In fact, she became an advocate for patients, fighting for the rights and needs of the poor and underserved, those whom the Royal Free Hospital saw as "unsuitable." The use of social workers spread throughout British Commonwealth hospitals, and their role soon broadened to include advocacy, referral to other community resources, patient education, and counseling.

The Emergence of Medical Social Work in the United States

The person who is generally considered the originator of medical social work in the United States is Ida Cannon. As a young woman, Ida Cannon had worked as a visiting nurse in the slum areas along the Mississippi River in St. Paul, Minnesota. Inspired by Jane Addams, the great settlement house worker, Cannon became interested in social work and went to Boston to pursue her studies at the Boston School of Social Work. In 1905 Dr. Richard Cabot, whose concerns about poverty and its impact on illness paralleled her own, asked Ida Cannon to join the staff of Massachusetts General Hospital.

In her professional practice, Cannon was not only a competent social worker but also a dynamic leader, a teacher of medical and social work students, and an articulate author. Health care social workers were the first among the various social work specialty groups to organize professionally. Ida Cannon was among the founders of the American Association of Hospital Social Workers in 1918. This organization, later known as the American Association of Medical Social Workers (AAMSW), published its own journal, *Medical Social Work.* The AAMSW eventually merged with other independent social work organizations to become the National Association of Social Workers (NASW) in 1955. Cannon's 1952 text, *On the Social Frontier of Medicine: Pioneering in Medical Social Service,* describes the early years of hospital social work.

Soon after Ida Cannon developed the social service department at Massachusetts General Hospital, Bellevue Hospital in New York hired a social worker. Slowly hospitals across the country, including specialized facilities, copied these examples. Public health concerns about patients with tuberculosis and venereal disease resulted in employment of social workers by state health departments and tuberculosis sanatoriums. The passage of the Social Security Act in 1935 resulted in entitlements that further encouraged the expansion of social work in health care settings. Both the American Hospital Association (AHA) and the American Public Health Association developed standards and requirements for social workers in the facilities they regulated.

THE POLITICS AND ECONOMICS OF HEALTH CARE

By 1905 when Ida Cannon initiated the first hospital social work department, the U.S. health care system had evolved from one delivered by women within their own households relying primarily on homemade medical preparations, to an industry dominated by specialized professionals, pharmaceutical corporations, and institutions. Massive hospitals, first built during the Civil War, utilized new techniques of hygiene and by the early 1900s vastly increased the number of surgical procedures performed, thanks to the development of diagnostic X-rays and anesthesia.

By the 1940s "former charity hospitals transformed themselves into profit-making, or surplus-generating (among the nonprofit institutions) businesses, increasingly dependent on cash-paying customers and third-party payers (for example, insurers)" (Weiss, 1997, p. 13). Blue Cross and Blue Shield, instituted in the 1930s, were controlled by hospitals and physicians, thereby ensuring payment for medical services delivered by the private sector. Public health services, which had served the nation through several waves of infectious diseases and provided health care to low-income populations, were politically crushed by the strength of the entrepreneurial health care industry.

> By the 1960s, however, it was clear that private health insurance was not capable of providing benefits to large numbers of people and that it was not capable of containing costs. At the same time, nationwide pressure was building for national health insurance. (Weiss, 1997, p. 86)

Medicare

The federal government's involvement in health care financing became a reality in the 1960s with the enactment of the programs known as Medicare and Medicaid. Medicare was created in 1965 with an amendment, Title XVIII, to the Social Security Act. Labor unions strongly supported this legislation while the American Medical Association (AMA), the AHA, "and the insurance industry engaged in a bitter, vitriolic battle to keep government out of health care. These interests perceived government involvement as a threat to the realization of maximum profit and to professional autonomy" (Weiss, 1997, p. 153). It may be that the compromises made to secure passage of Medicare are partially responsible for some of the program's current problems with skyrocketing costs, fraudulent charges by health care providers, and mismanagement. Compromises won by the AMA and the AHA included limiting government control over reimbursements for services and, a major victory, allowing for Blue Cross and Blue Shield (and other insurance companies) to be the conduit for payments made to providers.

Medicare currently covers 39 million Americans who are:

- People who are 65 years old.
- People who are disabled.
- People with permanent kidney failure (Medicare, p. 1).

Medicare is divided into two parts. Part A provides insurance for hospital care and 100 days in a nursing home. Medicare comes from payroll taxes paid while people are working; however, it is definitely not free. It requires substantial co-payments (approximately $200 a day for hospitalization beyond 60 days and $100 a day after 20 days of nursing home care). Hospice care is provided for terminally ill persons but only if they are expected to die in six months. Many qualifications must be met before a person may receive home health care under Medicare.

Part B is different from Part A. It closely resembles a private health insurance program. It is entirely voluntary, but it is vital to most people because it pays for some of the health care expenses not covered by Part A. Like private insurance, there are monthly payments ($50 monthly in 2001). The payment amount is almost always increased when there is a raise in Social Security. Part B is often thought of as outpatient insurance since it provides payment for physicians, laboratory services, medical equipment such as wheelchairs or walkers, and outpatient surgeries.

To the surprise of some people, Medicare does not cover all medical expenses of the elderly. In fact, with growing concern about the cost of this program, recent legislation has decreased Medicare coverage substantially. Often social workers must explain the limitations of Medicare to disbelieving elderly persons who have trusted that the money they paid into Social Security would take care of all of their medical needs in old age. (Could concern about the cost of her medical care have caused some of Katherine Lewandowski's depression in the case study at the beginning of this chapter?) Services not provided by Parts A or B include:

- Long-term nursing or custodial care.
- Dentures and dental care.
- Eyeglasses.
- Most prescription drugs.

It should be noted, however, that Medicare provides an option in the form of managed care plans that sometimes do cover some of the services listed above. These are **capitated plans,** prepaid by Medicare, in which comprehensive health care is provided and services are coordinated by the plan. Clients may not receive any health care services outside the plan.

While officially Medicare has just two parts, some people refer to the numerous additional options, initiated in 1997, as Part C. Also known as the Medicare+Choice program, it opens the door to an ever growing list of options. Included are various managed care and HMO plans plus Medical Savings Accounts. The Medical Savings Accounts are very complex, but basically they require a very high deductible payment (approximately $6,000 each year) in addition to monthly premiums. If illness occurs, the $6,000 (amount is likely to change over time) must be paid before the plan will take over, but when it does, it pays all remaining medical expenses. The premiums paid go into a "savings account," which can be used to pay the $6,000 annual deductible. The Center for Medicare Advocacy, which provides legal advocacy for Medicare-related problems, urges extreme caution about the Part C plans. They suggest: "Wait to see what experience tells about these new options. As it is, many beneficiaries have experienced difficulties with Medicare managed care plans and appeals. . . . Managed care plans are changing their benefit packages, many are disbanding, leaving some geographic areas with no managed care options at all; appeal systems are being challenged; physicians are losing their independence. . . . We do not know how the new Medicare+Choice options will work or what limitations will unfold" (Center for Medicare Advocacy, 2001, p. 1).

An advantage of the Medicare+Choice programs is that many include prescription drug coverage. A critical complaint of Part A and B of Medicare is their failure to provide coverage for prescriptions. People who qualify for Medicaid do have their prescriptions covered, but persons who are not poor enough to qualify for Medicaid frequently have no insurance prescription coverage. The cost of medication for chronic illnesses that elderly people encounter may be as much as $500 or more per month. People sometimes try to deal with this by not getting prescriptions filled or by cutting in half the recommended amount of medications they should be taking.

Pain, misery, and economic downfall from expensive hospitalizations are the outcome. Prescription drug coverage has emerged as such a strong political issue that numerous legislative proposals have been advanced. Early in 2001 President George W. Bush proposed a plan to cover only low-income seniors. By July 2001, he introduced a drug discount card plan to be available for a minimal charge to all seniors. His plan is market-driven, meaning that it will be offered by private corporations that will compete for seniors' business. The discounts offered may range upwards from 10 percent (HCFA, Medicare, 2001). Opponents support a broader plan that will cover all persons receiving Medicare and that will not create yet another layer of for-profit corporations but will, instead, operate within the existing Medicare program.

Medicare, despite its failings, is a remarkable program. It provides health care to millions of people, many of whom could otherwise not afford it. It is expensive and it has problems, one of which is the millions of dollars lost each year in fraud that is perpetrated not by Medicare recipients but by laboratories, managed care plans, physicians, hospitals, nursing homes, and others.

Medicaid

Social work as a profession has a special commitment to people who are poor or vulnerable. Of course, this includes people who are at risk of or who have existing physical and mental health problems. Since Medicaid is the largest U.S. financial aid program for poor people, it is obvious that social workers need to know something about Medicaid. Most social workers, however, will not need to know all of the intricate details; they do need to know where they can find information about Medicaid. One of the best sources is the Medicaid website, currently at http://www.hcfa.gov/medicaid/meligib.htm. Some very basic information about the Medicaid program follows.

Medicaid, also known as Medical Assistance, was enacted in 1965 as Title XIX of the Social Security Act. It is administered and partially funded by states, but the federal government also partly funds Medicaid and provides some oversight of the program. Initially designed to provide health care funding for poor older people, it was expanded over time. It now covers 36 million people, including people who receive SSI (Supplemental Security Income) because they are blind, aged, or have disabilities. Pregnant women and children with a family income below 133 percent of the poverty line, in general, are also eligible. Medicaid is a lifeline for poor people because it pays for prescriptions, laboratory tests and X rays, inpatient and outpatient hospital care, skilled nursing home care, and home health care.

Medicaid is a means-tested program. Applicants must provide proof of poverty according to their state's definition. Many people find the application procedure humiliating. Since all persons become eligible for Medicare at age 65, there is no means test. This dramatically differentiates Medicare from Medicaid.

In recent years, the states' power over Medicaid has increased considerably. Now each state:

- Establishes its own eligibility standards.
- Determines the type, amount, duration, and scope of services.
- Sets the rate of payment for services.
- Administers its own program (HCFA, Medicaid, 2001, p. 1).

An Analysis of the Politics of Medicaid

EXHIBIT 4

Business interests—typically a well-organized lobby—generally want to discredit Medicaid and cut benefits in order to reduce their tax burden. . . . Hospitals and providers, also with well-organized lobbies, are interested in maximizing Medicaid income through high reimbursements on the one hand but want to weaken federal and state oversight as much as possible on the other. Medicaid beneficiaries—low income persons, female-headed single parent families, disproportionately minority, elderly, or disabled—are among those with the least political power to influence Medicaid inequities. Legislators commonly want to pass laws that appear to benefit the poor, elderly and disabled but that objectively meet the needs of the business community and providers.

Source: Quoted from L. D. Weiss. (1997). *Private medicine and public health: Profits, politics, and prejudice in the American health care enterprise.* Boulder, CO. Westview Press, pp. 180–181.

As political pressure mounts to cut the costs of Medicaid, states have been given special authority to design their own programs. Some have trimmed Medicaid to its bare bones while others have provided more generous benefits. Cost-cutting methods have included eliminating some health care benefits, moving people out of nursing homes, putting all persons into managed care programs, and cutting mental health services.

Myths that minority, low-income women with many children accounted for most of the expenditures were unfounded; in fact, data indicate that approximately $1,000 is spent per year on children while over $12,000 is spent per person for long-term care and home health care (Waid, 1998, p. 18). One author's analysis of the politics of Medicaid is shown in Exhibit 4. The future of the Medicaid program depends, ultimately, upon the political and economic decisions Americans will make concerning the financing of health care.

Financing Health Care

In 1983 the federal government instituted a hospital payment program that almost overnight changed the way hospitals provided service. The program came to be known as the **diagnostic related group (DRG) plan.** It provided payment to hospitals based on a specific dollar amount per diagnosis. The implementation of DRGs resulted in reduction of hospital stays, increased use of outpatient care, and some level of cost containment. Although designed for Medicare, the DRG plan has evolved into today's **prospective payment system (PPS).** It is widely used by managed care organizations and private insurance plans as well. The PPS sounds more confusing than it really is. With this system, hospitals are paid a fixed amount, a lump sum of money, based on the patient's diagnosis. If the hospital can discharge the patient early, it makes a profit. If the patient outstays the fixed amount, the hospital could lose money. Obviously this system of health care financing offers powerful incentives to hospitals.

Katherine Lewandowski, the client in this chapter's case study, is an example of an elderly person whose discharge from the hospital was dictated, at least in part, by the PPS hospital reimbursement plan. Social workers are among the health care professionals who have expressed concern about the impact of the DRG hospital payment plan on similarly vulnerable patients.

Over the last decade, HMOs evolved from nonprofit, consumer-oriented plans into managed care, for-profit organizations. In an effort to stem rising costs, HMOs were supported by federal financing in order to "break the hold of the insurance industry and fee-for-service physicians on health care delivery. Seeing both a potential threat and an economic opportunity, the insurance industry simply purchased the competition, and it now owns the lion's share of HMOs" (Weiss, 1997, p. 93). Weiss believes that HMOs are inefficient and he questions the quality of health care they provide (p. 93).

Health Care Reform Efforts

Health care reform has pushed its way to the top of the political agenda, it would seem. Medicare and Medicaid are frequently in the news. A "Patient's Bill of Rights" passed in the U.S. Senate in summer 2001 after fierce opposition. That bill was important because it would reform managed care by ensuring patients access to a speedy appeal process when access to care is denied and by giving patients the right to sue managed care corporations when injury or death occurs as a result of the corporation's decisions or actions. The Patient's Bill of Rights legislation, however, is basically consumer rights protection, not large-scale health care reform and certainly not reform in the sense of the Clinton Health Security Act of 1993, which would have achieved **universal coverage.** Universal coverage means that every citizen would receive health care benefits at the same rate and without regard to their economic status.

Hillary Rodham Clinton campaigned across the country seeking support for the Clinton Health Security Act. Her message was not well received. According to one magazine, she "invokes the rhetoric of rights and morality. Health care is the 'right' of all Americans, she says, and assuring that they get it is a matter of 'social justice.' " (Barnes, 1994, p. 15). Opponents argued that universal health care was so expensive that it would destroy the country's economy. Liberals failed to support the Clinton proposal because it retained private insurance corporations as program administrators (hence huge administrative costs and built-in profitability) and failed to require a single-payer system. A **single-payer system** exists when either the government or a selected corporation administers the insurance program. The Clinton Health Security Act would have given states control over the system, including the right to select and use a private enterprise single-payer system, but the federal government would have had oversight.

What happened to defeat this major piece of health care reform legislation? Gorin's analysis (2000) provides insight:

> Although the Health Security Act would have preserved the employer-based system of coverage and the private insurance industry, it also would have transformed our health care and political systems. Establishing a right to health care would have dealt conservatives a severe blow and strengthened efforts to expand the social safety net. Interestingly, conservatives had a clearer understanding of this relationship than many progressives did. William Kristol, a key Republican strategist, warned that the Health Security Act posed "a serious *political* threat to

the Republican Party" (Skocpol, 1997, p. 145). He warned that the plan's enactment would revive faith in government and enable the Democrats to pose as the "protector of middle-class interests." Conversely, the act's defeat would be a "watershed in the resurgence of a newly bold and principled Republican politics" (Skocpol, p. 146). (Gorin, 2000, p. 141)

So the Health Security Act went down in defeat. Even before the act was voted down, managed care was expanding rapidly and moving with dizzying speed into all segments of the health industry. Once the Clinton national health care reform was clearly dead, "vast sums of federal money (Medicare and Medicaid) were already flowing through private, for-profit MCOs [managed care organizations]" (Davidson, Davidson, & Keigher, 1999, p. 164). The failure of the Health Security Act proved to be a watershed indeed. A **national health insurance** plan would not be politically acceptable again in the near future.

What made the failed piece of legislation a national insurance plan? National insurance plans are those systems of a given country that ensure participation in comprehensive health care insurance for all citizens. Sometimes there is confusion, especially in the political rhetoric, between **national health service** and national health insurance. A national health service is a country's ownership and administration of health care facilities and services where all citizens may receive care. England and Germany, for example, have such systems. In the United States the Veteran's Administration operates health care facilities that serve veterans; the U.S. military also administers and provides health facilities for military families. A national insurance plan, by contrast, is merely the insurance that is provided to ensure that citizens can access health care. In national health insurance, the government may operate the insurance program or it may contract with one (a single-provider system) or multiple private insurance companies. National insurance plans and national health services both provide universal coverage. In fact, most industrialized countries except the United States do have some form of universal coverage.

Change   There is no doubt that our health care system is changing. Many Americans are not satisfied with the way the health care system is evolving, but they feel powerless to effect change. Workers who only a few years back received free or low-cost health insurance as a fringe benefit of employment are finding that employers are shifting more of the health insurance costs to them. They now make co-payments each time they see a doctor or get a prescription refilled. They also pay much larger monthly fees for employer-sponsored health care insurance. Yet these employees are lucky. Employees of small businesses may receive no employee health insurance at all. Health care has become increasingly impersonal. Small, private hospitals have merged into giant corporations that own not only the hospital but also the outpatient clinics, pharmacy, behavioral health system, and nursing homes. Doctors have lost control over hospital admissions and discharges, since they are increasingly determined by the corporation's business office. Freedom to choose one's health care provider—once a hallmark of the American system, a factor that separated it from the systems of other countries—has quietly vanished. More importantly, vast numbers of Americans (42,554,000 according to the 2000 census) have no health insurance at all (U.S. Census Bureau, 2000).

Many people believe that change is needed. Hillary Rodham Clinton is not alone in questioning the social justice of the present situation. Because of their commitment to social justice, social workers are among the groups seeking change, but the process of change is a complex one. According to Gorin, health care reform can occur through incremental change or through fundamental change. If social justice is to be achieved, the end result of change would be that all Americans would have access to health care (universal coverage). Large-scale health care reform would need to take place. Can that occur quickly? Gorin cites polls taken during the 2000 election that showed 45 percent of registered voters supporting extension of coverage to people who currently have no health care insurance (Kaiser/Harvard Poll, 2000). In a focus group of Democratic voters (Lake et al., 1999), a majority were unsure that it would be feasible to provide health insurance coverage to all who are uncovered; they saw incremental change as the best approach. We don't know if there were people in that focus group whose families had no health insurance coverage. Would their position be different? What kind of change would they have supported? Were there social workers in the focus group? Would they, too, have supported relatively minor incremental change such as the Patient's Bill of Rights legislation?

Cost-Benefit Analysis   Health care costs are likely to continue to rise despite cost containment measures, so it is instructive to see what benefits we achieve from our health care dollars. Today, as Exhibit 5 shows, the United States spends considerably more on health care per citizen than other industrialized countries. But what has this investment purchased?

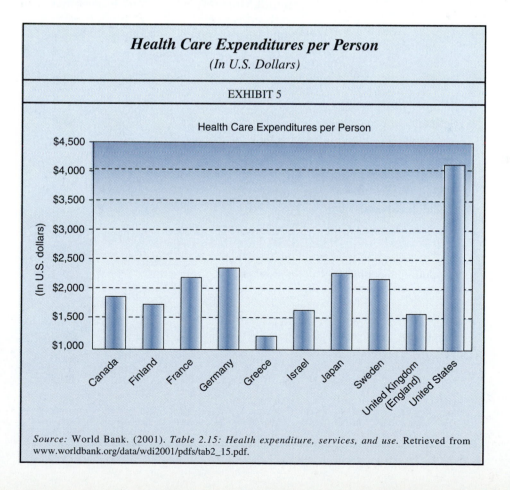

Health Care Expenditures per Person
(In U.S. Dollars)

EXHIBIT 5

Source: World Bank. (2001). *Table 2.15: Health expenditure, services, and use.* Retrieved from www.worldbank.org/data/wdi2001/pdfs/tab2_15.pdf.

For many years health-index statistics have been tracked by country, and so it is now possible to compare critical indicators of health across many nations. Two prominent measures traditionally used to evaluate health systems' performances are infant mortality rates and life expectancy. Compare the health-index data in Exhibit 6 with the per person health care expenditures in Exhibit 5. Even though other factors such as healthier lifestyle may account for some of the differences seen, it is apparent that in the United States the cost per citizen is not achieving the results on these important indicators that national health care systems attain in the other industrialized countries. Less developed countries generally have much higher infant mortality rates and also a briefer life expectancy. Sierra Leone, for example, reported 146 infant deaths per 1,000 live births, and Afghanistan had a

Measures of Health Systems' Performance

EXHIBIT 6

Country	Infant Mortality (Deaths per 1,000 Live Births)	Life Expectancy at Birth (Years) Male	Female
Japan	3	77.8	85.0
Sweden	3	77.6	82.6
Hong Kong	4	77.3	82.8
Belgium	4	75.7	81.9
(2 additional countries)	4		
Canada	5	76.2	81.8
Singapore	5	75.9	80.3
(3 additional countries)	5		
Israel	6	77.1	81.0
Slovenia	6	72.3	79.6
(5 additional countries)	6		
Malta	7	75.9	81.0
United States	7	74.6	80.4
Cuba	7	74.8	78.7
Macao	8	76.9	81.6
Cyprus	8	76.0	80.5

Source: Mortality rates and life expectancy at birth, by sex, for selected countries, 2000. Indicators on health. United Nations Statistics Division. Retrieved July 24, 2001, from http://www.un.org/Depts/unsd/social/health.htm.

tragic rate of 161 infant deaths in year 2000 reports. The lowest rates of infant mortality came from Sweden and Japan (only 3 deaths). The United States, which ranked 22 among countries in 1998, had slipped to 26 by 2000. Exhibit 6 provides data for selected other countries.

As United States citizens seek answers to the health care dilemmas of this country, some look to the Canadian system. Enacted in 1971 and known as Medicare, it is of considerable interest, since Canadians share many of the values and beliefs of Americans. An overview of the basic principles of the Canadian system is provided in Exhibit 7. It is also possible to look at data that challenges some of the myths and misinformation about the U.S. and Canadian health care systems.

Americans ask: How can we possibly afford the cost of a universal health care system? The dollar differences between what the United States and Canada spend on health care can be seen in Exhibit 5. It is useful to remember, too, that since the Canadian system is mostly publicly financed, there is no need for hospitals to determine costs of individual tubes of toothpaste, bandages, aspirins, surgical supplies, and so on. Because Canada has a single-payer system, there are minimal expenses for billing. It is estimated that approximately half of the differences in costs between Canadian and U.S. hospital costs relate to administrative expenses. Canada also expends only minimal time and costs in determining who is eligible for care and what the extent of their insurance coverage is; Canadians merely present their provincial health identification card. Hospitalization is covered so they are not billed (Armstrong, Armstrong, & Fegan, 1998).

Access   Although no Canadian is denied health care based on financial ability, what happens for the many uninsured or underinsured Americans is that they postpone preventive or diagnostic care. The result is more expensive care, debilitation, and even premature death. The underinsured are also discharged from care prematurely, which also brings long-range health (and cost) hazards.

Basic Principles of the Canadian Health Care System

EXHIBIT 7

1. *Universality.* Everyone is covered and has the same benefits.
2. *Portability.* Benefits are not linked to employment or province of residence.
3. *Comprehensiveness.* Benefits include full coverage of medical and hospital care, long-term care (covered separately and differently, depending on the province), mental health services, and prescription drugs for people over 65 and for people with catastrophic illnesses, and other services.
4. *Public, nonprofit administration.* The system is publicly run and publicly accountable, with provincial governments as the single payers of physicians and hospitals.
5. *Freedom of choice of provider.*

Source: T. Mizrahi, R. Fasano, & S.N. Dooha, (1993). National health line: Canadian and American health care: Myths and realities. *Health & Social Work, 18*(1), pp. 7–8.

It does seem likely that at present the United States has more technology for organ transplants, diagnostic imaging, and other complex procedures, but the Canadian system is not far behind and does routinely perform open heart surgeries and other major operations. Access to high-tech medical procedures is more uniformly available to Canadian citizens than to U.S. citizens. In terms of pioneering new technology, Canadian doctors, too, have made important contributions: the discovery of insulin for the treatment of diabetes, the pioneering of lung transplants and bone marrow transplants, and the development of very lightweight batteries to supply power for artificial hearts.

Waiting lines are another issue related to access. The myth is that Canadians must wait in long lines to see doctors but that Americans don't. The reality is that while waiting definitely can be a problem in Canada, it should be recalled that those Americans who cannot afford private doctors must use emergency rooms and clinics, where waiting lines do exist. Similarly, in rural areas and underserved metropolitan neighborhoods, waiting lines are long. Older Americans, who routinely travel hundreds of miles from U.S. border states to Canada to have their prescriptions refilled at Canadian prices, haven't complained about Canadian waits either. The Canadian government investigated reports that Canadian citizens were obtaining care in U.S. hospitals when urgently needed cardiac surgery, for example, was unavailable at home. It was found that less than 1 percent of Canadians had received care in the United States; for those who had sought surgery, their need was not urgent, but they had decided not to wait for treatment at home (Mizrahi, Fasano, & Dooha, 1993).

The last few years have been difficult ones for the Canadian health care system. The Canadian provinces are feeling pressure from American interests that would like to see the Canadian health care system opened up to free enterprise. Profit-focused insurance corporations, managed care companies, and even some Canadian doctors who would like to have the high income of U.S. physicians are seeking change in Canada's system. To this pressure, the newsletter of the Canadian Physicians for National Health Plan (PNHP) responds angrily:

> There is a great deal of money to be made by wrecking the Canadian system of Medicare. All the excess costs of an American-style payment system represent higher incomes for both the insurance industry and providers of care. The extra $45 billion it would cost us to match American expenditure patterns is a big enough carrot to motivate promotors of the illusion of American superiority. We are left with the question: what's really right about the Canadian health care system? Compared with the American system, just about everything. We do have problems, but the Americans do not have the solutions. (Evans & Roos, 2000, p. 3)

Part of the difficulty that is facing the Canadian system today is the failure of the Canadian government to sustain funding. Some Canadians suspect that the government is slowly moving toward increased privatization of health care. Social workers, among others, worry that Canadian health care may be moving toward increased inequality of care, downsizing of facilities, shifting patients into community-based programs (often returning them to their homes where the burden of care is borne by women relatives), and seeking increased payments from patients. They anticipate that if Canada does continue in this direction, the cost of health care will grow dramatically, quality of care will suffer, and there will be increased foreign ownership by private, for-profit health care providers (Armstrong, Armstrong, & Fuller, 2000). Some Canadians, it is said, think that "the grass is greener" on the other side of the border.

Bureaucracy   Americans are highly suspicious of bureaucracy. This generates fear about government regulation and centralized authority. It is a mistake, though, for Americans to think that our health care system is not bureaucratized and regulated: it is increasingly regulated by thousands of insurance and managed care corporations so impersonal that patients have not even had the right to appeal decisions or sue for malpractice. Our system isn't centralized. Sometimes that is an advantage, but when it leads to fragmentation and lack of access to needed care, it can be a serious limitation. The Canadian system is also not managed by a single government bureaucracy; instead the 10 Canadian provinces (similar to U.S. states) administer their own services. The Canadian federal government partially funds the system and requires that each province meet the system's principles (see Exhibit 7).

The growing state of crisis in the U.S. health care system suggests that change is necessary, either incremental change or large-scale, fundamental change. There are probably many different directions that the United States could go. The inequity and huge administrative costs of the present system suggest the inevitability of change despite the current lack of enthusiasm for wholesale reform. The "Up for Debate" box offers arguments for and against a national health plan for the United States that would be based on the Canadian system. In this plan private as well as public hospitals would continue to exist and doctors could be employed in public health or an HMO, or could operate private practices. A single-payer system (where one governmental insurance plan, perhaps by state, pays hospitals and providers directly) would eliminate private insurance and ensure universal coverage—health care for all citizens.

FUTURE TRENDS FOR SOCIAL WORKERS

The enactment of Medicare and subsequent legislation related to Medicare profoundly influenced the profession. One result was an expansion of the number of social workers hired by hospitals. Hospitals became increasingly alert to the credentials of the persons who provided social services as gradually all of the states passed laws requiring certification or licensure for social workers (some, however, only at the MSW level of practice). Other health care providers, such as nursing homes and home health care agencies, also increased their hiring of social workers.

In the 1980s, when Medicare cost containment became a serious concern, prospective pricing was introduced through the DRG procedure described earlier in this chapter. Many MSWs found the discharge planning responsibilities of the DRG program less appealing than the more therapeutic services they had been providing. As a result, some hospitals increased the number of BSWs and made discharge planning their primary responsibility. But other hospitals began using nurses as discharge planners. Then, as the 1990s brought increased pressure to cut costs, hospitals ceased expansion of social work departments and, in some cases, reduced the number of social workers.

Up for Debate
Proposition: The United States should adopt a national health insurance plan based on a single-payer system that would provide universal coverage.

Yes	No
1. Access to health care should not depend on one's economic status.	1. Persons who work hard and carry substantial responsibility are entitled to receive whatever level of health care their income affords them.
2. Use of a single, public system to process claims based on standardized forms would save billions of dollars in health care costs.	2. The nation's economy would be adversely affected by the demise of the health insurance industry.
3. The kind of competition that improves service and reduces waiting can be built into a national plan.	3. The likelihood of waits for nonemergency yet needed services, including surgeries, is a big risk.
4. All citizens would be covered even if they were between jobs, were employed part-time, or had a preexisting condition.	4. The current mix of public and private health care plans fuels the economy and generates diverse health plans that meet most people's needs.
5. Equal access to health care is a moral right of all citizens.	5. There is no constitutionally defined right of citizens to health care.

The Bureau of Labor Statistics' publication *Occupational Outlook Handbook* predicts that "employment for social workers is expected to increase much faster than the average for all occupations through 2008. The aged population is increasing rapidly, creating greater demand for health and other social services" (Bureau of Labor Statistics, 2001, p. 163). Their experts anticipate growth in the number of social workers needed for hospitals, long-term care facilities, and home health care as a result of the early discharge of patients from hospitals. The elderly, mentally ill persons, people with chronic health problems, and families in crisis are expected to need increased services in the future from health care providers. These are the very people that social workers will be seeing in long-term care facilities, subacute centers, home health care, hemodialysis units, rehabilitation and other specialized care centers, HMOs, and health clinics. Within hospitals, social work responsibilities will continue to shift toward emergency and trauma centers, cardiac and intensive care units, oncology and hospice programs, and perinatal centers. The growth of community-based centers, including outpatient surgeries and diagnostic centers, is predicted to provide more employment opportunities, too. With fewer services offered under some managed care plans and large numbers of families who are under- or uninsured, social work advocacy skills will be needed in both clinical and policy arenas (Poole, 1995). A new area for further development is social work within insurance companies: in community education, in prevention programs for new parents, in case management with frail older adults, and in management and policy-making positions.

Health care is one of the most rapidly changing fields of social work practice. It brings social workers into some of the most emotional and sensitive experiences of human lives—life-saving surgeries, births, minor as well as serious injuries, and deaths—some experiences welcomed and some filled with anger and despair. Social workers will need to sharpen their skills for work in these very challenging areas. Technology such as the Internet (see Internet Sites for some examples), distance education, and computer-based chat rooms and bulletin boards will afford social workers wider opportunities than in the past for professional communication and learning.

INTERNET SITES

http://www.napsw.org	The National Association of Perinatal Social Workers
http://www.nrharural.org/	National Rural Health Association
http://www.ahsr.org	Academy for Health Services Research & Health Policy
http://www.aosw.org	Association of Oncology Social Work
http://www.who.int/	World Health Organization
http://www.kidney.org/professionals/CNSW	Council of Nephrology Social Workers of the National Kidney Foundation
http://www.npaf.org/	The National Patient Advocate Foundation
http://www.medicareadvocacy.org/	Center for Medicare Advocacy, Inc
http://www.medicare.gov/	The Official U.S. Government Site for Medicare Information
http://www.kff.org/sections.cgi?section=kcmu	Kaiser Foundation on Medicaid and the Uninsured
http://www.aascipsw.org	American Association of Spinal Cord Injury Psychologists and Social Workers
http://www.homehealthsocialwork.org	American Network of Home Health Care Social Workers, Inc.

SUMMARY

Linda Sanders, a senior social work student in field placement, introduces the reader to the field of health care. Because her courses are preparing her for generalist social work practice, Linda is able to assess the tragedy of Katherine Lewandowski's death within the context of a whole population of frail elderly persons who might be at risk because of premature discharge from the hospital. The case study is designed to illustrate why it is necessary for social work students to acquire knowledge and skill not only in counseling and one-on-one work but also in advocacy and larger systems change. These practice skills are needed in health care as much as—perhaps even more than—in any other field of social work practice.

Social workers frequently serve as members of health teams that grapple with ethical dilemmas. Often decisions are made by the team as a whole, leaving no one person to make a decision alone. Ethics and values content pervade the social work curriculum and are also derived from philosophy, theology, and literature courses, giving social work students in health care settings a basis from which to examine ethical issues. In addition, the code of ethics of the National Association of Social Workers provides guidelines for ethical practice.

The health care field encompasses much more than hospitals. Indeed, social workers are employed in HMOs, nursing homes, hospices, outpatient clinics, home health care services, and insurance companies—in large cities, in small towns, and in rural areas. The community itself, including its economic well-being and its racial and ethnic characteristics, must be understood by the health care social worker in order to provide a bridge between the community and the health care facility.

The history of social work in health care is a proud one. Not only have social workers in this field helped patients and their families, but for 100 years they have worked to make health care organizations more responsive and more sensitive to the needs of people.

Today the impact of public policy is immense. The entire health field seems to be in crisis. At the center of the debate is health care financing. Increasing numbers of people are underinsured in the United States, and others have no health insurance coverage at all. As health care costs keep rising, business corporations and nonprofit organizations are less willing to pay for employees' health insurance. The cost containment procedures that have been implemented have the potential result of leading to inadequate medical care or premature discharge of hospital patients. Reform of the U.S. health care system is needed, but public support for a comprehensive national program is uncertain. Social workers, who witness the tragedy of inadequate health care, will undoubtedly continue to fight for comprehensive reform.

In order to meet the challenges of this exciting and evolving field of practice, social workers will need to sustain commitment to their professional values just as social workers have since the days of the lady almoners at the Royal Free Hospital in London.

KEY TERMS

acute care
capitated plan
cost containment
diagnostic related group (DRG) plan
health maintenance organization (HMO)
hemodialysis
hospice
lady almoner
long-term care
Medicaid

Medicare
national health insurance
national health service
osteoporosis
prospective payment system (PPS)
sickle-cell anemia
single-payer system
subacute center
universal coverage

DISCUSSION QUESTIONS

1. Why do you think that Katherine Lewandowski, the patient in the case study, was discharged from the hospital when she apparently did not want to leave?

2. Could the nursing home social worker have done anything to prevent Katherine Lewandowski's death? What could she have done?

3. Discuss the hospital policy changes that could result from social workers' intervention following the Lewandowski case.

4. Chapter 1 described generalist social work practice. What knowledge, values, and skills does a generalist social worker need in order to work effectively in health care?

5. In what ways is health care social work different in rural areas than in urban areas?

6. Social work is one of many professions providing health care. What are some of the others? How might these various professional roles overlap?

7. In the discussion of the emergency room as a health care setting, a young Puerto Rican woman who is pregnant experiences an *ataque*. How could the social worker's understanding of their culture help the family in this situation? Should Katherine Lewandowski's Polish culture have been of significance to social workers at the hospital (or at the nursing home)? Why?

8. Medicare and Medicaid have been presented in detail in this chapter. Outline the differences between the two programs.

9. What is the goal of managed health care? What are its strengths and weaknesses? Can you identify any managed care programs in your community?

10. Name the person who is generally considered the originator of medical social work in the United States. How did she come into social work? Explain the nature of her contributions to the history of the social work profession.

11. Analyze the costs and benefits of the present U.S. health care system. In what ways does the United States spend more than other countries on health care? Do these additional expenditures benefit American citizens?

12. What kind of incremental change do you think might take place in health care policies in the United States in the future? What are the prospects for fundamental health care system reform? How might this come about?

13. What do you expect the impact of the current administration to be on Medicare? Medicaid? Other components of the American health care system?

14. What are the prospects for social work employment in health care? In what types of health care settings is employment likely to increase for social workers in the future?

CLASSROOM EXERCISES

1. This chapter notes that over 42 million Americans are without health insurance today. Discuss possible reasons why this is so. Do you think a large uninsured population is good for the nation overall, in that it makes people more economically insecure and thus more willing to work, a classic conservative argument?

2. The chapter's case example regarding Katherine Lewandowski illustrates a policy or system known today as PPS, or prospective payment system, used not only by Medicare but by managed care organizations and private insurance plans. According to this sytem, a hospital is paid a fixed fee for a patient's care according to the diagnosis. Identify as many pros and cons of this policy as you can. Overall, do you think it is a good one for Americans in need of care? Why or why not?

3. The text compares and contrasts the Canadian health care system with the American system. What are the differences? The similarities? Overall, which nation's plan does the author believe better meets the health care needs of its citizens? Review the evidence provided in the text. Do you agree with the author? Why or why not?

4. Should health care be universal in the United States? Why or why not? If health care were to become universal, which approach do you believe would best serve the needs of Americans, a national health service or universal health insurance? If universal health insurance, which approach do you believe would be more cost-effective, a single-payer system coordinated by the government or multiple systems run by private insurance companies? Cite evidence provided in the text to support your position.

RESEARCH ACTIVITIES

1. Using library resources, identify five countries that have a universal health care plan and find out how each of these plans functions.

2. Explore the full range of health care settings in your community in which social workers are employed.

3. What professional social work periodicals does your school's library have that focus on social work in health care? Read the table of contents of a couple of the most recent issues. What topics appear to be of special concern to social workers in health care? Do any of these topics directly or indirectly relate to the profession's ultimate goal of social and economic justice, or to subjects that have ethical implications?

4. Identify several friends and/or family members who have been hospitalized recently or who have a serious health problem. Conduct a survey to determine if they have any concerns about the current U.S. health care system, concerns based on their own experiences or the experiences of other people they might have encountered. Then describe the Canadian system to them and determine their level of support for a similar system in the United States.

INTERNET RESEARCH EXERCISES

1. There is a Sickle Cell Information Center on the Web that provides information about that disease (http://www.emory.edu/PEDS/SICKLE/sicklept.htm). Click on "What Is Sickle Cell Anemia?"
   a. Why is the disease called "sickle cell" and what causes the cells to change?
   b. Is sickle-cell anemia found only in African Americans?
   c. What are six complications from sickle-cell anemia?

2. The Kaiser Family Foundation prepared a fact sheet on Medicaid's role in long-term care (http://www.kff.org/content/2001/2186).
   a. How many people in the United States need long-term care?
   b. How many people under age 65 require some form of long-term care?
   c. What does the term "spend down" mean with reference to Medicaid availability?
3. A very complete explanation and discussion of hemodialysis as a treatment method for advanced and permanent kidney failure is available on the website of the National Institutes of Health (http://www.niddk.nih.gov/health/kidney/pubs/kidney-failure/treatment-hemodialysis/treatment-hemodialysis.htm).
   a. What is kidney dialysis and when is it necessary?
   b. What is dialyzer?
   c. What are three conditions related to kidney failure and treatment?

REFERENCES

Armstrong, P., Armstrong, H., & Fegan, C. (1998). The best solution: Questions and answers on the Canadian health care system. *Washington Monthly, 30* (4), 8–12.

Armstrong, P., Armstrong, H., & Fuller, C. (2000, November). Health care, limited: The privatization of Medicare. Retrieved July 23, 2001, from New Rules Project-Equity website: http://www.newrules.org/equity/Cnhealthcare.html.

Auerbach, C., Rock, B. D., Goldstein, M., Kaminsky, P., & Heft-Laporte, H. (2000). A department of social work uses data to prove its case (88-99B). *Social Work in Health Care, 32* (1), 9–23.

Barnes, F. (1994, August 15). A White House watch: Left out. *New Republic, 211* (7), issue 4, 152, 15–17.

Bureau of Labor Statistics. (2001, April 12). Social workers. *Occupational outlook handbook*. Retrieved July 27, 2001, from http://stats.bls.gov/oco/pdf/ocos060.pdf.

Butler, D. J., & Beltran, L. R. (1993). Functions of an adult sickle cell group: Education, task orientation, and support. *Health & Social Work, 18* (1), 49–56.

Cannon, I. M. (1952). *On the social frontier of medicine: Pioneering in medical social service*. Cambridge, MA: Harvard University Press.

Center for Medicare Advocacy. (2001). The Medicare+Choice program (Medicare Part C). Retrieved July 20, 2001, from http://www.medicareadvocacy.org/Medicare+Choice%20Program.htm.

Davidson, T., Davidson, J. H., & Keigher, S. M. (1999). Managed care: Satisfaction guaranteed . . . Not! *Health & Social Work, 24* (3), 163–168.

Devore, W., & Schlesinger, E. G. (1987). *Ethnic sensitive social work practice* (2nd ed.). Columbus, OH: Merrill.

Egan, M., & Kadushin, G. (1997). Rural hospital social work: Views of physicians and social workers. *Social Work in Health Care, 26* (1), 1–23.

Evans, R., & Roos, N. P. (2000, March). What is right about the Canadian health care system? Retrieved July 23, 2001, from Third World Traveler website: http:www.thirdworldtraveler.com/Health/WhatsRight_CanadaHC.html.

Garner, J. D. (1995). Long-term care. In *Encyclopedia of social work* (19th ed., pp. 625–1634). Washington, DC: NASW Press.

Gorin, S. H. (2000). Progressives and the 2000 election. *Health & Social Work, 25* (2), 139–143.

HCFA: Health Care Financing Administration. (2001, July 11). The president's Medicare prescription drug discount program. Retrieved July 21, 2001, from www.hcfa.gov/news/pr2001/pr010711.htm; Overview of the Medicaid program. Retrieved July 21, 2001, from www.hcfa.gov/medicaid/mover.htm.

Health Key Medical Group: Medical Care Associates, Inc. (1986, December). *Society for Hospital Social Work Directors of the American Hospital Association: HMO Task Force report.* Chicago, IL: American Hospital Association.

Healy, T. C. (1998). The complexity of everyday ethics in home health care: An analysis of social workers' decisions regarding frail elders' autonomy. *Social Work in Health Care, 27* (4), 19–37.

Kaiser-Harvard Poll. (2000). The Henry J. Kaiser Family Foundation. Retrieved (n.d.) from http://www.kff.org/.

Keigher, S. M. (2000, February). Knowledge development. *Health & Social Work. Health & Social Work, 25* (1), 3–8.

Lake, Snell, Perry, & Associates, Inc. (1999). *Findings from recent focus group research.* New York: Author.

Mayden, R. W., & Nieves, J. (2000). Health care. In *Social work speaks: National Association of Social Workers policy statements 2000–2003* (pp. 147–155). Washington, DC: NASW Press.

McGinn, F. (1996). The plight of rural parents caring for adult children with HIV. *Families in Society, 77* (5), 269–278.

Medicare: The Official U.S. Government Site for Medicare Information (2001). Medicare basics. Retrieved July 20, 2001, from http://www.medicare.gov/Basics/Overview.asp.

Mizrahi, T., Fasano, R., & Dooha, S. M. (1993). National health line: Canadian and American health care: Myths and realities. *Health & Social Work, 18* (1), 8–11.

Mortality rates and life expectancy at birth, by sex, for selected countries, 2000. Indicators on health. United Nations Statistics Division. Retrieved July 24, 2001, from http://www.un.org/Depts/unsd/social/health.htm

NASW. (1993). *NASW clinical indicators for social work and psychological services in nursing homes* (brochure). Washington, DC: Author.

National Association of Social Workers Practice Research Network. (2000). Practice area. *PRN Datagram* (PRN 1, 3, 2000). Washington, DC: Author.

Oktay, J. S. (1995). Primary health care. In *Encyclopedia of social work* (19th ed., pp. 1887–1894). Washington, DC: NASW Press.

Pistella, C. L. Y., Bonati, F. A., & Mihalic, S. (1999). Social work practice in a rural community collaborative to improve perinatal care. *Social Work in Health Care, 20* (1), 1–14.

Poole, D. L. (1995). Health care: Direct practice. In *Encyclopedia of social work* (19th ed., pp. 1156–1167). Washington, DC: NASW Press.

Reamer, F. G. (1993, July). AIDS and social work: The ethics and civil liberties agency. *Social Work, 38*(4), 414–415.

Robert, S., & Norgard, T. (1996). Long-term care policy based on ADL eligibility criteria: Impact on community dwelling elders not meeting the criteria. *Journal of Gerontological Social Work, 25*(3/4), 71–91.

Rogers, J., Smith, M., Ray, J., Hull, G., Pike, C., Buchan, V., & Rodenheiser, R. (1999, November). *The revised outcomes instrument, report of findings: Total database (as of October 1, 1999).* Paper presented at the 17th Annual Program Meeting of the Association of Baccalaureate Social Work Program Directors, St. Louis, MO.

Shahar, I. B. (1993). Disaster preparation and the functioning of a hospital social work department during the Gulf War. *Social Work in Health Care, 18* (3/4), 147–159.

Slivinski, L. R., Fitch, V. L., & Wingerson, N. W. (1998). The effect of functional disability on service utilization: Implications for long-term care. *Social Work, 23* (3), 175–185.

Skocpol, T. (1997). *Boomerang: Health care reform and the turn against government.* New York: W. W. Norton.

U.S. Census. (2000, October 10). Health insurance coverage: 1999. Retrieved July 22, 2001, from http://www.census.gov/hhes/hlthins/hlthin99/hi99ta.html.

Waid, M. O. (1998). *Brief summaries of Medicare & Medicaid.* Retrieved June 25, 1998, from http://www.hcfa.gov/medicare/ormed.htm.

Weiss, L. (1997). *Private medicine and public health: Profit, politics, and prejudice in the American health care enterprise.* Boulder, CO: Westview Press.

Woolhandler, S. (2001, January 23). Quality of care research seminar series. Retrieved July 18, 2001, from http://www.hsph.harvard.edu/qcare/woolhandler.html.

World Bank. (2001). Table 2.15 Health expenditure, services, and use. Retrieved July 27, 2001, from http://www.worldbank.org/data/wdi2001/pdfs/tab2_15.pdf

FOR FURTHER READING

Cannon, I. M. (1952). *On the social frontier of medicine: Pioneering in medical social service.* Cambridge, MA: Harvard University Press.

Anyone who is interested in the history of social work will find Ida Cannon's classic text very informative. The book provides a rare opportunity to read about the development of an area of social work practice from the perspective of the woman who led the movement. Her sensitive analysis of the social problems of her time—problems such as poverty and industrial hazards—will give readers a perspective on contemporary social problems. It is difficult to read this book without gaining inspiration from the intellect, energy, and compassion of Ida Cannon.

Ejaz, F. K. (2000). The influence of religious and personal values on nursing home residents' attitudes toward life-sustaining treatments. *Social Work in Health Care, 32* (2), 23–39.

Older adults living in nursing homes often delegate to their families decisions about the kind of medical treatment that should be used when they become terminally ill, especially in the event that they become unable to make such decisions for themselves. The author's research of 133 nursing home residents points to the complexity of decisions about end-of-life treatment. In some cases older people did not wish to consider an advance directive (the end-of-life treatment directions to health care professionals). In other situations, it held great meaning and was significantly related to the older person's values about reliance on God (not merely on denominational affiliation). Education, the context of the nursing home itself, and death anxiety (fear of dying) were among other factors that appear to have practice implications for social workers in long-term care.

Goggin, K., Catley, D., Brisco, S. T., Engleson, E. S., Rabkin, J. G., & Kotler, D. P. (2001). A female perspective on living with HIV disease. *Health & Social Work, 26* (2), 80–89.

This research team discovered remarkable strengths among women living with HIV disease. Their interviews with 55 women diagnosed with HIV disease demonstrated that, despite fairly high levels of distress, the women had found in their disease a motivating force that enabled them to make changes in their behaviors, their relationships, their spirituality, and their valuing of themselves. The women had not been newly diagnosed; they had lived with HIV an average of five years. This article is consistent with the strengths perspective that has become so vital to the theory base of generalist social workers today.

Weiss, L. D. (1997). *Private medicine and public health: Profit, politics, and prejudice in the American health care enterprise.* Boulder, CO: Westview Press.

Weiss exposes the flaws, abuse, and deceit of the current for-profit health care system in the United States. Using research, trial documents, personal accounts, and statistical data, he uncovers the political power used by physicians' professional groups, hospitals, and the pharmaceutical and insurance industries to fend off a national health care program. This small book is highly readable yet sure to deliver new understandings about the forces that make systemic change so difficult—and so necessary.

White House Domestic Policy Council (1993). *The president's health security plan.* New York: Times Books, Random House.

This paperback book supplies both the original draft of President Clinton's Health Security Plan and a report prepared by the White House Domestic Policy Council. It is a fascinating source of information about a U.S. national health care plan that almost happened.

CHAPTER 8

Social Work in the Workplace

At 8:00 A.M. Staci started reviewing the forms that recorded nonemergency calls that had come in during the night to their office, a national employee assistance program. It had been an unusually busy night. Many calls needed the immediate attention of the on-call staff person, in this case a master's-level social worker. Staci had been assigned many of the nonemergency calls to follow up on. She began reading the first one.

Almost immediately the telephone rang. The caller identified herself as Gwen Knowles, an administrative assistant to a vice president at the Star Products Corporation. Gwen's voice was high pitched and she spoke rapidly, explaining that she and her daughter had a terrific fight the previous night. At the height of the battle her daughter ran out of the house screaming that she would never return. Gwen's description of the incident painted a vivid picture of two extremely upset persons. Staci listened carefully as Gwen's words slowed and she could hear forced intake of breath. Apparently the argument began with 14-year-old Erica's request that she spend the night with her boyfriend at his parents' home. Erica was angry with her mother's apparent inability to trust her. And, in truth, Gwen was terribly frightened for Erica. Gwen was only 14 when she herself had been raped while on a date. She just could not let anything like this happen to her beautiful daughter. She was still very, very angry with Erica for challenging her authority, for the bitter, hurtful words she used, and for storming out of the house, but now Gwen was mostly frightened. Should she call the police? She didn't know what to do.

Staci used a quiet, comforting tone of voice as she worked to bring calm to Gwen's disordered thinking. She reassured Gwen that together they could think through what had happened and they could develop a plan so that Gwen would know what to do next. Gwen responded quickly, saying that normally she was able to think very clearly but this was one time when she needed outside help. Staci established that the "fight" had not been a physical one; no one had been hurt. She was not surprised to learn that Erica hadn't come home. Staci helped Gwen to talk about what she had done so far. Around 3:00 in the morning Gwen had telephoned Erica's boyfriend's home. She was startled to learn that Erica was not there but used some excuse so as not to alarm Erica's boyfriend. Gwen could not sleep. She turned on every light in the house so that if Erica came back, she would know that she was welcome. Gwen's thoughts raced back to her own sexual assault. She had pushed it to the back of her mind but, she realized now, it had begun to lurk near the surface of many discussions she had with Erica. Until tonight she had been convinced that Erica would never be told. Now Gwen wasn't so sure. Gwen decided to stay off the phone in case Erica called.

By 6:30 A.M. Gwen began calling Erica's friends' homes. No one had seen Erica. Should she call the police? Erica had never before been in difficulty with the police. Staci listened carefully to Gwen's description of what had taken place, sometimes offering encouragement for Gwen to continue, sometimes asking questions for further clarification. Gwen responded, her thoughts becoming clearer. Staci then suggested that it would indeed be a good idea to telephone the local *police. It would also be a good idea to call Erica's school and ask that she be contacted if Erica arrived there. Gwen said that she was feeling a bit better now and would make the calls right away. Staci suggested that Gwen call her back when she completed this and that Gwen might then want to talk with a more experienced staff member who, having been filled in on the details of the situation, would be able to offer more help.*

Two hours later Gwen telephoned again. Gwen had followed Staci's advice and contacted both the police and the school. But shortly afterwards, Erica had come home on her own after spending the night with a classmate, someone that Gwen did not know. She and Gwen hugged each other, cried in relief, and had a good talk. Erica was taking a shower and would be going off to school shortly. The crisis was over, at least for now. Gwen was clearly very relieved. But this experience had forced her to do some serious thinking. She said that Staci's concern and her responsiveness had given Gwen courage to tackle the difficult job of facing her bad memories. She wanted to find out how to deal with her past experience so that she would not inadvertently use it in a way that would be hurtful to her daughter. Gwen said she was very grateful that her employee assistance plan at work would provide for some additional counseling. Staci let Gwen know how pleased she was that Erica was back at home and that Gwen had decided to pursue counseling. She informed Gwen about the family counseling program that would provide her at least five counseling sessions. A social worker would be available to see Gwen today if she wished.

As Staci returned to her stack of folders, she smiled. Her baccalaureate social work courses had provided her with skills that enabled her to help many people. This job also taught her a lot in the past year and its flexible hours would make it possible for her to enter graduate school next fall. Staci had enjoyed her break from college, but she was ready to begin an MSW program that would give her the advanced practice skills to provide more in-depth and complex services to people like Gwen and Erica.

THE WORLD OF WORK

For Staci Evans, the employee assistance program had become a fascinating and fulfilling environment in which to practice her profession, social work. Staci enjoyed the fast pace of her job, the challenge of crisis intervention work, and the endless variety of people and problems in living that she dealt with. One drawback, Staci found, was that her interviews with people were always by telephone, e-mail, or fax, never in person. Yet she knew that she was continually improving her ability to quickly assess the problem situations presented to her while at the same time conveying warmth and concern for the persons who contacted her.

Staci's friends from the university social work major were also employed now in child welfare, health care, or other fields of social work practice. They were quite surprised with her level of interest in employee assistance work. Staci explained to them that in this field she could experience nearly every kind of problem that they encountered in all of their different social work practice settings. Often she could help people to solve problems and, as a result, sustain their employment or improve the quality of their relationships with co-workers or employers. Problems in their personal lives or the problems of their families or communities also had impact on employees' work performance. Like a growing number of social workers and other human service professionals, Staci had come to appreciate the many and varied meanings that work and the work environment hold for people.

Work, for many of us has, indeed, come to define who we are and, to a considerable degree, how we feel about ourselves. Employment can contribute dramatically to the quality of our lives. In contemporary society, the personal relationships between employees sometimes are deeper and closer than those among family members, who may be dispersed within a state, across a nation, or around the world. Employment is also necessary to economic survival for most people. The threat of loss of employment may be perceived as a personal crisis of considerable magnitude. When a plant closes or moves out of the community, the result may be communitywide trauma.

Occupational social work is the field of social work practice that is conducted in or provides services to businesses, industry, governmental institutions, and unions and their employees.

This field is sometimes referred to as industrial social work. Specific workplace-related human services, known as **employee assistance programs,** have been developed for business, industry, and government organizations not just in the United States but around the world. The term "employee assistance program" has been defined by the Employer Assistance Program (EAP) Association as

> a worksite-based program designed to assist: (1) work organizations in addressing productivity issues, and (2) "employee clients" in identifying and resolving personal concerns, including but not limited to, health, marital, family, financial, alcohol, drug, legal, emotional, stress, or other personal issues that may affect job performance." (Macdonald, 1998, p. 14)

The key difference between the concepts of occupational social work and of employee assistance work is that the field of employee assistance is made up of many different professionals, while only social workers engage in occupational social work.

Some social workers, like Staci Evans in the case study, provide interdisciplinary service in organizations or programs that are specifically designated as employee assistance programs. Other social workers do not work in employee assistance programs but in the very broad world of work. They may serve as consultants to business corporations, counsel newly employed persons, assist former welfare recipients who have been transported to work sites long distances from their homes, or help immigrants and their employers to understand each other. As in other fields of practice, social workers in business and industry seek to prevent problems or to ameliorate or eliminate existing personal, family, group, organization, and community problems. Workplace social work practice should not be confused with psychotherapy; instead, it tends to be short-term and focused on immediate needs or problems.

Social worker in industrial plant gives young mother a referral to day care for her new baby.

THE CHANGING WORKPLACE

Worldwide the workplace is changing. Seeking a competitive advantage, corporations are moving their manufacturing sites from north to south in the United States, across national borders, or even halfway around the world to low-wage third world countries. The steel industry is threatened with the loss of thousands of jobs to China and Russia (Sharkey, 1998). The U.S. textile industry, once one of the largest, has relocated production to the Philippines, Indonesia, and eastern European countries. International economic trade agreements such as NAFTA (the North American Free Trade Agreement of 1994) and the evolution of the European Union have redefined commerce. Implementation of NAFTA will continue to occur on a planned basis over several years, but it has already resulted in a flow of U.S. investments, including relocation of business corporations and jobs, to Mexico and Canada.

Globalizing economies, corporate mergers and acquisitions, and rapid technological advancements are impacting the workplace forcefully. Nearly simultaneously, the United States and Japan shifted from manufacturing based to information and service economies over the past two decades. Both countries initially experienced huge economic growth, followed by financial setbacks, especially in the wake of the 2001 terrorist attacks on the World Trade Center and the Pentagon. In the United States, the shift was initially marked by plant closures and increasing nonavailability of the high-wage jobs that formerly existed in manufacturing. Instead, low-wage, part-time, temporary jobs flooded the marketplace as corporations sought to respond to changing markets while at the same time cutting the expenses associated with full-time employees. The new service economy grew rapidly, creating a huge demand for low-cost labor. Except for urban, inner-city areas, unemployment rates fell dramatically from a high of 9.9 in 1983 to 3.9 percent in 2000 (Bureau of

Labor Statistics, 2001) and increased again to 5.8 percent as 2001 (Bureau of Labor Statistics, 2002) came to a close. Wide fluctuations in the economy left employment opportunities primarily available in low-wage jobs.

Today, as the demand for low-cost labor continues to increase, a new idea is being promulgated by the National Center for Policy Analysis, a private organization located in Texas. This organization suggests that "the answer to all those problems [labor shortages, etc.] is the inmate workforce" (National Center for Policy Analysis, 2001, p. 1). To stem the flow of U.S. jobs to India, Mexico, and Asia, this organization suggests that private sector companies be encouraged to develop contracts and outsource jobs to prisons, thus creating prison-based production systems. The objective of this plan is to reduce prison costs by permitting the readily available prison workforce to compete for American jobs. They further suggest that faith-based organizations be used within prisons to train prisoners for their jobs. This is clearly an interesting new twist on the creation of an additional extremely low wage labor force, one that is indeed a captive workforce, without even having the expense and complications of moving corporations to other countries. Of course, it also raises numerous questions about the relationship between the religious organizations and the prison population.

In today's fast-paced and volatile economic environment, availability of a temporary work staff is also advantageous. **Contingency work** is the term that is emerging for jobs that are time-limited and devoid of any opportunity for ongoing, long-term employment. While contingency work is much more frequently associated with low wages, there are also highly paid consultants and high-tech troubleshooters whose lives revolve around mobile jobs in various parts of the United States or any number of other countries (Armour, 1998). The transitional nature of work is reflected in the Bureau of Labor's finding that the number of jobs held by workers over a period of time is increasing and today people hold an average of 9.2 jobs between age 18 to age 34 (Bureau of Labor Statistics, 2000). Currently 5.4 million persons hold contingent work jobs and 8.6 million are in other alternative work arrangements. Together they total 10.4 percent of the total U.S. workforce (Monthly Labor Review Online, 2001).

For many people, the workplace isn't a "place" any longer, as we will see in a discussion of home health care workers later in this chapter. Like home health care workers, persons employed in several expanding occupations transport themselves from location to location throughout their working day. Still others work within their own homes in child care (a growth area since welfare reform), telephone marketing, and computer-related work. Telecommuting, the "virtual" form of commuting to work via the Internet, has resulted in the "teleworkaholic," a home-based employee who tends to overwork. "Hotelling" is the developing practice of large corporations that make office space available on a prior reservation or sign out (like signing out a library book) basis to employees who spend part of each day in the field (Logophilia, n.d.). This enables corporations to cut costs by having as many as 50 percent fewer offices for their staff. The changing location of employment, then, is another characteristic of the service economy.

New tools have revolutionized today's workplace. "Retooling" and "work redesign" are terms associated with the challenging learning needs that accompanied the change in the kind of tools and equipment used today. Computer technology has replaced the machines used to make everything from beer to automobiles and motorcycles. Workers who once operated lathes and factory equipment have shifted, when possible, to complex computerized tools and robotics. Obviously not all workers could make this transition. The manual dexterity required in the past has been replaced by demands for computer competence and programming skills. The workplace now requires that employees become adept at mastering new, technology-driven skills on an ongoing basis. In addition to high-tech skills, employees now need verbal and mathematical skills as well as competence in time management and interpersonal relationship skills.

The workplace of the future will also stress increasing expectations for higher education. This is apparent in the U.S. Bureau of Labor Statistics analysis of employment trends and future projections, which are shown in Exhibit 1. The column

U.S. Department of Labor: Employment by Major Occupational Group: 2000 and Projected 2010
(Numbers in Thousands of Jobs)

EXHIBIT 1

Occupational group	Employment				Change	
	Number		Percent distribution			
	2000	2010	2000	2010	Number	Percent
Total, all occupations	145,594	167,754	100.0	100.0	22,160	15.2
Management, business, and financial occupations	15,519	17,635	10.7	10.5	2,115	13.6
Professional and related occupations	26,758	33,709	18.4	20.1	6,952	26.0
Service occupations	26,075	31,163	17.9	18.6	5,088	19.5
Sales and related occupations	15,513	17,365	10.7	10.4	1,852	11.9
Office and administrative support occupations	23,882	26,053	16.4	15.5	2,171	9.1
Farming, fishing, and forestry occupations	1,429	1,480	1.0	.9	51	3.6
Construction and extraction occupations	7,451	8,439	5.1	5.0	989	13.3
Installation, maintenance, and repair occupations	5,820	6,482	4.0	3.9	662	11.4
Production occupations	13,060	13,811	9.0	8.2	750	5.7
Transportation and material moving occupations	10,088	11,618	6.9	6.9	1,530	15.2

NOTE: Detail may not equal total or 100 percent due to rounding.

Source: D. E. Hecker. (2001, November). Occupational employment projections to 2010. *Monthly Labor Review* (p. 60). Retrieved January 8, 2002, from http://www.bls.gov/mlr/2001/11/art4full.pdf.

on the far right in Exhibit 1 reflects the increase in growth of the various occupational groups. Notice that the occupational groups that will be among the fastest growing in the near future are also primarily those that require the most education. The group that is expected to have the largest increase in employment through the year 2010 is the professional and related occupations group. (Social work is represented in this group, as are engineers, librarians, teachers, and psychologists, among others.) The left columns of Exhibit 1 show the actual number of people in the different occupational groups in 2000 and the projected increases by 2010. The declining needs in areas such as farming and maintenance occupations become most apparent when reviewing the middle (percentage distribution) columns (Hecker, 2001). Educational attainment tends to produce benefits for more highly educated workers, too, as Exhibit 2 demonstrates.

A trend in the workplace that is relatively recent is that of privatization. **Privatization,** the replacement of government organizations with private sector, often for-profit, services, is growing rapidly in the social service arena. This was apparent in the social work employment data shown in Chapter 1, where a shift away from public agency employment and toward private organizations was reported in the employment of baccalaureate-level social workers. Other areas of the human services are also experiencing privatization. Teachers, for example, are finding employment in charter schools and other alternative schools that are privately owned but funded to a large part by government grants. Prisons and jails, once the sole domain of government, are increasingly found in profit-oriented, private enterprise. There are some concerns related to privatization. Primary among them is the fact that the government has relinquished responsibility for oversight and the clients' or consumers' needs may become secondary to the profit motive of the corporation. In addition, salaries for workers in some privatized establishments may be lower than in comparable government organizations, and the commitment for long-range employment may be less in the private sector as well. In social work, privatization is sometimes associated with contracted services, where the

Education Pays: Average Weekly Earnings for Persons 25 and Over in 2000 by Education	
EXHIBIT 2	
Educational Attainment	**Dollars Earned per Week**
Less than a high school diploma	$360
High school graduates; no college	$506
Less than a bachelor's degree	$598
College graduates	$896

Source: MLR Online. (2001, June 27). Education pays. Retrieved August 3, 2001, from http://stats.bls.gov:80/opub/ted/2001/june/wk4/art03.htm.

duration and frequency of the social worker's contacts with clients is predetermined by the contract. Ethical dilemmas emerge when the contract ends yet the client is in need of continuing service.

A discussion of the workplace would not be complete without at least a brief examination of what a typical workday looks like. The work schedule depicted in Exhibit 3 was developed by the U.S. Department of Labor. Your own work schedule may look different from this, but it may cover the same total number of hours. Balancing family income with quality time for family members and friends has become a challenge. Employment is not the only pressure for families. It was estimated by the Department of Labor that by 1996, nearly 20 percent of American families provided care for a relative or friend age 50 or older (U.S. Department of Labor). The Department of Labor expects this percentage to double within the next five years. If child care were added to this equation, a more accurate picture of the pressures on families would be apparent. It would also explain the increase in number of meals eaten away from home and the growth in day care for older adults as well as young children.

For social workers there are many implications of the dynamic changes occurring in the workplace. Of course, there are issues of work site shifts, as noted in the gradual move away from governmental organizations as places of social work-

---

A Schedule for Today's Workday

EXHIBIT 3

5:30 A.M.	get up/get dressed/exercise
6:30 A.M.	make: breakfast, school lunches, grocery list
7:30 A.M.	get kids up, dressed, and fed
8:00 A.M.	drop off kids and dry cleaning
9:00 A.M.	on the job . . . 12 e-mail messages waiting for reply
1:30 P.M.	meeting at day care center (your child is biting!)
2:30 P.M.	back on the job . . . 8 voice-mails waiting
5:00 P.M.	forward office calls to cell phone
5:30 P.M.	pick up child from school aftercare
6:05 P.M.	pick up other child, pay late pickup fee at day care
7:00 P.M.	make dinner
8:00 P.M.	do: dishes, homework, laundry
8:30 P.M.	bathe kids
9:00 P.M.	read work memos to kids as bedtime story
9:30 P.M.	fold laundry/fall asleep

Source: Futuretime: The real workday. (n.d.). *Futurework: Trends and challenges for work in the 21st century, executive summary* (p. 6). Retrieved August 3, 2001, from http://www.dol.gov/dol/asp/public/futurework/execsum.htm.

ers' employment. The world of business and the workplace itself, however, has become a rapidly growing field of practice in social work. In this field, social workers have opportunities to work in counseling relationships with employees or to work with management on behalf of employees. This is an exciting field of practice with future opportunities that have yet to be imagined and implemented. It is also an area that holds many potential value conflicts for professional social workers. The issues and problems that are presented to social workers in this field of practice range from a runaway teenager and frightened mom, as in the chapter's case study, to problems of substance abuse, serious mental illness, family care needs, and violence.

SOCIAL WORKERS' ROLES AND RESPONSIBILITIES

A quick overview of the kinds of problems often seen by social workers in occupational social work or employee assistance programs could include any of the following:

- Abusive relationships
- Anger, anxiety, or problems with assertiveness
- Chemical dependency or substance abuse
- Eating disorders
- Inability to cope with change
- Interpersonal relationship difficulties
- Posttraumatic stress
- Sexual dysfunction
- Stress management
- Suicide prevention (O'Neill, 2002)

Dale Masi, who offered the listing of services above, also pointed out in an *NASW News* article that social workers offer a much broader array of services than many other behavioral health counselors, especially those employed by managed care organizations. Generally the counselors must restrict their services to clients whose problems fit a *Diagnostic and Statistical Manual of Mental Disorders (DSM)* category and deny services to people whose difficulties don't fit the *DSM* (O'Neill).

Indeed, the role of social workers is much broader than just a narrow focus on the problems of individuals. One role for social workers is helping to meet the needs of people within the family, work, and community environments in which they live. Another role is that of helping people to secure and sustain employment. Changing work and community environments to make them more responsive to the needs of people is yet another area of social work practice. Bringing social work values into the workplace, values such as appreciation for human diversity and nurturing of family, is another important role that is often overlooked. Occupational social workers also connect the work world to that of social policy. They do this by helping the work world to understand and carry out the mandates of social policies such as those related to the ADA (Americans with Disabilities Act) and by influencing social policy development from the perspective of what is good for the workforce (Mor Barak & Bargal, 2000).

Social workers at all levels—baccalaureate, master's, and doctorate—are found in occupational social work. The case study at the beginning of this chapter illustrated the kind of responsibilities that BSW social workers often carry. MSW and doctorate-level social workers provide clinical services. They also design, plan, evaluate, and administer human service programs in conjunction with other professional practitioners and corporate or union leadership. Often, too, they conduct research, write grants to obtain funding for new programs, and conduct community needs assessments.

PATHWAYS TO THE SOCIAL WORKER

One of the very rewarding elements of occupational social work is the wide spectrum of persons and life situations that social workers encounter. The range of problem areas and avenues for prevention was reflected in the previous paragraphs. The people who seek help from social workers in relation to workplace issues may be employees or managers at any rung of the corporate ladder. Their ethnicity, socioeconomic circumstances, religion, gender orientation, and health/mental health are likely to be widely varied. They may be angry, depressed, joyous, or frightened. But how do employees find their way to the social worker?

Now that obtaining help with personal problems is increasingly accepted by the larger society, employees are frequently self-referred. They also may be referred by supervisors or managers, whose referrals may be informal or formal. In an informal referral, an office manager may suggest to a despondent accountant: "I know how hard it is to get over a divorce. Sometimes it helps if you talk it over with someone. You might want to talk with one of the counselors in our employee assistance program."

A **formal referral**—one in which the employee is required to seek help or else face job termination or other disciplinary action—is used in some employee assistance programs. There is little doubt that this form of referral is coercive, but while some social workers in employee assistance work discourage this form of referral, others see it as a potentially valuable means to confront troubled employees. Dr. Dale Masi, a social worker who heads up her own firm, Masi Research Associates, and who initiated a doctoral program in industrial social work at the University of Maryland, takes the latter view, saying, "The threat of job loss is perhaps the most powerful tool that can be used to increase worker productivity and morale—an increase that results from a successful referral to the EAP" (quoted in Watts, 1988, p. 11).

Like others, Masi has found that careful training of managers and supervisors to recognize the indicators of employee problems is essential to the success of the employee assistance program. Even when problems are recognized, however, it is sometimes difficult for administrators to take the next step. The personal problems of employees are seen as very sensitive and potentially volatile issues and may therefore consciously be ignored by managers. In the absence of an employee assistance program, personal problems of employees are often ignored or tolerated until work performance degenerates significantly and the employee is fired. With training, however, managers learn to communicate openly with workers. They are encouraged to use a letter to accompany their discussion of problems in volatile situations or when there are threats to safety. Exhibit 4 is an example of a formal referral, even though it does not overtly threaten reprimand if the employee fails to seek counseling.

Formal Letter of Referral to an Employee Assistance Program

EXHIBIT 4

Mr. Paul White
Stone, Iowa

Dear Paul:

As you know from the discussion you and I have had, I am concerned with your work performance. I am writing this letter to you because of my high regard for you and for your contribution to the company. In the last few months it seems that your performance has increasingly shown signs of impairment. A summary of specific reasons for my concern includes:

1. On two occasions I have been notified that you violated company policy on entering the building at night. On the nights of May 5 and 27, you did not enter through the main entrance and did not sign in with security.
2. Your work quality has changed substantially in the last two months. On our last three reports, major data omissions occurred.
3. Your work attitude has altered. On several occasions I have heard you say your work doesn't matter to anyone anyway.
4. Your attendance at departmental meetings has been irregular. In the last two months you have missed all Monday meetings and only attended two Friday meetings. Your absence meant input from your unit was not received.
5. Relationships with co-workers have deteriorated. Kay Silver has told me no one in her unit is willing to work directly with you on joint projects because of your outbursts of anger. One of the company pilots has reported you were two hours late for a flight and offered no explanation to her. These behaviors are unusual and atypical of the valued worker you have always been.

Because of your drastic changes, I feel there may be some personal issues you are currently facing. Our company provides a resource, the Employee Assistance Program (EAP), to help employees whose job performance in the past has been fine and then gradually deteriorates, possibly because of a personal issue. I strongly suggest that you consider contacting the EAP to help you resolve whatever issues may be causing you concern at this time. The coordinator, Mary Green, has the job of helping you understand what may be interfering with your ability to do your job and then helping you locate resources that might deal directly with the issue. The program provides referral; it does not provide counseling.

The program is confidential; that is, the coordinator cannot and will not tell me anything you say unless you decide you want her to. Because this is a formal referral to the program, she will give me a yes or no answer as to whether or not you went to the program. Again, I urge you to contact the EAP at 999-1111 so you might obtain help in returning to your previous level of performance. If you make an appointment during working hours, you will need to advise me of the appointment. You will be given release time from your work to meet with the EAP counselor. My request is that you call by June 17 to make the appointment. Specific details of the EAP are presented in the attached brochure.

Again, Paul, we need your performance to return to normal and I very much hope using the Employee Assistance Program will be of benefit to you in your work and personally.

Sincerely,

S. Brown

Source: The Formal Letter of Referral to an Employee Assistance Program is used with permission from Judy Winkelpack and Michael Lane Smith, Identifying and referring troubled employees to counseling, Chap. 4 in *Social work in the workplace*, G. M. and M. L. Smith (Eds.). New York: Springer, 1988, pp. 57–58.

VIOLENCE IN THE WORKPLACE

Media reports of workplace violence occur almost daily. Gas station attendants are shot, convenience store clerks robbed, nurses assaulted, a stalker forces his way into a woman's office and beats her in front of her horrified coworkers. A federal building is bombed in Oklahoma City. The Pentagon in Washington, D.C., and the World Trade Center in New York are attacked by terrorists.

The data on workplace violence are horrifying. Two million persons are victims of violence in the United States each year, and the economic loss to employers is estimated at billions of dollars. Sadly, "homicide remains the third leading cause of fatal occupational injuries for all workers and the second leading cause of fatal occupational injuries for women" (IPRC, 2001, p. 4). **Sexual harassment** (abusive, discriminatory, or unwanted sexual behaviors) charges filed, according to the Equal Employment Opportunity Commission, have increased from 10,532 in 1992 to 15,836 in 2000, and monetary benefits paid as a result of sexual harassment claims reached $54.6 million in 2000 (EEOC, 2001).

Social workers are among the professionals who respond to workplace violence. Prevention efforts and training of supervisors are often their responsibility, too. In all social work practice settings, however, social workers may become involved with friends and family members of persons who have been victims or, possibly, the perpetrators (potential or actual) of workplace violence. It is important for all social workers to understand and appreciate the importance of workplace experiences in the lives of clients and of everyone around them.

Differentiating the types of violence that occur provides some insight into the nature of workplace violence. Four categories have been identified by the IPRC, the Injury Prevention Research Center (2001): criminal intent, customer/client, worker-on-worker, and personal relationship type.

Type 1: Criminal Intent. The perpetrator is usually unrelated to employees or the business establishment and approaches the premises with intent to commit a crime. Robbery and shoplifting are the most common forms of crime in Type 1 violence. A weapon such as a knife or gun is frequently involved. Not surprisingly, the greatest portion of workplace homicides (85 percent) occur with Type 1 incidents. The employees who are most at risk are those who must make change and handle cash at night or those that work alone, especially late night hours. Exhibit 5 illustrates Type 1 workplace violence.

Type 2: Customer/Client. Intent to commit a crime is not involved in Type 2 situations. Instead violence erupts in the exchange of service between an employee and a customer, nursing home or hospital patient, social service agency client, a prisoner, an airline passenger, or a student. Type 2 is illustrated in Exhibit 6

Type 3: Worker-on-Worker. Because this type of violence occurs between coworkers, it often is linked to a history of relationship problems between two or more employees and may follow a series of work-related disputes. See Exhibit 7 for further details regarding Type 3 violence.

Type 4: Personal Relationship. In Type 4 violence, the employee who is victimized has a personal relationship with the perpetrator that derives from outside the workplace. The perpetrator is not a coworker or employee. Domestic violence

Type 1: Criminal Intent

EXHIBIT 5

In May 2000, two men entered a Wendy's in Flushing, NY, with the intent to rob the fast-food restaurant. They left with $2,400 in cash after shooting seven employees. Five of the employees died and two others were seriously injured.

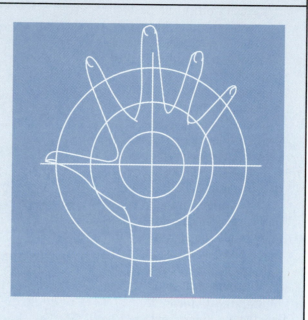

This is an extreme example of Type 1 workplace violence: violence committed during a robbery or similar crime in the workplace. Type 1 is the most common source of worker homicide. Eighty-five percent of all workplace homicides fall into this category. Although the shootings in Flushing drew a great deal of media attention, the vast majority of these incidents barely make the news. Convenience store clerks, taxi drivers, security guards, and proprietors of "mom-and-pop" stores are all examples of the kinds of workers who are at higher risk for Type 1 workplace violence.

Source: IPRC, Injury Prevention Research Center, The University of Iowa. (2001, February). *Workplace violence: A report to the nation,* p. 6. Retrieved August 4, 2001, from http://www.pmeh.uiowa.edu/iprc/ NATION/PDF?

is often involved. Women are more frequently targeted than men; however coworkers sometimes become victims of the perpetrator's rage. Type 4 violence is illustrated in Exhibit 8.

Categorizing the different types of workplace violence suggests that the causes, too, must vary. While further research is needed to provide more precise indicators of the causes of workplace violence, some causes can be understood. The workplace environment may be a source of stress that nourishes existing interpersonal conflicts between employees. The increasing human diversity of our society is reflected in workplace environments and may also trigger violence. Such conflicts may be related to any kind of human diversity but appear to be especially volatile when linked with allegations of sexual harassment

Type 2: Customer/Client

EXHIBIT 6

Rhonda Bedow, a nurse who works in a state-operated psychiatric facility in Buffalo, NY, was attacked by an angry patient who had a history of threatening behavior, particularly against female staff. He slammed Bedow's head down onto a counter after learning that he had missed the chance to go outside with a group of other patients. Bedow suffered a concussion, a bilaterally dislocated jaw, an eye injury and

permanent scarring on her face from the assault. She still suffers from short-term memory problems resulting from the attack. When she returned to work after recuperating, the perpetrator was still on her ward and resumed his threats against her.

In Type 2 incidents, the perpetrator is generally a customer or client who becomes violent during the course of a normal transaction. Service providers, including health care workers, schoolteachers, social workers and bus and train operators, are among the most common targets of Type 2 violence. Attacks from "unwilling" clients, such as prison inmates on guards or crime suspects on police officers, are also included in this category.

Source: IPRC, Injury Prevention Research Center, The University of Iowa. (2001, February). *Workplace violence: A report to the nation,* p. 7. Retrieved August 4, 2001, from *http://www.pmeh.uiowa.edu/iprc/ NATION/PDF?*

(Braverman, 1999). Enlightened organizations today increasingly recognize and value the "human capital" of their labor force, yet too often abusive supervision of workers poisons the work environment and sets the stage for violence. Abusive supervision is characterized by sustained verbal and nonverbal hostile behaviors by the supervisor toward one or more employees. Individual employees' responses to negative forms of supervision, however, may vary widely (Gummer, 2001; Tepper, 2000).

Type 3: Worker-on-Worker

EXHIBIT 7

Type 3 violence occurs when an employee assaults or attacks his or her coworkers. In some cases, these incidents can take place after a series of increasingly hostile behaviors from the perpetrator. Worker-on-worker assault is often the first type of workplace violence that comes to mind for many people, possibly because some of these incidents receive intensive media coverage, leading the public to assume that

most workplace violence falls into this category. For example, the phrase "going postal," referring to the scenario of a postal worker attacking coworkers, is sometimes used to describe Type 3 workplace violence. However, the U.S. Postal Service is no more likely than any other industry to be affected by this type of violence.

Type 3 violence accounts for about 7% of all workplace homicides. There do not appear to be any kinds of occupations or industries that are more or less prone to Type 3 violence. Because some of these incidents appear to be motivated by disputes, managers and others who supervise workers may be at greater risk of being victimized.

Source: IPRC, Injury Prevention Center, The University of Iowa. (2001, February). *Workplace violence: A report to the nation,* p. 9. Retrieved August 4, 2001, from *http://www.pmeh/uiowa.edu/iprc/NATION/PDF?*

Stress may also be transported to the workplace from workers' homes and from workers themselves. Sometimes the chemistry between this kind of stress and an existing problematic work environment is sufficient to create an explosive incident. Substance abuse is an example. Drug and alcohol abuse of individual workers or groups of workers can be an underlying threat. If it is tolerated or encouraged in the workplace, the likelihood of someone being injured is increased. Substance abuse very often occurs in conjunction with other factors,

Type 4: Personal Relationship

EXHIBIT 8

Pamela Henry, an employee of Protocall, an answering service in San Antonio, had decided in the summer of 1997 to move out of the area. The abusive behavior of her ex-boyfriend, Charles Lee White, had spilled over from her home to her workplace, where he appeared one day in July and assaulted her. She obtained and then withdrew a protective order against White, citing her plans to leave the county.

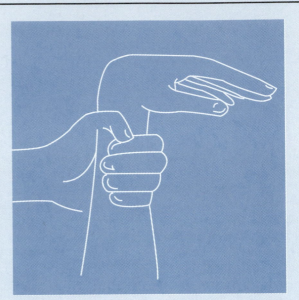

On October 17, 1997, White again appeared at Protocall. This time he opened fire with a rifle, killing Henry and another female employee before killing himself.

Because of the insidious nature of domestic violence, it is given a category all its own in the typology of workplace violence. Victims are overwhelmingly, but not exclusively, female. The effects of domestic violence on the workplace are many. They can appear as high absenteeism and low productivity on the part of a worker who is enduring abuse or threats, or the sudden, prolonged absence of an employee fleeing abuse. Occasionally, the abuser—who usually has no working relationship to the victim's employer—will appear at the workplace to engage in hostile behavior.

In some cases, a domestic violence situation can arise between individuals in the same workplace. These situations can have a substantial effect on the workplace even if one of the parties leaves or is fired.

Source: IPRC, Injury Prevention Center, The University of Iowa. (2001, February). *Workplace violence: A report to the nation*, p. 11. Retrieved August 4, 2001, from http://www.pmeh/uiowa.edu/iprc/NATION/PDF?

such as abusive supervision when violence is triggered. Domestic abuse issues transport violence from the home and community into the office, plant, or classroom. Similarly, workers' mental health or behavioral problems can erupt in ways that injure the worker or others (Braverman).

So, how would a social worker deal with an episode of workplace violence? Breadth of social work skills is imperative. Every social system level from individual to families, groups, the organization itself, and even the community may need attention from the social worker. The following example, one involving a murder at a utility company, portrays an occupational social worker in action (Walsh, 1987).

The case involved an employee of a Midwestern utility company who returned to work following a three-day disciplinary suspension and went to his supervisor to talk about work materials. When the supervisor was unable to talk with him immediately, the employee drew a gun and shot the supervisor four times, killing him. Amid the resulting confusion, the company's medical officer suggested calling in a social worker who was under contract as a consultant to the company.

On arriving, the social worker was briefed by management, and he advised the managers immediately to prepare and distribute to all employees a fact sheet providing accurate information about what had happened. This would offset rumors that were already surfacing and assure employees that they would have access to additional information as soon as it became available. Group sessions were begun. One group was formed for eyewitnesses to the murder, who were in trauma. Another group included friends and colleagues of the victim and of the assailant. The social worker also created groups for supervisors to help them deal with the reactions of the workers in their units. These groups continued to meet for several weeks.

Individual counseling sessions were conducted on-site as well. On the first day, group and individual participants expressed fear of the unknown, especially fear related to the potential behavior of the employee who shot the supervisor. This was considerably alleviated when that employee was subsequently taken into police custody. Family members and other persons who might be of support to emotionally upset employees were telephoned and were invited to come to the utility company and participate in the early individual and group sessions. This proved to be helpful.

The social worker was able to help the utility company develop a set of principles and guidelines to be used to prevent future trauma situations. Employee disciplinary procedures were examined as were early referrals for disciplinary problems. The utility company was also receptive to suggested ways of dealing with any future episodes of violence. This included designation of responsibility for decision making, identification of tasks related to communication with employees and the media, and approaches to intervention with distressed persons and their family members.

Physical trauma—such as accidental injury, rape, and fights—is not unusual in the workplace. In addition, employees are subject to **psychological trauma.** Some occupations, such as police work, place the employee in situations of psychological trauma almost daily. The specific work setting may be psychologically hazardous by nature; examples include hospice programs for the terminally ill, psychiatric facilities, and funeral homes. Threats to one's life during robbery attempts are increasingly common for such workers as gas station attendants, convenience store clerks, and bartenders. The impact of psychological trauma can be as great as that of physical trauma.

While the terrorist attacks on the World Trade Center and the Pentagon in 2001 took thousands of lives and injured hundreds of people, the bombing of the federal building in Oklahoma City in 1995 that killed 168 people also resulted in physical and psychological trauma for considerable numbers of people. The Oklahoma City bombing, too, propelled hospitals into emergency procedures, and the American Red Cross and Salvation Army were among the national organizations that arrived on the scene promptly to provide disaster assistance. Just as in the more recent New York City and Washington, D.C., disasters, social workers and social work students were also on the scene immediately. In Oklahoma City, for example, when telephone and other communications services were overloaded, a senior social work student at the University of Kansas in Lawrence used his computer to provide information about the disaster. Other students and faculty from the University of Oklahoma School of Social Work assisted in hospitals that had only small social work departments. At the Salvation Army students helped families find food or temporary lodging, made emergency travel plans with relatives, and assisted with funeral arrangements (Smith, 1995, pp. 3–5).

Michael Culotti, a social worker and senior account executive with the national employee assistance program, Family Enterprises, Inc., was also on the scene. Upon arriving in Oklahoma City, his first contact was with management personnel of the businesses his organization had contracts with; this included several HMOs that served the federal employees who had worked in the bombed building. Managers and supervisors identified high-risk people and employees who needed immediate individual help, those who wanted to be seen in a group, and those who preferred to be left alone to deal with the experience in their own way. Next, Michael Culotti organized **critical incident debriefing** sessions, in which participants were encouraged to talk about how the event affected them. They were helped to understand the normal and varied responses—physical, behavioral, and psychological—elicited by traumatic events. Culotti helped traumatized people to put their thoughts and feelings into an understandable framework. A single two-hour group often brought marked changes in employees' ability to think and talk about their experiences. Follow-up groups, Culotti knew, would be important in the weeks to come. Educational materials that explained trauma and the human responses to it, and also identified resources for help, were provided for those who chose to deal with the trauma on their own, as well as for others. Michael Culotti found that many people in Oklahoma City had wonderful family and church supports already in place (personal interview with Michael Culotti, Family Enterprises, Inc., Milwaukee, June 16, 1995).

OCCUPATIONAL SOCIAL WORK: FORMATS FOR SERVICE DELIVERY

Today, social work in the work environment is one of the fastest-growing segments of social work practice. It takes place in a myriad of locations and circumstances, but these can probably be sorted into five general areas: services offered by contract, services offered within corporations, those offered through unions, specialized services, and (the area showing the most rapid growth) services offered on the Internet.

Internet-Based Services

Private practitioners in social work and other human service professions as well as employee assistance programs are rapidly moving into cyberspace with information and counseling services targeted at workplace issues. Online counseling may be especially appealing for persons whose workdays are so full that they leave little time for after-hours regular sessions with a counselor or therapist. Many people have access to the Internet from work sites but not at home. A survey of an employee assistance company's clients by the University of Maryland School of Social Work showed a remarkably high level (93%) of satisfaction with the corporation's website. Many persons "used the Web site because they had issues too embarrasing to share face to face" (O'Neill, 2002, p. 14). Chat rooms permit questions to be raised and discussed with candor and in confidence or enable persons to "lurk" (listen in on discussions without getting involved) until they are comfortable to participate. Social workers hosting the chat rooms often focus discussion on specific topics that are announced in advance. Self-assessment for problems with substance abuse, depression, and stress is also made available on the Internet by some employee assistance companies. Information and educational services are provided, too, in areas such as stress reduction, caring for older adults, parenting, and personal finance (O'Neill, 2002).

Contracted Services

The most rapidly expanding format for the delivery of social work to the business world today is through services offered under contract by social workers in an employee assistance corporation. In this form of delivery, social work services are generally provided away from the workplace or union office. Instead, clients are referred by the union or business corporation, or they are self-referred, meaning they seek out the social worker voluntarily. The social worker's services are most frequently funded through a corporate employee benefit plan. The social service tends to be brief or focused on a crisis, rather than a long-term intervention.

Growth in this area of practice has been phenomenal. In large national employee assistance firms social workers and other professional staff provide services to people over the telephone rather than in office visits. Corporate employees, such as Gwen Knowles in the chapter case study, are provided a toll-free telephone number to call. If the brief telephone counseling or crisis intervention services are not sufficient, the employees are referred by the social worker or other employee assistance professional to preapproved social agencies or practitioners for more extensive assistance. Employee benefit plans specify the total number of contacts that will be paid by the employer. A strength of this service delivery plan is that there tends to be excellent follow-up by the social worker to confirm that needed care has been obtained.

Corporate Auspices

Social workers are also employed within business corporations and industrial plants to meet employees' human welfare needs. Conflicts of interest between employees and management do occur, and so social workers in this field of practice need to be especially alert to such ethical considerations as the use and assurance of confidentiality. They also need to work within existing legislation governing labor–management issues such as strikes and unions, and with benefit programs related to pensions and health care.

Social workers in corporations or industrial plants generally have offices located in the company's employee assistance or employee counseling program or in the human resources department. Assistance is provided to all levels of staff, and issues range from personal problems such as substance abuse or parent–child problems to preretirement planning.

Since employees are often referred to the social worker by supervisors, supervisory personnel are trained by social workers to make appropriate referrals and to do so in a way that preserves the dignity of the client. In addition, of course, many employees seek services themselves. Social work services are often available to the families of employees as well as to employees of the corporation. Although issues of confidentiality are a lingering concern when social workers are actually located in workplace settings, there is a strong advantage to being intimately present on-site, recognized and known by employees (Akabas, 1995). (See the "Up for Debate" box.)

Having ongoing opportunities to influence change in corporate decisions affecting employees is also a benefit. In addition to business firms, public and private nonprofit institutions have also developed services for employees patterned after this service delivery plan. Nevertheless, this "in-house" model of practice is declining as business corporations increasingly seek to cut costs by contracting out as many of their ancillary work units as possible.

Labor Union Auspices

The third form of service delivery is within a labor union. In this case the social worker is an employee of the union. The social worker's place of employment, usually located at the union office, is often known as the counseling or membership services office. Only members of the union and their families are eligible for service.

Unions are generally viewed by union members as having greater long-term interest in the well-being of employees than employers have. Union members are often more trusting of union social workers; these clients tend to be self-referred. This form of service delivery is most commonly found in the eastern United States and in those areas where unions remain strong.

Specialized Services

This is a miscellaneous group of services provided to corporations or unions usually via a contract for a defined period of time or for specific services such as retraining and referral programs that prepare people for job loss. Other types of spe-

Up for Debate

Proposition: When plants or corporations are large enough, employee assistance social work should be offered on the premises rather than through a contract organization.

Yes	No
1. When employees see the social worker daily and become familiar with him or her, they will be more trusting and likely to seek services.	1. Employees may not trust that private information will be treated with respect and that confidentiality is ensured.
2. When violence, personal crises, or traumatic events occur, the social worker is immediately available.	2. Contract services are generally available within 24 hours; therefore, in-house services are not needed.
3. Employees with long-term, complex problems can be seen over the span of their employment.	3. Corporations cannot afford to take responsibility for psychotherapy or long-term counseling.
4. Supervisors and managers are more likely to be provided with ongoing training to sensitize them to the stress, concerns, and needs of the workforce.	4. Employees prefer that supervisors and managers have no knowledge or involvement in individual employees' problems.
5. Sensitive issues related to the diversity of employees can be identified: prevention/intervention can be targeted appropriately.	5. Focusing on issues of diversity can be polarizing in the workplace.
6. The social worker who is on-site has ongoing access to key corporate decision makers.	6. A contracted EAP firm can have influence as an outside agent that is free from internal politics.

cialized services include consultation about personnel matters such as affirmative action or drug testing, stress-reduction courses (some designed for upper management), consultation to assist a supervisor with a worker's special needs or with co-workers' efforts to assist another worker (a rape victim, for example), preretirement groups, and assistance with community service projects.

It is important to note that employee assistance programs, regardless of their location, are staffed by a variety of professional as well as uncredentialed persons. In addition to social workers, psychologists, nurses, persons trained in personnel work, alcoholism counselors, union stewards, and counselors without formal credentials may all be found in employee assistance offices. Lawyers are also colleagues to social workers in the increasing number of employee assistance programs that provide legal services as well as social services.

THE FIGHT FOR SOCIAL AND ECONOMIC JUSTICE

Human diversity, populations-at-risk, the processes of discrimination—these are all important components of the professional social worker's knowledge base. Although all social workers expect to practice with diverse populations, there are special challenges in the workplace for persons who are at special risk because of age, ethnicity, or physical or mental abilities or because they are gay or lesbian. Long in the forefront of the fight for social and economic justice, the social work profession is committed to the development of employment opportunities and fair treatment for all persons.

Assisting employers to meet their federally mandated equal employment and affirmative action requirements has been a responsibility greatly valued by social workers who also advocate for fair employment practices for gays and lesbians, who are not currently included in federal protective legislation. The National Association of Social Worker's policy statement in support of affirmative action is shown in Exhibit 9.

Affirmative Action

In Chapter 4 of this text, the concept of affirmative action was introduced. You will recall that the Civil Rights Act of 1964 (as amended in 1972) prohibited employment discrimination based on race, color, religion, sex, or national origin; age and disability were added at a later date. It became the basis for the affirmative action and equal employment opportunity policies that changed the way workplace decisions were made. The Civil Rights Act was powerful legislation that had immediate and lasting impact on social policy, but vigorous opposition to affirmative action has persisted, and affirmitive action has never fully achieved its goal of ending discrimination in employment, housing, and other areas.

Although sometimes used interchangeably, creating confusion, the concepts of equal employment and affirmative action are different but related. **Equal employment opportunity** is the right of all persons to work and advance on the basis of merit, ability, and potential. Affirmative action (described in Chapter 4) can be seen as the process used by organizations in recruitment, hiring, and other areas to ensure or guarantee the right to equal opportunities. The intent of affirmative action is to end the discriminatory practices that had been put into place years ago and that continue even today in more subtle but insidious forms.

In the United States, social policy is created by legislation, court actions, executive orders of the president, and government regulations. Civil rights policy, especially affirmative action, reflects the influence of all these functions. Our Equal Employment Opportunity (EEOC) laws grew out of the Civil Rights Act of 1964. These laws prohibited making personnel decisions based on race, color, and all of the other protected categories, and their intent was to end discriminatory personnel decisions. Equal employment opportunity, however, did not commit employers to

NASW Policy Statement on Affirmative Action

EXHIBIT 9

NASW SUPPORTS AFFIRMATIVE ACTION

The intent of affirmative action is to correct the present effects of past discrimination and exclusion from opportunites (Myers, 1995) and to achieve future parity. Its purpose is to provide opportunities to a class of qualified individuals who have either historically or actually been denied opportunities and to prevent recurrence of discrimination (U.S. Commission on Civil Rights, 1977, 1981). Affirmative action has been effective in a broad spectrum of U.S. society's activities including, but not limited to, employment, education, housing, and federal contracting.

NASW supports affirmative action as a viable tool for upholding its ethical code to act to prevent and eliminate discrimination.

NASW supports the following principles:

- Full endorsement of local, state, and federal policies and programs that give all people equal access to resources, services, and opportunities that they require—everyone should be given equal opportunity regardless of age, disability, gender, language, race, religion, or sexual orientation.
- Social workers joining others to denounce attempts to end affirmative action initiatives.
- Changes in affirmative action that will strengthen practice and policy aimed at ending discrimination and its impact.
- A firm commitment to protect the gains realized by affirmative action.
- Working with others to develop more effective and cogent policies and strategies to guide society and communities to that end.

Source: R. W. Mayden & J. Nieves. (2000). Health care: Policy statement approved by the NASW Delegate Assembly, August 1999. In *Social work speaks: National Association of Social Workers policy statements 2000–2003* (p. 17). Washington, DC: NASW Press.

any specific action, and therefore they were not very controversial or very effective until President Lyndon Johnson's Executive Order 11246 in 1965, effectively creating what we now know as affirmative action. This executive order required corporations that had contracts with the federal government to specify and implement affirmative action goals for any racial, ethnic, or other imbalance existing in hiring or contracting procedures. (Women were added in 1967; sexual orientation has never been added, but half of the states now have nondiscrimination laws that protect the rights of gays and lesbians.)

Affirmative action goes beyond prohibiting discrimination. It promotes hiring of people from those groups who have experienced discrimination. Affirmative action is not a law; it is a voluntary action. Only organizations and institutions that seek to do business with the federal government are required to have affirmative action procedures. So, while not a law, affirmative action definitely carries clout. To implement affirmative action, a business, educational institution, union, or other organization develops recruitment procedures for hiring that widen the pool of applicants who will be considered for available positions. Affirmative action permits preference to be given to candidates from protected groups, women and those groups of people who have historically suffered discrimination in employment. It encourages openness in advertising and hiring and the development of hiring, retention, and promotion goals. Quotas are not part of affirmative action, but they can be used by the courts as a penalty when discriminatory employment practices, violations of EEOC laws, occur (Page, as cited in Finsterbusch, 1999).

Affirmative action is based on the belief that the reduction of socioeconomic inequality depends on the active creation of employment opportunities for groups of people who have experienced decades of discrimination. Affirmative action policies were not intended to be permanent but used as a tool to undo past wrongs and fight against existing discrimination. Opponents of affirmative action believe that these policies are inherently unfair.

The changing political climate in the United States has had considerable impact on affirmative action. As politically conservative presidents have been elected to office, they have appointed conservative judges to the U.S. Supreme Court. Gradually court interpretations eroded from their once-strong stance favoring civil rights and affirmative action. In a 1978 U.S. Supreme Court case, *Regents of the University of California v. Bakke,* the Court determined that quotas were illegal but that the university's use of race to achieve affirmative action goals in the recruitment of students was acceptable. In 1989 the U.S. Supreme Court ruled that employees who were adversely affected by affirmative action plans could also file lawsuits alleging discrimination. During the 1990s voters in California, Michigan, and Texas passed legislation substantially limiting or abolishing affirmative action. In 1998, despite clear opposition of the governor, the state of Washington also approved an initiative that would deny the use of preferences for women and minorities in government employment. According to Governor Gary Locke, it could "eliminate job training programs that help women and minorities make the transition from welfare to work" (Locke, 1998, pp. 1–2).

Recruitment and admissions are affirmative action issues for colleges and universities. For years many schools made concerted, specific efforts to diversify their faculty and student body. In light of growing skepticism about affirmative action in higher education, the former president of Princeton, William Bowen, and Harvard's Derek Bok conducted a comprehensive study of 45,000 students from 28 highly ranked colleges and universities. Bowen and Bok's findings, reported in 1998, supported their hypothesis that race-sensitive recruitment and admission policies really have worked. Among the indicators of success were data showing that the black students in the study finished college in the same amount of time as white students, were more likely than white students to complete graduate degrees in law and medicine, and following graduation were more likely than their white counterparts to be actively engaged in civic life. White students in the study reported that they were pleased to have experienced an ethnically diverse campus. The black students indicated that they had not been stigmatized by other students and faculty but, in fact, had good experiences while attending college. Not surprisingly, Bowen and Bok concluded that affirmative action admission procedures should remain in place in higher education (Bowen and Bok, 1998).

The changing interpretations of affirmative action and equal employment have had special meaning for social workers. The social work profession's support for affirmative action is based on the belief that it is an important tool in the fight for social and economic justice. So social workers assist corporations in writing their affirmative action plans and in developing procedures for monitoring the plans. Social workers in business and industry also train managers and supervisors in affirmative hiring and worker retention. Sometimes they also assist organizations in finding potential employees from among minority groups, women, the disabled, and the elderly. This is an area in which the social worker's knowledge of community groups and resources is especially valuable. None of these efforts, however, will ultimately meet the needs of corporations or employees unless business organizations are committed to creating a work environment that promotes opportunity.

Affirmative action, while supported by NASW and other groups, has developed strong opposition. The administration of George W. Bush and much of the business world support an end to affirmative action. The various components of social policy—especially state and federal legislative bodies and the courts—can be expected to engage in vigorous battles on issues of civil rights and affirmative action in coming months. Affirmative action may surface as an issue during the next presidential campaign.

Gender Issues

Social and economic workplace issues of concern to social workers also include gender discrimination in hiring and promotions and on-the-job sexual harassment of women. When attorney Anita Hill charged U.S. Surpreme Court nominee and now Justice Clarence Thomas with sexual harassment in 1991, awareness of this form of abuse was markedly heightened in the corporate world, but abuses continue. Sexual harassment tends to occur in two forms. In the first, "sexual favors are demanded to keep or advance on a job," and in the second, a hostile work environment exists "in which women are made to feel uncomfortable on the job through remarks and other messages from coworkers because of their gender" (Mayden & Nieves, 2000, p. 135). Although sexual harassment is a civil rights violation, research suggests that most women attempt to ignore it, try to find a way to deal with it without involving legal authorities, or leave their jobs (Miller, 1992). Unfortunately, sexual harassment exists within the social work profession just as it does elsewhere. The NASW *Code of Ethics* explicitly prohibits sexual relationships between social workers and clients (Section 1.09), sexual harassment of clients (Section 1.11), and sexual relationships with or harassment of supervisees and students (Sections 2.07 and 2.08). The NASW *Code of Ethics* appears in the Appendix of this book.

Lower salaries for women than for men have persisted over the history of our country. The U.S. Department of Labor's "glass ceiling report" (1991) that documented the pervasiveness of this problem in corporate America was described in Chapter 4 of this text. That report also focused attention on the difficulty experienced by women in seeking promotions into middle and upper levels of corporate management despite competitive credentials and work histories. The profession of social work, which comprises large numbers of women and which serves women, must be vigilant in its practice and policies as it seeks to avoid discriminatory behaviors that violate civil rights law and harm women. Indeed, social workers are called upon to value and empower women and to engage in political processes that will eliminate all forms of workplace discrimination.

Gay and lesbian employees also contend with many forms of insensitivity and outright discrimination. As previously indicated, the Civil Rights Act did not include homosexuality. Workplace discrimination has been openly practiced by no less than the largest employer in the United States, the federal government. In World War II, the military services declared that homosexuals were unfit for military service. The more recent "don't ask, don't tell" policy of the U.S. military mirrors common practice in much of corporate America, which strongly discourages people from honestly and forthrightly revealing their true identity. In the 1980s, unrealistic fears about HIV disease resulted in considerable workplace discrimination, including firings. Today it is not uncommon for gay men and lesbian women to be the butt of ugly jokes, to be assigned the least desirable work, to be passed over for promotions, and to be victims of workplace violence. Like women who experience sexual harrasment, gays and lesbians often just "take it" as long as they can, and then quit their jobs.

Social workers in corporate settings or employee assistance work can be effective on several different levels. Some of the issues that social workers help organizations and their workers to deal with include family leave and spousal benefits for same-sex partners, fears experienced by employees in anticipation of "coming out" to coworkers, and depression following death of a partner or breakup with a partner. Supervisor training can provide an excellent opportunity to create a tolerant work environment.

Probably the foremost role for social workers, though, is to influence organizational policy makers' and managers' thinking and conduct within the corporate environment. There has been an undeniable shift in the social climate of our country over the last decade in terms of increasing acceptance of sexual minorities. Although employment nondiscrimination legislation has not been passed, it has been introduced several times at the federal level and appears to be achieving broader support. In 1998, President Bill Clinton signed Executive Order 11478 adding sexual orientation to the list of protected groups for employment by civilian federal agencies. In addition, a growing number of states, counties, and municipalities have enacted ordinances prohibiting employment discrimination on the basis of sexual orientation. This, combined with an economic climate that makes it imperative for employers to retain skilled employees, sets the stage for potential improvement in the American workplace. It is increasingly a climate that will be open to social workers' efforts to secure policies and practices that will support gay men and lesbian women.

VALUES AND ETHICS

Business is based on the profit motive. Potential ethical and value conflicts exist when the profit motive takes precedence over the welfare of people (employees, consumers) or of social justice. Profit is the "bottom line" in business because failure to realize a profit means that the business ceases to exist. This does not necessarily imply profit at all costs, but it does imply a very basic difference in values and priorities between the world of business and the profession of social work.

Some social workers argue that social work cannot exist in a business environment without compromising professional ethics and values. These social workers tend to view business and industry as essentially exploitative. Others believe that coexistence is possible as long as the social worker is very clear about the innate differences in objectives and values between business and social work. Social workers who favor coexistence tend to believe that the profession has too long ignored workers and the ramifications of employment on clients' lives.

The fundamental concern is whether the social worker will ultimately serve the employee or the employer. Historically, social work has been committed to social change and has promoted the health and well-being of people. When dealing with violations of affirmative action, unsafe working conditions, corporate plans to decrease health insurance benefits, and plant relocation or closure, the industrial social worker needs to be especially clear about professional values: "In industrial social work, no less than in other fields of practice that appear to constrain options, practitioners must hold fast to their dual commitment to being providers of social services and agents of social change" (Kurzman, 1987, p. 907).

One area of special concern to both social workers and employees is confidentiality. For employees, breach of confidentiality could mean the loss of a job or loss of opportunity for advancement. This concern has led some unions to develop their own counseling programs at the insistence of employees who were reluctant to use the corporation's employee assistance program. Although instances of ethical violation of confidentiality are said to be rare, social workers nonetheless need to respond to this concern. In particular, social workers should be alert to signs of management's misunderstanding or potential mishandling of confidential materials. In contracting with business firms, social workers should be very clear about the boundaries of confidentiality. This is especially true when an employee assistance program is housed within the human resources department. Such an arrangement may heighten employees' anxiety about issues of confidentiality and may even convey an unintended message to management about the availability of personal information about employees.

Occupational social work sometimes poses an identity problem. In business and industry, social workers generally are not identified as such. Often, even in labor unions, they are referred to as counselors. The isolated social worker, practicing in an environment devoid of professional colleagues, needs to sustain her or his professional identification and to clearly understand the differences between the social work role and roles of other employee assistance or corporate personnel.

SOCIAL WORK AND INDUSTRY: A HISTORY

Evolution of Professional Practice

In the Middle Ages, generally the years 700 to 1500, the organization of labor became increasingly complex. **Guilds** (organizations of craftspeople, artisans, and merchants) evolved to protect the economic interests of their members. In time, the guilds became powerful social and political forces. They gradually assumed responsibility for providing for members and their families in cases of accident, death of the provider, or poverty. The guilds built elaborate meeting halls as well as schools and almshouses, taking over some of the functions formerly provided by churches. Thus, the first known employee benefit program was that provided by the guilds.

The Industrial Revolution, which began in England around 1760, substantially changed the nature of work and the work environment. Hand tools were replaced by power-driven machines. Most work was done in large factories or mills instead of in small shops or homes. Women, especially, were recruited for work in the mills. Workdays were long—12 or 13 hours—and people worked six days a week. In the early 1800s several industrialists developed factory towns in which the employees lived in dwellings owned by the factory and bought their food and supplies from company-owned stores. A few factory owners provided educational and health benefits. One industrialist, Robert Owen, added such important social welfare provisions as unemployment insurance, sick benefits, and child labor regulations to the housing, schools, and athletic fields that he provided in his factory town of New Lanark, Scotland.

In the late 1800s in the United States company owners hired persons, mostly women, known as **welfare secretaries,** who were responsible for providing services to employees. They managed existing employee benefit programs, obtained housing if necessary (especially for new immigrants who were brought to the United States by companies as cheap labor), and attempted to improve sanitation and working conditions. Aggie Dunn is recognized as the first industrial social worker. She was hired by the H. J. Heinz Company of Pittsburgh in 1875 in the position of social secretary. Her job was to hire, counsel, and watch over the 1,200 women employees of the company. "Mother" Aggie Dunn remained in this position for 50 years (Googins & Godfrey, 1985).

The Twentieth Century

The turn of the century saw an interesting development: a growing sense of sisterhood among women. Women like Margaret Dreier Robbins became leaders of trade unions and fought for improved working conditions. In the South, African American women's organizations evolved settlement houses based on the model of Janie Porter Barret's Locust Street Settlement in Hampton, Virginia. Southern communities often lacked the resources available in the industrial North. Instead of trained professionals such as nurses and elaborate programs such as those of Hull House in Chicago, they relied on local church volunteers, temporary housing, and the support and leadership of schools such as the Tuskegee Institute in Alabama. In Los Angeles, the Sojourner Truth Club was founded by Margaret Scott to provide boarding rooms for African American women from the rural South who emigrated in search of employment.

As schools of social work developed in the early 1900s, many of the industrial welfare secretaries obtained professional education. Gradually, methods of casework and group work were incorporated into the interventions used by the welfare secretaries.

The inhumane working conditions of factory employees, especially of minority employees, were exposed by social workers such as Emma Shields, who was appointed by the U.S. Department of Labor to study the conditions experienced by African American women in industry. She found many older black women—emancipated from slavery as youths—working in wretched, malodorous factories with no sanitary facilities: "Either standing all day, in some occupations, or, in others, seated on makeshift stools or boxes with no back support, they toil incessantly throughout the long, tedious hours of the work day" (Shields, 1921, p. 254). In the tobacco factories that Shields visited, black female employees were segregated from white female employees, who often toiled in newer and somewhat more sanitary buildings.

When the Great Depression struck the United States following the stock market crash of 1929, the corporations and businesses that managed to survive were forced to discontinue employee benefit programs and to lay off massive numbers of employees. Often this included the social work staff. The social work profession gradually moved away from practice in industry, and by 1935 social workers' places in industry were assumed by personnel officers and industrial nurses.

During World War II, industrial social work was revitalized. Huge airplane and munitions corporations needed social workers to assist a large labor pool of previously inexperienced industrial workers. Labor unions found social workers to be competent advocates for the labor movement as well as for individual employees. Bertha Reynolds, who was to become a leader in the social work profession, was hired by the United Seamen's Service, serving members of the National Maritime Union. Her work with the union won considerable support among union leaders for the social work profession. Until well into the 1940s, "labor and social work shared perspectives on corporate power, child labor, the right to organize, and the need for adequate wages and cooperated in political movements around those issues" (Scanlon, 1999, p. 590).

The U.S. armed forces also developed social work services to meet the needs of military families (Kurzman, 1987). With the end of World War II, defense industries shut down, women factory workers returned to their homes, and the human service professional workers once again turned to other areas of practice. For social workers, social change and union activism gave way to more conservative interests in mental health and psychiatric social work.

After two decades of decline, interest in industrial social work reemerged in the 1960s. One of the first schools of social work to develop a specialization in industrial social work was Columbia University in New York. In the early 1960s Hyman J. Weiner directed the development of the Industrial Social Welfare Center at Columbia. This program encompassed a strong union-based model in which social workers were prepared to work with and on behalf of unions. The program developed relationships with unions such as the American Federation of State, County, and Municipal Employees and the Amalgamated Clothing Workers (Jorgensen, 1981).

The 1970s saw the emergence of employee assistance programs, an evolution of the alcoholism-oriented programs that had developed earlier. Encompassing a much broader perspective than just substance abuse, their purpose was to intervene whenever employee work performance suffered, whether because of marital and family problems, mental or emotional problems, or substance abuse. Corporations such as General Motors in Detroit and the Xerox Corporation in Rochester, New York, found that staffing employee assistance programs with social workers was of benefit to the company. These firms valued both the direct services that social workers provided to employees and the consultation that they provided to corporate decision makers.

By the 1980s a considerable portion of the nation's businesses and industrial corporations had developed employee assistance programs. Governmental organizations also initiated such programs for their employees. Smaller corporations more often chose to contract with social workers in private practice or with family service agencies for their employee assistance services. Labor unions and corporate managers responded to employees' demands for programs to improve the quality of life, including wellness and stress-reduction programs, by contracting with or employing social workers to provide these services. The return of women to the workplace created needs for day care services for young children and for older adults, for flexible work hours, and for attention to family and community environments.

Plant closings and layoffs in northern states in the 1990s resulted when manufacturing and high-tech corporations relocated to southern states where wages were lower and fewer unions existed or relocated to underdeveloped countries where low-wage labor was available in abundant supply. Across the nation employment was readily available in service industry jobs, but it was often part-time, not well paid, and temporary. The result was a growing number of **working poor,** persons whose income from employment was insufficient to meet their survival needs.

Issues of the Twenty-First Century

The revolution in information technology has dramatically changed the world we live in. Because of nearly instantaneous communication and increased international travel, the world is perceived as a much smaller place today than it was a

HAZEL MANKIN

A heated discussion follows the announcement of a plant closing.

generation ago. Globalization of world economic markets is arguably the single most potent function driving workplace change in the twenty-first century. The whispers of change to come can perhaps best be heard in the voices of the youthful workers now working in low-wage jobs for multinational corporations in developing countries.

Interviews conducted with footware and clothing factory employees in Thailand, Vietnam, and Indonesia were the focus of a *Time International* article. These workers shared many characteristics of assembly line employees in the footware and apparel industry in developing countries: 80 percent were in their teens and twenties, single, and female. Most had little if any previous factory work experience or formal education. Although the factory employment offered shockingly low wages, the mere fact of their employment offered opportunities unthinkable even 10 years ago. Because they could earn a small income, these young women potentially have some alternatives to youthful marriages followed by years of child bearing. Their responses to questions about the kinds of training they would be interested in receiving reflected their aspirations for a new future. Knowledge of family and labor laws, skills for financial decision making and effective community leadership, management skills to advance in their current jobs, and training that would enable them to become small business owners were among their requests of their employers and any concerned organizations. The article concluded:

> Half the world's inhabitants are under the age of 25, and in the developing world, the majority of the population is under 20. . . . Many are already parents, workers, activists and consumers in the global economy. We ignore their plight and their limitless promise at our collective peril . . . we must listen to their voices. (Little, 2000, p. 42)

The very globalization that is producing a huge cheap labor supply in developing countries has cost jobs and lowered wages in the United States and other industrialized countries. On college campuses in Europe and the United States, protests and campaigns oppose sweatshop work conditions and the widening gap between "those reaping the benefits of globalism and those still struggling to survive" (Little, p. 42). Protests against the injustice of the evolving global economies and their use of human labor are increasingly disrupting world economic and trade conferences. Although it is likely that governments will attempt to silence these protests, the workplace in the next few years is likely to feel the impact of the gathering forces of young workers who are already gaining experience as social and community activists. Multinational corporations and world economic leaders, both very powerful forces, will also impact this scene. One can almost sense the energy that is growing.

Another kind of energy that will increasingly influence the workplace, especially in North America and Europe, is the energy that comes from human diversity. "The vast majority of new workers entering the workforce in the 21st century will be women, members of minority groups, and immigrants" (Johnson & Packer, 1987, as cited in Mor Barak, 2000, p. 49). Civil rights laws, the ADA (Americans with Disabilities Act), and, yes, affirmative action have been much more successful than is commonly acknowledged. Even a casual observer can recognize the increased presence of persons with disabilities, women, and other diverse populations in work environments. Diverse perspectives bring creativity and fresh insights, wonderful contributions to the world's economic well-being. But because diversity is sometimes threatening, a role for occupational social workers is one of assisting organizations to make diversity work. The social work profession's adoption of practice theory that fosters "goodness of fit" meets these needs very well. One strategy is to help corporate managers to resolve existing exclusion of diverse employee groups from workplace information communications, interpersonal relationships with decision makers, and advancements and promotions (Mor Barak, 2000). There are, however, no easy answers for complex issues.

The intensity and challenge of diversity-related workplace tension are seen in Keigher's report of violence experienced by home health workers as a result of institutionalized racism or religious discrimination. Home health workers are the persons who assist elderly persons to avoid nursing home placement by providing essential services such as bathing, cleaning, and meal preparation. Like child care workers, they are among the low-wage, temporary employees of the twenty-first century. Keigher's study compared home health care in Milwaukee, Wisconsin, and Belfast, Ireland. She found a remarkable level of "reticence to cross community boundaries: No Milwaukee White workers served Blacks. In Belfast, both Catholic and Protestant Home Helps [home health care workers] in working class areas fear serving the other community" (2000, p. 367). Black workers in Milwaukee and Catholic home health workers in Belfast experienced more threats and violence than workers from the dominant sectarian or ethnic group.

The issues of the twenty-first-century workplace, then, are complex and have ramifications that are at once global and personal. Like the youthful clothing and footware workers in developing countries, these issues are bristling with potential conflict and bursting with promise. Social workers will need to be prepared to counsel and advocate for individuals and families but also work with unions, corporations, and international coalitions to seek just solutions to problems and to create policies and programs that unleash human potential.

PREPARATION FOR PRACTICE WITH EMPLOYEES AND EMPLOYERS

The majority of social workers employed by corporations or working under contract with them hold master's degrees in social work. A few social work master's degree programs offer a concentration in occupational social work. The National Association of Social Workers recommends the master's degree, with field placement in an employee assistance program with an MSW field instructor. Some baccalaureate social work programs provide learning experiences in work settings for students who are interested in this field of practice.

Barbara Shank, in an article in *EAP Digest* (1985), identified the following routes to career preparation for industrial social work:

1. A concentration in occupational social work at an accredited graduate school of social work.
2. Coursework and field placement in occupational social work at an accredited baccalaureate program in social work.
3. A combined social work–business administration major.
4. A social work major and a business administration minor.

Most writers in the field of EAP or occupational social work encourage students considering a career in this arena to acquire an understanding of the nature and environment of business. The recommended course work includes economics, organizational psychology, history of the trade union movement, time management, conflict resolution, and personnel policy. It is also suggested that students acquire competence in research, statistics, and substance abuse counseling. Finally, there is general agreement that only experienced MSWs with clinical training should pursue positions in which they would be providing clinical assessments and psychotherapy. This would be consistent with the *Code of Ethics* that requires that social workers practice only within their area of expertise.

Because social workers in this field of practice often work in close teamwork relationships but with few other social workers at hand, they have an especially strong obligation to engage in continuing education programs and professional development on a career-long basis.

The EAPA (Employee Assistance Professionals Association) has come into existence to serve the needs of the diverse professionals who work in the field of employee assistance. Recognizing that most professional education programs in colleges and universities do not offer specific courses related to the field of employee assistance, the EAPA has created a certificate program. The EAPA sponsors courses at various universities, often through the university's continuing education division. The EAPA (not the university) awards a certificate, the CEAP (Certified Employee Assistance Professional), when the coursework has been completed (University Outreach, 1998). Additional information regarding the broad field of employee assistance and occupational social work is available on the Internet.

INTERNET SITES

http://stats.bls .gov/	U.S. Bureau of Labor Statistics
http://www.pmeh.uiowa.edu/iprc/ NATION.PDF?	Workplace Violence
http://www.dol.gov/_sec/gils/records/ 00187.htm	Futurework—Trends and Challenges for Work in the 21st Century (U.S. Department of Labor)
http://www.opm.gov/ehs/workplac/ index.htm	Dealing with Workplace Violence— A Guide for Agency Planners (U.S. Office of Personnel Management)
http://www.ccohs.ca/oshanswers/ hsprograms/eap.html	Canadian Centre for Occupational Health and Safety
http://www.osha-slc.gov/SLTC/ healthprofessional/	Occupational Health Professionals (OSHA) Behavior OnLine, the
http://behavior.net/	Gathering Place for Mental Health and Applied Behavioral Science Professionals
http://www.efr.org/	Employee and Family Resources

http://www.eap-association.com/	Employee Assistance Professionals Association
http://www.eapassociation.org/IAEAPE/	International Association of EAP's in Education
http://www.hr.upenn.edu/quality/wellness/managersupport.asp	Penn Friends Employee Assistance Program

SUMMARY

As reformers, activists, and counselors, social workers have been involved with workers and their work sites since the earliest days of the profession. The workplace is a natural setting for prevention and intervention. Yet the history of social work practice with business and industry is not one of steady, progressive growth. In the early 1900s, when schools of social work first emerged, some of the first students were experienced as welfare secretaries in textile mills and other industries. A decline of occupational social work in the 1930s was brought about by economic depression; the businesses that managed to survive were unable to provide employee benefits, including social services. During World War II, many women who were previously inexperienced in employment left their homes for full-time jobs in munitions companies and the aircraft industry. Industrial corporations and unions hired social workers to assist this newly recruited labor pool, but when the war ended, social workers left industry, along with female employees.

Freudian psychology captivated the profession, and interest shifted from the workplace to psychiatric facilities. Twenty years later, and with a renewed interest in client advocacy, the profession rediscovered the workplace and occupational social work quickly became one of the fastest growing areas of professional practice.

Today social services are delivered to workers and workplaces in a variety of formats. Internet-based services have been introduced fairly recently and are growing rapidly. Contracted services are the most rapidly expanding format, whereby social workers in private practice, in social agencies, or in private corporations assist employees of a firm or an organization that offers these services as an employee benefit. These social workers are generally located away from the place of employment, sometimes hundreds of miles away. Occupational social workers are also located within corporations or organizations; they may be more immediately available and intimately knowledgeable of workplace issues than in some other service delivery formats. Social work assistance is also available in some union offices; here the social worker is an employee of the union, not of the business corporation.

The pathways by which people come to the social worker vary. Some employees are referred by their supervisors or managers, while others are self-referred. In some cases there is coercion—loss of employment may be threatened if the person does not provide evidence of having obtained assistance. Events, often violent and traumatic, also bring the social worker and employee together. Issues of social and economic justice are distinctly workplace related. Professional values and ethics can be realized through the social worker's assistance to corporate decision makers regarding affirmative action procedures, valuing of human diversity in corporate policies, and training supervisors in conflict resolution.

The chapter describes the educational preparation needed by the occupational social worker. A generalist practice perspective is especially valuable because of the variety of tasks performed and of populations encountered. The master's degree in social work is required for all positions that involve provision of psychotherapy or in-depth counseling.

The brief case study at the beginning of the chapter drew attention to the ways in which baccalaureate social workers practice alongside MSWs in the world of work. Professional persons other than social workers—and persons who are not professionally trained, too—constitute the staff of some employee assistance programs. Teamwork skills, therefore, are especially useful in this field of practice.

Not all persons will be comfortable with the value dilemmas that must be confronted by the social worker employed in a business environment. Bakalinsky describes this as the "basic conflict between the [social work] profession's dedication to people's well-being and industry's dedication to profits" (1980, p. 471). She urged social workers to boldly confront this value dilemma and to create opportunities for serving the work world without loss of the basic mission of the profession.

The twenty-first century presents some interesting opportunities and challenges for social workers. Globalization of business and industry has brought huge profits to some individuals and corporations while job loss, wages below the poverty line, and temporary or contingency employment with minimal benefits have been the outcome for vast numbers of persons. Many social workers, along with other professional people and social activists, question the ethics of unjust economic systems. Social workers who truly want to "make a difference" will find that the twenty-first-century workplace environment will surely provide exciting opportunities to apply their practice skills and to advocate for organizational, community, and even global system change that will benefit the workplace and workers, their families, and their communities.

KEY TERMS

contingency work
critical incident debriefing
employee assistance program
equal employment opportunity
formal referral
guild
occupational social work

physical trauma
privatization
psychological trauma
sexual harassment
welfare secretary
working poor

DISCUSSION QUESTIONS

1. What were the responsibilities of the baccalaureate social worker in the chapter case study? Under what circumstances would the BSW social worker be likely to refer a client to a master's-level social worker? Was the BSW social worker effective?
2. What are the pros and cons of formal referrals in occupational social work?

3. Locate examples in the chapter of social workers helping victims of violence. Give examples of other forms of workplace-related violence that can result in physical or psychological trauma. How might employee assistance organizations and social workers providing Internet-based services have helped families of people affected by the World Trade Center and Pentagon terrorist attacks? Can you think of ways in which social workers could help corporations to prevent workplace violence or to plan for any future violent or traumatic events?

4. Does your school (or your place of employment if you are employed) provide an employee assistance program? Which form of service delivery does it represent? What are the credentials of the staff of the employee assistance program?

5. How does affirmative action differ from equal employment opportunity? What is the role of the social worker in relation to these concepts? Does your school have an equal employment opportunity policy? Does it also have an affirmative action procedure?

6. Provide examples that describe EAP or occupational social workers serving the needs of (a) an individual, (b) a family, (c) a group, (d) a corporation or other organization, and (e) a community or a special population.

7. What kinds of value conflicts are likely to emerge when social workers are employed by business corporations?

8. What can social workers teach to supervisors and managers of corporations?

9. What groups of people are vulnerable to discrimination in the workplace? What forms does such discrimination take?

10. Think about the globalization of the workforce. How is it related to poverty and affluence? How does a cheap labor supply in other countries affect the workers of the United States? Is there energy to create change that will lead to social and economic justice? Where might this energy come from?

CLASSROOM EXERCISES

It is suggested that students break into small groups of three or four to discuss these exercises. It may be helpful to choose a scribe to record and report interesting points to the class after the group discussion.

1. In Chapter 4, a classroom exercise suggested comparing and contrasting affirmative action and nondiscrimination policies for employment and university admission. While Chapter 8 uses the term "equal opportunity employment" rather than "nondiscrimination," these concepts are essentially the same. For this classroom exercise, divide again into small groups. Half of the groups should identify arguments promoting affirmative action as the more just social policy; half of the groups should identify arguments promoting "equal opportunity" or "nondiscrimination" as the more just social policy. Each group should then appoint a spokesperson to represent its arguments in a classroom debate or panel discussion.

2. This chapter introduces the idea of prison labor as a source of low-wage labor for American industry. In small groups, identify and discuss pros and cons of this proposition. Overall, do you think widespread use of prison labor by private industry is a good idea? Why or why not?

3. Social workers employed by employee assistance programs frequently accept clients who have been involuntarily referred by their supervisors. In light of the profession's core value of self-determination, what do you think about this practice? Pros? Cons? What safeguards do you think are necessary for this practice to be in accord with the *Code of Ethics?*

4. While people of color and women are protected classes under the federal Civil Rights Act, this is not true of people of minority sexual orientation. The social work *Code of Ethics* promotes protection for groups that suffer discrimination. What can happen to people of minority sexual orientation (and their families) if they are not protected? Why do you think discrimination against sexual minorities is not outlawed by the Civil Rights Act? What do you think can or should be done about this situation?

RESEARCH ACTIVITIES

1. If you were interested in obtaining employment in occupational social work after completing a BSW, where might there be opportunities to do this? Review your college or university catalog and identify the courses that you could take before graduating that would help to prepare you for a position in occupational social work or with an employee assistance program. If, instead, you wanted to pursue an MSW, you would need to obtain information about MSW concentrations in this field of practice. Locate information about MSW concentrations in occupational social work or employee assistance work. List the distinguishing features of these programs and compare them to determine which curriculum and program would better suit your potential career interests.

2. Various government agencies, such as the U.S. Department of Justice's Bureau of Justice Statistics and the U.S. Department of Labor's Occupational Safety and Health Administration, provide comprehensive reports on workplace violence and other issues of concern to social workers. Locate one report and prepare a summary of the type of information available.

INTERNET RESEARCH EXERCISES

1. Dr. Dale A. Masi is the founder of Masi Research Consultants, Inc., a corporation that assists companies in the United States and abroad to develop employee assistance programs. On her website (located at http://members.aol.com/drmasi/masi.html), locate the following information about this social work pioneer and leader:
   a. Her current teaching positions, publications, and awards, as well as the organizations she has consulted for.
   b. The topics covered in her book on international employee assistance.
   c. Her international experience as a consultant and educator on employee assistance programs.

2. The Sidran Foundation has a paper on psychological trauma on its website (http://www.sidran.org/whatistrauma.html).
   a. What key does the author provide to understanding traumatic events?
   b. The paper defines single blow versus repeated trauma. Which is the most damaging and why?
   c. What are the four self-protective coping strategies that people are likely to use to avoid psychic harm where traumatic situations are experienced?

3. The Canadian Centre for Occupational Health and Safety has an informational page on its website explaining employee assistance programs (http://www.ccohs.ca/oshanswers/hsprograms/eap.html).
   a. How does this agency define an EAP?
   b. What are three types of referral to an EAP listed on this information sheet?
   c. List four factors that make an EAP successful.

REFERENCES

Akabas, S. H. (1995). Occupational social work. In *Encyclopedia of social work* (19th ed., pp. 1779–1786). Washington, DC: NASW Press.

Armour, S. (1998, July 13). Short-term workers enjoy their freedom. [Electronic version]. *USA Today (Money)*. Retrieved Aug. 1, 2001, from www.nbta.org/Applications/News/ChangingWorkplace.cfm.

Bakalinsky, R. (1980, November). People vs. profits: Social work in industry. *Social Work, 25* (6), 471–475.

Bowen, W. G., & Bok, D. (1998). *The shape of the river: Long-term consequences of considering race in college and university admissions.* Princeton, NJ: Princeton University Press.

Braverman, M. (1999). *Preventing workplace violence: A guide for employers and practitioners.* Thousand Oaks, CA: Sage.

Bureau of Labor Statistics. (2000, April 25). *National longitudinal surveys. Number of jobs held, labor market activity, and earnings growth over two decades: Results from a longitudinal survey, summary.* Retrieved from http://stats.bls.gov/news.release/nlsoy.nr0.htm.

Bureau of Labor Statistics. (2001, January 23). *Household data annual averages, Table 2: Employment status of the civilian noninstitutional population 16 years and over by sex, 1969 to date.* Retrieved August 3, 2001, from http://stats.bls.gov/pdf/cpsaat2.pdf.

Bureau of Labor Statistics. (2002, January 4). *Employment situation summary.* Retrieved January 5, 2002, from http://stats.bls.gov/news.release/empsit.nr0.htm.

Finsterbusch, K. (Ed.). (1999). *Taking sides: Clashing views on controversial social issues* (10th ed.). Guilford, CT: Dushkin/McGraw-Hill.

Googins, B., & Godfrey, J. (1985, September–October). The evolution of occupational social work. *Social Work, 30* (5), 396–402.

Gummer, B. (2001). Abusive supervisors, competent workers, and (white) friends in high places: Current perspectives on the work environment. *Administration in Social Work, 25* (1), 87–106.

Hecker, D. E. (2001, November). Occupational employment projections to 2010. *Monthly Labor Review.* Retrieved January 7, 2002, from http://www.bls.gov/opub/mlr/2001/11/art4full.pdf.

IPRC: Injury Prevention Research Center. (2001, February). *Workplace violence: A report to the nation* (The University of Iowa). Retrieved August 4, 2001, from http:/www.pmeh.uiowa.edu/iprc/NATION/PDF.

Jorgensen, L. A. B. (1981). Social services in business and industry. In N. Gilbert & H. Specht (Eds.), *Handbook of the social services* (pp. 33–352). Englewood Cliffs, NJ: Prentice Hall.

Keigher, S. M. (2000). Violence in community care: An exploratory cross-national study of care in two segregated cities. *The Gerontologist, 40* (1), 367.

Kurzman, P. A. (1987). Industrial social work (occupational social work). In *Encyclopedia of social work* (18th ed., Vol. 1, pp. 899–910). Silver Spring, MD: National Association of Social Workers.

Little, R. (2000,). Workers of the world, speak up: At last, people on the factory floor have entered the globalism debate (Electronic version]. *Time International, 155* (25), 42.

Locke, G. (1998). Initiative Measure 200: Arguments for and against. *1998 online voter's guide: Office of the Secretary of State, State of Washington* (online). Available: http://wa.gov:80/sec/vote98/i200fa.htm.

Logophilia. (n.d.) *The word spy.* Hotelling (posted March 28, 1998) and Teleworkaholic syndrome (posted January 20, 1999). Retrieved January 5, 2002, from http:/www.logophilia.com/Word Spy.asp.

Macdonald, S. B. (1998, March–April). Clarifying the EAP-health care law connection. *EAPA Exchange, 12*–15.

Mayden, R. W., & Nieves, J. (2000). Gender-, ethnic-, and race-based workplace discrimination. In *Social work speaks: National Association of Social Workers policy statements: 2000–2003* (5th ed., pp. 132–140). Washington, DC: NASW Press.

Miller, D. C. (1992). *Women and social welfare: A feminist analysis.* New York: Praeger Press.

Monthly Labor Review Online. (2001, June). *Labor month in review, 124,* (6). Retrieved August 3, 2001, from http://stats.bls.gov.80/opub/mir/2001/06/lmir.htm.

Mor Barak, M. E., & Bargal, D. (2000). Social services in the workplace: Repositioning occupational social work in the new millennium. *Administration in Social Work, 23* (3/4), 1–12.

Mor Barak, M. E. (2000). Beyond affirmative action: Toward a model of diversity and organizational inclusion. *Administration in Social Work, 23* (3/4), 47–68.

Myers, S. L., Jr. (1995, July/August). Equity, fairness, and race relations. *Emerge, 6,* 48–52.

National Center for Policy Analysis. (2001, April 11). *Convicts could save U.S., jobs, reduce prison costs.* Retrieved August 3, 2001, from http://www.ncpa.org/press/nr041101a.html.

O'Neill, J. V. (2002). EAPs offer multitude of internet services. *NASW News, 47* (1), 14.

Scanlon, E. (1999). Labor and the intellectuals: Where is social work? *Social Work, 44* (6), 590–593.

Shank, B. W. (1985, July–August). Considering a career in occupational social work? *EAP Digest, 5* (5), 54–62.

Sharkey, A. G. (1998, September 16). Opinion: Let's save U.S. jobs. American Iron and Steel Institute. Retrieved August 3, 2001, from http://www.steel.org/news/oped/sharkey.htm.

Shields, E. L. (1921, May). Negro women and the tobacco industry. Life and labor. In G. Lerner (Ed.) (1972). *Black women in white America: A documentary history* (pp. 142–144). New York: Random House.

Smith, R. (1995, June). In the wake of the blast. *NASW News, 40* (6), 3–5.

Tepper, B. J. (2000). Consequences of abusive supervision. *Academy of Management Journal, 4* (2), 178–190.

University Outreach, University of Wisconsin-Milwaukee. (1998). *EAP Certificate Program in Employee Assistance* [Brochure]. Milwaukee, WI: Author.

U.S. Commission on Civil Rights. (1977). *Statement on affirmative action* (Clearinghouse Publication No. 54). Washington, DC: Author.

U.S. Commission on Civil Rights. (1981). *Affirmative action in the 1980s: Dismantling the process of discrimination* (Clearinghouse Publication No. 70). Washington, DC: Author.

U.S. Department of Labor. (n.d.). 7—Implications of workplace change. *Futurework: Trends and challenges for work in the 21st century.* Retrieved August 3, 2001, from http:www.dol.gov/dol/asp/public/futurework/report/chapter7/main.htm.

U.S. Department of Labor. (1991). *Report on the glass ceiling initiative.* Washington, DC: U.S. Government Printing Office.

U.S. Equal Employment Opportunity Commission. (2001, January 18). *Sexual harassment charges EEOC & FEBAs combined: BY 1992-FY 2000.* Retrieved January 8, 2002, from http://www.Eeoc.gov/stats/harass.html.

Walsh, J. (1987). Murder in the workplace: Responding to human trauma. *EAP Digest, 7* (5), 34–37, 66–69.

Watts, P. (1988). Management in practice: Effective employee assistance hinges on trained managers. *Management Review, 77* (1), 11–12.

Winkelpack, J., & Smith, M. L. (1988). Ch. 4 Identifying and referring troubled employees to counseling. In G. M. & M. L. Smith (Eds.), *Social work in the workplace* (pp. 45–62). New York: Springer.

FOR FURTHER READING

Herod, A. (2000, October). Workers and workplaces in a neoliberal global economy. *Environment and Planning A, 32* (10), 1781–1790.

Don't let the title scare you! This article provides a fascinating look at the forces that are transforming the workplace. The article is a continuation of the discussion at the end of this chapter concerning globalization and its impact on workers and the workplace of the twenty-first century. Herod reviews the apparently logical arguments that we hear daily about the need for a leaner, more flexible labor source in order for our corporate structures to meet the complex demands of the global economy. He then suggests that there are alternatives to the present approach of poverty-level wages, temporary work, and masses of exploited workers. His analysis suggests that there are indeed ways of connecting the factory workers of developed and developing countries in social action that has constructive potential. Read this article to learn how he understands the forces at work and the strategies that he sees as potentially useful to the achievement of a just economy.

Masi, D.A. (1997, July). Evaluating employee assistance programs. *Research on Social Work Practice, 7*(3), 378–390.

This is a very "nuts and bolts" article about implementing assessment procedures in employee assistance programs. Interestingly, the author's conceptual model incorporates the total quality management (TQM) approach, which seeks to ensure ever-increasing consumer satisfaction. One of the targets of evaluation recommended by Masi is the telephone referral procedure. In most EAPs, the first point of contact occurs on the telephone. With rapidly evolving telephone communication systems, increasingly effective technology is available so that it should be possible for callers to make quick contact with a professional and not have to make their way through complex menus and voice mail. The effectiveness of the responder is evaluated for communication of caring, and for clarity and efficiency. This is just the beginning of the process. Evaluation proceeds through physical observation of the facility, the management information systems used for monthly reports as well as the nature of data gathered, utilization rates, counselor credentials, employee feedback, cost benefit analysis, and a clinical review process based on case record reviews. Despite the challenges to evaluations, which Masi identifies, this author insists on and provides clear guidelines for the evaluation of employee assistance programs.

Raber, M. (1996). Downsizing of the nation's labor force and a needed social work response. *Administration in Social Work, 20*(1), 47–58.

That corporate downsizing has reached global proportions is no longer news. The reasons for this practice range from increased global competition to technological change. It is not confined to business and industry but is occurring with the government workforce as well. Job loss has serious ramifications in human terms—mental health suffers along with family incomes. Raber's article frames a social work response that is remarkably positive against such a bleak background. Raber proposes that social workers can serve as advocates with managers on behalf of employees, provide systematic procedures for referrals to outplacement agencies or to specific potential new employers, and attempt to humanize the process of layoff and job loss. Raber urges social workers to use the principles of empowerment to help employees to take control of their own careers though what she calls career management skills, skills that a team of social work and human resource personnel can deliver.

Solomon, C.M. (1998, February). Picture this: A safer workplace. Polaroid addresses family violence to combat workplace violence. *Workforce, 77*(2), 82–87.

This article describes the way that a specific corporation, Polaroid, decided to take on the issue of workplace violence. What is unique with the Polaroid example is that this corporation used the very product it manufactures, in addition to its employee assistance program, to seek solutions to workplace problems. When the corporation recognized the presence of domestic violence among its workers, the EAP program was asked to intervene. EAP staff helped in the usual ways, with counseling and community referrals to local shelters and other services. Then the company created the Polaroid School of Law Enforcement Imaging to teach police officers photographic technology to document the evidence of domestic abuse; also taught were skills in effective assistance to the victim of abuse. A subsequent hostage-taking incident in which an employee threatened to kill five other workers provided additional awareness that violence happening in the home—the employee, it turned out, had a history of battering his wife—could spill over into the workplace. Out of this incident came the corporation's commitment to create a safer work environment by actively combatting domestic violence. The Solomon article describes the extensive EAP program, personnel practices, and community efforts now underway at Polaroid.

Van Den Bergh, N. (1995). Employee assistance programs. In *Encyclopedia of Social Work* (19th ed., Vol. 1, pp. 842–849). Washington, DC: NASW Press.

Students who are considering a career that combines business and social work or students whose library research assignment includes occupational social work will find the Van Den Bergh article of value. A history section traces the development of employee assistance social work from its beginnings in the late 1800s to the present day. The pronounced focus on alcoholism is interesting to note. Van Den Bergh also discusses the varieties of program design for EAPs and identifies 11 specific components that are characteristic of most EAPs. These range from procedures to secure case records to data collection mechanisms and assessment and referral practices. Her section on future trends does not bode well for internal EAPs but suggests the possibility for evolution and growth of other forms of employee assistance programs, including expansion into the European market.

Social Work in the Schools: Lisa and Loretta Santiago, Children-at-Risk

LISA AND LORETTA SANTIAGO

Frank Haines, social worker for the Valdez Middle School, checked the memos in his mailbox as he did every weekday morning. Sure enough, there was a new referral concerning **truancy.** *Two sisters, Lisa and Loretta Santiago, had been absent for nearly two weeks.*

Children whose primary language was Spanish, such as Lisa and Loretta, could learn basic subjects like math and reading in their native language at this school, enrolling at the same time in English as a Second Language (ESL). Other Spanish-speaking children who had a better grasp of English could take most classes in English, and a bilingual teacher would assist them in Spanish as needed. Frank Haines, the social worker, was not Latino, but he spoke a fair amount of Spanish. In his former training to be a Catholic priest, Frank had traveled to two Latin American countries and had also served as a street worker among Latino youth. He recognized that there were great differences as well as similarities among Latino families and that linguistic dialects and cultural norms differed significantly among Spanish speakers from Mexico, Puerto Rico, Cuba, South America, and the Southwestern United States.

Frank had eventually changed his career goals to social work because he wanted to have a family of his own. He then earned the MSW, the degree most commonly required for this type of employment in the public schools. He also took courses in education to obtain certification in school social work, as required by his state's department of public instruction.

To begin his work with the Santiago sisters' case, Frank examined the girls' school files for records of attendance, conduct, and grades. He found that the two sisters had transferred from a school in Texas three years before. Their attendance had been regular until recently. The younger girl, Loretta, a seventh-grader, had good grades up to the most recent report. Lisa, an eighth-grader, had only fair grades the previous year, but her grades for the first quarter of this year were absolutely terrible. Frank wondered if something might have happened recently to upset the children, especially Lisa.

Frank then checked with the children's teachers. Loretta's teachers expressed concern for the girl and worried about her absence, but otherwise reported that she was a good student. Her home room teacher had sent the parents a note about attendance, but there had been no response.

Lisa's teachers reported that ever since summer vacation, the girl had seemed "different." The mathematics teacher and the ESL teacher said that Lisa stared at the classroom walls for long periods of time. Sometimes she would cry, or chew on her knuckles. Teachers had sent notes home, asking for a conference with the parents, but so far, no one had responded.

Frank's next step in his investigation was to try to talk with the parents. No one answered his first several telephone calls. Finally, a young woman answered who said that she was the children's stepmother. She told Frank that the girls had run away two weeks before. Frank made an appointment for a home visit late the next day, when Mr. Santiago would be home from work. He mentally crossed his fingers, hoping he would get his work done in time to have supper with his family. All too frequently, Frank's work hours conflicted with his precious time at home.

Fortunately, both Mr. and Mrs. Santiago were present when Frank arrived for his appointment. In the Latino culture it is often considered improper for an unrelated man to visit alone with a woman, even on official school business. Frank greeted the couple in Spanish, which warmed the atmosphere immediately. Mrs. Santiago served the two men coffee and then withdrew to manage several small children. Frank began the interview with Mr. Santiago in his best halting Spanish, but the latter, with a broad smile, responded in imperfect but much-better English. "Spanish is a beautiful language," he said, "but I think perhaps it will be easier for you to speak in English. I understand you are here because of my two older daughters, Lisa and Loretta. You see," he said, "they come from my first wife, who still lives in Texas, and sometimes they cause me a great deal of trouble."

Frank soon learned that Mr. Santiago had been battling with his former wife over custody of Lisa and Loretta for years. The court had awarded him custody because his second marriage was intact, whereas the biological mother was not legally married to her live-in boyfriend in Texas. Mr. Santiago loved Lisa and Loretta as well as his five younger children by his second marriage, but, like many urban men of Mexican descent, he translated his love for his daughters into powerful protectiveness and control.

The girls had run away, he said, because Lisa broke his rule against dating. Lisa had taken Loretta with her on the date as a family chaperone, but that was not enough to satisfy the father. When he learned what had happened, he became very angry, gave them both a severe lecture, and grounded them for two weeks. Then he locked them in their bedroom, but they broke out and ran away. Mr. Santiago knew where they were, he said: with his current wife's sister. They were afraid to come home, he said, because they knew he was so angry he "might be tempted to use the belt."

"How will the girls learn that you are ready to let them come home without that kind of punishment?" Frank said. "You know that's not a good way to discipline your children."

"Oh," Mr. Santiago replied breezily, "if I tell my wife it's OK, they'll be home soon enough."

Frank suspected that the father might be ready for an excuse to let his daughters come home, since he cared enough about them to let them stay in a safe place until he calmed down. The social worker seized the moment to tell Mr. Santiago that he was very worried; the father was breaking the law by allowing his daugh-

335

CHAPTER 9
*Social Work
in the Schools:
Lisa and Loretta
Santiago,
Children-at-Risk*

*ters to remain truant. If they stayed out of school much longer, a parental confer-
ence would have to be set up with the principal. That would mean Mr. Santiago
would miss work and could lose hours of pay.*

*After a few minutes, Mr. Santiago said he had decided it was time. He would
speak to his wife and she would bring the children home. Two days later, Lisa and
Loretta were back in school. Frank called them into his office for a conference. Both
girls moaned to Frank that they would never be able to lead a normal life. All their
friends were allowed to go out with boys when they were in junior high, they said.*

*"All of them?" asked Frank. "You know, I've heard that girls from Latino
families are often not allowed to date, at least without a brother or sister along."*

*"But I took my little sister," Lisa wailed, "even though I know lots of girls who
don't have to. None of the Anglo kids have to do that."*

*Frank empathized with the girls, but he pointed out that, since they lived with
their parents, they would have to obey their parents' rules.*

*"But we don't live with our parents," Lisa wailed again, "and these aren't our
parents' rules. We live with our father, and they are our father's rules. And I hate
him," Lisa said suddenly in a much different tone, intense and furious. "He was
mean to my mother, very mean. Last summer I was visiting her in Texas, and he
was staying with my grandparents there. I was walking with my mother when my
father saw us on the street. He came up and stood in her way and wouldn't let her
by. He called her horrible names and shoved her until she nearly fell. I thought he
was going to hit her. My mother was shaking all over. He made her cry, and I
heard every terrible word he said. I hate him."*

*Now Frank understood why Lisa was acting so troubled and defiant. She had
been through an emotionally traumatic experience. He let both girls talk at length.
He wondered out loud if they might want to see a counselor either by themselves
or with their father and stepmother. But they insisted a counselor wouldn't help.*

*A few weeks later, Lisa and Loretta violated their father's curfew again. When
they returned home, Mr. Santiago lost his temper and began shouting at his daughters, yelling that they were no good and would be grounded for a month. They would
not be allowed to go on a school trip they had been counting on. The girls retaliated
by calling their father every nasty name they could think of, in both English and
Spanish. Mr. Santiago locked them in their room, but they left through the window.*

*Soon afterwards, the girls showed up at Frank's office door at school, sobbing
angrily. Fortunately, no one else was there, so he invited them in right away. Before Frank could find out what was wrong, however, Mr. Santiago himself arrived,
clearly in a rage. Lisa immediately began to scream and curse. Mr. Santiago
shouted for her to be quiet and then yelled at Frank that he had had all the disre-
spect and disobedience from his daughters that he could take. "Listen to that!"
Mr. Santiago shouted, jabbing at Lisa and Loretta with a powerful forefinger.
"Listen to how my daughters defy me! Listen to the kind of language they use with
their own father! These girls are runaways, Mr. Haines! I want you to call the police! They are no longer welcome in my home!"*

*Lisa and Loretta continued to cry and yell. The more they carried on, the angrier
Mr. Santiago became. Suddenly, he turned abruptly and began to stalk out of the office.*

*Frank stopped him. "Obviously, Mr. Santiago," he said quietly, "you have had a
very difficult time. But I think we need to talk a little longer to decide what to do now."*

"I will not talk any more!" Mr. Santiago shouted. *"I have had all the disre-spect I can take from these children! They must be punished! I want you to call the police. I will not allow these girls to darken my door again."* He stormed out of the office and was gone.

After calming Lisa and Loretta as best he could and finding out what had happened at home, Frank determined that it would not be safe for the girls to return there. He called the protective services unit of the county social services department. No one was free to come to the school. Underfunding and understaffing are perennial problems of protective services programs. Frank thus took the girls to protective services in his own car, a personal risk for him, beyond his professional obligation. If he had had an accident, his automobile insurance company might not cover him, since he was doing work-related driving.

The social worker on duty tried to place Lisa and Loretta temporarily with their step-aunt, the person they requested. But the woman declined a formal arrangement, saying it might ruin her relationship with her brother-in-law. So the girls were placed with strangers. And unfortunately, soon afterwards, their foster father was charged with sexually molesting a former ward. The girls could not be left in that home. The protective services worker consulted with Frank. Should Lisa and Loretta be transferred to a different foster home, enduring another major adjustment, or should Mr. Santiago be approached about taking the girls back again? The worker said she had already looked into sending the girls to their mother in Texas, but lengthy court action would be required because of the prior custody battle and interstate regulations. Additional time in foster care would be required during that process.

Frank felt compassion for the children. They had been through a great deal. But he thought that Mr. Santiago and his second wife basically meant well. The problem was that Mr. Santiago set rigid rules that drove his daughters to disobey. The rules were within the bounds of his cultural norms, but different from those of many of the girls' Anglo friends. The father verbally assaulted Lisa and Loretta when they disobeyed and gave them lengthy punishments, but the girls provoked him further with their own harsh words. If the cycle of provocation could be stopped, Frank believed that this family could learn to live together more peacefully and happily. As the discovery of sexual abuse in the foster home illustrated, life elsewhere was no bed of roses either.

Frank felt the best plan for the girls would be to go back home, with family counseling to help improve communication and understanding among the generations. He knew, however, that the girls should be consulted first, and that the father would need some persuading. The protective services worker was more than willing to let Frank take on those tasks.

Frank talked with the girls the following day and learned they were ready to return to their father and stepmother. They were lonely and afraid in the foster home. He made an appointment with Mr. Santiago through the stepmother. When he arrived, he was not surprised to hear Mr. Santiago announce that the girls were no longer welcome in his home. Frank called on his former training for the priesthood to help accomplish his goal of having the children return. Given Mr. Santiago's cultural heritage, he expected that the man would be a devout Catholic. So he told the story of the Prodigal Son in somber, measured tones, inviting this father to forgive like the father in the Bible. Eventually, Mr. Santiago was persuaded to take his daughters back and to participate in family counseling if a Latino counselor could be found. Since Mr. Santiago's job provided very limited insurance benefits, however, a very low cost provider would have to be found.

Frank took on the challenge. He soon found a Latino social worker with expertise in family counseling, Ramon Garcia, who was willing to see the family free of charge providing that he could use the opportunity to train two graduate students in field placement. Mr. Santiago agreed, and Frank arranged the first session personally.

A week passed, and then another. Lisa and Loretta both attended school regularly. There were no more incidents of truancy. At a meeting with Frank, they explained that Ramon had helped family members talk to each other without fighting so much. At a follow-up home visit, Frank learned that the parents were pleased with the counseling experience as well. They believed they understood the girls better. They had become a little more flexible with their rules, and the children no longer tested them so severely. Life for the family was much happier.

337

CHAPTER 9
*Social Work
in the Schools:
Lisa and Loretta
Santiago,
Children-at-Risk*

SOCIAL WORK ROLES IN THE SCHOOLS

As noted by Boyle-Del Rio, Carlson, and Haibeck (2000), the role of the school social worker is constantly changing to meet shifting school, community, and societal needs. Social workers must be creative, innovative, and proactive in developing, implementing, and interpreting new roles in this challenging setting. Nevertheless, like all social workers, they utilize a variety of levels of intervention, as discussed below.

Working with Individuals

Social workers perform a variety of roles in the schools. First of all, as illustrated in the Santiago case, social workers frequently counsel with individual students. Students may be referred for a variety of reasons, among them, truancy, undesirable

BOB DAEMMERICH/THE IMAGE WORKS

Social worker discusses school attendance problem with youth.

behavior, and pregnancy. In schools where there is a guidance counselor, such cases may be assigned either to the counselor or to the social worker, depending on who has more time available.

School social workers today work with individual school personnel in a variety of ways as well: consulting with teachers about the needs of particular children, sharing with teachers and each other knowledge about cultural factors in the educational process, informing staff about important community resources, consulting with teachers about classroom relationships, and so on.

Some school social workers become involved in screening individual students for material aid, such as free or reduced-fee lunch programs. Some schools also distribute donated books, clothing, writing materials, and the like, to needy children. Often it is the social worker who identifies the children who need this material help.

Family Work

Another type of social work service in the school setting involves working with parents and families. The social worker is often the only person from the school who can make home visits. Parents are contacted to gain information that may help teachers work more effectively with particular children. The worker may also make suggestions about parenting techniques in the home.

When a student is referred to **special education** for evaluation, especially for suspected **emotional or behavioral disturbance,** the school social worker usually interviews the parents to learn more about that child's early development and about how he or she currently behaves in the home and community settings. This responsibility will be discussed in more detail in a later section of this chapter. When appropriate, school social workers refer families to community agencies for material assistance, counseling, or other services.

Group Work

School social workers also often develop and lead groups of students. Group work utilizes peer processes and other motivational techniques to help resolve attendance, academic, and social difficulties (Rose, 1998). Topics are sometimes controversial, such as pregnancy prevention, sexual orientation, preventing sexually transmitted diseases, and coping with parents who are drug abusers. Groups can become the focus of heated community debate, because some parents want these topics to be discussed only at home.

School social workers may also become involved in leading groups of parents and/or teachers, with topics depending on circumstance and need. Some school social workers become involved in leading groups to promote change in the school system or the wider community.

Working with Organizations and Communities

In accord with the generalist approach, educating and organizing school personnel and the wider community is an important part of school social work. This role is increasingly important today as children's problems grow and school resources shrink. For example, more and more children today find themselves with nothing to do and no place to go after school, since their parents all work outside the home. Social workers increasingly find themselves doing community assessments to try to find resources for after-school programs, only to end up organizing these programs themselves within the school setting using laboriously recruited volunteer staff, both parents and teachers (Wells, 1999).

339

CHAPTER 9
*Social Work
in the Schools:
Lisa and Loretta
Santiago,
Children-at-Risk*

Involvement with school-linked, integrated services (discussed below) is another undertaking that requires skill in working with organizations and communities.

Teamwork

Perhaps the most important thing to note about teamwork in the schools is that the school presents the social worker with a **secondary social work setting,** or host setting, for employment (see Exhibit 1). The primary purpose of the school system is educational. The position of the social worker within the school setting is to support the educational function of the institution. In contrast, a family service agency is an example of a **primary social work setting** for a social worker. The primary purpose of the family service agency is to enhance social functioning, which is also the primary purpose of the social work profession, so that the majority of the staff are social workers (see Exhibit 1).

Social workers almost always function as part of a team in school social work. That team might consist only of the social worker and a referring teacher, working together to try to meet the educational needs of a particular child. It might be a multidisciplinary team assessing a student referred for special education evaluation. Because social workers value cooperation and are trained to communicate well across disciplinary boundaries, they are often assigned to work as team coordinators and leaders.

The Secondary Social Work Setting

EXHIBIT 1

The social work job function is affected in major ways when it is performed in a secondary, or host, setting. For example, most of the employees in a school are teachers; if there is a social worker, usually there is only one employed in that setting. This can be a lonely position because nobody else is apt to have the same knowledge, values, and skills. In addition, many social workers are assigned to several schools. They may not have private offices but instead must share space with other staff, holding interviews in temporarily empty classrooms or even utility closets. Private telephones may be unavailable, so that scheduling home visits or discussing family problems by phone is difficult if not impossible. Organizing the political support required to secure needed changes is not easy in a secondary setting where one may be the sole representative of one's profession.

School-Linked, Integrated Services

A movement toward school-linked, integrated services is under way in many communities across the United States. The intent is to make schools "hubs" for the delivery of a full range of services, involving various health, mental health, and social service agencies from the wider community (Franklin, 2000). Sometimes these services are provided at the schools themselves, and sometimes they are simply coordinated by school personnel.

Schools where coordinated community services are actually delivered on site are sometimes called "full-service" schools. They have been developed in several states to help children-at-risk, those who arrive unprepared for the educational process and unable to concentrate on school work due to abuse, neglect, homelessness, poverty, and poor health. Services such as counseling, family intervention, and group work may be targeted toward children displaying specific at-risk behaviors. Other more broadly based services may also be available, such as case management, advocacy, child care, and transportation.

Sometimes community organizations place social workers and other staff of their own into school settings to provide health, mental health, and other services (Berrick & Duerr, 1998). Examples of such agencies include community youth services agencies, juvenile justice agencies, drug and alcohol prevention programs, big brother/big sister programs, crisis counseling agencies, and employment services (Burt, Resnick, & Novick, 1998).

Social workers who work in a school setting today thus may be employed by the school system itself or, in a full-service school, may be loaned to the school by other community agencies. Rarely, social workers hired by schools are "outposted" at other community agencies such as neighborhood centers.

THE IMPACT OF CULTURAL DIVERSITY IN THE SCHOOLS

Cultural diversity has been increasing rapidly in the United States over the past few decades. The impact of cultural diversity on the city school system where Lisa and Loretta Santiago attended was considerable. When Latino children first began attending the public schools, they were a small minority and were placed in classrooms where English only was spoken; some of these children swam, but many of them sank. No help was offered to those who could not handle the experience. This is still the situation in many schools in the United States today. Rural school systems are particularly devoid of resources for children whose native language is other than English. Yet in recent decades the Latino population has been growing more than seven times as fast as the rest of the nation, and by 2030 Hispanics are expected to constitute 25 percent of the total school population (Ginorio & Huston, 2001).

The American cultural myth of the melting pot has lulled many people into assuming that children who are not native speakers of English can assimilate the language effortlessly. Yet many children struggle, and cannot keep up in basic subjects like math and history. Crucial early learning time, the foundation for more advanced study, is lost (see Exhibit 2).

341

CHAPTER 9
*Social Work
in the Schools:
Lisa and Loretta
Santiago,
Children-at-Risk*

Children from Non-English-Speaking Homes: One in Five

EXHIBIT 2

(Approximately) 9.9 million children, or 22 percent of the school-age population, live in a house where a non-English language is spoken. . . . Children of racial minorities and non-English speaking children tend to come from families occupying a lower socioeconomic position. Their parents are often poorly educated and somewhat mystified by the educational process and all of the special programs. Moreover, their parents also may not have a command of the English language. These children generally find entry into the public school difficult because they lack the family resources and experiential background that usually lead to successful achievement in what has been called a middle-class institution.

Source: Quoted from Sandra Kopels (2000). Securing equal educational opportunity: Language, race, and sex. In P. Allen-Meares, R. O. Washington, & B. L. Welsh, *Social work services in schools* (3rd ed., p. 216). Boston: Allyn and Bacon.

Many schools have devised innovative programs to meet the needs of children from diverse backgrounds. The primary thrust came from educators, but social workers provided strong support. Two models for teaching children whose native language is not English have emerged. The **bilingual** model allows students to take courses like math and history in their native languages, while studying English. The other model plunges students immediately into intensive **English as a Second Language (ESL)** instruction to get them up to grade level in English and into regular classrooms as quickly as possible. Many teachers prefer the bilingual method, because it provides students the opportunity to learn ideas and concepts in the language in which they think. Later these can be translated into English. In some circumstances, however, appropriate bilingual teachers are simply not available for all students who need them. For example, 127 different native languages and dialects are spoken in the Washington, D.C., public schools (Gray, 1993). In situations like this, the ESL approach may be the only one feasible.

The model used at the Valdez school Lisa and Loretta Santiago attended was bilingual. Hispanic children could take all their classes in Spanish, if desired, enrolling concurrently in ESL courses. Students with more understanding of the English language were **mainstreamed,** or educated in English in as normal a fashion for an American child as possible, while still having bilingual teachers available who could assist them in Spanish when needed.

Around the nation today, however, bilingual education is being challenged. For example, in 1998, the state of California, which has a large Hispanic population, voted by a large margin to abolish bilingual education. Reportedly, about two-thirds of the state's Hispanic population supported the change. Why? Research is needed to better understand. Instead of bilingual education, California children who are not native English speakers will be provided a one-year English immersion program and then placed in regular classrooms. Many California teachers are concerned, believing that a single approach to a complex problem is too limited and will not meet the needs of many children (Wood, 1998).

Some experts argue that American schools need to go beyond language alone to help assist diverse populations to be more successful in the school setting. They recommend incorporating other aspects of the students' cultural traditions in the educational process (see Exhibit 3).

Bilingual teachers, social workers, and other staff are needed in schools where a large proportion of children speak languages other than English; however, these professionals also need to know about the cultural backgrounds of their students. Frank Haines, for example, secured his job at the Valdez Middle School partly because he spoke limited Spanish but also because he had direct experience working with various Hispanic peoples in his prior training for the priesthood. To work effectively at the Valdez school, for example, Frank needed to know about dating customs constraining young Hispanic girls, and to understand normal disciplinary practices within the Hispanic families who lived around the school. He needed to understand sex-role behaviors and authority patterns.

Changing the Culture of Today's Schools

EXHIBIT 3

Billions of dollars have been poured into everything from bilingual classes to school-based clinics, yet nearly a third of all Hispanic youths in America leave school without a diploma, according to a recent survey by the U.S. Department of Education.

This failure has some educators looking to create an entirely new classroom culture, one that changes far more than its textbooks. In fact, some experts argue the problem is not that Hispanic students are unfit for school; American schools may be unfit for Hispanic students.

The key may be a focus on group learning—as well as greater parental and church involvement in school affairs. "Hispanic families tend to teach children to respect elders," and often focus on the needs of the group, says Elena Lopez, an education professor at Harvard University in Cambridge, Mass. The consequence is that quiet students are often labeled apathetic or insolent. Many end up receiving less attention than do white peers.

As a result, hundreds of underperforming schools—from East Los Angeles to the Rio Grande Valley—are moving to build on cultural strengths of their Hispanic communities. If Latino hands aren't rising during question-and-answer time, for example, teachers try to put children into collaborative groups. If Hispanic parents are reluctant to speak out at parent-teacher meetings, or to inquire when their children falter, schools are taking extra steps to make parents feel like partners.

Source: Quoted from Scott Baldauf (1997, August 20), Schools try tuning into Latino ways, *The Christian Science Monitor,* pp. 1, 13.

Social workers can learn what behavior is appropriate in a given culture or **subculture** by talking with other workers who are knowledgeable, by observing behavior directly, by talking with members of the subculture in question, by taking classes, and by reading. Many sources of information are available, but they must be conscientiously pursued.

Another important impact of cultural diversity in the schools involves the fact that the children learn from each other. **Norms** that might go unquestioned within a single culture may be questioned as the children learn that there are other ways of doing things. On the positive side, this can lead to flexible, informed, tolerant citizens later on in life. On the negative side (as in the case of the Santiago sisters), it may lead to rebellion against family norms and expectations because other alternatives are readily in evidence.

Particularly during the teenage years, most children enter a period of rebelliousness as they attempt to define who they are. A major developmental task of adolescence is to differentiate one's emerging self from parents and other family members. Cross-cultural issues complicate this normal process. Social workers may need to reach out to contact children who are experiencing difficulty, because some cultural norms do not promote a tendency to seek professional help. On the whole, the value of exposure to differences and the learning that children must undertake to deal with conflicting information probably far outweigh the discomfort of temporary confusion or rebellious behavior. (See the "Up for Debate" box.)

Alternative Schools and Charter Schools

Another impact of cultural diversity in the schools is a proliferation of what are known as **alternative schools,** schools that operate outside the regular public system. Although these schools are usually privately run, at least two cities, Milwaukee and Cleveland, provide taxpayer money to poor parents to help finance tuition. In some places alternative schools develop formal agreements with public schools and even share staff. Alternative schools are not limited to children of ethnic minority background, but minority parents have become strong advocates. For example, a 1997 poll by the Joint Center for Political Studies found that 65 percent of Hispanics and 56 percent of blacks supported the concept of school choice (Baldauf, 1998).

Probably a reason many minority parents have become advocates for alternative schools involves the fact that cultural or religious teachings may be incorporated into the regular curriculum. Also, these schools frequently have much smaller classes than regular public schools, providing students with more personal attention. In alternative schools a full-time social worker is frequently on staff, sometimes more than one, whereas in the regular school setting, a social worker is usually shared among several schools. Baccalaureate social workers usually have a better chance to be hired in alternative schools than in regular public schools.

Charter schools are a type of alternative school growing rapidly in states that permit them. They are public schools (financed through tax revenues like regular public schools) that are operated independently (Coeyman, 2001, June). Arizona, which has a very liberal charter school law, had over 403 of them in 2001 (Coeyman, 2001, May). Their use of social work services has not yet been well-researched.

343

CHAPTER 9
*Social Work
in the Schools:
Lisa and Loretta
Santiago,
Children-at-Risk*

Up for Debate
Proposition: Bilingual education should be provided in the public schools.

Yes	No
Children learn more easily in their native language, especially complex concepts.	Children need to learn the language of the majority culture as quickly as possible.
Children feel more comfortable in an environment where their native language is spoken.	Children need to learn to feel comfortable in an English-speaking environment in the United States.
Teaching in one's own language affirms children's cultural identity and thus enhances self esteem.	Pride in one's cultural heritage and in oneself can be taught in English.
Some children simply fail when they must learn in a language that is not their own.	Some children will fail regardless of the language in which they are taught.

INVOLVEMENT IN SPECIAL EDUCATION

Since 1975 many social workers have been hired by schools to work with special education programs. Before that time, many students with special needs were simply refused admission to public school. In 1975, however, landmark federal legislation—Public Law 94-142, the Education for All Handicapped Children Act—changed public education forever. This law is now known as the Individuals with Disabilities Education Act, or IDEA. It promises free appropriate public education to all children with disabilities (Burrello and Lashley, 1992).

Public Law 94-142 requires that social workers be part of a **multidisciplinary team** (sometimes called an **M-team,** pupil planning team, etc.) that evaluates referrals. Students are referred to special education services for a variety of reasons: speech or language impairment, physical disability (including visual or hearing impairment), learning disability, cognitive disability or other developmental disability, emotional or behavioral disturbance, pregnancy or health impairment, autism, and traumatic brain injury. Many children who never would have received an education, or completed one, now have a much better chance.

Public Law 99-457 (Part H), federal legislation adopted in 1986, extends the right of special education services to infants and toddlers with disabilities. The law calls for cooperative planning among 10 different disciplines, requires interagency cooperation, and includes greater parental participation. In 1991, Part H became Subchapter VIII according to an amendment, but provisions for infants and toddlers remain intact. Participation by states is not mandated, but every state has participated due to powerful financial incentives (Saunders, 1998).

Social workers in special education programs assume many roles, but a prominent one involves evaluating children who are referred because of suspected "emotional disturbance" or "behavior disturbance." (Other terminology is used in various states, such as "behavior disorder" or "personal and social adjustment problem.") Essentially, these are the children who teachers believe behave in harmful or inappropriate ways. Their behavior ranges from extreme withdrawal to extreme acting out, or misconduct (Wells, 1999).

345

CHAPTER 9
*Social Work
in the Schools:
Lisa and Loretta
Santiago,
Children-at-Risk*

School social workers often need to become involved before evaluation of a referral can take place, because under special education law all parents must consent in writing. This is to safeguard the rights of the parents. Usually a child's referring teacher contacts the parents about a referral and the reasons why it was made. Then a permission slip is sent for the parents to sign. If the parents do not return the form, the social worker usually makes a home visit to explain the process and try to obtain permission.

Once permission to do an evaluation has been obtained, the social worker's next responsibility is to interview the parents to determine whether a referred child exhibits disturbance in the home or community environment. If a referred child misbehaves at school but gets along well in the home and community settings, then perhaps the problem lies with the school and not with the child.

Once a child has been accepted into special education, the law requires that the educational program be "definitely in the least restrictive appropriate environment and in an environment tailored to each handicapped child's needs. . . . An individualized education program (IEP) must be prepared by appropriate professionals with parental input" (Salzman & Proch, 1990, p. 229). Under the law children are also entitled to "related services" such as social work and psychological counseling. IDEA, Part H, requires not only an IEP for each child but also an individualized family service plan, or IFSP (Saunders, 1998).

Federal legislation regarding education for children with disabilities is enforced by funding regulations. Federal funds are provided only to schools that comply, and so most schools do. However, definitions of major terms in the law are still being hammered out in court. For example, what is the "least restrictive environment"? What is "appropriate" education? What are "related services"? For example, does education in the "least restrictive environment" mean that every child should be mainstreamed, or educated in a regular classroom, as proposed by advocates of the "full inclusion" movement? (see Exhibit 4). Recently, in the *P. J. v. State of Connecticut* case, Connecticut agreed to mainstream more of its 4,000 students with cognitive disabilities (Associated Press, 2001).

Students who are infected with the HIV virus or have AIDS (acquired immune deficiency syndrome) present a special population who may or may not be eligible for special education services. To be considered disabled under special education law, a child's disability must present symptoms that interfere with his or her ability to be educated. Freeman, Halim, and Peterson (1998) point out that these children often do not stand out at school. Many choose to keep their diagnosis private as long as possible to avoid social stigma. They must thus cope alone. Those who do become identified as HIV-positive may be ostracized and even more alone. Some school systems try to exclude them entirely out of fear of contagion. Social workers can be important advocates for these children and for the development of programs that emphasize AIDS prevention. Every level of intervention may be required, from individual counseling to community organizing.

Self-Determination and the Least Restrictive Environment

EXHIBIT 4

The profession would do well to listen to the people most affected by these educational policies—the families of children with disabilities. Before 1975 parent advocacy groups frequently sued school boards to include their children in regular education classrooms. Presently, parents are as likely to sue to maintain their children in special education classes as otherwise. Clearly, special education is doing something right. . . . Most parents do not want their children with disabilities mainstreamed because of an abstract agenda, but only after a careful biopsychosocial assessment of their individual child.

Source: Quoted from James C. Raines (1998). Appropriate versus least restrictive: Educational policies and students with disabilities. In E. M. Freeman, C. G. Franklin, R. Fong, G. L. Shaffer, & E. M. Timberlake (Eds.). *Multisystem skills and interventions in school social work practice* (p. 447). Washington, DC: NASW Press.

Educational Evaluations as Applied Research

What the evaluation team does when activated by a school special education referral is an example of applied research. Each member of the multidisciplinary team seeks information about the referred child in his or her area of expertise. Results of these research efforts are used in joint decision making. Within 90 days, the M-team must meet together to determine whether the child is indeed qualified to receive special services and, if so, what kind. This type of applied research has serious, immediate consequences for a given child.

The social worker researches the child's developmental history and also investigates his or her current behavior at home and in the community. When researching the child's developmental history, the social worker gathers information that will help determine if the child has developed "normally" or not. How did the parents feel about the child's birth? Did the child walk and talk at about the same age as most children? What kind of concerns about the child, if any, did the parents have in the past? How has the child related to the parents? How does he or she behave at home? What types of discipline seem to work best with this child? Are there any brothers or sisters? If so, what was the birth order? How has the child related to the siblings? Has the child been in any sort of trouble in the community? If so, what kind? What concerns do the parents have about the child today? About the school? These are only a few of the questions a social worker might ask.

Sometimes parents are anxious about having their child evaluated by the school. They become distressed about giving certain information that would be helpful in assessing the child because talking raises sensitive issues or painful memories. In these circumstances the social worker must use his or her best relationship skills and assure the parents that any information they provide will be shared only with the special education evaluation team. The assurance of confidentiality helps parents overcome their fear of providing sensitive information.

347

CHAPTER 9
*Social Work
in the Schools:
Lisa and Loretta
Santiago,
Children-at-Risk*

School social worker interviews parents in the home setting.

Sometimes a social worker must make many visits to the parents of a referred child, because time is needed to obtain the parents' trust and cooperation. The social worker may also assist the school in obtaining signed releases from parents to gather medical and other pertinent diagnostic information.

While the social worker is conducting his or her part of the investigation, other members of the evaluation team will also be at work. The psychologist may be conducting a battery of psychological tests designed to indicate evidence of emotional disturbance and may also administer an IQ test. The teacher for the emotionally disturbed will observe the child in the regular classroom, taking detailed notes to document the percentage of the time the child is doing assigned work ("on task"), as opposed to how much time the child spends misbehaving, wandering around, daydreaming, and the like.

After the various members of the multidisciplinary team have gathered their data, an M-team meeting will be held to which the parents are invited. At this meeting, the team will determine whether the child demonstrates needs that qualify him or her for special education services. Parents must then agree in writing for their child to receive these services. They may also refuse services, or they may appeal an M-team decision that has determined that the child does not need special services.

The social worker's role on the school's special education team then often involves securing cooperation and information from the family. Both BSWs and MSWs perform this type of work, although BSWs will usually find greater opportunities in rural areas, where the professional labor supply is limited. Additional training in child development and education is desirable for both BSWs and MSWs. Appropriate expertise is especially important in school social work, since the lives of children with special needs are affected so directly.

Unfortunately, the beliefs and actions of people in the wider society some-times create clients for social workers in special education. In an ideal society, special education evaluation would be a waste of time for these children because, given acceptance by others, they would have no problems to evaluate. The follow-ing is an example of such a circumstance, sadly all too common today.

School Social Work with Other Special-Needs Children: The Ordeal of Two Gay Brothers

Todd Larkin was about 11 years old when he began to sense he was different. As early as the sixth grade he sometimes felt very alone. His buddies made cracks and catcalls at the girls, and the girls flirted in return. Everyone seemed to share some sort of secret. Todd, who had many friends who were girls, couldn't grasp what it was all about. He liked girls as people, but the flirting and catcalls left him bewil-dered. However, he didn't talk to anyone about his confusion because he was afraid there might be something wrong with him. Since he was handsome, athletic, and gregarious, nobody noticed his pain.

When Todd was in his early teens, he noticed a strong attraction to his male friends. Since no other boy mentioned such an attraction, he felt confused and scared. Other boys were starting to date, but they dated only girls. Todd felt a de-sire to date boys. Increasingly, he wondered if something was wrong with him. He was afraid to talk with anyone about his fears, however. He didn't even have the words in his vocabulary to help him name his difference from other children.

Then, by chance, Todd saw a movie on television one evening at home. The movie was called *The Truth about Alex.* The movie's hero, Alex, was handsome, athletic, and outgoing, just like Todd. And also like Todd, he was physically at-tracted to boys, not girls. Alex kept his difference a secret for a long time, but eventually he told a close friend in high school. As a result, Alex was labeled **homosexual** and ostracized by all his former friends.

Todd began to believe that he was homosexual too; but, given Alex's experi-ence in the movie, he determined to remain absolutely silent. He even began to date girls to make sure no one would ever suspect. He "passed" very successfully. He was popular among the young ladies. But he graduated from high school with the whole burden of worry about his sexuality on his own shoulders. He didn't even talk with his parents about it.

Because Todd felt so lonely and misunderstood in high school in his small, rural town, he decided to go away to college in a large city. He hoped he might be able to talk with someone there about his concerns. Being extremely bright and an academic achiever, he was admitted to a prestigious private urban university. But his first days at college were disappointing. Right across the hall from his dorm room, for example, a large poster was displayed making fun of gay and lesbian people. And in theology class, Old Testament scriptures were quoted that rebuked gay people. Again, the boy felt lonely and afraid.

One day a hall director found Todd staring at the poster on the door across from his room. The director, a sensitive young woman who also served on the Campus Ministry staff, asked Todd if the poster offended him. Todd admitted that it did. The director agreed and suggested that Todd talk with a certain priest at the college, who felt the same way.

For several weeks, Todd tried to find the courage to call the priest. He was afraid, however, of being overheard in the dorm. Finally, he decided to call from a pay phone. Slumping down in the booth, Todd dialed the priest's number six times in a row. Each time his call was answered, he hung up in embarrassment and confusion. At last, on the seventh call, a warm, gentle voice spoke before the boy could hang up. "Come to my office today at 3 P.M.," Father Healy said.

Todd arrived at the priest's office door feeling sick to his stomach and not sure what to say. However, Father Healy's gentle sense of humor broke the ice. "Hello, son," the man began with a smile as he saw the boy's tense face. "I hate hang-ups. Come on in, and let's talk." Todd did just that. By the time he left Father Healy's office, he had been invited to attend a group of **gay** students run by Campus Ministry, co-led by the priest and Todd's own hall director.

When the boy didn't appear after a couple of weeks, Father Healy called to tell Todd he was sending a student to fetch him. In this way the priest gave Todd a chance to refuse, and yet actively expedited his appearance. The hall director met Todd at the door of the meeting and eased his way into the group by finding a place for him to sit. It took several weeks for the boy to tell his story. But in the nurturing environment provided by the Campus Ministry gathering, Todd began to understand that his worth and dignity as a spiritual being were not diminished by his sexual orientation. He began to open up. Six months into the school year, Todd decided that he was, indeed, gay and that it was time to come out of the closet.

Encouraged by his support group, Todd began by telling his mother about his sexuality. To his shock, Todd's mother told him that she had suspected he was gay for some time and that she was glad he was finally able to tell her. Todd's mother eased the boy's way toward acceptance in the family by telling his father and stepfather for him. Todd's stepfather accepted the news fairly well; his biological father was more ambivalent. Neither man, however, totally rejected Todd, as he had feared they would.

The one person Todd pledged his mother not to tell, however, was his younger brother Tim. Todd felt that Tim, having weathered his mother's divorce and remarriage, needed a stable male role model in his life. Todd believed he was that role model, and feared Tim would be upset at a critical time in his life if he learned that Todd was gay. The mother consented.

Ironically, Tim was struggling with questions about his own sexuality. Like his brother before him, he was afraid to talk to anyone. At age 11 the boy began to abuse drugs, perhaps to mask his worries and confusion about his sexuality. At age 13 Tim took a major overdose and had to be hospitalized to save his life. It was there, by Tim's bedside at the hospital, that Todd learned what his brother had been going through. As Todd sat in the visitor's chair and asked Tim what was wrong and why he had tried to kill himself, he heard the younger boy say things like "I'm all alone" and "No one understands me."

For a while, Todd could not understand what his younger brother was trying to tell him. But suddenly, he recognized his own feelings and experiences in high school. Was it possible that Tim had doubts about his sexuality too? Finally, Todd asked. Tim began to cry, and then Todd cried, and the two brothers shared as they never had before.

It would be nice if the story ended happily here, but life had more trials in store. Two weeks after the suicide attempt, Tim decided to confide in a close friend in junior high. He chose the friend carefully, hoping to be accepted.

349

CHAPTER 9
*Social Work
in the Schools:
Lisa and Loretta
Santiago,
Children-at-Risk*

But Tim was not accepted. A terrible replay of *The Truth about Alex* began to take place in his small, rural town. Within a week, everyone seemed to be pointing at him. The boy felt betrayed, angry, confused, ashamed, and scared. His family's house was pelted with eggs, and his mother's car tires were slashed. When the family appealed for help from the police, the police did nothing.

A couple of weeks after that, a boy in Tim's eighth-grade class pointed at him rudely and jeered loudly, "You're a fag, Tim Larkin! You're a fag!"

Tim's teacher should have protected him. But, instead, the man pointed a long finger at the boy. "Well, Tim," the man said, looking down his considerable nose, "Is it true?"

Tim couldn't speak at first. Then he took a deep, slow breath. "I don't know, Mr. Humphrey," he replied bravely. "I'm not sure yet."

The class roared with laughter. The teacher glared and said, "I thought so; I thought so."

Mr. Humphrey's tone was so harsh, and the laughter in the classroom so derisive, that Tim couldn't bear to stay in his seat. He leaped up and ran home, shut the window shades, and locked the door. He refused to go back to school. When his mother and stepfather were able to persuade him to go back a few days later, Tim found himself thrown against lockers, spat upon, and beaten up. The school principal refused to help. "We aren't in the business of protecting people from discrimination here," he said, when Tim's parents went to the school to complain.

When Tim continued to refuse to go to school, the school administration threatened to prosecute for truancy. At this point Tim's mother appealed for help at the state level, wanting to know her and her son's rights. She also took Tim to a social worker in private practice, an MSW who specialized in family counseling.

The social worker helped Tim and his mother understand that confusion about sexual orientation was a normal part of adolescence. She helped the mother provide Tim with much-needed understanding and support, so that despite the harsh daily reality of rejection from the outside world, Tim did not attempt suicide again. Instead, he brought his troubles and frustrations to the safe haven of home or a counseling session. On the suggestion of the state office of public instruction, Tim's mother also referred the boy for special education services at the school. The social worker counseling privately with the family wrote a powerful letter to the evaluation team describing the school as an environment hazardous to Tim's physical and mental health. The team then determined that Tim was a student at risk and authorized homebound instruction.

Tim continued to face difficulties, however. He was harassed when he went to school to pick up his assignments for homebound instruction. So the family enrolled him in a home-schooling organization. However, trapped in the house, afraid to go out even to the grocery store, Tim couldn't concentrate on his studies by correspondence. He then decided to work for his GED (general equivalency diploma) at a technical school in a neighboring town. Again, however, the boy suffered ridicule by students who had heard of his situation.

Discouraged, Tim dropped out of the GED program. About this time, hoping to help create positive social change, Tim's mother courageously agreed to take part in a public radio program discussing challenges for parents with homosexual children. When she returned to her job (she had been a caretaker for an elderly woman for more than 15 years), she found her belongings piled on the front porch, the door of the house locked, and a note telling her she was fired. She was never allowed to speak with her former client, a shut-in, again.

With such truly depressing experiences, one could hardly blame this family for becoming bitter and giving up. But instead, they maintained hope and overcame the odds with help from people who cared. For example, a dedicated teacher tutored Tim outside the regular GED program; he passed the exam! Tim's family, excited and relieved, gave him a formal graduation ceremony along with Todd's partner, who completed his GED at approximately the same time. Many celebrating friends and family members attended. Tim was accepted into college. Todd now has his MSW and counsels gay and **lesbian** youth.

Tim's mother explains that she maintains a safe haven for her two sons at home. It is still dangerous for them to walk alone in the neighborhood. She declares that antigay people, even long-term family friends, are not allowed in the house when her sons are present. This impressive woman has also paid attention to her own needs. Not only has she survived being fired from her job, but she has updated her nursing credentials and developed entrepreneurial skills as well. Today she runs her own bridal shop.

351

CHAPTER 9
*Social Work
in the Schools:
Lisa and Loretta
Santiago,
Children-at-Risk*

SOCIAL WORK VALUES IN THE SCHOOL SETTING: POLICY IMPLICATIONS

Social work professional values strongly affect the policies social workers promote in the school setting. The Santiago and Larkin cases will be used as illustrations followed by a discussion of other serious school issues that tend to be addressed in very different ways depending on value orientation.

The Santiago Sisters

Let us begin with the Santiago sisters. Years ago, truancy would have been viewed simply as bad behavior, and the response of the school system would have been punitive. However, over the years more enlightened values in the fields of education and social work together have led to the development of a more individualized approach to truancy. Today, many schools have a policy of assigning a social worker to approach the investigation not as an effort at social control but as a fact-finding task. The uniqueness of each child's personal circumstance is recognized, and the worth and dignity of each child is respected. Usually the truant child needs assistance with some underlying problem.

The very existence of bilingual education illustrates how values have affected policy in the schools. The primary thrust for the development of bilingual education came from the profession of education, of course, but social work values such as self-determination strongly support it if that is what minority people request. Recognition of minority languages and cultures in public schools not only helps children learn but also shows respect for the worth and dignity of all persons. Such attention helps minority children gain self-esteem and pride in their own heritage.

Values also were the fuel for development of special education programs in the public schools. Certainly it is easier for a school system simply to refuse admission or to expel children who bring with them special problems and needs. But over time, the values of fairness and individual worth and dignity have led to the recognition that children don't have much of a chance to make it in this society without an education. Even children with special problems should thus have a right to public education. Committed organizing and political strength were required to translate these values into public law, however.

The Larkin Case

The Larkin case is an example of what happens when conformity rather than diversity is valued by a school administration. Social work values, by contrast, honor the worth and dignity of all persons, and they teach respect for diversity. If social work values had been activated in Tim's school during his ordeal, new school policy would have been proposed, at the very least, to protect the rights of minorities. However, no one on the staff stepped forward to organize for change. Ideally, such a task would have been taken on by a school social worker (see Exhibit 5). Unfortunately, recent evidence suggests that many social workers themselves are **homophobic,** or at least **heterosexist** (Berkman & Zinberg, 1997).

Challenge of Gay Youth for Social Work

EXHIBIT 5

Educational systems need to develop programs that increase faculty and student awareness of homosexuality as a normal variation on sexual orientation. Accurate information about homosexuality should become a part of school sex education curriculums, and faculty in-service training must be provided in this area. School social workers, with their ethical commitment to the uniqueness and individuality of all people, can be instrumental in providing or arranging for such training. Administrative discrimination in the hiring of gay and lesbian teachers must cease; these teachers should be sought as positive role models for lesbian and gay youths in the same way that culturally diverse teachers are hired to serve as role models for their respective cultures. . . .

Sanctions need to be implemented to end lesbian and gay discrimination, harassment, and violence in the schools. These sanctions must be enforced for students, teachers, and administrative personnel alike. . . .

Finally, social workers must work to dispel negative stereotypes, myths, and discrimination aimed at lesbian and gay individuals. Social workers must become role models of respect and acceptance of diversity among people, including gay and lesbian people.

Source: Quoted from Deana F. Morrow (1993, November). Social work with gay and lesbian adolescents. *Social Work, 38*(6) pp. 655–660.

Who knows how many children with questions about their sexual orientation are currently hiding their pain, dealing with their confusion and fear all alone? Who knows how many parents are struggling with their own confusion and fear alone as well?

353

CHAPTER 9
*Social Work
in the Schools:
Lisa and Loretta
Santiago,
Children-at-Risk*

Punitive attitudes toward diversity, rather than respect, do not just hover in the abstract. They have concrete and horrific results. One study of gay and lesbian students, for example, found that 22 percent of males and 29 percent of females experienced physical injury by other students because of sexual orientation. Other studies have found that gay and lesbian students attempt suicide at a rate two to seven times higher than their heterosexual counterparts. Almost 40 percent have problems with truancy and 30 percent drop out of school. These are tragedies relating to harassment, yet school personnel rarely view stopping harassment as part of their job (Dupper, 2000).

How different life for gay and lesbian students would be if school personnel, including social workers, took a serious interest in this issue and worked hard to solve it! Schools can be ideal settings to provide education about sexual orientation because almost all children and families become involved in them. School programs can help teach understanding and acceptance of diversity to students and parents alike, given the commitment to do so.

Beyond the school setting, social work values support protective laws for people with homosexual orientation and their families. Without such laws, people like the Larkins may find it difficult to obtain police protection when harassed, and they may be without recourse when fired from their jobs.

Violence in the Schools

Almost everyone today is aware of violence in the schools. The mass shooting at Columbine High School in Littleton, Colorado, in April 1999 awakened everyone to its frightening reality. Murder, however, is a very unusual example of violence in the schools. School shootings account for less than 1 percent of firearm-related deaths of children under 19 in America, and children are more than twice as likely to be killed by lightning than to be shot at school (Koch, 2000).

On a more daily level, however, a recent study commissioned by the American Association of University Women found that 2 students in 10 feared being hurt or bothered in school, girls and boys almost equally, regardless of whether the school was urban, suburban, or rural. Eight in 10 students experienced some form of sexual harassment at some time during their school careers, 6 in 10 often or occasionally, one-quarter often (Harris Interactive, 2001). A study in Cleveland found that 22 percent of female students and 33 percent of male students had been beaten at school in a single year (Mathis & Diaz, 1995). The result can be PTSD, or posttraumatic stress disorder, the emotional disturbance suffered by Juan Attencio as described in Chapter 4. The effects of PTSD are devastating. The characteristic hypervigilance and hyperaggression can lead to further violence in the school setting. Other symptoms of PTSD such as low self-esteem and emotional numbness can sentence millions of students to academic failure.

In 1994, the federal government mandated **zero-tolerance** policies in schools under President Bill Clinton's Gun-Free Schools Act. Zero tolerance means that a student *must* be expelled from school for a calendar year if caught carrying a weapon (although administrators are given slight latitude according to the circumstance). After the mass shootings at Columbine, many schools began bringing in police, posting hall monitors, installing metal detectors and surveillance cameras, requiring student ID badges, and the like. Students began being disciplined for very minor infractions. For example, in Manalapan, New Jersey, 50 children were suspended in a six-week period in 2001, mostly kindergartners to third graders. An example of a typical infraction was a 10-year-old girl who muttered, "I could kill her!" after wetting her pants when a teacher refused to let her go to the bathroom (Zernike, 2001). The major response to safety concerns in many schools has thus been one of increased security and punitive measures.

The good news is that violence has been decreasing in schools in recent years. In fact, the number of high school seniors reporting being injured or threatened with a weapon was lower in 1996 than 1976 (Koch, 2000). In 1999–2000, there were no mass fatal shootings in U.S. schools, and only 9 shooting fatalities, down from 23 in 1998–1999, 35 in 1997–1998, and 43 in 1992–1993 (Savoye, 2000).

Is zero tolerance and strict disciplinary action therefore a policy supported by the social work profession? Is this the best way to prevent violence? Many social workers would disagree. Our professional values stress the worth and dignity of every person and the provision of options and choices, not repression. Many children who threaten or disobey in school have been bullied themselves by peers or teachers (such as the little girl mentioned above who was not allowed to go to the bathroom). Many students feel afraid at school, as evidenced by the recent AAUW study. Surveillance measures may only make them feel more afraid (see Exhibit 6). And what about the futures of the children who are expelled? What about the safety of the communities where they may be left to wander unsupervised?

Social work values counsel that there is a better approach to working with violence in the schools. From the profession's perspective, more preventive efforts such as conflict resolution and peer mediation programs, after-school programs,

---

Surveillance: Helpful or Harmful?

EXHIBIT 6

Even the increasingly ubiquitous presence of metal detectors, surveillance cameras, police officers, and emergency drills has left some educators feeling uneasy.

A study by two University of Maryland researchers found that the greater the physical security measures taken at a school, the greater the number of fights and thefts and the less safe kids reported feeling.

"The metal detectors have not necessarily had as great an impact as people would like to think," says Mr. Dwyer. "There's no research data that show those things have been effective. When I do focus groups with teenagers, they tell me how they get around those things anyway."

Source: Quoted from Craig Savoye (2000, June 13). Violence dips in nation's schools. *The Christian Science Monitor,* 4.

and family intervention programs are needed. The number of social workers, psychologists, and guidance counselors available to assist children to deal with their frustration and anxieties should be increased (Savoye, 2000).

355

CHAPTER 9
*Social Work
in the Schools:
Lisa and Loretta
Santiago,
Children-at-Risk*

Successful examples of school intervention programs in tune with social work values include Cleveland Elementary School in Tampa, Florida. In 1993, this school introduced social skills training in topics such as how to listen, how to resolve conflicts without fighting, dealing with losing, waiting one's turn, and the like. In 1992–1993, before the program began, there were 358 disciplinary referrals at the school; by 1996, the number had been cut to 85. Kennedy Middle School in Eugene, Oregon, is another example of a school with a successful preventive program. Prior to the beginning of this program, students with disciplinary problems were routinely sent to the vice-principal and then either suspended or sent back to class. In 1996–1997, there were 1,200 such disciplinary referrals. Under the preventive program, students were sent to meet with counselors instead. The number of disciplinary referrals fell 60 percent in just five years, to 500 (Kiefer, 2000).

Disciplinary action may be necessary to help create pro-social behavior. However, social skills training and counseling are far more lasting, transformative experiences and help create a more positive, trusting wider environment.

Sexuality and Teen Pregnancy

Sexuality and teen pregnancy are issues for schools because sexual behavior often begins while children are still students in school. Pregnancy can lead to dropping out and other school-related problems. Students are at risk for sexual activity at very young ages today: 8.3 percent report sexual activity before the age of 13. While sexual activity has decreased slightly for both males and females between the ages of 15 and 19 (in 1995, 51 percent of females and 55 percent of males 15 to 19 reported sexual experience, down from 55 percent and 60 percent, respectively, a few years earlier), sexual activity is actually *increasing* in frequency among children under 15. Sadly, the younger the girl when she first has sex, the less likely she is to have wanted it. Nearly 4 in 10 girls who had first intercourse at age 13 or 14 report that it was involuntary or unwanted (National Campaign to Prevent Teen Pregnancy, Recent Trends, 2001).

Early sexual activity is particularly risky among children today because girls are physically maturing earlier and thus at greater risk of pregnancy. As Dr. Jocelyn Elders (2001), former U.S. Surgeon General, puts it, "In the good old days the mean age of menstruation was 17—time to get married. In the 1800's it was 15 or 16—time to date. Now it's 11 years and 4 months—time to educate!"

Whether schools should get involved in sex education has been a controversial issue for decades. Many people insist that sex education should take place in the home only. Yet Dr. Elders reports that only 36 percent of teens surveyed said they had had a helpful conversation about sex with their parents (Dr. Jocelyn Elders, 2001). Many people oppose sex education in the schools because they fear it may increase sexual activity. However, a recent review of 250 programs teaching teens how to avoid pregnancy found that these efforts did *not* lead to increased sexual activity. Instead, many resulted in the opposite. The most successful programs employed an "abstinence plus" approach, promoting abstinence but also encouraging teens who were sexually active to protect themselves from sexually transmitted diseases and pregnancy (Study: Safe-sex programs don't increase sexual activity, 2001). (See Exhibit 7.)

The teen birth rate is at a record low today, having declined 20 percent between 1991 and 1999 for girls between the ages of 15 and 19. That is very good news. Still, nearly 4 in 10 young women become pregnant before they are 20; 80 percent of their pregnancies are unintended, and 70 percent take place to unmarried teens (*National Campaign,* 2001). Such figures are staggering. This nation, to its shame, has the highest teen birth rate in the industrialized world. Certainly we can do something about this, since other nations have.

One approach to the problem is simply to blame the teens and walk away, or else to inflict punishment such as expulsion (usually of the pregnant girl). This was the norm not so many years ago, justified as a deterrent to other students. Another approach, however, is to honor the worth and dignity of all youth and to provide them with more genuine choices and opportunities to maximize their potential. The latter is the approach in accord with social work values, and it is probably more effective in terms of school retention. For example, while statistics often correlate early pregnancy with dropping out of school, and many social scientists assume that pregnancy *causes* the dropping out, sometimes evidence indicates that the relationship may be the other way around. Instead, discouragement at school may lead to early pregnancy as a means of escape. A recent study, for example, found that girls with previous academic difficulties were more likely to become pregnant, use drugs and alcohol, and engage in delinquent behavior (Ginorio & Huston, 2001).

What can social workers do to help make schools more hospitable places for their students, so that they want to stay and learn? When the question is posed in this way, many creative ideas can be generated. For example, cultural events that help members of ethnic minority groups feel more comfortable can be organized.

Sex Education in the Schools?

EXHIBIT 7

One of the most difficult subjects schools teach is sex education. Pressure from parents and community members often results in sexual education ending up on the "evaded" curriculum—never discussed, and its side effects ignored and relegated to the area of "personal problems." Even if sex education is taught as part of the formal curriculum in health class, *meaningful* school-based support systems for teen mothers are still relatively rare. Teen mothers rarely have good options for child care and alternative scheduling that will allow them to work toward, and complete, their high school degree. "Sex education school initiatives tend to place primary responsibility for adolescent pregnancy on girls."

Source: Quoted from A. Ginorio and M. Huston (2001). *Si, se puede! Yes we can, Latinas in school.* Washington, DC: AAUW Educational Foundation, p. 26.

Family outreach and family life education programs can be developed, along with after-school tutorial and recreational programs, sex education and self-defense programs, support groups for pregnant teens and young mothers, day care for their children, and the like. A myriad of possible programs may help prevent early pregnancy or at least help young parents complete high school.

357

CHAPTER 9
*Social Work
in the Schools:
Lisa and Loretta
Santiago,
Children-at-Risk*

As the book *Si, Se Puede* puts it (2001, p. 26):

> School—enters the equation on education in three distinct ways: conducting sex education classes to discourage pregnancy, offering support services to pregnant teens and young mothers, and ensuring that girls are engaged in school.

Accountability, Standardized Testing, and Teen Dropout Rates

There has been a great deal of public discussion in recent years regarding accountability in the schools. Schools are to be held accountable for teaching their students; the extent of student learning is to be measured by standardized tests. In schools where students do not perform well on the tests, schools or teachers may be penalized in various ways, usually by the withholding of funds. Students who fail the tests may not be allowed to graduate. Both Presidents Clinton and Bush have pushed such policies at the federal level, and 24 states have implemented them or are in the process of doing so (Jonsson, 2001).

While no one can argue the importance of good schools and effective teachers, there is another side to this issue. Many students come to school unprepared to learn. They may be hungry. They may have had no parental supervision or assistance with homework because their single parent had to work two jobs to pay the rent. Lewin (2001) reports that adolescent children in three early studies of welfare-to-work programs had lower academic achievement and more behavioral problems than children in other welfare households. They may be suffering from posttraumatic stress syndrome because they witnessed a shooting on the street or lost a friend in a gang fight. Children do not perform very well on standardized tests when their neighborhoods resemble war zones. Holding schools accountable for what are in part results of national and state social policies that ignore the needs of the poor may be counterproductive. Now the schools that need funds the most will get even less, and children who badly need that first basic ticket to a job, the high school diploma, are more likely to fail in their attempt to secure it.

While evidence to date is not conclusive, many researchers believe that students who score poorly on early versions of the standardized tests become discouraged and drop out. Several states have seen an increase in dropout rates since the passage of standardized testing laws. Michelle Fine, for example, a researcher at the City University of New York, believes that new graduation standards may be spiking the dropout rate across the country. "For many kids it's a double assault," she says. "There's the recognition that they don't have the skills, and then there's the recognition that they're not going to be allowed to graduate" (Jonsson, 2001).

Other educators report that less school time than ever is being provided for counseling and tutoring students who need the most help, thus also tending to increase dropout rates. Standardized testing may actually lead some schools to encourage poor students to drop out, in fact, because then their scores will not have to be included in the overall school average (see Exhibit 8).

When Dropouts "Help" Districts

EXHIBIT 8

As teacher salaries and school perks become interwoven with test outcomes, critics say some educators now turn away failing students. As a result, they say, American high schools are less welcoming to students with a penchant for mechanics rather than Molière.

"A low scoring kid dropping out is no longer a problem for a school," says Ms. First. "In many districts, it's an advantage for the school to have them drop out."

Source: P. Jonsson (2001, May 15). Higher standards—and more dropouts? *The Christian Science Monitor,* p. 3.

Social work values, of course, promote the goal of assisting all students to succeed at school, to help them qualify for better opportunities in life, and to maximize their potential. Recent evidence demonstrates that *school failure itself* is far more predictive of teens ending up in trouble than race, income, or family structure. Marks (2000, p. 2) writes that for years, people assumed that if a teen was black, poor, and from a broken home, he was more likely to end up afoul of the law. However, the largest study of American teenagers to date, the National Longitudinal Study of Adolescent Health, "turned that assumption on its head." Marks notes that factors such as "school failure, large amounts of time spent 'hanging out,' and friends who engage in risky behavior themselves are three to eight times more likely to predict trouble for teens than race, income, and family structure combined."

Clearly, ways of helping children to succeed in school, *all* children, are required, not only for their own sakes but for that of society. Social workers may have to help lawmakers rethink the meaning of accountability and help the schools influence social policies that make sense for their students outside school walls as well as within.

THE HISTORY OF SOCIAL WORK IN THE SCHOOLS

Early Years

Social work in public schools in the United States has had a fairly short history. It began with efforts of voluntary organizations. In 1906 two New York City settlement houses, Hartley House and Greenwich House, assigned "visitors" to do liaison work with three school districts. One of these visitors, Mary Marot, was a teacher and a resident of Hartley House. A natural leader, she formed a visiting teacher committee at the settlement house. The Public Education Association of New York became interested in her work and asked her if she would make her committee part of their organization. She agreed, and the association publicized the concept of "visiting teacher." At about the same time, the Women's Education Association in Boston established a "home and school visitor" to improve communication between the home and school settings. In Connecticut, the director of the Psychological Clinic of Hartford hired a "special teacher" to assist him in making home visits and to act as a liaison between the clinic and the school (Hancock, 1982).

359

CHAPTER 9
*Social Work
in the Schools:
Lisa and Loretta
Santiago,
Children-at-Risk*

The fact that the concept of visiting teacher took hold at about the same time in three separate cities indicates that this was an idea whose time had come. Initially, visiting teachers were financed by settlement houses or other private associations or agencies. But from about 1913 to 1921 various school boards began hiring them, and the movement expanded from the eastern to the midwestern states. The early focus of these workers was community-based; settlement houses in particular lent an orientation toward finding ways to alter the environment to improve individual lives. Visiting teachers tried to find ways to intervene in the school and community settings to help prevent retardation and delinquency, improve attendance, and develop scholarship.

The passage of compulsory attendance laws during this time reflected growing societal awareness of the importance of education, and that every child had not only a right but an obligation to go to school. Compulsory education laws increased the employment of visiting teachers (Costin, 1987). Increasing numbers of visiting teachers led to the establishment of the National Committee of Visiting Teachers in 1921 (Freeman, 1995).

During the 1920s the initial emphasis on community liaison and change gradually shifted toward concentration on adjustment of the individual child. Attention was focused on reducing delinquency and improving mental health, not so much through improving school and community conditions as through helping the child personally to adjust. This shift in emphasis paralleled the growth in popularity of Freudian psychology, which strongly focused on individual treatment rather than social change.

The Great Depression of the 1930s drastically reduced employment for social workers in the schools. Early in this period, those who retained their jobs tended to become heavily involved in locating and distributing food, shelter, and clothing. When the federal government began to provide these necessities, social workers gradually resumed their trend toward becoming caseworkers with individual students and their families. This orientation was well in place by the 1940s.

Middle Period

Throughout the 1940s and 50s, with the federal government providing many basic financial and material needs to American families, social workers continued to focus on a clinical orientation, increasing their prestige in the school setting. Refinement of practice techniques to help individual students adjust to their environments became the primary goal. The 1960s, however, brought a number of social protest movements, and with them came a shift in emphasis to changing the school environment to help it better meet the needs of diverse students, in collaboration with other school personnel. Development of systems theory and an ecological perspective helped focus attention on the complex problems of schools and communities, including racism and students' rights, in the 1970s. Not all workers made the transition, however (Freeman, 1995). During this time, the term "visiting teacher" gradually changed to "school social worker."

Employment of school social workers expanded in the 1960s and continued to expand in the 1970s. One reason was that legislation provided a variety of new employment settings. For example, the Economic Opportunity Act of 1964 created Head Start programs, which often employed social workers full- or part-time. Moneys appropriated under the Elementary and Secondary Education Act, which sought to improve educational opportunities for disadvantaged children, sometimes were used to employ social workers. In 1975, as has been described previously, the Education for All Handicapped Children Act created new roles for social workers as part of the special education team.

In 1978 the National Association of Social Workers developed standards for school social work. This project was initiated by the NASW Task Force on Social Work Services in the Schools and completed by its successor, the Committee on Social Work Services in the Schools. The basic purpose of these standards was "to provide a model or measurement that school social workers can use to assess their scope of practice and their practice skills" (Hancock, 1982). The standards identify three major targets of service: pupils and parents, school personnel, and the community. Clearly, the intent of the standards is that school social work services maintain a strong preventive, ecological perspective.

Current Period

In the 1980s, school social work began to pay more attention to students' rights, cultural diversity, parental involvement in the schools, and school-community-family partnerships. The impact of IDEA legislation in particular encouraged active parental involvement in educational planning for their children. Social workers have assumed much of the responsibility to make this a reality. They frequently provide information to parents about programs and services, serve as mediators in conflicts regarding educational decisions, and provide mental health services in the classroom (Freeman, 1995).

Trends

Social workers are challenged today, and will continue to be challenged, by the many issues and trends discussed earlier in this chapter. These include meeting the needs of an increasingly diverse student population, especially greater numbers of children of ethnic minority heritage, children whose first language is other than English, and gay and lesbian students. It involves dealing constructively with violence, teen sexuality and pregnancy issues, and new school accountability measures (including holding those measures *themselves* accountable so as to find ways to make them fairer for children who are poor, underprivileged, and overstressed).

Since schools serve almost all children in this country today, they can be primary sites for preventive efforts and early intervention. What better locus for social work leadership? Not surprisingly, whenever possible social workers today are increasingly involved in macrolevel intervention to stretch scarce resources and prevent problems from arising. Efforts are myriad in scope, including organizing after-school programs, child care programs, weekend recreational programs, parenting classes, substance abuse prevention programs, and the like. Increasingly, efforts involve securing the funds to support these programs, requiring sophisticated grant writing skills (Wells, 1999).

Major new legislation pertaining to education was passed by Congress and signed into law by President George W. Bush at the end of 2001. It was intended to provide assistance to poor schools and included built-in accountability measures. At the time this chapter is being written, it is too early to tell what the impact will be. However, social workers in schools will probably need to become further involved in proactive "policy practice" to keep legislators informed of unintended side effects of this (or any other) legislation. Social workers may also need to lobby for changes. For example, increases in student dropout rates were already manifest in studies measuring effects of standardized testing *prior* to the above legislation. If rates continue to increase, and appear related to accountability measures such as standardized testing, prompt action may be needed.

361

CHAPTER 9
*Social Work
in the Schools:
Lisa and Loretta
Santiago,
Children-at-Risk*

Another issue looming on the horizon is that of advertising. More and more schools, strapped for funds, are allowing advertising on their websites, in their hallways, and in their classrooms via television stations such as Channel One, which combines news with ads aimed directly at high school students. A grassroots, bipartisan coalition is attempting to free schools from advertising, but as of September 2000, only 19 states had adopted any regulations. Of those 19 states, 14 had very limited statutes, such as Virginia's law prohibiting ads on school buses (Farah, 2001). Another serious problem relating to advertising aimed at school children is the fact that the Supreme Court recently struck down regulations in Massachusetts that prohibited tobacco advertisements within 1,000 feet of schools and playgrounds. The conservative court ruled that such regulations violated the First Amendment rights of tobacco companies (Richey, 2001). Teen smoking is on the rise today, so the battle against luring students into addiction to fatten corporate profits must be continued.

The trend toward increased numbers of alternative and charter schools has been discussed earlier. Increased summer school enrollment will also affect social work practice. Particularly in large cities, summer school enrollment has been burgeoning in recent years. Summer school enrollment in Chicago, for example, increased 10-fold over a five-years period, so that more than half of its student body was enrolled in summer school by 2001. This trend is partially fueled by standardized testing and the curbing of social promotion. Other factors involve increasing numbers of single-parent and two-working-parent households that welcome summer programming for their children (Sappenfield, 2001). So far teachers have been most affected, but it seems likely that school social workers too will find their employment contracts running more on a year-round basis soon.

Issues related to gender diversity remain serious. According to a report on gender gaps in the schools conducted by the American Institutes for Research, commissioned by the American Association of University Women Educational Foundation (1998), the cumulative effect of poverty, abuse, and other family or community problems is even worse for girls than for boys. The report notes that about 20 percent of girls have been sexually or physically abused, and 25 percent show signs of depression. Twenty-five percent do not receive needed health care. Sexual harassment interferes with the learning of both boys and girls in schools. Substance abuse is a widespread problem; in boys it is tied to a higher school dropout rate than for non-substance-abusing boys, in girls to a higher rate of criminality than for non-substance-abusing girls.

Special-needs populations today include children with developmental disabilities, emotional or behavioral disorders, cognitive disabilities, physical disabilities, and the like. Early assessment and planning for services in the least restrictive environment remain important tasks for the school social worker today. Assessing how home and community environments affect student development is another important focus of today's school social workers (Freeman, 1995).

School social work is a strong and growing field today. The number of state associations for school social workers has grown throughout the 1980s and 90s, and in the early 1990s, school social workers developed the first specialty practice section within the NASW, the School Social Work Section. Such associations are important because they provide forums for development and discussion of important issues in the field and for dissemination of current research findings. They can also, ideally, lead to the development of political action groups to lobby for needed legislation and funding.

INTERNET SITES

http://www.sswaa.org/	The School Social Work Association of America
http://www.faculty.fairfield.edu/fleitas/contents.html	Band-Aides and Blackboards
http://www.edc.org/urban/	National Institute for Urban School Improvement
http://www.ncsu.edu/cpsv/save.html	Students against Violence Everywhere
http://www.naswdc.org/practice/standards/school.htm	NASW Standards for School Social Work Services
http://internationalnetwork-schoolsocialwork.htmlplanet.com/	International Network for School Social Work
http://members.aol.com/_ht_a/lovetuls/skeelphobia.html	School Phobia?
http://www.ncbe.gwu.edu/	National Clearinghouse for Bilingual Education
http://www.ed.gov/offices/OBEMLA/	Office of Bilingual Education and Minority Affairs
http://www.nabe.org/	National Association for Bilingual Education
http://www.rong-chang.com/	English as a Second Language
http://www.newstimes.com/archive99/mar0599/rgc.htm	Support groups for homosexual teenagers, families, and friends

SUMMARY

This chapter begins with a case study of two Latino sisters who were referred to the school social worker because of attendance problems. The social worker approaches the referral from a generalist perspective, finding out what the girls' past

363

CHAPTER 9
*Social Work
in the Schools:
Lisa and Loretta
Santiago,
Children-at-Risk*

history of attendance had been and consulting with the parents, teachers, and the girls themselves to determine the nature of the problem. He does not assume that the problem lies with the girls, but he explores the possibility that family, school, or other environmental factors might be contributing to their truancy. After gathering and assessing data concerning the problem and determining appropriate goals (reducing conflicts at home, increasing school attendance), the social worker develops a plan of action, referring the children and their family to appropriate resources. The social worker thus mobilizes the resources of family, school, and community.

The impact of cultural diversity on the schools is clearly illustrated in this case study by the organization and planning invested in making a bilingual, bicultural program available for Hispanic children. Social work values such as self-determination support the development of such programs. Not only can the children learn better and faster in their own language, but self-esteem is enhanced in circumstances where the children's heritage is recognized and honored.

The public school is a gathering place for most of the children of America. For that reason, representatives of almost every minority will be found there. This chapter's second case study concerns two brothers with a homosexual orientation. It is offered to illustrate the serious challenge the social work profession faces in helping to expand tolerance for diversity in the school setting. Social work values affirming the worth and dignity of every person serve as a beacon to help guide the worker through circumstances involving ignorance and intolerance.

The school is a secondary, or host, setting for the social worker, so the social work role is often as a member of a team. In general, on the special education team, the social worker is the professional liaison between school and family; she or he gathers information about children's developmental histories and behavior patterns in the home and community settings. Special education evaluations can be seen as applied research with important consequences pertaining to multidisciplinary team decision making.

Social work values help orient social workers in influencing and implementing policies in the schools that deal with issues such as violence, sexuality and teen pregnancy, and accountability. How policies may differ according to value orientation (for example, the orientation toward educating, developing new social skills, and maximizing potential, rather than controlling or punishing) is discussed.

Social work roles in the schools must be generalist, ranging from working with individuals and families to working with small groups, organizations, and communities. Problems such as violence in the schools have their roots in the community as a whole, so that intervention on a single level will not suffice.

KEY TERMS

alternative schools
bilingual education
emotional or behavioral disturbance
English as a Second Language (ESL)
gay
heterosexism
homophobia

homosexual
lesbian
mainstreaming
multidisciplinary team (M-team, pupil
    planning team)
norms
primary social work setting

secondary social work setting
special education
subculture

truancy
zero tolerance

DISCUSSION QUESTIONS

1. What two major educational models to assist minority children at school have developed over the past several years? How are these models of education in accord with social work values? Why are they considered important?

2. Imagine you were a child entering public school with no knowledge of English. Which educational model do you think would have worked better for you? Why?

3. What were Frank Haines's initial hypotheses with respect to the truancy of the Santiago sisters? How accurate did his hypotheses turn out to be? How useful were they in shaping his initial investigation?

4. What is a culture? A subculture? Which cultures or subcultures are represented in the Santiago case example described in this chapter? Why is the concept of culture important in social work practice?

5. What are school-linked, integrated services? What kinds of services do full-service schools provide in addition to an education? What are some strengths of this kind of collaborative effort? Can you think of any problems that might arise?

6. What is the social worker's role on a special education evaluation team? How is this role an example of applied research? How does this role affect children and families referred to special education?

7. How did social workers originally become involved in work in the schools? How has the school social work role changed over time? In what ways has it remained the same?

8. According to NASW standards, what are three major targets of social work services in the schools? How do these standards compare with the generalist concept of social work practice?

9. If you could develop a policy pertaining to students with a homosexual orientation for your school, what key provisions would you include? Why?

10. Violence in the schools may relate to the fact that American communities themselves are violent. What has been your own experience? Do you agree? Disagree? Why?

11. Many social workers believe that sex education should be offered in the schools. What do you think about this? Why? If a student becomes pregnant, do you believe that services should be offered to help keep that student in school? If so, what kind of services do you think would be most helpful?

12. What are your views on standardized testing in the schools? What evidence is provided in this chapter that accountability measures such as these can have unexpected side effects? How do you think the social work profession should respond to accountability measures in the schools? Why?

CLASSROOM EXERCISES

While not required, it is suggested that students break into small groups of three or four to discuss these exercises. It may be helpful to choose a scribe to record and report interesting points to the class after the group discussion.

1. Think about something school-related that you did or considered doing that teachers or other staff would describe as at-risk behavior, something you are willing to share with the group. Examples might include truancy, substance abuse, withdrawn or disruptive

behavior, and the like. Given the perspective of time, why do you think you did what you did, or why *didn't* you? On reflection, what school policies do you think could have helped you? Do you think counseling individually or in small groups by a school social worker could have helped? Do you think the threat of punishment or the provision of positive incentives such as skills training and various rewards can best change troubled behavior?

365

CHAPTER 9
*Social Work
in the Schools:
Lisa and Loretta
Santiago,
Children-at-Risk*

2. In your high school, how prevalent were troubles such as violent behavior, sexual harassment or teen pregnancy? What policies, if any, did the school implement to address these issues? What policies do you believe could have been helpful?

3. Were accountability measures such as standardized testing practiced at your school? Describe measures you were aware of. What effects, if any, did they have on you? On your classmates?

4. If you were to develop policies to help develop the best possible atmosphere in your school to help enhance student learning and cooperation, what policies would you develop? What would be the role of the school social worker?

RESEARCH ACTIVITIES

1. Arrange to interview a social worker who works in a regular public school and another who works in an alternative school. Compare and contrast their educational backgrounds, satisfaction with their positions, and descriptions of their work roles and responsibilities.

2. If your town or city has a full-service school, arrange to talk with social workers employed by community agencies stationed at the school. What is their perception of the major needs of students at the school? How does their work help meet these needs? What needs of the students still are not met, from their point of view?

3. Find out about special education services in the school system in your town or city. Are there special classrooms for children with disabilities or is the full-inclusion model in operation? Interview both a teacher and a social worker who work with the special education program. What do they think about full inclusion as an educational model for students with disabilities? What are their reasons?

INTERNET RESEARCH EXERCISES

1. The impact of the shootings at Columbine High School is described in an article titled "Bound by a Trauma Called Columbine," by Frank M. Ochberg (http://www.sourcemain.com/gift/Html/Columbine.htm).
   a. How has the posttraumatic stress disorder (PTSD) evidenced its presence at Columbine?
   b. What types of emotions reoccur among the administrators of the school?
   c. As a school social worker, what type of services and help would you offer to ameliorate the situation in schools that have been victimized by violence?

2. A position statement on confidentiality was issued in March 2001 by the School Social Work Association of America (http://sswwaa.org/about/publications/confidentiality.html).
   a. The statement noted that in most states, the communication between a social worker and a client is privileged, but this privilege is not absolute. Please explain.
   b. Should information learned by the school social worker be available to other school personnel? Expand on your yes or no answer.
   c. What is the final determinant on whether or not to preserve confidentiality?

3. An organization called the Gay, Lesbian, and Straight Network addresses the problem of homophobia in schools (http://www.glsen.org/templates/resources/record.html).

    a. What are the real costs of bigotry on lesbian, gay, bisexual, and transgender (LGBT) students as cited for the Vermont and Massachusetts Departments of Education?

    b. Is "Don't Ask, Don't Tell" the best policy? Why?

    c. The article states that "change is a process, not an event." Explain this statement as you interpret it after reading this article.

REFERENCES

American Institute for Research. (1998). *Gender gaps: Where schools still fail our children.* Washington, DC: American Association of University Women Educational Foundation.

Associated Press. (2001, June 19). State agrees to mainstream more disabled kids. *The Christian Science Monitor,* p. 16.

Astor, R. A., Behre, W. J., Wallace, J. M., & Fravil, K. A. (1998, May). School social workers and school violence: Personal safety, training, and violence programs. *Social Work, 43*(3), 223–232.

Baldauf, S. (1998, September 8). Public schools at a crossroads. *The Christian Science Monitor,* pp. 1, 18.

Berkman, C. S., & Zinberg, G. (1997, July). Homophobia and heterosexism in social workers. *Social Work, 42*(4), 329–332.

Berrick, J. D., & Duerr, M. (1998). Maintaining positive school relationships: The role of the social worker vis-à-vis full-service schools. In E. M. Freeman, C. G. Franklin, R. Fong, G. L. Shaffer, and E. M. Timberlake (Eds.), *Multisystem skills and interventions in school social work practice* (pp. 334–339). Washington, DC: NASW Press.

Boyle-Del Rio, S., Carlson, R., and Haibeck, L. (2000, Fall). School personnel's perception of the school social worker's role. *School Social Work Journal, 25*(1), 59–75.

Burrello, L. C., & Lashley, C. A. (1992). On organizing for the future: The destiny of special education. In K. Waldron, A. Riester, and J. Moore, (Eds.), *Special education, the challenge of the future* (pp. 69–70). San Francisco: Mellon Research University Press.

Burt, M., Resnick, G., & Novick, E. R. (1998). *Building supportive communities for at-risk adolescents.* Washington, DC: American Psychological Association.

Coeyman, M. (2001, May 15). From experiment to institution. *The Christian Science Monitor,* p. 4.

Coeyman, M. (2001, June 11). A school of her own. *The Christian Science Monitor,* pp. 11, 14.

Costin, L. (1987). School social work. In A. Minahan (Ed.), *Encyclopedia of social work* (18th ed., pp. 536–539). Silver Spring, MD: National Association of Social Workers.

Dr. Jocelyn Elders urges comprehensive sexuality education (2001, Spring). *Moving Forward,* 1. (Milwaukee, WI, Planned Parenthood)

Dupper, D. R. (2000). The design of social work services. In P. Allen-Meares, R. O. Washington, & B. L. Welsh, *Social work services in schools* (3rd ed., pp. 243–272). Boston: Allyn and Bacon.

Farah, S. (2001, June 19). Coalition takes on TV—and its ads—broadcast in schools. *The Christian Science Monitor,* p. 15.

Franklin, C. (2000). The delivery of school social work services. In P. Allen-Meares, R. O. Washington, & B. L. Welsh, *Social work services in schools* (3rd ed., pp. 273–298). Boston: Allyn and Bacon.

367

CHAPTER 9
*Social Work
in the Schools:
Lisa and Loretta
Santiago,
Children-at-Risk*

Freeman, E. M. (1995). School social work overview. In R. L. Edwards (Ed.). *Encyclopedia of social work* (19th ed., pp. 2087–2097). Washington, DC: NASW Press.

Freeman, E. M., Halim, M., & Peterson, K. J. (1998). HIV/AIDS policy development and reform: Lessons from practice, research, and education. In E. M. Freeman, C. G. Franklin, R. Fong, S. G. Shaffer, & E. M. Timberlake (Eds.). *Multisystem skills and interventions in school social work practice* (pp. 371–377). Washington, DC: NASW Press.

Ginorio, A., and Huston, M. (2001). *Si, se puede! Yes, we can, Latinas in school.* Washington, DC: AAUW Educational Foundation.

Gray, P. (1993, Fall). Teach your children well. *Time,* pp. 69–70.

Hancock, B. (1982). *School social work.* Englewood Cliffs, NJ: Prentice Hall.

Harris Interactive (2001). *Hostile hallways, bullying, teasing, and sexual harrassment* in *school.* Washington, DC: AAUW Educational Foundation.

Jonsson, P. (2001, May 15). Higher standards—and more dropouts? *The Christian Science Monotor,* p. 3.

Kiefer R., and Irwin, N. (2000, May 2). How schools stop teen violence. *The Christian Science Monitor,* pp. 1, 4.

Kosh, K. (2000). School violence, are American schools safe? In D. Bonilla, *School violence* (pp. 5–33). New York: The H. W. Wilson Company.

Kopels, S. (2000). Securing equal educational opportunity: language, race, and sex. In P. Allen-Meares, R. O. Washington & B. L. Welsh, *Social work services in schools* (3rd ed., p. 216). Boston: Allyn and Bacon.

Lewin, T. (2001, July 31). Surprising result in welfare-to-work studies. *New York Times.* Available: http://nytimes.com/2001/07/31/WELF.html?ex=9975930&ei=1&en=14a580ab.

Marks, A. (2000, December 1). Clearer picture emerges of "at-risk" youths. *The Christian Science Monitor,* p. 2.

Mathis, S., & Diaz, M. (1995, Spring). Post traumatic stress disorder (inner city youth). *Race, Rights, Resistance, 5*(2), 73–76.

Morrow, D. F. (1993, November). Social work with gay and lesbian adolescents. *Social Work* 38(6), 655–660.

National Campaign to Prevent Teen Pregnancy (2001). *Fact sheet: Recent trends in teen pregnancy, sexual activity, and contraceptive use* (online). Available: http://www.teenpregnancy.org/rectrend.htm (May 2001).

National Campaign to Prevent Teen Pregnancy (2001). *General facts and stats* (online). Available: http://www.teenpregnancy.org/genlfact.htm (July 2001).

Richey, W. (2001, June 29). States can't ban antismoking ads. *The Christian Science Monitor.* pp. 1, 3.

Rose, S. (1998). *Group work with children and adolescents, prevention and intervention in school and community systems.* Thousand Oaks, CA: Sage Publications.

Saltzman, A., & Proch, K. (1990). *Law in social work practice.* Chicago: Nelson Hall.

Sappenfield, M. (2001, June 22). For more students, summer means—more school. *The Christian Science Monitor,* pp. 1, 9.

Saunders, E. J. (1998). Services for infants and toddlers with disabilities: IDEA, Part H. In E. Freeman, C. G. Franklin, R. Fong, G. Shaffer, & E. M. Timberlake (Eds.), *Multisystem skills and interventions in school social work practice* (pp. 402–410). Washington, DC: NASW Press.

Savoye, C. (2000, June 13). Violence dips in nation's schools. *The Christian Science Monitor,* pp. 1, 4.

Study: Safe-sex programs don't increase sexual activity (2001, May 30). *The Daily News,* p. A 10.

Wells, C. (1999). *Social work day to day, the experience of generalist social work practice* (3rd ed.). New York: Addison Wesley Longman.

Wood, D. B. (1998, June 4). Vote to eliminate bilingual education in California resonates nationwide. *The Christian Science Monitor,* p. 10.

Zernike, K. (2001, May 23). Schools rethink zero tolerance. *The Daily News,* p. 3.

FOR FURTHER READING

Allen-Meares, P., Washington, R. O., and Welsh, B. (2000). *Social work services in schools* (3rd ed.). Boston: Allyn and Bacon.

This text on school social work begins with a section on major contemporary issues in American schools in historical context. Part Two introduces conceptual frameworks for school social workers, emphasizing an ecological perspective. Part Three discusses educational policy and social work practice. Part Four explores planning, implementing, and evaluating social work services in the schools.

American Institutes for Research. (1998). *Gender gaps: Where schools still fail our children.* Washington, DC: American Association of University Women Educational Foundation.

This study, commissioned by the American Association of University Women Educational Foundation in follow-up to *How Schools Shortchange Girls,* finds that girls do not enroll in higher-level mathematics and computer courses at the same rate as boys, do not take as many advanced placement exams for college in these areas, and do not do as well on college entrance examinations. Recommendations are made concerning ways to encourage girls to take more advanced mathematics, science, and computer courses, and ways to make college entrance examinations measuring the strengths of young women more equitable.

The report also finds that poverty and abuse have strongly negative effects on school achievement for both boys and girls.

Burt, M., Resnick, G., & Novick, E. (1998). *Building supportive communities for at-risk adolescents.* Washington DC: American Psychological Association.

Various programs around the country that are integrating services for adolescents are reviewed. Since almost all American youth are served by the public schools, the school as a natural location for integrated services is discussed. The book notes that today, given massive cutbacks in federal aid, state and local communities are increasingly expected to do more with less. Integration of services is presented as a major strategy to meet this challenge.

Freeman, E. M., Franklin, C. G., Fong, R., Shaffer, G. S., & Timberlake, E.M. (Eds.). (1998). *Multisystem skills and interventions in school social work.* Washington, DC: NASW Press.

This useful anthology for those with a special interest in school social work contains an impressive number of articles about this field of practice. Sections are organized according to level of intervention. Part One explores work with individuals, Part Two provides examples of practice with families, Part Three presents work with groups and classrooms, Part Four examines skills and interventions in community practice, and Part Five discusses work with larger systems and examines policy development and reform.

Saltzman, A., & Proch, K. (1990). *Law in social work practice.* Chicago: Nelson-Hall.

Saltzman and Proch provide social workers with a substantial overview of law and the legal system. They examine social work roles in the hearing process as well as methods of locating and using the law. They then examine basic principles of criminal law, juvenile law, law and the family, legal aspects of health and mental health care, and legal aspects of social work practice such as credentialing and confidentiality. The most pertinent material relating to social work in the schools is the section on juvenile law—Chapter 10, "Primary and Secondary Education." This chapter explores discrimination, attendance, discipline, and education of handicapped children.

Wells, C. (1999). *Social work day to day: The experience of generalist social work practice* (3rd ed.). New York: Addison Wesley Longman.

Social Work Day to Day presents a year in the life of a school social worker as she introduces social work services in a rural setting. The book is written in a storytelling style to help students understand what this type of work is really like. The emphasis is on work with special education programs. The third edition presents case examples from the practice of two social workers who today hold the author's former position as school social worker in two rural towns, and discusses effects of changes in American social and educational policy. The book is further augmented by examples of contemporary school social work practice in an urban setting.

369

CHAPTER 9
*Social Work
in the Schools:
Lisa and Loretta
Santiago,
Children-at-Risk*

CHAPTER 10

Substance Abuse Services

Dan was so cold that he knew he might freeze. He looked down at his feet and remembered that he had given his boots to an old man by the train station. Now his broken shoes did little to protect his feet from the snow on the streets. If he could just keep walking, he would not freeze. If he could get a drink, he would feel warm. Dan saw a familiar figure, stooped and hacking with a cough, turn into the alley behind the library, his hand in his pocket. Dan followed, and soon both men were sitting in George's cardboard-box shelter, sharing a bottle of brandy. It warmed them as they talked about better times. George had been a preacher in Mississippi until he came north in search of a secure job. That was in the mid-1980s, and the secure job had never materialized. Alcohol had eased his disappointment, but it never erased the memories of the family he had left behind.

Dan, at 23, was much younger and was not ready to give up hope. True, he had left his wife . . . well, not really. Angela had told him to leave because of his drinking. He wouldn't believe that he had a drinking problem. He thought it was her imagination. But thinking about Angela hurt too much; he'd better have another drink of that brandy. George had fallen asleep, Dan noticed. Dan looked around for some newspapers to cover George, to keep the cold out, but he saw none. He was feeling sleepy himself, his body exhausted from walking all day on the cold city streets.

When the police found George and Dan, both men were unconscious. For the paramedics who were called, this was the third conveyance of street people to hospitals that evening. The first call had led them to a white woman with a baby, both with frostbite; the baby was listed in serious condition. The second call involved an African American man, but he had not been drinking, and—although suffering from malnutrition and exposure—he had been admitted in stable condition. George and Dan, also African Americans, were in more serious condition. George had no heartbeat; Dan's was very weak.

*St. Francis Hospital was very busy with emergencies that night, but when Dan and George were brought in, the staff rallied. Dan had **hypothermia** (extreme loss of body temperature) and frostbite; one foot looked very damaged. He was admitted to the hospital for further care. After 10 minutes of effort by the emergency room medical staff, George was pronounced dead. It was a bitter cold night in Chicago.*

Two weeks later, Dan was talking with the social worker at the Salvation Army Emergency Lodge. Dan had arrived at the shelter the previous afternoon, having been referred there by the alcoholism counselor at the hospital. Madeleine Johnson, the shelter's social worker, knew about the treatment program he had begun at the hospital, but she questioned him again to gather more information about his drinking history. Dan instinctively liked this African American social worker, but he found himself somewhat irritated by the persistence of her questions. He found he could talk fairly easily about his days drinking with high school friends when he was 17. It was much more difficult to talk about what happened later. Admitting that he had lost two good jobs as a computer programmer because of his drinking was definitely not pleasant. But it was true. Having to talk about all this was so hard!

But most difficult and painful to admit was what his drinking had done to his marriage. Angie was so beautiful, and their love had been so deep, so incredible. His pain was unbearable when he thought about Angie. The social worker probed this painful area too, and she made him talk about Angie and the last time he had spoken with her. For three months after Angie had asked Dan to leave and he had begun living on the streets, he would phone her from time to time. He tried to make her believe that he was managing just fine. But he had not telephoned her from the hospital, and he had not given anyone her name, even when he was in critical condition and needed surgery to remove the frostbitten toes of his left foot. Following surgery, he entered the AA program at the hospital. Here he realized and admitted out loud for the first time that he had let alcohol ruin him, that he was an alcoholic. Now, at the Salvation Army Emergency Lodge, he was determined to continue attending AA meetings. The program made sense to him even if it was humbling to have to admit, in front of a group, what alcohol had done to his life.

Madeleine Johnson, the Salvation Army social worker, described the AA meetings held every evening at the Emergency Lodge. Dan said that he was serious about ending his drinking. He planned to attend the meetings daily. They also discussed how they would work together to locate employment opportunities for Dan as soon as the doctors said he was well enough to work. When Dan missed an AA meeting on the third day of his stay at the Emergency Lodge, the social worker asked to see him. Dan knew that Madeleine was disappointed that he had missed the meeting; that was a goal he had set for himself. But he was angry too. He claimed that the meetings were not intended for black men and that he was not—and probably never would be—comfortable with the group. He told her about the comments made by several of the men. It was clear they did not want minority members, especially blacks, in their group. Stan, an older man, had been especially outspoken; most of the others, even the two Puerto Ricans, had sided with Stan.

Then Madeleine revealed that she herself was a recovering alcoholic. She too attended meetings and needed the support of others to prevent a return to active drinking. Some AA groups did not meet her needs as an African American woman and a professional person, so she had searched out and found a group that was right for her. Dan was stunned by her admission, her honesty. After further discussion Dan resolved to return to AA meetings, but he planned to explore other groups as soon as he was able to walk better on his healing foot.

In the weeks that followed, Dan did attend meetings faithfully. Through meetings and through his interviews with the social worker, Dan grew to better understand himself and his reaction to alcohol. Madeleine Johnson was a BSW with four years' experience at the Emergency Lodge. She was able to help Dan acknowledge his anger about the misunderstandings and prejudices against African American people that he encountered in the AA group and among other residents of the shelter. Dan's trust in Madeleine grew as he discovered that she shared his deep concern about the people like George, even families with children, who were living on the streets.

Dan learned from another Emergency Lodge resident that Madeleine and the other social workers had written a grant proposal that just last week had been approved for funding to begin a health care program for homeless people. They would need volunteers, Dan thought. Perhaps there was something he could do to help. He would silently dedicate his volunteer work to his friend George.

After Dan had lived at the shelter for three weeks, his doctor at St. Francis Hospital said that he could return to work soon. Madeleine and Dan had been talking about Dan's future plans. Now they developed a strategy that involved temporary employment in a service-industry job and evening classes to enable Dan to get back into the computer field. Dan was encouraged to find that the social worker did not want him to settle for a service-industry job for good. But he did need to start somewhere, and he would need income immediately to pay rent for a single room. Dan began searching the classified ads in the newspaper for a job that was near public transportation. Within a week he was hired at a fast-food restaurant. Dan knew that it was only temporary; he had other plans.

Dan registered for classes at the community college immediately. On the day that he began his computer class, he telephoned Angie. He had found a single room that he could afford with his minimum-wage job; he was leaving the shelter the next day. Angie was clearly reluctant to believe that Dan was really no longer drinking. She had heard that story before. Still, she was relieved to hear from him and to know that he was OK. She seemed excited about his computer class. Later, as he was leaving the shelter, Dan thanked Madeleine Johnson. She encouraged him to stay in touch with her when he returned for AA meetings and the volunteer work that he would soon begin. Dan sensed her sincerity when she wished him well in the new life he was beginning. In his heart Dan wished her well too, for now he understood the special lifelong demands imposed by addiction to alcohol.

ROLES FOR SOCIAL WORKERS

Case studies, like that of Dan Graves, are interesting, but they also pose some problems. One potential problem is that readers might make inappropriate generalizations. In this case study, for example, one might conclude that all street people are alcoholics, which, of course, is not true. By this point you have read many case studies throughout the text, and you probably have developed the ability to think about them carefully and critically. It is important not to draw inappropriate inferences from case studies.

Another incorrect conclusion based on this case study would be that a history of substance abuse is a necessary background for a social worker. Madeleine Johnson, after all, was able to use her own alcoholism effectively in working with client Dan Graves. In reality, however, a social worker's effectiveness is based on the application of skill and knowledge, and one's knowledge base is much broader and much deeper than one's personal history. The other social workers at the shelter, those with no history of addiction, were also effective with their clients.

There was a time in the past when professionals did not understand chemical dependency and preferred not to work in this field. As a result, alcoholism counselors were mostly people who had no professional credentials but instead used their own life experience with addiction. Today most counselors in the field are expected to obtain certification through substance abuse training programs. Most states have some form of counselor certification, but requirements vary from state to state, as does the designation of the certification. Certification generally requires up to two years of coursework and field work. Increasingly professionals in nursing, social work, psychology, occupational therapy, and other areas are adding state certification for alcoholism or other drug counseling to their credentials for working with this population.

Social workers in substance abuse treatment settings function as members of a team. The social worker may or may not assume primary leadership of the treatment team. Before any decisions about treatment are made, however, assessment occurs.

Assessment

In substance abuse work, assessment is complicated by the variety of substances used and abused. It is further complicated by the need to determine whether a pattern of addition is involved or whether the use/abuse might be related to other causes such as a person's response to experiencing disaster or trauma. An understanding of the causes of addiction is only now evolving. Alcoholism, for example, has been known and studied for many years. Although initially it was thought to be "sinful" and a sign of "weak" character development, it is increasingly understood to be a constellation of many types of problems that have genetic, neurochemical, psychological, and environmental contributing mechanisms. Biological causative factors are not as well understood for addictions other than alcoholism (Leukefeld & Walker, 1998).

Multiple approaches to assessment exist. The *Social Work Dictionary* offers a helpful framework for assessment that has fairly clear indicators for intervention. Three types of alcoholism are proposed: primary, secondary, and reactive. **Primary alcoholism** is characterized by heavy drinking, often "in response to physiological withdrawal symptoms" (Baker, 1999, p. 375). The person with primary alcoholism "lives to drink." Primary alcoholism generally becomes apparent between age 25 to 35. A strong family history of alcoholism is common. This form of alcoholism may be genetically linked. **Secondary alcoholism** differs markedly from primary alcoholism in that a major psychiatric disorder precedes heavy alcohol use. **Reactive alcoholism** occurs shortly after severe trauma from a disaster such as the 2001 World Trade Center terrorist attack or the murder or accidental death of a loved one. According to Barker, "After the traumatic event, the individual may or may not become and remain addicted to alcohol" (p. 401).

Generally the person with primary alcoholism will benefit from a period of hospitalization followed by counseling and/or group therapy as an outpatient. If secondary alcoholism exists and the patient has been drinking heavily, a brief period of hospitalization for detoxification may be needed, but the primary mental illness must then become the major focus of treatment. The person experiencing reactive alcoholism needs intervention that will help her or him to deal with the emotions and life situation resulting from the crisis that occurred; this client may need no hospitalization but may need intensive counseling and support. The drinking behavior will need to be closely monitored.

Although Madeleine Johnson, the social worker in the case study, was not employed in a substance abuse setting, she frequently encountered clients who were alcoholic. Alcoholism is more commonly found in social work practice than other forms of substance abuse are, and so this chapter gives more attention to alcoholism than, for example, cocaine abuse.

Medical facilities that treat substance abuse tend to rely on the American Psychiatric Association's *Diagnostic and Statistical Manual of Mental Disorders (DSM-IV-TR)* approach to assessment. The *DSM-IV-TN* identifies 11 substances—

drugs that can be abused, such as alcohol—and describes criteria that differentiate abuse of these substances from dependence (a more serious condition). These criteria are explained in Exhibits 1 and 2. **Alcohol dependence,** using the criteria, is characterized by compulsive drinking that produces such symptoms as tolerance for alcohol, withdrawal from it, ineffective efforts to cut back on its use, and failure to change the drinking behavior despite evidence that it is causing serious difficulty. **Alcohol abuse** is the recurrent use of alcohol to the extent that repeated use results in an inability to fulfill normal role functions, or presents legal or social/interpersonal problems, or creates a hazard to self or others (American Psychiatric Association, 2000). Note that alcohol abuse does not produce the physiological ramifications that occur with alcohol dependence.

Criteria for Substance Dependence

EXHIBIT 1

A maladaptive pattern of substance abuse, leading to clinically significant impairment or distress, as manifested by three (or more) of the following, occurring at any time in the same 12-month period:

1. Tolerance as defined by either of the following:
   a. A need for markedly increased amounts of the substance to achieve intoxication or desired effect.
   b. Markedly diminished effect with continued use of the same amount of the substance.
2. Withdrawal, as manifested by either of the following:
   a. The characteristic withdrawal syndrome for the substance. [Each substance has two criteria for withdrawal: (1) cessation or reduction of use that has been heavy and prolonged and (2) specified mood and physiological changes.]
   b. The same (or closely related) substance is taken to relieve or avoid withdrawal symptoms.
3. The substance is often taken in larger amounts or over a longer period than was intended.
4. There is a persistent desire or unsuccessful efforts to cut down or control substance use.
5. A great deal of time is spent in activities necessary to obtain the substance (e.g., visiting multiple doctors or driving long distances), use the substance (e.g., chain-smoking), or recover from its effects.
6. Important social, occupational, or recreational activities are given up or reduced because of substance abuse.
7. The substance use is continued despite knowledge of having a persistent or recurrent physical or psychological problem that is likely to have been caused or exacerbated by the substance (e.g., current cocaine use despite recognition of cocaine-induced depression, or continued drinking despite recognition that an ulcer was made worse by alcohol consumption).

Source: American Psychiatric Association. (2000). *Diagnostic and statistical manual of mental disorders* (4th ed., text rev.). Washington, DC: American Psychiatric Association, p. 197.

Criteria for Substance Abuse

EXHIBIT 2

A. A maladaptive pattern of substance use leading to clinically significant impairment or distress, as manifested by one (or more) of the following, occurring at any time in the same 12-month period:
1. Recurrent substance use resulting in a failure to fulfill major role obligations at work, school, or home (e.g., repeated absences or poor work performance related to substance use; substance-related absences, suspensions, or expulsions from school; neglect of children or household).
2. Recurrent substance use in situations in which it is physically hazardous (e.g., driving an automobile or operating a machine when impaired by substance use).
3. Recurrent substance-related legal problems (e.g., arrests for substance-related disorderly conduct).
4. Continued substance use despite having persistent or recurrent social or interpersonal problems caused or exacerbated by the effects of the substance (e.g., arguments with spouse about consequences of intoxication, physical fights).
B. The symptoms have never met the criteria for Substance Dependence for this class of substance.

Source: American Psychiatric Association. (2000). *Diagnostic and statistical manual of mental disorders* (4th ed., text rev.). Washington, DC: American Psychiatric Association, p. 199.

The American Medical Association has considered alcoholism a disease since 1956, and yet there has been no universally accepted definition of alcoholism. This text, then, defines **alcoholism** as the compulsive use of alcohol characterized by evidence of abuse or dependence, as defined by the *DSM-IV-TR,* and resulting in some level of personal and social malfunctioning.

It is, essentially, this understanding of alcoholism that underpins Madeleine Johnson's and other social workers' practice as they gather information for an assessment. The actual process of data collection, especially in substance abuse treatment facilities, is increasingly a multidimensional one. The biological dimension is assessed by reviewing the person's medical history and current health and nutrition. (Nutritional needs may be neglected during heavy and prolonged bouts of drinking.) A drinking history is obtained that incorporates responses to the following questions: "What does the client drink, how much, how often, when, where, and in conjunction with which other substances? What are the eating, sleeping, and drug-taking patterns? When did the drinking begin? Is the pattern daily or binge drinking? How about blackouts, tolerance, DTs, and hallucinations? (Van Wormer, 1995, p. 312). The biological assessment provides clues to medical treatment needs.

The psychological dimension reviews the client's mental health history to determine the possible presence of underlying mental disorder. Questions are asked about current level of anxiety, depression, and suicidal thinking as well as unresolved trauma or grief. The connection between alcohol and psychological functioning emerges when questions about psychological functioning shift to "reasons for starting, stopping, and resuming drinking" (Van Wormer, p. 312).

The Brief MAST

EXHIBIT 3

Questions	Circle Correct Answers	
1. Do you feel you are a normal drinker?	Yes (0)	No (2)
2. Do friends or relatives think you are a normal drinker?	Yes (0)	No (2)
3. Have you ever attended a meeting of Alcoholics Anonymous (AA)?	Yes (5)	No (0)
4. Have you ever lost friends or girlfriends/ boyfriends because of drinking?	Yes (2)	No (0)
5. Have you ever gotten into trouble at work because of drinking?	Yes (2)	No (0)
6. Have you ever neglected your obligations, your family, or your work for two or more days in a row because you were drinking?	Yes (2)	No (0)
7. Have you ever had delirium tremens (DTs), severe shaking, or heard voices or seen things that weren't there after heavy drinking?	Yes (2)	No (0)
8. Have you ever gone to anyone for help about your drinking?	Yes (5)	No (0)
9. Have you ever been in a hospital because of drinking?	Yes (5)	No (0)
10. Have you ever been arrested for drunk driving or driving after drinking?	Yes (2)	No (0)

Score your own responses by adding all the points shown in parentheses for the items you have circled. A score of 6 or above identifies persons who may be alcoholic. Note that the points assigned to each question usually would not be shown to the person completing the assessment.

Source: Quoted from A. D. Pokorny, B. A. Miller, & H. B. Kaplan. (1972). The brief MAST: A shortened version of the Michigan Alcoholism Screening Test. *American Journal of Psychiatry, 129* (3), 344.

The social dimension of assessment engages the client in a review of family, friends, coworkers, and other social network relationships. Who has or currently provides friendship and support? Where do stresses and tensions exist? Which relationships have been impacted by the person's drinking? Are there religious or other organizations or community memberships or involvement that serve to protect against drinking? What about spiritual beliefs and practices? Who and what matters to the client? A careful, thorough multidimensional assessment provides insight for the client as well as the professional staff (Van Wormer).

The assessment process usually involves informal discussion as well as structured, predesigned questionnaires. The Michigan Alcoholism Screening Test (MAST) is one of several rapid assessment instruments that have been carefully tested for reliability and used for many years. (You might find it interesting to score yourself on the brief form of MAST shown in Exhibit 3.) Engaging people in their own assessment, perhaps including close family members or friends along with the social worker or counselor, can build effective team relationships that give energy and focus to the next steps of the treatment process.

Generalist Interventions

Once the social worker has made an assessment of the situation, the next step in the problem-solving process is to develop an intervention plan, sometimes referred to as a treatment plan. Because the problem, the person, and the situation are all unique, the intervention must be creative. An early decision that must be made is: Where should the social work action be targeted? Is the person who is actively drinking or abusing another substance the appropriate "client"? Perhaps the entire family should be seen as a unit. Perhaps an organization, possibly a work site, inherently promotes substance abuse (a brewery that encourages its employees to drink on the job, for example); if so, quite a different intervention plan would be needed. Are new programs needed in the community? Perhaps vulnerable populations can best be reached through community outreach work.

Many different and sometimes overlapping interventions are available to the generalist social worker. The social worker selects one or more strategies based on compatibility with client needs, culture, and goals. Some possible intervention approaches include:

- Behavioral approaches
- Self-help groups
- Family intervention
- Group therapy
- Chemical treatment (prescribed medications)
- Therapeutic communities
- Program development
- Community outreach

Behavioral approaches to intervention seek to change behaviors that are harmful or to encourage positive behaviors; the focus is less on understanding the causes or contributing factors of the behavior and more on effecting an immediate behavioral change. Self-help approaches generally involve groups of persons with similar problems who use what they have learned to help each other. Social workers may initiate and lead such groups, or they may refer people to existing groups.

Interventions that include work with the family can confront patterns of interpersonal relationships and family communications that subtly encourage or excuse excessive alcohol consumption or drug use and abuse. Securing the family as an ally in treatment and support for the client can be highly beneficial. Group therapy conducted by social workers, psychologists, or other professionals focuses on the "whys" of drinking and chemical addiction. Feelings are also explored and worked with in a group environment that is at once supportive and confrontational.

Prescription medications are sometimes used alone or in conjunction with one of the other intervention approaches; they may produce unpleasant effects such as nausea if alcohol is used (Antabuse), or they may block the pleasurable sensation of opiates (Methadone). Therapeutic communities are live-in programs where the resident is intensely and repeatedly confronted by staff and other residents when his or her thinking or behavior is inappropriate. Always alert to the needs of the community, generalist social workers may focus their intervention on building bridges between vulnerable persons, such as people living in isolation or on the streets, and the services that can help them with substance abuse problems. Sometimes it is first necessary to create new services or to put established treatment programs into entirely new areas; suburban communities and rural areas are examples. Social work interventions typically do focus on work at several different systems levels, as Chapter 1 explained.

Individuals and Families   Hospitalized patients who have undergone detoxification (medical treatment to remove or reduce the dangerous level of alcohol or drugs in the body) often initially need help with practical financial matters and with decisions such as where to live following discharge. The most effective intervention at this time occurs if clients are actively involved in decision making. People often are sick and uncomfortable during detoxification, and hospitalization is brief. Only very brief counseling takes place during hospitalization. Use of behavioral approaches, therapeutic communities, or other forms of intervention usually occurs in the recovery period following hospitalization. The focus of this intervention depends on the assessment, but it always incorporates the goal of helping the client to cope with everyday life without resorting to substance abuse.

Research has demonstrated that families are significant in motivating and sustaining members during recovery (Stanton & Heath, 1995). Family involvement often proves to be an effective adjunct to individual counseling. In fact, in our case study, one would hope that at some point Angie would be brought into counseling with Dan. Alcoholism and drug dependency have a serious negative impact on family relationships and on the family system. As Dan began treatment, he recognized the damage that his drinking had done to his relationship with Angie. He valued that relationship and wished to restore it. Angie, like many spouses and children of recovering alcoholics, was frightened and unsure of what to believe. Would Dan begin drinking again? Could she risk emotional commitment by going back to Dan again? Family or couple counseling requires that the social worker have a clear understanding of family dynamics as well as of addiction.

Case management has been found to be a useful approach in practice with chemically dependent persons. Rapp describes his experience using a strengths-based model of case management with persons whose substance abuse has primarily been with crack cocaine. This approach was so different from and contrary to the medical models previously used with the clients that initially they were confused. It was very difficult for some of them to identify any personal strengths, any competence, even any good decisions that they had made. Rapp found that they responded well to this approach—case managers met with them in their own environments, developed relationships with them, and helped them to obtain needed resources (Rapp, 1997). The generalist practice knowledge and skills of BSW social workers are a sound basis for case management using a strengths perspective.

Groups   Although empirical research has not yet demonstrated the superiority of group treatment over other forms of intervention, practical experience has shown that groups offer many advantages. Among the potential advantages of group intervention are the facts that they "alleviate the social stigma associated with addiction by providing social acceptance from peers and they facilitate identification with peers who are further along in recovery" (Smyth, 1995, pp. 2329–2330). Groups can also be confrontational, making denial of drug dependence less possible, and can help members achieve a level of self-awareness that is essential to the development of self-control.

Social workers use a variety of intervention approaches in their work with groups. Psychoeducational groups, often co-facilitated by a social worker and physician, frequently use a lecture format to teach members about addiction, including the body's reaction to alcohol and other chemical substances, the signs and symptoms of addiction, and the stress-reduction and other coping techniques that can be used in recovery. Therapy groups, on the other hand, use member involvement to provide feedback, confrontation, and support. Role-playing is sometimes used to help members learn new behaviors (Smyth, 1995).

Despite the advantages of group intervention, groups are not the best choice for all chemically dependent persons. Clients must be able to function well enough to tolerate the emotional intensity of group encounters. Chronically mentally ill persons, for example, might find some groups devastating. Usually, however, social workers can structure their groups to meet the needs of specific populations or persons.

Self-help groups such as Alcoholics Anonymous and Narcotics Anonymous, which will be discussed in further detail later in this chapter, typically involve persons who share the same problem and meet together for mutual assistance. Until recently most self-help groups avoided involvement with professional people. After many years of antipathy between professional groups and such organizations as Alcoholics Anonymous, social workers and other professionals now

Social workers help group members to confront each other and also offer support and encouragement.

recognize the value of self-help groups for specific clients, and they frequently refer people to them or combine another form of therapy with self-help group participation. Sometimes, too, social workers will initiate a group for this purpose, and then guide the group in developing its own leadership and group processes.

Changing Organizations and Communities   Effective organizational change can potentially benefit a far larger population than one-on-one counseling or group work. Social workers practicing from a generalist perspective often target an organization for change rather than an individual or a group. Social workers on the faculty of colleges and universities, for example, sometimes help to initiate support groups for students, faculty, and staff with chemical dependencies. Organizational change can result in new or improved prevention or treatment programs. Serving as consultants, social workers help businesses, industrial corporations, and unions to implement employee assistance programs (EAPs) that offer help to people involved in chemical abuse. Within alcoholism and drug rehabilitation centers, social work staff attempt to effect policies and procedures to ensure that service will be provided in a humane manner. Educational programs are also offered by the social work staff to help other staff of the rehabilitation center better understand and serve the patients, their families, and the community.

In addition to working with individuals, families, groups, and organizations, social workers often view the community as the target of their intervention. In fact, drug and alcohol abuse prevention is linked to community education. Seminars and informational exchanges, for example, are offered by some social workers in community centers, churches, or schools. Other social workers staff local and state mental health associations and alcoholism councils that distribute informational materials and develop media messages (such as "Don't drink and drive!") designed to prevent problem drinking and drug use.

Community outreach is another role for generalist social workers. Contact can be made with homeless persons who are abusing alcohol or chemical substances by "street workers," social workers who visit sites where homeless people live or gather. Coffee and hot food are a good entrée, especially in cold weather. If community outreach had been available, Dan Graves's friend, George (from the case study), might not have died. Community outreach social workers do save lives through early detection and strong emotional support that brings people who are at risk into treatment centers. Ability to form trust relationships and engage even hard-to-reach people is critical to successful outreach work with homeless people and also with teen gangs. Recognizing that a considerable portion of health crises are related to (even generated by) substance abuse, social workers have also begun initiating assessment procedures in hospital emergency rooms in suburbs as well as central city areas. A physician's forceful recommendation for treatment can be a strong motivator.

Program development is another powerful intervention in the substance abuse field. In Louisville, Kentucky, for example, a substance abuse prevention program was brought to five sites, including two rural area sites 40 and 45 miles from Louisville, two suburban sites, and one inner-city site. Interestingly, all were church sites; program development involved securing the cooperation and sponsorship not just of individual churches but of interdenominational groups.

Research subsequently demonstrated the effectiveness of the program in moderating drug and alcohol use of youths as well as increasing parental knowledge of alcohol and other drugs. The program also decreased the parents' own use of alcohol, improved family communication, and strengthened bonding relationships within the families (Johnson et al., 2000).

AT-RISK POPULATIONS

Generalist practice theory directs social workers to develop intervention plans based on a careful assessment of the individual client within the totality of her or his life situation. Logan, McRoy, and Freeman (1987) underscore the need for social workers to take into consideration the client's "age, ethnicity, gender, availability of other supports, and other factors such as the particular client's orientation to change and principal mode of learning" (pp. 183–184) when developing intervention plans for chemically dependent clients.

When people abuse alcohol or other substances as a reaction to grief or the overwhelming trauma of disaster or war, this seems understandable to society. Less well understood are the socioeconomic stressors that also exist. Of the various professionals who work in the substance abuse arena, social workers probably have the best understanding of this. As Roffman (1987) states, "Regardless of their negative consequences, psychoactive drugs [and alcohol] are used excessively precisely because they are effective, if only temporarily, in reducing pain—including the pain of being poor" (p. 482).

Women and Children

Among the most vulnerable populations in the United States are addicted women and their children. Findings from the 2000 National Household Survey on Drug Use demonstrate that a smaller percentage of women than men use alcohol, engage in binge drinking, or use alcohol heavily (see Exhibit 4), yet women and their children are at risk. It is estimated that only a small portion of addicted women receive services. The reasons for this vary but include the outmoded societal attitude that it is acceptable for men to drink to excess but for women, especially mothers, to do so is immoral.

Turnbull's research demonstrated that women who were depressed often self-medicated with alcohol, thus becoming even more depressed. (Alcohol depresses the central nervous system.) Suicide ideation and marital disruption were sometimes present at the point at which the women sought treatment. Turnbull concluded that careful assessment and early treatment of depression in women who would be likely to turn to alcohol might decrease the occurrence of alcohol dependence and associated risk factors (1988).

Some women need counseling, probably with a female social worker, that focuses on childhood or current experiences with violence and victimization. Family and couple therapy are helpful to many women, as is parent training, given the guilt that addicted women experience because of their failures in this area. Rhodes and Johnson (1994) found that teaching women to accept that alcohol has taken power over their lives—which is a tenet of Alcoholics Anonymous and may be

Alcohol Use and Abuse: Demographic Characteristics

EXHIBIT 4

Demographic Characteristic	Any Alcohol Use		"Binge" Alocohol Use		Heavy Alcohol Use	
	1999	2000	1999	2000	1999	2000
TOTAL	46.4	46.6	20.2	20.6	5.7	5.6
AGE						
12–17	16.5	16.4	10.1	10.4	2.4	2.6
18–25	57.2	56.8	37.9	37.8	13.3	12.8
26 or older	48.7	49.0	18.6	19.1	4.9	4.8
GENDER						
Male	53.2	53.6	28.1	28.3	9.2	8.7
Female	40.2	40.2	12.9	13.5	2.4	2.7
HISPANIC ORIGIN AND RACE						
Not Hispanic						
White only	50.3	50.7	21.1	21.2	6.2	6.2
Black only	34.3	33.7	16.3	17.7	3.6	4.0
American Indian or Alaska Native only	33.9	35.1	20.0	26.2	5.8	7.2
Native Hawaiian or other Pacific Islander	*	*	*	*	*	*
Asian only	30.7	28.0	10.8	11.6	2.5	1.4
More than one race	41.4	41.6	20.2	17.5	7.7	5.2
Hispanic	38.6	39.8	21.7	22.7	5.4	4.4

The above columns fall under the spanning header **Type of Alcohol Use**.

* Low precision; no estimate reported.

Note: "Binge" alcohol use is defined as drinking five or more drinks on the same occasion on at least 1 day in the past 30 days. By "occasion" is meant at the same time or within a couple hours of each other. Heavy alcohol use is defined as drinking five or more drinks on the same occasion on each of 5 or more days in the past 30 days; all heavy alcohol users are also "binge" alcohol users.

Source: Substance Abuse and Mental Health Services Administration. (2001). *Summary of findings from the National Household Survey on Drug Abuse.* Office of Applied Studies, NHSDA Series H-13, DHHS Publication No. (SMA) 01-3549. Rockville, MD, Table F.43, p. 177.

more useful with men—is potentially devastating to women. Instead, they encourage the use of empowerment approaches, helping women to acquire competence and self-esteem. Then, because addicted women are less likely than men to have health insurance, substance abuse intervention is needed in the places such women frequent: shelters, public health departments, and even jails.

Health care systems tend to be particularly punitive toward homeless women because they lack health insurance. Based on their experience with homeless women in hospital emergency rooms, Boes and van Wormer argue for use of a strengths perspective within a feminist framework for social work services to these vulnerable women (1997). If inpatient addiction care can be obtained, women's guilt may be compounded by the need to place their children temporarily in foster care. Much support is needed, and social workers can help the mothers to understand that they are making painful but good decisions. Children who were neglected or abused are especially confused and vulnerable. The needs of these children must be addressed, and the children must be provided a safe environment, too. Group homes or community centers can sometimes be found that will offer nurturing posthospital care for recovering mothers and their children (Finkelstein, 1994).

Fetal alcohol syndrome (FAS), the name given to the abnormalities in children that can result from heavy alcohol consumption during pregnancy, also places both women and children at risk. One Seattle study, for example, found that 75% of the mothers of the more severely damaged FAS children had died of alcohol-related causes within six years of their births (Streissguth, Clarren, & Jones, 1985).

Among the abnormalities that accompany FAS are growth deficiencies, mental retardation, characteristic facial features, cleft palate, small brain, and behavioral problems. These children require special care—sometimes institutional care—for many years. Physicians who have studied FAS persons into adolescence and adulthood have found that they sustained significant attention deficit and diminished intellectual ability and had problems with judgment. According to the National Women's Health Information Center, "Prenatal alcohol exposure is one of the leading known causes of mental retardation in the Western world" (2000, p. 2).

Recognizing that some unborn children will be damaged by even a very small amount of alcohol, many physicians are recommending complete abstinence during pregnancy; others suggest that possibly one drink every 10 days might be safe (Jacobson & Jacobson, 1994). From a prevention perspective, much greater effort should be expended on informing the public about the potentially profound effects of alcohol consumption during pregnancy.

Youths

Adolescents and young adults frequently use, even abuse, drugs and alcohol as a part of their developmental process. While this may not necessarily result in adult dependency, it may be associated with unsafe sexual activity leading to sexually transmitted diseases (such as HIV infection), and/or pregnancy as well as car accidents, drownings, and illegal activities. Government reports showed marked increase in the use of illicit drugs by 12- to 17-year-olds—from 5.3 percent in 1992 to 11 percent in 1997—followed by a gradual downward trend to 9.7 percent in 2000. The 18- to 25-year-old cohort, consistently the heaviest users of illicit drugs, also showed an increase in usage—from 13.1 percent in 1992 to 16.4 percent in 1999 and then a decline to 15.9 percent in 2000 (Substance Abuse and Mental Health Services Administration, 1998, Table 11; and 2001, Tables F.3 & F.4).

These "youth at risk" are the focus of Malekoff's study of preventive programs. He asks the question, "What differentiates youth who become alcohol and drug abusers from their contemporaries from similar backgrounds who do not?" (1997, p. 228). Among the protective factors his research suggests is the bonding that occurs between adolescents, especially those who are non-drug users, and bonding with adults. Malekoff suggests use of group work with at-risk youths—groups that are well planned, that engage the youths in activities that promote development of skill and competence as well as relationships, and groups that also involve family activities.

Native Americans

The case study at the beginning of this chapter suggests that racism and poverty can be factors in substance abuse. Native American women clearly belong to several at-risk groups and, perhaps not surprisingly, they have a high rate of children born with fetal alcohol syndrome (FAS). In a North Dakota study researchers found that of 132 cases of children diagnosed with FAS, 106 (80.3%) were from Native American families and 24 (18.2%) were Caucasians (Bagheri et al., 1998). Prevention efforts, including the screening of all pregnant women for alcohol use, were urged. (See Exhibit 5.)

EXHIBIT 5

Source: A. P. Streissguth, R. A. LaDue, & S. P. Randels. (1988). *A manual on adolescents and adults with fetal alcohol syndrome with special reference to American Indians* (2nd ed.). Washington, DC: U.S. Department of Health and Human Services, Indian Health Service.

A hospital-based program at the Tuba City Indian Medical Center in Arizona was successful in achieving abstinence from alcohol in 19 of 21 pregnant Navajo women who were at risk of delivering alcohol-affected infants. Statistically, more Navajo women abstain from alcohol than women in the general U.S. population, but heavy alcohol consumption exists among those women and families where poverty and social problems abound. The Tuba City program is noteworthy because of the incorporation of cultural sensitivity and respect, as was demonstrated in the hiring of Navajo staff and use of the Navajo language (Masis & May, 1991). This comprehensive ethnic- and gender-sensitive program had a remarkable level of acceptance among the women it served.

FAS, associated with excessive alcohol consumption, is not the only risk factor for American Indian or Alaska Native Peoples. They also have one of the highest rates of all illicit drug use. The result is exceptionally high rates of suicide, homicide, car accidents, and deaths associated with cirrhosis.

Hispanic Americans

The Hispanic population in the United States, according to the last census, is increasing more rapidly than most other population cohorts. The higher birthrate of this population results in a large youth cohort. The number of Hispanic youths aged 12 to 17 increased from 1,225,000 in 1996 to 3,671,000 in 2000. Although Hispanic people have one of the lowest rates of illicit drug use for all ethnic groups (5.3 percent past-month use reported in 2000), the 12- to 17-year-old youth group reported 10.4 percent past-month use in 1999 and 9.5 percent use in 2000 (Substance Abuse and Mental Health Services Administration, 2001, Tables E.3, p. 123, and F.15, p. 161). The youth rate of illicit drug use, while significantly lower than that of many other populations, is of concern to Hispanic families.

Melvin Delgado, a social worker, reiterates the need for culture-specific services. Of special concern to him is the lack of understanding of the variances in Hispanic culture among treatment facilities and their failure to acknowledge the impact of acculturation. Delgado (1988) suggests five culturally specific content areas that should be explored in intake interviews with youthful Hispanic substance abusers:

1. Attempt to understand the patterns alcohol and drugs play in the context of the family: ceremonial use? religious prohibition?
2. Find out the extent to which the client identifies with ("owns") her or his Hispanic heritage. Does it represent pride or is it viewed as a deficit?
3. In what language can the client best express herself or himself? (This has important ramifications for counselor or group treatment assignment.)
4. How does the youth's social network relate to drinking or substance use? Does it support or fight against treatment?
5. What prior assistance, through both formal and informal mechanisms, has been attempted, and with what results?

African Americans

Ethnic sensitivity acquires new dimensions when the client is African American. There are few black Americans, regardless of education or socioeconomic status, who have escaped the experience of racism, of being treated with unequal status.

Sensitivity to this component of the client's social reality permits the social worker to help the substance-dependent client to understand how alcoholism actually contributes to his or her own experience of oppression. An approach that objectifies the substance abuse behavior—separating it from the person who engages in that behavior—is useful because it makes the behavior the focus for aggressive change, rather than threatening or attacking the person.

Helping African American substance abuse clients to strengthen skills in negotiating between the dominant European American culture and the African American culture in which they live is also very empowering for clients who are struggling to build an existence beyond chemical dependency (Beverly, 1989). Intervention that uses this approach values the client's own culture. But it also recognizes that in everyday life minority people often engage in a **dual perspective,** a "conscious and systematic process of perceiving, understanding, and comparing simultaneously the values, attitudes, and behavior of the larger societal system with those of [their own] immediate family and community system" (Norton, 1978, p. 3).

Community education and the prevention efforts of churches and schools have resulted in a marked decline in the use and abuse of alcohol by African Americans: from a high past-month use approximating 59 percent in 1979 to 33.7 percent in 2000. African Americans now show a lower rate of use of alcohol than white or Hispanic people (Substance Abuse and Mental Health Services Administration, 2001, Table F.43, p. 177). Use of illicit drugs, although higher than for whites or Hispanics, has shown a decline over the past several years, from 7.9 percent in 1995 to 6.4 percent in 2000 (Substance Abuse and Mental Health Services Administration, 1998, Table 11; 2001, Table F.14, p. 144). Despite this, African Americans continue to experience barriers to treatment facilities associated with lack of funds or health insurance. White professional staff often lack the cultural understanding needed to work successfully with African Americans.

Exhibit 6 provides data demonstrating the variations in illicit drug use according to age and ethnicity. For African Americans as well as many of the other ethnic and age cohorts, there has been a continuing decline in illicit drug use (does not reflect alcohol use). There are some exceptions, however. Past-month use of illicit drugs shows a slight increase in 2000 for the age-26-and-older population, women, whites, American Indians/Alaska Natives, Hawaiian/Pacific Islanders, and persons of more than one race. The period of declining illicit drug use corresponded roughly with a period of economic growth in America. Will the illicit drug use data from 2001 forward, following the terrorist attacks on the United States and subsequent economic decline, show a continued decline? Or will illicit drug use patterns begin to increase? The National Household Survey on Drug Abuse, a good source for this data, can be accessed on the Internet at http://www.samhsa.gov.

Despite the recent decline in illicit drug use, drug abuse has had a devastating impact on African American families. Drug-related family violence and crime have resulted in the need for shelter care for women and children, imprisonment, and foster care for children. Cocaine abuse has led to addictions to other drugs, and also to HIV/AIDS and other infections and diseases. Families struggle to remain intact under the pressure of drug abuse. Grandparents and even elderly great-grandparents carry heavy burdens as they take on the care of children whose parent or parents are absent from the home (Ruiz, 2001).

Let us now turn to some other populations who are at risk for substance abuse but for whom data on use and abuse are less readily available. (See Exhibit 6.)

Use of Illicit Drugs by Persons Aged 12 or Older: By Demographic Characteristics: 1999 & 2000 (in Percentages)

EXHIBIT 6

Demographic Characteristic	Lifetime		Past Year		Past Month	
	1999	2000	1999	2000	1999	2000
TOTAL	39.7	38.9	11.5	11.0	6.3	6.3
AGE						
12–17	27.6	26.9	19.8	18.6	9.8	9.7
18–25	52.6	51.2	29.1	27.9	16.4	15.9
26 or older	39.2	38.5	7.4	7.1	4.1	4.2
GENDER						
Male	43.6	43.5	13.8	12.9	8.1	7.7
Female	36.0	34.7	9.3	9.2	4.6	5.0
HISPANIC ORIGIN AND RACE						
Not Hispanic						
White only	42.0	41.5	11.4	11.2	6.2	6.4
Black only	37.7	35.5	13.2	10.9	7.5	6.4
American Indian or Alaska Native only	51.0	53.9	18.3	19.8	10.4	12.6
Native Hawaiian or Other Pacific Islander	*	*	*	*	*	6.2
Asian only	20.8	18.9	6.1	5.2	3.2	2.7
More than one race	42.2	49.2	15.5	20.6	10.3	14.8
Hispanic	31.2	29.9	11.0	10.1	6.1	5.3

* Low precision; no estimate reported.

Source: Substance Abuse and Mental Health Services Administration. (2001). *Summary of findings from the National Household Survey on Drug Abuse.* Office of Applied Studies, NHSDA Series H-13, DHHS Publication No. (SMA) 01-3549. Rockville, MD, Table F.14, p. 144.

The government statistical reports cited for other groups record no data regarding alcohol or drug use or abuse by gay men and lesbian women. The absence of reliable data does not eliminate the possibility that "oppression of gay men and lesbian women and subculture support of drinking could produce higher rates of alcoholism among them. Internalized homophobia results in tremendous anxiety and self-hatred, sometimes assuaged by alcohol" (Anderson 1995, p. 209). Gay bars have served as places to socialize and, until the recent development of substance-free establishments, this has hampered the efforts of gays and lesbians who are in treatment.

The open hostility that lesbian women and gay men sometimes experienced at Alcoholics Anonymous meetings resulted in 1970 in the founding of Alcoholics Together, another 12-step program. But 12-step programs are no longer well accepted by many women, including lesbian women, because of the focus on admitting loss of control over one's life, identifying one's moral and character defects, and so forth. Some women find empowerment-based models more useful, and, for lesbian women at least, treatment models that incorporate political awareness and concepts of oppression may prove more effective (Saulnier, 1991).

Among the homosexual community, black male alcoholics are at special risk of encountering misunderstanding and negative attitudes that can interfere with treatment. Not only do some substance abuse programs and professional staff display negativity, but the African American community is sometimes not accepting of homosexuality, and some members of the gay community are racially biased. Social work intervention must help these clients to deal with their substance abuse and also help them to locate and link with a positive support system and to integrate their sexual identity with their racial identity (Icard & Traunstein, 1987).

Persons with Disabilities

Persons with disabilities—physical, cognitive, or psychiatric—may use or abuse drugs (sometimes their own prescriptions) and alcohol just to make their lives more bearable. If they become dependent on chemical substances, treatment is complicated because it must be adapted to the situation of the specific client. Coexistence of mental illnesses and chemical dependence, known as a **dual diagnoses,** requires well-coordinated treatment from both mental health and substance abuse programs. When these are not available within the same facility, careful attention must be given to ensure responsible interrelationship of treatment.

Among the homeless or people living on the streets it is estimated that roughly 10 percent to 20 percent are persons with dual diagnosis. Some are chemically dependent and have health problems and disabilities other than mental illness. Clearly it is extremely difficult for them to comply with treatment regimes or to keep scheduled appointments. Outreach work by social workers, other professionals, and volunteers is undertaken to try to bring some forms of health care to the streets. Concern about transmission of HIV infection through sharing of dirty needles has prompted needle exchange programs in some communities. The largest program, in San Francisco, is estimated to reduce HIV infection by approximately 30 percent (SFAF HIV Prevention Project, 2001).

PREVENTION AND TREATMENT PROGRAMS

Prevention and Treatment in the United States

Prevention of chemical dependence focuses on education and research. All levels of society are targeted but colleges and universities, business corporations, health care settings, and school children are the primary populations served. Three large federal government organizations have assumed leadership in the prevention field.

The National Institute on Alcohol Abuse and Alcoholism (NIAA) is a part of the National Institutes of Health. It supports and conducts research into the causes and consequences of alcohol abuse. It publishes *Alcohol Health and Research World,* a good source of current research.

The National Institute on Drug Abuse (NIDA) is responsible for research on drug abuse. Its Medications Development Program specifically focuses on research pertaining to the use of medication in the treatment of drug addiction.

A third organization, the Center for Substance Abuse Prevention (CSAP), is the unit within the large Substance Abuse and Mental Health Services Administration (SAMHSA) that focuses on prevention efforts. It funds prevention programs, including the Community Partnership Program, which encourages coalitions of agencies to work together to implement substance abuse prevention programs. The National Clearinghouse for Alcohol and Drug Information (a good source of substance abuse materials for student term papers) is operated by CSAP. See the Internet Sites at the end of this chapter for the Internet addresses of these three organizations.

In local public schools, educational programming is aimed at preventing the use of drugs and alcohol by children of all ages. Substance abuse prevention is a role for school social workers (school social work was described more fully in Chapter 6). Social group work with school children, whether oriented toward socialization or therapy, routinely contains content related to drugs. This is also true of parent education or family life seminars presented by school social workers.

The treatment of substance abuse often begins with a brief hospitalization for detoxification to safely withdraw the person from drugs or alcohol. Detoxification may also be done on an outpatient basis, depending on the drugs used by the person and the risks involved in the medical treatment. Withdrawal from barbiturates, for example, requires hospitalization because it may result in life-threatening seizures. Until recently, a 30-day inpatient treatment program routinely followed detoxification. Cost containment policies of managed care have resulted in briefer inpatient treatment for most people today.

Outpatient or follow-up care is available in a wide range of settings: mental health centers, substance abuse clinics, "drunk-driving" programs, halfway houses, prisons, social service agencies, employee assistance programs, college and universities, and through private therapists in the community. Treatment tends to be highly multidisciplinary but often involves social workers. The approaches used in treatment also vary widely but may include education programs, biofeedback training, group therapy, family therapy, and intensive short-term programs. The goal of these programs is abstinence.

European Approach: The Harm Reduction Model

The two models of substance abuse prevention and treatment used most commonly in the United States are the abstinence model and the 12-step recovery program. Both seek a complete and total end to substance use. An alternative but controversial program that is used far more frequently in Europe and Australia than in the United States is known as the **harm reduction model.** The focus of this approach is to reduce the harm that can be caused while people are using chemical substances. It is based on the philosophy that people can be withdrawn more safely, effectively, and humanely from chemicals if this process is done slowly. Because it attempts to prevent the spread of disease, it is sometimes referred to as a public health model. The harm reduction model seeks to prevent overdose deaths, suicide, spread of HIV and other infections through shared needles, even domestic violence enacted while under the influence of drugs (Des Jarlais, 1995).

European children grow up in a culture that incorporates alcoholic beverages in everyday life. "There is no negative stereotype attached to the act of drinking" (Loebig, 2000, p. 1). Some of these European countries have a more open attitude toward the rights of people to use other substances and many, but not all, have been prescribing methadone for the treatment of addiction for a long time. Needle exchange programs, in which used needles are exchanged for sterile ones, are much more common in Europe than in the United States. A program in Frankfurt am Main, Germany, that emphasizes harm reduction is described as follows:

> Frankfurt am Main is the first German city to open consumer rooms where drug users are allowed to use drugs under hygienic and stress-free conditions. Since December 1st 1994, Integrative Drogenhilfe, a non-profit organization,

©MATT SUMNER/FROM THE HIP/THE IMAGE WORKS

San Francisco, California: Needle exchange program, volunteer (facing camera) talks with drug user.

was the first of these facilities in Frankfurt's largest crisis center, the "Schielestraae". A maximum of eight people can use the room at the same time. Two senior workers in the drug field who are also skilled in first aid are always present to provide help in cases of emergency. At the door, clean needles and syringes as well as alcohol-pads, clean water, citric acid, filters and candles are handed out. For legal reasons, all clients have to sign a declaration that they are at least 18 years old and do not participate in the methadone program (Loebig, 2000, p. 3).

Does the harm reduction model work? As previously mentioned, San Francisco's AIDS Foundation HIV Prevention Project estimates that its needle exchange program has reduced new HIV infection by 30 percent (SFAF HIV Prevention Project, 2001). In 1998, U.S. Department of Health and Human Services Secretary Donna Shalala announced that, based on extensive empirical research, the HHS Department had determined that needle exchange programs could be an effective strategy to reduce transmission of HIV infection. The research had demonstrated, too, that needle exchange programs did not encourage use of illicit drugs (HHS Press Office, 1998). Does harm reduction increase or decrease addiction? Data on the number of addicts per country show that countries with liberal harm reduction programs tend to have fewer drug addicts. The Netherlands, for example, had 1.66 drug addicts per 1,000 persons in its population, Belgium had 1.75, Germany had 1.38, compared with the United States that had 6.36 (Loebig). Much more research is needed to evaluate the harm reduction model, but it does pose another alternative to the present prevention and treatment approach used in the United States.

Alcoholics Anonymous

Although it began in the United States, Alcoholics Anonymous has spread throughout the world. Also known as the "12-Step Program," this organization has been the model for the creation of many other self-help groups: SIDS (Sudden Infant Death Syndrome) groups, numerous groups for people who wish to lose weight, and One Day at a Time (groups for people suffering from cancer). Alcoholics Anonymous has also spawned mutual aid groups for friends and relatives of alcoholics (A1-Anon) and groups for the adolescent children of people with alcoholism (A1-Ateen). In addition, the Adult Children of Alcoholics organization assists people struggling with past childhood experiences that continue to damage their present adult relationships.

Narcotics Anonymous (NA) is structured like Alcoholics Anonymous and uses the same principles and philosophy as AA, including the 12 steps. Cocaine Anonymous functions similarly but is probably not as well known as NA. Alternative self-help groups have borrowed some of the AA philosophy but use other strategies. Rational Recovery, for example, is based on cognitive-behavioral theory that seeks to change self-defeating thinking patterns. Women for Sobriety emphasizes self-respect for women who abuse alcohol. Some groups have emerged that avoid the spirituality of AA and instead focus on personal responsibility. A brief history of Alcoholics Anonymous is provided in Exhibit 7.

The Legacy of "Bill W."

EXHIBIT 7

The history of the founding of Alcoholics Anonymous is an interesting one. Bill Wilson was a stockbroker with a string of failed business ventures and years of alcohol abuse when he met Dr. Robert Holbrock Smith, a proctologist and surgeon, who was a graduate of Dartmouth College and of Rush Medical College in Chicago. Dr. Bob's alcohol abuse was beginning to interfere with his medical practice. Talking together, they discovered, helped Bill Wilson to deal with his compelling desire for a drink, and it helped Dr. Bob to face and begin to deal with his own alcoholism. Bill W.—his "anonymous" name to others in the organization that came to be known as Alcoholics Anonymous—was gregarious, impulsive, and an inspirational speaker. Dr. Bob, a man of few words, avoided public speaking and left that function to Bill W. Dr. Bob's authority, however, molded the new Alcoholics Anonymous organization in many ways. Women were not admitted to AA for years because Dr. Bob opposed their inclusion, preferring to keep AA an exclusively male organization (Robertson, 1988).

Without media publicity, the notion of a person-to-person supportive network spread only gradually, and yet its appeal touched the lives of many people. By 1939 about 100 persons belonged to Alcoholics Anonymous. They pooled what they had learned from their own experiences and created the book *Alcoholics Anonymous,* a classic that is still known as "The Big Book." It describes the 12 steps, which is the basic process by which members had learned to keep themselves sober. After the publication of The Big Book, Alcoholics Anonymous grew rapidly. Five thousand people attended the twentieth-anniversary convention in St. Louis in 1955; by 1957 Alcoholics Anonymous had grown to 200,000, with groups meeting in 70 countries. Today Alcoholics Anonymous has over 2 million members throughout the world.

RESEARCH

Much research has been undertaken to explore the effectiveness of different interventions. Walsh's 1991 research with clients who were given a choice in treatment programs demonstrated the effectiveness of inpatient treatment followed by mandatory AA attendance. The Gibbs and Hollister study of 1993 made an important contribution to the scientific literature by isolating four distinct types of alcoholic clients based on measures of social stability and intellectual functioning. Their attempt to determine which form of treatment best fit each typology was unsuccessful because of difficulties such as inability to randomly assign clients to inpatient versus outpatient treatment. Their findings, however, suggested that clients with strong social stability and intellectual functioning were 25 percent more likely to achieve sobriety at six months through outpatient as opposed to inpatient treatment.

The largest clinical research trial ever to be implemented regarding alcoholism, Project MATCH, attempted to match clients with the most effective treatment. This eight-year, rigorous, multidisciplinary research effort sought to determine which of its three treatment approaches was most effective with specific configurations of characteristics. The surprising result was that each of the three forms of treatment—cognitive-behavioral therapy, motivational enhancement therapy, and therapy aimed at facilitating clients' involvement in a 12 step program— "appeared to do quite well and, perhaps more importantly, patients' gains were well sustained throughout 39 months' follow-up" (Allen, 1998, p. 43).

In the United States, it is estimated that approximately 7 million people are not receiving needed alcohol treatment and another 4 million are not currently receiving needed intervention for drug abuse. Research has been federally funded to determine effective procedures to fill this treatment gap (Substance Abuse and Mental Health Services Administration, 2001). Worsening tobacco-related diseases worldwide have prompted the World Health Organization to call for research into effective approaches to treat tobacco dependence (Tobacco: A pandemic, 2001). Research breakthroughs on many fronts in the past 10 years have demonstrated that prevention and treatment efforts can have impact. Future research can now be more targeted and refined.

BUILDING A KNOWLEDGE BASE

Social workers in virtually every setting encounter substance abuse. Students entering any of the social service or human service fields must prepare themselves to work with clients who abuse chemical substances and with others who have been victimized by parents, spouses, friends, or employers who are dependent on drugs or alcohol.

Where do students find curriculum content on substance abuse? The response is that it permeates many of the courses in the liberal arts (courses such as sociology and psychology) and the courses taken in the social work major. Field placements may also expose students to practice with or on behalf of chemically dependent and alcoholic persons. Some field placements will be in substance abuse treatment programs in which the entire client population has abused alcohol and/or drugs. Elective courses on alcoholism or substance abuse may also be available.

Awareness of community resources for the prevention and treatment of substance abuse is also necessary. The case study used in this chapter portrays a social worker in an emergency shelter and her very effective work with an African American male alcoholic. A part of Madeleine Johnson's effectiveness was her ability to link Dan Graves to appropriate resources, not only to substance abuse treatment programs but also resources for employment and educational opportunities.

Their generalist professional education prepares BSWs to enter practice in a variety of settings with the expectation that they will continue to develop and refine their knowledge, especially in reference to the client population they serve. MSW candidates, on the other hand, add a specialization—possibly in substance abuse treatment—to their generalist practice base. An MSW with this area of specialization is more likely to take courses entirely devoted to substance abuse than is a BSW student or an MSW student who has chosen another specialization. Social workers meet their responsibility to continue their education through their own research, reading, seminars, and workshops.

SUBSTANCES OF ABUSE

Because substance abuse is encountered by social workers throughout social work practice, social workers need to have an understanding of the substances that are most frequently misused and abused. Exhibit 8 provides basic information about these drugs. Exhibit 8 is a modified version of the classification created by the National Clearinghouse for Alcohol and Drug Information. Exhibit 8 does not include all possible substances that people abuse but, instead, focuses on those most in use.

Exhibit 8 begins with alcohol because it is by far the most abused substance today. The other substances appearing in Exhibit 8 are not arranged in order of frequency of use. Alcohol, often mistakenly believed to be an "up" drug, is, in reality, a depressant. It has potentially serious side effects—withdrawal from alcohol can actually result in death. Although there has been a decline in the use of alcohol over the past 10 years, it continues to be used excessively.

The next major category of substances that social workers should be familiar with is that of **narcotics.** They are derived synthetically or naturally and are used medicinally to deaden pain. The most commonly used opioids in the United States are heroin, morphine, and codeine. In the 1990s heroin use began to rise, after having declined for many years. The spread of AIDS among intravenous drug users is a major concern to public health authorities. Death can result from overdose.

New production methods have resulted in increased purity and potency of heroin, raising the possibility of overdose. Sometimes heroin, like cocaine, is diluted with other substances to lower its cost to users and to increase profits for drug dealers; the user cannot immediately tell if the drug has been diluted. Morphine is illegal (when not prescribed by a physician), addictive, and hazardous because of the frequent use of unsterile needles for injection. Malnutrition often occurs because of the depressant nature of the drug and because addicts become so dependent on it that they are unable to take care of their own basic needs.

Depressants are drugs that depress the central nervous system. Physicians rely on these drugs to treat various conditions, such as epilepsy and anxiety, and for their anesthetic properties. Barbiturates, ("downers") are generally obtained through a physician's prescription (or several physicians' prescriptions). Most frequently, barbiturates are taken in pill form. If injected, they are most dangerous because of their immediate effect. Withdrawal has the potential for mental disorder, seizures, and even death. Barbiturates are often the drug used in suicides and mercy killings of animals as well as humans.

Tranquilizers and sleeping medications are milder depressants of the central nervous system. They are among the most frequently prescribed substances in the United States. These drugs can create psychological dependence, but they

Substances of Abuse

EXHIBIT 8

Drug	Method of Administration	Desired Effect	Hazards and Side Effects
Alcohol	Oral ingestion	Increased sociability; sense of pleasure, good feelings; mood alteration; relief of anxiety	Depression; liver damage; intoxication; loss of consciousness; psychological dependence; physical addiction; possibly fatal withdrawal
NARCOTICS			
Opium	Oral, smoked	Euphoria	Physically addicting; psychological dependence
Heroin	Injected into vein or under skin; inhaled	Euphoria	Withdrawal symptoms resemble flu, but not life-threatening; physical addiction; death
Morphine	Injected into vein	Euphoria; pain relief	Depression; withdrawal; anxiety; elevated blood pressure; physical addiction
Codeine	Oral as pill or liquid	Pain relief	Less addicting than heroin or morphine; withdrawal discomfort not as severe
DEPRESSANTS			
Barbiturates	Oral, injected	Pain relief; reversal of effects of stimulants such as amphetamines	Confusion; mental disorder; seizures; death from suicidal overdose
Tranquilizers	Oral, injected	Reduction of anxiety	Psychological dependence; severe, unpredictable results if taken with alcohol or other drugs

(Continued)

Drug	Method of Administration	Desired Effect	Hazards and Side Effects
STIMULANTS			
Amphetamines Methamphetamines	Oral, injected Oral, injected	Increased alertness; relieves fatigue; used to counteract the "down" feelings of tranquilizers, alcohol	Elevated blood pressure; high doses: anxiety, suicidally severe depression; overdose: hallucinations, seizures, coma, death
Ice	Smoked, oral, injected, inhaled	Mood elevation, exhilaration, alertness	Extremely addictive, high blood pressure, depression, anxiety, paranoia; overdose: can cause coma and death
Cocaine Crack "coke"	Inhaled ("snorted"); injected; smoked	Euphoria: carefree feeling; relaxation; sexual prowess	Anxiety; severe depression; persecutory delusions; paranoia
INHALANTS			
Gasoline Toluene (correction fluid, glue, marking pens)	Inhaled	Cheap high, sense of euphoria, fun	Eye infection; loss of muscle control; loss of consciousness, lung and brain damage
HALLUCINOGENS			
PCP "Angel Dust" "Loveboat"	Oral, smoked	Dreamlike experience with beautiful illusions and hallucinations	Panic attack; confusion; hallucination with frightening visions; flashbacks; suicide
LSD	Oral	As above	As above
Mescaline	Oral, injected	As above	As above
Peyote	Oral, injected	As above	As above
Psilocybin	Oral, injected, smoked, sniffed	As above	As above
Designer drugs Ecstasy, PCE	Oral, injected, smoked	As above	As above

(Continued)

Drug	Method of Administration	Desired Effect	Hazards and Side Effects
CANNABIS			
Marijuana	Oral, smoked	Sense of well-being; relaxation; euphoria	Psychological dependence; impaired judgment; overdose: paranoia, psychosis, disorientation
Tetrahydro-cannabinol	Oral, smoked	As above	As above
Hashish	Oral, smoked	As above	As above
Hashish oil	Oral, smoked	As above	As above
STEROIDS			
Dianabol	Oral	Increase in strength, muscle size, weight, athletic performance	Aggressive behavior; combativeness; skin rash including purple or red spots; impotence
Nandrolone	Oral	As above	As above

Source: The National Clearinghouse for Alcohol and Drug Information. (n.d.). *Drugs of abuse.* Retrieved October 11, 2001, from http://www.health.org/govpubs/rpo926/.

are most hazardous when combined with alcohol or other drugs, causing a condition referred to as **potentiation.** This term denotes the dramatically increased potential for serious consequences to the health and well-being of the user. Social workers have learned to inquire about prescription drug use when obtaining a drinking history. When central nervous system depressants are combined or taken with alcohol, they can be truly lethal. Women—perhaps because they see physicians more frequently than men do—are more likely than men to have prescriptions for the minor tranquilizers. They are more likely to become involved in **cross-addiction,** that is, addiction to two or more substances at the same time.

The next category is the central nervous system **stimulants.** These are drugs that produce energy, increase alertness, and provide a sense of strength and well-being. The primary drugs are amphetamines. They are sometimes taken for weight loss. Illegally obtained methamphetamines are used by students and truck drivers, among others, to avoid sleep in order to complete work. The resulting errors in judgment range from a poor exam grade to highway fatalities. Ice is a form of methamphetamine that can be administered by injection, orally, inhaled, or smoked. An overdose can cause coma and death. Addiction occurs very rapidly, sometimes after only a single use.

Cocaine is sometimes classified as a narcotic but more often as a stimulant. Cocaine is well known to social workers as a cause of child abuse and neglect, family violence, suicide, and unprovoked shootings. Repeated or prolonged use of cocaine can produce physical and psychological intoxication and withdrawal symptoms, including suicide. Use of contaminated needles is of great concern. Cocaine combined with alcohol results in a dangerous level of toxicity. Crack is a less expensive pellet form of the more expensive and relatively pure powder forms of cocaine hydrochloride.

The next class of substances is inhalants. People have inhaled such products as gasoline, ether, and glue with mixed results. Sometimes they hope for a "high," and sometimes they seek improved sexual performance; the actual result may be blindness, conjunctivitis (an infection of the eyes), euphoria, or simply disappointment. Youths age 10 to 17 are especially vulnerable. A survey by the American Academy of Pediatrics found 62 percent of children in this age group to be aware of "huffing," yet only half had talked with their parents about it (Preboth, 2000). Parents' relative lack of information about inhalants is significant since so many of the products currently inhaled are readily available at home: cooking sprays, model cement, aerosol sprays, and deodorant.

Hallucinogens, drugs that produce sensory distortions (dreamlike experiences, visual and/or auditory effects), are increasingly used once again. Heavy users of hallucinogens report flashback experiences months after the drug use. LSD (lysergic acid diethylamide), the well-publicized drug of the 1960s, is being used again today. More frequently, however, people are using a variety of other hallucinogenic chemicals that are synthesized in black-market and home laboratories and are sold on the streets.

"Designer drugs" are a form of hallucinogens. They are chemically produced drugs that differ slightly from the illegal drugs that they were formulated to replicate. Often they are many times stronger than the drugs they imitate. Initially treated as legal drugs, they, too, are now illicit. Their potential danger is often underestimated. In some cases a single use can cause irreversible brain damage. Ecstasy is the designer drug used—sometimes in combination with marijuana, heroin, and cocaine—in rave parties that have spread across Europe and America. Rave parties of 750,000 (Zurich) or 1.3 million persons (Berlin) occur in Europe each year, along with numerous small parties in more rural areas. For the most part they are tolerated in Europe, though five deaths and two rapes at the same party in France have recently prompted discussion of legislation to crack down on rave parties (Keaten, 2001).

Cannabis, most commonly used as marijuana, is grown throughout the United States and is also a lucrative but illegal import. Marijuana, the leaf of the hemp plant, may produce a sense of well-being and relaxation, but it also may result in social withdrawal, anxiety, and even paranoia. It has been found useful in the treatment of diseases such as glaucoma. Yet marijuana use is controversial. Its advocates seek legalization of its use; its opponents request stiffer penalties for using it illegally.

Abuse of steroids surfaced prominently in college athletics in the 1990s. Although no physical dependence on steroids has been clearly documented, psychological dependence has been noted. Of concern are the aggressive behaviors and the physical changes that occur with the use of steroids.

"Club drugs" comprise a wide combination of drugs used at college parties, bars, and dance clubs. Some are used to enhance the highs produced by cocaine or to reduce the negative effects of crack. One of these is rohypnol, the "date rape" drug, a tablet that can be easily crushed and put into a drink. Its immediate effect is a sense of intoxication, relaxation, and drowsiness that can last for many hours. It can be fatal when used in combination with alcohol or another depressant (The National Clearinghouse for Alcohol and Drug Information, 2000).

One of the latest new substances used by children, teens, and young adults in the United States is embalming fluid. This substance typically has a formaldehyde base but is mixed with ethanol, methanol, and other solvents. Tobacco or pot cigarettes are soaked in the fluid and then dried. Street names for the drug include "wet," "fry," and "illy." Embalming fluid can produce a high, auditory hallucinations, pain tolerance, and euphoria that can last from several hours to three days. Suburban areas and college campuses are typical sites for its use (Loviglio, 2001).

Despite the focus of this chapter, chemical substances are not the only forms of addiction. Worldwide, compulsive gambling has lead to bankruptcy for millions of persons. Sexual addictions have wreaked havoc in many families. Computer addiction is on the rise.

SOCIAL WELFARE POLICY RELATED TO SUBSTANCE ABUSE

No one can doubt that the economic, societal, and personal impact of alcohol and drug abuse is staggering. In recent years, the major research sites in the United States have not even attempted to estimate all the direct and indirect costs, but it is clear that billions of dollars are consumed. Indirect costs include health care for heart disease, cirrhosis of the liver, and other diseases; car accidents; costs to industry related to absenteeism and lost wages for employees; crime; fetal alcohol syndrome; foster care and domestic abuse shelter costs; and so many more. The hidden costs to the state of Montana for alcoholism alone have been estimated at approximately $53 million (Newhouse, 1999). In Europe research indicates that the cost of alcoholism alone represents 2 percent to 6 percent of the gross national product, depending on the specific country (Cost of alcoholism, n.d.). How did this come about? Some insight can be gained by examining the societal context in different periods of civilization.

Early History

Throughout recorded history, alcoholic beverages have been used and abused. Mythology from the Greeks and the Romans tells of such gods of wine as Bacchus. The New Testament provides ample evidence of the multiple uses of wine during the time of Christ; in fact, both Old and New Testament passages demonstrate the use of alcohol for mood changing and for medicinal as well as social purposes. Vineyards in Europe today were developed by the Romans during the reign of the Caesars. By the Middle Ages alcohol consumption was a daily routine in most European countries.

Quindara, California: Members of the Temperance movement
smashing the contents of a saloon.

The ship's log appears to provide evidence that the Pilgrims' diminished supply of food and beer resulted in their decision to land at Plymouth in 1620 rather than spending additional time exploring the coast of the New World (Kinney & Leaton, 1995). During the late nineteenth century, the Industrial Revolution brought social turbulence and imposed strains on normal family life in the United States. Morphine, cocaine, and alcohol became available through new means of production, distribution, and marketing. Hollow needles were first used at this time to inject chemical substances. The chaos of the times was mirrored in disrupted family life. In the view of many who joined the social reform movement that had begun in the mid-1800s, domestic violence was incited by alcohol abuse. Women in those years were almost totally dependent on their husbands as providers for themselves and their children. Letters and diaries from the 1870s provided ample evidence of the wife and child abuse that brought thousands of women into the temperance movement (Lacerte & Harris, 1986).

Reform and Regulation

The Woman's Christian Temperance Union (WCTU) was founded in Cleveland in 1874 to pursue social reform, education, and legislation regarding alcohol abuse, which came increasingly to be seen as the root of all evil. Together with another powerful prohibitionist organization, the Anti-Saloon League, the WCTU rallied the vote and was largely responsible in 1919 for passage of the Eighteenth Amendment (commonly referred to as the Volstead Act), which prohibited the manufacture and sale of alcoholic beverages in the United States. However, Prohibition of the 1920s proved to be neither enforceable by the authorities nor fully acceptable to American society. It was repealed in 1933 by the Twenty-First Amendment.

With the repeal of Prohibition, alcohol use increased steadily until the 1970s, when it began to level off. After some ups and downs into the 1980s, alcohol consumption began to decline.

Drug regulation in the United States was also influenced by the social reform movement that brought the WCTU into existence and that resulted in Prohibition. Opium was widely used in many parts of the world by the 1850s, and U.S. merchants joined in the lucrative opium trade. Drug use in general was common. Before 1900 narcotics were available from grocery stores and over the counter in pharmacies. Women used them to relieve discomfort related to menstruation and gave their children cough syrup containing opium. In fact, Coca-Cola's original formula contained cocaine.

Although the first U.S. tax on crude opium imports occurred in 1842, it was not until the Harrison Narcotics Act of 1914 that the use of narcotics for nonmedical purposes was prohibited. The public, which never completely supported the banning of alcohol, did support the suppression of narcotics. Federal laws resulted in increasing control of narcotics, with the 1956 Narcotic Drug Control Act providing the stiffest of penalties, including the death sentence for anyone convicted of selling heroin to a minor (Ray & Ksir, 1993).

Politics and Policy

The 1960s saw a massive increase in the use of drugs. Social reform efforts by the end of the decade resulted in the Comprehensive Drug Abuse Prevention and Control Act of 1970. This law shifted authority for control from the Department of the Treasury to the Department of Justice's Drug Enforcement Administration. The result was recodification of the substances, which separated alcohol and tobacco from drugs with a high potential for abuse; this left heroin, LSD, and marijuana in a category that brought penalties, including imprisonment, for their sale (1988 legislation added penalties for possession). Prevention and treatment funding was appropriated by the 1970 act, although alcoholism treatment centers had actually been developed shortly after the founding of Alcoholics Anonymous in 1935.

When the introduction of psychoactive drugs made methadone and antabuse available to treat heroin and alcohol abuse, new treatment programs emerged. The public became increasingly convinced that substance abuse was treatable. With the advent of the Reagan administration in the 1980s, however, the role of the federal government shifted away from a leadership role in treatment funding. Increasingly states were given responsibility for substance abuse treatment.

The use of law enforcement to curtail the supply of drugs became a primary focus of government. Given the major focus on the prosecution and incarceration of drug users and suppliers, more prison facilities were constructed. Already overcrowded correctional facilities could not accommodate a rush of new offenders, and new facilities soon filled to capacity. In election after election, the public supported prison sentences as an answer to the perceived drug problem.

Despite the perception of the public, the "drug problem" has actually become less of a problem since the early 1980s. Back in 1979, just under 26 million people in the United States had used illicit drugs in the previous month (Substance Abuse and Mental Health Services Administration, 1998). By 2000 that rate fell to an es-

Up for Debate
Proposition: Use of marijuana should be legalized for medical purposes.

Yes	No
1. Legalization would allow doctors to practice medicine more humanely, relieving pain and reducing nausea and vomiting caused by anticancer drugs.	1. There is no empirical evidence that affirms the medicinal value of marijuana to humans.
2. Hundreds of patients and their doctors have filed applications seeking compassionate use of marijuana.	2. If use of marijuana for medical purposes were legalized, there would immediately be a demand to legalize it for recreational purposes.
3. A synthetic form of marijuana, Marinol, is available, but patients have found it to be less effective than marijuana in relieving pain.	3. Tax dollars should be spent on research to find new alternatives to marijuana.
4. Marijuana isn't nearly as potentially harmful as numerous other prescription medications in current use.	4. The Drug Enforcement Administration (DEA) is firmly opposed to making this illicit, potentially addictive drug available.

timated 14 million people (Substance Abuse and Mental Health Services Administration, 2001). Marijuana was used by 76 percent of all drug users in the United States in 2000, making it the most frequently used of the illegal drugs. Ecstasy had been tried by 6.4 million persons at least once in their lifetime; this was an increase from 1999. Because the research design used in obtaining these data had changed somewhat in 1998, comparisons between current and earlier years should be considered with some caution; nevertheless, they do provide some indication of illicit drug use trends.

The most constructive handling of alcohol and drug concerns remains a potent issue in politics, especially in the current politically conservative environment. Substance abuse is often linked in the media with crime and has been used to promote lengthy prison sentences. Legalizing the use of marijuana remains an unresolved issue. Struggle over the legalization of marijuana for medical purposes (see the "Up for Debate" box) is a reflection of the interconnectedness of health and drug policies. As these debates continue, it is useful to recall how, over past years and leading up to contemporary times, social policy relating to drug and alcohol use has vacillated so widely in our country and worldwide.

THE PROFESSION'S HISTORY
IN THE SUBSTANCE ABUSE FIELD

Social workers need to value their clients as unique human beings and to believe in the potential growth and contribution of each client. Dan Graves's social worker did this well. Madeleine Johnson was not burned out by the broken promises of numerous alcoholic clients. Unfortunately, however, social workers and other human service professionals in the past often held very negative attitudes toward this client population. As a result, potential clients and their families sometimes were refused treatment or were shunted to the least experienced staff. One reason for professionals' avoidance of substance abuse clients was the frustration of working with abusers who regularly denied drinking to excess or who denied abusing other substances. Today this attitude is giving way—somewhat—to a better understanding of why and how people (and not just substance abusers) use resistance and denial. To gain a perspective on the change that is taking place, let us review the history of social work in the field of substance abuse.

Mary Richmond: An Early Leader

In 1917 in her now classic text *Social Diagnosis,* Mary Richmond described alcoholism as a disease that requires skillful medical as well as social work attention. She proposed use of the word "inebriety" to replace "drunkenness" and the word "patient" to replace "culprit" in social work practice. She incorporated the new terminology in an interview guide that she devised for assessment of clients. This instrument has much to recommend it even today. Sections of Richmond's interview guide focused on heredity of the inebriate, duration of the drinking behavior, causal factors, drinking habits (when, where, and so forth), the physical condition of and any current medical treatments needed by the person, and a description of the social conditions in which the person lived. Richmond's insights into the human condition enabled her to elicit information about the client's employment, home and family life, use of drugs in combination with alcohol, and even the potential use of alcohol by women to help them nurse their babies (Richmond, 1917).

As the director of the Russell Sage Foundation's Charity Organization Department in New York City, Mary Richmond was a highly respected and influential social worker. She was also noted for her work as a writer and teacher and is said to have contributed substantially to the acceptance of social work as a profession. Her sensitive discussion of social work practice with "the inebriate" may have helped to move social workers away from the extremely rigid, moralistic view of substance abusers that was held by contemporary society in the early 1900s.

An Uneven Evolution for the Profession

Social work literature from 1920 to 1950 contains little reference to intervention aimed at helping alcoholic or drug-dependent persons. Instead of working with the chemically dependent client, social workers tended to work with the spouses or families of such persons. In 1952, when New York University was requested by the U.S. Public Health Service to investigate juvenile drug use, the faculty felt as though they were "exploring a virtually unknown territory" (Chein, 1956, p. 50).

Similarly, in 1956 Catherine M. Peltenburg wrote in *Social Casework* that the few psychiatrists, psychologists, and social workers who did work with alcoholic patients in clinic settings had to deal with their own attitudes—with their feelings that alcoholism was a moral weakness and that alcoholic patients were morally depraved and lacked character. Jean Sapir's 1957 article urging social workers to help change public attitudes toward alcoholism is a classic in the field of social work and substance abuse; it was also one of the first articles that described an effective working relationship between social work and Alcoholics Anonymous and an attempt to differentiate those clients who could benefit from referral to AA from those who would not be appropriate candidates for this form of intervention.

In 1970 important legislation was passed that was to affect the delivery of services, including social work services, to alcoholic clients. The Comprehensive Alcohol Abuse and Alcoholism Prevention, Treatment, and Rehabilitation Law was the first piece of legislation that recognized alcohol dependence as an illness in need of treatment. The law established the National Institute on Alcohol Abuse and Alcoholism at the federal level, and it authorized grants to help the states develop alcoholism prevention and treatment programs. With such strong leadership from the federal government, many programs were initiated across the country.

Responding to the new federal initiative, the Council on Social Work Education commissioned a text to assist social work educators; the book, *Alcoholism: Challenge for Social Work Education,* was published in 1971 (Krimmel). This innovative work was useful to the schools that began offering courses on alcoholism, for it provided excellent content about working with alcoholic clients and their families, community resources, and alcoholism and poverty.

With the election of Ronald Reagan as president and the new era of diminished federal funding of substance abuse prevention and treatment, crime, drugs, and immigration began to be lumped together. Funding was increasingly shifted to military and police crackdowns on the import and sale of illegal substances and also to housing immense numbers of prison inmates whose sentences were drug-related. Insurance corporations' decisions to pay only for substance abuse care delivered in general hospitals led to closure of many residential treatment centers. In the 1990s, however, some new, short-term, community-based programs began to be developed. Social workers designed, implemented, and staffed many of these organizations.

Managed care has presented a challenge for substance abuse programs because of its reluctance to cover care. In fact, managed care is one of the powerful forces seeking to prevent incorporation of alcohol and substance abuse treatment in an updated federal Mental Health Parity Act when it is reviewed by Congress in the near future. As one program executive explained, "There has to be more recognition that addiction is a disease prone to relapse." He added, "With few exceptions, managed care doesn't get this as yet" (Surviving managed care, 1997, p. 17). The National Association for Addiction Professionals is one of many professional organizations currently fighting to ensure parity in health insurance coverage for addiction treatment. (This organization's website is included in the Internet Sites at the end of this chapter.) NASW has a policy statement that also supports parity. In part, it states:

"NASW advocates that comprehensive insurance coverage for alcohol, tobacco, and drug addiction treatment be mandated for all insurance policies at the federal and state levels. . . . Such comprehensive insurance should include coverage for the treatment of the substance abusers and their children (minors or adults), spouses, parents, and significant others who are affected" (Mayden & Nieves, 2000, p. 23). This policy statement reflects the shift made over time in social workers' attitudes toward persons involved with substance abuse. The current position is much more consistent with the NASW *Code of Ethics.*

DISASTER RELIEF, SOCIAL WORKERS, AND SUBSTANCE ABUSE

Social workers provided substance abuse treatment services for people affected by the bombing of the federal building in Oklahoma in 1995. American Red Cross social workers continued to provide services to survivors of fire, flood, tornado, and other disasters in the following years. In 2001, however, the entire nation's attention was riveted to the horrific devastation and loss of human life following terrorist attacks on the World Trade Center and the Pentagon. Massive numbers of volunteers sought to help, including social workers. Then, as the nation plunged into a war against terrorism and geared up for more attacks on the United States, American Red Cross offices across the country increased disaster relief training, with some sessions delivered at NASW state and local conferences.

The link between response to disaster and abuse of alcohol and other drugs was clearly articulated by Alan Leshner, director of the National Institute on Drug Abuse. Stressful times, he said, when there has been "large-scale damage and loss of life, and uncertainty of what may happen next . . . may be particularly difficult for people who are more vulnerable to turn to substance abuse or may be recovering from an addictive disorder" (2001, p. 1). He noted that there was evidence in New York City following the 2001 terrorist attack of increasing sale of street drugs. Disasters of this magnitude surely compound stress that can trigger relapse for addicted persons, even after many years of abstinence. Leshner also pointed out that of the millions of people across the world who witnessed the devastation of the World Trade Center, some were also likely to experience emotional reactions that could result in efforts to escape reality through substance abuse.

Terrorism and the threat of global war have brought new challenges to social workers. New knowledge and increased competence will be required. The concepts of crisis intervention and disaster relief have taken on new and deeper meanings.

INTERNET SITES

http://www.samhsa.gov	SAMHSA Center for Substance Abuse Prevention
http://www.naadac.org/	The National Association for Addiction Professionals
http://www.nida.nih.gov	NIDA (National Institute on Drug Abuse)

http://www.niaaa.nih.gov/	National Institute on Alcohol Abuse and Alcoholism
http://www.marijuana-as-medicine.org/alliance.htm	Alliance for Cannabis Therapeutics
http://www.treatment.org/	The Treatment Improvement Exchange
http://www.ecstasy.org/	Ecstasy.org
http://www.alcoholics-anonymous.org/	Alcoholics Anonymous World Services, Inc.
http://www.paihdelinkki.fi/english/serviceinfo/info/216.html	Paihdelinkki—Addiction Link (Finland)
http://www.aphanet.org/development/Hungary.htm	Prevention and Treatment of Alcohol Use Disorders in Hungary
http://www.nationalhomeless.org/addict.html	Addiction Disorders and Homelessness
Http://www.ca.org	Cocaine Anonymous

SUMMARY

The setting for the chapter's case study is an emergency shelter, and the social worker is a BSW who is herself a recovering alcoholic. Madeleine Johnson's disclosure that she, too, is a recovering alcoholic helps Dan Graves to trust her. Dan decided to continue AA attendance while at the shelter. The client's housing, social, medical, financial, and educational needs are addressed, and the social worker then extends her concern to Dan's relationship with his wife, Angie.

Social workers in all fields of practice are likely to work with persons who abuse chemicals or whose lives are otherwise touched by substance abuse. Because of this social workers need to understand those populations, such as women and children, who are at risk and the types of chemicals that are most abused.

Social workers also need an understanding of the prevention and treatment programs that are available and the goals and philosophy of those programs. As programs evolve and change in the United States, it is often helpful to look at services being offered in other countries, services such as those in some European countries that emphasize the harm reduction model. This chapter introduces Alcoholics Anonymous, a program that has become international in scope.

The substances most frequently abused in the United States are identified. In addition to alcohol, the most commonly abused substance, some of the current "designer drugs" and "club drugs" are described.

Social welfare policy and the provision of funding for prevention and treatment programs are described in relation to the political context of U.S. society. A brief history of the profession of social work in this field of practice is presented.

Today there is a resurgence of interest in substance abuse among social work students. This is hopeful because the profession will look to them in the future to create humane programs that will be sensitive to the needs of women and children, minority groups, homosexual and lesbian clients, the disabled, and other at-risk persons. Through research they will be able to add to our understanding of chemical dependency. They will have opportunities to educate the public, which, in turn, will affect political policy regarding prevention and treatment programs.

KEY TERMS

alcohol abuse
alcohol dependence
alcoholism
cross-addiction
depressants
dual diagnosis
dual perspective
fetal alcohol syndrome (FAS)
hallucinogens

harm reduction model
hypothermia
narcotics
potentiation
primary alcoholism
reactive alcoholism
secondary alcoholism
stimulants

DISCUSSION QUESTIONS

1. In the case study, what are Dan Graves's chances for successfully dealing with alcoholism? Identify the factors that might help him to attain success. What may prevent him from attaining a successful recovery?
2. What is a recovering alcoholic? How long does recovery take?
3. How have the patterns of drug and alcohol abuse changed over the history of the United States?
4. Identify substances discussed in this chapter that, if abused, can result in death.
5. Which populations or groups of people are at high risk in relation to substance abuse? Why?
6. Explain the differences between primary, secondary, and reactive alcoholism. Which kind of alcoholism did Dan Graves have?
7. What are some of the generalist practice interventions social workers may use in their work with chemically dependent clients?
8. What is the harm reduction model in the area of substance abuse services? How does it differ from the abstinence approach? Would there be any value in integrating the harm reduction model in U.S. programs?
9. Can you think of ways in which a generalist social worker with an understanding of substance abuse could be helpful to persons affected by crisis or disaster?

CLASSROOM EXERCISES

It is suggested that students break into small groups of three or four to discuss these exercises. It may be helpful to choose a scribe to record and report interesting points to the class after the group discussion.

1. Why do you think people become addicted to alcohol and other drugs in the United Staets today?
2. Do you view substance abuse as a moral issue, a medical issue (physical illness), a law enforcement issue, or something else? What policies do you believe could best reduce drug use and abuse in this country?

3. How does the harm reduction model of substance abuse treatment in Europe differ from the abstinence model and the 12-step program of Alcoholics Anonymous in the United States? Which approach makes most sense to you? Why?

4. What do you think are the major reasons for the shortage of substance abuse treatment programs in the United States today? What do you think can or should be done about this issue?

RESEARCH ACTIVITIES

1. Gather information about your community's substance abuse programs. What are the names and locations of these organizations? What is the nature of the treatment provided? What is the cost? Will people who are uninsured be accepted?

2. Survey people of different ages and political persuasions on the issue of legalization of marijuana for medical purposes. Do your survey results suggest stronger support for or stronger opposition to legalization? Are the survey responses related to age or political preferences?

3. Review available local and national newspapers. Cut out all articles that pertain to substance abuse. Identify themes that relate to current or emerging political issues. (Example: Automobile accidents caused by drunk drivers might relate to lack of substance abuse treatment resources, and that might connect with a political issue such as federal mental health parity legislation.) Then note how these themes might relate to the at-risk populations discussed in this chapter. Do any of these issues create concern for you as a potential social worker? Is there anything you can do in the political arena to advocate for the at-risk population?

4. Do library research to further your understanding of binge drinking, weekend rave parties, and drug abuse on college campuses. Then survey students on your campus and interview administrators such as the director of security about the prevalence of this activity on your campus.

INTERNET RESEARCH EXERCISES

1. On October 2, 2001, the Substance Abuse and Mental Health Services Administration issued a press release entitled "HHS Announces First Wave of Emergency Fund Grants for Disaster-Related Mental Health and Substance Abuse Services" (http://www.health.org/newsroom/releases/2001/oct01/2.htm).
   a. What was the purpose of granting the funds?
   b. For what use were the funds designated for substance abuse prevention and treatment programs intended?
   c. Why were only eight states and the District of Columbia given grants?

2. The National Coalition for the Homeless has an interesting fact sheet, *Addiction Disorders and Homelessness*, on its website http://ww.nationalhomeless.org/addict.html.
   a. What does this article say regarding the prevalence of addiction among the homeless?
   b. Cite three barriers to treatment of addiction noted in this article.
   c. What is your opinion of the law signed by President Bill Clinton relative to denying Supplemental Security Income (SSI) and Social Security Disability Insurance (SSDI) to people with addictions? Why?

3. The National Commission Against Drunk Driving has an article on its website entitled *Alcohol on Campus* (http://www.ncadd.com/youth/campus.cfm).
  a. Where did the term "binge drinking" first appear? What is its definition?
  b. Describe the "social norms approach" to behavior modification. Describe its use in relation to student drinking.
  c. An international association of colleges and universities whose goal is to work with potential alcohol problems on campus is cited in the article. What is the name of this group? What is its URL?

REFERENCES

Allen, J. P. (1998). Project MATCH: A clarification. *Behavioral Health Management, 18* (2), 42–44.

American Psychiatric Association. (2000). *Diagnostic and statistical manual of mental disorders* (4th ed., text rev.). Washington, DC: American Psychiatric Association.

Anderson, S.C. (1995). Alcohol abuse. In *Encyclopedia of social work* (19th ed., pp. 203–215). Washington, DC: NASW Press.

Bagheri, M. M., Burd, L., Martsolf, J. T., & Klug, M. G. (1998). Fetal alcohol syndrome: Maternal and neonatal characteristics. *Journal of Perinatal Medicine, 26*(4), 263–269.

Barker, R. L. (1999). *The social work dictionary* (4th ed.). Washington, DC: NASW Press.

Beverly, C. (1989). Treatment issues for black, alcoholic clients. *Social Casework, 70*(6), 370–373.

Boes, M., & Van Wormer, K. (1997). Social work with homeless women in emergency rooms: A strengths-feminist perspective. *Affilia, 12*(4), 408–426.

Chein, I. (1956). Narcotics use among juveniles. *Social Work, 1*(2), 50–60.

Cost of alcoholism. (n.d.). *Alcohol, Health.* Retrieved October 13, 2001, from http://www.alcoweb.com (*Hint:* click on genl info in English; click on contents and go to entry #4.)

Delgado, M. (1988). Alcoholism treatment and Hispanic youth. *Journal of Drug Issues, 18*(1), 59–68.

Des Jarlais, D. C. (1995). Editorial: Harm reduction—A framework for incorporating science into drug policy. *American Journal of Public Health, 85* (1). Retrieved October 4, 2001, from http://www.drugtext.org/articles/harmred2.html.

Finkelstein, N. (1994). Treatment issues for alcohol- and drug-dependent pregnant and parenting women. *Health and Social Work, 19*(1), 7–15.

Gibbs, L. E., & Hollister, C. D. (1993). Matching alcoholics with treatment: Reliability, replication and validity of a treatment typology. *Journal of Social Science Research, 17*(1/2), 41–72.

HHS Press Office. (1998, April 20). *Research shows needle exchange programs reduce HIV infections without increasing drug use.* Retrieved October 7, 2001, from http:/www.hhs.gov/news/press/1998pres/980420a.html.

Icard, L., & Traunstein, D. M. (1987). Black, gay, alcoholic men: Their character and treatment. *Social Casework, 68*(5), 267–272.

Jacobson, J. L., & Jacobson, S. W. (1994). Prenatal alcohol exposure and neurobehavioral development. *Alcohol Health & Research World, 18*(1), 30–36.

Johnson, K., Noe, T., Collins, D., Strader, T., & Bucholtz, G. (2000). Mobilizing church communities to prevent alcohol and other drug abuse: A model strategy and its evaluation. *Journal of Community Practice, 7* (2), 1–27.

Keaten, J. (2001, August 9). *Authorities find parties nothing to rave about.* Retrieved October 13, 2001, from http://www.theage.com.

Kinney, J., & Leaton, G. (1995). *Loosening the grip: A handbook of alcohol information* (5th ed.). St. Louis: Mosby.

Krimmel, H. (1971). *Alcoholism: Challenge for social work education.* New York: Council on Social Work Education.

Lacerte, J., & Harris, D.L. (1986). Alcoholism: A catalyst for women to organize: 1850–1980. *Affilia, 1*(2), 41–52.

Leshner, A. I. (2001, October 10). A message from the director. *NIDA: National Institute on Drug Abuse.* Retrieved October 13, 2001, from http://www.nih.gov/leshner note.html.

Leukefeld, C. G., & Walker, R. (1998). Substance use disorders. In J. B. W. Williams & K. Ell (Eds.), *Mental health research* (pp. 182–202). Washington, DC: NASW Press.

Loebig, B. J. (2000). *European alcoholism and drug abuse perceptions.* Retrieved October 4, 2001, from http://www.geocities.com/bourbonstreet/2640/topic.htm.

Logan, S., McRoy, R. G., & Freeman, E. M. (1987). Current practice approaches for treating the alcoholic client. *Health and Social Work, 12* (3), 176–186.

Loviglio, J. (2001, July 27). Embalming fluid latest drug for users seeking new high. *Dayton Daily News,* p. 11A. Retrieved October 13, 2001, from http://proquest.umic.

Malekoff, A. (1997). Group work in the prevention of adolescent alcohol and other drug abuse. In G. L. Greif & P. H. Ephross (Eds.), *Group work with populations at risk* (pp. 227–243). New York: Oxford University Press.

Masis, K. B., & May, P. A. (1991). A comprehensive local program for the prevention of fetal alcohol syndrome. *Public Health Reports, 106* (5), 484–489.

Mayden, R. W., & Nieves, J. (2000). Alcohol, tobacco, and other substance abuse. In *Social work speaks: National Association of Social Workers policy statements, 2000–2003* (5th ed.) Washington, DC: NASW Press.

The National Clearinghouse for Alcohol and Drug Information. (2000, August 4). Prevention works! *Prevention Alert, 3* (26). Retrieved from http://www.health. org/govpubs/prevalert/v3i26.htm.

National Women's Health Information Center. (2000, October 23). *Alcohol abuse and treatment.* Retrieved October 6, 2001, from http://www.4woman.gov/faq/sa_alcoh.htm.

Newhouse, E. (1999, November 21). Alcoholism levies huge hidden cost. *Great Falls Tribune.* Retrieved October 13, 2001, from http://www.pulitzer.Irg/year/2000/ e. . .tory-reporting/works/alcohol111.html.

Norton, D.G. (1978). *The dual perspective: Inclusion of ethnic minority content in the social work curriculum.* New York: Council on Social Work Education.

Peltenberg, C. (1956). Casework with the alcoholic patient. *Social Casework, 37* (2), 81–85.

Pokorny, A. D., Miller, B. A., & Kaplan, H. B. (1972). The brief MAST: A shortened version of the Michigan Alcoholism Screening Test. *American Journal of Psychiatry, 129* (3), 342–345.

Preboth, M. (2000). Mental health: Addiction: Recreation drugs. *Excite Health.* Retrieved July 3, 2001, from www.excite.com/guide/health/mental_health/addiction/recreations/drugs/marijuana/newsandguides/.

Rapp, R. (1997). The strengths perspective and persons with substance abuse problems. In D. Saleebey (Ed.), *The strengths perspective in social work practice* (2nd ed., pp. 77–96). New York: Longman.

Ray, O., & Ksir, C. (1993). *Drugs, society, & human behavior* (6th ed.). St. Louis: Mosby.

Rhodes, R., & Johnson, A. D. (1994). Women and alcoholism: A psychosocial approach. *Affilia, 9*(2), 145–154.

Richmond, M. E. (1917). *Social diagnosis.* New York: Russell Sage Foundation.

Robertson, N. (1988). *Getting better: Inside Alcoholics Anonymous.* New York: Ballantine.

Roffman, R. A. (1987). Drug use and abuse. In *Encyclopedia of social work* (18th ed., Vol. 1, pp. 477–487). Silver Spring, MD: NASW Press.

Ruiz, D. S. (2001). Ch.16: Traditional helping roles of older African American women: The concept of self-help. In Carlton-LaNey (Ed.), *African American leadership: An empowerment tradition in social welfare history* (pp. 215–228). Washington, DC: NASW Press.

Sapir, J. V. (1957). The alcoholic as an agency client. *Social Casework, 38* (7), 355–361.

Saulnier, C. L. (1991). Lesbian alcoholism: Development of a construct. *Affilia 6* (3), 67–84.

SFAF HIV Prevention Project (Needle Exchange). (2001, May 20). Retrieved October 7, 2001, from http://www.sfaf.org/prevention/needlesexchange/.

Smyth, N. (1995). Substance abuse: Direct practice. In *Encyclopedia of social work* (19th ed., Vol. 3, pp. 2328–2337). Washington, DC: NASW Press.

Stanton, M. D., & Heath, A. W. (1995). Family treatment of alcohol and drug abuse. In R. H. Mikesell, D. D. Lusterman, & S. H. McDaniel (Eds.), *Integrating family therapy: Handbook of family psychology and systems theory* (pp. 529–544). Washington, DC: American Psychological Association.

Streissguth, A. P., Clarren, S. K., & Jones, K. L. (1985, July 13). Natural history of the fetal alcohol syndrome: A 10 year follow-up of eleven patients. *Lancet, 2,* 85–91.

Streissguth, A. P., LaDue, R. A., & Randels, S. P. (1988). *A manual on adolescents and adults with fetal alcohol syndrome with special reference to American Indians* (2nd ed.). Washington, DC: U. S. Department of Health and Human Services, Indian Health Service.

Substance Abuse and Mental Health Services Administration (1998). Table 1A: Estimated numbers of persons (in thousands) in the U.S. population aged 12 and older, by age group, race/ethnicity, and sex: 1979–1997; Table 11: Percentages reporting past month use of any illicit drug, by age group, race/ethnicity, and sex: 1979–1997; Table 14: Percentages reporting past month use of alcohol, by age group, race/ethnicity, and sex: 1979–1997. *Preliminary Results from the 1997 National Household Survey on Drug Abuse* [Online]. Available: http://www.samhsa.gov/oas/nhsda/hnsda97/97tab.htm.

Substance Abuse and Mental Health Services Administration. (2001). *Summary of findings from the National Household Survey on Drug Abuse.* Office of Applied Studies, NHSDA Series H-13, DHHS Publication No. (SMA) 01-3549. Rockville, MD.

Surviving managed care: CD treatment providers speak out. (1997, November–December). *Behavioral Health Management, 17* (6), 16–19.

Tobacco: A pandemic. (2001). International Council on Alcohol and Addictions. Retrieved July 17, 2001, from http://icaa.ch/icaaintro.html.

Turnbull, J. E. (1988). Primary and secondary alcoholic women. *Social Casework, 69* (5), 290–297.

Van Wormer, K. (1995). *Alcoholism treatment: A social work perspective.* Chicago: Nelson-Hall Publishers.

Walsh, D. C., et al. (1991). A randomized trial of treatment options for alcohol-abusing workers. *New England Journal of Medicine, 325* (11), 775–782.

FOR FURTHER READING

About AA: A Newsletter for Professional Men and Women.

Published quarterly, this single-sheet newsletter provides a wealth of information about current alcoholism research. It also keeps professional people attuned to the ways in which AA cooperates with the professions and the areas in which AA seeks to retain its own identity and philosophy. The newsletter and other Alcoholics Anonymous materials are available from Box 459, Grand Central Station, New York, NY 10163.

Doweiko, H. E. (1999). *Concepts of chemical dependency* (4th ed.). Pacific Grove, CA: Brooks/Cole.

Doweiko's work is characterized by a remarkable degree of objectivity and an engaging style of writing. He does not necessarily agree that our nation is experiencing an epidemic in drug use. He cites his resources so thoroughly that it is easily possible to pursue additional research in a variety of areas. This text is a comprehensive introduction to chemical dependency. Content includes all of the substances of abuse described in this chapter and much additional content.

Lewis, J. A., Dana, R. Q., & Blevins, G. A. (2002). *Substance abuse counseling* (3rd ed.). Pacific Grove, CA: Brooks/Cole.

Although this is a text that focuses on counseling skills and, therefore, is somewhat advanced for students of an introductory social work course, it would be an excellent resource for term papers related to substance abuse treatment. For persons considering pursuing a career in social work, this book might provide a glimpse of future practice. The approach of the text authors is one that emphasizes respect for persons who are struggling with addictions. Strategies have been selected that fit a collaborative model in which clients' goals and needs drive the counseling process.

Lowery, C. T. (1998). American Indian perspectives on addiction and recovery. *Health and Social Work, 23*(2), 127–135.

Lowery's article offers a unique perspective on the integration of spirituality and ecology from a Native American perspective. She incorporates content on the trauma experienced by native people globally, a kind of spiritual trauma that at least in part accounts for the high rates of alcoholism found among American Indians. Lowery believes that it is necessary to integrate the spiritual into social work intervention especially when working with alcohol abuse among women.

Member named to head SAMHSA. (2001, October). *NASW News, 46* (9), p. 1, 10.

After reading about the federal organization known as SAMHSA (the Substance Abuse and Mental Health Services Administration), readers of *The Social Work Experience* text might find this announcement of interest. Charles Curie, President George W. Bush's appointee for administrator of SAMHSA, as the *NASW News* article reports, is a social worker and a longtime member of NASW. In his new position, Charles Curie is responsible for the organization that houses the Center for Substance Abuse Prevention (CSAP), the Center for Substance Abuse Treatment (CSAT), and the Center for Mental Health Services (CMHS). Curie's career in the profession of social work is described.

Palmer, N. (1997). Resilience in adult children of alcoholics: A nonpathological approach to social work practice. *Health and Social Work, 22*(3), 201–209.

Palmer has chosen to pursue research and practice with adult children of alcoholics from a strengths model rather than from a medical or pathology conceptual model. She presents for consideration a "differential resiliency model" that affirms varying degrees of competence and life skills achieved by persons as they seek to cope with experiences derived from their status as adult children of alcoholics.

Social Work with Older Adults

ROSE BALISTRIERI

Jake Jacobs, BSW, hung up the telephone and sat back in his chair with a thoughtful look on his face. He had just been talking with Ms. Rose Balistrieri, an older widow whom he knew well from prior contacts. Now Rose was having trouble with the neighbors who lived above her tiny apartment. Noisy parties had kept her awake for several nights. She had already asked her landlord for help, but he had done nothing.

Jake was a social worker employed by a private nonprofit agency funded by a group of inner-city churches. The specific social service the agency offered was to help maintain frail, elderly people in their own homes or apartments. Jake believed in the work of his agency, found his role personally and professionally rewarding, and was often able to make a real difference in people's lives.

Most of Jake's clients were women in their late seventies and older; most were white, including many European immigrants, although blacks and Hispanics were moving into the neighborhood. This area of the city was deteriorating, with an aging population clinging to aging apartments and churches.

The churches in the area, including Catholic, United Church of Christ, Presbyterian, Lutheran, and Methodist, did what they could to meet the changing needs of a population growing older and more diverse in ethnic background. The church that donated office space to Jake's agency ran a senior center in another part of the building. People who attended the senior center frequently requested Jake's services because he was well known to this group.

The agency provided services to all the older adults who applied, without regard to religious affiliation or ethnic background. It offered a variety of services to those who lived nearby in an area that included several city blocks. Probably its most important service was **case management,** *or coordination of assistance from a variety of resources. People came to Jake for help with all sorts of problems. He did whatever he could to assist them, from* **advocacy** *with negligent landlords to helping people find new homes or new sources of income.*

415

*Jake was especially concerned about Rose Balistrieri because she had several health problems, including high blood pressure and osteoporosis (brittle bones) related to her advanced age of 82. Living in an apartment building where noisy upstairs neighbors kept her awake night after night could result in further deterioration of her health. Ms. Balistrieri had already survived a very difficult shock only two years before, when she had been forced out of her small quarters in an aging downtown hotel where she had lived since the death of her husband several years before. As part of a project to revitalize the downtown area, the hotel had been converted into luxury condominiums. A niece had helped Rose find her current apartment, but the rent was more than two-thirds of her small income, a **pension** left by her husband and Social Security survivor's benefits.*

Rose Balistrieri was somewhat unusual for an elderly Italian woman in that she had little family to turn to. Typically, an Italian extended family maintains very strong ties, with the younger generation taking in older relatives who reach advanced age. But Rose and her husband had emigrated from Italy, bringing with them two young children. They settled near Mr. Balistrieri's brother's family, who had previously emigrated. The couple had a third child, a daughter, shortly after they arrived in the United States.

Rose's three children were now in their late fifties and early sixties; sadly, two of them were severely disabled. The oldest was unmarried and had been wheelchair-bound since an industrial accident in his twenties. He and his mother had a close, affectionate relationship, but he was unable to help Rose physically or financially. He lived in an apartment for people with disabilities and worked in a sheltered workshop.

The older of Rose's two daughters had worked hard as a young woman to assimilate into her adopted country; she had attended college and worked as a teacher. But then she had had a serious mental breakdown. She had never recovered and lived in a nursing home. When her mother visited, the two would speak only Italian. The daughter seemed to have lost her English-speaking skills. Rose Balistrieri's other daughter had moved to a distant state many years ago. She had married very young to a man not of Italian descent. According to Rose, this was her greatest tragedy—that her youngest child had left her. A daughter's duty, according to Italian custom, is to take care of her parents, but this daughter lived more than a thousand miles away and rarely visited. She had raised children who spoke no Italian at all; she wanted them to be "real" Americans.

Rose Balistrieri's only family help came from nieces (children of her deceased husband's brother), who were now mostly in their sixties, and from some great-nieces and nephews. These youngest relatives weren't very interested in Rose; they spoke primarily English and had busy lives of their own. The nieces, on the other hand, spoke Italian fluently and cared about Rose sincerely. But they were all getting on in years and had health problems of their own. Their primary duty, as they saw it, was to care for their mother, a widow in her nineties.

So when Ms. Balistrieri needed assistance to allow her to remain in her own apartment, she turned to Jake Jacobs's agency. Actually, what happened was that she fell and broke her right wrist, spraining her other wrist at the same time. The social services department of the hospital that treated her referred her to a visiting nurse, who made the referral to Jake's program. The visiting nurse was worried because Ms. Balistrieri's injuries made it very difficult for her to dress herself, shop, and prepare meals.

Jake made a home visit to assess Ms. Balistrieri's needs. When he learned how much rent she was paying, he asked if she would be interested in applying for subsidized housing for the elderly. In Jake's city, several such projects were managed by the federal Department of Housing and Urban Development (HUD). Rent was set at 30% of the tenant's gross income, about half what Ms. Balistrieri was now paying. "I don't want **charity,**" was her immediate response.

Jake concentrated on providing Ms. Balistrieri with services she needed to continue in her current living situation. He described the services his agency could provide. He could assign a volunteer to visit two or three times a week, he explained, to provide companionship and to monitor her needs. The volunteer could provide transportation for doctor's visits and help with food shopping. The volunteer could also call on the telephone every day to make sure she was all right. However, Jake continued, the volunteer couldn't do the daily meal preparation; there wasn't enough agency staff to provide that kind of service. He suggested that Ms. Balistrieri apply for the Meals On Wheels program. He thought he might be able to get her some financial assistance for this purpose, and perhaps he could secure a homemaker aide from the county department of social services to help with the housework until her wrists healed.

Ms. Balistrieri protested strongly that all these things sounded like charity to her and that she had faith that God would provide. She didn't want to be a burden. Jake was not surprised at the older woman's response. In his experience, most older adults maintained pride, dignity, and a strong religious faith to help them through the hard times. Jake admired and respected these feelings and beliefs, but he also wanted to help ease people's lives.

"Now, Ms. Balistrieri," he responded, "for how many years did you work hard raising your children, cooking, cleaning, and keeping house? Nearly 30? Do you have any idea how much it would have cost your husband to pay for all those services? And wasn't your husband working hard all that time too, earning money and paying taxes? You helped him pay those taxes, with your work at home. Why do people pay taxes? So that public services are available for people who need them. You need them now. Public services to eligible people are not charity; they are a right."

At first Ms. Balistrieri was willing to accept only the volunteer visitor from Jake's own agency, but within a couple of weeks she had been gently persuaded to apply for other services. Jake had noted her obvious weight loss, and so he had continued to express his concern about her basic nutritional needs. He then assisted her in applying through the county department of social services for a subsidized Meals On Wheels program and a homemaker aide. The county could provide the meal service immediately, but not the homemaker aide, given a long waiting list. Jake then sought homemaker services through a private agency. Ms. Balistrieri was soon eating regularly and living in a clean apartment, and she was much happier. Jake also checked with the Social Security office to find out if she could qualify for SSI (Supplemental Security Income) to augment her small monthly income. He found, however, that the combined income from her deceased husband's pension and from Social Security exceeded the limit allowed.

There remained the problem that, although Ms. Balistrieri's income exceeded the limits for monetary assistance from SSI, she was still terribly poor. The eligibility rules for the SSI program consider only an applicant's monthly income, and do not take into account their fixed expenses such as rent. Jake felt that Ms. Balistrieri did an amazing job of budgeting her money, but now there was the additional expense of Meals On Wheels and the homemaker aide. Jake believed that Ms. Balistrieri would be much better off in subsidized housing. Although there were long waiting lists for HUD apartments throughout the city, the projects for older adults had frequent openings simply because tenants died.

But Ms. Balistrieri had already moved in the recent past and she didn't want to do it again. Jake, respecting her wishes, didn't press her. He understood that moving can be traumatic for anyone, much less a **frail elderly** *person of 82 with high blood pressure, brittle bones, and little family support. He occasionally reminded her of the option of moving, however, and today, when she called about her problems with the noise upstairs, he wondered again if she wouldn't be better off applying for a HUD unit and moving as soon as she could.*

When Jake stopped to talk with Ms. Balistrieri that afternoon, he found she was exhausted from lack of sleep and apprehensive about talking with the landlord again. She was willing to face the man, though, with Jake's support. Jake reviewed her lease agreement and found it specified that noise was to be kept low at all times. He called for an appointment with the landlord and learned that he and Ms. Balistrieri could see the man in the downstairs office right away.

With the lease under his arm, Jake assisted his elderly client to the elevator. Ms. Balistrieri protected the sling around her broken wrist with the fingers of her other hand. She pulled at the sling, her face, and her hair with anxious fingers. Inside the main office, the two greeted the landlord, a middle-aged man impeccably dressed. He sat behind a large desk drumming his fingers. Jake introduced Ms. Balistrieri, then himself, and he gave the name of his agency as well. Then he asked Ms. Balistrieri to tell the landlord what was bothering her, and he helped her get started when she hesitated. Finally, Ms. Balistrieri told her story about the frequent noisy parties that went on in the apartment above her throughout the night, keeping her awake and exhausted. Pointing to the sentence in the lease prohibiting such noise, she asked the landlord to speak to the offenders.

The landlord was polite. He told Ms. Balistrieri that he would talk to the people upstairs. But, he added, he didn't know if it would do any good. The tenants were good working people, he said, and paid their rent regularly. He couldn't be on the premises in the middle of the night to enforce the lease. He suggested that Ms. Balistrieri might consider moving to a building with older tenants like herself who would want things more quiet.

At this point Jake intervened to remind the landlord that he had some tools at his disposal to enforce the lease; he could threaten noisy tenants with eviction, for example. But Ms. Balistrieri clutched at Jake's arm anxiously and said, "Oh no, no, no! I don't want to make trouble, I don't want to make trouble." She clearly feared that the person who might be threatened with eviction was herself.

Jake talked with the landlord for a few more minutes, urging him to talk sternly with the tenants upstairs. The landlord promised to do so. Still, Jake felt angry because he thought the message the man conveyed most strongly to his client was that she wasn't particularly welcome. Back in Ms. Balistrieri's apartment, Jake asked what the elderly woman thought would happen now. "Oh, maybe they'll be quiet upstairs for a few nights," she said, obviously discouraged, "but I don't think the landlord wants me here."

"Ms. Balistrieri, we can't be sure what will happen yet," Jake said gently. "Maybe things will improve. The landlord has promised to speak to the people upstairs. If that doesn't help, we can keep complaining." He paused for a few moments. "But," he continued, "what would you think about putting your name on the waiting list for one of the HUD apartment buildings, just in case? You don't have to take an apartment when it becomes available. But you'd have the choice."

"Well, Mr. Jacobs," Ms. Balistrieri said softly, "perhaps it wouldn't hurt to put my name on that waiting list. Perhaps by the time an apartment becomes available, I'll be ready."

THE IMPORTANCE OF GENERALIST SOCIAL WORK

Work with older adults requires practitioners who can operate from a generalist framework; every level of intervention is required, from individual to community. The generalist approach is illustrated well by the work of Jake Jacobs, BSW, who assisted Ms. Balistrieri.

Jake's agency provides ongoing services to help maintain elderly people in their own homes: companionship, transportation to medical and other important appointments, assistance with grocery shopping, and telephone reassurance. Assisting Jake in providing these services are two part-time "senior aides" over 60 years of age, two undergraduate social work students in field placement from a nearby state university, and various volunteers.

Jake routinely provides case management for his clients, coordinating needed services and service providers. To this end, he maintains records for all clients, including assessments of need, plans of action, and results. He makes sure that the volunteers provided by his agency carry out their visiting and telephone-monitoring roles. He informs clients about other resources such as Meals On Wheels, homemaker services, and public housing programs, and helps link clients with these resources when necessary. He follows up to make sure his clients actually receive the services to which he refers them. In the course of working with Ms. Balistrieri, Jake also engages in family work. He contacts various members of Ms. Balistrieri's family, for example, to assess their potential roles and resources for assisting her. He also encourages Ms. Balistrieri to participate in various groups that gather at the senior center in the church housing his agency. He frequently assists in running group programs at the senior center himself. He engages his organizational skills in recruiting volunteers, supervising staff, and administering his agency.

In addition to working with individuals, families, groups, and organizations, Jake sometimes becomes involved in social action and community organizing. For example, he recently led a successful fight to extend a cab service for people with disabilities, partly financed by the county, to include frail elderly people. Many older adults had been having a difficult time climbing into city buses and private cabs because they used canes and walkers. These frail elderly didn't qualify for special cab services for the disabled, however, because they did not use crutches or wheelchairs, and weren't sufficiently visually impaired.

The fight to obtain county-run cab services for frail elderly people took over a year and required lobbying with every county supervisor. Jake did a good deal of lobbying in person, but he also organized input from other staff, volunteers, students, and the elderly themselves. He strongly believes in empowering people to advocate on their own behalf, and so he encouraged his older adult clients who needed special cab services to attend legislative hearings and tell their own stories. The strategy worked. For a small payment, the elderly now have access to a county-run, subsidized cab service with specially modified vehicles to accommodate people with minor physical impairments.

A true generalist, Jake utilizes social work skills at every level of intervention.

SOCIAL WORK ROLES AND SERVICES FOR OLDER ADULTS

Social workers like Jake Jacobs must take on many roles, even inventing a few in the course of solving the complex problems that come their way. Creativity, flexibility, and dedication of purpose are required by the professionals in this field. In return, their work is constructive, rewarding, and often exciting. Results may be tangible and immediate, as older adults are often stimulating and appreciative clients.

Bellos and Ruffolo (1995) identify a variety of roles that social workers with older adults may assume and services in which they may become involved: case management (or coordination of care), advocacy, individual and family counseling, grief counseling, adult day care services, crisis intervention services, adult foster care services, adult protective services, respite care services, support and therapeutic groups, transportation and housing assistance, counseling, therapy, and advocacy services. These authors find that social workers constitute a significant portion of the network of service providers for older adults. (See Exhibit 1.)

Social Work Roles with Older Adults	
EXHIBIT 1	
Case management	Adult foster care services
Advocacy services	Adult protective services
Individual and family counseling	Respite care services
Grief counseling	Support and therapeutic groups
Adult day care services	Transportation and housing assistance
Crisis intervention services	Psychotherapy

Case management is probably the primary role utilized today by social workers in working with frail or ill older adults. Rosengarten (2000, p. 100) describes the goals of this kind of case management as:

1. Helping older adults remain safely, independently, and happily within their own homes and communities for as long as possible.
2. Helping older adults and their families to cope with transitions to more dependent status when needed (such as living with a family member or aide on a part-time or full-time basis; accepting nutritional and health care interventions; assisting with finances, transportation, and so on).
3. Helping those older adults and their families who need to consider a move to a more protected living environment, such as senior housing, enriched housing, a continuing care facility, or a nursing home.

Pierce, Gleason-Wynn, and Miller (2001) note that older adults who need assistance with psychosocial issues such as nursing home placement are often referred to social workers today by their attorneys. Older persons and their families frequently turn first to attorneys for assistance in estate planning, guardianship and probate issues, and qualifying for Medicaid payment for nursing home placement. Qualifying for Medicaid involves a tremendous task of locating and sorting through myriad financial documents and coping with highly complicated rules. Attorneys have found that social workers can be of great assistance in this task, providing counseling and support to their clients while helping to clarify complex rules and regulations.

Social workers who provide case management throughout the Nursing Home Medicaid Benefit certification process also usually monitor caregiver care plans throughout the process as well. Wherever possible, however, they will assist their elderly clients to find and utilize resources in the wider community that will enable them to remain at home. Most older adults treasure their independence and want to keep it as long as possible.

WHO ARE OUR OLDER ADULTS?

In terms of both total number and percentage of the population, more and more Americans are reaching the age of 65. In 1900, there were approximately 3.1 million Americans over 65, or about 4 percent of the population. Today, there are approximately 35 million, and they constitute about 13 percent of the population. It is expected that their number will double to 70 million in the next 30 years (Associated Press, 2000). The population of older adults is also growing worldwide. For example, while they constitute about 10 percent of the global population today, they are expected to reach 34 percent by the end of the twenty-first century, given trends toward increasing longevity and falling birthrates. (The world's population, 2001).

Should a person over 65 be considered "old"? This question is new. Traditionally, 65 has been considered the age of retirement. Life expectancy at the turn of the century was only 47 years, so that 65 was considered old indeed. Life expectancy in the United States today is 76, and the longer one lives, the longer one can expect to live. A 75-year-old has a life expectancy of over 84, for example. There are roughly 61,000 people who are 100 years or older living in this country today, and 1 in 26 baby boomers is expected to live to 100. This number will probably increase greatly in the future, as people over 85 are the fastest growing segment of the U.S. population (Living longer, 1999).

Today mandatory retirement is no longer legal for most positions. What seems "old" is clearly changing. Popple and Leighninger (1999) note that some researchers distinguish between the "young old" (those 65 to 74), and the "old-old" (those 75 and older). The former group tends to maintain health and independent living, whereas the second is more likely to contain individuals who are frail and require significant social, health, and other services. Almost half of all older adults today are over 75.

Geographical Distribution

When some people retire, they move to warmer climates. Florida, for example, has a distinctly higher proportion of elderly people than the national average (more than 18%). In general, however, older adults are less likely to move than any other age group. Studies indicate that 90 percent of seniors do not want to move more than 100 miles after they retire; 80 percent of respondents to a recent survey planned to stay in-state (Axtman, 2001).

Apparently the pull of the Sun Belt does not outweigh the benefits of remaining near family and friends for many. Older people tend to be concentrated in certain areas of the country today. More than half live in nine states: California, New York, Florida, Pennsylvania, Texas, Ohio, Illinois, Michigan, and New Jersey (Popple & Leighninger, 1999).

Marital Status

Marital status is an important factor for older adults because at this stage of life a spouse is a significant resource for independent living. Women live longer on the average than men, helping create differences in marital patterns among older men and women. A 65-year-old woman can expect to live another 19 years, for example, whereas a man averages only about 15.5 more years. On the one hand, longer life may seem a blessing for women, but on the other, wives care for husbands until the husbands die. Then, like Ms. Balistrieri, they spend the rest of their lives coping alone. Almost half of all women over 65 are widowed; there are about five times as many widows as widowers (Popple & Leighninger, 1999).

Even if women should want to remarry, there are few men available. This situation worsens with age. For example, among the very old (age 85-plus), fewer than one man in five lives alone; 70 percent are still married, living with their wives. But only 22 percent of women are still married and living with their husbands at this age; nearly half (45.1%) live alone. Women in this age group outnumber men 10 to 4. Women in Ms. Balistrieri's age group (75 to 84) outnumber men 5 to 3.8 (Cox & Parsons, 1994).

Employment

In general, labor force participation by older people has been falling. At the turn of the century, for example, two-thirds of older men were employed; today, only 12 percent of men over 65 are employed (Popple & Leighninger, 1999). Cox and Parsons (1994) note a difference in the employment patterns of older men and women. While labor force participation of men aged 55 to 64 has been falling in recent years, employment of women has been increasing. In the future, an even greater percentage of women may work into their later years, both because of economic necessity due to lower wages and early widowhood and because of personal choice.

Recent decades have seen an increase in part-time work among older adults of both sexes (Maldonado, 1987). Over half who are employed today work part-time. This may reflect Social Security regulations, which require a decrease in benefits if earnings exceed a specified limit. It may also reflect job discrimination, in that part-time work may be the only employment available to older people (see Exhibit 2).

Michael Mor-Barak and Margaret Tynan (1993) note that encouraging older workers to stay in the work force makes good sense, because the baby boom generation is aging and a declining number of young people are entering the work force. Yet employers in general are not "user-friendly" to elderly workers. They rarely provide flexible hours, for example, that could allow older workers to meet such special needs as caring for an ailing spouse or relative.

Economic Status

Statistics reveal increased economic security among people aged 65 and over in recent years. In 1960, fully a third of older Americans were poor. Their economic situation today is improved in large part due to federal government initiatives such as indexing Social Security benefits to inflation, Medicare, and Supplementary Security Income (see Chapters 3 and 7). The greater financial stability of older adults today has been widely publicized and unfortunately tends to pit the elderly against other groups competing for resources. However, having adequate income describes only some older adults, those of the middle and upper classes. Many retired people experience great difficulty making ends meet.

In 1999, 9.7 percent of older Americans had incomes below the official U.S. poverty line, less than the overall U.S. poverty rate of 11.8 percent for all persons for that year (Greenstein, Primus, & Kayatin, 2000). However, it must be remembered that the poverty line for older people assumes that they eat less than younger

---

Age Discrimination

EXHIBIT 2

Despite the Age Discrimination Act of 1967, which was designed to promote employment of older people according to ability rather than age, discrimination against hiring the elderly is still a fact of life. This seems to reflect a societal attitude that older people live in the past and cannot be trained to meet contemporary needs. Yet some older people want to work and are qualified and able to do so. Some must work, out of economic necessity.

people. (The poverty line is determined by multiplying the cost of the Department of Agriculture's emergency food basket times three). This, of course, may or may not be true for any given older adult.

Drawing on 30 national studies covering 66,000 older adults, Nancy Wellman, director of the National Policy and Resource Center on Nutrition and Aging at Florida International University, calculates that three out of every five Americans age 65 or older are at high to moderate nutritional risk. They exhibit three to five warning signs on a 10-point checklist that incudes eating fewer than two meals a day, eating poorly, and experiencing economic hardship. Malnourished people are known to become ill more frequently and to spend more time in hospitals, so that providing adequate nutrition is cost-effective. However, monies available at the federal, state, and private-sector levels do not come close to serving all who are hungry. For example, the New Orleans Council on Aging has over 1,000 names on a waiting list for hunger relief, and 30 more are added every week (Weaver, 2000).

Members of ethnic minority groups and women are especially likely to be poor among older adults. For example, in 1999 the median net worth of households headed by older African Americans was $13,000, compared with $181,000 for households headed by older whites (Associated Press, 2000). The percentage of elderly Hispanics and Native Americans with incomes below the poverty level (22 percent and 20 percent, respectively) is over twice as high as that for older whites. Poverty increases with age and is highest among women. For example, among women 75 and older, 33.2 percent of Latinas have incomes below the poverty line as do over 37 percent of African American women (Greene, 2000).

Social Security provides an income for over 90 percent of older adults today, lifting many out of poverty. Without government benefits, 47.7 percent of older adults would fall below the poverty line (Greenstein, Primus, & Kayatin, 2000). The average benefit for a retired worker is about $8,500 per year (Segal & Brzuzy, 1998) and is indexed to inflation. As Judith Gonyea (1994) notes, Social Security benefits by themselves are not enough to lift persons without additional pensions and other financial resources out of poverty. She writes that ethnic minorities and women are the most likely to remain poor in old age because they have worked for lower wages, thus contributing fewer dollars in Social Security taxes, which results in lower monthly benefits. Gonyea reflects:

> Social security lifts a much smaller percentage of women and minorities out of poverty as compared to white men. For the young-old (ages 65–74), social security was 84% effective in helping white men escape the official poverty rate, but only 64% effective for black men. For white women it was 69% effective in raising them above the poverty line, yet for black women it was only 48% effective.

When the Social Security Act of 1935 was passed, it was not intended to be a sole source of income but rather to supplement people's pensions and savings. However, for many older adults pensions and savings are nonexistent. According to Katz (2001), fully half of today's elderly are entirely dependent on Social Security, and nearly another third receive 90 percent of their income from the program. The poorest elderly, approximately 6 percent, receive Supplemental Security Income (SSI, see Chapter 3), but SSI does not raise its recipients above the poverty level.

Older adults who are minorities bear a double burden—the devaluation in status associated with old age and the disadvantages imposed by their ethnic minority group status (Greene, 2000). Women who are members of ethnic minority groups face the greatest risk of poverty in old age, since they are subject to discrimination on three bases: age, ethnicity, and gender. White males and married white females face the least risk.

Physical and Mental Health

To some degree, health is something that money can buy. At least good medical care, which costs money, helps. In 1994, nearly 70 percent of the elderly rated their health as good or excellent, an encouraging finding that is probably related to the availability of health care under Medicare and Medicaid (see Chapter 3). Only about 5 percent of persons over 65 are severely disabled. Members of racial minority groups report less satisfaction with their health than whites, probably because lower incomes on the average decrease their ability to purchase quality health care (Popple & Leighninger, 1999).

Despite the improvement in availability of medical care through the Medicare and Medicaid **insurance** programs, older adults still face substantial health costs that are not covered. A significant problem is that Medicare does not cover prescription drugs. A fact sheet prepared by the American Association of Retired Persons (AARP, 2001) reports that the average Medicare beneficiary fills a prescription drug 18 times a year, and 80 percent of retirees use a prescription drug on a daily basis. Prescription drugs can be extremely costly, so that in many cases elderly people must simply go without them. In the case of blood pressure medications, for example, which must be taken regularly, this problem can be fatal.

The AARP reports that Americans 65 and over account for more than 40 percent of all drug spending in this country today, at an average out-of-pocket cost of $480 per year. While 70 percent of Medicare beneficiaries have some type of drug coverage, it is often inadequate; nearly half lack coverage at some point during the year due to low caps on benefits. Fewer than 10 percent of older adults who have purchased Medigap plans (private health insurance plans aimed at older adults on Medicare) have drug coverage, and only 3 of the 10 major Medigap plans offer it. Of employers who offered retiree benefits to Medicare-eligible retirees in 2000, 21 percent did not offer coverage for prescription medications (AARP, 2001).

In addition to the problem of coverage for prescription drugs, Medicare premiums and **co-insurance** make appropriate medical care out of reach for many older Americans This is an important problem because among the elderly, chronic health conditions, those that are persistent and possibly lifelong, afflict a large percentage. Most older adults suffer from at least one, and among the elderly, chronic health conditions tend to limit activities more than acute illnesses do. Those most frequently reported are arthritis (49%), hypertension (37%), hearing impairments (32%), and heart disease (30%). Other common disorders include diabetes, sinusitis, visual impairments, and orthopedic impairments (Nathanson & Tirrito, 1998). They can become long-term if not permanent conditions, requiring adjustments in lifestyle and continuing care and attention. Health-related habits acquired earlier in life such as diet, exercise, and smoking and drinking patterns can have important consequences for health in later life.

Approximately 11.8 percent of older adults between 65 and 74 have difficulties performing their **activities of daily living (ADLs),** such as cooking, eating, dressing, and toileting, but the percentage increases to 26.5 percent for those between 75 and 84 and rises to 57.6 percent for people over 85 (Mui, Choi, & Monk, 1998).

Alzheimer's Disease   Alzheimer's disease is one of the most serious chronic conditions afflicting elderly people today. It affects both physical and mental functioning. First described by Alois Alzheimer in 1907, the disease produces tiny lesions in the brain. The disease cannot currently be prevented or cured. It causes irreversible dementia, or loss of one's mental faculties. People as young as 20 have been affected, but most victims are much older. Symptoms of Alzheimer's disease are progressive. Eventually, the afflicted person loses use of both body and mind.

From 2 percent to 15 percent of people over 65 eventually contract Alzheimer's disease, with a significantly higher incidence in people over 80 (Popple & Leighninger, 1999). The diagnosis is difficult to substantiate. The first indication may be a slight loss of memory. Physical symptoms may involve weakness or partial paralysis, loss of bowel and bladder control, a shuffling gait, and stooped posture. But all these conditions can be caused by other conditions: stroke, tumor, depression, and the like. Only a biopsy of the brain can confirm a diagnosis of Alzheimer's disease. Because the procedure is dangerous, biopsies are done only when all other possibilities have been ruled out (Beaver & Miller, 1992).

Symptoms of Alzheimer's disease progress at different rates for different people. They may stabilize for long periods of time. Types of symptoms vary with the individual; one person may have difficulty with speech, for example, while another has difficulty with spacial relations and gets lost easily. Some people become severely depressed or agitated. Researchers speculate that symptoms vary because different areas of the brain are affected by the disease process. Unfortunately, over time, every patient gets worse and eventually dies.

Despite the dismal long-term prognosis for Alzheimer's patients, social workers in nursing homes can help maximize the functioning of afflicted elderly people by helping them exercise whatever faculties they have left. Structured small-group activities are excellent for this purpose. Today, with more older people being cared for in the community, those who are admitted to nursing homes tend to be sicker than in the past. It is estimated that 30 percent to 50 percent of people living in nursing homes today have Alzheimer's disease (Beaver & Miller, 1992).

Mental Health Challenges   Of the elderly who become institutionalized in nursing homes, it is known that well over half suffer from cognitive deficit, or loss of mental acuity; only about 5 percent of community-based elderly people suffer from this condition. Alzheimer's disease is an increasing cause of mental confusion in older adults.

Nathanson and Tirrito (1998) point out that the aging process is accompanied by important personal losses. Body strength declines with age, for example, and one tends to suffer more chronic illness. Spouses, family members, and friends may die. Retirement brings loss of income and loss of the worker role, and age discrimination limits one's ability to secure additional work. The older adult gradually loses the necessary resources to remain independent. Independence, of course, is a major cultural measure of personal worth, and its loss undermines self-esteem. Chronic depression can follow.

Cox and Parsons (1994) suggest that social workers use an **empowerment** model when working with older adults, assisting them to use and develop their coping skills to their best advantage through consciousness raising, education, and support. This approach is consistent with Jake Jacobs's assisting Ms. Balistrieri to understand that she had a right to complain about the noise in her apartment building, and going with her to advocate with her landlord. Encouraging older adults to join advocacy groups such as the American Association of Retired Persons (AARP) or the Gray Panthers can also aid in the process of empowerment. The socialization and advocacy groups that are available at senior centers can also increase opportunities for empowerment.

Ethnicity

Because U.S. Bureau of the Census data in the past have tended to lump together whites and nonwhites without distinguishing subcategories, it is difficult to determine exactly who the elderly are with respect to race and ethnicity. However, black and Hispanic elderly are increasing at a faster pace than white elderly.

African Americans today constitute approximately 8 percent of older adults aged 65 and above. The current average life span of an African American male is about nine years less than that of a white male; the African American woman is most likely of all older women to become widowed. Asian and Hispanic elderly, on the other hand, have longer life expectancies than whites, and percentages of Asian and Hispanic elderly are growing faster than percentages of white. In 1995, approximately 85 percent of all older adults were white, but that percentage is expected to decline to 67 percent of all older adults by the year 2050 (Popple & Leighninger, 1999).

Living Arrangements

Despite the popular belief that most elderly people live in nursing homes, in fact, only about 5 percent reside in one of these institutions at any given time. Most older adults live alone or in an independent household; about 13 percent reside with children, siblings, or other relatives. Nearly three-quarters of older adults own their own homes, reflecting a very strong American belief in home ownership. Many of these are mortgage-free.

The good news is that a large majority of elderly homeowners enjoy relatively low-cost, independent accommodations. The bad news is that the housing occupied by people over 65 is considerably older than housing occupied by people under 65 and may be substandard or in serious need of repair (having, for example, broken plaster, peeling paint, exposed wiring, roofing leaks, and worn-out furnaces). Those who must rent their accommodations, especially ethnic minorities or people living in rural areas, run the greatest risk of substandard housing (Popple & Leighninger, 1999).

Although many older Americans need safe, low-cost housing, the federal government has not invested in constructing additional units for decades. This omission is not likely to be rectified in the foreseeable future, given Congress's continued pursuit of budget cuts, particularly in social programs.

Research on Family Strengths

There has been a myth in our times that Americans abandon their elderly parents, callously storing them away in nursing homes, never to see them again except perhaps at funerals. Although such tragedies undoubtedly do occur, research consistently refutes this myth with respect to most families. For one thing, older adults in need of long-term care have been relatively rare until recent times. Stories about families caring for parents until death in the early days of this country may have been true, but that death would probably have occurred rather quickly. The average life expectancy in 1900 was more than a quarter century less than it is today. More families are caring for elderly members today than ever before, and for many more years. The four-generation family is common; some families have five. Conner (2000) even offers a term for this type of structure: the "beanpole family."

Greene (2000) points out that traditionally, family developmental tasks have centered around the nuclear family and child rearing. Families, however, also encounter developmental tasks in later life. Establishing a mutually satisfying parent–child relationship in later years involves the issue of dependency, a normal and important family process. Dealing with issues of dependency constructively involves both a realistic acceptance by the older adult of strengths and limitations, and the ability of the adult child to accept a caregiving role. The adult child must also recognize strengths and limitations in his or her capacity to carry out this role.

GETTY IMAGES

A proud family of four generations.

A recent national study of "baby boomers," adults 45 to 55, commissioned by the AARP, found that 44 percent of respondents had children under 21 as well as living parents, in-laws, or both (Belden, Russonello, & Stewart, 2001). These are the people sometimes referred to as the "sandwich generation," because they are pulled in different directions by the needs of both children and parents. The initial expectation of the AARP was that people in this situation would feel extremely burdened. Certainly, many did. But surprisingly, most welcomed involvement with their loved ones, and over 70 percent felt that they could comfortably handle their responsibilities.

Unpaid informal support from family and friends is by far the most prevalent form of long-term care for older adults today. Over two-thirds rely exclusively on family and friends, and over 90 percent of noninstitutionalized older adults receive some form of informal care. In all, family members—spouses, adult children, siblings, and broader kin networks—provide fully 80 percent of the long-term care needed by older adults who reside outside nursing homes. Many take on significant out-of-pocket financial expenses (Mui, Choi, & Monk, 1998).

Given that families today have many responsibilities, with most able-bodied adult members required to participate in the paid workforce to make ends meet, these figures are impressive indeed.

Older Adults as Caregivers

Family members do not just assist their older adult relatives. Older adults are often caregivers themselves. First of all, many care for each other. Married elderly, for example, particularly women, frequently take care of a spouse through long-term illness, including dementia, right up until death brings release. Many others also care for relatives and friends.

Older people also frequently care for children. Sometimes they provide child care for grandchildren while the children's parents work. But more than that, today many families are headed by older adults who are assuming increasing responsibility for raising grandchildren. Between 1990 and 1997, for example, grandparent-headed households increased by 19 percent to more than 2.4 million. They now constitute 6.7 percent of U.S. households with children under 18 (Mays, 1998). Some of these households include three generations (grandparents, parents, and children); a significant proportion include grandparents and grandchildren only.

The primary reason compelling many children to be cared for by their grandparents is substance abuse by the parents, followed by neglect and illness due to AIDS. Grandparents often suffer increased health problems of their own because of their additional responsibilities. Others experience increased psychological distress and social isolation. Innovative programs have been developed in a few places to help support their caretaking efforts, such as visiting nurse services, in-home assessments by social workers, support groups, parenting skills groups, respite care, and assistance with legal concerns such as adoption and welfare benefits (Mays, 1998).

Today older adults are adopting children more often. Many, for example, who were serving as foster parents in 1997, the year of the Adoption and Safe Families Act, decided to adopt their wards. This act encouraged states to speed up adoptions of children unlikely to have the opportunity to return to their biological families. Rather than risk losing the children in their care, many foster parents over the age of 60 decided to adopt. Since children older than five are considered hard to place, many of the older adults who applied were given legal permission to do so. Even an 80-year-old received permission to adopt. She had been foster parenting a 10-year-old. This elderly woman planned to adopt a second foster child as well. Longevity is an issue in such situations, of course. Late life adoptions bring the risk of additional loss by the children at an early age. But perhaps a shorter than ideal period of love and stability is the best than can be offered in many circumstances (Stevens, 2001).

An unusual caretaking service by older adults is taking place in prisons today. Given the very long prison terms that are all too common today, more and more inmates are growing old and dying behind bars. Some prisons have developed hospice programs, and the response has been heartwarming. Not all inmate hospice volunteers are older adults themselves, but many are (see Exhibit 3).

Intergenerational Stress and Cultural Conflict

Although families provide an enormous amount of aid to elderly parents and relatives, not every member of the younger generation has an equal commitment or ability to do so. In the case of Ms. Balistrieri, her older daughter was institutionalized as a result of mental illness, and her son was physically disabled. Ms. Balistrieri herself, at age 82, was the primary caretaker among the three. She regularly

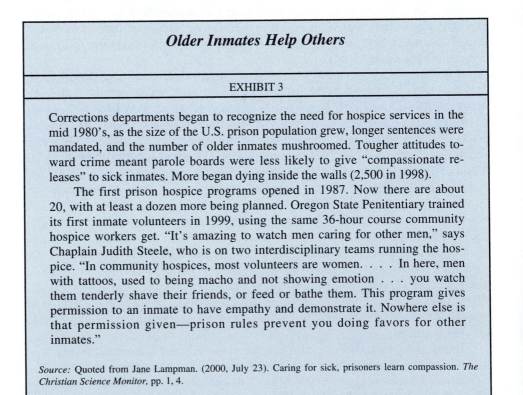

Older Inmates Help Others

EXHIBIT 3

Corrections departments began to recognize the need for hospice services in the mid 1980's, as the size of the U.S. prison population grew, longer sentences were mandated, and the number of older inmates mushroomed. Tougher attitudes toward crime meant parole boards were less likely to give "compassionate releases" to sick inmates. More began dying inside the walls (2,500 in 1998).

The first prison hospice programs opened in 1987. Now there are about 20, with at least a dozen more being planned. Oregon State Penitentiary trained its first inmate volunteers in 1999, using the same 36-hour course community hospice workers get. "It's amazing to watch men caring for other men," says Chaplain Judith Steele, who is on two interdisciplinary teams running the hospice. "In community hospices, most volunteers are women. . . . In here, men with tattoos, used to being macho and not showing emotion . . . you watch them tenderly shave their friends, or feed or bathe them. This program gives permission to an inmate to have empathy and demonstrate it. Nowhere else is that permission given—prison rules prevent you doing favors for other inmates."

Source: Quoted from Jane Lampman. (2000, July 23). Caring for sick, prisoners learn compassion. *The Christian Science Monitor,* pp. 1, 4.

visited her adult children with disabilities, fulfilling the responsibilities of parent-hood well into old age. In her concern and care for others, Ms. Balistrieri was like many older adults today, who courageously provide assistance to others including grandchildren, over extended periods of time.

Ms. Balistrieri had a third child, a younger daughter who was able-bodied. As an Italian-born woman who maintained a strong identification with her Old-World heritage, Ms. Balistrieri's cultural expectation was that her younger daughter should care for her. However, this daughter had a family of her own over a thousand miles away and no interest in returning to care for her mother. Many grown children leave their homes to pursue an education or a job or to fol-low a spouse. Differences between the hopes and expectations of parents and the preferences of children can result in severe intergenerational stress. Problems can be exacerbated in situations where the parents' cultural identification—including preferred language, clothing style, eating habits, and so on—differs from those of the children, who may have more fully assimilated into the wider American culture.

Caregiver Stress

Providing help to older adults is often experienced as stressful by younger family members. Activities of daily living such as shopping, cooking, cleaning, helping with laundry, and bathing all take time and money. Even more time is required when an elderly relative is ill. Women are especially under stress as they provide about 75 percent of all caregiving (Caring for caregivers, 1993).

Currently, approximately 2 million Americans employed outside the home also provide significant unpaid care to older relatives. Many also have children (Mui, Choi, & Monk, 1998).

According to a 1998 study of previously identified female caregivers by the National Alliance for Caregiving, three-quarters of respondents reported that infor-mation about dealing with the stress of caregiving would be very helpful. Many in-dicated stress that involved time factors: the average respondent spent 22 hours per week in caretaking responsibilities. About a third reported moderate financial hardship related to their caregiving role, and 17 percent reported high levels of hardship (National Alliance for Caregiving, 1998).

While family caregivers often give of their time and financial resources will-ingly, the strain can take its toll (see Exhibit 4). And because parents and in-laws may need help at different times, many people are long-term caregivers more than once (Elders' caregivers, 1998).

Caregiving can be stressful enough to undermine the health of the caregivers themselves. Concerning this problem, Sobel (1998) writes:

> Millions of Americans are caring for a chronically ill spouse, parent, or other loved one. New research shows that this stressful endeavor can be hazardous to the caregiver's own health—especially in cases where the chronic disease in-volved is severe. Some caregivers begin to neglect their own health. Others un-knowingly experience stress-induced changes that can lead to heart disease, can-cer, or other ailments. As the number of people living with chronic conditions continues to rise, health care providers must learn to identify and help the at-risk caregivers upon whom so much depends.

The "Sandwich" Generation

EXHIBIT 4

At issue is the cost of providing care to greater numbers of elderly. . . . The phenomenon is also putting a squeeze on more families, who find they are unprepared to handle the financial and emotional challenges of aging parents, growing children, and their own retirement. . . .

Colleen Galligan has first-hand knowledge of the challenges that can confront the sandwich generation. Last year her mother became physically unable to care for herself. Ms. Galligan and her three siblings shared the responsibility of caring for her, preparing meals, scheduling doctor's appointments, and finding someone to help during the day. Money was also tight.

"The most stressful thing to me was having small children and caring for mom at the same time because it put so much extra work on my husband," says Galligan, who also had a full-time job.

Source: Quoted from E. L. Spaid. (1996, November 4). Florida leads states in effort to provide more elder care. *The Christian Science Monitor,* p. 3.

A recent study of baby-boom generation caretakers finds that members of different ethnic groups respond differently to the challenges of caregiving. For example, 42 percent of Asian Americans in this study helped care for or provided financial support for their parents, in-laws, or other relatives. That compares with 34 percent of Hispanics, 28 percent of African Americans, and only 19 percent of non-Hispanic whites. Perhaps not surprisingly, non-Hispanic whites were least likely to feel "squeezed" by the needs of their children and parents. They were also least likely to feel stressed or guilty about their caregiver roles (AARP Research Center, 2001).

Perhaps this difference reflects the greater financial security of many older non-Hispanic whites, who are more likely to have the means to finance and manage their own care. It may also reflect a difference in cultural expectations, however. For example, three-fourths of the older Asian Americans in the study said that children *should* care for their elders, whereas only half of the other older "boomers" in the study agreed.

Elder Abuse

Most families do their best to provide for their older members. But given the pressures of caregiving, it may not be surprising that reports of elder abuse are rising nationwide. Exact statistics are not available, since reporting laws differ from state to state, but it has been estimated that 4 percent to 6 percent of older adults may suffer some form of abuse (Ansello, 1996).

Abuse may occur in several ways (Kosberg & Nahmiash, 1996):

- Physical maltreatment, in which pain or injury is inflicted.
- Verbal or emotional abuse, in which a person is insulted, humiliated, or threatened.

- Material or financial abuse, in which money or property is misused.
- Passive or active neglect, or not providing adequate food, shelter, and other necessities for daily living.
- Violation of civil rights, or forcing someone to do something against his or her wishes.
- Self-neglect, in which a person retains responsibility for his or her own care but manages poorly in areas such as nutrition and hygiene.

Self-neglect, which is especially common among the elderly, can raise ethical dilemmas for social workers who serve this population. Many elderly people choose, for example, to live in their own homes, but they may grow too frail to cope well alone. Some, like Ms. Balistrieri, suffer injuries that temporarily prevent them from being able to provide adequate self-care. Some elderly people in need refuse assistance even when it is offered; their reasons include financial concerns, pride, and worry about losing independence. Social workers face difficult decisions when honoring the value of a client's self-determination can result in severely inadequate living conditions.

Increased social services to older adults, including day care for frail elderly and **respite care,** or temporary relief for their caregivers, could help prevent a large proportion of the elder abuse occurring today.

WORKING WITH OLDER ADULTS OF DIVERSE BACKGROUNDS

Ethnic and Cultural Minorities

The number of older adults who are members of ethnic minority groups is growing faster than average. Because of discrimination and other factors, minority elderly people are especially vulnerable to poverty and are likely to have an increased need for social services. The NASW (*Social work with older people,* 1994, pp. 17–18) has made the following recommendations for effective practice with minority elderly persons:

1. Presenting problems should be defined in terms of family and community systems and the culture, ethnicity, and heritage of the client.
2. Social work interventions should be based on the client's and the family's definition of problems, goals, needs, and solutions. Service plans should be based on the older person's strengths rather than deficits.
3. Programs should be preventive in nature whenever possible.
4. Services should be family- and community-based.
5. Service planning should be designed to enhance choices offered. For example, program options should include home health services, respite care, family support groups, and in-home care, along a continuum to nursing home care. Resource and program development activities should be undertaken to ensure the availability of services.
6. Services must be tailored to fit older people rather than forcing older people to fit into categorical services.
7. Services must be accessible.
8. Development of services should reflect appropriate roles for the life cycle of individuals.

The R-E-S-P-E-C-T Model for Serving Older Gays and Lesbians

EXHIBIT 5

R—Review existing policies and practices at one's agency. How are lesbian/gay consumers treated at the present time?

E—Educate administration, staff, and residents about a range of taboo topics such as human sexualities and gender differences.

S—Share ideas and experiences for the unlearning of homophobia and heterosexism.

P—Promote diversity and prevention of homophobic practices. Illustrate the comparison between heterosexism and other "isms" such as racism, sexism, and classism.

E—Explore and evaluate areas for continued learning and teaching.

C—Change belief systems and taboos that devaluate diversity, including sexual diversity.

T—Transition to a diversity-friendly facility that offers support and attention to older gays and lesbians.

Source: P. Metz. (1997). Staff development for working with lesbian and gay elders. In J. K. Quam (Ed.), *Social services for senior gay men and lesbians* (pp. 35–45). New York: Hawthorn Press.

Gay and Lesbian Older Adults

Another minority that has had to learn to live in at least two different cultural systems simultaneously comprises gay and lesbian older adults. If they are female, persons of color, or poor, they have had to survive multiple barriers. Many have chosen not to reveal their sexual orientation in fear of rejection by family and friends. Yet many serve as caregivers for parents, spouses, or partners.

Gay and lesbian older adults have the same concerns as all older adults: health care, housing, employment, transportation, and so forth. They need support, both formal and informal, to help cope with the ongoing concerns of old age. This represents a challenge for social workers because many gays and lesbians choose to remain invisible due to fear of social stigma and prejudice. Many remain isolated and alone (Kochman, 1997).

Metz recommends a model called R-E-S-P-E-C-T in serving this population (see Exhibit 5).

SOCIAL WORK WITH OLDER ADULTS: A BRIEF HISTORY

While in the early 1800s, older adults in the United States were viewed in a positive light as survivors who had mastered the secrets of long life, by the turn of the century this view had changed. Reasons are not well understood, but the rise of social Darwinism in the mid to late 1800s, with its stress on survival of the fittest, probably played a part. Professionals began to focus on the problems and ills of elderly people, rather than their wisdom and strengths.

In addition, by the early 1900s most residents of "poor houses" were 60 or older, since younger people with disabilities had been sent to training schools or mental hospitals. An institutionalized concentration of poor older adults maintained at public expense helped solidify the concept of old age as a social problem (Popple & Leighninger, 1999).

Social workers in the early years of the profession worked with older adults in institutions and in their own homes where possible, but such work was not emphasized as a special field until recent decades when the numbers of elderly people began to increase significantly. Nathanson and Tirrito (1998) note that social work with older adults has shifted focus over time. In the early years, the profession focused on alleviation of social ills through pursuit of social programs. Then, during the 1920s, the focus shifted to developing practice methods for work with individuals. One school, using Sigmund Freud's psychoanalytic theories, focused on treating individual psychopathology among older adults. A second school, the functional, emphasized utilizing health, growth, and self-determination along with social programs to help alleviate problems of older adults.

In the 1960s, the War on Poverty helped inspire another shift in social work's focus from working primarily with older individuals toward developing programs to alleviate the social disadvantages they experienced. Today, however, while the profession maintains an interest in alleviating social ills, developing improved practice methods with older individuals is again a priority (Nathanson & Tirrito, 1998).

SOCIAL POLICY AND OLDER ADULTS: PAST TO PRESENT

Family Care

Historically, before governmental social policies dealing with older adults were developed, services to the elderly were provided almost entirely by the family. This was workable because of the short life-span that was the norm until the turn of the century. In addition, in earlier times there were many more tasks that an elderly parent or relative could perform as a way of reciprocating. For example, on the farm an older adult could assist with gardening, feeding animals, and so on. Similarly, elderly relatives today are economic assets in households where child care is a necessity if a mother is to work outside the home.

By the late 1800s, however, industrialization of society had changed family patterns. Grown children tended to move to the cities. Individual achievement as a value took precedence over loyalty to one's extended family. The nuclear family supplanted the extended family as the primary locus of responsibility. Changes such as these undermined family support systems for older adults. The need for new forms of support began to appear. In early times the only alternatives were the church or almshouse. Later, **pension plans** were established in some countries.

Early Pension Plans

Germany initiated a compulsory pension program in 1889 that provided a regular source of income for older, retired workers. Employers, workers, and the state each contributed equal amounts to the financing. Britain introduced a pension program in 1908, which permitted general tax revenue to be transferred to elderly poor persons (Huttman, 1985). By comparison, the United States has been slow in developing universal pension plans for the elderly. Some states had pension plans by the 1920s, but they all required a means test (only people with very low incomes could qualify).

Not until the Great Depression did this country enact a nearly universal pension plan for the elderly, via the Social Security Act of 1935. The intent of Title II of this act was to stabilize income for older Americans without the appearance of the "dole," or a government handout. People were required to contribute to Social Security through a special tax during their working life. Thus, they could perceive the program as a contributory "insurance" plan, not charity. Workers who were required to pay Social Security taxes were later eligible to receive benefits after retirement, whether rich or poor. In 1939, coverage expanded to include widows and their children. Eventually many other categories such as self-employed people, farm and domestic workers, government workers, the military, and religious personnel were brought under the provisions of the act (Huttman, 1985).

Social Security Today

Today, almost all retired persons receive Social Security benefits, and these benefits keep approximately two-fifths of older adults out of poverty. Social Security was never intended to provide the sole source of income for elderly people, however, but rather to supplement personal savings and private pensions. But only about half of American workers are employed at companies that offer pension plans today (Popple & Leighninger, 1999), and many people will change jobs or become laid off before becoming eligible to receive them. Moreover, pensions usually provide fixed incomes, while the cost of living climbs with inflation.

Social Security benefits are indexed to inflation, which can help keep poverty at bay for increasingly older Americans, yet indexing has become a political football in recent years. Worries have arisen that the Social Security program cannot meet its obligations in the future. That is because the number of retirees continues to grow while the relative number of younger workers is declining.

Katz (2001) writes that the implication that this decline foreshadows an economic crisis is misleading. He points out that the fall has been much greater in the past (for example, from 8.6 workers per retiree in 1955 to 3.3 today) with no economic disaster. Furthermore, increases in productivity make dependency care more affordable. For example, the workforce in agriculture has fallen about 80 percent as compared to 40 years ago, but agricultural production has actually increased.

The Social Security program is not in any immediate danger financially, although it is politically. Social Security taxes generate an enormous surplus today. This surplus is invested in government Treasury bonds. By 2016, income from Social Security tax revenue will be less than benefits paid out, so that the program will have to cash some of its bonds. By approximately 2038 the bonds will be used up, and at that time income from Social Security taxes are projected to cover about 72% of the benefits owed. (Lipman, 2001). However, before 2038 there are a number of ways to take corrective action without fomenting a crisis.

Conservatives, including the commission appointed by the Bush administration, argue that the program should be privatized to allow maximum returns to investors (those, at least, who happen to be lucky). They argue that, otherwise, a crisis will occur in 2016. Critics of this view say the real deadline for action is 2038, because the Treasury bonds held by the Social Security program are just as real as the Treasury bonds held by private investors, who consider them an extremely safe investment.

How this program should be modified is the subject of national debate as this text goes to press. The AARP identifies several possible options (Social Security, the facts, 2001). Should the cost-of-living adjustments be reduced? Should the taxes paid on benefits be raised? Should the benefits be means-tested and available only to poor people, or benefits reduced for the affluent? Should the retirement age be raised further, say from 67 today to 70? Should the payroll tax rate be raised, or the income limit on which taxes are paid be raised ($80,400 in 2001)? Should coverage be expanded to new employees of state and local governments who are not currently part of the system? Should trust funds be invested in the stock market? Should Social Security be privatized by replacing all or part of the program with individually managed accounts?

Whatever decision is made is extremely important. About half of older adults, and particularly elderly widows, rely entirely on the program. Along with 35 million retirees, the program supports 7 million survivors (widows and dependent children) and nearly 7 million disabled adults and their dependents (Lipman, 2001). Most people of liberal political persuasion argue that Social Security is sound as is and can be saved with very slight adjustments in the tax base.

Other Federal Entitlement Programs

An **entitlement program** is one in which a legal right to receive benefits has been bestowed by law on people who meet certain eligibility criteria. (These criteria vary with the law and the program.) Social Security, briefly described above and also in Chapter 3, is a federal entitlement program created under the Social Security Act. Other major entitlement programs include Supplemental Security Income (SSI), housing assistance, and the programs described below.

Supplemental Security Income was initiated in 1972 as an amendment to the Social Security Act, replacing Old Age Assistance. As explained in Chapter 3, this program was developed to reduce the stigma of public assistance for poor people falling into three categories: the elderly, the blind, and the disabled. It established uniform national eligibility requirements and benefits. Stigma was reduced by allowing people to apply for SSI benefits through federal Social Security offices, rather than through state or local "welfare" offices. Benefits, although federally established and administered, remain low. For example, Ms. Balistrieri, of this chapter's case example, had an income too high to qualify for SSI, although she was obviously struggling to make ends meet.

Housing Assistance

Older adults tend to pay a higher percentage of their income for housing than younger people. Ms. Balistrieri's paying two-thirds of her monthly income to her landlord is not unusual. To assist with this problem, the Federal Housing Assistance Program, through the U.S. Department of Housing and Urban Development (HUD), subsidized nearly 2 million apartments for poor people, about half of them for the elderly, for many years (Salamon, 1986). However, the Reagan administration slashed HUD funding after his election in 1980, and the funding losses have never been restored. In addition, many units of public housing have been demolished as unsafe. Thus, affordable housing has been increasingly out of reach for all of the nation's poor, including older adults. A Republican Congress has tried to cut HUD funding entirely in recent years; to save the department, the Clinton administration converted its programs into a system of block grants to the states. But in 1996, Clinton signed a bill permitting no new applications for rental assistance. Today, the hope for affordable housing for poor older adults resides almost entirely with local communities (Popple & Leighninger, 1999).

Health Insurance

Before 1965, most health care costs for older adults were paid by the elderly themselves, with the result that many lacked any care at all. This situation greatly improved after the 1965 passage of Medicare, Title XVIII of the Social Security Act. As noted elsewhere in this book, all persons over 65 qualify for benefits whether they have paid into the Social Security system or not, and whether they are poor or not.

Part A of Medicare pays for hospital care and some follow-up care. Part B pays for some outpatient hospital care and some physicians' services (the elderly must pay a special premium to receive Part B coverage). Neither Part A nor Part B of Medicare pays for prescription drugs, however—a major problem for many older adults with chronic health issues. Nor is nursing home care covered unless licensed nursing services (such as drawing blood) are required. Even then, the number of days partially covered for nursing home care is limited to 100.

Because of rising costs of the Medicare program, benefits frequently change. Medicare, Part C, has recently been enacted, offering new options designed to cut costs. In general, elderly persons today are being asked to pay an increasingly large **deductible** (the portion of a given medical expense that must be paid up front before the Medicare program will contribute) and increasing co-insurance (percentage of the overall bill). See Chapter 7 for a more complete discussion.

Title XIX of the Social Security Act, an amendment passed at the same time as Title XVIII in 1965, was added specifically to aid older adults with low incomes. As explained in Chapter 3, Title XIX, or Medicaid, is administered under each state's public welfare system. Costs are shared between state and federal governments. An elderly person must be very poor to qualify; how poor one must be depends on each state's eligibility requirements. Benefits also differ from state to state. Many needy older adults avoid applying because of stigma.

Medicaid pays for certain hospital expenses, physicians' expenses, prescription drugs, nursing home fees, and other health-related services. Benefits recently have been changing, and in general poor people are being required to pay more of their own fees as part of cost containment legislation. This means, of course, that medical services available to the elderly poor are becoming scarcer.

The Clinton administration attempted to create a universal program of national health care that might have eliminated the need for Medicaid and Medicare programs. However, health care reform was rejected by Congress in 1994 despite a Democratic majority. Older adults, like other adults, can purchase private health insurance if they have the financial means. Many private plans are designed to coordinate with federal insurance programs.

Food Stamps

Food stamps, also discussed in Chapter 3, are another federal entitlement program available to the most poor older adults. Eligibility requirements involve both one's income and the number of persons in a given household who presumably share income. Elderly immigrants were denied eligibility under the welfare reform law in 1996, but, thankfully, eligibility has been restored to those who were 65 or older on the day the law was signed (Bills tackle welfare, patients' rights, 1998).

Current Innovative Programs and Alternative Lifestyles

Because of the growing number of older adults needing services, along with cuts in government assistance, innovative programs, both public and private, are trying to fill the gap at the local level. For example, in Florida a new group called the Commission on Aging with Dignity organizes forums bringing together leaders in government, business, and religion as well as ordinary citizens. The purpose of the commission is to educate the public about care and funding issues concerning older Americans, to help find solutions before intergenerational stress accelerates (Spaid, 1996).

In Los Angeles, an innovative private initiative called Alternative Living for the Aging builds cooperative residences for older adults. Residents have their own private bedrooms and bath, but kitchen facilities, living areas, and a courtyard are shared. Home-cooked meals are prepared and served by residents every evening, meeting needs far beyond physical nutrition. Home sharing programs are growing. A 1993 survey by the National Shared Housing Resource Center found 350 already in existence (Freeman, 1998).

Seniors themselves are experimenting with new lifestyles. For example, in spite of the fact that most choose to stay close to home, others are taking to the highways. It is estimated that approximately 750,000 senior citizens travel and work out of their RVs (recreational vehicles) for all or part of the year, forging their own alternative lifestyles. Support networks such as RV associations, magazines, and Internet sites posting job listings are developing. Employers targeting seniors include campgrounds, guest ranches, public parks, private theme parks, and tour operators. Salaries are generally offered in the range of $6 to $7 an hour, but benefits include guest passes and perks such as gas money. Some of these older travelers work because they need to supplement their Social Security benefits, but many volunteer their services at places like state and national parks (Terry, 2001). (See Exhibit 6.)

Seniors on the Road
EXHIBIT 6

John Szekley, in his eighth year at Wall Drugs, is also in his tenth year of full-time work camping. "I got tired of the rat race," he says, referring to the days he lived in Anaheim, California. "This is like coming back to family," Mr. Szekley says of the store and the town of 800 people.

His advice to anyone contemplating the rolling work life: "Don't wait. I started when I was 50 years old, and I wish I'd started sooner. It's a less stressful life."

For some senior citizens, seasonal work is a way to supplement their Social Security income. For others, it's a way to cut costs while traveling to places they've always wanted to visit. For many, the work is pure pleasure—a way to enjoy life, make new friends, and see the world.

Source: Quoted from Sara Terry. (2001, June 18). Seasonal seniors. *The Christian Science Monitor,* pp. 15, 18–20.

MORE FEDERAL LEGISLATION RELATING TO OLDER ADULTS

The Older Americans Act

The mid-1960s were important years for the elderly. The Older Americans Act of 1965 focused on coordinating comprehensive services for all people over 60, not just the poor. It established the Administration on Aging at the federal level, and authorized state units and local area agencies on aging. These units assess the needs of the older adults and try to develop programs to meet them. State and local autonomy is permitted within federal guidelines. In 1993, President Clinton raised the position of commissioner of the Administration on Aging to an assistant secretary level (Torres-Gil & Puccinelli, 1995).

Amendments to the act in 1981 established priorities: information and referral services (including those for non-English-speaking elderly); transportation; in-home assistance (homemakers, health aides, visiting and telephone reassurance efforts); and legal services. Nursing home ombudsman programs (programs to investigate complaints) were required, as were nutrition programs.

Funding under the Older Americans Act has always been low. Still, it supports nutrition programs, senior centers (which often house the nutrition programs, consisting of low-cost congregate meals for all persons over 60), and information and referral services. In these times of social service cutbacks, many argue that services should be provided only for older adults who are also poor or disabled. However, others point out that two-tiered services separate people according to economic status, place a stigma on services, and result in competition for scarce resources instead of cooperative self-help efforts. National organizations such as the American Association for Retired Persons and the Gray Panthers support offering services to all seniors. (See the "Up for Debate" box.)

Up for Debate
Proposition: Services under the Older Americans Act should be means-tested.

Yes	No
Funding under this act is low, so that services should be limited to the most needy.	All older Americans benefit greatly from balanced meals and an opportunity for social interaction.
Taxpayers are unwilling to **subsidize** services for all elderly.	All taxpayers will one day be elderly. Services for all can help make old age a rewarding experience for everyone.
Poor elderly need help the most.	Services limited only to the poor separate people according to economic status and place a stigma on services.
Since money is scarce, it should be targeted to poor people.	Limiting services to the poorest people pits the nonpoor against the poor, rather than encouraging all older adults to develop cooperative self-help efforts.
Taxpayers may resist using tax dollars to provide universal services for all older adults.	If most taxpayers know they will be denied services when they get old because they are not poor enough, no wonder they protest using tax money to provide these services for others.

The Social Services Block Grant

Before the 1970s, people who applied for financial assistance received services from social workers in public welfare departments, who routinely assessed social service needs while determining eligibility for financial aid. However, beginning in the early 1970s, eligibility for financial aid was determined by clerical staff who made no further assessment of need (Cox & Parsons, 1994).

Social services for older adults began to be funded by the Social Services Block Grant in the mid-1970s. It is a limited source of financing for homemaker services and adult day care. Originally known as Title XX of the Social Security Act, implemented in 1975, this program was renamed and modified significantly under the Omnibus Budget Reconciliation Act of 1981 (Eustis, Greenberg, & Patton, 1984). Funding is very limited today, and states are allowed a great deal of freedom in determining how to use it (Karger & Stoesz, 1998).

Funding for programs for older adults involves national policy choices; such policy choices translate into dollar terms the values of those who determine the policy. Should all American older adults be offered tax-supported services such as congregate meals, for example, or only the poorest, frailest elderly? Is it important for all older adults to have access to balanced meals along with a social group experience, or should these services be limited to the poor? Research can provide helpful data, but even the selection of questions for research is guided by values.

The debate around privatizing Social Security relates much more to value than to real financial concerns. Conservatives who want to privatize the program are primarily interested in promoting the free enterprise system so that the stock market gets the money contributed for retirement rather than the government. Under their plan, people who invest the most successfully will benefit the most. Liberals are more concerned about providing a decent standard of living for all older adults, their survivors, and people disadvantaged under the capitalist system due to disabilities.

Torres-Gil and Puccinelli (1995) write that a "politics of the new aging" is emerging. Increasing diversity among older adults means increasing complexity of issues and values, as well as intensified competition for scarce public resources. In addition, young and old populations compete against each other, creating strong intergenerational tensions. Whose interests should be served?

The "Continuum of Care": Prolonging Independence

Most older adults want to maintain independence as long as possible. Recognition of this preference has led to the concept of the **continuum of care.** Highly relevant is the principle of "least restriction: the least that will get you the most is the appropriate intervention" (Huttman, 1985). Generally, whatever can be done to enable the elderly person to remain in his or her own home setting (the **least restrictive environment**) is appropriate.

Exhibit 7 illustrates the major components of a long-term continuum of care for older adults. The diagram illustrates how many services for the elderly can fit into more than one category; for example, nutrition programs can be offered either in the home or in the community, perhaps at a senior center. The following sections briefly describe each major category of care.

In-Home Services   Monitoring services usually involve telephone calls to make sure that an elderly person is alive and well and to provide support and reassurance. Jake Jacobs's agency offered monitoring services to Rose Balistrieri, for example. In fact, the agency's service went beyond telephone calls; volunteers made weekly home visits.

Homemaker services involve housecleaning, laundry, shopping, minor home repairs, yard work, and other routine chores. A more intensive kind of homemaker service may involve personal care, such as help with bathing and dressing. Home health aides provide medically oriented care, under the supervision of a skilled nurse. Home health aides may change bandages, give injections, and take a client's blood pressure.

Components of Long-Term Care for the Elderly

EXHIBIT 7

Least Restrictive

Monitoring services

Homemaker — In-Home

Home health care

Nutrition programs

Legal/protective services

Senior centers

Community medical services — Community

Dental services

Community mental health

Adult day care

Respite care

Hospice care

Retirement village

• Life care services

Domiciliary care

Special Housing — Foster home

Personal care home

Group home

Congregate care — Institutional

• Meals

• Social services

• Medical services

• Housekeeping

Intermediate care

Skilled nursing care

Mental hospitals

Acute care hospitals

Most Restrictive

Source: Quoted from R. R. Greene. (1986). *Social work with the aged and their families* (p. 177). New York: Aldine de Gruyter.

Medicare and Medicaid pay for some of these services, but eligibility requirements are complicated and restrictive. For example, Ms. Balistrieri could not qualify for a home health aide under Medicare, even though one of her wrists was broken and the other was sprained. To qualify for Medicare, she would have had to require active medical care, not just assistance with personal care.

Sometimes elderly people can receive homemaker services at very low cost by applying to an agency partly funded by the Older Americans Act or the Social Services Block Grant. Ms. Balistrieri received services of a homemaker aide through Jake Jacobs's referral to a private agency partly funded in this way.

Community Services Nutrition programs can help older adults remain in their own homes. For example, without Meals on Wheels, Ms. Balistrieri might have been forced to go to a nursing home, since she could not cook with her injured wrists. In some communities, programs funded under the Older Americans Act provide congregate meals at senior centers or other sites five days a week.

Sometimes an older adult becomes mentally or physically incapacitated to the point of needing protection by the community. Occasionally, family or other caretakers abuse or neglect older people. Protective services for the elderly are a fairly new phenomenon; in 1968 fewer than 20 communities had such programs (Dunkel, 1987). Today, however, almost every state requires helping professionals to report suspected abuse or neglect of older adults (Ansello, 1996).

Elderly people themselves rarely request protection. Often legal guardianship must be assumed by the community for effective intervention, stripping away legal rights. An older adult's need of protection should be balanced with the important principle of self-determination. Limited options in the community, however, often result in imperfect solutions.

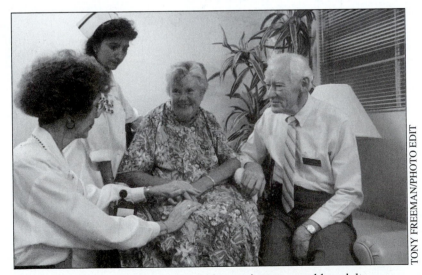

Senior center activities promote social interaction among older adults.

Senior centers are important means for older adults to maintain social interaction. Many are privately funded and administered by organizations such as churches, or by local cities or counties. Some centers receive funding through the Older Americans Act or Social Service Block Grants.

Community medical and dental services include private-pay arrangements that older adults finance themselves as well as public services financed partly by Medicaid and Medicare. An important public policy issue involves how much of their own medical costs the elderly should have to finance themselves.

Community mental health services can help older adults cope with various stresses of living, including the stress of caring for a spouse who is ill. Mental health services also can assist other family caregivers. For example, a daughter or a daughter-in-law may have to give up a paying job and most personal freedom in order to provide round-the-clock care for an elderly relative. Mental health services may assist the caretaker in coping with this consuming task (see Exhibit 8).

Adult day care services provide regular programming outside the home to supervise and maintain elderly persons who cannot get through the day alone. Many older adults who spend their days in adult day care programs live with relatives who regularly assist them but must work during the day. While adult day care can be expensive (it costs about $6 per hour, or about $200 to $250 per week, in 2001), it can allow a family caregiver to hold a paying job while providing a home for a frail elderly person.

Rural versus Urban Issues   Services to assist older adults to live independently in the community are scarce almost everywhere, but gaps in the continuum of care are far more likely to occur in rural areas (see Exhibit 7). Even where important programs such as congregate meals and adult day care exist within a given rural county, transportation over long distances may be required to obtain them, so that

---

Common Community Settings for Working with Frail Older Adults

EXHIBIT 8

- Home bound services such as Meals on Wheels
- Outreach/case-finding programs
- Elder abuse programs
- Financial management programs
- Legal services programs such as legal aid and eviction prevention programs
- Mental health programs
- Adult protective services
- Guardianship programs

Source: Karen Bassuk & Janet Lessem. (2001). Collaboration of social workers and attorneys in geriatric community based organizations. *Journal of Gerontological Social Work 34*(3), 103, 104.

many seniors and their families are effectively blocked from participating in their benefits. Many rural areas are lacking in crucial services such as senior centers with congregate meals, Meals on Wheels, affordable housekeeping help, medical screening services, adult day care programs, and the like. The result is that too many seniors in rural areas who become frail and ill find that their only option is to enter a nursing home, unless they are fortunate enough to have relatives or friends willing to take them in.

Social HMOs   Social HMOs for older adults are an exciting and relatively new development in the United States. Traditional HMOs, health management organizations that are an option for many older adults under Medicare, provide medical care only. Many are cutting back on services today, or pulling out of the program entirely, because of financial problems. Social HMOs, on the other hand, are operating in the black or breaking even. There are only four of them so far, but they are expanding and serving as a hopeful model for other areas (Marks, 2001).

Social HMOs differ in two important ways from tradional HMOs. First, they offer social services to help people continue living at home. Services include such practical assistance as shopping and even replacing lightbulbs, to help prevent injuries (which would be more costly to treat). Second, Medicare allows social HMOs a slightly higher fee for frail older adults, and less for healthy ones.

Critics fear that seniors would "come out of the woodwork" if such services were available to all, and bankrupt Medicare. But the oldest and largest social HMO, Senior Care Action Network (SCAN), in Long Beach, California, appears to belie this concern. SCAN has been in operation for nearly 20 years and has 44,000 subscribers. Fully 20 percent of them meet all state criteria for nursing home admission. Yet more than 95 percent are still able to live at home. Given that nursing home care would cost at least $30,000 per year for each frail elderly person, the savings involved in assisting them to stay independent are enormous. The average cost for the social HMO client is about $5,000, no more than that of the average Medicare recipient in a traditional program, yet social HMOs provide full prescription drug benefits as well as social services. Clearly, this is a model for health care reform nationwide.

Institutional Services   Some institutions, including nursing homes, administer a service called respite care, whereby an elderly person resides in the institution for a few days, a week, or even a month. This temporary arrangement allows family caretakers to take a break, go on vacation, or otherwise "recharge their batteries" physically and emotionally. After the respite, the elderly person returns home to their care. Many institutions also offer day care services as described above.

The next several categories in Greene's continuum of care (Exhibit 7) are institutional, in that they involve long-term care outside the elderly person's home, but Greene also places them in the subcategory of special housing. The first of these is hospice care, an institutional service that, when available, is provided to elderly people (and others) who are dying. Medicare will pay for hospice care for elderly persons whose prognosis indicates that they have six months or less to live. Many hospices are contained entirely within hospitals or nursing homes. However, hospice care is sometimes provided in small homelike facilities or even in patients' own homes; that is why Greene also includes it as special housing. The purpose of hospice care is to help the patient die with dignity, with as little pain as possible.

The next item with both institutional and special housing aspects is the retirement village. Many retirement villages offer lifetime care with a continuum of services; many are private, nonprofit arrangements established by religious denominations. Elderly persons who are economically advantaged may purchase lifetime rights to an apartment or other housing unit. Some such programs offer the option of purchasing congregate meals. Many include a domiciliary option, or a large housing unit where a number of elderly people live and are offered personal assistance and meal services. The most advanced retirement villages include skilled nursing home care as needed.

Some older adults reside in foster homes or in small group homes, where they can receive individual attention and protection if needed, as long as ongoing medical attention is not required. Others live in larger **personal care homes,** which usually provide meals and are sometimes called nursing homes because the services of nurse's aides are available to help with bathing, eating, dressing, and the like. Technically speaking, however, a personal care home is not a nursing home, because very limited nursing care is available.

The institutional settings that provide the most restrictive environments for care of older adults are nursing homes and hospitals. Most elderly people do whatever they can to avoid them. However, since living into one's eighties and nineties is becoming common, an increasing number of older adults do face an eventual move to nursing home. These facilities provide the only reasonable alternative to 24-hour family or hospital care when an elderly person is very ill or very frail.

Fortunately, nursing homes now are professionally organized and staffed. Many provide responsible services along with opportunities for older adults to enjoy the companionship of peers. However, nursing homes should be utilized only when less restrictive alternatives have been exhausted. "Intermediate care" and "skilled nursing care" are categories that reflect the level of nursing care provided in a nursing home setting. The former is less intensive care than the latter, and the monthly fees are generally lower.

Coming to Terms with Long-Term Care

We usually do whatever we can, both personally and collectively as a society, to live longer lives, and we are succeeding. Life spans are increasing and show every indication of continuing to do so. That is the good news. Ironically, however, it is also bad news in some ways. Longer lives present new problems. Long-term care is a major one. It requires considerable financial outlay for which most of us are unprepared and raises important issues regarding quality of life.

As discussed earlier in the chapter, Americans are living about a quarter of a century longer than they did in 1900. Many people today face years of chronic illness and increasing frailty and will eventually be unable to carry on without assistance. Yet a recent survey found that nearly one-third would rather die than move to a nursing home. While pioneers have made major efforts to improve nursing home quality (see Exhibit 9), the focus in most places is still on "nursing" rather than "home." Nationwide, 18% of nursing home residents take antidepressants (Culhane, 2000).

Making a Home Out of a Nursing Home

EXHIBIT 9

(Dr. William) Thomas believes that the three plagues of loneliness, helplessness, and boredom afflict most nursing homes. "Often medications are used to make deficiencies in the environment less noticeable," he says. "We try to cover up the loneliness with pills."

With this research behind him, Thomas and his colleagues brought 12 dogs, 20 cats, and more than 600 birds to live in three nursing homes in upstate New York in 1993. (Other programs offer weekly or monthly pet visits, but Thomas wanted to provided permanent companions.) Employees filled the halls with hundreds of plants and invited elementary school students to join junior-senior gardening clubs. By 1995, the death rate at all three locations had dropped 25 percent and the residents used half as much medication. "People had a reason to get up each day," says Thomas. "They simply got hooked on living again."

Source: Quoted from Kari Watson Culhane. (2000, April). A real home. *Natural Health,* 80.

Nearly 1.5 million older adults reside in America's 17,000 nursing homes today. Nearly a third of these facilities, fully 5,283, were cited for physical or verbal abuse violations between January 1999 and January 2000, according to a congressional report (Elderly people were abused, 2001). Understaffing and staff turnover are chronic problems that contribute to improper care and unacceptable levels of abuse, particularly in for-profit nursing homes where the bottom line is the primary concern, resulting in low wages and frequent staff cuts (see Chapter 7). Yet nursing homes in general are extremely costly. While various sources cite differing average costs, the AARP states that the national average is nearly $50,000 per year (AARP, 2001).

Most elderly adults today cannot afford these prices. So almost 70% receive help from Medicaid. A few have private long-term care insurance. Medicare is not a serious resource because it covers only short periods of skilled nursing home care after a hospital stay (AARP, 2001).

Medicaid payments to nursing homes are lower than the fees charged to private clients, and they do not usually cover the full cost of care. Most nursing homes, therefore, accept private-paying clients first. When their money runs out, they turn to Medicaid. Most nursing homes will allow them to stay, but had they originally applied as Medicaid clients, their chances of admission would have been small. Frail older adults who have experienced lifelong poverty thus may find nursing home care very difficult to obtain.

Other types of long-term care are costly as well. For example, care at home can run between $12 and $25 an hour. Assisted living ranges between $20,000 and $40,000 per year, depending on the location. Total outlays for elder care in the United States now run well in excess of $90 billion annually, according to many studies. Yet one-half of all American households possess less than $1,000 in net financial assets, according to a study by the Consumer Federation of America (Halverson, 2000).

Clearly, there is a mismatch between the reality of the cost of aging and the ability of many elderly to finance it. In response to this dilemma, private long-term care insurance policies are becoming available and are widely recommended. However, many cannot afford to purchase the policies. As Halverson (2000) writes:

The elder care challenge calls out for action on three fronts, experts say:

1. Making affordable elder care insurance more widely available
2. Providing adequate financial help for elder care needs
3. Ensuring that there are affordable assisted living or extended care facilities in most metropolitan communities

SOCIAL WORK WITH OLDER ADULTS: A GROWING FUTURE

Older adults in this country are growing in number and proportion day by day. Even with the predictable waxing and waning of public financing for social services for the elderly, reflecting shifts in the values of the politicians in power and the people who elect them, older adults are developing growing political sophistication. As a group, they are making themselves heard at all levels of government. Their needs are many. Thus, employment for social workers in the field of aging will probably continue to grow well into the foreseeable future.

Social workers who work with older adults encounter a varied and challenging client population. These are people who have led full lives and have developed the wisdom and perspective that come with many years on this planet. Elderly people are fascinating, enriching clients who can enlighten social workers as well as command their skills.

On the other hand, probably no other field of social work requires so much soul-searching on the part of the practitioner. Older adults are manifestly nearing the end of their journey on earth, and this fact makes many thoughtful workers ponder the "meaning of it all."

INTERNET SITES

http://www.aahsa.org/	American Association of Homes and Services for the Aging
http://www.alz.org/	The Alzheimer's Association
http://www.agesocialwork.org/	The Association for Gerontology Education in Social Work
http://www.cswe.org/sage-sw/	Strengthening Aging and Gerontology Education for Social Work
http://www.elderweb.com/	ElderWeb (a research site for both professionals and family members looking for information on elder care and long-term care)

http://www.caregiver.org/	Family Caregiver Alliance
http://www.geron.org/	The Gerontological Society of America
http://www.ncoa.org/	The National Council on the Aging
http://www.ifa-fiv.org/menu1.htm	International Federation on Aging
http://www.nih.gov/nia/	National Institute on Aging
http://www.aoa.dhhs.gov/	Administration on Aging

SUMMARY

The case study of Rose Balistrieri, an elderly widow of Italian descent, illustrates not only several of the common problems that older adults face but also the response of a private, nonprofit agency designed to assist this population, especially those elderly who are frail. The case study describes the work of Jake Jacobs, BSW, a social worker with strong generalist skills.

Currently, approximately 13 percent of the population of the United States is over 65, or more than one person in eight. People over 65 are expected to constitute about 20 percent of the population by the year 2030, or one person in five. This growing group, while resilient and self-sufficient in many cases, challenges the nation's social service system. The risk of poverty increases with age, and is especially serious for members of ethnic minority groups and women. Those with lower incomes suffer the greatest problems in terms of health and adequate housing.

Families are increasingly active in helping older adults to cope with their special needs. Because people are living longer, more families are contributing to the care of elderly relatives than ever before, and for many more years. Middle-aged children, especially middle-aged women, often find themselves part of the "sandwich generation," those who have children to care for in addition to elderly relatives. Social workers can help many families cope with the stresses involved in intergenerational care.

Social workers are encouraged to use an empowerment model when working with older adults, assisting them to advocate for themselves and to utilize whatever resources are available. Pension plans and federal entitlement programs such as Social Security, Supplemental Security Income, housing assistance, health insurance, and food stamps help elderly people meet financial and material needs to some extent. Limited services such as information and referral, congregate meal programs, low-cost homemaker aids, and protective services are provided under the Older Americans Act and the Social Services Block Grant. However, need for services far outstrips supply, and a large burden of care today falls upon families, creating intergenerational stress.

The concept of the continuum of care, designed to help older adults maintain independence for as long as possible, includes in-home services, community services, special housing, and institutional services. Whenever possible, older adults should be helped to remain in the least restrictive environment.

Given increasing longevity, the need for careful attention to long-term care is growing in importance, not only for individuals but for families and society as a whole. While an impressive continuum of care has been developed, we have not yet managed to come to terms with financing and quality of life issues.

Social work practice with older adults is likely to grow rapidly in the future because of rapidly increasing numbers of people who are frail and require ongoing services.

KEY TERMS

activities of daily living (ADLs)
advocacy
case management
charity
co-insurance
continuum of care
deductible
empowerment
entitlement program

frail elderly
insurance
least restrictive environment
pension
pension plan
personal care home
respite care
subsidy

DISCUSSION QUESTIONS

1. Approximately what percentage of the U.S. population is over the age of 65 today? About what percentage will be over 65 in the year 2030?
2. Why is it more likely that older women will live alone than older men? Who are more likely to be poor: older men or older women? Why?
3. What is meant by the statement "More families are caring for elderly members than ever before, and for many more years"? Why is this happening?
4. In what ways can cultural expectations both aid and complicate care for elderly people in one's own extended family?
5. Is Social Security intended to be the sole source of support for older adults? What does this mean about the level of benefits provided? How likely do you think it is that older adults will have other sources of income in the future?
6. What types of programs are funded by the Older Americans Act of 1965? In general, has funding for these services been adequate? Why or why not? What major questions does the chapter raise about the funding of these services?
7. How do national values affect federal policies relating to the elderly? What major questions are being debated today? How will the answers to these questions affect specific services for the elderly? How might policy relating to the elderly in general affect social work practice options (or resources) available to assist particular elderly people in need?
8. Describe the continuum-of-care services that can help older adults maintain independence as long as possible.
9. How does the concept of the "least restrictive environment" reflect the social work ethical principle of self-determination?
10. If community care is cheaper per person than care in a nursing home, do you think that more community care could still end up costing the nation more overall? If so, how? Do you think the social work profession would support more funding for community care even if it did end up costing more? Why or why not? Support your answer with a discussion of professional values.

CLASSROOM EXERCISES

It is suggested that students break into small groups of three or four to discuss these exercises. It may be helpful to choose a scribe to record and report interesting points to the class after the group discussion.

1. Review the arguments pro and con means-testing services provided under the Older Americans Act. One or more groups should then develop as many additional arguments as possible to support means testing, and one or more groups should develop as many additional arguments as possible against it. Then, each group should choose a spokesperson to represent its ideas in a classroom debate or panel discussion.
2. Discuss various policy options for making Social Security more financially sound. Include those identified by the AARP and any other options you can think of. Which policies make the most sense to you? Why? Which make the least? Why?
3. Imagine that you have the power to establish national policies that will solve the long-term care problem for older adults in the United States. What policies will you implement? Why?

RESEARCH ACTIVITIES

1. Find out if your community, or one nearby, has a local area agency on aging established under the Older Americans Act. Visit the agency and find out about the services it offers. Interview a staff member to learn about staff roles. What was the educational background of the staff person you interviewed?
2. Visit a local nursing home. Interview a social worker on staff. What are the roles of this worker? Next, interview a nursing home resident. What does the resident think about the services he or she receives? What would the resident like to be different at the home?
3. Find out if there is a retirement village near your community that provides a range of residential options for older adults. What is the range of services offered? Are there any gaps in service that you can identify? Interview a resident. How does resident satisfaction compare with that of the nursing home resident you interviewed earlier?

INTERNET RESEARCH EXERCISES

1. Like most areas of human endeavor, social work has its share of acronyms. One of these is SAGE-SW (http://www.cswe.org/sage-sw/whoweare.htm).
   a. What is SAGE-SW?
   b. What are its objectives?
   c. What is the John A. Hartford Foundation? (*Hint:* Double-click on the name link on the SAGE-SW site.)
2. The Census Bureau and National Institute on Aging have a report: *An Aging World: 2001*. This can be downloaded at the site http://www.trinity.edu/~mkearl/geron.html. At the beginning of that paper is a quiz about global aging. Try to answer the questions and then check yourself on the following page. How did you do?
3. The National Institute on Aging addresses many problems of older people (http:/nia.nhi.gov/about/history.htm).
   a. How long has the NIA been in existence?
   b. Subsequent legislation made it the primary federal agency for what disease research?
   c. In addition to its research, what other mission does the NIA serve?

AARP. (2001). *Medicaid: Paying for nursing home care* (online). Available: http://www.aarp.org/confacts/health/medicaidnurse.html.

AARP. (2000). *Medicare prescription drugs: Just the fact* (online). Available: http://www.aarp.org/prescriptiondrugs/facts.html.

AARP. (2001). Social Security, the facts (online). Available: http://www.aarp.org/socialsecurity/issues.home.html.

AARP Research Center (2001). *In the middle, a report on multicultural boomers coping with family and aging issues* (online). Available: http://www.aarp.org.

Ansello, E. F. (1996). Causes and theories. In L. Baumhover & S. C. Beall (Eds.), *Abuse, neglect, and exploitation of older persons* (pp. 9–27). Baltimore: Health Professions Press.

Associated Press. (2000, August 10). Inequities seen in elderly health advances. *The Daily News,* West Bend, WI, p. A9.

Axtman, K. (2001, January 23). Retirees not just after fun in sun. *The Christian Science Monitor,* pp. 1, 4.

Karen Bassuk and Janet Lessem, "Collaboration of Social Workers and Attorneys in Geriatric Community Based Organizations," *NAELA Quarterly,* National Academy of Elder Law Attorneys, Spring 2000. Reprinted with the permission by the National Academy of Elder Law Attorneys.

Beaver, M. L., & Miller, D. A. (1992). *Clinical social work practice with the elderly* (2nd ed.). Belmont, CA: Wadsworth.

Bellos, N. S., & Ruffolo, M. S. (1995). Aging: services. In R. L. Edwards (Ed.), *Encyclopedia of social work* (19th ed., Vol. 1, pp. 165–171). Washington, DC: NASW Press.

Bills tackle welfare, patients' rights. (1998, September). *NASW News.*

Caring for caregivers. (1993, summer). *The Extended Family of Family Service of Milwaukee, 12*(2), 3.

Conner, K. A. (2000). *Continuing to care.* New York: Palmer Press.

Cox, E., & Parsons, R. (1994). *Empowerment-oriented social work practice with the elderly.* Pacific Grove, CA.: Brooks/Cole.

Culhane, K. W. (2000, April). A real home. *Natural Health,* 79–81.

Denzer, S. (1999, January–February). Raising the stakes; how will you fare when Congress makes its move? *Modern Maturity,* 43–57.

Dunkel, R. E. (1987). Protective services for the aged. In A. Minahan (Ed.), *Encyclopedia of social work* (18th ed., Vol. 2, pp. 393–395). Silver Spring, MD: NASW Press.

Elderly people were abused in almost one-third of the U.S.'s nursing homes. (2001, July 31). *The Christian Science Monitor,* p. 20.

Elders' caregivers also are growing in number. (1998, November). *NASW News,* p. 11.

Eustis, N., Greenberg, J., & Patton, S. (1984). *Long term care for older persons, a policy perspective.* Monterey, CA: Brooks/Cole.

Freeman, M. S. (1998, December 2). Sharing a roof and a way of life. *The Christian Science Monitor,* pp. 11, 14–15.

Gonyea, J. G. (1994, January). The paradox of the advantaged elder and the feminization of poverty. *Social Work, 39*(1), 37.

Greene, R. R. (2000). *Social work with the aged and their families* (2nd ed.). New York: Aldine de Gruyter.

Greenstein, R., Primus, W., & Kayatin, T. (2000, revised October 10). *Poverty rate hits lowest level since 1979 as unemployment reaches a 30-year low.* Washington, DC: Center on Budget and Policy Priorities (online). Available: http://www.cbpp.org/9-26-00pov.htm.

Halverson, G. (2000, January 3). Coming to terms with long term care. *The Christian Science Monitor,* pp. 11, 14–15.

Huttman, E. (1985). *Social services for the elderly.* New York: Free Press.

Karger, H. J., & Stoesz, D. (1998). *American social welfare policy: A pluralist approach* (3rd. ed.). New York: Addison Wesley Longman.

Katz, M. B. (2001). *The price of citizenship.* New York: Metropolitan Books.

Kochman, A. (1997). Gay and lesbian elderly: Historical overview and implications for social work practice. In J. K. Quam (Ed.), *Social services for senior gay men and lesbians* (pp. 1–10). New York: Haworth Press.

Kosberg, J. I., & Nahmiash, D. (1996). Characteristics of victims and perpetrators and milieus of abuse and neglect. In L. A. Baumhover and S. C. Beall (Eds.), *Abuse, neglect, and exploitation of older persons* (pp. 31–45). Baltimore, MD: Health Professions Press.

Lampman, J. (2000, July 23). Caring for sick, prisoners learn compassion. *The Christian Science Monitor,* pp. 1, 4.

Lipman, L. (2001, August 6). There's still no agreement on Social Security's woes. *The Daily News,* West Bend WI, p. A5.

Living longer. (1999, January). *Mayo Clinic Health Letter, 17*(1), 1–3.

Maldonado, D. (1987). Aged. In A. Minahan (Ed.). *Encyclopedia of social work* (18th ed., Vol. 1, pp. 97–100). Silver Spring, MD: NASW Press.

Marks, A. (2001, May 1). In social HMOs, a model for health care reform. *The Christian Science Monitor,* 1, 4.

Mays, P. J. (1998, October 10). Grandparents caring for young children face more health woes and stress. *The Daily News,* West Bend, WI, p. A7.

Metz, P. (1997). Staff development for working with lesbian and gay elders. In J. K. Quam (Ed.), *Social services for senior gay men and lesbians* (pp. 35–45). New York: Hawthorn Press.

Mor-Barek, M. F., & Tynan, M. (1993, January). Older workers in the work place: A new challenge for occupational social work. *Social Work 38*(1), 47–50.

Mui, A. C., Choi, N. C., & Monk, A. (1998). *Long term care and ethnicity.* Westport, CT: Auburn House.

Nathanson, I. L., & Tirrito, T. T. (1998). *Gerontological social work: Theory into practice.* New York: Springer Publishing.

National Alliance for Caregiving (1998, September). *The caregiving boom: Baby boomer women giving care* (online). Available: http://www.caregivers.org.

Pierce, C., Gleason-Wynn, P., & Miller, M. G. (2001). Social work and the law: A model for implementing social services in the law office. *Journal of Gerontological Social Work, 34*(3), 61–71.

Popple, P. R., & Leighninger, L. L. (1999). *Social work, social welfare, and American society.* Boston: Allyn & Bacon.

Rosengarten, L. (2000). *Social work in geriatric home health care.* New York: The Hayworth Press.

Salamon, M. (1986). Mind/body health in practice, taking care of the caregivers. *Mindbody Health Newsletter, 7*(3), 3.

Segal, E., & Brzuzy, S. (1998). *Social welfare policy, programs, and practice.* Itasca, IL: Peacock Publishers.

Sobel, D. (1998). Mind/body health in practice, taking care of the caregivers. *Mindbody Health Newsletter, 7*(3), 3.

Social Security, the facts (2001) (online). Available: http://www.aarp.org/socialsecurity/issues/home.html.

Social work with older people: Understanding diversity (1994). Washington, DC: NASW Press.

Spaid, E. L. (1996, November 4). Florida leads states in effort to provide more elder care. *The Christian Science Monitor,* p. 3.

Stevens, D. G. (2001, May 23). Elderly help fill adoption gap. *The Daily News,* West Bend, WI, p. A5.

Terry, S. (2001, June 18). Seasonal seniors. *The Christian Science Monitor,* pp. 15, 18–20.

The world's population, now at 6.1 billion, will peak at 9 billion over the next 70 years. (2001, August 2). *The Christian Science Monitor,* p. 20.

Torres-Gil, F. M., & Puccinelli, M. A. (1995). Aging: Public policy issues and trends. In R. L. Edwards (Ed.), *Encyclopedia of social work* (19th ed., Vol. 1, pp. 159–164). Washington, DC: NASW Press.

Weaver, P. (2000, June). Going hungry: It still happens. *The States, Regional News of Interest to AARP Members,* pp. 9–11.

FOR FURTHER READING

Beaver, M. L., & Miller, D. A. (1992). *Clinical social work practice with the elderly* (2nd ed). Belmont, CA: Wadsworth.

Intended primarily for social work practitioners, this book is packed with information pertaining not only to clinical aspects of working with the elderly but also to social welfare policy factors that have an impact on the elderly and those who work with them. The book is organized so that it discusses intervention on primary, secondary, and tertiary levels.

Cox, E. O., & Parsons, R. J. (1994). *Empowerment-oriented social work practice with the elderly.* Pacific Grove, CA: Brooks/Cole.

This book offers an empowerment model for working with older adults. Part I provides the framework, Part II describes empowerment-oriented interventions appropriate for use at various levels, and Part III provides selected practice examples. The book also provides a wealth of demographic and policy information that is useful in working with the elderly.

Greene, R. R. (2000). *Social work with the aged and their families* (2nd ed.). New York: Aldine de Gruyter.

This well-written book provides a model for implementing comprehensive assessments and social work interventions based on a clinical understanding of older adults within a family and social systems perspective. The first part of the book focuses on assessment issues and processes, and the second part focuses on intervention and treatment.

Morris, R., Caro, F. G., & Hansan, J. E. (Ed.). (1998). *Personal assistance: The future of home care.* Baltimore: The Johns Hopkins University Press.

Not limited to a discussion of home care needs of older adults, but rather of all people with disabilities who require assistance, this interesting volume provides a historical background for home care, a discussion of family roles in providing personal assistance, roles for both volunteers and professionals, financial aspects of home care, assistive devices, and linkages between home care and medical services.

Mui, A. C., Choi, N. G., and Monk, A. (1998). *Long term care and ethnicity*. Westport, CT: Auburn House.

Mui and colleagues provide valuable information regarding differences in long-term care needs and utilization of services by white, African American, and Hispanic elders. Within the Hispanic populations, differences are documented among Mexican American, Cuban American, and Puerto Rican elders. Ethnicity, informal caregiving services, and caregiver burdens are discussed.

Nathanson, I. L., & Tirrito, T. T. (1998). *Gerontological social work: Theory into practice*. New York: Springer Publishing Company.

This book provides an integrative model for social work with older adults. Practice methods for work with individuals constitute the primary focus. The book also presents an overview of special needs of older adults and discusses the formal social service network. Issues involving legal, religious, work, and political environments are presented.

Quam, J. K. (Ed.). (1997). *Social services for senior gay men and lesbians*. New York: Haworth Press.

This slim volume contains a valuable anthology of articles reviewing various aspects of social service needs and actual service utilization by gay and lesbian older adults. The book begins with a historical overview, proceeds to examine programs and services, provides research data about and treatment of gay elders, and concludes with comprehensive case studies.

Rosengarten, L. (2000). *Social work in geriatric home health care*. New York: The Hayworth Press.

This idea-packed little book describes how a professional social worker drew on traditional social work values, knowledge, and skills to create a new model of home health care for the sick and frail elderly in the city of New York. The author shifts services from a nursing-oriented perspective to one that is more consumer-oriented, cooperation-based, and democratic.

CHAPTER 12

Criminal Justice Settings

OUTLINE

ALAN MARTIN

Alan Martin slumped in his chair and sighed. Then he picked up the file again. Another new case had just been added to his already overloaded caseload. You're letting yourself burn out, he thought. Then, reminding himself that he was just tired but he could go home soon, he picked up the telephone and dialed the number he had found in Brian Cook's folder. He talked briefly with Brian's mother, Laura Cook, scheduling an office appointment with Brian for Friday. The file showed that Brian had been released on parole from the state juvenile corrections center just five days ago. He had served two years of a four-year sentence for selling illicit drugs. He had apparently been a model prisoner.

The telephone rang and Alan reached for his notepad . . . an emergency; the police had just arrested another of his clients, a 13-year-old, for selling cocaine at the bus stop across the street from a school. There had been a scuffle, weapons were involved; one officer and the 13-year-old were badly injured and being transported to the hospital by ambulance. A picture of 13-year-old Ramon flashed through his mind: a bright, defiant, angry kid whose father died six months ago. Without hesitation Alan replied to the voice on the phone: "I'll be at the hospital in 10 minutes." It was very late when Alan finally got home that night.

Alan Martin was an experienced BSW social worker who had worked in the criminal justice field for six years now, initially in adult probation and parole and, for the past six months, in Youth Correctional Services. Alan was respected by his colleagues, police, and the judges. Among his clients he was viewed as tough, demanding, and fair. Once actively involved with NASW and careful to sustain continued professional learning activities, Alan had gradually drifted away from identification with his profession and, in fact, had forgotten to renew his NASW professional membership. Alan felt vaguely unsettled with his life and his work.

On Friday, minutes before Brian Cook's scheduled appointment, Alan pulled out his file. Brian's 14-year-old face stared back from the photo taken at the time of his arrest two years ago. This image was quite a contrast to the older-looking, broad-shouldered, passive but mistrustful person he had met at the correctional facility two weeks ago. Kids who weren't criminals before they arrived at that place were quite likely to be so by the time they were released, Alan thought as he snapped the file closed and went out to get Brian from the drab, vaguely filthy waiting room.

Their first session in Alan's office included a review of the parole contract. Brian's cool, almost sullen expression was annoying. Alan found himself talking loudly, lecturing Brian about the consequences of failure to abide by the terms of the contract. He told Brian about the procedure for providing a urinalysis to check for drugs each time he came in. He was angered by Brian's comment: "So, you don't trust me. I told you I don't do drugs." "No, I don't trust you," he responded, using the very words he didn't like but often heard other parole officers use. Further annoyed with himself for having said this, Alan changed the subject to school. Brian said that he had enrolled and started attending classes this week but hated the school. Alan ignored this, instead warning Brian about associating with anyone related to his conviction, especially Shari, the girl for whom he had purchased drugs.

After Brian left the office Alan returned the telephone call that had come in from Ramon's mother. She was at the hospital; Ramon was not doing well but she couldn't understand the doctor's explanation about what was happening to him. Alan decided to stop by the hospital during his lunch break. The expression of the policeman guarding the room told Alan that all was not well. One look at Ramon's face, contorted with pain and discolored by jaundice, confirmed that Ramon was in serious condition. Alan beckoned Ramon's mother to follow him. Tearfully she told him that in her heart she did not think that Ramon was going to live. She didn't know what was wrong; she was terrified. Alan searched frantically for a nurse, finally finding one who would talk with them. The nurse was dignified but cold. Ramon had developed an infection related to the gunshot wound in his abdomen. He was not responding to antibiotics. His lab reports this morning were very bad. She certainly didn't know why these teenage criminals thought they could get away with fooling around with guns. As she turned to leave, Alan heard her say, "Sometimes they have to pay the price." Struck to the core by her remark and instantly, painfully aware of the negative attitudes he had been developing, he turned to Ramon's mother, hugging her to defend her from the added pain of the nurse's remark. He took her to a quiet corner, explained what the nurse had said about the seriousness of the infection, and sat with her for a time while she cried. Alan left when Mrs. Perez's sister arrived. That night Ramon died.

Thoughts about Ramon's tragic death and the judgmental attitude of the nurse remained with Alan for weeks. Attending Ramon's funeral service both refreshed him spiritually and strengthened his determination to fight for real justice, a justice built on dignity and respect for people, not on retribution and various prejudices. Alan made time at night to do a bit of reading—some light short stories that were delightful and refreshing and some professional articles from social work journals. Rereading the NASW Code of Ethics renewed Alan's awareness that as a professional person he was responsible for the quality of his own practice. In his work with his clients Alan consciously struggled to become more self-aware and more attuned to the reality of their lives.

On the day that Brian Cook was scheduled to see him again, Alan received a report from the school indicating that Brian was not attending classes. This was a violation of his parole contract, and it also raised questions about what he was doing with his time. Was he back into the drug scene again? Alan confronted Brian with all of this. To his annoyance, Brian insisted that he was attending school. Brian added: "I know you won't believe me about this. You don't believe anything that I say." Alan showed him the report, but Brian still insisted that he was attending school even though he hated it. Then, despite the report, Alan decided to suspend his disbelief until he and Brian could check out the report together. Brian was quite surprised when Alan proposed this but readily agreed to wait while Alan met with his next client. Then they drove to the school in Alan's car.

On the drive Alan encouraged Brian to talk about his classes. By the time they reached the school it seemed more and more likely that Brian really had attended at least some of his classes. They were fortunate in being able to meet briefly with two of Brian's teachers, who affirmed that Brian had indeed been in class. Both gave Brian suggestions about how to improve his work. When Alan presented their case to the school attendance clerk, she reviewed her records and found that a mistake had been made.

Back in the car, Brian smiled for the first time. He said, "This time truth was on my side." Alan agreed. Suddenly Brian's expression changed. He said, "I can understand better now about truth. . . . I was lied to and I actually did lie to you, too." He explained that Shari had promised him when he was convicted that she would be true to him while he was away. He counted on that. Since getting out he had been trying to contact her but she wasn't returning his phone calls. Today he found out that she was pregnant and due to have a baby shortly. So he had been lied to. And he had lied to Alan, too, when he agreed not to contact Shari. When Brian looked up at Alan, there was pain in his eyes. It was quiet in the car for several minutes; Alan let the silence hang in the air unbroken, feeling Brian's pain. Then he said, "OK, Brian let's start over now . . . and we'll begin by trusting each other."

COMPONENTS OF THE CRIMINAL JUSTICE SYSTEM

Alan Martin, the social worker in the chapter case study, was experienced in the adult as well as juvenile corrections systems. In his practice Alan Martin worked with all of the subsystems of the criminal justice system. Sometimes referred to as the three Cs (cops, courts, and corrections), the criminal justice system in the United States grew out of the system brought to this country by colonists from England. Over time it developed into a complex and somewhat fragmented system, with separate subunits that did not always interact effectively. It acquired a strange and somewhat inconsistent combination of goals: to punish, to deter crime, to rehabilitate, and to remove criminals from society. Today social workers are engaged in all three areas of the U.S. criminal justice system.

Specific laws and regulations pertain to each of the criminal justice system areas. Social workers can expect to learn the laws and regulations that guide the area of the criminal justice system in which they work. A police social worker will develop an understanding of arrest procedures, statutory rape laws, and laws pertaining to child and spouse abuse. A social worker serving as a parole agent, such as Alan Martin in the case study, will become familiar with the administrative law that defines the responsibilities of probation and parole agents, with parole contracts, and with revocation procedures.

Two terms that will be used in the remainder of this chapter, and that should be understood by informed citizens, need further definition: *misdemeanor* and *felony*. A **misdemeanor** is a relatively minor offense but certainly more serious than a misdeed; it is punishable by fines, probation, or a relatively brief jail or prison sentence unless taken to extreme or done repeatedly. A **felony** is a serious crime. Murder, rape, and armed burglary are felonies, while defacing public property is a misdemeanor. Assault could be a misdemeanor, while aggravated assault (involving deadly force or intent to rob, kill, or rape) would be considered a felony. Under federal law and also in many states, the consequence of a felony is a prison sentence of one or more years; the most extreme penalty for a felony is the death penalty. Professional people, such as social workers, may be prohibited from being licensed or certified to practice in their state if they have a criminal record.

Two additional terms, *probation* and *parole,* were encountered in the Alan Martin case study, and these terms will be used frequently in this chapter. It is important to understand the differences between the two. **Probation** is a sentence, following conviction for a crime, in which the offender is ordered to undergo supervision for a prescribed period of time instead of serving that time in prison. The supervision is provided by a court-designated probation officer who may be a social worker. **Parole** is defined as "the release of a prisoner before completion of full sentence because of good conduct in prison, promised good conduct, and continued supervision by an officer of the legal system (often a social worker) once out of prison" (Barker, 1999, p. 350). Note that the person who has been paroled has served time in prison; probation normally does not require prior imprisonment.

Let us now examine the three major components of the criminal justice system in the United States and the interesting ways in which social work as a profession has found a niche in each of these areas.

Law Enforcement

When we speak of law enforcement, we are essentially referring to the police. The police, as law enforcement officers, comprise the first of the three areas of the criminal justice system. What exactly is the role of the police? It is much broader than most citizens realize.

Police are responsible for responding to citizens' complaints and for questioning and apprehending persons. Before charging a person with a crime, however, police have considerable decision-making responsibility. Exhibit 1, for example, illustrates the decisions made by police in 1999 for the juvenile offenders that they took into custody. Note that more than two-thirds of these youths were turned over to the juvenile courts, 22.5 percent were handled within the police department and released, and 6.4 percent were referred to criminal or adult courts; this compares with 50.8 percent of juveniles referred to juvenile courts, 45 percent handled within the police department and released, and 1.3 percent referred to criminal or adult courts in 1972 (Maguire & Pastore, 2001, Table 4.26). Police decide whether a charge is warranted or another alternative might be considered. Current law determines the officer's decision. Prevailing public sentiment or the political climate might also be influential. Often it is a matter of chance, of visibility (as in a "high-crime" neighborhood that is under greater scrutiny than other areas), or of past behavior that determines whether a violation of the law even results in contact with the police. Shopkeepers, school authorities, and neighbors may be more prone to call the police in some parts of the city or community than in others.

In addition to responding to criminal complaints, police are also responsible for keeping the peace. In this role they encounter families in crisis, domestic violence, suicidal behavior, and substance abuse. One of the frustrations of police officers is that they receive little recognition by the community or even by the police system itself for the human services they routinely provide.

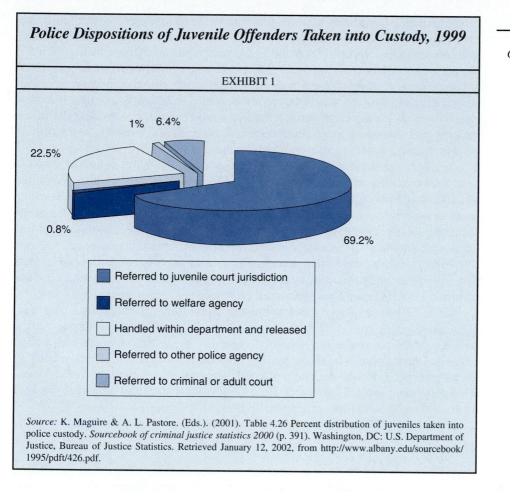

Police Dispositions of Juvenile Offenders Taken into Custody, 1999

EXHIBIT 1

1% 6.4%

22.5%

0.8%

69.2%

- ■ Referred to juvenile court jurisdiction
- ■ Referred to welfare agency
- □ Handled within department and released
- ■ Referred to other police agency
- ■ Referred to criminal or adult court

Source: K. Maguire & A. L. Pastore. (Eds.). (2001). Table 4.26 Percent distribution of juveniles taken into police custody. *Sourcebook of criminal justice statistics 2000* (p. 391). Washington, DC: U.S. Department of Justice, Bureau of Justice Statistics. Retrieved January 12, 2002, from http://www.albany.edu/sourcebook/ 1995/pdft/426.pdf.

Police social work is the practice of social work within police departments, courthouses, or in jails. Police social work is still a relatively underdeveloped area of social work practice, but it appears to be an expanding area of the profession. Police and social workers share a common concern about personal and family crisis situations. A considerable portion of police calls is of a social service nature, for people are most likely to call the police when they don't know where else to turn for help. In communities where police social workers are available, dispositions of cases frequently results in redirection from the criminal justice to the social service system.

When social workers were first employed by police departments, they were assigned to youth services. Their tasks included resolution of parent–child conflicts; referral of children to child guidance or child psychiatric clinics; assessment of child abuse, neglect, and abandonment situations; and a variety of crisis roles. Police social workers have proven their value in domestic dispute situations. Since these are some of the most dangerous cases for police, police social workers' ability to ease the tension in such situations, as well as to assess and intervene, has impressed police departments.

Nonetheless, conflicts of roles and values remain sources of difficulty between police and social workers. Police did not initially welcome "interference" from police social workers. Over the years, police had found satisfaction in helping persons in crisis, and they were not always eager to relinquish this role. Even today, police and social workers may occasionally differ on the appropriate disposition of a case, or they may disagree about who has authority to make the decision. Police social workers continue to have concern about maintaining their own integrity and sustaining their values, especially the values of dignity and worth of all persons and clients' rights to self-determination.

In recent years police social workers' responsibilities have expanded. Assessment and counseling are increasingly provided for police officers when the pressures associated with police work threaten to create mental or physical health problems or result in inability to make rational judgments in tense situations. Police officers are vulnerable to the same kind of posttraumatic stress that other people experience following encounters with violence, disasters, or other life-threatening events.

Police social workers are not confined to desks in police departments. In fact, they are increasingly involved in crime prevention work in the community. Often, as in the DARE (Drug Abuse Resistance) Program, a team consisting of a social worker and a police officer seeks to prevent crime through educational programs provided to youth groups, in the schools, or to civic associations. Today, suburban police systems are in the forefront of community organization work, with police personnel participating in and often leading community action efforts related to crime prevention, the development of youth services, and even the reform of mental commitment laws. Their professional education makes police social workers especially well suited for such responsibilities.

The Courts

Courts exist at the federal, state, and local levels, and they range from municipal courts to the highest court in the land, the U.S. Supreme Court. Courts have two primary functions: civil and criminal. Civil functions deal with the rights of private citizens and may result in fines or monetary damages. Criminal functions involve determination of guilt or innocence; punishment such as a prison sentence may result. In the criminal court system, a case begins with an arrest.

Some persons may have charges against them dropped, and therefore they discontinue their involvement in the criminal justice system. In fact, at each step along the way—from the point of police questioning through arrest, charging, and sentencing—a certain percentage of persons exit the system. Only a fraction of those initially detained for questioning are actually found guilty and incarcerated. In this "criminal justice funnel," the top of the funnel represents all the crimes that have been committed. The people who exit the system along the way are found in the slanting sides of the funnel. At the bottom of the funnel are those persons actually prosecuted and sent to prison—a mere 3 percent (Mauer, 1994). As research studies described later in this chapter suggest, racial biases may be among the factors that influence decisions at each step from questioning through incarceration.

Social workers are increasingly found in the courts of America, where they serve in several interesting ways. One role for social workers is work with and on behalf of victims of crime. Social workers were among the pioneers of victim/witness programs. These programs, often housed in the local district attorney's office, assist people who are intimidated by the legal process. Programs to help battered women through the court system were among the first to emerge. Today social workers assist victims of domestic abuse to obtain restraining or harassment no-contact orders, and they serve as client advocates in the courts. Persons who are injured in crimes are also provided services that emphasize compassion, affirmation, and emotional support.

Testifying in court is a responsibility for social workers in child and family services, corrections, and many other fields. NASW has a variety of resources that help to prepare social workers, beginning with how to deal with receipt of a **subpoena** (an order to appear in court on a specified date). The NASW's guidelines for social workers who receive a subpoena describe the social worker's and client's rights, and recommendations are made about sources of legal assistance for social workers (Landers, 1997). Guidelines have also been written by NASW attorneys to assist social workers with court testimony, especially when they serve the court as expert witnesses (Take the stand, 1998). In addition, NASW's training videos improve social workers' skill in providing court testimony; these are all available through the annual NASW publications catalog.

Another role for social workers in the court system is that of work on behalf of the court in conducting a **presentence investigation.** If a case goes to court and the offender is convicted, a presentence investigation may be requested by the judge. This is more likely to occur if imprisonment in excess of one year is probable. Presentence investigations are conducted by probation officers, many of whom are social workers (in some jurisdictions, nearly all probation workers are social workers); the investigations typically involve both office and home visits with family members, the client, and other collaborative sources. The report is likely to be very detailed and comprehensive, including a social history, descriptions of the offender's home and work environment, education and employment, and physical or mental health problems, as well as an identification of existing social supports. The concluding recommendation often evaluates "the merits and risks of keeping an offender in the community. Recently this has been especially important in cases involving the physical and sexual abuse of children, where the needs of the victim constitute a major factor in the presentence investigation" (Isenstadt, 1995, p. 71).

When the court decides to sentence a convicted person, the result will be a jail term, probation, or imprisonment. Note that there are significant differences between jail and prison. A **jail** is a correctional facility used for short sentences or for detaining persons while they await a court hearing. A **prison** is used for lengthier sentences, generally for a number of years. In passing sentence, judges are required to abide by the legal code, which provides parameters for length of imprisonment; therefore, judges' options are somewhat limited.

In recent years, courts have used various alternatives to prison. They are less costly than prison and they are a good deal more humane than a prison sentence. Any alternative program mandated by the court is usually attached to a sentence of probation. **Community-service sentencing** is an alternative that has come into use in many areas. It usually requires the offender to work without pay in a private or governmental human service organization for a specified period of time. **Restitution** programs require that offenders, adult as well as juvenile offenders, compensate their victims (usually monetarily) for the losses suffered as a result of the criminal offense. Restitution is most frequently used in conjunction with property crimes, which are the most prevalent of all crimes committed (Butts, 1995). It has often been the experience of social workers that the monetary payment made by the offender has less long-range meaning than the experience of facing the victim, explaining the offense, and seeking to restore the loss.

The Correctional System

The **correctional system** is that part of the criminal justice system that uses imprisonment, probation, parole, and various alternatives to change the behaviors of persons convicted of crime. The two major components of the correctional system in the United States are prisons and community-based programs. Each of the 50 states has its own correctional system with varying structures, sanctions, and administrative laws. The federal government has the Bureau of Prisons, which operates the federal prison system and is a component of the U.S. Department of Justice, and a federal probation system operated by the courts. In addition, the Department of Defense maintains military prisons. States have their own correctional systems; at the local level, some counties and cities also operate correctional facilities and probation departments. There is considerable variety of organizational structures as well as weak linkages among these many systems.

Prisons   Across jurisdictional systems, prisons tend to be classified as minimum-, medium-, and maximum-security facilities. Until recently, all prisons were owned and administered by governmental bodies, but private enterprise has created a very profitable prison industry in some parts of the country. There has been considerable construction of new prisons, yet they tend to be extremely overcrowded, housing populations in excess of their capacity day in and day out. Juvenile facilities are separate from prisons for adults and are often located in newer structures. They too are seriously overcrowded, presenting the same health, safety, and security problems found in adult facilities. Smaller, community-based correctional programs serve as prerelease centers, halfway houses, and group homes.

The various jurisdictions have different procedures for assigning persons to correctional facilities. Often newly sentenced persons are observed in specially designated reception facilities for several weeks while vocational and psychological testing is done to help select the most appropriate prison facility. Social workers participate in the evaluation procedure, gathering social-history data or supplementing information already available if a presentence investigation was done.

With the burgeoning rate of imprisonment of women (see Exhibit 2), the classification of women prisoners is receiving increased attention. Farr, for example, notes that the same classification system tends to be used for both male and female prisoners, yet research demonstrates that women prisoners are significantly less of a threat to other inmates or to the outside community, should they escape. Instead of basing the system on risk, Farr calls for a prison classification system for women based on need. She recommends substance abuse treatment, obstetric and gynecological health care, improving the connections between women and their children, instituting parenting skills training, and treatment for the mental disorders that appear to be more prevalent among women prisoners (Farr, 2000).

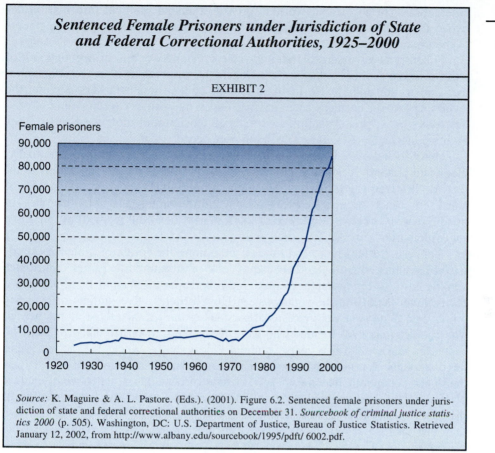

Sentenced Female Prisoners under Jurisdiction of State and Federal Correctional Authorities, 1925–2000

EXHIBIT 2

Female prisoners

Source: K. Maguire & A. L. Pastore. (Eds.). (2001). Figure 6.2. Sentenced female prisoners under jurisdiction of state and federal correctional authorities on December 31. *Sourcebook of criminal justice statistics 2000* (p. 505). Washington, DC: U.S. Department of Justice, Bureau of Justice Statistics. Retrieved January 12, 2002, from http://www.albany.edu/sourcebook/1995/pdft/ 6002.pdf.

Prison social workers are prisoners' links to their home community. In women's prisons, for example, it is often the prison social worker who communicates with the foster care agency when children have been placed in care pending the mother's release from prison. Family members often have great difficulty accepting the imprisonment. Feelings of anger, abandonment, fear, and denial have to be worked with. Just as families need to make very difficult adjustments when a member is imprisoned, other social, emotional, and economic adjustments are required when release from prison is anticipated. It would be wonderful if all prisons had social workers with sufficient time to provide these services. The reality is that some prisons have no social work staff at all, and other prisons have so few social workers that staff must carefully prioritize their tasks.

Although social workers are members of the prison staff, they do serve as communication facilitators between inmates and other prison staff. As advocates for prisoners, social workers attempt to secure resources, such as access to scarce educational or vocational programs. Social workers advocate with prison administrators for changes in policies or procedures affecting the inmate population. They also promote an exchange of information between families of inmates (especially children in foster care) and the prisoners. During medical emergencies, prison social workers provide updated medical information between family members and prisoners and, if appropriate, with other segments of the prison community.

Prison riots have demonstrated the role of social workers in negotiation. Social workers have been selected by prisoners to present their issues to administrators and to the outside world. At the same time, social workers become the spokespersons for hostages taken in riots. Given the serious overcrowding of prisons today, most prison facilities experience tension and violence almost daily. Fighting between prisoners is a common occurrence.

Hans Toch's 1977 description of the prison environment remains true today: "Jails and prisons . . . have a climate of violence which has no free-world counterpart. Inmates are terrorized by other inmates, and spend years in fear of harm. . . . Such fears cause problems beyond the immediately obvious ones. In prison, fear is a stigma of weakness, and it marks men [and women] as fair game for exploitation" (p. 53).

Robbery, assault, rape, and murder are among the forms of violence experienced by inmates. Boredom because of lack of structured activities contributes significantly. In his research Wooldredge found that 20 percent of inmates in a correctional facility in the southwestern United States were victims of property crime, and 14 percent were victims of personal crime within a three-month period. The characteristics of inmates who were most likely to inflict violence included sentences longer than five years; minimal time spent in educational activities but large amounts of time watching television; and visits from family or friends less than once per month. The most likely victims of personal violence were younger prisoners who had prior histories of incarceration, spent few hours weekly in prison recreational programs, had few close friends in the facility, and had less than one visitor per month. Wooldredge recommended closer surveillance of the prisoners most likely to be victimized (the younger prisoners) and those most likely to perpetrate injury (those with sentences longer than five years). He strongly emphasized educational programming, developing recreational programs beyond television, placement of prisoners in facilities close to home, and increased efforts to facilitate visitation of prisoners (1994).

Violence in prisons is not limited to inmate-inflicted abuse, nor is it only a function of modern times. Inmates of some of the early prison facilities were forced to work as servants in the homes of wardens, where many abuses were suffered, including beatings and death for disobedience. Female prisoners have always been subject to sexual abuse. Lawsuits filed on their behalf and public investigations into such abuses have resulted in the implementation of procedures that require a formal hearing and response to the complaints of inmates in correctional facilities, but this has not eliminated exploitation or violence.

The absence of heterosexual outlets encourages same-sex relationships in prisons and jails. These relationships may provide some level of comfort and closeness, but they may also produce jealousies, heated altercations, and acts of reprisal for unfaithfulness. Especially in prisons that are overcrowded, rape also occurs, sometimes with extensive physical injuries.

In prison and jail facilities social workers seek to reduce violence by building bridges between inmates and staff, by helping prisoners develop or enhance their sense of self-worth, and by reducing the inmates' sense of powerlessness. In their practice with prisoners, social workers often focus on creating behavioral change, seeking to improve problem-solving skills and to apply these skills in day-to-day institutional decision making. Behavior rehearsal and role-playing are used to teach new behaviors or to modify existing actions. Educational and skill-building programs are implemented. Alcohol and substance abuse group treatment is provided for persons with problems in these areas. Techniques including reality therapy, behavior modification, transactional analysis, and educational programs are used, depending on the social worker's level of skill and on inmates' needs.

Community-Based Corrections   Community-based corrections are programs that provide an alternative to incarceration. Probation and parole, the major community-based programs, require ongoing supervision until the original sentence is concluded. The person providing that supervision is generally referred to as a parole (or probation) agent or officer. Preferences regarding the use of "agent" or "officer" vary among the many federal, state, county, and city jurisdictions; we will use "agent." Very often, although not always, the probation or parole agent is a BSW or MSW social worker. The federal system specifies a minimum of a bachelor's degree in social work, criminology, psychology, sociology, or law, and states tend to require similar credentials (Allen, 1995).

While parole provides for the early release of a prisoner from a penal institution, probation permits the offender to avoid imprisonment, remaining in the community to serve her or his sentence. Both parole and probation are conditional; that is, if the terms of the probation or parole agreement are violated, the offender may be subject to **revocation** (may be returned to prison for the remainder of the sentence). The terms of the agreement are identified in a contract signed by the client and the agent. A typical contract is shown in Exhibit 3. Note that space is provided for specific terms for the individual client. Exhibit 4 illustrates a set of specific terms that might be used with someone convicted of a sex offense.

Helping the person to meet the terms of the probation or parole agreement is a key function of the social worker. In truth, the client's life is subject to almost continuous scrutiny by the social worker. Developing a relationship of trust with a corrections client is not always easy. It requires skill and commitment from the social worker.

Alan Martin, the social worker in the case study, carried many of the responsibilities of both parole agent and probation agent. As a professional social worker in the role of parole agent, Alan Martin sought to apply the knowledge, values, and skills that he had learned while in college. He used the same problem-solving steps cited in Chapter 1, a process that underpins all generalist social work practice. If Brian Cook had been sentenced by the judge to probation instead of prison, Alan Martin might have been assigned as his probation agent. Since the role of the probation agent is very similar to that of the parole agent, Alan would have engaged Brian in the same problem-solving work that was done during Brian's parole.

The correctional system requires the agent, in this case Alan Martin, to assist the client in meeting the terms of the probation agreement. The same contract form, citing the very same terms, may be used for both probation and parole, as is the case with the contract shown in Exhibit 3. Some correctional systems, however, use separate forms. The probation client generally has not left his or her

Probation/Parole Rules

EXHIBIT 3

DEPARTMENT OF CORRECTIONS
Division of Community Corrections
DOC-10 (Rev. 2/01)

Probation/Parole Rules

WISCONSIN
Administrative Code
Chapter DOC 328 & 332
Federal Law
42 U.S.C. ss 290DD-3, 290ee-3
Federal Regulation
42 C.F.R. Part 2

OFFENDER NAME

DOC NUMBER

Notice: If you are on parole and sentenced for crimes committed on or after June 1, 1984, or have chosen to have the new Good Time Law apply to your case and you violate these rules, the highest possible parole violator sentence will be the total sentence less time already served in prison or jail in connection with the offense.

As established by Administrative Rule DOC 328.11, you have an opportunity for administrative review of certain types of decision through the offender complaint process.

The following rules are in addition to any court-ordered conditions. Your probation or parole may be revoked if you do not comply with any of your court-ordered conditions or if you violate any of the following rules.

1. You shall avoid all conduct which is in violation of federal or state statute, municipal or county ordinances, tribal law or which is not in the best interest of the public welfare or your rehabilitation. Some rules listed below are covered under this rule as conduct contrary to law and are listed for particular attention.
2. You shall report all arrests or police contact to your agent within 72 hours.
3. You shall make every effort to accept the opportunities and counseling offered by supervision.

   The confidentiality of drug and alcohol treatment records is protected by Federal laws and regulations. Generally programs you are involved in may not say to a person outside the Department of Correction that an offender is attending the program, or disclose any information identifying him/her as a drug/alcohol abuser unless: 1) You consent in writing; or 2) The disclosure is allowed by a court order; or 3) The disclosure is made to medical personnel in a medical emergency or to a qualified personnel for research, audit, or program evaluation; or 4) You commit or threaten to commit a crime either at the program or against any person who works for the program. Programs that contract with the Wisconsin Department of Corrections can release information to Wisconsin Department of Corrections staff.

   Violation of the Federal law and regulations by a program is a crime. These regulations do not protect any information about suspected child abuse or neglect from being reported under state law to appropriate authorities.

   Refusal to sign the consent for releasing information, including placement for treatment, shall be considered a refusal of the program.
4. You shall inform your agent of your whereabouts and activities as he/she directs.
5. You shall submit a written report monthly and any other such relevant information as directed by your agent.
6. You shall make yourself available for searches or tests ordered by your agent including but not limited to urinalysis, breathalyzer, DNA collection and blood samples or search of residence or any property under your control.
7. You shall not change residence or employment unless you get approval in advance from your agent, or in the case of emergency, notify your agent of the change within 72 hours.
8. You shall not leave the State of Wisconsin unless you get approval and a travel permit in advance from your agent.
9. You shall not purchase, trade, sell or operate a motor vehicle unless you get approval in advance from your agent.
10. You shall not borrow money or purchase on credit unless you get approval in advance from your agent.
11. You shall pay monthly supervision fees as directed by your agent in accordance with Wis. Stats. s.304.073 or s.304.074, DOC Administrative Rule Chapter 328.043 to 328.046 and shall comply with any department and/or vendor procedures regarding payment of fees.
12. You shall not purchase, possess, own or carry any firearms or any weapon unless you get approval in advance from your agent. Your agent may not grant permission to carry a firearm if you are prohibited from possessing a firearm under Wis. Stat. s.941.29, Wisconsin Act 71, the Federal Gun Control Act (GCA), or any other state or federal law.
13. You shall not, as a convicted felon, and until you have successfully completed the terms and conditions of your sentence, vote in any federal, state or local election as outlined in Wisconsin Statutes s.6.03(1)(b).
14. You shall abide by all rules of any detention or correctional facility in which you may be confined.
15. You shall provide true and correct information verbally and in writing, in response to inquiries by the agent.
16. You shall report to your agent as directed for scheduled and unscheduled appointments.
17. You shall submit to the polygraph (lie detector) examination process as directed by your agent in accordance with Wisconsin Administrative Code 332.15.
18. You shall pay fees for the polygraph (lie detector) examination process as directed by your agent in accordance with Wisconsin Administrative Code 332.17(5) and 332.18 and shall comply with any required Wisconsin Department of Correction procedures regarding payment of fees.
19. You shall follow any specific rules that may be issued by an agent to achieve the goals and objectives of your supervision. The rules may be modified at any time, as appropriate. The specific rules imposed at this time are stated below. You shall place your initial at the end of each specific rule to show you have read the rule.

I have reviewed and explained these rules to the offender.		I have received a copy of these rules.	
AGENT SIGNATURE	AREA NUMBER	OFFENDER SIGNATURE	DATE SIGNED

Source: Provided by Peggy Kendrigan, State of Wisconsin Department of Corrections, Division of Community Corrections. (2001). Wisconsin Administrative Code. Madison, WI.

EXHIBIT 4

DEPARTMENT OF CORRECTIONS
Division of Community Corrections
DOC-10SO (4/01)

Standard Sex Offender Rules

WISCONSIN
Administrative Code
Chapter DOC 301, 328 & 332
Federal Law
42 U.S.C. ss 290DD-3, 290ee-3
Federal Regulation
42 C.F.R. Part 2

OFFENDER NAME

DOC NUMBER

Notice: If you are on parole and sentenced for crimes committed on or after June 1, 1984, or have chosen to have the new Good Time Law apply to your case and you violate these rules, the highest possible parole violator sentence will be the total sentence less time already served in prison or jail in connection with the offense.

As established by Administrative Rule DOC 328.11, you have an opportunity for administrative review of certain types of decision through the offender complaint process.

The following rules are in addition to any court-ordered conditions. Your probation or parole may be revoked if you do not comply with any of your court-ordered conditions or if you violate any of the following rules.

1. You shall have no contact with _____ nor any prior victims of your offenses nor their family members without prior agent approval. This includes face-to-face, telephone, mail, electronic, third party, or "drive by" contact.
2. You shall have no contact with anyone under the age of 18 without prior agent approval and unless accompanied by an adult sober chaperone approved by your agent. This includes face-to-face, telephone, mail, electronic, third party, or "drive by" contact.
3. You shall not establish, pursue, nor maintain any dating and/or romantic and/or sexual relationship without prior agent approval.
4. You shall fully cooperate with, participate in, and successfully complete all evaluations, counseling, and treatment as required by your agent, including but not limited to sex offender programming. "Successful completion" shall be determined by your agent and treatment provider(s).
5. You shall not reside nor "stay" overnight in any place other than a pre-approved residence without prior agent approval. "Overnight" is defined as the daily period of time between the hours of _____ p.m. and _____ a.m. unless redefined by your agent in advance.
6. You shall permit no person to reside nor stay in your designated residence between the hours of _____ p.m. and _____ a.m. without prior agent approval.
7. You shall not possess, consume, nor use any controlled substance nor possess any drug paraphernalia without a current prescription from a physician from whom you are receiving medical treatment. Verification must be provided to your agent as directed.
8. You shall not possess nor view any sexually explicit material—visual, auditory, nor computer-generated—without prior agent approval.
9. You shall seek, obtain, and maintain employment as directed by your agent. You shall obtain agent approval before accepting any offer of employment and prior to beginning any volunteer work.
10. You shall not purchase, own, nor manage any residential rental properties without prior agent approval.
11. You shall fully comply with all sex offender registry requirements as applicable and directed by your agent and/or required by statute. You shall immediately respond to all correspondence from the Sex Offender Registry Program.
12. You shall fully comply with Wisconsin Statute 165.76 requiring a biological specimen to be submitted to the State Crime Lab for DNA testing as applicable and as directed by your agent.
13. You shall pay all court ordered financial obligations and treatment co-payments as directed by your agent in accordance with your established payment plan.
14. You shall not purchase, possess, nor use a computer, software, hardware, nor modem without prior agent approval.

I have reviewed and explained these rules to the offender.		I have received a copy of these rules.	
AGENT SIGNATURE	AREA NUMBER	OFFENDER SIGNATURE	DATE SIGNED

Source: Provided by Peggy Kendrigan, State of Wisconsin Department of Corrections, Division of Community Corrections. (2001). Milwaukee, WI.

home community as a result of the conviction and sentence; therefore, the agent has the advantage of working with a person who is still connected to family, neighborhood, and job or school. The pressing need to find housing or employment—so often the case with parole clients—is not usually present, nor is reintegration into the community an issue to be worked through.

The problem-solving process serves the social work probation agent well. The central problem is that a crime has been committed and future criminal activity is to be avoided. In probation work, many additional problems may be present. Often the client's environment is filled with drugs, guns, and violence. Family, school, and even employment (if the client is employed) may actually promote rather than deter criminal activity. Sometimes neighborhoods are so unsafe that even police do not visit them alone. The social worker must assess all these factors in developing an intervention plan. The plan may involve removing the person from the environment, but in many cases that is not possible. When no alternative exists, the social worker and client must do the best they can with whatever resources are available, or they can try to create new resources.

Placement in a group home may be an option. In this arrangement the client lives in a large home in a residential neighborhood with 10 or 12 other corrections clients. Group homes may be operated by the corrections department or may be privately owned and under contract with corrections. Group homes offer the advantage of a supervised program and a known environment. Neither government nor private enterprise has been able to provide as many group homes as are needed today, nor will such intervention solve the problems of poverty and violence in the community—problems that contribute to crime.

Probation and parole agents often have extremely large caseloads. They range widely, from 30 to 400 clients. This makes it difficult for some agents to know their clients well. Often they use much of their time managing crises and barely spend more than 15 minutes with the client who reports for scheduled monthly meetings. With rapidly increasing prison populations, more agents will be needed.

Probation and parole departments have analyzed the work load and have found that there are identifiable corrections populations that need more time and greater expertise than others. Accordingly, some jurisdictions have created separate units to work with mentally ill offenders, for example, or those whose crime involves substance abuse or sex offenses. Social workers in specialized units usually have a smaller caseload; frequently they have MSW degrees plus experience.

One approach to minimizing **recidivism** (the repetition of criminal behavior resulting in return to prison or reinstatement of a prison sentence) is **risk rating** in which clients with higher risks of recidivism are placed under closer and more frequent supervision. According to Christopher Baird, at the National Center for Crime and Delinquency, the risk-rating assessment form similar to the one shown in Exhibit 5 is now used in most state and county probation and parole departments as well as in Canada and Australia. Considerable work by the National Center for Crime and Delinquency and other corrections agencies has been done to validate the risk assessment instruments that are used (Baird, 1991; Allen, 1995). A score of 15 or higher on the form in Exhibit 5 would suggest the need for a maximum level of supervision; scores of 7 to 14 support a median level; and a

Admission to Adult Field Caseload
Assessment of Offender Risk

EXHIBIT 5

DEPARTMENT OF CORRECTIONS
Division of Community Corrections
DOC-502 (Rev. 7/96)

ADMISSION TO ADULT FIELD CASELOAD
ASSESSMENT OF OFFENDER RISK

WISCONSIN

OFFENDER NAME	Last	First	MI	DOC NUMBER	A

DATE PLACED ON PROBATION OR RELEASED ON PAROLE IN WISCONSIN (MM/DD/YY)	AGENT LAST NAME	AREA NUMBER

FACILITY OF RELEASE	CODE	DATE COMPLETED (MM/DD/YY)

(Select the appropriate answer and enter the associated weight in the score column.)

SCORE

Number of Address Changes in last 12 Months:
(Prior to incarceration for parolees)
- 0 — None
- 2 — One
- 3 — Two or more

Percentage of Time Employed in Last 12 Months:
(Prior to incarceration for parolees)
- 0 — 60% or more
- 1 — 40% - 59%
- 2 — Under 40%
- 0 — Not applicable

Alcohol Usage Problems:
(Prior to incarceration for parolees)
- 0 — No interference with functioning
- 2 — Occasional abuse; some disruption of functioning
- 4 — Frequent abuse; serious disruption; needs treatment

Other Drug Problems:
(Prior to incarceration for parolees)
- 0 — No interference with functioning
- 1 — Occasional abuse; some disruption of functioning
- 2 — Frequent abuse; serious disruption; needs treatment

Attitude:
- 0 — Motivated to change; receptive to assistance
- 3 — Dependent or unwilling to accept responsibility
- 5 — Rationalizes behavior; negative; not motivated to change

Age at First Conviction:
(or Juvenile Adjudications)
- 0 — 24 or older
- 2 — 20 - 23
- 4 — 19 or younger

Number of Prior Periods of Probation / Parole Supervision:
(Adult or Juvenile)
- 0 — None
- 4 — One or more

Number of Prior Probation / Parole Revocations:
(Adult or Juvenile)
- 0 — None
- 4 — One or more

Number of Prior Felony Convictions:
(or Juvenile Adjudications)
- 0 — None
- 2 — One
- 4 — Two or more

Convictions or Juvenile Adjudications for:
(Include current offense, Score must be either 0,2,3, or 5.)
- 0 — None of the Offense(s) stated below
- 2 — Burglary, theft, auto theft, or robbery
- 3 — Worthless checks or forgery
- 5 — One or more from the above categories

Convictions or Juvenile Adjudication for Assaultive Offense within Last Five Years:
(An offense which involves the use of a weapon, physical force or the threat of force)
- 15 — Yes
- 0 — No

TOTAL _____   Total all scores to arrive at the risk assessment score

CASE FILE

Source: Provided by Peggy Kendrigan, State of Wisconsin Department of Corrections, Division of Community Corrections. (1996). Milwaukee, WI.

score of 6 or below would normally result in a minimal level of probation or parole supervision. According to D. Schneider (personal communication, Jan. 15, 1999), the levels of supervision are defined as follows:

maximum = face-to-face contact every 14 days; one home visit every 30 days
  medium = one face-to-face contact every 30 days; one home visit every 60 days
minimum = face-to-face contact every 90 days with mail-in reports as required;
                    no home visits required

An offender may also be placed in a specialized category of probation known as **intensive probation.** Offenders who have committed violent crimes or who have displayed violence or hostility and are considered to be of high risk are candidates for intensive probation. As the name implies, this form of probation utilizes frequent client contacts—daily or at least several contacts per week. Intensive probation is more cost-efficient than imprisonment and provides a relatively high level of community protection. It is also useful with special client populations such as chronic abusers of alcohol or drugs (Butts, 1995).

Before concluding this discussion of probation and parole, it is important to note the considerable policing power of the corrections social worker. No other area of social work practice gives the social worker so much police authority. "In most jurisdictions the probation and parole officer not only performs supervision, surveillance, and counseling roles, but also has the authority to handcuff, search, arrest, and seize property and otherwise restrict clients' freedom" (Netherland, 1987, pp. 356–357). The agent also has the right to recommend a client's return to prison if terms of parole are not met. Agents may require clients to participate in treatment such as substance abuse counseling or batterers' group therapy. This power cannot be taken lightly.

Several other forms of community-based corrections programs exist. Some, such as victim–offender mediation and restitution, have already been described. Several others are informal diversion, community service, and house arrest. Informal diversion is used with first offenders or for minor offenses and is most common in juvenile justice systems. With informal diversion, an authorized intake worker (sometimes a social worker) or officer obtains agreement from the offender to abide by the law and, possibly, to make restitution, in lieu of being prosecuted for the offense. This is humane and cost-effective. Community service may be a component of diversion, or it may be the sentence following conviction. It requires unpaid labor that is useful to the community and that, when possible, utilizes the offender's knowledge or skills. With house arrest, offenders are confined to their homes with electronic surveillance ensuring that they do not leave. Wrist or ankle bracelets are widely used and effective in confining offenders. Advances in telephone and computer in-home surveillance are expected to expand the use of house arrest as a form of community-based corrections.

Public opinion has not supported community-based corrections based on the belief that criminal justice programs are generally not effective. The reality is that research is able to demonstrate what works and what doesn't in both prison and community-based programs. University of Maryland researchers, for example, have developed an innovative technique to examine the effectiveness of programs that seek to reduce crime or prevent recidivism. Their review of previously conducted research showed that prison-based intensive treatment targeting drug use was effective, as was prison-based drug treatment combined with postprison follow-up treatment. Sex offender treatment based on cognitive-behavior methods and provided outside of prison was effective in reducing further offenses, but prison-based sex offender treatment was shown to be ineffective. Shock probation and Scared Straight (programs that attempt to prevent or reduce crime through imposing fear) and correctional boot camps were also found to be ineffective (MacKenzie, 2000). Another recent review of research reported on an especially carefully designed empirical study in Switzerland where persons convicted were randomly assigned to various sentencing options. Short-term imprisonment of 14 to 30 days (short-term imprisonment is commonly used in Europe) was clearly effective in reducing criminal behavior; an alternative, community service sentencing, was even more effective (Killias, Aebi, & Ribeaud, 2000).

The Juvenile Justice System

The juvenile court system evolved from quite a different philosophy than the adult court system and came out of the pioneering and social reform work of Jane Addams and Hull House workers, among others. Established in 1899 in Chicago, it was born of the belief that children were not fully developed human beings capable of making judgments about their behavior or controlling their lives in the same way adults were expected to do. Juvenile courts were designed to intervene when children misbehaved or were in need of protection. There was a strong belief that children could be rehabilitated. Treatment was stressed, as well as separation of the child from adult court systems. Juvenile court proceedings were conducted informally, often without legal representation.

While Jane Addams and her Hull House colleagues in Chicago spearheaded social reform including the founding of the first juvenile court in 1899, Margaret Murray Washington (wife of Booker T. Washington) was actively pursuing similar goals in the South. The pioneers of this movement were later referred to as the "child savers," for their efforts led to the establishment of child labor laws, kindergartens, compulsory school attendance, and, perhaps their most ambitious project, the development of a juvenile justice system (Moon, Sundt, Cullen, & Wright, 2000). Removing children from the adult court and prison system was a major breakthrough. It required the skill of noted civic leaders like Margaret Murray Washington, whose personal involvement led to the development of Mt. Meigs Reformatory for Juvenile Law-Breakers in Alabama, which became a state institution in 1911, and the Mt. Meigs Rescue Home for Girls (Dickerson, 2001).

Children's courts and juvenile justice systems were gradually implemented in all parts of the country, and social workers were soon a major presence in the day-to-day operation of many of these programs. The juvenile justice system continued to grow into the 1960s. At this time, however, a major philosophical shift occurred. After two landmark Supreme Court decisions, primarily the 1967 case, *In re: Gault,* formal legal processes were instituted within juvenile courts, affording children increased legal protections. No longer could the courts imprison or detain children without due process. An **adversarial court** evolved in which attorneys representing the prosecution and attorneys representing the defense were permitted to engage in cross-examination. Children's courts quickly lost their former informal environment in which parents, children, judges, and social workers talked across a table. Constitutional rights and legal processes increasingly became paramount. Legal issues emerged relating to detention, search and seizure, and, most recently, questions about transfer of children to adult courts.

Youth encounters with the juvenile justice system proceed through several phases: arrest, intake, detention, adjudication, and disposition. Behaviors in violation of the law bring youths into contact with the police. The officer determines whether to take formal action, to file charges. While there is considerable variability across states in the United States, most youths who come in contact with police are not arrested but are instead given a warning or the problem is resolved in some other way. The Juvenile Justice and Delinquency Prevention Act of 1974 discontinued the earlier practice of jailing youths for offenses such as curfew violations and truancy, and required that arrested youths be separated from adults in jails or prisons. As a result, juvenile detention centers were constructed. They are now the locations that receive arrested youths. In rural areas, where juvenile facilities do not exist, youths may be held in jails, but they are kept in cells separate from adults.

Following arrest an intake process is begun. It may take only a few minutes or may take up to several days to complete. The intake process will conclude with a decision to detain, dismiss, or make some other disposition of the case. The risk-and-needs assessments that are increasingly part of the intake process may affect the disposition decision. Juvenile court or probation officers (often social workers) generally conduct the intake-and-assessment process. The data collected include any history of past offenses, violent or aggressive behavior, mental health or substance abuse needs, family or peer problems, educational deficits, medical problems, and sexual abuse history. In addition, standardized assessment instruments are used, and information is gathered from parents, police, schools, and other health and social service organizations (Mears & Kelly, 1999).

Sometimes **detention** (placement in a juvenile jail facility) is used on a temporary basis while the intake process is being completed. It is also used when there is reason to believe that the youth will not return for the assigned court date. Home detention, possibly supplemented with use of an electronic wrist or ankle monitor, may be used as an alternative. Social workers in juvenile detention centers provide individual and group counseling, often with a behavior change focus. Juvenile court work ideally includes service to families as well, but significant staff shortages often preclude the provision of significant family service.

Adjudication, the next phase, refers to the decisions made by the juvenile court judge when the charge against the youth is reviewed. The court may decide to drop all charges, but if instead the youth is found guilty, sentencing follows. The **disposition** of a case entails the carrying out of the court order. Probation is the most common sentence in juvenile courts. It is similar to adult probation and may require regular monthly contacts or more intensive and frequent meetings with a probation agent, who is often a BSW social worker. Restitution and/or community service may be a component of probation or may be court ordered as an alternative to probation (Barton, 1995). If the assessment done at intake identified need for mental health or substance abuse treatment, placement in a community-based residential treatment program or group home may be court ordered. Serious crimes or frequent offenses may result in sentencing to a secure juvenile prison, commonly referred to as a training school. Sentencing is for a specified number of years. Training schools are typically designed as a series of cottages, a school, and administrative facilities, all enclosed by walls topped with razor wire. Parole, which resembles probation, typically follows incarceration. Another possible disposition of a juvenile justice case is waiver to adult court for sentencing. This action, which is used with increasing frequency, is generally reserved for serious or violent criminal behavior. Serious and violent crimes, however, have actually declined.

VALUE DILEMMAS FOR SOCIAL WORKERS

Opportunities abound for social workers in the field of criminal justice. Not only does this field offer stimulating practice, but also there are employment opportunities at all levels of federal, state, and local government as well as with private organizations. Salaries tend to be very good, and there are additional opportunities for advancement to administrative positions. But refer back to Exhibits 5 and 7 in Chapter 1 and you will find that only a small percentage of social workers enter this field, although a larger percentage of BSWs than MSWs do so. One of the reasons for this may be the value dilemmas that confront practitioners.

The use and abuse of authority represent one of the most consistent value dilemmas for social workers in correctional settings. For one thing, the legal system within which the corrections social worker functions gives the probation or parole agent substantial policing authority and responsibilities, and this may well conflict with—or at least appear to conflict with—the professional obligations to a client that are defined in the *NASW* Code of Ethics.

In his article "Social Work Ethics in Probation and Parole," Scheurell examined value dilemmas of social work practice in correctional settings, using the *NASW* Code of Ethics as a guide (1983). He looked, for example, at the section of the code that addresses social workers' ethical responsibility to clients. A major consideration is the client's right to self-determination. Although the code obliges social workers to foster maximum self-determination in clients, in correctional settings clients' rights to self-determination are often severely limited by their offenses and subsequent legal status.

Scheurell cited the case of a parole client who left the state, accompanied by his wife and children, to visit his wife's seriously ill mother, without the consent of his parole agent, thereby violating his parole agreement. According to law, it was the task of the agent to determine how serious this violation really was and what action should be taken. In this case, the social worker determined that the client's behavior had not been of danger to others (he had not used drugs, been in possession of weapons, and so forth). The agent decided to reconfirm with the client the conditions of his parole, but not to send him back to prison. In making this decision, the social worker exercised his judgment without abusing the legal authority he held. In addition, the social worker respected the dignity of the client and his natural right to determine that it was proper to make the trip out of state in a time of family crisis.

The Code of Ethics's strong emphasis on confidentiality presents a dilemma since social workers in criminal justice settings are required to testify, as requested by the courts, regarding their contacts with offenders and to report any new or suspected offenses. This requirement may place special strain on the relationship between social worker and client. Hard decisions sometimes have to be made by the social worker. In one of Scheurell's examples, a teenaged girl, on probation for running away, admitted to the probation officer that she had been running away because of her father's sexual abuse. The social worker felt sad about having to violate the confidence so painfully shared by the teenaged girl, but there was no doubt that this situation had to be reported and assessed further.

The profession of social work has long struggled with the issue of coercion in help-seeking. Mandatory, or involuntary, clients, for example, are people who are required by the law to see a social worker or other professional person. Social workers believe that motivation for change is not encouraged when the client is coerced to seek help. Forcing a client to see a social worker on a regular basis, as occurs in probation and parole situations, can result in "conning," where clients learn to "play the game," telling social workers just what they want to hear and nothing more. Sometimes it seems that the criminal justice system has succeeded remarkably well at educating offenders in such avoidance behaviors.

On the other hand, many of the clients seen by social workers and other human service professionals have been forced by some circumstance to seek help. Although a couple may seek marriage counseling from a family service agency voluntarily, the chances are good that one of the marital partners has insisted on counseling as a condition for the continuance of the relationship.

Mandated services can result in a very difficult issue for social workers: the issue of social control. In correctional settings social workers become agents of social control, enforcing specified behaviors from unwilling clients. Social workers ask: Is this a professional, even an ethical role? Hutchison responds that "social workers in mandated settings must acknowledge that they represent society's need, as well as desire, for a functional level of social stability" (1987, p. 587). She further suggests that there are always limits to individual self-determination, since human beings live in societal systems that are defined by their attempt to meet the greater good of the entire community. Sometimes societal systems are repressive, abusive, and unjust. Social workers do not wish to become agents of repression or even of a system that enforces a questionable status quo. Provided this is not the case, Hutchison believes that the social control role is legitimate if it is practiced with care and critically analyzed and if the social worker also seeks changes within the organization needed to humanize it and make it responsive to the needs of its clients as well as the larger society.

SOCIAL WORK WITH GROUPS AND ORGANIZATIONS

Although the case study and most of the discussion to this point have focused on correctional social work practice with individuals and families, there is a growing trend toward work with groups and with entire organizations.

Group work has been shown to be especially useful in prisons. Unfortunately, social workers in prisons are few in number compared with the burgeoning population of new prison admissions. Historically women's prisons have provided even fewer social services than have prisons that house men. As a result, opportunities for individual counseling in prison facilities are limited. Group work has been found to be a useful alternative, and some believe that it is the treatment of choice in institutional settings.

Problems with anger management may have led to the offense that precipitated incarceration, but it may also be a complication of daily life in prison. In prison, for example, it is not uncommon for guards to demand that a work task, such as scrubbing a floor, be repeated several times even though it was satisfactorily completed initially. An inmate's personal possessions may be taken by other inmates or even by guards when similar prison materials (a radio, for example) are missing. An inmate may have to share a small cell with a mentally ill or disabled person who is verbally or physically abusive, or an inmate who urinates in bed. Anger, frustration, depression, and mental deterioration are common in prisoners.

Groups can help prisoners to verbalize their upset and dissatisfaction. Groups can sometimes be used for advocacy purposes too. Wardens and other prison authorities may be more open to hearing complaints from a group, especially one with a professional staff leader, than from individual prisoners. In this case, the social worker can use generalist practice skills to help make the organization—the prison—more humane, more just, and more responsive to the needs of its client population.

Group work can also be the primary problem-solving approach used in community-based homes for adolescents just released from correctional institutions. Since peer influence is so significant during adolescence, group work can sometimes be more beneficial than individual work with this age cohort. Establishing communication and relationships with withdrawn, socially immature teenagers is often an important goal for social workers in group homes.

Group home placement can be a desirable intervention plan, but a limitation is the high rate of staff turnover. In order to keep the group home or community-based correctional facility functioning, the social worker must tackle organizational tasks such as training the youth care staff, helping them to understand and work more effectively with the residents. Youthful residents of group homes are often violent, impulsive, and very difficult for staff to work with; therefore, group sessions, in which problems of the home or the unit are discussed by staff and residents, are beneficial. The ability of the staff and the group home as an organization to meet the needs of this complex resident population depends heavily on the effectiveness of the social worker.

Social workers work with organizations in other ways as well. When social workers are the administrators of community-based correctional facilities and group homes, they are responsible for the budget, for recruitment and supervision of staff, and for the quality of care provided. A BSW holding the middle-management position of house manager is responsible for the day-to-day operation of the home, for direct supervision of staff, and for program planning for the residents. Whether serving as a house manager, an administrator, or a parole agent, the social worker has a professional responsibility to help make her or his organization as humane, just, and responsive to clients as possible.

PROMOTING SOCIAL JUSTICE

If the promotion of social and economic justice is truly a goal of the social work profession, the profession has an enormous challenge in the criminal justice system and with the larger society to ensure fair and humane treatment for prisoners. Social workers can work with other professions such as journalists, lawyers, and physicians to effect change when there is indication of improper treatment.

Amnesty International is a private, nonprofit organization that operates worldwide to secure human rights. It has a large international membership base of individuals as well as student chapters on university campuses around the globe. This organization has exposed inhumane treatment in prisoner of war camps, the detention of political prisoners of conscience, and executions without trial by the Taliban in Afghanistan. In 2000 Amnesty International filed a briefing with the United Nations, alleging that treatment of prisoners in the United States was in violation of the United Nations Convention against Torture and Other Cruel, Inhuman or Degrading Treatment or Punishment. When the United States had ratified this UN convention in 1994, it had agreed to abide by the principles of the convention.

Amnesty International's listing of concerns included the following:

- Beatings, excessive force and unjustified shootings by police officers
- Physical and mental abuse of prisoners and detainees by prison guards, including use of electroshock equipment to inflict torture or ill-treatment, and cruel use of restraints
- Sexual abuse of female prisoners by male guards
- Prisoners held in cruel conditions in isolation units
- Ill-treatment of children in custody
- Failure to protect prisoners from abuses by staff or other inmates
- Inadequate medical or mental health care and overcrowded and dangerous conditions in some facilities
- Racist ill-treatment of ethnic or racial minorities by police or prison guards
- Ill-treatment of asylum seekers held in detention, including in adult jails
- Cruel conditions on death row and violations of human rights standards in the application of the death penalty (Amnesty International, 2000, p. 1)

Amnesty International (AI) made numerous recommendations for improvement in U.S. correctional facilities. The development of standards for care of prisoners based on internationally accepted human rights standards, improvements in training of correctional officers, prohibition of torture and ill-treatment, and banning of dangerous restraint procedures were among the recommendations. AI also recommended that only female officers be used to guard female prisoners and that routine shackling of pregnant prisoners during labor and immediately after birth be discontinued. Further, AI recommended that children be incarcerated only as a last resort and that solitary confinement of children be used only as a last resort and the death penalty be discontinued for children and the mentally retarded (2000).

Social workers can promote social justice for prisoners by supporting Amnesty International's efforts. Indeed, social work students on many college and university campuses are working with AI campus chapters to secure humane treatment of prisoners. Action is also being targeted at specific areas of injustice. The New Mexico Chapter of NASW, for example, has developed a coalition of social workers, clergy, and other human rights activists to target the New Mexico state death penalty. According to the chapter executive director, "If we do not take a position against state-sanctioned capital punishment, then we become part of the problem" (Beaucar, 1999, p. 13).

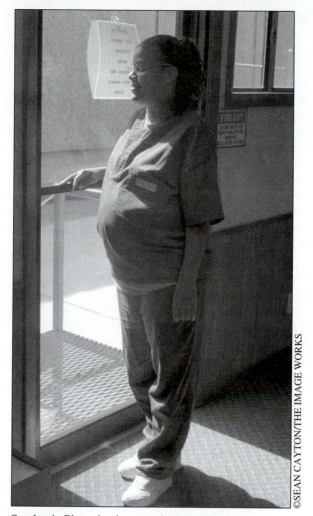

©SEAN CAYTON/THE IMAGE WORKS

Stephanie Pierre is nine months pregnant and is
serving time at the Colorado Women's Correctional
Facility. She will give her baby to the New Horizons
Ministries, a Mennonite ministry that cares for
children who have parents in prison.

Using another approach to address the rights and needs of prisoners, a respected author of social work ethics books, Frederic Reamer, serves on his state's
parole board. As a member of the Rhode Island parole board Reamer believes that
he can make a difference for prisoners by using his social work skills to "assess
what the inmate needs after release to succeed on the outside" (Social work in the
public eye, 2001, p. 13). Residential living (possibly in an adult group home),
treatment for gambling or addictions, mental health services, and employment
training are among the parole recommendations made by Reamer.

In Michigan the increasing imprisonment of women, especially drug-dependent
pregnant women, resulting from nationwide tougher sentencing for drug-related
crime concerned social workers. They were aware of the lack of prenatal care in

prisons, the high rate of infant mortality, the serious complications of pregnancy for women prisoners, and the inhumane treatment of women prisoners during labor and following delivery. A group of Michigan social workers engaged a Detroit city council member, a coalition of community leaders, and the state Department of Corrections in the development of WIAR, the Women and Infants at Risk program. Social work students did much of the research and organizing work for this project. Especially alarming to them was their finding that in Michigan "women in labor were secured in 'belly chains' while being transferred to the hospital, and a corrections officer—male or female, depending on who was on duty— remained with the client through the birth and the entire hospital stay" (Siefert & Pimlott, 2001, p. 130). The mothers were separated from their babies after a brief hospitalization and returned to the prison. The WIAR project was housed in a residential facility in a Detroit neighborhood. The women who qualified for the program were moved to the WIAR home, provided with maternity clothes (not normally available to prisoners), engaged in prenatal classes, linked with prenatal health care in the community, and given nutritional supplements. When the women went into labor, they were admitted to the local hospital where they delivered their babies. They were not chained or shackled during transport, labor, or following delivery. They returned to the WIAR facility and were able to care for their babies for a full month before returning to a reduced level of work responsibilities. The WIAR program, which continues now after 10 years of operation, also provides GED classes, substance abuse treatment, and counseling. Referring to poor, drug-dependent, pregnant women prisoners, two of the social workers involved with this project concluded: "We hope that social workers in all states will take leadership in addressing the needs of this growing population by reforming punitive and ineffectual policies and instituting constructive and humane programs" (Siefert & Pimlott, p. 133).

PUNITIVE JUVENILE JUSTICE POLICIES: IMPLICATIONS FOR MINORITY YOUTH

Social justice issues also permeate the juvenile justice system. In a recent report the U.S. Justice Department clearly acknowledged a disproportionate overrepresentation of minority youth in the juvenile justice system (Poe-Yamagata & Jones, 2000). This report "leaves no doubt that we are faced with a very serious national civil rights issue, virtually making our system juvenile injustice," said National Urban League president Hugh B. Price in a *New York Times* article (as quoted in Butterfield, 2000, p. A1).

The report, entitled *And Justice for Some,* noted that until recently, the most severe punishment for youths was sentencing to a residential correctional facility. Now public sentiment supports waivers to adult court, punishment over rehabilitative goals, and court decisions based on age or offense seriousness rather than on the unique circumstances of each case. The authors believe that "as the blurring of the line between juvenile and criminal court increases, so does the likelihood that these trends will disproportionately affect minority youth" (Poe-Yamagata & Jones, 2000, p. 28). Their research demonstrated that minority youths were locked up twice as often as nonminority youths, and that African Americans were the largest ethnic/racial youth population incarcerated. They also found that when youths were charged with the same crime, "African American youth with no prior admissions were six times more likely to be incarcerated in public facilities than White youth with the same background. Latino youth were three times more likely than White youth to be incarcerated" (p. 3). Exhibit 6, which comes from the *And Justice for Some* report, looks at the African American youth population in the United States, the percentage that are arrested (26%), of that group the percentage (31%) that are referred to juvenile court, and subsequent decisions that might ultimately lead to imprisonment.

Disparities in juvenile justice occur in other countries, too. Research conducted in Israel looked at ethnic differences in determining whether to close the file or to prosecute young people suspected of crime (Mesch & Fishman, 1999). Arab and Jewish youths aged 12 to 18 who were suspected of involvement in delinquent acts were the focus of this study. The findings indicated that file

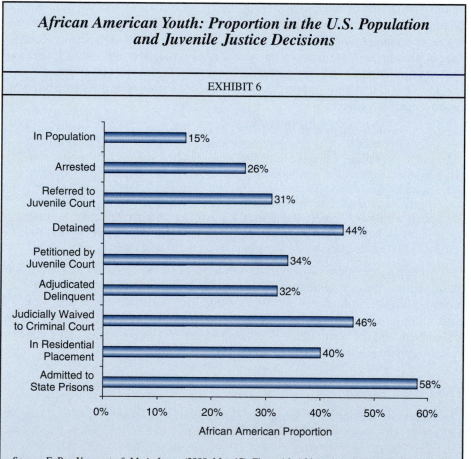

African American Youth: Proportion in the U.S. Population and Juvenile Justice Decisions

EXHIBIT 6

Category	African American Proportion
In Population	15%
Arrested	26%
Referred to Juvenile Court	31%
Detained	44%
Petitioned by Juvenile Court	34%
Adjudicated Delinquent	32%
Judicially Waived to Criminal Court	46%
In Residential Placement	40%
Admitted to State Prisons	58%

African American Proportion

Source: E. Poe-Yamagata & M. A. Jones. (2000, May 17). Figure 16: African American proportion of youth (p. 28). *And justice for some.* Retrieved November 17, 2001, from http:www.buildingblocksforyouth. org/justiceforsome/jfs.pdf Note: This data reflects 1998 population, 1998 arrests, 1997 information on referrals, detentions, petitions, adjudications, waivers; 1997 residential placements; 1997 state prison admissions.

closure was much higher for Jewish youths, even when multiple legal and demographic factors were considered. The results showed that, despite the general belief in Israeli society, Arab youths were really not involved in more serious crimes but, like the African American youths in the previous study, they were much more likely to be prosecuted by the juvenile justice system. The researchers concluded that the juvenile justice system indeed applied different criteria, criteria based on stereotypical thinking about the ethnic and nationality characteristics of youths.

Injustice of the kind described—whether in Israel, the United States, or any other country—has serious implications for young people. Mark Solar, president of the Youth Law Center, sums it up well: "These disparities accumulate, and they make it hard for members of the minority community to complete their education, get jobs" and be good parents (as quoted in Butterfield, 2000, p. A1).

SOCIAL WELFARE POLICY IN CRIMINAL JUSTICE

Punitive programs or rehabilitative programs—what do we want for our country? What type and location of prisons do we want: community-based or massive prisons far from population centers? Decisions about these social policies are made by the people we elect to office. The way we vote and how we interact with our elected representatives determine the nature of our criminal justice system.

The liberal and conservative political ideologies concerning incarceration are summarized by McNeece:

> *Liberals* assume that most of the defects of human behavior have their origins in the social environment. . . . Liberals assume that incarceration should provide treatment to rehabilitate, reeducate, and reintegrate offenders into the community. *Conservatives* support the notion of retribution or just deserts, not necessarily as vengeance, but because it serves utilitarian purposes as well. Punishment is not only proper, but necessary, because it reinforces the social order. Deterrence is an expected outcome of incarceration, because punishing offenders for their misdeeds will reduce both the probability of their repeating the act (specific deterrence) and the likelihood of others committing criminal acts (general deterrence). (1995, p. 61)

The strength of political conservatives in recent years has resulted in more use of imprisonment, longer sentences, and less concern about rehabilitation. This approach, however, ignores the simple fact that after a severe prison sentence and with minimal rehabilitation or preparation, most prisoners will someday be released back into the community. What kind of security or protection does this provide our communities? Is this true social or criminal justice?

The Prison Population

The increasing rate of incarceration is demonstrated in Exhibit 7. Comparing the 1970 data with those of 1999 shows an astounding rise in the prison population: from 200,000 persons in state and federal prisons to 1,276,688, or a rate of 96 per 100,000 persons in the population to 468 by 1999. At the end of 2000, "state prisons were operating between full capacity and 15 percent above capacity, while federal prisons were operating at 31 percent above capacity" (Beck, 2001, p. 1).

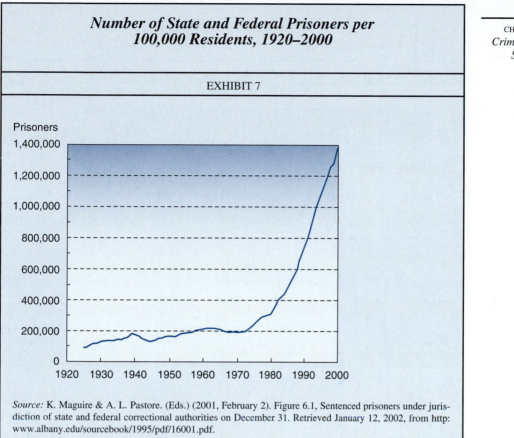

**Number of State and Federal Prisoners per
100,000 Residents, 1920–2000**

EXHIBIT 7

Source: K. Maguire & A. L. Pastore. (Eds.) (2001, February 2). Figure 6.1, Sentenced prisoners under jurisdiction of state and federal correctional authorities on December 31. Retrieved January 12, 2002, from http: www.albany.edu/sourcebook/1995/pdf/16001.pdf.

The rate of imprisonment always varies from state to state. In 1999 Minnesota and Maine had imprisonment rates of only 120 and 128 while Texas had a rate of 704 and Louisiana had a rate of 763 persons imprisoned per 100,000 people in their resident population (Maguire & Pastore, 2001).

One result of increasing taxpayer support going to prison construction, staffing, and maintenance is that decreasing portions of governmental budgets become available for allocation to universities, social service programs, health care, and other needs. Another result is that an entire new industry has evolved: private, for-profit prisons. In 1999 over 138,000 prisoners were held in private prisons, 71,250 in prisons owned by Corrections Corporation of America alone. By 2000 the total number of persons in private prisons dropped to 119,449 as states opened new prison facilities (Maguire & Pastore, 2001, Table 1.92). Public pressure for mandatory sentences, "truth in sentencing" (an end to parole), and waivers of juvenile offenders to adult courts suggest vastly increasing prison populations in coming years. Why is this? Have crime rates, especially violent crimes, increased in the past several years? The data would suggest quite the opposite (see Exhibit 8). The U.S. Department of Justice announced that violent crime rates reached "the lowest level ever recorded in 2001" (p. 1).

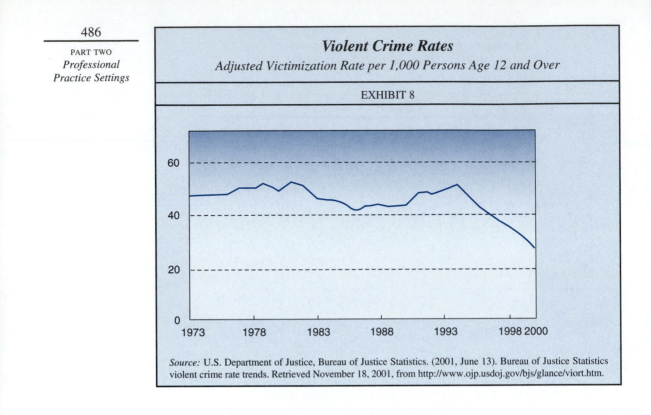

Violent Crime Rates

Adjusted Victimization Rate per 1,000 Persons Age 12 and Over

EXHIBIT 8

Source: U.S. Department of Justice, Bureau of Justice Statistics. (2001, June 13). Bureau of Justice Statistics violent crime rate trends. Retrieved November 18, 2001, from http://www.ojp.usdoj.gov/bjs/glance/viort.htm.

An increasing rate of imprisonment is not unique to the United States, but the United States did have the highest rate of all countries in the world in 2001, according to the International Centre for Prison Studies at King's College in London. Comparative figures for selected other countries are provided in Exhibit 9. It is interesting to note that recently Russia's rate of imprisonment was higher than that of the United States and, before apartheid ended in South Africa, that country had the highest incarceration rate in the world (Mauer, 1994).

The world prison population rate was approximately 140 for 100,000 persons in 2001, quite a contrast to the U.S. imprisonment rate of 702 per 100,000 persons! In the 1990s the prison rate grew in many parts of the world, not just in the United States. European countries saw a growth rate of approximately 20 percent. In the United States the rate was around 85 percent, while in Canada it was only 12 percent. There was an increase of 33 percent in South Africa. Japan and Finland, where the imprisonment rate declined through the 1990s, had an increase of 13 percent in 2000. In a report delivered at a United Nations conference in 2001, an international authority on prison studies indicated that rising crime rates were not the cause of increasing incarceration (crime rates were actually declining, not rising), nor was the nature of crime committed. Instead, it was believed that the cause was related to an increased fear of crime and strong desire for retribution, especially among some political policy makers (Walmsley, 2001).

Incarceration Rates for Selected Nations, 2001
(per 100,000 Population)

EXHIBIT 9

United States of America	702
Russian Federation	635
South Africa	406
Singapore	383
Poland	183
Zimbabwe	168
Mexico	148
New Zealand	145
South Korea	137
Libya	127
England/Wales	125
Brazil	113
China	112
Argentina	107
Canada	103
Germany	97
Sweden	64
Norway	59
Cambodia	49
Japan	44
India	39

Source: International Centre for Prison Studies. (2001, July 17). *World prison brief of the International Centre for Prison Studies.* Retrieved September 4, 2001, from http://www.kcl.ac.uk/depsta/rel/icps/home.html.

The Death Penalty

Another social policy issue relates to **capital punishment,** the death penalty. Since its founding, the ultimate penalty for criminal conduct in the United States has been death. According to the American Civil Liberties Union, "13,000 people have been legally executed since colonial times" and approximately 2,000 people are on death row today (*Briefing paper,* n.d.). Public sentiment regarding use of the death penalty, however, has vacillated over time. It remains a hotly debated issue. Comments in favor of the death penalty and in opposition to it include:

> "There are plenty of innocent people being killed by those on parole. . . . The only cure for this kind of sickness is death. I know I may sound hard and cruel—but I for one, have had enough!" (From a feedback forum, *Detroit News,* March 2, 1999)

> "I like it the way it is." (Comment by Governor George W. Bush of Texas at the time that a law prohibiting execution of the mentally disadvantaged was defeated)

> "We oppose the death penalty not just for what it does to those guilty of heinous crimes, but for what it does to all of us: It offers the tragic illusion that we can defend life by taking life." (Most Rev. Joseph A. Fiorenza, President, National Conference of Catholic Bishops/U.S. Catholic Conference, 1999)

> ". . . in Canada, the death penalty has been rejected as an acceptable element of criminal justice. Capital punishment engages the underlying values of the prohibition against cruel and unusual punishment. It is final and irreversible. Its imposition has been described as arbitrary and its deterrent value has been doubted." Supreme Court of Canada. (Robinson, 2001, p. 2)

As the preceding quote suggests, Canada does not have capital punishment. Nor do many of the other industrialized nations of the world. Some nations refuse to extradite prisoners to the United States because of the U.S. death penalty. Many U.S. organizations—including the National Association of Social Workers, the American Bar Association, the American Civil Liberties Union (ACLU), and various religious organizations—are now calling for the suspension or discontinuation of the death penalty. Inadequate legal representation for poor persons, racial bias, execution of child criminals, execution of mentally impaired persons, and execution of innocent persons are among the concerns of opponents to the death penalty. In recent years, DNA testing has confirmed the innocence of a number of persons sentenced to death. The ACLU has called for a moratorium on capital punishment in the United States. In the meantime, the number of prisoners on death row is increasing.

Social Policy and Juvenile Justice

Juvenile crime, like adult crime rates, has declined, yet the same forces that support punitive policy for adult offenders also support waiving juvenile cases to adult court, allowing youths to be jailed with adults, and using the death penalty for youths. Considerable public opinion supports such policies and momentum appears to be growing. This chapter's "Up for Debate" box provides a flavor of the arguments in the juvenile justice policy arena.

Meanwhile, Jensen and Howard (both social workers) propose that juvenile justice decisions should be based on our knowledge "about the social conditions that place youths at risk of delinquency" (1998, p. 331). This includes such factors as poverty, family instability, and substance abuse. They suggest developing prevention programs targeted at youths known to be at high risk for antisocial behavior and investing in community economic development aimed at providing opportunities for young people. Jensen and Howard warn that "juvenile justice policy reform should not be solely determined by the characteristics of a relatively small number of violent and chronic offenders" (p. 332).

> ### *Debate Box*
> ### *Proposal: Juveniles who commit heinous crimes should be subject to the same consequences as adults.*
>
> | **Yes** | **No** |
> |---|---|
> | 1. If a crime as serious as murder, for example, is committed, the consequences should be severe. | 1. A crime as serious as murder is not committed by young people unless circumstances are extraordinary. |
> | 2. Severe punishment of violent crimes is necessary to deter other people from committing them. | 2. Empirical research does not support the theory that deterrence is accomplished for adolescents through severity of punishment. |
> | 3. The victims of violent crimes often request the most severe penalty possible, including the death penalty, to relieve their own sense of loss. | 3. The vast majority of youths who commit even violent crime during adolescence are statistically unlikely to commit offenses as adults. |
> | 4. If youthful offenders are given lengthy sentences, they will be incapacitated—unable to commit additional crimes for a long time. | 4. With little rehabilitation provided, young people leaving correctional facilities will be more rather than less likely to commit crime. |

Scott and Grisso write from their perspectives as an attorney and a psychiatrist when they express concern that "the current landscape of juvenile justice reform suggests a view of delinquent youth as appropriately subject to adult punishment and procedures and thus as indistinguishable in any important way from their adult counterparts" (1998, p. 1). They urge the incorporation of understandings from developmental psychology in social policymaking. Scott and Grisso point to statistics that show that delinquent behavior is both fairly common in adolescence and likely to conclude as youths become young adults. Adolescents' knowledge base and decision-making abilities are sufficiently immature, they state, that it impairs their ability to make sound judgments when they are read their rights, at arrest, and in their ability to stand trial. Sometimes immature judgment is also involved in the behavior that leads to arrest. They conclude that severe sanctions (transfer to adult courts, imprisonment in adult jails, severe sentences) on youths for first offenses, even for serious crimes, will be in the best interests neither of the youths nor of society. Not surprisingly, they are opposed to the termination of separate juvenile and adult justice systems in the United States.

Issues of social justice also arise concerning the safety and well-being of juvenile offenders who are waived to adult courts. In one study, adolescents were eight times as likely to commit suicide in adult jails as in juvenile detention, five times as likely to be sexually assaulted, and much more likely to be beaten by staff in adult facilities (Flaherty, 1980; Forst, Fagan, and Vivona, 1989, as cited in Schiraldi and Soler, 1998).

Of special concern is the growing number of girls, some serving long sentences, in adult jails and prisons. These girls tend to be isolated and not well supervised in adult facilities. A 16-year-old interviewed in a California prison in 1995 stated that

> during the six weeks she was incarcerated in a women's jail, she was so frightened and depressed that she stopped eating and lost 20 pounds. Although her physical appearance became frighteningly fragile and her behavior increasingly withdrawn, she was given no medical or psychological assistance. (Acoca, 1995; as cited in Acoca, 1998, p. 582)

Our juvenile justice policy discussion concludes with the observation that the practices described above are inconsistent with the 1989 United Nations Convention on the Rights of the Child. The United States did sign the United Nations Convention, but only one other of 190 countries besides the United States has yet to ratify it; the other country is Somalia (Acoca, 1998).

Populations-at-Risk

The demographics of crime and crime victimization are not very well understood. Which populations are most at risk of being victims of crime? Data from the 2000/ Bureau of Justice Statistics demonstrated racial disparity among victims of violent crime; 35.3 out of 1,000 black persons experienced violent crime compared with a rate of 27.1 for whites and 20.7 per 1,000 persons of other races. In all categories of violent crime—rape/sexual assault, robbery, assault, and personal theft—African American persons experienced higher victimization rates than whites or persons of other races. Poor people, too, were more likely to be victims of violent crime than nonpoor persons. Those households with incomes of less than $75,000 in 2000 had a violent crime rate of 60.3 compared with a 22.3 rate for households with incomes of $75,000 or more. It should be noted, however, that the overall rate of violent crime fell 15 percent between 1999 and 2000, making this the lowest annual rate of violent crime since 1973. Another piece of good news: the decline in crime victimization was statistically greatest for poor households and African American persons (Rennison, 2001).

Imprisonment rates provide another perspective on the demographics of crime and of victimization. In the United States the rate of incarceration of African American males is shocking: 3,457 per 100,000 persons in the population compared with 449 for white males and 1,220 for Hispanic males (Beck, 2001). Does this mean that black males actually commit more crime? What does all this mean to social workers? Social workers are committed to working with poor people. Given the huge overrepresentation of minority groups among the poor and the fact that crime is one way of surviving poverty, then perhaps the data may represent reality. If this is the case, then social workers must be aware of this reality. On the other hand, racially discriminatory behavior from the time an arrest decision is made through sentencing may also profoundly affect the data.

Racial profiling is one example of discriminatory behaviors that lead to arrest. **Racial profiling** "occurs when the police target someone for investigation on the basis of that person's race, national origin, or ethnicity" (American Civil Liberties

Union Freedom Network, n.d., p. 1). Initially racial profiling emerged in relation to police decisions concerning arrests for traffic violations. This came to be known as "driving while black." More recently it has emerged in relation to airport passenger searches where, again, the apparent race or ethnicity of a person triggers search action on the part of security personnel. Racial profiling that substitutes skin color or ethnic characteristics for evidence puts minorities at increased risk of search, arrest, and ultimately imprisonment.

Many other at-risk populations exist within the criminal justice system. Women, for example, are a growing segment of the prison population and, as was demonstrated in an earlier section of this chapter, women prisoners have many unmet health needs.

Paralleling the increase of older persons in the general population is an increase of the elderly in prisons. One study of older male prisoners in Iowa found that they had few visitors. Health care problems included incontinence (the inability to control bowel movements or urination), hearing and vision loss, stiffness and inflexibility, cardiac disease, and high blood pressure (Colsher, Wallace, Loeffelholz, & Sales, 1992). Most prisons are not adequately staffed to deal with problems of advancing age and disability.

DISASTER, TRAUMA, AND THE CRIMINAL JUSTICE SYSTEM

September 11, 2001, was a day of trauma and tragedy for people across the United States. Persons who only experienced via television the terrorist attacks and nearly instantaneous deaths of over 4,000 innocent persons were nonetheless profoundly affected. Fear, horror, panic, and an overwhelming desire to reach home and family engulfed masses of people. Men and women in prison, too, were impacted. For some an immense sense of helplessness was compounded by the reality that they were captives and totally unable to be with or to nurture their families through this time of extraordinary stress. "Lock downs" were instituted in some prison and jail facilities because of the anxious, hyperactive, unpredictable behavior of prisoners following the disastrous events of September 11, 2001 (J. Barczak, personal communication, October 9, 2001).

Traumatic experiences occur inside prisons, too. A *Time* magazine article reported over 100 serious physical injuries in a two-month period at a private juvenile correctional facility in Louisiana. In one incident a 17-year-old "who wore a colostomy bag as a result of gunshot wounds was hospitalized after an altercation with a guard. The nurse at the prison's infirmary noted that about 5 in. of the boy's intestines were in the colostomy bag" (Stein, 2000, p. 84). In addition to injuries inflicted by correctional staff, inmates may be victims of fights or physical abuse of other inmates, rape or sexual assault, even murder. "Postincarceration syndrome" is the term that has recently come into use to describe posttraumatic stress from both preimprisonment trauma and institutional abuse. Sensory deprivation from prolonged exposure to solitary confinement may also be associated with this set of behaviors, along with personality traits associated with learned helplessness and personality traits developed in response to institutional abuse. It is speculated that postincarceration syndrome may account for the high rates of recidivism in the United States. Recommendations flowing from study of this syndrome include diverting some offenders into drug and mental health treatment, the elimination of lengthy mandated sentences, and conversion of correctional facilities into rehabilitation programs focusing on education and development of vocational skills (GORSKI-CENAPS Corporation, 2001).

In a study of incarcerated male adolescents, rates of posttraumatic stress disorder were found to be even higher than those in the classic studies of posttraumatic stress in Vietnam combat veterans (Erwin, Newman, McMackin, Morrissey, & Kaloupek, 2000). Among the youths studied, 82% had witnessed homicide, 55% had witnessed family domestic violence, and 45% had themselves experienced family physical assault or a serious accident prior to imprisonment. Over half reported a fear of dying. The researchers suspected that the life experiences of these adolescents were linked to the kind of impulse control and emotional problems that resulted in their criminal behaviors. Treatment during incarceration for posttraumatic stress disorder and lifetime exposure to potentially traumatic experiences was recommended. Disaster and trauma, it seems, may have been so interwoven in the criminal justice system that until very recently they were overlooked. A rehabilitative approach that recognizes these factors may benefit society as well as those persons who have entered the criminal justice system.

HISTORY OF SOCIAL WORK IN CRIMINAL JUSTICE

The history of the profession in the very interesting field of criminal justice is one that has slowly evolved out of a distant past when punishment for misdeeds was instantaneous and severe. Archaeological findings have provided evidence of the use of beatings and slavery for those who violated societal norms in ancient times. In the enlightened period of Greek civilization, around 400 B.C., new ways of looking at criminal behavior emerged. Hippocrates insisted that natural causes, rooted in the environment and in the family, shaped behavior more significantly than did evil spirits.

Evidently such enlightenment failed to continue, for by the Middle Ages in Europe severe punishments were being used: branding, cutting out an offender's tongue, public hanging, beheading, or burning at the stake. In the 1600s many of these punishments were brought to America by the colonists. Following the Revolutionary War in America, the Pennsylvania Quakers became alarmed about the harshness of punishments being used. "They argued that offenders might be reformed through segregation from the evil influences of other persons and the opportunity to become penitent (thus the term *penitentiary*)" (Galaway, 1981, p. 259). This, then, was the precursor of the present prison system.

In France the Napoleonic Code of 1807 created a new and more humane approach to Western society's thinking about criminal justice for children. The Napoleonic Code established a minimum age at which children could be charged and punished for offenses. Thus was born the principle of differentiating juvenile from adult crime. Separate correctional facilities for children—facilities then known as refuges—began to be provided for children in the United States in the early 1820s. These privately funded, supposedly charitable organizations unfortunately grew into large institutions characterized by severe discipline.

John Augustus, a Boston shoemaker, is credited with the establishment of probation. In 1841 Augustus requested permission of the courts to serve as surety—to accept personal responsibility and provide supervision—for a man charged with

FRANK SITEMAN/THE PICTURE CUBE

Women's prison: social worker engages clients in prison release planning.

drunkenness. That first successful experience led Augustus to continue his work with other offenders. In 1869 the first formal position for probation work was created by the Commonwealth of Massachusetts; the agent was required to appear at criminal trials of juveniles, to locate suitable homes for them, and to supervise them. In 1878 Boston began to provide probationary supervision for adult offenders.

During the mid-1800s persons in England began to realize that the concept of transporting convicts to other lands was not an effective approach to the problem. Captain Alexander Maconochie, who was responsible for the British penal colony on Norfolk Island in the South Pacific, devised and promoted a concept of conditional release for prisoners. The first correctional system in the United States to experiment with the concept was the Elmira Reformatory in New York State in 1877. The use of parole soon became an accepted principle in corrections in the United States.

By the early 1900s juvenile courts began to be established across the United States. A special concern of juvenile courts was provision of competent, professional service for children. These courts looked to the new profession of social work for staff to assist juvenile court judges. In contrast, the adult probation and parole agents of the time represented a variety of disciplines but tended to use sheriffs and persons with police experience. Gradually this area too was professionalized, but even today probation and parole agents come from a variety of disciplines with quite different philosophical approaches to criminal justice.

Women such as Jane Addams of Hull House and Edith Abbott, dean of the School of Social Service Administration at the University of Chicago, provided much of the leadership, teaching, and research in correctional social work in its early days. Abbott, for example, studied crime and incarceration of women during the Civil War and World War I.

Social casework was introduced within the U.S. Bureau of Prisons in the 1930s. By that time society had begun to accept Freudian concepts of causation of behavior. Increasingly, counseling for prisoners incorporated some of this theory. The federal prisons were fraught with riots resulting from overcrowding, understaffing, and overall poor prison conditions. Reform efforts introduced social casework as part of a rehabilitation effort. Kenneth Pray, a community organizer and educator, helped to clarify the role of social casework in the prisons with his writings in the 1940s (1945).

Police social work programs grew out of demonstration projects initially funded by the federal government, generally by the Law Enforcement Assistance Administration in the 1970s. Harvey Treger, of the Jane Addams School of Social Work at the University of Illinois, is probably the most significant figure in the development of this field. Victim/witness programs were also initially created through governmental funding.

Innovations that occurred in probation and parole in the 1980s and 1990s included the use of home confinement, electronic monitoring, intensive supervision as a substitute for incarceration, and restitution. All of these programs brought opportunities for new approaches to practice for social workers in the corrections field. The expansion of privatization in the 1990s focused on custodial care with minimal attention to prisoner rehabilitation. Many of the private prison facilities were located in southern states but were frequently used to house prisoners from northern states. The frail linkages between prisoners and their families became even more tenuous.

Today the criminal justice system is reacting to public sentiment through harsh sentencing and long prison terms, but there are calls for reform. The social work perspective that looks at poverty, prejudice, housing, education, and family support needs to become a part of public policy debate. Hopefully the social work profession will join with other professions such as law, psychiatry, and criminal justice to challenge the punitive and ultimately destructive direction criminal justice policy has taken. The field of criminal justice could be a very exciting arena for new social justice activism and reform!

INTERNET SITES

http://www.aclu.org	American Civil Liberties Union
http://www.ncjrs.org/	National Criminal Justice Reference Service
http://thomas.loc.gov/	Thomas (legislative information on the Internet)
http://www.undcp.org/crime_prevention.html	United Nations Office for Drug Control and Crime Prevention
http://www.sentencingproject.org/	The Sentencing Project
http://www.nofsw.org/	National Organization of Forensic Social Work
http://angelfire.lycos.com/doc/general/angelfire_popunder.html	Native American Inmates and Families Support Group
http://www.religioustolerance.org/execut3.htm	Religious Tolerance: Facts about Capital Punishment

http://www.ojp.usdoj.gov/	Bureau of Justice Statistics
http://www.kcl.ac.uk/depsta/rel/icps/home.html	International Centre for Prison Studies
http://www.buildingblocksforyouth.org/justiceforsome	Building Blocks for Youth: And Justice for Some
http://www.albany.edu/sourcebook	Sourcebook of Criminal Justice Statistics Online
http://www.cswf.org/law.html	Committee on Clinical Social Work and the Law/ Forensic Practice
http://www1.umn.edu/irp/publications/racialprofiling.html	Institute on Race & Poverty
http://www.recidivism.com	Recidivism Site

SUMMARY

Alan Martin, the social worker in the case study, was experienced in the field of criminal justice. He had worked in the adult justice system before taking his current position with juvenile justice. In fields of social work practice such as criminal justice, where social work is not necessarily the primary profession, it takes special effort to sustain professional self-awareness; Alan Martin had begun to lose his professional identification and was becoming tired and unmotivated. Fortunately for Brian Cook and for Alan's future clients, he was able to confront and not to become lost in the pain of one client's tragic death. Instead, Alan Martin forced himself to reconnect with his professional knowledge base, including a strengths perspective that did not devalue his clients.

The complexities of the criminal justice system are introduced with an examination of its three major components: law enforcement, the courts, and the correctional system. The juvenile system, including its own courts and correctional programs, is also presented. While both BSWs and MSWs are employed in police departments and the courts, it is correctional systems that offer most of the social work employment opportunities today. In fact, many more social workers are employed in probation and parole than in prison facilities.

This chapter offers readers not only an introduction to the population served but also the value dilemmas and role conflicts that social workers in the correctional field experience. Generalist social work practice with individual clients as well as practice with groups, organizations, and within the community are described. Special attention is given to the juvenile justice system and work with youthful offenders since this is an area that often appeals to social workers and that has historically held more career opportunities for social workers.

The social policy context of corrections is frustrating and challenging for social workers with the current emphasis on punishment (even execution) of offenders rather than prevention and rehabilitation. Issues of poverty and racism that impact both the victims and the perpetrators of crime call out for social justice. Populations that were shown to be at special risk were African American males and the youths, especially young women who are now increasingly housed in adult prisons.

The impact of disaster and trauma on prisoners was explored. Disasters, such as the terrorist attacks on the World Trade Center in New York in 2001, are experienced in unique ways by persons who are imprisoned. Prison, too, can become the source of trauma for inmates. The chapter also explained how traumatic life experiences can potentially lead to criminal behavior and incarceration.

A brief historical overview of criminal justice efforts was provided as a context for the evolution of social work within this field of practice. The perspective of social work, rooted in its knowledge of community and social as well as psychological systems, is somewhat unique within criminal justice. It is, nonetheless, a perspective that is needed, one that could challenge the system to seek new approaches and the kind of reform that would ensure true social as well as criminal justice. This field of practice offers career opportunities and exciting challenges for social workers.

KEY TERMS

adjudication
adversarial court
capital punishment
community-based corrections
community-service sentence
correctional system
detention
disposition
felony
intensive probation
jail
misdemeanor

parole
police social work
presentence investigation
prison
probation
racial profiling
recidivism
restitution
revocation
risk rating
subpoena

DISCUSSION QUESTIONS

1. Speculate about the future of Brian Cook. What are his chances of leading a law-abiding life and avoiding return to prison?
2. What will the social worker, Alan Martin, need to do to prevent burnout?
3. How does probation differ from parole?
4. What is the benefit to a community of having police social workers? Are there police social workers in your community? What are their roles?
5. Why does a court request a presentence investigation? How detailed is this kind of report? What would be the outcome for the client if the social worker's presentence investigation report were poorly written or inaccurate or failed to include significant data?
6. Explain the function of a prison social worker.
7. What trends have emerged in the rate of imprisonment in the United States? How does the U.S. rate of imprisonment compare with that of other countries?
8. What racial or ethnic group has been most victimized by crimes of violence? What group has the highest rate of imprisonment? How can this be explained?
9. In what ways might prisoners experience and respond to trauma? How could this be constructively addressed?
10. What social justice issues exist in the field of criminal justice?

CLASSROOM EXERCISES

It is suggested that students break into small groups of three or four to discuss these exercises. It may be helpful to choose a scribe to record and report interesting points to the class after the group discussion.

1. This chapter states that only a small percentage of social workers enter the field of criminal justice, possibly due to value dilemmas. Identify major social work values that might interfere with practice in the criminal justice area and discuss ways in which they could be put into action to the fullest possible extent.
2. Minorities are disproportionately incarcerated not only in this country but abroad. Discuss evidence cited in this chapter pertaining to the United States and to the nation of Israel.
3. Discuss concerns with U.S. prisons that have been identified by Amnesty International and this organization's recommendations for improvement. How can social workers promote social justice for prisoners?
4. What are some unforeseen results of increased taxpayer support going to the building and maintenance of prisons? For example, how does prison spending affect public support of universities? Hospitals? Other important social institutions? Do you think this is a good trade-off? Why or why not?

RESEARCH ACTIVITIES

1. Use community resource directories and focused telephone contacts to identify the various organizations that are directly or indirectly involved with criminal justice in your community. Which of these employ social workers? Consider interviewing a social worker to learn about his or her professional responsibilities.
2. Based on the findings from your research of the community, determine whether private (for-profit) enterprise has entered the correctional field in your community or whether your local/state corrections programs send prisoners to private enterprise facilities in other areas. What effects, if any, do you expect this trend to have on offenders and their families?
3. Review and analyze current media reports related to criminal justice. How are victims of crime presented? How are the persons who committed the crimes presented? In media coverage of criminal justice programs or proposed policies or programs, is funding for rehabilitation programs described? Based on your media research, what kind of actions should social workers (and students) be taking to fight for social justice?

INTERNET RESEARCH EXERCISES

1. A discussion of the "Effects of Race on Sentencing in Capital Punishment Cases" may be found at the http://www.geocities.com/bigmike_75/aessays/a14.html.
   a. What are two of the rationalizations to justify the role of race in death penalties?
   b. Please comment on the observation that 41% of death row inmates are black and 48% are white.
   c. What does the article say is required to eliminate the bias in capital punishment cases?

2. The British Association of Social Workers has a briefing on the Internet relating to criminal justice social work services (http://www.basw.co.uk/scotland/policy/commsent.htm).
   a. What circumstances led to the ongoing problems that the client, John, has had throughout his life?
   b. Consultation Point 3 addresses the need for communication of what information on the local level?
   c. In the "Conclusion," the report makes a point of the fact that victims as well as offenders require the services of qualified social workers. Please comment on this.

REFERENCES

Acoca, L. (1998). Outside/inside: The violation of American girls at home, on the streets, and in the juvenile justice system. *Crime and Delinquency, 44*(4), 561–589.

Allen, G. F. (1995). Probation and parole. In *Encyclopedia of social work* (19th ed., pp. 1910–1916). Washington, DC: NASW Press.

American Civil Liberties Union. (n.d.). *Briefing paper number 8: The death penalty.* Retrieved November 23, 2001, from http://www.soci.niu.edu/~critcrim/dp/dppapers/aclu.brief.

American Civil Liberties Union Freedom Network. (n.d.). *Arrest the racism: Racial profiling in America.* Retrieved November 23, 2001, from http://www.aclu.org/profiling/.

Amnesty International. (2000, May). *A briefing for the UN Committee against Torture.* Retrieved October 30, 2001, from http://www.web.amnesty.org/ai.nsf/indes/AMR510562000.

Baird, C. (1991). *Validating risk assessment instruments used in community corrections.* Madison, WI: National Council on Crime and Delinquency.

Barczak, J. (2001, October 9). Personal communication.

Barker, R. L. (1999). *The social work dictionary* (4th ed.). Washington, PC: NASW Press.

Barton, W. H. (1995). Juvenile corrections. In *Encyclopedia of social work* (19th ed., pp. 1563–1573). Washington, DC: National Association of Social Workers.

Beaucar, K. O. (1999). Effort against death penalty alters views. *NASW News, 44*(6), 13.

Beck, A. J. (2001). Prisoners in 2000. In *Bureau of Justice Statistics Bulletin.* Washington, DC: Office of Justice Programs.

Butterfield, F. (2000, April 26), Racial disparities seen as pervasive in juvenile justice. *The New York Times,* p. A1.

Butts, J. A. (1995). Community-based corrections. In *Encyclopedia of social work* (19th ed., pp. 549–555). Washington, DC: NASW Press.

Colsher, P. L., Wallace, R. B., Loeffelholz, P. L., & Sales, M. (1992). Health status of older male prisoners: A comprehensive survey. *Public Health Briefs, 82*(6), 881–884.

Dickerson, J. G. (2001). Margaret Murray Washington: Organizer of rural African American women. In I. B. Carlton-LaNey (Ed.), *African American leadership: An empowerment tradition in social welfare history.* Washington, DC: NASW Press.

Erwin, B. A., Newman, E., McMackin, R. A., Morrissey, C., & Kaloupek, D. G. (2000). PTSD, malevolent environment, and criminality among criminally involved male adolescents. *Criminal Justice and Behavior. 27*(2), 196–215.

Farr, K. A. (2000). Classification for female inmates: Moving forward. *Crime & Delinquency, 46*(1), 3–15.

Galaway, B. (1981). Social service and criminal justice. In N. Gilbert & H. Specht (Eds.), *Handbook of the social services.* Englewood Cliffs, NJ: Prentice Hall.

GORSKI-CENAPS Corporation. (2001, October 26). *Post incarceration syndrome (PICS).* Retrieved November 23, 2001, from http:www.cenaps.com/training/pics.cfm.

Hutchison, E. D. (1987). Use of authority. *Social Service Review, 61* (4), 581–598.

International Centre for Prison Studies. (2001, July 17). *World prison brief.* Retrieved November 21, 2001, from King's College, London site: http:www.kcl.ac.uk/depsta/rel/icps/worldbrief/world_brief.html.

Isenstadt, P. M. (1995). Adult courts. In *Encyclopedia of social work* (19th ed., pp. 68–74). Washington, DC: NASW Press.

Jensen, J. M., & Howard, M. O. (1998). Youth crime, public policy, and practice in the juvenile justice system: Recent trends and needed reforms. *Social Work, 43*(4), 324–334.

Killias, M., Aebi, M. F., & Ribeaud, D. (2000). Learning through controlled experiments: Community service and heroin prescription in Switzerland. *Crime & Delinquency, 46*(2), 233–251.

Landers, S. (1997). Subpoenas 101: Leaping a legal chasm. *NASW News, 42*(3), 3.

MacKenzie, D. L. (2000). Evidence-based corrections: Identifying what works. *Crime & Delinquency, 46*(4), 457–471.

Maguire, K., & Pastore, A. L. (Eds.) (2001, February 2). Figure 6.1, Sentenced prisoners under jurisdiction of state and federal correctional authorities on December 31; Table 1.92, Private adult correctional facility management firms; Table 4.26, Percent distribution of juveniles taken into police custody; Table 6.2, Sentenced female prisoners under jurisdiction of state and federal correctional authorities on December 31; Table 6.27, Rate (per 100,000 resident population) of sentenced prisoners under jurisdiction of state and federal correctional authorities on December 31. *Sourcebook of criminal justice statistics 2000.* Retrieved January 12, 2002, from http://www.albany.edu/sourcebook.

Mauer, M. (1994). *Americans behind bars: U.S. and international use of incarceration, 1992–1993.* Washington, DC: The Sentencing Project.

McNeece, C. A. (1995). Adult corrections. In *Encyclopedia of social work* (19th ed., pp. 61–68). Washington, DC: NASW Press.

Mears, D. P., & Kelly, W. R. (1999). Assessments and intake processing: Emerging policy considerations. *Crime & Delinquency, 45*(4), 508–529.

Mesch, G. S., & Fishman, G. (1999). Entering the system: Ethnic differences in closing juvenile criminal files in Israel. *Journal of Crime and Delinquency, 36*(2), 175–193.

Moon, M. M., Sundt, J. L., Cullen, F. T., & Wright, J. P. (2000). Is child saving dead? Public support for juvenile rehabilitation. *Crime & Delinquency, 46*(1), 38–60.

Netherland, W. (1987). Corrections system: Adult. In *Encyclopedia of social work* (18th ed., pp. 351–360). Silver Spring, MD: NASW Press.

Poe-Yamagata, E., & Jones, M. A. (2000, May 17). *And justice for some.* Retrieved November 17, 2001, from http:www.buildingblocksforyouth.org/justiceforsome/jfs.pdf.

Pray, K. (1945). Place of social casework in the treatment of delinquency. *Social Service Review, 19* (2), 235–248.

Rennison, C. M. (2001, June). Criminal victimization 2000: Changes 1999–2000 with trends 1993–2000. *National crime victimization survey.* Washington, DC: Bureau of Justice Statistics.

Robinson, B. A. (2001, February 16). *Capital punishment: The death penalty.* Retrieved November 23, 2001, from http://www.religioustolerance.org/ececute.htm.

Scheurell, R. (1983). Social work ethics in probation and parole. In A. R. Roberts (Ed.), *Social work in juvenile and criminal justice settings* (pp. 241–251). Springfield, IL: Charles C. Thomas.

Schiraldi, V., & Soler, M. (1998). The will of the people? The public's opinion of the Violent and Repeat Juvenile Offender Act of 1997. *Crime and Delinquency, 44*(4), 590–602.

Scott, E. S., & Grisso, T. (1998). The evolution of adolescence: A developmental perspective on juvenile justice reform. *Journal of Criminal Law and Criminology, 88*(1), 137–189.

Siefert, K., & Pimlott, S. (2001). Improving pregnancy outcome during imprisonment: A model residential care program. *Social Work, 46*(2), 125–134.

Social work in the public eye. (2001, June). *NASW News, 46*(6), 13.

State of Wisconsin Department of Corrections. (2001). Form DOC-10 (Rev. 2/01): Probation/Parole Rules. Form DOC-10SO (Rev. 4/01): Standard Sex Offender Rules. Form DO-502 (Rev. 7/96): Admission to Adult Field Caseload: Assessment of Offender Risk. Wisconsin Administrative Code. Madison, WI: Author. Provided by Peggy Kendrigan, Division of Community Corrections.

Stein, J. (2000, July 10). The lessons of Cain. *Time,* pp. 84–85.

Take the stand: Primer for the expert witness. (1998). *NASW News, 43*(1), 16.

Toch, H. (1977). *Police, prisons, and the problem of violence.* Rockville, MD: National Institute of Mental Health, Center for Studies of Crime and Delinquency.

U.S. Department of Justice, Bureau of Justice Statistics. (2001, June 13). *Violent crime rates.* BJS home page (p. 1). Retrieved November 18, 2001, from http://ww.ojp.usdoj.gov/bjs/glance/viort.htm.

Walmsley, R. (2001). *An overview of world imprisonment: Global prison populations, trends and solutions.* Paper presented at the United Nations Programme Network Institutes Technical Assistance Workshop, Vienna, Austria. Retrieved November 21, 2001, from the International Centre for Prison Studies (King's College, London) website:http:www.kcl.ac.uk/depsta/rel/icps/worldbrief/north_Records_php?code=4.

Wooldredge, J. D. (1994). Inmate crime and victimization in a southwestern correctional facility. *Journal of Criminal Justice, 22*(4), 367–381.

FOR FURTHER READING

Acoca, L. (1998). Outside/inside: The violation of American girls at home, on the streets, and in the juvenile justice system. *Crime and Delinquency, 44*(4), 561–589.

Unlike most research articles, this reading makes ample use of dialogue from interviews conducted as a part of the author's investigative study of abuses, past and present, suffered by girls incarcerated in California juvenile correctional facilities. Acoca connects the girls' painful descriptions of their trauma with her review of the literature and with her data analysis. She concludes with challenging questions about how our nation wishes to allocate its resources when significant problems of child abuse exist, especially for the young women who will be the mothers of the future.

Blanchard, C. (1999). Drugs, crime, prison and treatment. *Spectrum: The Journal of State Government, 72*(1), 26–28.

The premise of this article is that the coercive power of correctional systems to require participation in drug treatment programs can be used effectively with both inmates and persons living in the community. Outcome studies cited by the author suggest that such programs can result in decreased recidivism.

Scott, E. S., & Grisso, T. (1997). The evolution of adolescence: A developmental perspective on juvenile justice reform. *Journal of Criminal Law and Criminology, 88*(1), 137–189.

The authors, a professor of law and a professor of psychiatry, make a remarkably compelling argument for the continuation of separate juvenile and adult court systems in the United States. They apply a coherent, in-depth analysis of the understandings derived from developmental psychology to the criminal proceedings that occur at all phases from arrest to incarceration in juvenile justice systems.

Siefert, K., & Pimlott, S. (2001). Improving pregnancy outcome during imprisonment: A model residential care program. *Social Work, 46*(2), 125–134.

This article might well be a catalyst, generating enthusiasm for needed social activism on behalf of imprisoned pregnant women. The cruel treatment women experience and the inadequacy of health services provided during pregnancy are well documented in this article. The unique feature of the article, however, is its description of the planning, implementation, and evaluative research regarding a residential program developed in Michigan for a select group of pregnant, drug-dependent women. Of great interest to the readers of this text is the fact that it was social work students in field placement who were the driving force behind the coalition of government officials and human service agencies that developed and implemented this remarkably humane program.

Victor, J. L. (Ed.). (2000). *Annual editions: Criminal justice 00/01.* Guilford, CT: Dushkin/McGraw-Hill.

An advisory board assists in the selection of articles pertaining to criminal justice in this annual publication. Of special value for student or faculty research is the topic guide, which immediately follows the table of contents. Among the topics covered in the 2000 Annual Editions were battered families, community policing, death penalty, ethics, guns, juvenile justice, probation, and parole. Social work students interested in criminal justice will find articles attempting to explain the sudden drop in the crime rate, one critically examining the DARE Program, and another examining the enormous impact of drug abuse on the criminal justice system. This publication also included brief but fascinating accounts of 39 of the 82 persons sentenced to death who were exonerated and released in the 1990s.

Developmental Disabilities and Social Work: Mary and Lea Perkins

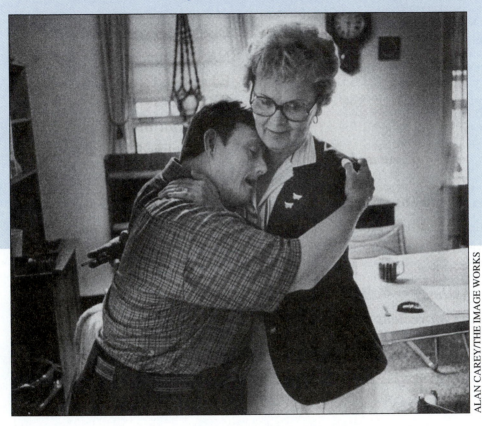

ALAN CAREY/THE IMAGE WORKS

MARY AND LEA PERKINS

Mary Perkins called the Department of Social Services (DSS) early one morning. Her daughter, Lea, 14, had been sexually assaulted by an unknown assailant during the night. The attack had taken place on the front steps of the family apartment. Mary had already called the police, but she decided to call the DSS as well, because she believed that Lea was out of control and needed help. The girl had disobeyed Mary's curfew rules again, contributing to her traumatic experience. She had skipped school almost daily for months. Mary asked the DSS for help in supervision. She knew the department offered these services because her older daughter, Lorraine, 16, already received them. Lorraine had been arrested for drug possession the year before. DSS supervision had been ordered by the court under a CHIPS petition (child in need of protection).

Shortly after Mary's call for help, a neighbor called to report Mary herself for neglect, complaining that the mother was rarely home and allowed her children to "run wild all day." The case was scheduled for investigation. The social worker making the initial contact regarding Lea found a mother who was overwhelmed by the demands of parenting three children, Lorraine, Lea, and Jeff, 11. Mary was openly seeking assistance. The children's father was not a resource for her. Alcoholic and unemployed, he had abused Mary physically and emotionally for years. Mary had recently secured a divorce; social workers at a local women's shelter had assisted her. With the children to support, Mary worked long hours every day to try to make ends meet and took overtime work whenever she could get it.

Because of Mary's admitted lack of control and other family difficulties, Lea was at risk for foster placement. The case was contracted out to a private agency according to a service agreement reflecting the current trend toward privatization. The agency assigned the case to its Home Base program, which provided intensive in-home intervention designed to prevent foster placement. According to the agency's contract with DSS, services could be provided in the home setting for up to three months, for four hours per week. If in-home intervention failed, foster care would follow. The Home Base program assigned the case to one of its social work student interns, Jenny Chambers.

Jenny felt anxious when she read the referral information, as the Perkins family seemed to have so many issues, but she tried to make an appointment right away. The telephone had been disconnected, however. Jenny sent a note to schedule a late-afternoon appointment, when the mother should be home from work. Mary met her at the door and invited her in. The apartment was a mess. Clothes lay scattered all over the floor and dishes overflowed the sink. Jenny took a deep breath and greeted the mother warmly, complimenting her on the one item she could see giving her an excuse to do so, a family picture hanging on the wall.

Mary began to talk about her troubles. Jenny soon learned that the family not only lacked a telephone but had no heat. The rent was three months overdue, and the landlord was threatening eviction. As Mary's bills piled up, she became so fearful she threw them into a plastic bag and tossed the bag into a bedroom closet. The children made Mary so nervous she withdrew into the bedroom early in the evening and shut the door. Two teenaged boys, Lorraine's boyfriend and one of his buddies, stayed in the apartment most of the time and added to the general confusion. They had been rejected by their own families and Mary felt sorry for them. Lea had recently thrown a frying pan at a friend's mother during an argument and had been arrested for assault. The neighbor had taken out a restraining order. There would be a court appearance soon.

Jenny's social work courses at school had prepared her to look for strengths and resilience. She was grateful, as otherwise she suspected she would feel overwhelmed listening to Mary's situation. She began consciously searching for strengths. She already knew of one: Mary had read Jenny's note and kept her appointment. There were several others. Mary wanted to hold her family together. Two of her three children were attending school. Prior to the neglect charge, Mary had had the strength to request assistance for Lea. Now that the DSS was considering foster placement, Mary was willing to do whatever she could to prevent that from happening. She worked long hours due to economic necessity, not because she wanted to neglect her children. She was managing a full-time job responsibly. Like many poor people, she was generous, sharing her meager resources with two needy teens who were not even related to her.

Jenny next talked with Mary about Lea. Mary felt sorry for her daughter about the sexual assault but was also angry with her, as Lea had been out after curfew. Jenny asked how Lea usually behaved. Mary described Lea as "out of control, disrespectful, and nasty." Mary frankly stated that she felt exhausted from trying to function as a parent. She didn't want to "lose" her daughter, however, as so many of her neighbors had lost their children. Lea could be killed or injured on the street, for example. She could end up in foster care due to the neglect charge or to repeated truancy. Mary said that Lea probably refused to go to school because she was a very poor student.

On a hunch, Jenny asked Mary about her own experience as a student. To her surprise, she learned that this mother had an intellectual disability. School had been a desperate struggle for her, but a special education program had been opened when she was in her early teens. A teacher had referred her for evaluation, and she was placed in a class for children with mental retardation. While ashamed at first, Mary began to blossom. During her senior year, she participated in a school-to-work program where she learned to assist in a physician's office. That education had served her well: Mary worked in a physician's office still.

Was it possible that Lea had an intellectual disability too, Jenny wondered? Could a special education placement make a positive difference for her? Certainly a referral for assessment was in order. And what about Mary's unusual coping style? Could her disability help explain the bag of unopened bills? The latter question would probably never be answered with certainty, as Jenny also learned that Mary was taking prescribed medication for anxiety. Anxiety too could affect coping skills.

Before Jenny left her appointment with Mary, she made another to talk with Lea. When she returned two days later, Lea was waiting for her, dressed in baggy jeans, an old sweatshirt, and torn sneakers. Lea told Jenny straight away that she was tired of being poor and wanted to move out of the "ghetto," as she described her neighborhood. People who lived there were looked down upon as "criminals or bums." Lea admitted that she used alcohol to feel better and had been drunk the night of the sexual assault. She was having difficulty sleeping now because of flashbacks and nightmares. She was fighting a lot at home and had recently been arrested for attacking a friend's mother.

Jenny recognized the emotional turmoil Lea was expressing and the associated behavioral problems. However, she also recognized many strengths. Lea had kept her appointment with Jenny and talked to her with surprising candor for a first interview. She could express her feelings verbally. She was aware that some of her behavior was inappropriate. In addition, she expressed strong interest in sports. Jenny thought that might help lure Lea back to school.

Jenny met next with Mary and Lea jointly. Together an intervention plan was developed, including a contract that was signed by all parties. The contract called for (1) school attendance and educational testing for Lea; (2) house rules for Lea; (3) consequences for Lea if she did not follow the rules, which Mary must enforce; (4) therapy for both mother and daughter; and (5) convincing DSS not to place Lea in foster care (this was the component that motivated Lea to agree to the other conditions).

To make the contract feasible, Jenny assisted the family in dealing with some very practical matters: the rent, the telephone, and the heat. She reviewed with Mary every bill in the plastic bag. She role-played talking with the landlord and encouraged Mary to approach the man in person. A payment plan for the back rent was successfully negotiated. Next, Jenny encouraged Mary to talk with the telephone company. A payment plan was worked out and service restored. Jenny found a state energy assistance program and encouraged Mary to call for more information. Mary's heating bill was substantially reduced with funds from the energy assistance program, and a payment plan was worked out. Heat was restored.

Jenny also painstakingly helped Mary develop a budget. While many single mothers are unable to make ends meet due to inadequate wages, Jenny suspected that Mary might have an especially difficult time due to her intellectual disability. So she showed Mary how to write her income and expenses on paper and how to record her payments. To help cut expenses, she shopped for groceries with Mary

505

CHAPTER 13
*Developmental
Disabilities and
Social Work: Mary
and Lea Perkins*

and showed her how to compare prices and use coupons. She even helped Mary plan simple meals, demonstrating how she could save money by avoiding fast-food takeouts.

Through these efforts, Jenny and Mary together realized that feeding two extra teenagers was impossible on Mary's income. Mary admitted to Jenny that their presence had a lot to do with her withdrawing to her bedroom every evening. With Jenny's coaching, she found the courage to tell the boys that they would have to find another place to stay. Jenny offered to help them approach their parents or to refer them for foster care. The boys opted for help in talking to their parents, and soon went back home.

Now Jenny decided it was time to clean up the Perkins apartment, if Mary was interested. She was. Jenny moderated a family meeting where Mary assigned regular chores to herself and the children. Together, they drew up a chart to record their accomplishments, displayed conspicuously on the refrigerator. While Jenny did much of the initial cleanup work with the family, gradually they took over.

Getting Lea to go to school or to attend therapy was not easy. The girl finally agreed to attend school only after her probation officer threatened to put her in juvenile detention if she didn't (Lea had been put on probation for assault shortly after Jenny began working with the family). She then agreed to go if Jenny would accompany her. Jenny agreed, but also referred Lea for a special education evaluation. Only after several meetings between Jenny, the special education staff, and Lea would Lea attend school on her own. Jenny also found she had to accompany Lea to her first few therapy sessions.

Assessment by the special education program determined that Lea did not have an intellectual disability. Her intelligence tested well above average, in fact. However, she did have another disability, emotional disturbance (ED). Lea demonstrated disturbance in three environments: school (truancy), home (disobedience), and community (fighting behavior). Moreover, Lea's therapist submitted a diagnosis of PTSD, or posttraumatic stress disorder. The PTSD related not only to the recent sexual assault but to prior physical and sexual abuse by her father, which the therapist reported to DSS for further investigation. Lea soon began receiving special services at the school and became a much happier person. She joined the girls' basketball team, making new friends.

To Jenny's dismay, however, Mary Perkins initially did not follow through with parts of her contract, either. She did not attend therapy, nor did she often enforce consequences when Lea broke house rules. Lea continued to roam the streets at night, and since the rapist remained at large, danger was real. Jenny sometimes wondered if foster placement might not be appropriate after all. Mary seemed to say one thing and do another with respect to her daughter. Jenny later wrote, in an assignment for school, "At these times I was forced to trust in the love between daughter and mother and hope that they, with assistance, could find balance and safety. I had to believe in the process of treatment, in healing, and in resiliency" (Stites, 2001, p. 23).

Believing in the power of a strengths-based approach, Jenny continued to talk with Mary regularly. She learned that Mary had suffered physical and sexual abuse from her own father. Jenny was then able to help the mother understand Lea's trauma (and need for parental protection) in terms of her own. Jenny also

507

CHAPTER 13
*Developmental
Disabilities and
Social Work: Mary
and Lea Perkins*

helped Mary understand that she needed to serve as a role model for her daughter and to maintain consistent discipline to help Lea gain a sense of security and importance. Finally, Mary began to attend therapy, which helped her deal with long-term anxiety and develop the strength to enforce her own house rules.

As the initial three-month contract with DSS came to a close, Jenny did not believe that either Mary or Lea was ready to carry on without assistance. She applied for, and received, a six-week extension. By the end of that time, the situation had stabilized. Lea was attending school every day on time, participating in the ED program, and actually earning A's. Mother and daughter were attending therapy regularly, reporting that it was useful. Mary was writing down on paper her behavioral expectations and consequences for Lea and enforcing them. She was discussing possible alternative living situations for Lea if her expectations were not met. Lea was following the house rules.

Termination wasn't easy for anyone. Lea, in fact, said she felt "sad and out of control" when Jenny reminded her that their time was coming to a close. Jenny helped Lea to recognize that she had many other caring people in her life now, such as her therapist and the special education staff. She reminded Mary and Lea that they could call the agency for services again if needed, but that she herself would no longer be an intern there. Jenny was sad at the end of her allotted time with the family, as she had grown fond of every member.

A few weeks later, Jenny's supervisor visited the family to evaluate Jenny's work. In response to her questions, Mary replied, with tears in her eyes, that Jenny had been "an awful nag, but we miss her terribly."

SOCIAL WORK ROLES WITH PEOPLE WHO HAVE DISABILITIES

Smart (2001) reminds us that there are four resources that professionals can bring to their work with clients who have disabilities: hope, ideas, understanding of the prejudices and discrimination they face, and a willingness to stand by them. Jenny Chambers, in her work with Mary and Lea Perkins, exemplifies these resources well. The results of her intervention demonstrate what an enormous difference professional help can make in people's lives.

Social workers have worked with people with disabilities in a variety of roles over many years. Early in the history of the profession, for example, Charity Organization Society (COS) workers investigated the needs of disabled people. Their work was described by Mary Richmond in her classic text, *Social Diagnosis*. Richmond, a leader in the COS, devoted an entire chapter to "The Insane—The Feebleminded" (Richmond, 1917).

Traditionally, social workers have tended to work with people with disabilities in institutional settings such as hospitals and nursing homes. Many are employed in these settings today. Their roles are multifaceted, including providing direct services to clients, program development, administration, and evaluation. As direct service providers, social workers usually function as members of a **rehabilitation** team, engaging in assessment and referral, education, and advocacy. Usually they are the only members of the team with knowledge and responsibility to focus on the *social* needs of their clients (Beaulaurier & Taylor, 2001).

Today more and more social workers are working with people who have disabilities and are living out in the community, as illustrated by this chapter's case example. As the service system continues to shift from an institution-based model toward a community-based one, social work roles have evolved to encompass increasing amounts of "boundary work," or intervention between and among social systems. Such work includes educating people with disabilities and their families about their civil rights and about appropriate programs and services in the community that may be of assistance. Important social work roles involve information and referral services, social brokerage between families and larger systems, and advocacy (Freedman, 1995). Assisting in the development of new or additional services and programs that are widely needed is another important role.

Beaulaurier and Taylor (2001, p. 81) offer an overall framework for services intended to assist people with disabilities:

1. Expand their range of options and choices.
2. Prepare them to be more effective in dealing with professionals, bureaucrats, and agencies that often do not understand or appreciate their heightened need for self-determination.
3. Mobilize and help groups of people with disabilities to consider policy and program alternatives that can improve their situation.

Within the community, then, social workers need to assist clients with disabilities to advocate for programs and services that will allow them to maintain their sense of personal dignity and maximize their independence. Within the family, social workers can be helpful in assisting parents to develop positive expectations toward their children with disabilities and to cope with the ongoing stresses of daily living. Individual, group, and family counseling may be helpful, as can parent training groups and parent-to-parent programs. Respite care opportunities and other supportive services such as day care may be crucial in assuring the success of family care. A systems-based, empowerment approach that recognizes and builds on family strengths is recommended (Freedman, 1995).

Traditionally, professionals who have coordinated services for people with long-term, complex needs have been known as "case managers." However, partly due to influence of the disability rights movement, terminology has been changing. (This movement has been active since the early 1970s. Both the movement and related legislation will be discussed later in the chapter.) For example, Part H of the Individuals with Disabilities Act (the section pertaining to infants and toddlers up to age three) uses the term **service coordinator** for professionals who provide case management services. The service coordinator providing early intervention services under Part H coordinates evaluations and assessments of a particular child, facilitates the development of an "individualized family service plan," helps the family identify relevant service providers, coordinates and monitors the delivery of services, informs families of the availability of advocacy services, coordinates medical and other health providers, and develops transition plans as a child approaches the age of three (Patton, Blackbourn, & Fad, 1996).

509

CHAPTER 13
*Developmental
Disabilities and
Social Work: Mary
and Lea Perkins*

Up for Debate
*Proposition: Genetic testing should be encouraged
for people planning to have children.*

Yes	No
Genetic testing can help reduce the overall incidence of developmental disabilities.	Any life is worthwhile, even one with a disability.
A life with a disability may bring much struggle and little satisfaction.	Many people with disabilities express strong satisfaction with their lives.
Family members, especially caregivers of people with disabilities, experience heavy burdens.	Many families find special rewards in providing care to members with disabilities.
Society as a whole is burdened by the special needs of people with disabilities.	People with disabilities are citizens who have the right to full participation in society like all other citizens.

A fairly new potential role for the social worker in the area of disabilities is that of **job coach,** or employment specialist in a supported employment setting. **Supported employment** is a vocational option that provides individualized supports to people with disabilities so that they can achieve their goals in the workplace. The role of job coach helps assure the success of supported employment. This specialist provides direct services to the consumer such as skill assessment, locating jobs, contacting employers, making job placement arrangements, providing on-site training, assisting with work-related issues, and providing other types of support as needed (Parent, Cone, Turner, & Wehman, 1998).

Genetic counseling is another important role for social workers in this field. Scientific knowledge of genetics and its impact on birth defects is expanding exponentially. Genetic counseling translates scientific knowledge into practical information. Genetic counselors work with people who may be at high risk for inherited disease or abnormal pregnancy, discussing their chances of having children who are affected (Public health information sheets, genetic series, 1998). (See the "Up for Debate" box.)

NASW STANDARDS FOR SERVICE

The NASW's standards for service reflect the need for social workers who are involved with disabled people to have generalist knowledge and skills. In 1982 the National Association of Social Workers collaborated with the American Association on Mental Deficiency to develop specific standards. These are summarized in Exhibit 1.

NASW Standards for Service

EXHIBIT 1

1. All social workers working with developmentally disabled clients shall possess or acquire and develop knowledge about developmental disabilities.
2. All social workers shall subscribe to a set of principles regarding developmental disabilities which should underlie their practice.
3. Social work practice and research shall seek to prevent or reduce the incidence of developmental disabilities.
4. All social workers shall participate in an interdisciplinary approach to serving the needs of developmentally disabled people.
5. The functions of the social work program shall include specific services to the client population and the community.

Source: Quoted from Ruth Freedman. (1995). Developmental disabilities, direct practice. In R. L. Edwards (Ed.). *Encyclopedia of social work* (19th ed., Vol. 1, p. 724). Washington, DC: NASW Press.

The NASW provides extensive interpretations of these standards. Services described include outreach, identification of individuals at risk, community liaison work, coordination of services, advocacy, and discharge planning. Services also include policy development, program planning and administration, research, and program evaluation.

EDUCATION FOR WORK WITH PEOPLE WHO HAVE DISABILITIES

Social Work

Various articles in the *Journal of Social Work Education* assert that more should be done in schools of social work, both graduate and undergraduate, to prepare future social workers for the field of developmental disabilities. DeWeaver and Kropf (1992), for example, point out that although the Council on Social Work Education requires curriculum content about various ethnic and minority groups and women, no such requirement exists regarding content about persons with mental retardation. Their observation could be extended to include persons with developmental disabilities in general and is still true at the beginning of the twenty-first century.

Despite the need for expansion of classroom content, social work education can offer an excellent background for working with developmentally disabled people because of its "person in environment" perspective. Many social work programs currently offer field placements in settings with people who have developmental disabilities. Students who aspire to work in this field can augment their formal education through outside reading, discussion with experienced professionals, attending workshops, and the like.

Qualified Mental Retardation Professional (QMRP)

511

CHAPTER 13
*Developmental
Disabilities and
Social Work: Mary
and Lea Perkins*

Most states now offer a special credential, the Qualified Mental Retardation Professional (QMRP), which certifies that the social worker (or other professional) is qualified to work with people who have mental retardation. The QMRP is authorized under the Code of Federal Regulations, Chapter 42, Subpart D, Section 483.430. Qualifications are flexible and include various bachelor's degrees in areas such as social work and the human services (*Habilitation plan administrator,* 2001). Many states, in addition, require at least one year's practice experience working with people with mental retardation.

People with the QMRP are usually the professionals responsible for developing individual habilitation plans (IHPs), written plans specifying goals for work, recreation, and leisure for disabled residents of institutions such as intermediate care facilities for the mentally retarded (ICF/MRs). ICF/MRs today are largely occupied by people with severe to profound mental retardation who require ongoing supervision and protection. The IHPs are important to ensure that these persons receive individualized, active treatment and are not just left to vegetate (see the case study of Stephanie Hermann and Sandra McLean in Chapter 2).

TYPES OF DEVELOPMENTAL DISABILITIES

According to U.S. Department of Education estimates from school-based data, over 5 million, or approximately 6.4 percent of Americans 21 and younger, have developmental disabilities. While figures on adults are even more difficult to determine, various studies estimate that approximately 49 million Americans have a disability of one kind or another (Patton, Blackbourn, & Fad, 1996).

Some disabilities are so obvious that everyone agrees the person so affected is, indeed, "disabled." A clear example of such a disability might be a bone deformity making it impossible for an afflicted individual to walk. On the other hand, some disabilities, while just as real, are much less visible. For example, today certain children are diagnosed with "learning disabilities" through painstaking assessment of problems in reading, spelling, writing, and so on. These disabilities would not be evident in a preliterate society.

In addition, some disabilities are truly disabling but are not "developmental." A person seriously injured in midlife as a result of an automobile accident may be disabled, but the disability is not defined as developmental. According to the federal definition of **developmental disability,** the condition must occur before the affected individual has reached the age of 22.

How "developmental disability" is defined is not just an academic exercise. The definition affects real people in very real ways. For example, funds reserved for special education services for people with developmental disabilities may be spent only for those who qualify for that funding under the legal definition. A person who needs reeducation in midlife due to injury from severe physical or sexual abuse will not qualify for the same services in the public schools that assisted both Mary and Lea Perkins.

Some states define developmental disabilities according to category—for example, mental retardation or cerebral palsy. Persons who fall into these categories are eligible for whatever financial aid is provided by state law for such classifications.

The federal definition of disability, on the other hand, is functional. The current revision of the Developmental Disabilities Assistance Bill of Rights defines developmental disabilities as

> disabilities that are severe and chronic in nature. Furthermore, they are caused by either mental or physical impairment, or both; present themselves before the person becomes 22; have a strong probability of continuing for the rest of the person's life; and significantly limit a person's ability to carry on major life activities, including the ability to live independently and earn a living. Developmental disabilities also include disabilities that require some kind of intervention, care, or treatment for a long duration, if not for life. (Mackelprang & Salsgiver, 1999, p. 147)

For a given person to qualify for federal funds, his or her disability must be severe in function, and the functional impairment must be chronic (of extended duration). Therefore, a person who might qualify categorically for state aid because of a mild disability might not qualify for federal aid.

With the above considerations of definition in mind, let us examine nine diagnostic categories of developmental disabilities (see Exhibit 2). We will also discuss fetal alcohol syndrome and cocaine-affected babies.

Intellectual Disability or Mental Retardation

Mental retardation is caused by a wide variety of factors. Sometimes it results from injury at birth, as in the case of Sandra McLean in Chapter 2's case study. Sometimes the mother has had a serious illness during pregnancy (measles is a well-known example). Sometimes, as in Down's syndrome, the cause is genetic and involves chromosomal abnormalities. Sometimes the problem involves inadequate nutrition for the pregnant mother, a terrible potential side effect of poverty. Early infant nutrition has an effect as well, as does early sensory stimulation. A mother's drinking, smoking, or drug use may result in retardation of her child. Some conditions are reversible with early intervention. Myriad factors—some identifiable, some not—may affect a young child's mental development.

A child who has an intellectual disability is unable to learn at the rate most children do or cannot apply what is learned in the normal way to requirements of daily living. Preschoolers with this diagnosis tend to learn more slowly than other children to crawl, sit, walk, and talk. Such school-aged children have difficulty de-

Major Categories of Developmental Disabilities	
EXHIBIT 2	
Mental retardation (intellectual disability)	Epilepsy
Cerebral palsy	Traumatic brain injury
Autism	Learning disabilities
Orthopedic problems	Co-occurrence of disabilities
Hearing problems	

veloping academic skills and often social skills as well. Such adults have trouble living and working independently in the community, although they may do well with supervision and other assistance.

513

CHAPTER 13
*Developmental
Disabilities and
Social Work: Mary
and Lea Perkins*

Mental retardation should be distinguished from mental illness, a temporary or chronic condition primarily involving emotional disorders. People with mental retardation may be very well adjusted emotionally. In 1992, the American Association on Mental Retardation (AAMR) published a new definition of mental retardation (quoted in Patton, Blackbourn, & Fad, 1996, pp. 91–92):

> Mental retardation refers to substantial limitations in present functioning. It is characterized by significantly subaverage intellectual functioning, existing concurrently with related limitations in two or more of the following applicable adaptive skill areas: communication, self-care, home living, social skills, community use, self-direction, health and safety, functional academics, leisure and work, Mental retardation manifests before age 18.

While in the past intellectual disabilities were usually classified according to IQ scores as mild, moderate, or severe, the AAMR recommends discontinuing this practice as IQ clearly does not tell the whole story. The AAMR definition focuses on how well people actually function. For example, some children with rather low IQs adapt well to the environment, both socially and physically, even better than some children with higher IQs. IQ tests, it must be kept in mind, were developed by middle-class white psychologists to measure the performance of middle-class white children. They do not always measure ability accurately, especially for children from minority backgrounds who may have learned entirely different things than the information sought by the tests.

If IQ scores alone were considered, about 2 percent of Americans (approximately 1 percent of school-age children) would be considered to have mental retardation. Children with mental retardation constitute about 13 percent of students with developmental disabilities (Patton, Blackbourn & Fad, 1996). (See Exhibit 3.)

Four Assumptions Essential to the Application of the Definition of Mental Retardation

EXHIBIT 3

- Valid assessment considers cultural and linguistic diversity, as well as a difference in communications and behavioral factors.
- The existence of limitations in adaptive skills in the context of community environments typical of the individual's age peers is indexed to the person's individualized needs for supports.
- Specific adaptive limitations often co-exist with strengths in other adaptive skills or other personal capabilities.
- With appropriate supports over a sustained period, the life functioning of the person with mental retardation will generally improve.

Source: Quoted from *AAMR fact sheet: What is mental retardation?* (2001, March 6). (Online). Available: http://161.58.153.187/Policies/faq_mental_retardation.shtml.

Cerebral Palsy

Cerebral palsy results from damage to the brain, usually before or during birth. It takes three major forms: spasticity, dyskinesia, and ataxia (described below). Some people manifest elements of all three forms. Cerebral palsy may affect the entire body or only parts, such as various limbs. Spasticity is the most common form of cerebral palsy. Movement is difficult, slow, and stiff, and sometimes jerky. Dyskinesia, on the other hand, is a manifestation in which movement may be continuous but random and uncontrolled, especially under stress. Facial features may move in an uncontrolled manner as well. The walking gait is lurching. Ataxia is the least common form of cerebral palsy and is primarily a balance disorder.

Approximately 2 to 3 children in 1,000 have cerebral palsy, but only about half of the people with this condition were born with it. Approximately 500,000 children and adults in the United States have it today (*Cerebral palsy,* 1999). Risk is particularly great with premature and low-birthweight children. For those who develop cerebral palsy after birth, head trauma and brain infection are the most frequent causes.

Cerebral palsy is often accompanied by other disorders. For example, about half the victims suffer mental retardation. Perceptual and language disorders are also common (Baroff, 1991).

Autism

Autistic children are often described as being in a "world of their own." No one knows the reason why. At birth these children may appear perfectly normal, and they may continue to appear perfectly normal for the first year or two. Then the parents will become disturbed by the child's repetitive motions and apparent inability to hear. Hearing tests will reveal, however, that the child does hear but pays attention to random sounds rather than to meaningful words. Language development is delayed, and the child may only repeat back exactly what is said, without apparent comprehension of meaning (such repetition is called echolalic speech). Mental retardation often accompanies autism, although intellectual functioning is difficult to test because of the child's language delays and behavior abnormalities. Autistic children do not respond positively to attention; instead, they withdraw and often behave violently or fearfully when approached. Such behavior, of course, can be heartbreaking to the parents (McDonald-Wikler, 1987).

According to the Autism Society of America (*What is autism?,* 2001), autism is a complex developmental disability that results from a neurological disorder of unknown cause. It affects approximately 1 in 500 individuals and is four times as common in boys as in girls. Autism is one of several related disorders classified by the *DSM-IV* as a "pervasive developmental disorder" (see Chapter 9 for a discussion of the *DSM-IV*). All persons who fall under this category exhibit communication and social deficits, but symptoms differ in terms of severity. Over one-half million Americans today have autism or some form of pervasive developmental disorder. Although autism is diagnosed according to a characteristic set of behaviors (for example, little interest in social interaction, delayed language development, lack of imaginative play, frequent tantrums or unusual passivity), these behaviors present themselves in myriad combinations and degrees of severity.

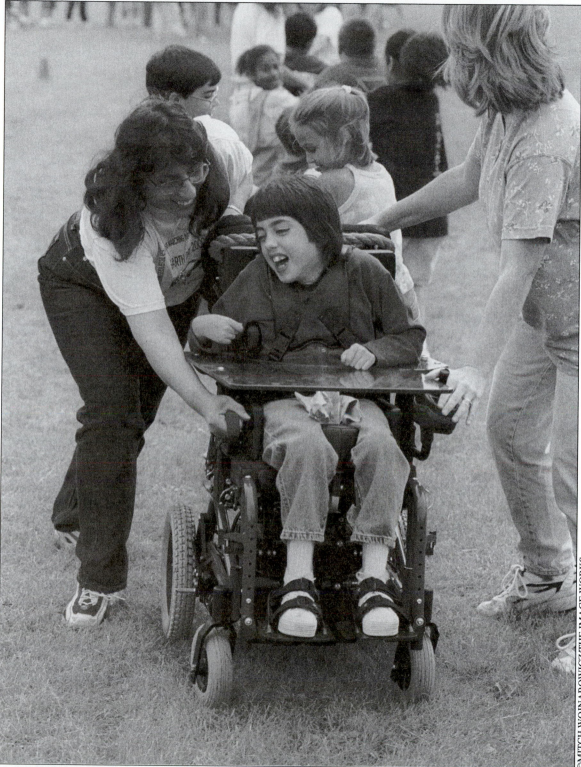

A mainstreamed fifth grader with cerebral palsy participates in a tug-of-war in her wheelchair helped by teachers during a school field day competition.

The cause of autism is not understood. At one time parents were blamed for being aloof and unresponsive, but this theory has been proved false. Today complex genetic factors are suspected. Early intensive interventions can make an important positive difference. With appropriate services and supports, most families are able to raise their autistic children at home.

Orthopedic Problems

Orthopedic problems include a wide variety of physical disabilities, such as problems with physical functioning of bones, joints, and muscles. Spina bifida is a well-known example. A child with this condition is born with an incomplete spinal column so that nerve impulses cannot reach the legs and the child cannot walk. Other examples of orthopedic problems include bone deformities, missing limbs, or extra fingers and toes. Some such problems can be corrected at birth by surgery or more gradually by corrective appliances such as braces.

Children with minor orthopedic problems may not be classified as developmentally disabled because functional impairment is not severe enough to meet the definition. Other children with severe orthopedic problems may receive services under a different classification (for example, cerebral palsy). For this reason, the exact prevalence of orthopedic problems in the United States is difficult to determine.

It should be kept in mind that children with physical impairments may experience rejection, embarrassment, feelings of insecurity, stigma, and so forth (Patton, Blackbourn, & Fad, 1996). Social workers need to be sensitive to the emotional challenges that these children face in addition to the physical ones.

Hearing Problems

Not widely known is the fact that hearing problems can cause massive developmental disabilities. This happens because speech and language are so important to cognitive development and social functioning and because hearing loss impedes language development. Children who are hearing-impaired are often diagnosed incorrectly as being mentally retarded, because their language development is so grossly delayed that they cannot be tested accurately. Without language development, the thinking process may be hampered as well.

Hearing loss may range from mild to profound. Conductive hearing loss is caused by various pathologic conditions in the outer and middle ear, so that sound cannot mechanically reach the inner ear. Such conditions may include wax, infections, or ruptures of the eardrum, and they are usually treatable. Sensorineural hearing loss is caused by pathologic conditions affecting the inner ear structure and/or the auditory nerve, which is much more difficult to treat effectively. Other causes of hearing loss include mechanical injuries and various birth defects (Talbott, 1992).

According to Mackelprang and Salsgiver (1999), approximately 21 million Americans today are deaf or hard-of-hearing, about 8.5 percent of the population as a whole. Most of these individuals experience their hearing loss as adults, and only about 1.35 million are completely deaf. About 190,000 were born deaf, however, or became deaf before acquiring verbal language. Another

113,000 became deaf as children. The more limited the exposure to verbal language, of course, the more likely that communication will take place through sign language.

517

CHAPTER 13
*Developmental
Disabilities and
Social Work: Mary
and Lea Perkins*

Approximately 5 percent of school-aged children suffer some degree of hearing impairment, but only about 0.13 percent receive special education services (Patton, Blackbourn, & Fad, 1996).

Epilepsy

Epilepsy, or seizure disorder, results from excessive electrical discharges in the brain. Seizures may be partial (originating from an electrical impulse on one side of the brain only) or general (originating simultaneously on both sides of the brain). Epileptic seizures have several common features. First, they are recurrent. Young children may suffer occasional seizures that disappear by age six or seven, but these are generally not regarded as epilepsy. In addition to their recurrent nature, epileptic seizures tend to have (1) a sudden onset, (2) an altered state of consciousness, (3) a similar length of time per type of seizure, (4) abnormal movement or postural change, (5) spontaneous cessation, and (6) a lapse of time before returning to the preseizure state (Baroff, 1991).

Although data on the prevalence of epilepsy are conflicting and vary with the definition used, approximately 2.5 million Americans have conditions resulting in recurrent seizures (Mackelprang and Salsgiver, 1999). Mental retardation occurs in only about 10 percent of persons with this disability (Patton, Blackbourn, & Fad, 1996).

Two types of seizures are particularly well known: grand mal and petit mal. A grand mal seizure is also called a convulsion. The afflicted person thrashes around on the ground for a few minutes and may be unconscious for a period of time afterward. A petit mal seizure is less dramatic. There is a lapse of consciousness for a few seconds, during which the person appears to be staring or daydreaming. Petit mal seizures may occur several times a day. They disturb the afflicted person because they interrupt ongoing activities and thinking and tend to result in memory loss.

In another type of seizure, called a "drop attack," the legs simply give way and the afflicted person drops to the ground. The attack lasts only a minute or two. Children with this disorder usually wear protective helmets.

Traumatic Brain Injury

Traumatic brain injury includes any trauma to the head that causes brain damage. Brain injuries generally occur in three ways: through blunt injuries, as when the head is hit by a fixed or moving object (such as a windshield or a baseball bat); penetrating injuries, as when the head is penetrated by an object such as a bullet; and compression injuries, as when the head is crushed.

Head injuries may result in fractures, or broken or dented skull bones. Loose bone fragments may place pressure on the brain. Concussion, or temporary loss of consciousness, may occur. Severe blows may cause contusions, or bruising of the brain tissue. Lacerations of the head may tear brain tissue.

Traumatic brain injury may result in a variety of disabling conditions such as impaired judgment, memory loss, agitation, confusion, lack of inhibition, and short attention span. (*Fact sheet on traumatic brain injury,* 1999).

Learning Disabilities

Some children have disabilities that interfere with their ability to read, write, spell, or do mathematical calculations. They may also have trouble listening, speaking, or thinking. Often these children appear perfectly normal until they go to school, where they encounter a whole new set of demands. They score normally on IQ tests, but somehow they do not seem to perceive written language in the same way that other children do. While they may be able to read written words, many cannot translate their meaning. No matter how hard they try, these children seem unable to learn in the usual way. Although there is much about learning disabilities that we do not understand, a number of techniques have been devised to help children so afflicted.

The definition of learning disability (sometimes called perceptual disorder) varies from state to state. In general, according to legal definitions for regulatory purposes, the inability to learn cannot be the result of low intelligence, socioeconomic circumstances, or poor sensory skills. The most frequent method of identifying learning disabilities involves measuring and comparing ability and achievement in the school setting. Thus, the disabilities are rarely identified before a child goes to school.

Learning problems are amazingly diverse. They may involve language skills, visual and auditory perception, the ability to combine information obtained from several senses (such as touch, sight, and hearing), limited attention span, hyperactivity, and memory skills. Such disabilities are considerably more common among males than among females, although the reasons are not understood (Bender, 1992).

Fetal Alcohol Syndrome and Cocaine-Exposed Babies

Babies who are born affected by alcohol, cocaine, and other drugs are a growing concern in the United States. Each year, more than 50,000 newborns show some degree of alcohol-related damage, and alarmingly, studies show that drinking among pregnant women is increasing. Many women are aware that heavy drinking can cause harm, but far fewer realize that light to moderate drinking can be harmful depending on the developmental stage of the fetus. Between 2,000 and 12,000 babies have fetal alcohol syndrome (FAS) annually, a combination of physical and mental birth defects, and the rest have fetal alcohol effects (FAE), or lesser degrees of alcohol-related damage (*Drinking during pregnancy,* 1999). In addition, according to the National Institute on Drug Abuse, approximately 45,000 women use cocaine during pregnancy, also placing their unborn children at serious risk of birth defects (*Cocaine use during pregnancy,* 1998).

Fetal alcohol syndrome involves both physical and mental birth defects. Babies born with FAS are abnormally small at birth and remain below normal in size. They usually have flat cheeks, small eyes, and short, upturned noses. Most have small brains and a degree of mental retardation. Poor coordination, a short attention span, and behavioral problems are characteristic of FAS. Babies born with FAE have some but not all of these difficulties. The effects of FAS and FAE are lifelong.

Mothers who drink heavily (four to five drinks daily or more) have a very high risk of giving birth to an infant with FAS, but even an occasional drink at a critical time during pregnancy can cause damage. Alcohol passes through the mother's placenta into the developing fetus, whose immature organs cannot break the substance down as fast as the mother's can. Hence, the alcohol level in the baby's blood may exceed that of the mother's and may result in irreversible damage. Unfortunately, cocaine also passes through the mother's placenta into the fetus. The drug can trigger labor so that many cocaine-exposed babies are born prematurely. Those who survive are likely to have brain damage causing mental retardation, cerebral palsy, and visual and hearing impairments. The babies tend to have small heads, which possibly indicates a small brain. Many appear to experience drug withdrawal; they are irritable and jittery, making it difficult to bond with parents or other caretakers.

While substance abuse during pregnancy clearly places a mother's infant at risk, there is increasing evidence today that substance abuse by fathers also increases the risk. More research is needed.

Co-occurrence of Disabilities

Many children suffer from more than one disability at the same time. For example, Sandra McLean, introduced in Chapter 2, suffered from both epilepsy and mental retardation. Children with cerebral palsy and autism frequently experience mental retardation as well. Children with FAS and those who are cocaine-exposed characteristically suffer multiple disabilities. In addition, it is important to remember that all disabilities, even those that appear to be entirely physical, involve psychological and social dimensions. Professional intervention must involve attending to the whole person.

SERVICES FOR PEOPLE WITH DISABILITIES: A BRIEF HISTORY

Throughout most of history, very little has been done for persons with disabilities. At one extreme (ancient Sparta), such unfortunate individuals were left outside to die of exposure. Native Americans, on the other hand, allowed people with disabilities to live unharmed as children of the Great Spirit.

There are a few early recorded efforts to make special provisions for persons with disabilities. In the 1300s a colony of persons with mental retardation was established in Belgium, and in 1325 King Edward II of England issued a statute distinguishing between people with mental retardation and those afflicted with temporary mental illness. He established guidelines to protect the rights of "idiots" and to provide for their daily care (Dickerson, 1981). Later on, the Elizabethan Poor Law of 1601 provided limited food and shelter for people with disabilities (along with the poor, the mentally ill, and the sick). Apparently, no thought was given to providing services or education to improve the lives and opportunities of such individuals.

France provided the pioneers who first educated persons with disabilities. Jacob Rodriguez Pereira demonstrated that people with speech and hearing problems could be taught to read words and to add simple numbers. By the late 1700s Pereira had become so famous for his work that he was honored at the court of King Louis XV. Later, in the early 1800s, Jean-Marc-Gaspard Itard took on the education of a young boy, about 12 years old, whom he named Victor. The boy had been discovered living in a forest in France in 1799, and Itard hoped to help him learn how to function as a normal human person. Itard worked intensively on this goal for about five years. The extent of Victor's mental retardation was too great, however, and Itard initially considered the project a failure. However, he was able to teach Victor basic self-care skills such as feeding and dressing. The boy remained mute but learned to read and write a few words. The French Academy of Science, impressed by Itard's accomplishments, recognized him and asked him to write a report. The result became a classic, *The Wild Boy of Aveyron* (Patton, Blackbourn, & Fad, 1996).

Another Frenchman, Itard's student Edouard Seguin (who was also influenced by Pereira), worked with small groups of children with mental retardation in a hospital in Paris in the mid-1800s. Seguin demonstrated that these children could be taught to speak, read, obey instructions, and accomplish simple tasks.

Training Schools

At the same time that Seguin was working with retarded children in Paris, a Swiss physician named Johann Guggenbuhl started a residential facility for people afflicted with cretinism. Cretinism is common in mountainous regions of Europe. Caused by a thyroid deficiency, it results in severe mental retardation and physical crippling. Guggenbuhl was inspired by a religious vision; he was determined to prove that these people could be taught. Guggenbuhl succeeded in his long-term goal, stimulating further work with people with disabilities all over the world, including the development of training schools in the United States. In the short run he ran into trouble, however, partly because he misunderstood the causes of cretinism. Like others of his time, Guggenbuhl thought the condition was caused by poor diet, unclean air and water, and lack of sunlight. He corrected these problems in his training school but promised too much in too short a time. His facility was closed in 1858.

In 1848 Dr. Samuel Gridley Howe, an American reformer, traveled to Europe and visited Guggenbuhl's training school and Seguin's hospital program. Back in the United States he lobbied for funds to begin similar work. He established training schools for children with disabilities in Massachusetts, New York, and Pennsylvania during the late 1840s and early 1850s. These schools were small and usually served fewer than 20 children each; their goal was to prepare children with disabilities (such as vision impairment or mild mental retardation) for productive adult lives in the community. Admission was limited to those children who were considered to have the most potential for rehabilitation and eventual discharge.

Seguin emigrated to the United States in 1848 after the rise of Napoleon III, a dictator with whom he had political and religious differences. As Seguin became active in the early movement establishing training schools for children with disabilities in America, he advocated for small facilities, each ideally serving no more than 200 children so that each child could receive individual attention and planning. He suggested that these institutions be built near cities and towns, so that younger children could receive instruction by parents, who, in turn, could be coached by the training staff of the school. Seguin's intent was that children should be returned to the community when they gained sufficient skills (Switzky, Dudzinzki, Van Acker, & Gambro, 1988).

Protective Asylums

Because of the lack of other resources for people with developmental disabilities in the community, the vision of the training school as a small institution to educate a few disabled children for community living soon was overwhelmed by demand for protective shelter for disabled people of all kinds. By the 1870s parents and relatives were begging the schools to take on the daily care of their family members with disabilities. The training schools quickly turned into huge impersonal institutions. They tended to be built in rural areas, which isolated the residents from the rest of society. To reduce costs, higher-functioning residents were to set to work the land, so that their education was abandoned in favor of using their abilities as a means of producing income for the asylums. Other talented residents were required to cook, clean, and provide personal care for the less able. Thus, tax input to support the institutions could be kept low, reducing taxpayers' complaints.

Custodial care, rather than education or rehabilitation, became the purpose of these large asylums. By the late 1860s Samuel Gridley Howe was advocating that the institutions be closed. He urged that their residents be reintegrated into society rather than being segregated into the cheaply built, warehouse-style, oppressive facilities designed to provide mass care rather than individualized care.

The Eugenics Movement

The institutions were not closed, however. The next period of history was one that demeaned people with developmental disabilities and tended to keep them not only socially isolated but also despised. By the 1880s social Darwinism was in full swing. Its advocates took Charles Darwin's fascinating discoveries regarding evolutionary trends in whole physical species and inappropriately applied them to individuals within the single species called *Homo sapiens* in a way Darwin never intended. Social Darwinists preached that since persons with disabilities were "inferior," they were second-class citizens, and taxpayers should not be required to assist them. In fact, it was better that they be allowed to die off according to "natural law."

Along a similar vein, members of the eugenics movement whipped up a hysteria of fear regarding people with disabilities. A book in 1883 by the English scientist Francis Galton, a cousin of Darwin, asserted that people with mental retardation committed terrible crimes and that "morons" were multiplying like rabbits compared with the rest of the population. Galton insisted that retarded people were spreading venereal diseases and sexual immorality. Frightened by such assertions, eugenicists (people committed to improving the genes of the population) clamored successfully for massive sterilization of people with retardation (Patton, Blackbourn, & Fad, 1996). They called for confinement of people with disabilities in segregated, jail-like institutions from which there could be no escape without sterilization. Obviously, social Darwinists and eugenicists found natural allies in one another.

A third social influence tending to demean people with disabilities was the development of the standardized intelligence test. The most famous IQ test of the time was devised by the French psychologists Alfred Binet and Théodore Simon. It was in widespread use by the early 1900s. The intelligence tests placed powerful labels such as "moron" on individuals with mental retardation and tended to set in stone other people's ideas of the potential of a person with disabilities. "Once feebleminded, always feebleminded" became a belief of the times. With such an outlook, why establish educational or rehabilitative programs for people with handicapping conditions?

Between 1880 and 1925 institutions for people with disabilities grew into huge facilities designed for subhuman "animals"; the model was that of the hospital, where everyone residing therein was viewed as "sick," where living units were called "wards," and where the residents were prevented from "hurting themselves" by being confined to locked wards with barred windows, little or no furniture, and nothing in the way of comfort or hope. Dehumanizing routines removed almost all opportunity for persons with disabilities to learn to live like people without disabilities, so that the "inmates" or "patients" truly seemed subhuman by the time the institution was through with them (Switzky, Dudzinski, Van Acker, & Gambro, 1988).

New Research, New Attitudes

In 1919 W. E. Fernald published a study of what happened to 1,537 residents with disabilities who were released from institutions between 1890 and 1914. He delayed publication of his results because they astonished him; he had previously supported the "social menace" theory. Fernald found that most of the men and women released exhibited socially acceptable behavior. Few married or bore children; many became self-supporting. Fernald conducted another study in 1924 of 5,000 children with mental retardation in Massachusetts schools and found that fewer than 8 percent exhibited any kind of antisocial behavior (Switzky, Dudzinski, Van Acker, & Gambro, 1988).

Other studies of the time demonstrated similar results. For example, Z. P. Hoakley investigated people discharged from public institutions in 1922 to determine how many had to be readmitted within one year; his results demonstrated that only 6 percent of males and 13 percent of females had to be readmitted. H. C. Storrs investigated 616 adults discharged from an institution in New York State in 1929 and found that only 4 percent had to be readmitted (Willer & Intagliata, 1984).

Attitudes toward people with disabilities began to improve in the 1920s, partly as a result of research but mostly because of the passage of time and the gradual dying down of the eugenics hysteria. Institutions made attempts to "parole" their highest-functioning residents into the community, at first to relatives' homes and later, by the 1930s, to family care homes. Some institutions developed "colony" plans that relocated residents to smaller institutions intended to provide more nearly normal, but still supervised, living arrangements. Some of the "colonies" were farms where residents could be nearly self-supporting; some were located in towns where residents could work in factories.

Economic factors interfered with the process of **deinstitutionalization.** The Great Depression of the 1930s made it impossible to find community-based jobs for all who could perform them. World War II improved public attitudes toward

523

CHAPTER 13
*Developmental
Disabilities and
Social Work: Mary
and Lea Perkins*

the disabled because so many war veterans came home with disabilities, but the war effort itself drained money away from other pressing social needs. Although the rate of institutional growth slowed during the 1940s, admissions to institutions continued to exceed discharges during this entire period, despite attempts at community placement (Willer & Intagliata, 1984).

Normalization and the Deinstitutionalization Movement

Normalization is a concept that was first developed in the Scandinavian countries in the 1950s. The principle can be summarized as "making available to persons with mental retardation, as well as to persons with other handicapping conditions, patterns and conditions of everyday life that are as close as possible to the norms and patterns of mainstream society" (Switzky, Dudzinski, Van Acker, & Gambro, 1988, p. 32). The idea took shape in the 1950s and continues to evolve today.

Normalization involves the recognition that people with disabilities are people first—people who simply happen to have physical or mental disabilities with which they must cope. They deserve caring, humane assistance. Parent groups such as the National Association for Retarded Citizens (organized in 1950 and known today as the Association for Retarded Citizens U.S.), as well as professional organizations such as the NASW, have provided leadership in this direction. The goal has not yet been achieved, but steps are being taken in the right direction, as illustrated in the case of Sandra McLean in Chapter 2 and Mary and Lea Perkins in this chapter's case example.

Normalization for a person with disabilities requires a plan of care providing for education, training in daily living skills, community-based rather than institutional care, and an opportunity for employment or some other occupation designed to maximize one's potential for independent living. Deinstitutionalization of persons with disabilities came to be perceived as part of the overall thrust of the 1960s toward upholding the rights of minority groups. Funding has been a continual problem in achieving this goal, however, as also is illustrated in the McLean case. Zoning is another barrier keeping group homes for people with disabilities out of residential neighborhoods. Both problems illustrate that people without disabilities still discriminate against those who are less fortunate.

Deinstitutionalization as a Goal

An important piece of legislation, the Developmental Disabilities Act of 1969, called for establishing planning councils and advocacy agencies in every state. The act helped create a service structure that could help make deinstitutionalization a realistic goal (Parkinson & Howard, 1996).

The deinstitutionalization movement accelerated during the 1970s and 1980s. This acceleration was spurred in part by court decisions. For example, in 1971 a class action lawsuit was initiated on behalf of patients with mental illness at Bryce State Hospital and residents with mental retardation at the Partlow State School, both in Alabama. The decision of the U.S. Supreme Court in *Wyatt v. Stickney* (1972) affirmed not only that institutionalized people have a constitutional right to **habilitation** services (services designed to help one achieve and maintain one's maximum level of functioning) but also that mildly or moderately retarded persons should be admitted to institutions only if this is the least restrictive environment available (Willer & Intagliata, 1984).

The economic climate of the early 1970s also helped the deinstitutionalization movement. The economy was strong, helping to provide funding for staff to organize community placement and permitting employment for the more independent of those discharged. That deinstitutionalization occured at a dramatic rate has been well documented by research. Between 1967 and 1988, for example, the percentage of people with development disabilities residing in institutions dropped from 85 percent to 34 percent (Wolfe, 1992).

Figures such as these probably overstate the reality experienced by people with disabilities, however. As inflation became a severe problem in the late 1970s, the coalition fueling community placement (political conservatives who desired reduced government spending, liberals who wanted more humane care) fell apart (Segal, 1995). Many people simply were shifted from large state institutions to private custodial settings such as nursing homes that were cheaper. Many of the new settings provided inadequate services for the population they absorbed. It has been suggested that "reinstitutionalization" better describes what actually happened to many people (Johnson & Surles, 1994).

HUMAN DIVERSITY AND POPULATIONS-AT-RISK: UNFINISHED BUSINESS

The best way to accomplish deinstitutionalization for people with developmental disabilities, a population-at-risk, is to prevent institutionalization in the first place. Such prevention, however, requires a continuum of care available in the community. Fortunately the service system moved from a primarily institution-based model in place prior to the late 1960s to a community-based model in the 1970s and 80s (Freedman, 1995). The change was advanced by the Developmental Disabilities Act of 1969, mentioned above. Community-based planning made a continuum of care at least a theoretical possibility for people with disabilities, although the task has never been completed.

The Continuum of Care

The **continuum of care** begins at home, the least restrictive, most normal environment in which children can be raised. **Respite care** to help prevent burnout of family caregivers can be crucial to the success of care in the home. Adults with disabilities may be able to live independently in homes or apartments of their own with appropriate assistance. Other reasonably independent adults may do well in boardinghouse-type arrangements, with room, board, and a minimum of supervision. Days may be spent in activity centers, regular employment, or **sheltered workshops** (places of employment that provide special training and services for people with disabilities).

Foster homes, or **family care homes,** are the next step along the continuum of care. They provide familylike settings with foster parents. Lea Perkins would have been placed in one had her own mother not been able to improve her parenting skills. Next, somewhere near the middle of the continuum of care, are small group homes. These facilities are staffed by aides and skilled professionals who provide care, supervision, and training for up to eight people.

525

CHAPTER 13
*Developmental
Disabilities and
Social Work: Mary
and Lea Perkins*

Nearing the institutional end of the continuum are nursing homes. Nursing homes range from those providing only room, board, and minor personal assistance to those offering skilled nursing care for persons with extensive physical needs. When large numbers of people with disabilities were moved to nursing homes in the 1970s, many of these facilities developed special programs for them. Unfortunately, however, many did not, and almost 20 years passed before federal Medicaid regulations required special certification and appropriate programming.

At the far end of the continuum of care are the large state institutions where people with disabilities reside in highly restrictive, regulated environments. Today, most people who live in these facilities have severe and multiple disabilities.

Research Suggests Direction for Service Improvement

For family care to have the best chance for success, specialized services are often needed. However, a study by Christopher Petr and David Barney (1993, May) found that parents received limited help from professionals (see Exhibit 4) and may even experience adversarial treatment. For example, some professionals recommended institutional placement when the family desired additional home-based services. Sometimes, however, home-based services were recommended but simply did not exist or were financially out of reach because private insurance refused to pay.

Parents in the study identified several pressing needs. The first was increased access to respite care, temporary care to relieve regular caregivers. Another was more information about and access to other community resources, including financial aid. In addition, parents wanted policies and programs to promote normalization and community integration for their children. They wanted these programs to

---

How Parents View Professionals

EXHIBIT 4

Parents of developmentally delayed children stressed the need for professional commitment to the child and family. Too often, workers seemed overwhelmed by caseloads and burned out, so that the family saw them only in a crisis. . . . Many of the parents also felt that professionals were too guarded and pessimistic about the child's potential. They felt that their own higher expectations were generally more accurate. . . . Parents are often dismayed at having to be such strong self-advocates to professionals. Rather than experiencing a helpful, concerned, and cooperative relationship, parents sometimes experience the parent–professional relationship as conflictual and adversarial.

Source: Quoted from Christopher Petr and David Barney, (1993, May). Reasonable efforts for children with disabilities: The parent's perspective. *Social Work, 38*(3), pp. 251–252.

be staffed by professionals who treated them as peers. They also wanted input into the design, implementation, and evaluation of these programs (Petr & Barney, 1993).

Providing Supportive Services to Diverse Families

Barnwell and Day (1996) point out that to intervene successfully, social workers and other professionals must understand that the values and experiences of the families they deal with may be very different from their own. Moreover, family needs change over time. Services required to cope successfully with infants with disabilities, for example, are very different from those required to meet the needs of adolescents, adults, or older adults.

These authors note that different ethnic and cultural groups utilize professional services at different rates, and provide professionals with different amounts and types of information. They point out that service systems tend to be designed according to white, middle-class values that emphasize self-reliance, whereas Hispanic values, for example, emphasize the importance of the extended family. Cultural sensitivity is required to help develop service systems that are responsive to the needs of diverse families with members who have disabilities. Moreover, cultural perspectives differ as to the meaning of disability, the causes of disability, and the appropriate roles of families with respect to disability. What may be experienced as a terrible tragedy in one culture may in another be experienced as God's will and an opportunity to serve. Professional intervention must take account of these cultural differences as well as differences in communication styles, child rearing practices, and the like.

To assess the impact of culture on disability services, the National Council on Disability conducted a public hearing in San Francisco in 1998 on "Meeting the Unique Needs of People with Disabilities from Diverse Cultural Groups." The council found extensive barriers to employment involving significant racial disparities in the delivery of vocational rehabilitative services. Barriers to special education services in schools were also widespread, involving difficulties in communicating with school personnel, particularly for persons whose primary language was other than English. In addition, cultural diversity factors increased the impact of disability on many minority group members. For example, the council found significant differences in the *perception* of disability. Many members of minority groups viewed disability as a reflection upon their entire family and, unfortunately, as a negative and shameful one.

According to its report (Lift every voice, 1999, p. 15) The National Council on Disability finds that:

> There is a tremendous need for education and outreach to minority individuals, their families, and their communities in order to support them in dealing with the impact of disability and, in turn, to increase their awareness about available resources and ways to integrate the experience of disability into one's life, one's family, and one's community without shame or unnecessary sacrifice of one's goals.

The council also found that citizens without disabilities frequently exhibited intolerant behavior toward citizens with disabilities and documented many unfortunate examples (see Exhibit 5). Professionals needed a better understanding of

527

CHAPTER 13
*Developmental
Disabilities and
Social Work: Mary
and Lea Perkins*

Riding the Bus:
Experiences of Blind Persons

EXHIBIT 5

When we get on the bus, if there are too many people, even though there is a public notice on seating the disabled first, people don't give up their seats, especially those young people. The drivers don't say a thing. They should talk out and ask people to give up their seats. Once, I came up and nobody said a word, neither did the driver. I couldn't reach the handle bar. I almost fell down when it started to move. If, indeed, I fell and got hurt, who could have been responsible for it? So I hope the government will keep on telling people—even though there have been public notices. The drivers should be told to tell people to help those disabled. Everyone can tell those who are in the wheelchair are disabled, but many people will kick the canes of the blind till they are broken. So this is a problem. It has caused us a lot of pain. We, the blind, only know it ourselves.

Source: Lift every voice, modernizing disability policies and programs to serve a diverse nation. (1999, December 1). Washington, DC: National Council on Disability, 50.

minority cultures and fluency in languages other than English (or access to skilled interpreters). Language-appropriate materials were also needed to better serve members of diverse cultural groups.

Empowerment, Self-Determination, and Self-Advocacy

Empowerment is an attitude, a process, and a set of skills involving the ability to gain some control over valued events, outcomes, and resources. Empowerment requires genuine choices and the power to make one's own decisions (Gilson, 1998), and is strongly in accord with social work's professional value of self-determination.

People with disabilities, like other people, want to have as much control over their own lives as possible. Segal, Silverman, and Tomkin (1993, p. 706) point out that even people with severe disabilities have "potential for self-determination, provided that they have access to support services, barrier-free environments, and appropriate information and skills." The desired outcome is independent living wherever possible.

The empowerment model strongly encourages self-advocacy among people with disabilities, both as individuals and in groups. Self-advocacy in fact has become a national movement, modeled after the civil rights movement. The American Association on Mental Retardation (AAMR) describes some of the goals (*Self advocacy fact sheet*, 2001, March 6):

The self-advocacy movement has redefined the "disability problem" as being less about rehabilitation and more about equality. People involved in the movement are very clear about not wanting to be called retarded, handicapped or disabled or to be treated like children. They are clear that self advocacy represents "rights" not "dependence"—the right to speak out, the right to be a person with dignity, the right to make decisions for themselves and others.

The concepts of empowerment, self-determination, and self-advocacy do not mean that society (or social workers) should abandon people with disabilities to struggle alone. It means, instead, that society must recognize that the impaired individual is not the problem; the problem is an environment that discriminates, does not provide viable choices, and does not meet the special needs of all its citizens.

Self-advocacy goes beyond individuals advocating for themselves alone. It also involves groups of people with disabilities working together to fight discrimination, to gain more control over their lives, and to work together toward greater justice in society. According to the AAMR, a national organization called Self-Advocates Becoming Empowered was formed in the United States in 1991. By 1993, there were at least 37 statewide self-advocacy organizations. Numbers of local chapters continue to grow, with some states having as few as 3 and others as many as 75. In addition, many other self-advocacy groups operate independently or are attached to different organizations assisting people with disabilities. Such collective efforts can lead to important new legislation bringing changes in social policy. The disability rights movement described below is an example.

THE DISABILITY RIGHTS MOVEMENT, SOCIAL POLICY, AND APPROPRIATE TERMINOLOGY

Disabilities have been viewed historically as medical problems or personal tragedies. This prevailing view began to be challenged in the 1960s, when, along with other minority groups, people with disabilities sought to redefine their identities and to change popular perceptions of the sources of their problems (Christensen, 1996). By the late 60s, first in Scandinavia and then in the United States, a disability rights movement developed advocating that people with disabilities should be seen as "subjects in their own lives rather than simply as objects of medical and social regimes of control" (Meekosha & Jakubowicz, 1996, p. 80). Community prejudice and discrimination were overtly identified as major barriers preventing people with disabilities from taking control of their own lives, as were stereotypes portrayed in the popular media.

The crux of the new thinking, as noted by Beaulaurier and Taylor (2001), was that an individual's impairment in itself was not so much the problem as the lack of **accommodation** provided by the wider society. Lack of accommodation was not so much a result of hostility as from simple failure to consider everyone's needs. So those who became involved in the disability rights movement determined to get the requirements of people with disabilities onto the national agenda.

In the United States, the disability rights movement promoted deinstitutionalization and independent living, and helped secure the passage of the Developmental Disabilities Act of 1969. The movement was strengthened in the late 1960s and early 1970s when thousands of veterans returned from the Vietnam War with extensive disabling conditions, both physical and emotional. Their added influence

529

CHAPTER 13
*Developmental
Disabilities and
Social Work: Mary
and Lea Perkins*

A social worker with severe disability displays sophisticated interviewing skills.

helped achieve passage of the federal Rehabilitation Act of 1973. Title V of this act prohibits recipients of federal funds from discriminating against people with disabilities in employment, education, or services.

The Rehabilitation Act of 1973 was followed in 1975 by the Developmentally Disabled Assistance and Bill of Rights Act, and the Education of All Handicapped Children Act, which later became the Individuals with Disabilities Act (Meekosha & Jakubowicz, 1996; Asch & Mudrick, 1995; Pardeck, 1998).

As publicly signaled by the changing terminology in the Individuals with Disabilities Act (IDEA), sensitivity is needed with respect to terminology. Certain commonly used phrases and adjectives can be experienced as demeaning and inappropriate. For example, as in IDEA, the word *handicap* should be replaced by the more neutral term *disability*. Biased phraseology such as *suffer from, crippled by,* and *victim of* should be avoided; a person "has" a disability; he or she isn't necessarily "afflicted" with it or "suffering" from it. A "client" becomes a "consumer" (Pardeck, 1998).

Another major piece of legislation promoting disability rights, the Americans with Disabilities Act (ADA), was passed in 1990; it was greatly strengthened by the Civil Rights Act of 1991. These acts are described below.

THE AMERICANS WITH DISABILITIES ACT OF 1990 AND THE CIVIL RIGHTS ACT OF 1991

The Americans with Disabilities Act was designed to assist all people with disabilities, not just those with developmental disabilities. Its purposes are identified in its Section 2 as providing a mandate for ending discrimination, providing enforceable standards of treatment for disabled people, and creating a central role for the federal government in enforcing these standards (see Exhibit 6).

The Americans with Disabilities Act Recognizes Discrimination

EXHIBIT 6

Section 2 of the Americans with Disabilities Act states, among other things, that:

. . . historically, society has tended to isolate and segregate individuals with disabilities, and, despite some improvements, such forms of discrimination against individuals with disabilities continue to be a serious and pervasive social problem; discrimination against individuals with disabilities persists in such critical areas as employment, housing, public accommodations, education, transportation, communication, recreation, institutionalization, health services, voting, and access to public services.

Unlike individuals who have experienced discrimination on the basis of race, color, sex, national origin, religion, or age, individuals who have experienced discrimination on the basis of disability have often had no legal recourse to redress such discrimination. . . .

Source: Quoted from Section 2, "Findings and Purposes," Public Law 101–336, Americans with Disabilities Act of 1990.

The Americans with Disabilities Act can help people in very concrete ways, as illustrated by the following true story:

A young woman employed at a Milwaukee Target store sat quietly in her wheelchair by the employee entrance before work one day. Unable to open the door by herself, she waited for someone to walk by and hold the door open for her. The individual who helped her that day happened to work for the State of Wisconsin.

After asking the woman how long she had been waiting to enter the building, the man instructed the store management to address the problem. Shortly after the incident, plans to install an electronic door opener began. (ADA rules out discrimination, 1993, October)

Without the Americans with Disabilities Act, neither the young woman in question nor the state employee would have had the legal clout to insist on an electronic opener for an employee of this Target store. However, Title I of the act makes new requirements of employers. One is that "employers with 15 or more employees may not discriminate against qualified individuals with disabilities." Another is that "employers must reasonably accommodate the disabilities of qualified applicants or employees, including modifying work stations and equipment, unless undue hardship would result" (*Americans with Disabilities Act Fact Sheet,* 1990, September). The law intends that required accommodations should be reasonable. Existing physical barriers, for example, need to be remedied only if this can be done without much difficulty or expense.

Other titles of the Americans with Disabilities Act call for reasonable access to public services (for example, special accommodations as needed to allow usage of buildings, buses, and trains) and accessibility to public accommodations such as

531

CHAPTER 13
*Developmental
Disabilities and
Social Work: Mary
and Lea Perkins*

restaurants, hotels, theaters, schools, day care centers, and colleges and universities. Also, telephone companies must provide telecommunications services for hearing-impaired and speech-impaired persons.

Students may be interested to know that the ADA requires educational institutions to make reasonable modifications if these would not fundamentally alter a program or cause undue financial hardship. Such modifications could include reassigning classrooms to assure accessibility, providing exams at different times or places, or offering early registration for classes (Pardeck, 1998).

The Civil Rights Act of 1991 greatly strengthened the ADA by allowing jury trials and compensatory and punitive damages in accord with those available to minorities under the Civil Rights Act of 1964. Complaints are handled by the Equal Employment Opportunity Commission (EEOC). By the fall of 1996, fully 70,000 complaints had been filed. Interestingly enough, a large number of job discrimination suits were filed with the EEOC by people with disabilities that no one anticipated because they were previously, to all intents and purposes, hidden. The first plaintiff to win a monetary award, for example, experienced job discrimination related to a diagnosis of cancer (Pardeck, 1998).

More recent legislation coming before the Supreme Court represented setbacks for the disability rights movement in two cases and a victory in another. One setback involved the case of *Alabama v. Garrett* (2001). Patricia Garrett, a nursing supervisor, claimed that she was demoted at a state-run hospital for taking time off for cancer treatments. Milton Ash, a security guard at a state youth agency, filed in the same case, claiming he was forced to work in a smoke-filled environment that triggered severe asthma. The U.S. Court of Appeals for the Eleventh Circuit sided with the workers, but the Supreme Court, in a 5 to 4 ruling, declared that employees do not have the right to sue states under the ADA. This setback was, obviously, a very serious one. The second setback involved the case of Edna Williams, who was diagnosed with carpal tunnel syndrome. She sued her employer, Toyota Motor Corporation, seeking accommodation at work under the Americans with Disabilities Act. The U.S. Court of Appeals for the Sixth Circuit ruled in favor of Ms. Williams, but the Supreme Court overturned that decision in early 2002, stating that since Ms. Williams's disability did not restrict her from performing a broad range of manual tasks central to daily life, her disability was not serious enough to qualify her for the protections of the ADA (Richey, 2001).

The victory involved the case of Casey Martin, a professional golfer. Martin was unable to walk a full course because of a severe circulatory condition in his right leg. A professional golfing association had allowed him to use a golf cart during qualifying trials, but denied him the right during tournaments, claiming that the fatigue of walking the course was part of the challenge of the game. On May 29, 2001, the U.S. Supreme Court, by a 7 to 2 decision, ruled that Martin could use his golf cart during tournaments.

VALUE DILEMMAS AND ETHICAL IMPLICATIONS

Both personal and professional values come into focus in social work with people with developmental disabilities. Today, because of new knowledge of genetics and new medical procedures, value issues in this field are more complex than ever. For example, genetic counseling makes it possible for a couple to know beforehand if they run a substantial risk of abnormality in a pregnancy. Should a concerned couple seek this type of information? What should they do if a substantial risk is identified?

A procedure called amniocentesis can identify many types of fetal abnormalities during a pregnancy. Sometimes corrective measures may then be taken in utero. Sometimes, however, nothing can be done for a deformed or otherwise abnormal fetus. Should such a pregnancy be continued? Does this question involve absolute principles? Or can it involve consideration of probable quality of life for the fetus and the family?

Social workers advocate self-determination. But who is the client engaging in self-determination? The person with the disability (such as Sandra McLean, in Chapter 3) or the family providing necessary care (such as frail Mrs. McLean and college-bound Susan)? Both are legitimate systems for intervention and might make different choices. Whose choice should be honored?

But perhaps those aren't the right questions. Perhaps if society provided sufficient supports to family caregivers, sufficient options such as universal access to respite care and day care services, choices could be made that would satisfy every member of a family, including the person with disabilities. Increasing options requires action in a larger arena. The social work code of ethics provides a guide to expanding choice (see Exhibit 7).

The Americans with Disabilities Act of 1990 and the Civil Rights Act of 1991 are important examples of legislation aimed at improving social conditions and promoting social justice for people with developmental disabilities. This minority group was publicly recognized and provided with significant legal protections under these laws. People with disabilities themselves, their families, social workers, and many, many others, participated in the effort that resulted in these new laws.

Social and Political Action

EXHIBIT 7

The social work Code of Ethics, provision 6.04, as quoted in part below, strongly advocates expansion of choice to make self-determination a more realistic opportunity for client systems.

(a) Social workers should engage in social and political action that seeks to ensure that all people have equal access to the resources, employment, services, and opportunities they require to meet their basic human needs and to develop fully. Social workers should be aware of the impact of the political arena on practice and should advocate for changes in policy and legislation to improve social conditions in order to meet basic human needs and promote social justice.

(b) Social workers should act to expand choice and opportunity for all people, with special regard for vulnerable, disadvantaged, oppressed, and exploited people and groups.

Social workers may assume policy-oriented roles directly by taking on administrative positions such as that of Stephanie Hermann described in Chapter 2. Even from direct-service positions, however, social workers may help create change by doing such things as writing informed letters to their agency administrators or to influential legislators. They may serve as expert witnesses at legislative hearings. Social workers may be even more active in creating policy by running for and holding public office. There is a great deal of work that still needs to be done with, and on behalf of, people with disabilities.

533

CHAPTER 13
*Developmental
Disabilities and
Social Work: Mary
and Lea Perkins*

Current Trends

Because community care today so often means ongoing care by the family, a major trend is respectful collaboration between families and professionals. The strengths, or empowerment, model has helped encourage a new paradigm in which families are viewed as competent, full partners in professional service, as illustrated in this chapter's case example with Mary and Lea Perkins. The role of social workers is primarily to assist families and consumers of services to meet their own goals. Mutual respect, trust, and open communication are imperative, as well as an atmosphere in which cultural traditions, values, and diversity are acknowledged and honored (Freedman, 1995).

Another major trend is the increasing life span of people with disabilities, made possible by advances in medicine. It is estimated that there are at least 526,000 adults over the age of 60 who have developmental disabilities, and this number is expected to double by 2030 when the entire baby boom generation reaches this age. Families today are the primary providers of care; in the last 20 years there has been a 70 percent reduction in the number of people with disabilities residing in institutions. Now, for example, 80 percent of people with mental retardation live at home (*Aging,* 2001, March 6). Yet the majority of state and federal funding still goes to institutional care (Hooyman & Gonyea, 1995).

As family caregivers themselves age and foresee a time when they will no longer be able to care for their offspring, future planning becomes a major concern for them. A recent survey found over 60,000 people with developmental disabilities on waiting lists for residential services in 37 states (*Aging,* 2001, March 6). Housing for people with disabilities is thus in very short supply. The Older Americans Act provides important family supports in some areas of the country: senior centers, nutrition sites, homemaker services, home delivered meals, and case coordination. But funding remains very low, and in many places waiting lists are long (see Chapter 11). Typically, even disabled persons who have worked their entire lives have little or no retirement income to help finance their own futures, having worked for minimal wages or no pay at all in sheltered workshops.

As a further potential problem for older workers with disabilities, a recent study by the General Accounting Office, an investigative arm of Congress, concluded that if the Social Security plan pushed by President George W. Bush were adopted by Congress, people with disabilities would lose out. The income from individual investment accounts would not be sufficient to compensate for the decline in insurance benefits that disabled beneficiaries would receive. On the average, benefits over a lifetime would be approximately 4 percent to 18 percent less (Pear, 2001).

Families thus are bearing increasing burdens of the cost of care for elderly people with disabilities, and as family caregivers themselves age, how long they will be able to carry on is an unanswered question. Only about 25 percent of non-institutional care is publicly subsidized (Hooyman & Gonyea, 1995).

In addition to families bearing increasing burdens of costs of care for elderly people with disabilities, they are also bearing a greater proportion of costs of children with disabilities. According to Mannes (1998), approximately 14 percent of the projected savings from welfare reform was expected to come from reductions in SSI (Supplemental Security Income; see Chapter 3) payments formerly provided for families with disabled children. The rationale was that eligibility criteria for disabilities were considered too lenient. Soon after passage of the welfare reform law, over 135,800 children with disabilities lost their benefits. They had disorders that were primarily "mental," including retardation, learning disabilities, and attention deficit disorders. The average benefit lost was $410 per month, which was originally intended to help families meet the higher costs associated with raising children with disabilities (Feldmann, 1997, Oct. 24).

As in so many areas of need today, the general trend is to rely on families to finance or provide care for their own, whether they can actually do so or not.

INTERNET SITES

http://www.ahead.org/	Association of Higher Education and Disability
http://www.bu.edu/cpr/reasaccom/	Reasonable Accommodation for People with Psychiatric Disabilities
http://ici.umn.edu/ncset/	The National Center on Secondary Education and Transition
http://www.rit.edu/~easi/	Equal Access to Software and Information
http://www.nichcy.org/	The National Information Center for Children and Youth with Disabilities
http://dimenet.com	Access Center for Independent Living
http://www.heath.gwu.edu/	Heath Resource Center
http://www.thearc.org/	The Arc
http://www.HydroAssoc.org/	The Hydrocephalus Association
http://www.wapd.org/	The World Association for People with Disabilities

SUMMARY

This chapter begins with a case study that illustrates contemporary, community-based social work with people with disabilities. Mary Perkins has an intellectual disability. She has been served in the past by a special education program that prepared her for gainful employment; Mary's daughter, Lea, has suffered traumatic abuse resulting in emotional disturbance and ongoing truancy. The family is experiencing myriad other difficulties as well. Through intensive family-based intervention, a young social work intern, Jenny Chambers, assists Mary to develop the skills required to keep her family together and to remain in their own apartment. She engages Lea in a special education program at school where the girl begins to excel.

While social workers traditionally have worked with people with disabilities primarily in institutional settings, today their services are becoming increasingly community-based. Social workers assist families to expand their options so that far more often today, children with disabilities are raised at home. Social workers assist individuals with disabilities and their families to advocate for their own ideas and choices, to deal constructively with bureaucratic agencies, and to join with others in promoting new policies and programs that can maximize their options.

By examining the differences between categorical and functional definitions of disability, we see why such differences are important in terms of funding resources and eligibility for service. Nine major categories of developmental disability are then discussed: intellectual disability or mental retardation, cerebral palsy, autism, orthopedic problems, hearing problems, epilepsy, traumatic brain injury, learning disabilities, and co-occurrence of disabilities. Fetal alcohol syndrome and cocaine-affected babies are also described.

Until comparatively recently, little has been done for persons with disabilities. For centuries people with mental retardation and other disabilities were cruelly incarcerated. Reformers such as the Frenchmen Pereira, Itard, and Seguin worked to demonstrate that people with disabilities can be taught. Huge institutions replaced training schools, however, and not until the 1920s did research contribute to a change in public opinion. In recent years the concept of normalization has spurred efforts toward removing people with disabilities from large institutions and placing them back in the community, ideally in homelike settings with special provisions to meet their needs.

Efforts toward home care have been hampered by lack of resources in the community. The Education for All Handicapped Children Act of 1975 (currently known as the Individuals with Disabilities Act), its 1986 amendment extending service to infants and toddlers, The Americans with Disabilities Act of 1990, and the Civil Rights Act of 1991 were discussed as examples of enabling legislation providing legal bases for equal opportunity and empowerment for people with disabilities. However, competition for scarce resources makes implementing the full intent of these laws difficult.

The NASW has developed standards for service for working with people with disabilities and their families. The chapter presents these standards and also discusses how professional values and ethics guide contemporary practice efforts in this field.

Opportunities for social workers to work with people with disabilities are growing. More community-based services are needed not only for younger people with disabilities but for ever-increasing numbers who survive into old age. A continuing problem is underfunding for community-based services, however, and recent legislation known as welfare reform has decreased rather than increased funding.

KEY TERMS

accommodation
continuum of care
deinstitutionalization
developmental disability
empowerment
family care homes
habilitation

job coach
normalization
rehabilitation
respite care
service coordinator
sheltered workshop
supported employment

DISCUSSION QUESTIONS

1. Discuss the concept of in-home intervention for families experiencing such severe difficulties that placement of a child outside the home is a strong possibility. Do you think the cost of providing these services to the Perkins family was worthwhile to the wider community that financed them? Why or why not? Do you think foster placement for Lea would have been a better plan? Why or why not?

2. Not many years ago, most children with disabilities were placed in institutions. How do you think this plan would have worked for Mary Perkins? For Lea? Explain your reasons.

3. What are nine major diagnostic categories of developmental disability? Describe. What types of disabilities are found in babies with fetal alcohol syndrome and those who have been exposed to cocaine? By what age must a disabling condition be diagnosed to be considered "developmental" according to the federal definition?

4. Some states define developmental disabilities by category, but the federal government defines them by function. Using the federal government's definition, what kind of disabled person do you think may tend to be ineligible for assistance in the United States? Why?

5. How did social Darwinism, the eugenics movement, and the development of the IQ test all tend to influence society's treatment of people with developmental disabilities?

6. How did research findings during the 1920s and World War II influence perceptions of the disabled? What changes were initiated in overall societal treatment goals?

7. Explain the concept of normalization. When and where did it develop? How does it affect care-planning efforts for disabled people in the United States today? Why?

8. Why is the generalist approach appropriate for social work practice with people with disabilities?

9. In what ways does the Americans with Disabilities Act of 1990 recognize people with disabilities as a minority group in need of protection? How is this act strengthened by the Civil Rights Act of 1991?

10. What are some of the major contemporary roles for social workers involved with the disabled?

11. How do social work values and the Code of Ethics guide practice in the field of developmental disabilities, according to this chapter?

CLASSROOM EXERCISES

While not required, it is suggested that students break into small groups of three or four to discuss these exercises. It may be helpful to choose a scribe to record and report interesting points to the class after the group discussion.

1. The author notes in this chapter that while most children with developmental disabilities are being raised at home today, the bulk of government funding still goes to

care in institutions. Many people believe that families are *supposed* to provide for their own, so that low levels of government assistance to those with disabled members living at home are not a problem. What do you think? Why?

2. People involved in the disability rights movement believe that their primary problem is not the disability itself but the failure of the environment to provide satisfactory accommodations. The movement teaches that in order for people with disabilities to be empowered, realistic options and choices must be available, and that these should be a right, not a privilege. Many people without disabilities, however, disagree, due to the cost and inconvenience of providing accommodations. What do you think? Why?

3. Many older people with disabilities are facing destitution in old age as their family caregivers grow too old to care for them, and alternative housing is in short supply. Their earnings have been too small to provide for retirement. Imagine that you have the power to create ideal social policies to deal with this situation. What policies will you develop? Why?

RESEARCH ACTIVITIES

1. With permission of your campus administrators, spend a day on your college campus using a wheelchair. Find out how easy or difficult it is for you to get around campus and attend your classes. Write a report about your experience and submit it to the administrators (and perhaps your campus newspaper).

2. Visit a local nursing home that has a specialized unit for people with disabilities. Talk with some of the residents about how they like living there. Interview the social worker to find out how well he or she thinks the services offered at the home meet the needs of the residents.

3. Interview various members of a family caring for a person with a disability, including the person with the disability. How do the perspectives of the different family members differ? What resources from the community are available to assist? What resources are needed but not available?

INTERNET RESEARCH EXERCISES

1. The National Information Center for Children and Youth with Disabilities (NICHY) has a site concerning respite care (http://www.nichcy.org/pubs/newsdig/nd12.htm).
   a. Why is this article subtitled "A Gift of Time"?
   b. When and why was the concept of respite care first used according to this article?
   c. What are the seven words suggested in the publication for the spelling of "respite"?

2. A sheltered workshop with the appropriate name of "Capabilities Inc." has a site on the Internet (http://www.capabilities.org).
   a. What is the primary mission of this type of workshop?
   b. What sort of work do they do?
   c. On the home page locate the index. Then go to "About Us." What is "supported employment"?

3. An Australian website, Centre for Developmental Disability Studies, presents some useful information about developmental disability (http://www.cdds.med.usyd.edu.au).
   a. What is the mission of this organization?
   b. What is their definition of "developmental disability"?
   c. List five conditions cited as resulting in potential developmental disability.

REFERENCES

ADA rules out discrimination. (1993, October). *Update,* p. 1 (West Allis, WI: Advocates for Retarded Citizens)

Aging, older adults and their aging caregivers. (2001, March 6). AAMR fact sheet (online). Available: http://161.58.153.187/Policies/faqaging.shtml.

Americans with disabilities fact sheet. (1990, September). Washington, DC: U.S. Architectural Board, 1.

Asch, A., & Mudrick, N. R. (1995). Disability. In R. L. Edwards (Ed.), *Encyclopedia of social work* (19th ed., Vol. 1, pp. 752–760). Washington, DC: NASW Press.

Barnwell, D. A., & Day, M. (1996). Providing support to diverse families. In P. Beckman (Ed.), *Strategies for working with families with disabilities* (pp. 47–65). Baltimore: Paul H. Brookes.

Baroff, G. S. (1991). *Developmental disabilities: Psychosocial aspects.* Austin, TX: ProEd.

Beaulaurier, R. L., & Taylor, S. H. (2001). Social work practice with people with disabilities in the era of disability rights. *Social Work in Health Care 32*(4), 67–91.

Bender, W. N. (1992). Learning disabilities. In P. J. McLaughlin & P. Wehman (Eds.), *Developmental disabilities: A handbook of best practices* (pp. 82–87). Boston: Andover Medical Publishers.

Cerebral palsy. (1999). March of Dimes fact sheet (online). Available: www.modimes/Healthlibrary2/Factsheets/Cerebral.Palsy.htm.

Christensen, C. (1996). Disabled, handicapped, or disordered: What's in a name? In C. Christensen & F. Rizvi (Eds.), *Disability and the dilemmas of education and justice* (pp. 63–78). Buckingham: Open University Press.

Cocaine use during pregnancy. (1998). March of Dimes fact sheet (online). Available: http://www.modimes.org/HealthLibrary2/factsheets/Cocaine_use_during_pregnancy.htm.

DeWeaver, K., & Kropf, N. (1992, Winter). Persons with mental retardation: A forgotten minority in education. *Journal of Social Work Education, 28*(1), 38–40.

Dickerson, M. U. (1981). *Social work practice with the mentally retarded.* New York: Free Press.

Drinking during pregnancy. (1999). March of Dimes fact sheet (online). Available: http://www.modimes.org/HealthLibrary2/factsheets/Drinking_during_pregnancy.htm.

Fact sheet on traumatic brain injury. (1999). Milwaukee, WI: ARC Milwaukee.

Feldmann, L. (1997, October 24). Fraud-busters cut benefits for disabled children. *The Christian Science Monitor,* p. 4.

Freedman, R. (1995). Developmental disabilities: Direct practice. In R. L. Edwards (Ed.). *Encyclopedia of social work* (19th ed., Vol. 1, pp. 721–728), Washington, DC: NASW Press.

Gilson, S. F. (1998). Choice and self-advocacy, a consumer's perspective. In P. Wehman & J. Kregel, *More than a job: Satisfying careers for people with disabilities* (pp. 3–23). Baltimore: P. H. Brookes.

Habilitation plan administrator. (2001). Washington State Department of Personnel (online). Available: http://hr.dop.wa.gov/lib/hrdr/speca/50000/56980.htm.

Hooyman, N. R., & Gonyea, J. G. (1995). Family caregiving. In R. L. Edwards (Ed.), *Encyclopedia of social work* (19th ed., Vol. 1, pp. 951–957). Washington, DC: NASW Press.

Johnson, A. B., & Surles, R. C. (1994). Has deinstitutionalization failed? In S. A. Kirk and S. D. Einbinder (Eds.), *Controversial issues in mental health* (pp 213–216). Boston: Allyn and Bacon.

539

CHAPTER 13
*Developmental
Disabilities and
Social Work: Mary
and Lea Perkins*

Lift every voice: Modernizing disability policies and programs to serve a diverse nation. (1999, December 1). Washington, DC: National Council on Disability, 50.

Mackelprang, M., & Saisgiver, R. (1999). *Disability: A diversity model approach in human service practice.* Pacific Grove, CA: Brooks/Cole.

Mannes, M. (1998). The new psychology and economics of permanency. *The prevention report # 2.* Iowa City: The University of Iowa National Resource Center for Family Centered Practice.

McDonald-Wikler, L. (1987). Disabilities, developmental. In A. Minahan (Ed.), *Encyclopedia of social work* (18th ed., Vol. 1, pp. 423–431). Silver Spring, MD: NASW Press.

Meekosha, H., & Jakubowicz, A. (1996). Disability, participation, representation and social justice. In C. Christensen and F. Rizvi (Eds.), *Disability and the dilemmas of education and justice* (pp. 79–95). Buckingham: Open University Press.

Pardeck, J. T. (1998). *Social work after the Americans with Disabilities Act.* Westport, CT: Auburn House.

Parent, W. S., Cone, A. A., Turner, E., & Wehman, P. (1998). Supported employment, consumers leading the way. In P. Wehman & J. Kregel (Eds.), *More than a job: Securing satisfying careers for people with disabilities* (pp. 149–166). Baltimore, MD: Paul H. Brooks.

Parkinson, C. B., & Howard, M. (1996). Older persons with mental retardation/developmental disabilities. In M. J. Mellor (Ed.), *Special populations and systems linkages* (pp. 91–101). New York: The Haworth Press.

Patton, J. R., Blackbourn, J. M., & Fad, K. (1996). *Exceptional individuals in focus* (6th ed.). Englewood Cliff, NJ: Prentice Hall.

Pear, R. (2001, February 7). Study says disabled would lose benefits under new Social Security plan. The *New York Times* (online). Available: http://nytimes.com/2001/tml?ex=982562510&ei=1&en=140c6f7cf3ebdcbe.

Petr, C., & Barney, D, (1993, May). Reasonable efforts for children with disabilities: The parents' perspective. *Social Work, 38* (3), 252–255.

Public health information sheets, genetic series. (1998, November). Wilkes-Barre, PA: March of Dimes Birth Defects Foundation.

Richey, W. (2002, January 9). In workplace, tougher standards on job-related injuries. *The Christian Science Monitor,* p. 2.

Richmond, M. (1917). *Social diagnosis.* Philadelphia: Russel Sage Foundation, 26.

Segal, S. P. (1995). Deinstitutionalization. In R. L. Edwards (Ed.), *Encyclopedia of social work* (19th ed., Vol. 1, pp. 704–711). Washington, DC: NASW Press.

Segal, S., Silverman, C., & Tomkin, T. (1993, November). Empowerment and self-help agency practice for people with mental disabilities. *Social Work, 38*(6), 705–708.

Self advocacy (2001, March 6). AAMR fact sheet (online): Available: http://161.58.153.187/Policies/faq_movement.shtml.

Smart, J. (2001). *Disability, society, and the individual.* Gaithersburg, MD: Aspen Publishers, Inc.

Stites, S. (2001). *Allyse* (unpublished paper). Northampton, MA: Smith College.

Switzky, H., Dudzinski, M., Van Acker, R., & Gambro, J. (1988). Historical foundations of out-of-home residential alternatives for mentally retarded persons. In L. Heal, J. Haney, & Amado, A. (Eds.), *Integration of developmentally disabled individuals into the community* (2nd ed., pp. 19–35). Baltimore: Paul H. Brooks.

Talbott, R. E. (1992). Communication disorders. In P. J. McLaughlin & P. Wehman (Eds.). *Developmental disabilities: A handbook for best practices* (pp. 98–100). Boston: Andover Medical Publishers.

What is mental retardation? (2001, March 6). AAMR fact sheet (online): Available: http://161.58.153.187/Policies/faq_mental_retardation.shtml.

What is autism? (2001). Autism Society of America (online). Available: http://www.autism-society.org/whatisautism/autism.html.

Willer, B., & Itagliata, J. (1984). *Promises and realities for mentally retarded citizens.* Baltimore: University Park Press.

Wolfe, P. S. (1992). Challenges for service providers. In P. J. Mclaughlin & P. Wehman (Eds.), *Developmental disabilities: A handbook for best practices* (pp. 125–130). Boston: Andover Medical Publishers.

FOR FURTHER READING

Baroff, George S. (1991). *Developmental disabilities: Psychosocial aspects.* Austin, TX: Pro-Ed.

This book describes several disorders of development: mental retardation, autism, cerebral palsy, and epilepsy. It explores the continuum of care required to assist people with disabilities to maximize their functioning in the wider environment. The book's particular strength lies in its use of multiple case studies to assist readers in understanding how various disabilities affect the lives of real people.

Kirk, S. A., & Einbinder, S. D. (Eds.). (1994). *Controversial issues in mental health.* Boston: Allyn & Bacon.

Various salient debates in mental health are presented in a "Yes–No" format. Topics covered include how mental disorders are identified, how they should be understood, and how professions dealing with them should relate. The book also presents debates about policy issues in mental health. The debate between Ann Braden Johnson and Richard C. Surles regarding whether deinstitutionalization has failed is particularly relevant to the area of developmental disabilities.

Mackelprang, R., & Salsgiver, R. (1999). *Disability: A diversity model approach in human service practice.* Pacific Grove, CA: Brooks/Cole.

This text is written primarily for students preparing for careers in the human services with people with disabilities, including social work. The book is organized into three sections. The first creates a context that recognizes social devaluation of people with disabilities and suggests a need for an aggressive political action to overcome oppression. The second examines various groupings of disabilities and provides personal accounts from people who experience them. The third section discusses human service practice with persons with disabilities in social context.

Mellor, M. J. (Ed.). (1996). *Special aging populations and systems linkages.* New York: The Haworth Press.

This unique anthology presents contemporary articles about people who are aging who also have disabilities. Various aging populations with disabilities are discussed, along with issues in kinship care. Different chapters are then presented dealing with various special needs: AIDS, cancer, alcohol, mental retardation, and other developmental disabilities. A chapter on elder abuse is also provided. The book concludes with a chapter on developing linkages among important systems serving the elderly with special needs.

Pardeck, J. T. (1998). *Social work after the Americans with Disabilities Act: New challenges and opportunities for social service professionals.* Westport, CT: Auburn House.

Pardeck's goal in writing this book was to inform social workers about the mandates and requirements of the Americans with Disabilities Act of 1990. He has done so well, including chapters that explain the provisions of the act, discuss its impact on social service agencies in particular, and explore the importance of advocacy with respect to the act. The book also describes the impact on education.

Patton, J. R., Blackbourn, J. M., & Fad, K. (1996). *Exceptional individuals in focus* (6th ed.). Englewood Cliffs, NJ: Merrill.

This well-written text is intended as an introduction to ideas and issues in special education. The book presents multiple case examples and thought-provoking questions to help readers identify with people experiencing various disabilities. Topics covered include learning and behavior disorders; physical, sensory, and communicative impairments; giftedness and cultural diversity; and the rationale for special education with children and adolescents.

Smart, J. (2001). *Disability, society, and the individual.* Gaithersburg, MD: Aspen Publishers, Inc.

This book examines the disability experience from the point of view of the individual with the disability. It also discusses how disabilities are viewed by the wider society and then considers the relationship between the two perspectives. Part I provides a detailed definition of disability. Part II examines the impact of social prejudice on people with disabilities, and Part III examines the impact of the disability itself on people with disabilities and their families.

Sutton, E., Factor, A. R., Hawkins, B. A., Heller, T., & Seltzer, G. B. (Eds.). (1993). *Older adults with developmental disabilities: Optimizing choice and change.* Baltimore: Paul H. Brookes.

Responsive to demographic shifts, this book discusses people with developmental disabilities who survive into middle and late adulthood. Like the population at large, a greater proportion of people with disabilities are now living into old age, so that services must be developed to meet their needs. Topics discussed include health and medical issues, lifestyles, community living options, and trends in service delivery.

Wehman, P., & Kregel, J. (Eds.). (1998). *More than a job: Securing satisfying careers for people with disabilities.* Baltimore: Paul H. Brookes.

A number of provocative articles are included in this book, taking a strong self-advocacy stance for consumers with disabilities who wish to engage in meaningful employment. Various issues and strategies in obtaining supported employment are discussed, as well as the roles of the employment specialist or job coach in facilitating the success of supported employment.

PART THREE

A Look at the Future

The future: what will it hold? The world sometimes seems utterly chaotic but, in fact, existing forces are the catalysts for powerful change that will drive and define our evolving future. We will begin this final section of the book by exploring several powerful forces that are energizing, shaping, and propelling transformation in the world. We will think about how social workers are involved in this change and consider implications for the profession of social work and for the people we serve. We will also identify some of the emerging issues that will create ethical and value dilemmas for social workers.

Chapter 14 begins by looking at the remarkable human diversity that is rapidly changing the face of America, a diversity flavored by culture, race, ethnicity, age, spirituality, and numerous other facets of humanity. Next, the political scene is considered: how are strong political currents shaping the opportunity system for people, especially for the poor? Connected to political trends are economic forces: how will a volatile economy impact people in the United States and elsewhere in the world? Chapter 14 also explores technological advances in computer usage in social work, considers the ethics of evolving technology for practice, and poses a futuristic scenario of computer-enhanced child welfare. The final but powerful force changing the future, biomedical advances, will challenge humanity and will impact the social work profession in countless ways. Chapter 14 focuses on biomedical advances in the areas of human reproduction, genetics, and organ replacement.

Our consideration of the future would not be complete without at least a glance at the future of the social work profession in terms of professional employment. The text authors suspect that students who are considering social work as a career will have interest in predictions about future employment opportunities. So, the text concludes with social work employment projections offered by the U.S. Department of Labor.

CHAPTER 14

Future Challenges and Closing Notes

RESETTLEMENT OPPORTUNITY SERVICES, INC.

Saying good-bye is always difficult, but when a social worker leaves her agency, even when a new future beckons, there are many feelings, many memories. Jeanne paused as she was about to close another box. This had been her first job after completing her MSW. It had been a great experience working for an organization that aided Southeast Asian refugees to find employment. Jeanne was going to miss Resettlement Opportunities, Inc., the staff, and the clients very, very much.

Jeanne smiled as she thought about this small town's business community. Working with the business community had been unexpectedly interesting for Jeanne. Although she had worked part-time for years when her children were young, she thought that she had left the business world for good when she returned to college to complete her baccalaureate and master's degrees in social work. Yet her job with Resettlement Opportunity Services involved Jeanne in many contacts with businesspeople.

In her small town Jeanne had opportunities to represent her agency with local economic development organizations, such as the chamber of commerce and the downtown business association. Jeanne's role with the business community was primarily one of advocating to obtain jobs for her clients. It was important for her to establish good relationships with area employers. In advocating for her clients, Jeanne often found that she had to fight discrimination and misunderstanding of many kinds—racial, gender, age—and to overcome a general reluctance in the business community to trust people whose language and lifestyle differed from the majority population.

Jeanne's clients were self-referred or were brought to the agency by a friend or family member. Jeanne also reached out to the refugee community by attending weddings, funerals, and community celebrations. She used every available opportunity to speak to groups of people from the refugee community.

Jeanne enjoyed her clients immensely. Intake with new clients involved an assessment that explored their current social, psychological, and family situation. The focus of the assessment, however, was on employability. But before many refugee parents could work, resources had to be identified and obtained. Child care was one problem; so were transportation, health care, and sometimes emergency housing and food assistance. Using the curriculum developed by her agency, Jeanne provided preemployment training in job seeking and job retention skills. Jeanne and her clients worked together in the job search, and, when employment was obtained, she provided intensive follow-up assistance to help each client sustain employment and economic self-sufficiency. Jeanne was amazed by the group support provided by Hmong, Laotian, and Cambodian extended families. The way in which the families pooled their resources and helped each other made child care, care of the elderly, and economic survival possible.

So many families, so many people to remember. Jeanne would never forget them and how they had enriched her own life. She placed another stack of file folders in a cardboard carton. Next, she turned her attention to the bookshelf. There, on a bottom shelf, was the photo album. How precious these pictures were now! She opened the album, and there was Mai's smiling face. Mai was one of Jeanne's first clients at the agency. With Jeanne's help, Mai was able to obtain employment as a teacher's aide. Jeanne was amazed at Mai's stamina. During the school year, Mai had to get her children up and dressed and to a relative's home before arriving at her assigned school by 7:30 A.M. From that time until noon she worked at one of the high schools; in the afternoon she worked at an elementary school. After school she picked up her children and returned home to prepare the family meal. After dinner Mai completed housework before bathing the children and getting them ready for bed.

The photo album showed Mai, her sisters, and other women from the family preparing food for a special event, one of the happiest in Mai's life. Mai's father was arriving from Thailand, where he, like so many Southeast Asian refugees, had lived in a refugee camp for many years. Mai had not seen her father for 10 years. She was only a child of 12 when she was separated from him, but she remembered him fondly. Mai's children had never met their grandfather. Jeanne West remembered being in the joyful crowd at the airport that welcomed the frail, beaming elderly man. Tears welled up in Jeanne's eyes. She closed the album and put it on her desk.

As Jeanne continued sorting through files, forms, and descriptive materials, she absentmindedly began cataloging facts she had learned about the beliefs, values, and behavior patterns of the Southeast Asian people who were her clients. Hmong people were a minority population who lived in Laos; the children grew up speaking Hmong but learned Laotian when they entered school. Hmong was not a written language until 1955. Jeanne had discovered for herself that Hmong was a very difficult language to learn. She had mastered a few simple phrases that enabled her to greet clients and convey her respect to them.

Learning English was not easy for the Hmong, either. Jeanne frequently relied on the paraprofessional refugees who worked for the agency for interpretation. She also discovered that Americans' tendency to shout at non-English-speaking persons in an effort to make themselves understood was offensive to Southeast Asians, who were quiet, soft-spoken people. Because the language barrier often made verbal communication difficult, smiles took on special meaning for many of Jeanne's clients. A cold response, with few genuine smiles, raised anxiety for many refugees. In working with Hmong, Cambodian, and Laotian people, Jeanne learned to limit her eye contact with clients. Among Southeast Asians, limited eye contact was a behavior intended to convey respect, not resistance.

The Southeast Asians highly valued their families. Several generations often shared the same home and resources such as a car. Money was pooled. Decisions were based on the best interests of the entire extended family. There was little confidentiality within the extended family; everything was shared openly. The family, however, protected its privacy from the outside world. Certain family matters were not discussed outside the family. Jeanne learned to ask, "Is it okay to talk about . . . ?" If the answer was no, she had to respect this.

Jeanne had difficulty with the gender consciousness of her clients. Husbands, Jeanne found, generally spoke for their wives. Women were not permitted to meet with a male social worker or any male professional person unless accompanied by their husbands. But the role of women, even in this group, was changing. Women were entering the workforce, which would not have been acceptable in the past. Husbands were sometimes suspicious and jealous. Marriages were still arranged by families, but Jeanne had found that the Hmong families tended to be sensitive and loving and would take into consideration a child's feelings about a potential marriage partner. Since there were only 12 to 14 extended Hmong families in the United States, most Hmong people knew each other at least by reputation.

Jeanne had learned so much in her three years with Resettlement Opportunity Services. She had become a more experienced, skilled social worker. She felt very privileged to have worked with her clients and looked forward to experiencing an even broader diversity of clients in her next position. Jeanne felt very ready for new challenges.

[Since there are so few Hmong family names, last names were not used in the case study. The authors are indebted to Jeanne West, MSW, of La Crosse, Wisconsin, for sharing her story and providing case illustrations that were combined and fictionalized by the authors.]

SOCIAL WORK: PROFESSION AT THE EDGE OF CHANGE

Jeanne West exemplifies social work practice that clearly values and respects differences in cultures. You see this in her effort to learn the Hmong language, her awareness of behaviors that are respectful to Hmong people (cautious use of eye contact, for example), even her presence at Hmong celebrations and special events. Jeanne West's work with Hmong people can be contrasted with the story from Merced, California, where a Hmong family's culture collided with western medicine and the result was the death of a young girl, Lia Lee. The story of Lia Lee, including conflicting cultural understandings of epilepsy, removal of Lia from her home, and her tragic death, is told by Anne Fadiman in her 1997 book, *The Spirit Catches You and You Fall Down.* In the preface Fadiman describes her position as the storyteller, a perspective very much like that of the social worker:

I have always felt that the action most worth watching is not at the center of things but where edges meet. I like shorelines, weather fronts, international borders. There are interesting frictions and incongruities in those places, and often, if you stand at the point of tangency, you can see both sides better than if you were in the middle of either one. (p. viii)

Indeed, a stream of exciting, sometimes frightening, highly energized forces is rapidly reshaping our world. Perhaps Jeanne West represents the social work profession at this confluence of change. Like Jeanne West, social workers live with change every day. Social workers also create change. Key to much of the change taking place in the world today is cultural transformation. Cultural misunderstandings were frequently at the heart of the problems that Jeanne West helped her Hmong clients and her community to work through.

In the next 10 years, the United States will become far more culturally diverse than it is today, and social work practice will be at that confluence of change. This is not an easy or comfortable place to be. The profession of social work will be challenged by a society that still does not understand it or its clients well. Education will be needed to dispel the stereotype of the welfare worker (social worker) dispensing "the dole" to lazy, fraudulent recipients (clients). This book attempts to destroy such stereotypes by providing extensive case studies that illustrate the true nature of social work practice and the people social workers work with. The people in the case studies—the clients as well as the social workers—were drawn from real-life situations. In fact, it would be quite easy to shift many of the clients from one case study to another as their lives and needs changed. These are people of dignity. They do not fit into stereotypes. Instead, the varying circumstances of their lives lead naturally into an exploration of the values, social policy issues, research findings, practice, and history of the profession of social work.

Just as the clients did not fit into any preconceived stereotype, neither did the case-study social workers. Certainly they did not fit old stereotypes such as the welfare worker or the lady bountiful. Neither, however, does social work fit the image of a glamorous, high-status profession. In reality, social work is not the right profession for everyone. This will be more true in the years to come than it has ever been in the past. At the heart of the social work profession lies a set of values that ultimately guide practice. Concern for the poor, the oppressed, those discriminated against, and those in pain and most at risk is central to the mission of social work. Belief in the dignity and worth of every human being is not merely a philosophical stance; it is—and must be—inherent in all social work practice. Social workers of the future will need to fight to make social institutions more humane and more responsive to human needs. Their commitment to social and economic justice will need to be carried out in action, not just in silent intent.

Many persons considering a career in social work will find that the value base of the profession is inconsistent with their own values, and they will need to look for another career. Those who enter social work will find that the profession is strongly influenced by various outside forces: demographic trends, political trends, economic conditions, and technological advances, just to name a few. These sources of energy are not separate but overlap and intermingle. They are among the forces that futurists analyze when they seek to forecast change that will take place in the next 5 to 25 years on this planet. This chapter will look at change that is predicted and at the implications this change will have for the profession of social work and the people that social workers serve.

Globalization and Terrorism

The term "**globalization**" has been a part of our language and thinking for at least the past decade. While it refers to the interconnectedness of all regions and people of the world as a result of technological advances in communication and transportation, it was probably most often thought of in terms of international commerce. In the aftermath of the terrorist attacks on the United States, however, globalization took on new meaning. Americans came to realize that, even as a world superpower, they were vulnerable to international terrorism. In addition, the military campaign to end terrorism has not satisfactorily answered important questions about why terrorism exists. What nourishes, supports, and sustains it? Of course, social workers don't have answers to all of these questions, but social workers do understand that frustrations related to poverty, economic exploitation, differences in religion and in worldview, among others, are driving forces in the global environment in which we all live. Social workers are also among the first professional persons to respond to disaster.

September 11, 2001, was a day of such dramatic violence and disaster that its impact reverberated around the world. At 8:48 A.M. that day American Airlines Flight 11, commandeered by terrorist hijackers, struck a tower of the World Trade

American Red Cross social workers help organize relief efforts
following terrorist attacks on the World Trade Center in 2001.

Center in New York City. Fifteen minutes later a second tower was struck, this
time by United Airlines Flight 175. Thirty-five minutes after that, another hijacked
American Airlines flight struck the Pentagon in Washington, D.C. Twenty-five
minutes later, a United Airlines plane crashed into a field in Pennsylvania, this
crash following an attempt by passengers to subdue the terrorist hijackers. The
World Almanac reports the following facts of this horrendous day:

- The exact number of fatalities may never be known. As of October 12, the
  toll of dead and missing in the attacks was reported as 265 on the four hijacked planes (including the 19 hijackers), 125 at the Pentagon, and 5,080 at
  the World Trade Centers, for a total of 5,470.
- Citizens of at least 62 countries perished in the attack.
- At least 50 Arabs, including Arab Americans, were believed dead or missing
  in the WTC attack (Facts about September 11 attack, 2002, p. 35).

The response to the September 11, 2001, terrorist attack was instantaneous. In addition to an outpouring of monetary contributions, blood donors exceeded the supply of blood needed, and the American Red Cross alone reported the involvement of over 39,000 volunteers. The Red Cross also provided shelter to 4,179 persons and served over 8,000,000 meals or snacks to disaster victims, rescue workers, and others (American Red Cross, 2001). Thousands of social workers responded. According to *NASW News,* some social workers staffed the Red Cross's Compassion Center in Washington, D.C., while others worked on-site at the Pentagon, participated in crisis-response debriefing teams, worked on the Red Cross's national disaster hotline, or counseled flight attendants at a walk-in center at Dulles Airport (O'Neill, 2001).

It is increasingly clear that posttraumatic stress and grief counseling will continue to involve social workers, possibly for years in the wake of this disaster. Social work practice will also be impacted in myriad ways with other ramifications of the 2001 terrorist attacks. The involvement of the American military in strikes against terrorist perpetrators and training camps in Afghanistan, for example, engaged American Red Cross and military social workers with the needs of military families, especially when injuries and deaths occurred. The sharp decline in the U.S. economy in early 2002 and ensuing unemployment increased the number of requests for food, shelter, and counseling related to financial crisis. Today ongoing threats of additional terrorism, including chemical and biological terrorism, and the potential for expansion of war, create additional fears.

Globalism and Healing

Terry Mizrahi, the president of NASW, speaks of the compelling need for social workers to adopt an international perspective. Recognition of the interdependence of people around the world is another and much more constructive form of globalism. As president of NASW, Mizrahi plans to "increase NASW's leadership in international affairs and strengthen our international relationships." She urges "social workers to understand that our fate is connected to the circumstances of the rest of the world" (2001, p. 2). Mizrahi anticipates the contributions that social workers can offer

> to help heal individuals, family and community wounds as mental health providers, resource specialists and community builders; to put a human face on otherwise abstract inhumane conditions and treatment; to demonstrate successful models of conflict management and inter-group relations; to comfort and connect people to the material and human resources they need to rebuild their lives; to advocate the adequate funding of and destigmatization of mental health services, given the anticipated long-term traumatic stress and economic distress that will affect millions of Americans; and to advocate an anti-violence, rather than only an anti-terrorist, policy agenda. . . . We will need to launch a new initiative that links our international, peace and social justice, and cultural competency agendas. (Mizrahi, 2001, p. 2)

Social workers, in concert with other health and human service professionals, will play a key role in the healing and transformation of our world that will go on for years. One of their greatest assets will be the strengths already existing in individuals, families, and communities. The remarkable sense of interdependence and outpouring of resources from around the world following September 11, 2001, reflected these strengths. Challenges for the future abound, as Exhibit 1 suggests, but there is hope, too, that both peace and social justice can prevail.

EXHIBIT 1

WIDER GAPS, WIDER CONFLICTS BY W. WARREN WAGAR (DISTINGUISHED TEACHING
PROFESSOR OF HISTORY AT BINGHAMTON UNIVERSITY)

Whatever the United States and its allies do in response to the September 11 attacks, there is little chance that they can eliminate all terrorist networks or prevent the formation of new ones. As the experience of Israel suggests, the struggle against terrorism is never-ending. It cannot be brought to a successful conclusion without removing its root causes, which lie deep within the structure of the modern world system.

In fact, the long-term prospects are for widening conflict between the rich and poor nations of the world, for widening conflict among the poor nations themselves, and for increasing destabilization worldwide. A system that routinely rewards the few who are rich and powerful at the expense of the many who are poor and weak—especially given the range of weapons and terrorist strategies available to the poor and weak—is a system that cannot stand. It is programmed for self-destruction, and its eventual collapse, if my guess is right, will be the principal event of the twenty-first century.

NEEDED: A MASSIVE PEACE MOVEMENT BY JOHAN GALTUNG
(ESTABLISHED THE INTERNATIONAL PEACE RESEARCH INSTITUTE IN OSLO IN 1959;
FOUNDER OF TRANSCEND, A GLOBAL NETWORK OF CONFLICT ANALYSTS)

With talk of Crusades from the United States, and of Holy War from Islamic quarters, the world may be heading for the largest violent encounter ever.

Dialogue and global education to understand how others think, and to respect other cultures—not debate to defeat others with stronger arguments—can lead the way toward healing and closure.

Governments in the West, and also in the South, cannot be relied upon to do this; they are too tied to the United States and also too afraid of incurring U.S. wrath. Only people can do this, only the global civil society. What is needed, as soon as humanly possible, is a massive peace movement, this time North–South. It worked last time, East–West.

The future of the world is more than ever in the hands of the only source of legitimacy: people everywhere.

GLOBALIZATION AND TERRORISM: THE LONG ROAD AHEAD BY VICTOR FERKISS
(EMERITUS PROFESSOR OF GOVERNMENT AT GEORGETOWN UNIVERSITY
AND MEMBER OF THE WORLD FUTURE SOCIETY BOARD OF DIRECTORS)

The tragedy of September 11 revealed in bloody horror that globalization is a two-edged sword. Bitter arguments exist as to whether globalization has on balance improved the lot of the people of the world economically. But many millions in the world are convinced that it is a cultural, political, and religious disaster. As a result, there is now no question but that terrorism, like trade, extends beyond national borders.

What can the United States do about it? Our economy has been struck a major blow. We will need all of our economic strength for the end game if we are to dry up the roots of terrorism in a lasting victory.

(Continued)

Bush has said that we "are not into nation-building." But we must be, because our long-term inter-est—extirpating terrorism—demands it. We will need to create many Marshall Plans for poor nations and the political equivalent to sustain their benefits. If we defeat the Taliban we must extend economic and political aid to Afghanistan so as to enable it to take the first halting steps toward globalization.

Even more problematic, we must somehow spur democratic governments and equitable economic globalization in such nations as Pakistan, Egypt, and Saudi Arabia, among others.

The choice is ours and must be made very soon.

DAY OF REMEMBRANCE BY BRUCE LLOYD (PROFESSOR OF STRATEGIC MANAGEMENT AT SOUTH BEND UNIVERSITY, ENGLAND)

Unfortunately, there is little prospect of the human race suddenly transforming itself into a utopian state, even if we could all agree on how we define that utopian state. In reality, there is little prospect of us being able to "rid this world of this evil," however defined. All we can reasonably expect to achieve is to reduce the incidents of "evil acts" through millions of small positive "good" acts by every one of us showing, even more conspicuously, our commitment to a better future for us all.

Perhaps one initiative the United Nations might consider is to declare September 11 as worldwide "day of Remembrance, Reflection, Reconciliation, and Peace."

A POSITIVE OUTCOME? BY MICHAEL MARIEN (FOUNDER AND EDITOR OF FUTURE SURVEY, PUBLISHED MONTHLY SINCE 1979 BY THE WORLD FUTURE SOCIETY)

Many commentators have already emphasized that any serious "war on terrorism" must attack the roots of terrorism. To counter the growing divisions of rich and poor within and between societies, this means extensive action to end poverty and despair, realize human rights for all, enhance human secu-rity and civil society, improve education and health care, fight global crime and corruption, develop democracy at national and global levels, ensure safe and abundant drinking water, promote greening of the market system, stabilize currency systems, reconsider damaging government subsidies, pursue sus-tainable development, and encourage environmentally benign technology.

No one has argued against undertaking these global reforms; rather, the many arguments for doing so are simply ignored. The new focus on terrorism, however, has already quickly and radically changed U.S. foreign policy from unilateralist to multilateralist. This initial step may lead to at least some of the numerous global reforms that are needed. And thus the acceleration of globalization and widespread global reform could very well be the most positive outcome of the September 11 terrorist attack.

The overall long-term benefits from this acceleration could possibly surpass the many costs of the terrorist attack and counterattack, likely to total hundreds of billions—if not trillions—of dollars.

Broad reform toward "a world that works for all" is thus a *futurible* that deserves our serious con-templation, and our heartfelt efforts to realize.

Source: Michael Marien. (2002, January–February). The new age of terrorism: Futurists respond. *The Futurist, 36* (1), 16–22.

DEMOGRAPHIC TRENDS

For peace and justice to prevail, there must be a new and respectful attention to human diversity. You will find reflections of this in the words of futurists in Exhibit 1. The case study at the beginning of this chapter, too, was chosen because of its focus on a population that is not widely known in the United States. Hmong fami-lies are just one of many immigrant population groups that are contributing to the evolving diversity in the United States. Jeanne West's practice with Hmong people reflected the shift in the social work profession from a "casework" approach that focused on individual people to emphasis on practice that is able to move comfortably across social systems. This more nimble generation of practitioners works with individuals, families, groups, organizations, communities, or even larger societal systems, often with several systems at once, depending on what is needed to prevent or resolve problems. Adapting to the needs of changing client populations is essential to effective practice in an increasingly diverse society.

Demographics, statistical data on population characteristics and trends, is an area of considerable interest to researchers and scholars who monitor patterns of change from which they develop forecasts of the future. Perhaps one of the most significant forces creating change today, change that will carry into the next 40 or 50 years, is that of the demographics of the United States. The U.S. Census Bureau, which charts population shifts, predicts that by the year 2050 whites will become a minority (*Projections*, 2000). In reality, the "new" multicultural world that is predicted may be new for some people, but not for all. Already, in some parts of the country, there is so much diversity that there is no single majority population. Other parts of the United States have few nonwhite residents. Rapidly changing demographics, however, will become increasingly apparent in the next few decades. The social work profession, with a value system that respects diversity and with historical roots in practice across cultures, should be well positioned to take on the challenges that lie ahead. Other demographic trends that will influence social work practice are the increase in our elderly population, evolutions in American family structures, and the changing immigrant and refugee population.

A Multicultural America

Although white Americans made up 85 percent of the U.S. population in 1950 (U.S. Bureau of the Census, 1950, pp. 90–91, 109–111), they constituted 75 percent in 2000 (U.S. Census Bureau, 2000). The ethnic makeup of the country is continuing to change, rapidly. Writing about the ramification of this shift, Farai Chideya observes:

> This is uncharted territory for this country, and this demographic change will affect everything. Alliances between the races are bound to shift. Political and social power will be reapportioned. Our neighborhoods, our schools and workplaces, even racial categories themselves will be altered. Any massive social change is bound to bring uncertainty, even fear. But the worst crisis we face today is not in our cities or neighborhoods, but in our minds. (1999, p. 5)

Her vision is that the new generation, the millennium generation of 15- to 25-year-olds that is already far more culturally diverse than any previous generation, will create a future that is less negatively biased on issues of race. In 1997, Nancy Gordon, Associate Director for Demographic Programs, U.S. Bureau of the Census, reported to the House Committee on Government Reform and Oversight that the number of mixed-race persons in the U.S. quadrupled between 1970 and 1990 (as cited in Chideya, p. 38). Even the matter of classifying persons by the U.S. Census Bureau is more complex today because many people are not able to identify with any single racial category. After a hard-fought battle, the Census Bureau declared that for the first time in its history, the 2000 census would permit people to "check more than one box under race—for example, 'white' and 'Asian'" (Chideya, p. 40). The result was that 6,826,228 persons did check the "two or more races" box. Although this represented only 2.4 percent of the total population, it was double the number of American Indian, Alaskan Native people, Native Hawaiian, and all other Pacific Island people combined (U.S. Census Bureau, 2000).

As for the millennium generation, is there really hope that the children of baby boomers will be more open to multiculturalism? In a poll of 12- to 17-year-olds, *Time*/CNN reported that "a startling number of youngsters, black and white, . . . seem to have moved beyond their parents' views of race" (Farley, 1999, p. 360).

The poll compared responses from the teens with responses to the same questions from adults. Both black and white teens indicated that race was less important to them than it appeared to be for adult respondents. When asked if they personally had experienced discrimination, only 23 percent of black teens but 53 percent of black adults replied affirmatively. When asked if race relations in the United States will ever get better, the teens (76 percent of white and 55 percent of black teens) said yes, while smaller portions (60 percent of whites and 43 percent of black adult respondents) said no. Obviously innocence and inexperience but also optimism and hope are reflected in these responses (Farley, 1999).

Like the *Time*/CNN poll, Americans have typically thought about race in terms of black and white. This tends to be how race is covered in the media. The reality, though, is that today 12.3 percent of our population is black (12.9 percent black or black plus another race) and 12.5 percent is Hispanic or Latino. Asian Americans made up 3.6 percent of the U.S. population in 2000 (4.2 percent Asian plus another race). Asian Americans are another rapidly growing segment of the U.S. population (U.S. Census Bureau, Census 2000).

The social work profession was birthed in a spirit of reform and celebration of multiculturalism, as revealed in the history sections of past chapters of this text. The Council on Social Work Education has written curriculum standards that ensure inclusion of human diversity content in all baccalaureate and master's degree programs. **Ethnic sensitive approaches** to social work practice are now taught in schools of social work that link knowledge of culture and ethnicity with understandings of social class differences (Devore & Schlesinger, 1999). In many ways, social work as a profession has meant being an advocate and supporter of human diversity.

But there is much more for social work to do to create a just society, and the predicted transformation of our country's ethnic and cultural makeup will challenge the profession to become much more proactive. An **ethnoconscious approach** might be the strategy of the future for the social work profession. This theoretical construct incorporates ethnic sensitivity with empowerment tactics that build upon appreciation for the strengths already existing in ethnically diverse communities (Gutierrez & Nagda, 1996). An ethnoconscious approach would insist, for example, that the organizations that deliver social work services reflect the ethnic makeup of the community served by the agency. From agency board members to executives, supervisors, and staff, human diversity would be clearly present. This organization of the future would be "dually focused on bringing about social change and providing empowering programs and services to its clientele" (Gutierrez & Nagda, 1996, p. 206). Linked not only to its service community, but

also to the region, nation, and other countries, the organization and its social workers could take on human problems in the lives of people as they live in families,
and function in groups, organizations, and entire communities.

The Graying of America

As indicated in Chapter 11, "Social Work with Older Adults," a significant shift in
the age of the population has also taken place in the United States. During the
colonial period of American history, approximately half the population was under
the age of 16, and relatively few persons lived to age 65. By 1900 about 4 percent
of the population was 65 years of age or older. In 1970 the proportion of persons
65 or older had grown to 9 percent, by 2000 this had increased to 12.4 percent
(34,991,733 persons), and estimates for the year 2050 indicate that the population
aged 65 and older is expected to reach 82 million; this will represent 20.3 percent
(U.S. Census Bureau, *Projections,* 2000). A surprise in the 2000 census was the
finding that the aged-65-and-older population was actually found to have increased "at a slower rate than the overall population for the first time in the history
of the census" (U.S. Census Bureau, *Nation's median age,* 2001).

Although it can be argued that people at age 65 are healthier now than in the
past and perhaps should not even be considered elderly, society increasingly deval-
ues older adults. Janet George, a social work writer, finds that social workers view
older adults differently: "Social work specifically articulates values of social justice in its work at all levels of intervention. Of particular concern in work with
older adults are the values of autonomy, equity and participation" (cited in Hokenstad & Midgley, 1997, p. 65). Today social workers provide financial counseling,
recreation and wellness programs, housing assistance, advocacy (especially in relation to health care), adult protective services, counseling, and case management.
People who compose the oldest cohort of the elderly, those 85 years and older, require the greatest number of services. As Exhibit 2 indicates, this segment of the
elderly population is growing most rapidly. Because of advanced age, these people
are more likely to have cognitive disorders such as Alzheimer's disease as well as
physical disabilities, so they require care that is physically and psychologically demanding for caregivers. The frailty of these older adults may require social workers of the future to reconceptualize the life course as one that acknowledges advanced age as a norm, a time in life that may include frailty, both physical and
mental (George, as cited in Hokenstad & Midgley). Intervention, then, would seek
to strengthen bonds of intergenerational caregiving as well as economic and social
service policies to ensure good quality of life.

A demographic characteristic that influences the planning and delivery of
social services to the elderly is the lifespan of women. Women tend to outlive
men by several years and they also tend to marry men who are several years
older, so it is common for women to outlive their husbands by 10 years or more.
Women are more likely than men to have to deal with the complex health, economic, and housing problems of old age, first as caregivers of others and later as
receivers of care.

The complex problems of aging require social workers to have both a sound
understanding of the aging process and a broad generalist practice background
that enables them to work simultaneously with individual clients, families, and

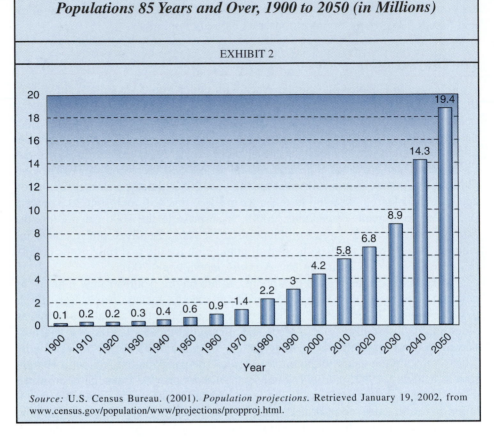

Populations 85 Years and Over, 1900 to 2050 (in Millions)

EXHIBIT 2

Source: U.S. Census Bureau. (2001). *Population projections.* Retrieved January 19, 2002, from www.census.gov/population/www/projections/propproj.html.

community systems. Jake Jacobs, the social worker in the case study in Chapter 11, effectively modeled such social work practice with his client, Rose Balistrieri. In addition to working with individual elderly clients, Jake became involved in community organizing efforts on behalf of the elderly. He lobbied city officials, collected research data to support his requests, and engaged elderly citizens in legislative hearings. Jake's work with students was especially encouraging, since many social workers will be needed in the future to work with older people.

The Evolving American Family

The American family has undergone considerable change and it continues to evolve. In the 1980s, some writers predicted the imminent collapse of the traditional American family. Such gloomy reports, however, were replaced in the 1990s by analysts' recognition of a renewed valuing of family life. In a 1994 article in *The Futurist,* for example, Cetron pointed out that family issues such as "long-term health care, day care, early childhood education, anti-drug campaigns, and drug-free environments" had come to dominate the 1990s (p. 8). Families were valued once again by society. The authors of *Megatrends for Women* agreed. Noting that families have evolved into numerous shapes (stepfamilies, lesbian or gay couples, single parents, grandparent families, etc.), they predicted that family members would continue to make conscious choices in order to spend more time together and to stay intact. They also found business corporations in the 1990s much less resistant to developing "family-friendly" policies (Aburdene & Naisbitt, 1992).

Interesting patterns have been developing in families. There were 105 million households in the United States in 2000, up from 99.6 million in 1996. The share of family households, which stood at 81 percent in 1970, had fallen to 68.1 percent in 2000. This was a continuing, though relatively small, decline from the 1990 rate of 71 percent (U.S. Bureau of the Census, 1998, and U.S. Census Bureau, 2000). Since 1990, too, nonfamily households have become a fairly steady 30 percent of all households; the vast majority of these are persons living alone. Nearly 60 percent of all households in the United States in 2000 included either children under the age of 18 or persons 65 years or older (U.S. Census Bureau, 2000).

As other chapters in this text have reported, there are many grandparents raising children today because drugs and AIDS have left parents unable to care for their children. Among the poor, especially since the implementation of welfare reform legislation, many grandparents provide live-in day care to enable the parents to continue their education. Loss of family income, such as many families experienced in the economic downturn following September 11, 2001, also accounted for adult children returning to their parents' home, sometimes with their young children.

New York City, in particular, suffered a considerable economic shock in the wake of the terrorist attacks of 2001. Approximately 100,000 jobs were lost by the end of 2001. Additional job losses followed as the economic downturn drifted into 2002. Unemployment benefits proved to be woefully inadequate for low-wage earners. Workers who were earning $8 an hour, for example, received only $140 per week, an amount that surely would not permit a very comfortable lifestyle in this city with its high cost of living. Organizations such as the Community Service Society of New York provided direct relief to assist families through the postdisaster period. They also proposed long- and short-term solutions, advocating for a transitional employment program, rent assistance, extended health insurance benefits, and provision for child care, food, and shelter (Jones & Hubbard, 2001). Social workers and social work agencies across the United States responded similarly, advocating for the needs of individuals and families who experienced hardships of many kinds during the economic downturn that began in 2001.

Since its beginnings, the profession of social work has provided service to the American family. As families and societal conditions changed over time, the profession found that it needed to rethink how it worked with families. In the past two or three decades, for example, the profession switched from strongly encouraging unmarried mothers to place their babies for adoption to helping families to remain together. Federal legislation, much of which was promoted by social workers, also resulted in renewed efforts to keep families together. The 1978 Indian Child Welfare Act, for example, discouraged adoption of Indian children into non-Indian families and gave tribes limited funds for family support services. The 1980 Adoption Assistance and Child Welfare Act was considered benchmark legislation for its attempt to ensure permanent families for children. The 1997 Adoption and Safe Families Act furthered commitment to adoption rather than long-term foster care by shortening the time limits of foster care and speeding up the adoption process.

This sounds quite wonderful, but there is another perspective on adoption that social workers must consider. Some cultures define family differently from the nuclear family concept that is valued by people of white, European descent. African Americans, for example, have traditionally valued the extended family. The Association for Black Social Workers has articulated clear preference for **kinship care** over adoption. Kinship is a broad concept, incorporating persons related by blood or legal ties, plus persons related by strong affectional ties (Holody, 1999, p. 7). Poverty is often a factor in preventing or discouraging biological parents from meeting agency behavioral demands that would allow them to reunite with children placed in foster care. Especially for minority families, poverty is also a factor in discouraging relatives from seeking legal adoption. But bonding with family members, permanency of care, and uninterrupted cultural identity are all potentially available through kinship care, which often occurs as long-term foster care (Holody, 1999).

Kinship care versus adoption is only one of many challenges that social workers of the future will confront. Families clearly are changing. The family of the future is likely to be diverse in culture and ethnicity, in age, and in structure (single-parent, two-parent, gay- or lesbian-parented, or a kinship unit). Nonrelative members of households may continue to increase in low-income families. Family income, especially if the gap between rich and poor widens, will have major impact on the educational opportunities and technological skills of young people. In thinking about social work with families in the years ahead, Karen Holmes suggests that in the future, social work practice

> will be characterized by a renewed professional commitment to social and economic justice. As the gap between the haves and have-nots widens, we will be challenged to move more assertively toward achieving a just and equitable society. . . . In our work with families of all kinds, we will be challenged to accept and appreciate diversity in its many forms. (1996, p. 178)

The Changing Immigrant and Refugee Population

The case study at the beginning of this chapter offered insight into the struggles of immigrant people. Immigration is one of the dynamics that will contribute to the dramatically increasing multiculturalism of the U.S. in the near future. Actually, throughout history patterns of human migration have evolved, often reflecting events such as war, famine, natural disasters, and religious or political persecutions. The early history of the United States is replete with descriptions of waves of immigrations. People arrived on U.S. shores to seek a fortune, for adventure, or as indentured servants, slaves, or promised brides. When the Cold War that followed World War II ended, the breakup of the former Soviet Union created massive poverty, prompting large numbers of persons to seek a better life in other parts of the world, including the United States. In the 1990s, war in Kosovo brought masses of new refugees to western European countries, many of which were already tense from episodes of antirefugee ethnic violence. Precipitated by civil unrest, thousands of additional people around the globe have become displaced in recent years. The United States has admitted some of these refugees. Canada and several European countries have also done so, and they have provided the newcomers with quite generous welfare programs.

People, in general, enter another country through three legal means: immigration, asylum, or as a refugee. An **immigrant** is someone who moves to another country for the purpose of settling there permanently. **Asylum** is a protected status that is granted only on a case-by-case basis to persons who can substantiate serious, possibly life-threatening political persecution. "**Refugees** are people who flee to another country out of a fear of persecution because of religion, political affiliation, race, nationality or membership in a particular group" (Ahearn, 1995, p. 771). The United States takes in only a small portion of the world's refugees, a total of approximately 70,000 per year. Asylum is typically granted to less than 10,000 persons per year.

In addition to these legal forms of entry there is, of course, illegal immigration. The United States has implemented border patrols, specialized policing, and considerable legislation to stop illegal immigration from Mexico, El Salvador, Guatemala, Cuba, and Haiti. While many people do enter the United States over guarded land or water routes, which is the way illegal immigration is often portrayed in the media, others arrive quite legally. They simply overstay the expiration of their employment, student, or other legal visa. The disparity between countries' standards of living and economic well-being will remain the catalyst for continued immigration, legal and illegal, into the United States and other industrialized countries for years to come.

The foreign-born population of the United States for several selected years is depicted in Exhibit 3. In 1850 and earlier years the foreign-born came primarily from European countries. Note, however, that the statistical data in those years excluded slaves, many of whom were born in other countries. Gradually the percentage of the population in the United States that was foreign-born increased until 1900, when it reached 13.6% of the total population. After a high of 14.7 percent in 1910, that portion of the population decreased until about 1960. Then it once again began to slowly increase through 2000. The North American foreign-born persons that are shown in all except the 2000 chart came overwhelmingly from Canada. Most dramatic, however, is the increasing percentage of persons coming to the United States from Latin America (many from Mexico) and the declining percentage of foreign-born persons from Europe. Significant increases in Asian newcomers are also apparent (Lollock, 2001).

The foreign-born population both historically and currently tends to be young, to have less education than the native population, and, not surprisingly, to be at increased risk of poverty (U.S. Census Bureau, *The foreign-born,* 2000). Kemp, writing in *Futures Research Quarterly,* predicts that increasing numbers of immigrant persons in U.S. cities "will create new demands for more specialized public services such as the need to hire more bilingual employees, implement cultural diversity programs, and evidence equity in the delivery of existing services to citizens" (2000, p. 23). There is a message in this prediction for social work students and for social workers. Bilingual social workers may be in even greater demand in the future than they are currently. The profession also needs to be able to recruit people who reflect the culture of the immigrant newcomers. Kemp anticipates that East and West Coast port cities will see an influx of immigrant groups. Existing

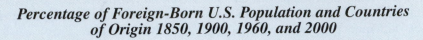

Percentage of Foreign-Born U.S. Population and Countries of Origin 1850, 1900, 1960, and 2000

EXHIBIT 3

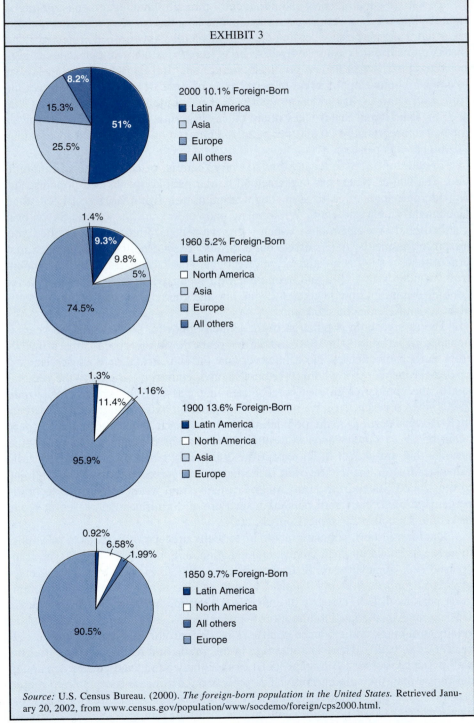

Source: U.S. Census Bureau. (2000). *The foreign-born population in the United States.* Retrieved January 20, 2002, from www.census.gov/population/www/socdemo/foreign/cps2000.html.

ethnic communities will likely expand, and new ethnic communities may emerge. Kemp expects that day care for children, youth and teen programs, community policing, and low-cost health care programs will be implemented. Throughout the United States—in schools, health care centers, shelters, and advocacy programs—social workers like Jeanne West in the chapter case study are among the first professional persons to assist new residents with resettlement.

Even prior to the September 11, 2001, terrorist attacks in the United States, futurists were predicting an increase in international terrorist activity. Cetron and Davies (from the United States) and Moller (ambassador of the Royal Danish Embassy in Singapore) expressed concern. According to Cetron and Davies, "On balance, the amount of terrorist activity in the world is likely to go up, not down, in the next 10 years" (2001b, p. 41). Moller observed that long-standing ethnic conflicts are likely to erupt, leading to dangerous situations involving multiple nations. "This could easily lead to immigration and/or refugees of a scale and magnitude we have rarely seen in recent times. The closest parallel was the flow of refugees in the aftermath of the two world wars in this century" (2000, p. 35).

Pressure to increase the numbers of immigrants and refugees admitted to the United States and other countries may prove to be intense if the U.S. experience following the infamous September 11 terrorist attacks persists. "Increased racist and xenophobic attacks, harassment and threats against Muslims, Sikhs and people of Middle Eastern and South Asian descent have been reported in the U.S." (*No safe refuge,* 2001). The U.S. attorney general sought authorization to "detain any non-citizen, including an asylum-seeker, legal permanent resident, or a refugee" if he suspected them of assisting or harboring terrorists or being in any way involved with terrorist activities or supporting groups that in any way aided terrorists. The potential for arbitrary action against innocent foreign-born persons was of concern to human rights advocates.

As advocates for at-risk and vulnerable populations, social workers may be called on increasingly in coming years to assist immigrants, refugees, and asylum-seekers. Social workers will be involved in resettlement work similar to that portrayed in the chapter case study. Social workers may also help organizations such as church groups to sponsor new immigrants or asylum-seekers. In international social service agencies such as the Red Cross, social workers will communicate across borders to keep relatives linked, especially during disasters or in the event that a person becomes a prisoner of war. Program planning will be undertaken, too, to assist communities in providing for the child care, health, and other needs of new immigrants.

POLITICAL TRENDS

As the twentieth century came to a close, a gradual shift in the political climate was apparent in many parts of the world. Politically conservative parties were gaining power in elections in many countries, including the United States, where the political liberalism of the Kennedy and Johnson administrations during the 1960s gave way, even when Democrats were elected to office. As Chapter 2 of this text explains, the neoliberals such as Bill Clinton and Al Gore took a more favorable stance toward big business and supported reduction of government aid to poor people. In this more politically conservative climate, taxpayers' support for social services in general, especially governmental social services, declined.

Welfare Reform

Welfare reform emerged as a popular political theme and, in 1996, the former AFDC (Aid to Families with Dependent Children) program that guaranteed cash benefits to low-income families was abolished. The TANF (Temporary Assistance for Needy Families) that replaced AFDC provided federal money to states, giving states considerable discretionary power to administer their own financial assistance programs. The TANF program has been referred to frequently in this text. A feature of TANF that did not exist in AFDC was a lifetime limit of 60 months on benefits. Under TANF, too, parents may be required to work after 24 months of assistance, and TANF assistance could be cut off for a variety of reasons—if a family failed to cooperate with the work requirement, for example, or if a teen mother stopped attending school. Discontinuation of benefits for failure to comply with TANF requirements became known as **sanctioning**. If another child was born while a family was receiving TANF, the state was not obliged to provide any additional assistance for the newborn. With a significant level of funding provided to states to design and administer their own TANF programs (which most states renamed to reflect their state's philosophy), some states provided child care funding and other services to encourage rapid transition to work from welfare.

The TANF program has achieved success by most counts. The U.S. Department of Health and Human Services 2000 report to Congress cited a decline in welfare caseloads of 7.8 million between 1993 and the end of 1999. During the same time there was a decrease in the percentage of the U.S. population receiving welfare—from 5.4 percent in 1992 to 2.3 percent by December 1999. Out-of-wedlock births declined and child poverty rates also declined, though less dramatically, from 41.5 percent in female-headed families in 1995 to 38.7 percent three years later. Child support payments also increased (U.S. Department of Health and Human Services, 2000).

Could the favorable economic conditions of the 1990s have accounted for this decline in welfare caseloads? Some observers suggest that the 1990s economy certainly played a role in the apparent success of the TANF program. Critics of the current program are concerned about the ability of state governments to sustain financial assistance after TANF terminates for the "hard core poor," those persons who were unable to transition to employment for a variety of reasons. They are calling for a rethinking of the TANF time limits. Late in 2002 the TANF program must be reauthorized by Congress. Research studies to evaluate the TANF program are under way. One study, completed by Case Western Reserve University, found that the majority of families forced off welfare when they reached their five-year time limit in 2001 were living well below the poverty line. Not surprisingly, many were living in overcrowded housing, often with relatives with whom their relationships were deteriorating (Marks, 2001). The economic recession that began in 2001 and deepened following the terrorist attacks resulted in thousands of layoffs. How many persons affected by the recession were former recipients of TANF benefits? What does this tell us about the TANF program?

When the law authorizing the TANF program was passed in 1996, it was not only a victory for persons seeking welfare reform but also an immense victory for conservative politicians whose objective was to return power to the states and to eliminate federal regulation and control. As social workers Gilbert and Terrell note, "TANF incorporates a sweeping decentralization of authority, eliminating in one swoop a structure of federal legislation that over the course of 30 years had endeavored with at least some modest success to liberalize welfare arrangements and provide a measure of reliable economic protection to a great many poor Americans (2002, p. 250). States' power in administering the TANF program, as it currently exists, is considerable. States may provide benefits or not. They may set the lifetime limit for financial assistance anywhere up to five years (several have opted for 24- or 36-month limits). Providing child care to assist parents in securing and sustaining employment is also the state's choice. They may also choose to extend benefits beyond the five-year period, but if they do so, the states will become responsible for financing these payments. When recession struck in 2001 and 2002, the state budget surpluses of the 1990s evaporated and the "welfare issue" suddenly seemed much more complex. Political forces once again began to polarize.

TANF is, of course, one of many important political issues of concern to social workers and to NASW that will require attention in the near future. In the aftermath of the September 11 tragedy, Congress attended to fears of renewed terrorist attacks, airline security, the military strikes in Afghanistan, and the threat of anthrax or other chemical, biological, or even nuclear terrorism. Domestic issues related to child welfare, mental health parity, the patient's bill of rights, and the future of Social Security all remained to be dealt with. Social work organizations at state and national levels, including NASW, remained actively involved, especially as the war in Afghanistan appeared to be reaching a military conclusion.

In the future, political forces, of course, will continue to determine the availability of human services in our country and in the nations of the world. If social workers truly care about people and about social change, they will not sit idly by, merely providing psychotherapy for the emotional and physical pain suffered by the victims of politics and poor public policy; instead, they will assume responsibility for their own political behavior and will also empower their clients to engage in the democratic process. Toward the end of this chapter we will discuss the kind of action social workers can take if they are truly motivated to help people, to make a difference in the world they live in. Next, however, we shall take a look at the result of one political trend on the delivery of social services.

Privatization

Privatization (turning government systems designed to meet the needs of people over to the private sector) has grown worldwide with the breakup of communist and totalitarian regimes. In the United States, increasing privatization emerged as a significant force by the end of the 1990s. In social work, privatization became especially apparent in the growth of for-profit human service organizations and in state human service agencies providing professional services through contracts with private nonprofit and for-profit agencies.

The case study in Chapter 8 is just one example of social work within a private corporation, in this case an employee assistance program. Group homes are another example. Twenty years ago, foster group homes for teenagers, developmentally disabled adults, and the elderly were almost exclusively operated by state and county welfare departments or nonprofit agencies. In most communities today, only a small portion of the group homes are run by nonprofit organizations. Instead, most are owned and operated by private corporations, often headed by social workers. The same is true of residential treatment centers for emotionally disturbed children. Substance abuse programs—once provided almost exclusively by tax-supported hospitals or denominational facilities—have become big business and are being marketed aggressively. Chapter 12 described the marked growth of a for-profit prison industry in the United States.

The entrepreneurial practice of social work has also expanded significantly, especially for MSWs. Social workers in private practice offer their services for a fee in much the same way that physicians or attorneys in private practice do. Often health insurance policies cover the cost of counseling through social workers. *The Social Work Dictionary* defines **private practice** as "the process in which the values, knowledge, and skills of social work, acquired through sufficient education and experience, are used to deliver social services autonomously to clients in exchange for mutually agreed payment" (Barker, 1999, p. 377).

Privatization has undoubtedly benefited the private practice of social work and nonprofit agencies as well by providing both clients and income. The most significant ramification of privatization, however, is a change in philosophy regarding the provision of service to clients. With privatization, public investment is shifted away from administering and sustaining public social service programs to purchasing the same service from a private source. Often this involves the purchase of a service contract between a state department of social services, for example, and a social worker in private practice, or a privately operated group home or residential treatment center, or a nonprofit agency. Service is provided for a specified period of time or until an agreed-upon goal is achieved. Service is terminated when the contract is completed, often with no provision for follow-up care. On the surface, this may look like economic efficiency, but when vulnerable populations such as the frail elderly or emotionally disturbed children are involved, such apparent efficiency may actually be detrimental to clients. Neither economic nor human justice interests are served when clients' well-being suffers because of disrupted or prematurely discontinued service. What is needed instead is service that is efficient, effective, humane, and readily available whether it is delivered through a public or private agency or through a professional person in private practice.

The trend toward privatization in human services, whether prisons or family therapy, breaks with a long tradition of tax-supported public services delivered without the cost and the potential conflicts of interest of the for-profit, entrepreneurial enterprise. This trend raises concerns about the inherent values of human service organizations, a concern very much like that described in the section about industrial social work in Chapter 3. Is monetary profit the primary goal, or are the best interests of the client the real goal? While moving more and more into for-profit practice, the profession of social work nevertheless maintains a somewhat skeptical stance about it. Of concern is the potential that social workers might lose their traditional commitment to advocacy, to social change, to social and economic justice, and to service to vulnerable populations.

Privatization in social services also risks high turnover rates for social workers. This was the finding of a study reported in 2002 conducted by three prestigious social work organizations, the Child Welfare League of America, the American Public Human Services Association, and the Alliance for Children and Families. Over 90 agencies were surveyed. The study found that private agencies had a turnover rate of 40 percent for child protective service workers compared with 19.9 percent for protective service workers in public agencies. When the researchers looked at the turnover rate in direct service areas other than child protective services, the findings were remarkably similar: 19.4 percent turnover in public agencies versus 40.8 percent in private agencies. (The comparability of findings for protective service and other direct service work suggests that the nature of child protective services work, often suspected as an especially high "burnout" area, was not a factor.) A primary reason given for the higher turnover rate in private agencies was their lower salaries. At the time of the study, the private agencies in the study paid an average of $28,646 to child protective service social workers while the state agencies averaged $33,436. The lower caseloads of the private agencies (13 compared with 24 for state social workers) did not appear to offset the salary discrepancy in preventing loss of staff (O'Neill, Private agency, 2002).

The political drive to shift public health and social services to the private sector remains very strong. Yes, it can save money for taxpayers by reducing personnel costs and fragmenting services, but at a substantial cost of the quality of services. When politicians again wish to locate funds for other uses (prison construction, for example), the next step might be a shift away from professional staffing of social services to reliance on volunteers. Community needs, especially the needs of abused and neglected children and other vulnerable populations, must be protected better than this! Although professional people may be accused of being self-serving, they will need to become proactive to ensure that the quality of professional services provided in the private sector is not further jeopardized and that public social services continue to exist. An important responsibility of government is to ensure the quality of life and well-being of its citizens.

Women's Issues

The profession of social work, because it serves many poor and vulnerable women and comprises significant numbers of women, is awakening to the needs of women and their struggle for equality. Even in the past, social work pioneers such as Jane Addams and Florence Kelley of Chicago's Hull House were leaders in the struggle for the right to vote and for equality for women. Despite public ridicule and even imprisonment in the early days of the women's movement, these women and the men that supported them succeeded in obtaining passage of the Nineteenth Amendment to the U.S. Constitution—the right to vote for women.

The next effort of women, to pass the **Equal Rights Amendment (ERA)** prohibiting discrimination on the basis of gender, was not as successful. The effort to achieve the ERA was immense, with huge political rallies, statewide and regional conventions, parades, and much demonstration of public support. In 1972 Congress did pass the ERA, but it was defeated when the necessary number of states failed to ratify this proposed amendment to the U.S. Constitution.

Other gains for women's rights, however, were achieved. In 1972 Title IX of the Education Act was passed, prohibiting most forms of gender discrimination in educational institutions that receive federal funds. Since then women's admissions to professional education programs have increased markedly (Gottlieb, 1995).

Another gain for women, although a painfully slow one, has been the narrowing of the wage gap between men and women. Using the most current data available at the time of writing, Exhibit 4 documents the progress that has taken place in narrowing the wage gap between American women and men. In reading this exhibit it is important to note that real annual wages have actually fallen for both men and women since 1980 because dramatically increased international trade has expanded the supply of low-skill, low-wage workers producing goods for the American market.

Also contributing to the current supply of low-wage workers is the "welfare reform" that replaced AFDC with TANF (described earlier in this text). Under the TANF welfare program, severe penalties are exacted when people do not accept employment, any employment that is available and quite possibly at minimum wage. In analyzing political trends, it is interesting to note that the TANF program, as it currently exists, will ensure a supply of low-wage workers to fuel the U.S. economy.

Wage Gap by Gender
Median Annual Earnings of Full-Time Workers by Sex: 1960–2000

EXHIBIT 4

| Year | Women's Earnings as a % of Men's | Earnings in Real Dollars | |
		Women	Men
1960	60.7%	$11,003	$18,175
1970	59.4	13,719	23,105
1980	60.2	13,589	22,587
1990	71.6	15,166	21,177
1995	71.4	14,762	20,667
1996	73.8	15,112	20,487
1997	74.2	26,720	36,030
1998	73.2	27,290	37,296
1999	72.2	27,208	37,701
2000	73.0	27,355	37,339

Source: U.S. Department of Labor. (2000). Retrieved January 22, 2002, from Feminist.com website. www.feminist.com/Fairpay/f_change.htm.

Because of low birthrates in the United States, in the 1960s and 1970s, there will be a decline in the number of young people available to the job market for entry-level low-wage jobs and there will be much need for low-wage workers. It is predicted that "this problem could be acute between 2000 and 2010, especially in the service sector" (Cetron & Davies, 2001b, p. 37). Recipients of TANF, even with potential modifications made when TANF is reauthorized, are likely to suffer sanctions if they do not accept the low-wage, minimal-benefit jobs that the service-driven U.S. economy will provide. The recipients of TANF are overwhelmingly women and their children.

Not surprisingly, inequality in wages became a political issue that women's organizations in particular targeted for change. As women's professional groups such as the 70,000-member Business and Professional Women/USA (BPW/USA) joined with labor unions and other politically active women's groups, the pragmatic concept of **pay equity** emerged. Pay equity is defined by the National Committee on Pay Equity as

> a means of eliminating sex and race discrimination in the wage-setting system. Most women and people of color are still segregated into a small number of jobs—such as clericals, service workers, nurses and teachers. These jobs have historically been undervalued and continue to be underpaid because of the gender and race of the people who hold them. Pay equity means that the criteria employers use to set wages must be sex and race neutral. (*Questions and answers on pay equity,* 1998, p. 1)

Does pay disparity have to exist? Perhaps not. Research comparing gender composition and wages in the United States and Canada found "no evidence that female jobs are systematically poorly paid in Canada" (Baker & Fortin, 1998, p. 1).

A coalition of women's groups including the BPW/USA established Equal Pay Day (generally early in April) to give special attention to efforts to obtain pay equity. Two bills that were introduced in Congress in 1997–98, the Paycheck Fairness Act and the Fair Pay Act, were not acted upon in that Congressional session. With more women than ever in the workplace, pay equity is one political issue that will be on the agenda of women in the future.

As women begin to pay more attention to legislative agendas, they are likely to seek greater representation in local and state offices as well as the U.S. Congress and other key political positions. The next decade seems poised to produce some exciting political races with high-powered women running effective campaigns for key offices. In 1984 the United States had its first female vice presidential candidate, Geraldine Ferraro. Meanwhile, in developing countries as well as industrialized parts of the world, women have been elected as presidents and prime ministers. Countries such as Switzerland, Pakistan, Ireland, Norway, and Great Britain have had women presidents and prime ministers. The 1992 elections swept 28 women into the U.S. Congress, a remarkable gain, but only two women were added in 1994 and by 1998 progress slowed with women totaling a mere 13 percent of congressional seats. (Knickerbocker, 1998). In the 2000 elections, women began to make a more impressive showing. Three women were elected to office as state governors, bringing the number of women governors to five. Three women were also elected as U.S. senators, bringing that number to 12 (Knickerbocker, 2000). The 2002 elections will be of considerable interest since that will be the first election year after **reapportionment,** the mandated redrawing of congressional districts, following the 2000 census.

ECONOMIC CONDITIONS

The people served by social workers, especially generalist baccalaureate social workers, are often poor people. Of course, social workers work with all sectors of society and all people are affected by the economy, but poor people and near-poor persons are likely to be most dramatically impacted by economic conditions. Not surprisingly, political forces and economic conditions are strongly interrelated. And now more than ever, events and conditions in other parts of the world affect our lives. In the past decade there has been an expansion of industrialization around the globe, especially in third world countries, in eastern Europe, and in the former Soviet Union. Some of the industrialization exploited the masses of poor people in emerging countries, luring them into urban areas and leaving their villages and farms bereft of able-bodied workers. In the United States, economic development has increasingly moved from central-city areas to suburbs and from northern to southern states.

During the late 1980s in the United States, the combination of economic stress coupled with a large federal budget deficit and a conservative administration led to major reductions in federal funding of social service programs. Social service programs were, in fact, among the first government programs to be cut back as the Reagan administration attempted to deal with recession. A significant change was taking place in the economy of the country. **Underemployment**—which is employment at or near minimum wage, often part-time and without health insurance or other benefits—had begun to replace unemployment. The numbers of employed persons receiving financial and medical assistance and food stamps increased, while the unemployment rate decreased dramatically. Food pantries provided groceries, and community feeding programs served meals to the families of employed persons whose income was inadequate to meet their daily needs. Advocates of the poor spoke out against the administration's cuts in social services, especially programs for the poor. One such advocate wrote:

> What first appeared as the Reagan Administration's war against the poor and the welfare state has now emerged as a broader national policy of social underdevelopment that affects most Americans. The deliberate policy of disinvesting in social programs has created a skyrocketing social deficit (the gap between met and unmet social needs), a bipolar structure of income distribution and a shrinking middle class. . . . It affects not only the social welfare system but the broader quality of life in urban and rural America, the way income is distributed, and the structure of U.S. social classes. (Iatridis, 1988, p. 11)

Meanwhile, a very small portion of the U.S. population had doubled its income in a single decade, ending in the late 1980s; the poorest 20 percent of the population, however, saw their share of the national income fall from 5.1 percent in 1980 to 4.5 percent by 1991. By the mid-1990s these economic conditions resulted in increased homelessness, which had become shockingly visible even in the nation's capital. The *New York Times* reported:

> Attention to homeless issues had been heightened in Washington, D.C., by the Nov. 29 discovery of the body of a homeless woman, Yetta Adam, outside the headquarters of the Department of Housing and Urban Development, the federal agency in charge of housing policy. (Major new spending, 1994, p. A18)

Using newly learned political action strategies, social work students seek an end to violence.

For many Americans the 1990s brought increased prosperity and a surge in consumer products. The number of households with telephones, televisions, cars, computers, and air-conditioning increased. Noting that an improved standard of living was occurring in Third World countries, too, one financier predicted that "as the twenty-first century unfolds, our children and our children's children will live lives of unprecedented comfort and wealth" (Templeton, 1999, p. 22).

When the federal welfare reform law, Temporary Assistance for Needy Families, was passed in 1996, it was heralded as an end to poverty in the United States. Four years later, the U.S. Department of Health and Human Services was able to report that employment of welfare recipients had increased to 33 percent compared to less than 7 percent in 1992, and welfare caseloads had dropped from 5.5 percent in 1993 to 2.3 percent by the end of 1999. Average hourly wages for TANF recipients was $6.60 to $6.80. This was definitely an increase for families that had been on welfare for a long time, but it was equal to or less than the hourly wages received by people who had only recently begun to receive TANF assistance (U.S. Department of Health and Human Services, 2000). Concerns began to be voiced about whether TANF recipients were really receiving an adequate income. The Children's Legal Defense Fund and the National Coalition for the Homeless jointly investigated the life experiences and well-being of the families who left welfare and discovered hardship and much deprivation. Their study included both employed and unemployed former recipients of TANF. They found that "across the country, there are indications that former recipients face large—and growing—problems feeding their families" (Sherman et al., 1998, p. 14). There were also numerous reports of utility shutoffs, frequent moves, eviction, and homelessness. Of 161 homeless families in Atlanta, 46 percent had been cut off from TANF in the past year. Social workers often know about these families, but their stories do not often grab headlines in the media quite as quickly as the headlines that read: "Welfare Rolls Down. Welfare Reform: A Success!"

The exceptionally healthy economy of the United States in the 1990s led even noted futurists to predict that "widespread affluence, low interest rates, low inflation, and low unemployment will be the norm" into the next century (Cetron & Davies, 2001a, p. 31). The reality, however, was that unemployment began to creep upwards early in 2001. From 4.2 percent in January, the unemployment rate increased to 4.9 percent in August and by October, following the terrorist attacks, the rate jumped to 5.4 percent. By the end of 2001 it had reached 5.8 percent, and across the country layoffs were continuing (U.S. Bureau of Labor Statistics, 2002). The terrorist strikes against the United States had an immediate impact on the economy of much of the rest of the world, which was just beginning to come out of an economic downturn.

With the success of the U.S. military operation in Afghanistan, the tide seemed to change and optimism again began to be expressed about economic conditions. Wartime military and homeland security expenditures, however, resulted in budget deficits that threatened funding for social programs, especially the programs that serve poor people.

In this world of mixed economic signals, poor people are most vulnerable. They tend to be the first people to be effected by layoffs. When rents cannot be paid, poor people are evicted and soon become homeless. Social programs are needed to find food, shelter, and medical care. Hopefully the increased sense of interdependence and compassion that was so evident following the terrorist attacks in 2001 will be sustained and reflected in public support for the social programs that are so necessary to the well-being of all people.

TECHNOLOGICAL ADVANCES

Technology is the fourth area that will have impact on the future of social work. The high-tech era that we live in will continue to influence the profession—sometimes directly, sometimes indirectly. Technology touches social work in terms of both computerization and its result: the need for humanization.

Computerization

Today's social work students are not naive about the future and its incorporation of computer technology. Instead, they are polishing their skills in word and data processing, running statistical analyses for their research papers, and relaxing by communicating with friends on the Internet. The Internet is also a valuable tool for library searches as are databases such as NASW's *Social Work Abstracts,* which is available in many college and university libraries.

Ethical Issues for Social Workers   As a profession, however, social work was slow to adopt computers, and some small agencies are still, only now, beginning to use databases, spreadsheets, and word processing to manage their administrative work and case records. A legitimate concern of some agency directors was that storage of clients' records in computer databases might be very efficient, but it could also present risks to confidentiality. On the other hand, computerized databases, e-mail, chat rooms, and other technology resources actually help to keep social workers connected and may remedy one of the most serious problems in social work: fragmentation of services.

Stephen Marson, of the University of North Carolina at Pembroke, conducted research that rank-ordered computer use by social workers. He found that the most frequently cited use of the computer was for networking, communicating with other professionals. Social work students ranked the Internet highly as a vital information resource for research and term papers. Social work computer users ranked highly the availability of resource information suitable for client referrals, especially the availability of recovery and support groups for people with alcohol or other addictions, people with AIDS, people adopting a child, and so on (Marson, 1998).

In Chapter 8 of this text we discussed the multiple ways in which professionals in workplace settings, such as employee assistance organizations, use electronic technology. This included many of the areas identified in Marson's survey but added the provision of information about problems such as substance abuse, domestic violence, work stress, and the use of computerized client self-assessments to screen for anxiety, depression, and chemical dependence. A survey of EAP consumers showed that some used websites "because they had issues too embarrassing to share face to face" (O'Neill, EAPs, 2002, p. 14). This poignant description of vulnerability, added to the fact that Internet counseling is rapidly increasing, underscores the importance of adhering to strict ethical guidelines when using electronic technology.

In her book *Social Work Values and Ethics* (1999) Elaine Congress provides a case study that depicts some of the ethical issues that are triggered by use of technology. In her case study Nancy, a social worker with a mental health clinic, is seeing Rhoda, a 32-year-old woman with depression. When Rhoda first came to the clinic, she completed a computerized assessment that showed her to have a dysthymic (chronically depressed mood) disorder. In addition to diagnosing the disorder, the computer program recommended brief treatment using a cognitive-behavioral approach. Nancy requested a client treatment history from the therapist who had assisted her two years previously, and this was sent promptly via office fax. After seeing Rhoda a couple of times, Nancy realized that she needed more extended treatment than the computerized assessment instrument recommended. Rhoda's insurance would not pay for additional visits under this diagnosis. What should Nancy do? Her agency has a right to be paid for Nancy's services and cannot continue offering services if it is not reimbursed.

Here the *NASW Code of Ethics* is instructive. It will hold the social worker responsible for advocating with the insurance or managed care company to obtain reimbursement for Rhoda's continuing mental health care. The code also makes Nancy and all social workers responsible for engaging in social or political action to secure equal access for all people to the care and services they need. Nancy's office provides her with state-of-the-art technology for receiving telephone messages, recording her interviews with clients, and sending and receiving information by fax. But this technology also presents ethical dilemmas. Nancy was out of the office on the day the fax arrived with Rhoda's previous mental health history. The fax sat on a desk, visible to all who passed by, until

GARY PORTER/MILWAUKEE JOURNAL SENTINEL

Social work programs empower young adults by enhancing computer skills.

Nancy returned the next day. Rhoda also tried to reach Nancy by phone on another occasion when Nancy was out sick; the office phone equipment did not enable Rhoda to talk with other staff or to reach Nancy. Nancy, of course, records each of her sessions with Rhoda on her computer. This avoids the likelihood of Rhoda's or any client's file being left on her desk and accessible to anyone entering her office when she goes to lunch. In solving one potential risk of confidentiality, however, another is created: the possibility that other staff can access Rhoda's file on the office computer network where all client files are stored (Congress, 1999).

Today's office technology—including computers, fax machines, cell phones, telephone answering machines or answering services, voice mail, and all other electronic equipment—is a potential source of ethical problems. The current *NASW Code of Ethics,* located in the Appendix of this book, holds social workers responsible for protecting confidentiality for clients; that would include accepting responsibility for the careful use of current technology in handling client records. According to Congress, "Social workers like Nancy must continually struggle to maintain confidentiality in a nonconfidential world" (1999, p. 41). What a challenge! Robert Vernon and Darlene Lynch's book, *Social Work and the Web* (2000), however, offers step-by-step directions for developing security systems within your computer or computer network to avoid some of the more serious technology-related ethical problems that beset social work practitioners.

The practice of social work in the future will be strongly influenced by computerization. Even today systems based on artificial intelligence are becoming more available to assist in assessing client problems, developing intervention plans, and evaluating the results of social work practice. Online groups dealing with specific issues such as breast cancer or children who are schoolphobic are being designed to provide mutual assistance as well as professional help. Such groups are likely to continue to increase because they are relatively inexpensive for computer owners and they function within a time frame that fits today's hectic lifestyles. E-mail is used increasingly, too, as an adjunct to private counseling or as the preferred mode of delivery. Virtual reality approaches, parent training videos, and computer-delivered bibliotherapy (treatment employing literature and poetry) were among the technological adaptations found to be effective in empirical studies of short-term therapies (Dziegielewski, Shields, & Thyer, 1998).

Marson's research of current social work computer users noted the relative absence of computer use for community organizing and natural network building (Marson, 1998). Clearly this is an area for future development for the social work profession. Social action, advocacy, and policy research will benefit dramatically in the future from the availability of shared databases and from programs that permit analysis of massive amounts of statistical data. Online databases available through the Internet contain rich sources of data useful to social workers. Internet home pages of U.S. senators and congressional representatives are readily accessible (see the Internet Sites), as are those of many other local and state elected officials. Computer technological advances, when coupled with advances in facsimile (fax) and long-distance telephone access, enhance the immediacy of communication. These tools are fostering globalization at a rapid rate, and for creative social workers, their potential uses in organizational, community, and even global systems change are phenomenal.

Computerized Practice in 20 Years   Because technology is advancing so rapidly, relatively few predictions have been made in the preceding paragraphs about how computer technology will impact social work practice beyond roughly the next 10 years. Short-range predictions are, in fact, increasingly the case in the entire field of futurist studies (Rubenstein, 2000). Vernon and Lynch, however, have ventured some guesses about the future 20 years from now. They believe that advanced technology will enable social workers to work out of their homes rather than being based in offices, though the "hotelling" practice mentioned in Chapter 8 of this text may operate, too. This decreased administrative cost of social service programs will be welcome politically because of its diminished impact on tax revenues. Social workers will have much better quality information and far greater access to information than we do currently. Foster homes, for example, may be readily accessed on the social worker's home computer screen. In fact, computers will be everywhere in 20 years—in every appliance, every piece of office equipment, even everywhere in homes. Unfortunately, as Vernon and Lynch peer into their 20-year crystal ball, they see a continuation of male dominance, even in the world of social work practice. Males, they speculate, will be dominant because they were more likely to have acquired mastery of computer skills in their earlier education; women students in the early 2000s, after all, were not as drawn to the computer sciences as their male classmates. Any group that has been left behind in acquisition of computer skills will be disadvantaged. Professional education in social work will be dramatically changed in 20 years, Vernon and Lynch predict. They anticipate that students will take whole components of their curriculum—social welfare policy, for example, or human diversity courses—from a variety of institutions in various countries. Curricular components may be accredited by the Council on Social Work Education (yes—it will continue to exist) rather than social work programs within single institutions. Continuing education, which will still be needed to sustain licensure, will be taken online. Vernon and Lynch see many technology changes awaiting us in the future, but they predict that the human problems and issues that social workers confront today will remain central to practice 20 years from now. Twenty years from now, they say, "kids still need protection" (2000, p. 279). Social workers will still be needed.

Biomedical Technology

Technological advances in medicine continue to startle the world—and to bring both hope and havoc to the lives of patients and their families. Social workers in health care settings very quickly encounter the ethical and personal dilemmas precipitated by advances in medicine, but across social work settings all social workers can anticipate working with people whose lives are impacted by advances in medical technology.

Organ Replacement Organ transplantation, an area that continues to evolve, involves social workers as key members of the medical team. Social workers are called upon to bridge the communication gap between the highly specialized medical professionals and the persons so vitally affected—such as organ recipients and family members of the potential organ donor. Social workers help family members to understand the medical situation, the decisions that need to be made, and the potential ramifications. Simultaneously, they help people deal with the overwhelming emotions of such health crisis situations.

Because sufficient replacement organs have not been available from human donors, biomedical research is moving at a rapid pace to design better artificial organs and to create human-generated replacement organs. Tissue engineers are working to produce cells that will reproduce or heal organs. One such scenario involves growing new blood vessels to bypass existing blockages in, for example, coronary arteries. Engineering to develop man-made organs, known as **neo-organs,** is already under way but in early stages of development. To develop neo-organs, individual cells are grown in labs where they multiply in cultures. Then, when attached to a synthetic scaffolding, they can be made to take on the structure and growth qualities of human organs. Cells can be taken from the person's own body to grow replacement organs, or in other future scenarios, "off the shelf," premanufactured organs will become available for immediate transplant when vital organs need immediate replacement, following traumatic injury in a car accident, for example (Mooney & Mikos, 1999). Research is moving rapidly, but especially for people with terminal illness or severe traumatic injury, these advances may not be ready soon enough. Social workers need to help people balance hope against unrealistic expectations.

Skin cell transplants, however, are already being used. The next area of rapid development in tissue engineering is cartilage replacement. Cartilage is used to repair damaged joints or for head and face reconstructive surgery. The current impediment to engineering of large-scale, complex replacement organs is the challenge of growing the blood vessel networks needed to feed and nourish such organs. Artificial cells made of polymers (plastics), collagens, and other materials available from nature are another approach in biomedical engineering. "Structural tissues, such as skin, bone and cartilage, will most likely continue to dominate the first wave of success stories, thanks to their relative simplicity" (Mooney & Mikos, 1999). Research currently under way promises continued developments in the near future.

Complex ethical questions, however, already abound in the area of human organ replacement. In the United States, historically, society has approved the donation or selling of blood, sperm, and bone marrow, but selling vital body organs that cannot be easily replaced, organs like kidneys or livers, is not legal in the United States. In some other parts of the world, especially in very poor countries, people desperate for income sell their vital organs at considerable risk. Moldova, a country that was formerly a part of the Soviet Union, is such a place. Here poor people sell their kidneys for $3,000, mostly to prosperous Asians. They may be paid in full, as promised, but often they are not. Lacking adequate medical care, the donor may encounter prolonged illness following surgery or may die. Other countries that are sources of human "spare parts" are Brazil, the Philippines, and Argentina. There seems to be evidence that China may be selling the vital organs of its prisoners (*Human organs for sale,* 2001). If the United States were to change its policy about sale of vital human organs in the future, this would undoubtedly be a concern for social workers. Shouldn't we also be concerned about these practices in other parts of the world?

Ethical issues regarding human embryo stem cell research also have been intensely debated in the media for the past several years. An ABCNEWS/Washington Post poll in 2001 showed 63 percent of Americans supporting federal government funding for human embryo stem cell research, despite the declared opposition of many conservative Christian religious groups (Derris, 2001). Harvesting of human tissues from aborted fetuses, nonetheless, remained a very distasteful consideration for many people in spite of the potential benefits these cells might offer. Then, in early 2002, it was announced that a researcher had discovered adult human cells, referred to as multipotent adult progenitor cells (MAPCs), that had the potential to "turn into a myriad of tissue types: muscle, cartilage, bone, liver and different types of neurons and brain cells" (Westphal, 2002, p. 2). The media heralded this breakthrough as an alternative to harvesting human embryos. In addition to human "spare parts," adult human stem cells procured from bone marrow demonstrated potential for treating disorders ranging from diabetes and heart disease to Alzheimer's and Parkinson's diseases (Henderson, 2002). The scientific community welcomed the discovery of adult stem cells but cautioned that considerable additional research would be needed to ensure the accuracy and safety of the adult cell findings. Biomedical ethics groups, too, urged that research involving adult human stem cells proceed cautiously (Dooley, 2001).

Genetic Research   Significant advances have also been made in genetics, thanks to the **Human Genome Project.** The Human Genome Project is a research effort coordinated by the U.S. Department of Energy and the National Institutes of Health. Begun in 1990, this project to determine the makeup of human DNA was scheduled for completion in 2005 but is now 90 percent completed, although half of the data produced are not yet sufficiently refined to be applied (*UCSC,* 2002). The findings coming from this project on an almost daily basis are presenting contemporary society and future generations with challenging ethical, social, and legal dilemmas. **Genetic testing** has been one of the first applications of this project. There are now genetic tests to determine the existence or potential for such conditions as cystic fibrosis, Huntington's disease, sickle-cell anemia, and certain kinds of cancer (some forms of ovarian, colon, and breast cancer). Testing that detects genetic mutations associated with certain forms of cancer can alert people to the need for early and frequent cancer screening tests, such as mammograms, and can provide alternatives to disease management (*Medicine and the new genetics,* 2001).

The ethical and social quandaries of women seeking genetic testing for breast or ovarian cancer were studied by Freedman, a social worker. Two segments from her research interviews reveal the emotion experienced by these women:

> I do not want to carry on another generation of cancer. Should my daughter be told not to have children? It feels like a death sentence. There is uncertainty and the never knowing.
>
> There is tyranny involved because the technology is available. I feel that it would be stupid of me not to avail myself of it. If there is anything that I can do to assure myself that I do not have to share my mother's fate, that I won't die a horrible death from ovarian cancer, I will do it. I don't want to be in the position down the road of beating my head against the wall and saying, "Why didn't I do this?" (1998, pp. 216–217)

Social workers help people to understand what genetic testing means, the kinds of information that can come from the tests, and how it can be used. They help family members to resolve the issues that testing results bring, the multigenerational consequences of information suggesting susceptibility to disease. The social worker is not usually the actual genetics counselor—that person is a medical specialist. But the social worker provides the supportive relationship, assists with panic or psychological crises that result, and assists the family after the information is given to them. Genetic testing is commercially available and costly. Its current lack of availability to all socioeconomic groups raises ethical questions for social workers. Ethical, moral, and spiritual questions are also inherent in the decisions made as a result of genetic testing (Freedman, 1998).

Gene therapy, unlike genetic testing, lies in the near future but is not available today. Research, however, is under way, and cures may become available for certain genetic and acquired diseases such as AIDS and some forms of cancer. Gene therapy introduces new genetic material into the human body to modify or "fix" existing genes that may cause, or potentially already have caused, disease. Yet another by-product of the Human Genome Project that is predicted to be available within the next decade is the application of DNA findings to pharmacology.

This will result in medications that are more sophisticated. Using genetic information, medications will be designed for specific individuals, for designated sites in the body, and they will be programmed to cause fewer side effects. This anticipated new specialty is already termed "pharmacogenomics" (*Medicine and the new genetics*, 2001).

Human Reproduction   The area of human reproduction has been impacted dramatically, too, and future advances may result in quite complex moral and ethical issues. Currently multiple for-profit organizations exist (many are advertised on Internet websites) that offer infertile persons alternatives for parenthood. Among the alternatives are surrogate parenting, human egg donation (or sale), and embryo transfer. In **surrogate parenting** a woman agrees to be impregnated and to release the baby that she delivers to the person(s) who contracted with her for this purpose. In human **egg donor programs,** the egg, also called ovum, of a donor is surgically implanted in anther woman who is unable to produce her own ovum; she may then be able to conceive a baby through sexual intercourse. **Embryo transfer** involves surgical implantation in a woman of another woman's egg that has been fertilized by her husband's, partner's, or a donor's sperm (*Glossary,* 2001).

In the United States alone in 1999, 30,000 babies were born as a result of one or more forms of assisted reproductive technology, according to the American Society for Reproductive Medicine (2001). While respected specialists in medicine, psychology, law, and social work are involved with reproductive medicine, there are also corporations whose staffs' credentials are less than sterling. In fact, a considerable amount of money is involved even in "donor" programs. Typically a surrogate mother is paid approximately $18,000, and as much as $3,000 is paid for a human ovum. The United States does not currently regulate the economically lucrative, for-profit fertility clinic industry. Even in European countries, where legal regulation does exist, there is concern about the increased probability of major birth defects with the use of poorly researched fertility enhancement processes (Ackerman, 1997).

Cloning is an asexual, as compared with a sexual, form of reproduction. Animals have been cloned, so why not humans? That, at least, is a question asked by futurists. In human cloning an embryo grows from either a male or female stem cell and then is implanted in a woman so that it can be brought to term and delivered as a newborn infant. This "clonal embryo" does not carry the genetic makeup of two persons; it consists of the genes of only the person who donated the stem cell. Obviously these genes could also be scientifically engineered or altered so that the child will not carry a predisposition to known diseases. There could potentially also be alterations to determine sex of the child, hair color, intelligence, body type, and numerous other traits. Or the child might be a true clone, identical to the "parent." Another type of cloning that is also likely to be developed is therapeutic cloning, where the tissue that results from the stem cell growth is used to replace organs or held indefinitely to permit creation of future organs, should there be a need (*Human cloning,* 2002). The "Up for Debate" box suggests some of the arguments that are inevitable as cloning possibilities draw near. What a strange and fascinating future awaits us!

Up for Debate
*Proposal: In the future, humans should be cloned
the way animals are now.*

Yes	No
1. Children would not be born with inheritable diseases or defects.	1. Cloning may not totally prevent defects and may, in fact, result in tragic malformations.
2. Regulating human reproduction has so many benefits to humankind that it should be mandatory.	2. Moral and spiritual values that view God as the creator should prevail over procedures that science makes possible.
3. Cloning should be allowed in order to obtain the most perfect human specimen.	3. Who is to determine the "perfect" human? Is the perfect human a mighty warrior or a peace maker, an intellectual giant, or a nurturer?
4. The health, longevity, and economic benefits of cloning are obvious.	4. Human variety and diversity are such valuable traits that they should be cherished, not obliterated.

THE SOCIAL WORK PROFESSION: FUTURE EMPLOYMENT OPPORTUNITIES

In the previous sections of this chapter, we have explored several powerful forces—demographic and political trends, the economy, and technological advances—that will impact life on our planet in the next 5, 10, 20 years or more. We have speculated about how these forces will affect the people that social workers serve and, for that matter, the profession and practice of social work. Now we will narrow our focus and briefly examine the future employment outlook for social workers.

Economic conditions, the political climate and resulting social welfare policy decisions made by our government, even changing demographics and technological advances—all of the forces we previously discussed—affect evolving employment prospects in social work and other fields. So, too, do new requirements for educational upgrading of positions or downgrading of credentials sought for specific employment positions. Replacement needs as workers retire or leave for other reasons also influence the number of positions available. In social work, the trend toward privatization described in previous chapters will likely mean that there will be a continuing shift away from governmental employment opportunities and toward employment opportunities in the private sector.

"Social Worker Shortage: Illusion or Reality" was the headline for a *Social Worker Today* article that reflected the very question that is of great interest to many in the profession. In California, a fact-finding state assembly hearing was called because of that state's shortage of social workers. The *Social Worker Today* article quoted concerns expressed during the hearing:

- A severe shortage of trained social workers and the lack of a candidate pool to fill empty positions.
- An insufficient number of graduates and enrollees at state schools of social work.
- An increasing demand accompanying a growing population.
- Heavy workloads and low morale caused by insufficient staffing and high turnover.
- Increasingly stringent licensing requirements. (Harvey, 2001, p. 11)

The article concluded that, indeed, there do appear to be severe shortages of social workers in some parts of the United States, but not in others. Clearly, the most serious shortage of social workers was in the child welfare area. An insufficient number of social workers to fill available and anticipated child welfare positions is a problem that is not unique to the United States. The government of Scotland, in a 1999 report, expressed concern about the need to recruit social workers across all fields of practice, noting that even at present, "overall, there are not enough social workers to meet current needs" (Changing for the future, 1999, p. 20). The special needs of child welfare were of greatest concern in Scotland.

Turning to the U.S. Department of Labor for data, we find that 468,000 social work jobs existed in 2000, with only one in three of those positions located in governmental organizations. Private sector social work positions tended to be largely in health care and social service agencies. The Department of Labor's *Occupational Outlook Handbook, 2002–03* listed the following categories of social workers for 2000 (2002, p. 162):

Child, family, and school social workers	281,000
Medical and public health social workers	104,000
Mental health and substance abuse social workers	83,000

The *Occupational Outlook Handbook*, perhaps in answer to the question about social work shortages, reported that there tends to be more competition in cities for social work jobs, especially in cities where professional educational programs are present. In rural areas, however, the need for social workers is often very great. Rural areas appear to have great difficulty attracting and retaining social workers. In view of their data, what employment projections does the U.S. Department of Labor make for social workers? "Employment for social workers is expected to increase faster than the average for all occupations through 2010" (2002, p. 162). This prediction is a remarkably strong statement!

The U.S. Department of Labor categorizes social work, along with psychology and other human service professions, within the Professional and Related Occupations area. The Labor Department's *Occupational Outlook Quarterly* predicts that from 2000 to 2010, total employment in the United States will increase by 22 million, a growth rate of about 15 percent. "Nearly half of all job openings are projected to be in service and professional and related occupations, accounting for 13.5 and 12.2 million jobs, respectively. These openings will result from employment growth—the creation of new jobs—and from the need to replace existing workers who retire or leave an occupation permanently for other reasons" (2001, p. 3).

The employment outlook for many other professions within the general category of professional and related occupations is not as positive. Employment positions in psychology, for example, "are expected to grow about as fast as the average for all occupations through 2010," according to the Labor Department (2002, p. 6). This would suggest a relatively slow rate of growth for a profession that, in 2000, recorded only 182,000 total positions. The Labor Department also notes that in psychology, a doctorate degree is required for most clinical work, although the master's degree is acceptable for some positions in schools and industry. Few opportunities are projected for persons holding only a bachelor's degree in psychology.

Why will social work positions increase in the future? The increasing population of older persons is one reason. Anticipating an acute shortage in social workers prepared to "enhance the quality of life for older adults and their families and to assist them in navigating ever-changing and increasingly complex health, mental health, social service and community environments," the Council on Social Work Education recently spearheaded a special initiative. It will seek to improve gerontological training for social workers and also improve incentives that will encourage social workers to enter this field of practice (Rosen, 2001). The U.S. Department of Labor agrees that rapid increases in social work positions will occur in this field. The baby-boomer generation is a somewhat younger age cohort that the Labor Department also anticipates will require services, services to assist with the stresses that accompany midlife crises related to career as well as personal issues. "In addition, continuing concern about crime, juvenile delinquency, and services for the mentally ill, the mentally retarded, the physically disabled, AIDS patients, and individuals and families in crisis will spur demand for social workers," according to the Department of Labor (2002, p. 162).

The Internet Sites list contains several sites that offer considerable additional information about employment in social work. Social work faculty members and college and university libraries are also good sources of information about career opportunities, especially employment positions available in the local community. Professional organizations such as the National Association of Social Workers and the Council on Social Work Education can also be contacted for additional information.

INTERNET SITES

http://www.socialworkers.org	National Association of Social Workers
http://www.cswe.org	Council on Social Work Education
http://www.bpdonline.org	Association of Baccalaureate Social Work Program Directors, Inc.
http://www.joboptions.com	Job Options

http://socialservice.com	Socialservice.Com (job and employment information
http://www.ornl.gov/hgmis/	Human Genome Project Information Site
http://gdbwww.gdb.org/	The Genome Database
http://www.nhgri.nih.gov/	The National Human Genome Research Institute
http://www.federalreserve.gov/ boarddocs/speeches/1998/19980116.htm	Greenspan Speech: The Underemployment of Minorities
http://www.feminist.com/fairpay/	National Committee on Pay Equity
http://www.now.org/issues/economic/ alerts/03-03-00.html	NOW Action Alert re: Pay Equity Act
http://www.ifg.org/	The International Forum on Globalization
http://www.surrogate-solutions.com/	Surrogate Mothers International
http://www.cnn.com/2001/HEALTH/ 01/15/growing.bone/	CNN Report on Neo-organs
http://rex.nci.nih.gov/NCI_PUB_ INDEX/GENBRST/INDEX.HTM	Genetic Testing for Breast Cancer Risk

CLOSING NOTES

Contemporary social work has been illustrated in these pages by social workers such as Madeleine Johnson of the shelter for homeless persons, Jake Jacobs from the frail-elderly social services program, Roberta Sholes with the mental health center, and many others. The social workers we have met are culturally diverse, men as well as women, students as well as experienced practitioners, and BSWs as well as MSWs. They practice in state and county departments of social service, hospitals, prisons, shelters, and family agencies, and in private as well as tax-supported agencies. Some of the social workers are employed in large bureaucratic organizations, while others work in small community-based programs. Small communities as well as large urban areas were the settings of the case studies. The people who were served by these social workers were remarkably diverse. This kaleidoscope of color, gender, background, age, and setting is, in fact, the pattern of social work today; and this will be true to an even greater degree in the future.

This book was written for students interested in selecting a career that will enable them to help others. It describes the profession of social work as it has developed throughout history and as it is practiced today. Case studies have been used not only to illustrate contemporary social work practice but also to answer the question, "What do social workers do?" By introducing readers to the people, problems, and programs that social workers care about, the book seeks to demonstrate the vital connection that exists between social policy and the availability of resources that enable people to have a reasonable quality of life.

The profession of social work is committed to social and economic justice, to equality, and to social change. In order to make change happen, social workers need to add the dimension of policy practice to their intervention roles. This means that while working with individual persons, families, or groups, social workers are simultaneously seeking to create or improve policies or programs. To do so, they may actively support legislation or organizational policies that will result in the resources and programs that are needed to ensure a good quality of life for clients and, indeed, for all Americans. Policy practice might also include voter registration, speaking before a city council meeting, giving testimony at a state legislative committee, and community education efforts. Social workers of the future will actively and effectively participate in their communities.

To prepare for the exciting challenges of the future, social work education will need to retain a firm hold on its values and ethics but change some parts of the curriculum. Practice courses will need to incorporate more content on empowerment, advocacy, coalition building, and legislative lobbying. Field placements should engage students in direct services to clients but also ensure that all students learn about and take appropriate action to create or support (or in opposition to) legislation that will affect the lives of the people they serve. Social work courses will need to broaden the human diversity content they incorporate, paying increased attention to spirituality, economic differences, ability/disability, new immigrant and refugee populations, and evolving family systems. Fluency in Spanish may become a requirement in some social work programs as Spanish-speaking populations become a larger presence in many parts of the United States. Computer and technology skills will expand students' access to information. The social work curriculum will develop students' ability to organize, analyze, and effectively use information as well as the technology tools that will increasingly be used to deliver services. Social work courses of the future will also increasingly incorporate global content and will build upon multicultural, international, and historical content from courses taken in the liberal arts. As military might is built in many parts of the world and security technology is developed to defend against possible biological and chemical terrorists, the social work curriculum may add a new dimension of study. Peace studies—alternatives to the use of violence to resolve conflict in families, communities, and worldwide—could become a focus for social work education of the future.

The profession of social work is probably one of the most difficult to practice. It is demanding and frustrating. It is not always well understood. Sometimes it is poorly paid. But it is potentially the most rewarding and enriching profession that anyone could choose. It also provides a unique opportunity to participate in the creation of a future society, one that we would choose for ourselves as well as for the people we serve.

KEY TERMS

asylum
cloning
demographics
egg donor program

embryo transfer
Equal Rights Amendment (ERA)
ethnic sensitive approach
ethnoconscious approach

gene therapy
genetic testing
globalization
Human Genome Project
immigrant
kinship care
neo-organs
pay equity

private practice
privatization
reapportionment
refugee
sanctioning
surrogate parents
underemployment

DISCUSSION QUESTIONS

1. How do you respond to people who think that social workers are welfare workers who dispense "the dole" to lazy, fraudulent people?

2. Identify several personal values that would be inconsistent with the values of the social work profession. Speculate about what might happen if persons with these values prepared for a career in social work.

3. What demographic changes are occurring in the United States? Why is this relevant to social work practice? How are the planning and delivery of social work services influenced by demographic trends?

4. Outline the political shifts that have taken place in the past 25 years. How would you characterize the current political environment? Identify current key political issues that have consequences for the people that social workers serve. Thinking about political forces, what implications do you see for the future of the social work profession?

5. What is the difference between unemployment and underemployment? Which of the two is most likely to be an issue in the United States in the next five years? In other parts of the world?

6. In what ways is the American family changing? What implications does this change have for social work practice?

7. Who are America's newest refugees? Where do they come from? Why are they fleeing their homeland? Are they seeking haven in other countries, too? Can you think of ways in which social workers will be able to assist them in the United States? In what ways might they enrich our country?

8. The privatization of social services has been discussed in several chapters in this book. Explain what is meant by privatization. How does it affect social work practice? Can you cite examples of conflicts between social work professional values and the movement toward privatization? Can you think of any advantages of privatized or entrepreneurial social services?

9. How do women's wages in the United States compare with those of men? How do you explain this discrepancy? Do you think that this will change? How? When?

10. What are the various ways in which social workers and social work students use computer technology? Are there risks in the use of computers and other technology in social service agencies? How can the risks be minimized? How do you think technology will affect social work practice in the next decade?

11. As you complete this text, you may be thinking about your own future career plans. Considering what you now know about the social work profession, is this a career area that you wish to pursue? What concerns do you have? What satisfactions might a social work career hold for you?

12. Almost every day there seems to be an announcement of yet another breakthrough in medical science. What biomedical advances do you think will occur in the next decade? What implications might they have for social work practice? Would you anticipate any ethical or moral dilemmas relative to these new technologies?

CLASSROOM EXERCISES

It is suggested that students break into small groups of three or four to discuss these exercises. It may be helpful to choose a scribe to record and report interesting points to the class after the group discussion.

1. Why does the author of this chapter believe that social work is not the right profession for everyone? What qualities, characteristics, or commitments help make a good fit between person and profession?
2. Globalism took on a new meaning for most Americans after September 11, 2001: a realization of vulnerability to international terrorism. What conditions in our current world situation do you think may support and sustain terrorism? How might social workers become involved in healing individual, family, and community wounds that occur as a result of terrorism? How might social workers help heal and transform the world, so as to eliminate conditions that lead to the development of terrorism?
3. If conditions of poverty, inequality, and conflict continue to worsen in this world, immigrants are likely to increase in number and in need. How might social workers become involved in addressing this worldwide issue?
4. Why do many political conservatives consider TANF a success, while many liberals, especially traditional liberals, do not? What is your own perspective? In particular, what do you believe is the more important goal, to eliminate welfare programs or to eliminate poverty? Why?

RESEARCH ACTIVITIES

1. Experiment with being a policy practitioner. Select an issue or a piece of legislation that will have impact on at-risk or vulnerable people. Review newspaper and news media coverage of your issue, noting the arguments in favor and those in opposition. Look at the historical development of the issue. Use the *NASW Code of Ethics* as a screen to filter the various perspectives and arguments related to your chosen issue. Think through what you have learned and determine what your position is. Then communicate your position to a legislator who should be involved with this issue. State your position convincingly and seek the appropriate action from your legislator. Request a response.
2. The text provided information about the changing demographics of the United States. Is your community also experiencing increasing diversity? What data can you obtain about the demographics of your community (or your university) over the past 10 years?
3. Interview one social worker each from the public sector (perhaps a county or state social services office), the nonprofit sector (a denominational agency or the American Red Cross, for example), and a social worker in a private for-profit practice or agency setting. Obtain information about the populations they serve and the nature of the services they provide. Note any discernible differences in their attitudes about their clients. Ask them to identify any changes they have experienced in the past five years regarding the financing or funding of their services.

INTERNET RESEARCH EXERCISES

1. How are older Americans doing in the new century? The Federal Interagency Forum on Aging Related Statistics website has some answers. Go to http://www.agingstats.gov, and then click on the Older Americans 2000 Key Indicators of Well-Being link. Examine each of the "indicator" subsections as you look for answers to the following questions:
   a. What will be the changes in the makeup of the racial and ethnic cohorts of older Americans in the future?
   b. What is the projected life expectancy for persons age 65 in 2000? What was it in 1900?
   c. In spite of the fact that most older people are socially active, what social behaviors threaten health and well-being?

2. The subject of genetic testing is briefly explained on a government laboratory website (http://www.lbl.gov/Education/ELSI/genetic-testing.html). Use that site to locate answers to the following questions:
   a. Is genetic testing highly reliable? Why?
   b. List and explain briefly three types of genetic testing.
   c. What are the three ethical, legal, and social issues in genetic testing as specified at this website?

3. A radical analysis of social work is one that challenges the status quo and engages us in thinking about the social class structure that exists in most industrialized contemporary societies. In the United States, we tend to prefer not to acknowledge the existence of class structure. In England and various other countries, the ramification of social class is more readily discussed in social work texts and professional conferences. The Barefoot Social Worker website (http://homepage.dtn.ntl.com/terence.p/barefoot/) will give you an opportunity to consider a radical perspective.
   a. Why does the radical perspective believe that social workers themselves have become distant from working-class people?
   b. What do you think the writer means by the statement that social work has become a form of "social engineering"?
   c. Compare the radical perspective reflected in this website with current economic trends, especially with the trend toward privatization in social work. What differences do you detect?

REFERENCES

Aburdene, P., & Naisbitt, J. (1992). *Megatrends for women.* New York: Villard Books.

Ackerman, E. (1997). Newfangled babies, newfangled risks. *U.S. News & World Report, 123* (24), 63–65.

Ahearn, F. L., Jr. (1995). Displaced people. In R. L. Edwards (Ed.), *Encyclopedia of social work* (19th ed., pp. 771–780). Washington, DC: NASW Press.

American Red Cross. (2001, October 21). Disaster services: Fast facts. [Informational sheet].

American Society for Assisted Reproductive Medicine. (2001, December 14). *More than 30,000 babies born in '99 as a result of ART procedures.* Retrieved January 28, 2002, from http: //www.asrm.org/Media/Press/99art.html.

Baker, M., & Fortin, N. M. (1998, September). *Gender composition and wages: Why is Canada different from the United States?* [online]. Available: www.chass.utoronto.ca/ecipa/archive/UT-ECIPA-BAKER-98.

Barker, R. L. (1999). *The social work dictionary* (4th ed.). Washington, DC: NASW Press.

Cetron, M. (1994). An American renaissance in the year 2000: 74 trends that will affect America's future—and yours. *The Futurist, 28* (2), 27, 1A–11A.

Cetron, M. J., & Davies, O. (2001a). Trends now changing the world: Economics and society, values and concerns, energy and environment. *The Futurist, 35* (1), 30–43.

Cetron, M. J., & Davies, O. (2001b). Trends now changing the world: Technology, the workplace, management, and institutions. *The Futurist, 35* (2), 27–42.

Changing for the future: Social work services for the 21st century. (1999). Retrieved January 30, 2002, from the Scottish Executive Publications online website: http://www.scotland.gov/uklibrary3/social/swor-00.asp.

Chideya, F. (1999). *The color of our future.* New York: William Morrow.

Congress, E. P. (1999). *Social work values and ethics: Identifying and resolving professional dilemmas.* Belmont, CA: Wadsworth.

Derris, J. F. (2001, August 3). *Life support? Stem-cell backing holds at six in 10.* Retrieved January 26, 2002, from http://abcnews.go.com/sections/politics/DailyNews/poll01803.html.

Devore, W., & Schlesinger, E. G. (1999). *Ethnic-sensitive social work practice* (5th ed.). Boston: Allyn and Bacon.

Dooley, T. P. (2001, July). *The dilemma of embryonic stem cell research.* Retrieved January 26, 2002, from the Altruis Biomedical Network website: http://www.e-stem-cell.com.

Dziegielewski, S. F., Shields, J. P., & Thyer, B. A. (1998). Short-term treatment: Models, methods, and research. In J. B. W. Williams & K. Ell (Eds.), *Mental health research: Implications for practice* (pp. 287–308). Washington, DC: NASW Press.

Facts about the September 11 attack. (2002). *The world almanac and book of facts.* World Almanac Education Group, 35.

Fadiman, A. (1997). *The spirit catches you and you fall down: A Hmong child, her American doctors, and the collision of two cultures.* New York: Farrar, Straus and Giroux.

Farley, C. J. (1999). What do kids really think about race? In B. Brunner (Ed.), *Time almanac 1999* (pp. 360–362). Boston, MA: Information Please.

Freedman, T. G. (1998). Genetic susceptibility testing: Ethical and social quandaries. *Health & Social Work, 23*(3), 214–222.

Gilbert, N., & Terrell, P. (2002). *Dimensions of social welfare policy* (5th ed). Boston: Allyn and Bacon.

Glossary of terms. (2001). Retrieved January 28, 2002, from The Fertility Institutes website: http://www.fertility-docs.com/glossary.html.

Gottlieb, N. (1995). Women overview. In *Encyclopedia of social work* (19th ed., pp. 2518–2529). Washington, DC: NASW Press.

Gutierrez, L., & Nagda, B. A. (1996). The multicultural imperative in human services organizations: Issues for the twenty-first century. In P. R. Raffoul & C. A. McNeece (Eds.), *Future issues for social work practice* (pp. 203–213). Boston: Allyn and Bacon.

Harvey, D. (2001). Social worker shortage: Illusion or reality? *Social Worker Today, 1* (7), 10–12.

Henderson, M. (2002, January 24). *Stem cell alternative to embryo.* Retrieved January 26, 2002, from http:/www.thetimes.co.uk/article/0,,2-20020397077,00.html.

Hokenstad, M. C., & Midgley, J. (Eds.). (1997). *Issues in international social work: Global changes for a new century.* Washington, DC: NASW Press.

Holmes, K. A. (1996). Headed for the future: Families in the twenty-first century. In P. R. Raffoul & C. A. McNeece (Eds.), *Future issues for social work practice* (pp. 172–179). Boston: Allyn and Bacon.

Holody, R. (1999). Toward a new permanency planning: How kinship care can revitalize the foster care system. *Areté, 23* (1), 1–10.

Human cloning and genetic modification: The basic science you need to know. (2002, January 24). Retrieved January 28, 2002, from http://www.arhp.org/cloning/.

Human organs for sale. (2001, July 21). Retrieved January 24, 2002, from the Newsweek website: http://www.msnbc.com/news/603127.asp.

Iatridis, D. S. (1988). New social deficit: Neoconservatism's policy of social underdevelopment. *Social Work, 33* (1), 11–15.

Jones, D. R., & Hubbard, B. A. (2001). *Back to work: Addressing the needs of New York's working poor since September 11th.* Retrieved on January 19, 2002, from http://www.cssny.org/ pdfs/whitepaper.pdf.

Kemp, R. L. (2000). Cities in the 21st century: The forces of change. *Futures Research Quarterly,* 21–30.

Knickerbocker, B. (1998, November 30). Women's march to political equality marked by short steps. *Christian Science Monitor* [online]. Available: www.csmonitor.com/durable/1998/11/30/fp3sl-csm.shtml.

Knickerbocker, B. (2000, November 9). Women grab more governorships and U.S. Senate seats. Retrieved January 22, 2002, from *The Christian Science Monitor* website: http://www. csmonitor.com/durable/2000/11/09/p11s1.htm.

Lollock, L. (2001, March). The foreign-born population in the United States: Population characteristics. *Current population reports.* Retrieved January 20, 2002, from the U.S. Census Bureau website: http://www.census.gov/population/www/socdemo/foreign/cps2000.html.

Major new spending urged for homeless. (1994, May 18). *New York Times,* p. A18.

Marien, M. (2002, January–February). The new age of terrorism: Futurists respond. *The Futurist, 36* (1), 16–22.

Marks, A. (2001). Welfare reform's biggest test begins. *The Christian Science Monitor, 94* (22), 3.

Marson, S. M. (1998). Major uses of the Internet for social workers: A brief report for new users. *Areté, 22* (2), 21–28.

Medicine and the new genetics: Gene testing, pharmacogenomics, and gene therapy. (2001). Retrieved January 28, 2002, from the Human Genome Project Information website: http://www.ornl.gov/hgmis/publicat/primer2001/6.html.

Mizrahi, T. (2001). International issues come home. *NASW News, 46* (10), 2.

Moller, J. O. (2000). Globalization and resistance to Western imperialism. *Futures Research Quarterly,16* (24), 31–42.

Mooney, D. J., & Mikos, A. G. (1999, April). Growing new organs. Retrieved January 24, 2002, from the *Scientific American* website: http://www.sciam.com/1999/0499issue/0499/mooney.html.

No safe refuge. (2001, October 16). Retrieved January 19, 2002, from Human Rights Watch website: http://www.hrw.org/backgrounder/refugees/afghan-bck1017.htm.

O'Neill, J. V. (2001). Chapters play helping role. *NASW News, 46* (10), 14.

O'Neill, J. V. (2002). EAPs offer multitude of internet services. *NASW News, 47* (1), p. 14.

O'Neill, J. V. (2002). Private agency turnover high. *NASW News, 47* (1), 11.

Questions and answers on pay equity. (1998). [online]. Available: www.feminist.com/ fairpay.htm [1999, January 25].

Rosen, A. L. (2001). *A blueprint for the new millennium* [Project Report]. Retrieved January 9, 2002, from http://www.cswe.org/sage-sw/whoweare.htm.

Rubenstein, H. (2000). Strategic planning tools for futurists. *Futures Research Quarterly, 16* (3), 5–17.

Sherman, A., Amey, C., Duffield, B., Ebb, N., & Weinstein, D. (1998). *Welfare to what: Early findings on family hardship and well-being.* Washington, DC: Children's Defense Fund and National Coalition for the Homeless.

Templeton, J. M. (1999, January). A worldwide rise in living standards. *The Futurist, 33* (1), 17–22.

The world almanac and book of facts, 2002. (2002). New York: World Almanac Education Group, Inc.

UCSC Human Genome Project working draft. (2002, January 27). Retrieved January 28, 2002, from http://genome.ucsc.edu.

U.S. Bureau of the Census. (1950). *Census of population: 1950* (Vol. II, Pt. 1, U.S. Summary, Table 38, pp. 90–91 & Table 61, pp. 109–111) and *U.S. census of population: 1950* (Special Reports: Nonwhite Population by Race, Table 2, p. 16, Table 3, p. 17, Table 4, p. 18, and Table 5, p. 19).

U.S. Bureau of the Census. (1998). Annual population estimates by sex, race and Hispanic origin, selected years from 1990 to 1998. *The official statistics.* Washington, DC: U.S. Government Printing Office.

U.S. Bureau of Labor Statistics. (2002). Table B. Seasonally adjusted unemployment rates and changes due to revision, January–December 2001. *Employment situation summary.* Retrieved January 22, 2002, from http://www.bls.gov/news.release/ empsit.nr0.htm.

U.S. Census Bureau. (1999, March 9). *Table 4 Region and country or area of birth of the foreign-born population, with geographic detail shown in decennial census publications of 1930 or earlier: 1850 to 1930 and 1960 to 1990.* Retrieved January 19, 2002, from http://www.census.gov/population/www/documentation/twps0029/ tab04.html.

U.S. Census Bureau. (2000). *Census 2000 national data. Projections of the resident population by age, sex, race, and Hispanic Origin: 1999 to 2100.* Retrieved January 18, 2002, from http://www.census.gov.

U.S. Census Bureau. (2001). *Nation's median age highest ever, but 65-and-over population's growth lags, Census 2000 shows.* Retrieved January 19, 2002, from http://www.census.gov/PressRelease/www/2001/cb01cn67.html.

U.S. Department of Health and Human Services. (2000, August). *Temporary Assistance for Needy Families (TANF): Third annual report to Congress.* Retrieved January 21, 2002, from http:www.acf.dhhs.gov/programs/opre/director.htm.

U.S. Department of Labor. (2001). Charting the projections: 2000–10. *Occupational Outlook Quarterly.* Winter 2001–02, 2–3. Retrieved January 30, 2002, from the Occupational Quarterly Online website: http://www.bls.gov/opub/ooq/2001/ winter/art01.pdf.

U.S. Department of Labor. (2002, January 10). Psychologists. Social workers. *Occupational outlook handbook 2002–03 edition.* Retrieved January 30, 2002, from http://www.bls.gov/oco/ocos060.htm.

Vernon, R., & Lynch, D. (2000). *Social work and the Web.* Belmont, CA: Wadsworth.

Westphal S. P. (2002, January 2). *Ultimate stem cell discovered.* Retrieved January 26, 2002, from http://www.newscientist.com/news/news.jsp?id=ns99991826.

FOR FURTHER READING

Abramovitz, M. (1998). Social work and social reform: An arena of struggle. *Social Work, 43*(6), 51–526.

Abramovitz's works are always an inspiration, and this article is no exception. Of special interest in this article is a remarkably comprehensive history of social work activism, rich historical material that should be treasured and nourished by the profession but that is largely undocumented in current social work texts. The author concludes by challenging social workers to forgo silence in the face of inhumane social conditions, and instead to keep the voice of change alive by active political involvement.

Finn, J., & Marson, S. M. (2001). Social work programs' use of the World Wide Web to facilitate field instruction. *Advances in Social Work, 2* (1), 26–37.

This article extends the discussion in Chapter 14 about social workers' use and future use of the Internet. In their article, Finn and Marson analyze the information about field instruction that schools of social work provide to students and others on their websites. Although the authors found that BSW programs tended to provide less information than MSW programs, the 292 websites they reviewed did contain information that could be very useful to students. Half or more of these sites provided the names of faculty in the program, the fieldwork requirements, and both fieldwork course and field seminar course outlines. Schools of social work are just beginning to use their websites as a communication tool for students, field instructors, faculty, and potential applicants to their programs. This use of the Internet is growing very rapidly, and it promises to be an excellent resource in the very near future. So, students, do take advantage of this resource as you think about and plan your junior or senior year field learning experiences.

Meenaghan, T. M., & Gibbons, W. E. (2000). *Generalist practice in larger settings: Knowledge and skill concepts.* Chicago: Lyceum Books, Inc.

This 160-page text succinctly but cogently addresses social work practice that aims to create change in larger social systems such as communities and social service organizations. There are other texts that address larger system practice, but the advantage of this text is that it is written by people who have worked with larger systems and who have a strong commitment to generalist practice principles. The three case studies at the end of the text nicely illustrate the kind of work that generalist social workers can engage in as they seek to create change that will affect large numbers of people.

Hopps, J. G., & Morris, R. (Eds.). (2000). *Social work at the millennium: Critical reflections on the future of the profession.* New York: The Free Press.

Social work as a profession is now 100 years old. The editors of *Social Work at the Millennium* have gathered and organized 12 experienced, respected social work educators' reviews of the past 100 years and their thoughtful perspectives on the future of the profession. Seven of the articles focus on specific fields of practice. The most clear, focused, and precise of these is the article entitled "Social Work and Health Care: Yesterday, Today, and Tomorrow" by Helen Rehr and Gary Rosenberg. It is especially highly recommended for additional reading. Taken as a whole, though, this text offers some optimistic perspectives on the future but poses even more challenges.

Reamer, F. G. (2001). *The social work ethics audit: A risk management tool.* Washington, DC: NASW Press.

Frederic Reamer is known across the United States as an authority on social work ethics. He has authored multiple other works and has made numerous conference presentations pertaining to social work ethics. Although his current book comes with a manual and a computer disk that are useful in conducting an ethics audit, social work students may find greatest value in the sections of the book that describe the nature of ethics audits and explain the reasons for conducting an audit. (In essence, an ethics audit is a procedure that systematically assesses an organization's actual risks of violating ethical standards and an evaluation of the agency's existing policies and practices that protect clients' rights.) Reamer believes that because malpractice litigation is increasing and social work's code of conduct has been more comprehensively developed, ethics audits will be used increasingly in the near future. This book is remarkably clear and well organized. It provides a compelling argument for careful adherence to professional ethics.

Van Hook, M., Hugen, B., & Aguilar, M. (Eds.). (2001). *Spirituality within religious traditions in social work practice.* Pacific Grove, CA: Brooks/Cole.

The rapidly increasing diversity of religions in the United States has caught the social work profession off guard. Consistent with Freudian perspectives adopted early in the profession's history, social work has tended to avoid the religious or faith dimensions of people's lives. Now the profession is awakening to its responsibility to understand, appreciate, and utilize the beliefs of clients as a resource in meeting their needs. The editors clarify the differences between spirituality and religion. Social work contributors representing 11 different religions present an introduction to faith and religious practices as diverse as Lakota, Hinduism, Confucianism, Catholicism, Judaism, Islam, African American Baptist, and Seventh-day Adventist. They write of their own personal religious experiences, and they offer implications for the ways in which the religion can be a source of help and healing for its believers. This book provides refreshing insight and begins to fill a gap that must be addressed by social work education.

Appendix: Code of Ethics of the National Association of Social Workers

As adopted by the 1979 NASW Delegate Assembly and revised by the 1990, 1993, 1996, 1998, and 1999 NASW Delegate Assemblies.

OVERVIEW

The *NASW Code of Ethics* is intended to serve as a guide to the everyday professional conduct of social workers. This *Code* includes four sections. The first section, "Preamble," summarizes the social work profession's mission and core values. The second section, "Purpose of the *NASW Code of Ethics,*" provides an overview of the *Code*'s main functions and a brief guide for dealing with ethical issues or dilemmas in social work practice. The third section, "Ethical Principles," presents broad ethical principles, based on social work's core values, that inform social work practice. The final section, "Ethical Standards," includes specific ethical standards to guide social workers' conduct and to provide a basis for adjudication.

ABOUT NASW

The National Association of Social Workers (NASW) is the largest organization of professional social workers in the world. NASW serves nearly 160,000 social workers in 56 chapters throughout the United States, Puerto Rico, the Virgin Islands, and abroad. NASW was formed in 1955 through a merger of seven predecessor social work organizations to carry out three responsibilities:

- strengthen and unify the profession
- promote the development of social work practice
- advance sound social policies.

Promoting high standards of practice and protecting the consumer of services are major association principles.

PREAMBLE

The primary mission of the social work profession is to enhance human well-being and help meet the basic human needs of all people, with particular attention to the needs and empowerment of people who are vulnerable, oppressed, and living in poverty. A historic and defining feature of social work is the profession's focus on individual well-being in a social context and the well-being of society. Fundamental to social work is attention to the environmental forces that create, contribute to, and address problems in living.

Social workers promote social justice and social change with and on behalf of clients. "Clients" is used inclusively to refer to individuals, families, groups, organizations, and communities. Social workers are sensitive to cultural and ethnic diversity and strive to end discrimination, oppression, poverty, and other forms of social injustice. These activities may be in the form of direct practice, community organizing, supervision, consultation, administration, advocacy, social and political action, policy development and implementation, education, and research and evaluation. Social workers seek to enhance the capacity of people to address their own needs. Social workers also seek to promote the responsiveness of organizations, communities, and other social institutions to individuals' needs and social problems.

The mission of the social work profession is rooted in a set of core values. These core values, embraced by social workers throughout the profession's history, are the foundation of social work's unique purpose and perspective:

- service
- social justice
- dignity and worth of the person
- importance of human relationships
- integrity
- competence.

This constellation of core values reflects what is unique to the social work profession. Core values, and the principles that flow from them, must be balanced within the context and complexity of the human experience.

PURPOSE OF THE NASW CODE OF ETHICS

Professional ethics are at the core of social work. The profession has an obligation to articulate its basic values, ethical principles, and ethical standards. The *NASW Code of Ethics* sets forth these values, principles, and standards to guide social workers' conduct. The *Code* is relevant to all social workers and social work students, regardless of their professional functions, the settings in which they work, or the populations they serve.

The *NASW Code of Ethics* serves six purposes:

1. The *Code* identifies core values on which social work's mission is based.
2. The *Code* summarizes broad ethical principles that reflect the profession's core values and establishes a set of specific ethical standards that should be used to guide social work practice.

3. The *Code* is designed to help social workers identify relevant considerations when professional obligations conflict or ethical uncertainties arise.
4. The *Code* provides ethical standards to which the general public can hold the social work profession accountable.
5. The *Code* socializes practitioners new to the field to social work's mission, values, ethical principles, and ethical standards.
6. The *Code* articulates standards that the social work profession itself can use to assess whether social workers have engaged in unethical conduct. NASW has formal procedures to adjudicate ethics complaints filed against its members. In subscribing to this *Code,* social workers are required to cooperate in its implementation, participate in NASW adjudication proceedings, and abide by any NASW disciplinary rulings or sanctions based on it.

The *Code* offers a set of values, principles, and standards to guide decision making and conduct when ethical issues arise. It does not provide a set of rules that prescribe how social workers should act in all situations. Specific applications of the *Code* must take into account the context in which it is being considered and the possibility of conflicts among the *Code's* values, principles, and standards. Ethical responsibilities flow from all human relationships, from the personal and familial to the social and professional.

Further, the *NASW Code of Ethics* does not specify which values, principles, and standards are most important and ought to outweigh others in instances when they conflict. Reasonable differences of opinion can and do exist among social workers with respect to the ways in which values, ethical principles, and ethical standards should be rank ordered when they conflict. Ethical decision making in a given situation must apply the informed judgment of the individual social worker and should also consider how the issues would be judged in a peer review process where the ethical standards of the profession would be applied.

Ethical decision making is a process. There are many instances in social work where simple answers are not available to resolve complex ethical issues. Social workers should take into consideration all the values, principles, and standards in this *Code* that are relevant to any situation in which ethical judgment is warranted. Social workers' decisions and actions should be consistent with the spirit as well as the letter of this *Code.*

In addition to this *Code,* there are many other sources of information about ethical thinking that may be useful. Social workers should consider ethical theory and principles generally, social work theory and research, laws, regulations, agency policies, and other relevant codes of ethics, recognizing that among codes of ethics social workers should consider the *NASW Code of Ethics* as their primary source. Social workers also should be aware of the impact on ethical decision making of their clients' and their own personal values and cultural and religious beliefs and practices. They should be aware of any conflicts between personal and professional values and deal with them responsibly. For additional guidance social workers should consult the relevant literature on professional ethics and ethical decision making and seek appropriate consultation when faced with ethical dilemmas. This may involve consultation with an agency-based or social work organization's ethics committee, a regulatory body, knowledgeable colleagues, supervisors, or legal counsel.

Instances may arise when social workers' ethical obligations conflict with agency policies or relevant laws or regulations. When such conflicts occur, social workers must make a responsible effort to resolve the conflict in a manner that is consistent with the values, principles, and standards expressed in this *Code.* If a reasonable resolution of the conflict does not appear possible, social workers should seek proper consultation before making a decision.

The *NASW Code of Ethics* is to be used by NASW and by individuals, agencies, organizations, and bodies (such as licensing and regulatory boards, professional liability insurance providers, courts of law, agency boards of directors, government agencies, and other professional groups) that choose to adopt it or use it as a frame of reference. Violation of standards in this *Code* does not automatically imply legal liability or violation of the law. Such determination can only be made in the context of legal and judicial proceedings. Alleged violations of the *Code* would be subject to a peer review process. Such processes are generally separate from legal or administrative procedures and insulated from legal review or proceedings to allow the profession to counsel and discipline its own members.

A code of ethics cannot guarantee ethical behavior. Moreover, a code of ethics cannot resolve all ethical issues or disputes or capture the richness and complexity involved in striving to make responsible choices within a moral community. Rather, a code of ethics sets forth values, ethical principles, and ethical standards to which professionals aspire and by which their actions can be judged. Social workers' ethical behavior should result from their personal commitment to engage in ethical practice. The *NASW Code of Ethics* reflects the commitment of all social workers to uphold the profession's values and to act ethically. Principles and standards must be applied by individuals of good character who discern moral questions and, in good faith, seek to make reliable ethical judgments.

ETHICAL PRINCIPLES

The following broad ethical principles are based on social work's core values of service, social justice, dignity and worth of the person, importance of human relationships, integrity, and competence. These principles set forth ideals to which all social workers should aspire.

Value: *Service*

Ethical Principle: *Social workers' primary goal is to help people in need and to address social problems.*

Social workers elevate service to others above self-interest. Social workers draw on their knowledge, values, and skills to help people in need and to address social problems. Social workers are encouraged to volunteer some portion of their professional skills with no expectation of significant financial return (pro bono service).

Value: *Social Justice*

Ethical Principle: *Social workers challenge social injustice.*

Social workers pursue social change, particularly with and on behalf of vulnerable and oppressed individuals and groups of people. Social workers' social change efforts are focused primarily on issues of poverty, unemployment, discrimination, and other forms of social injustice. These activities seek to promote sensitivity to the knowledge about oppression and cultural and ethnic diversity. Social workers strive to ensure access to needed information, services, and resources; equality of opportunity; and meaningful participation in decision making for all people.

Value: *Dignity and Worth of the Person*

Ethical Principle: *Social workers respect the inherent dignity and worth of the person.*

Social workers treat each person in a caring and respectful fashion, mindful of individual differences and cultural and ethnic diversity. Social workers promote clients' socially responsible self-determination. Social workers seek to enhance clients' capacity and opportunity to change and to address their own needs. Social workers are cognizant of their dual responsibility to clients and to the broader society. They seek to resolve conflicts between clients' interests and the broader society's interests in a socially responsible manner consistent with the values, ethical principles, and ethical standards of the profession.

Value: *Importance of Human Relationships*

Ethical Principle: *Social workers recognize the central importance of human relationships.*

Social workers understand that relationships between and among people are an important vehicle for change. Social workers engage people as partners in the helping process. Social workers seek to strengthen relationships among people in a purposeful effort to promote, restore, maintain, and enhance the well-being of individuals, families, social groups, organizations, and communities.

Value: *Integrity*

Ethical Principle: *Social workers behave in a trustworthy manner.*

Social workers are continually aware of the profession's mission, values, ethical principles, and ethical standards and practice in a manner consistent with them. Social workers act honestly and responsibly and promote ethical practices on the part of the organizations with which they are affiliated.

Value: *Competence*

Ethical Principle: *Social workers practice within their areas of competence and develop and enhance their professional expertise.*

Social workers continually strive to increase their professional knowledge and skills and to apply them in practice. Social workers should aspire to contribute to the knowledge base of the profession.

ETHICAL STANDARDS

The following ethical standards are relevant to the professional activities of all social workers. These standards concern (1) social workers' ethical responsibilities to clients, (2) social workers' ethical responsibilities to colleagues, (3) social workers' ethical responsibilities in practice settings, (4) social workers' ethical responsibilities as professionals, (5) social workers' ethical responsibilities to the social work profession, and (6) social workers' ethical responsibilities to the broader society.

Some of the standards that follow are enforceable guidelines for professional conduct, and some are aspirational. The extent to which each standard is enforceable is a matter of professional judgment to be exercised by those responsible for reviewing alleged violations of ethical standards.

1. SOCIAL WORKERS' ETHICAL RESPONSIBILITIES TO CLIENTS

1.01 Commitment to Clients

Social workers' primary responsibility is to promote the well-being of clients. In general, clients' interests are primary. However, social workers' responsibility to the larger society or specific legal obligations may on limited occasions supersede the loyalty owed clients, and clients should be so advised. (Examples include when a social worker is required by law to report that a client has abused a child or has threatened to harm self or others.)

1.02 Self-Determination

Social workers respect and promote the right of clients to self-determination and assist clients in their efforts to identify and clarify their goals. Social workers may limit clients' right to self-determination when, in the social workers' professional judgment, clients' actions or potential actions pose a serious, foreseeable, and imminent risk to themselves or others.

1.03 Informed Consent

(a) Social workers should provide services to clients only in the context of a professional relationship based, when appropriate, on valid informed consent. Social workers should use clear and understandable language to inform clients of the purpose of the services, risks related to the services, limits to services because of the requirements of a third-party payer, relevant costs, reasonable alternatives, clients' right to refuse or withdraw consent, and the time frame covered by the consent. Social workers should provide clients with an opportunity to ask questions.

(b) In instances when clients are not literate or have difficulty understanding the primary language used in the practice setting, social workers should take steps to ensure clients' comprehension. This may include providing clients with a detailed verbal explanation or arranging for a qualified interpreter or translator whenever possible.

(c) In instances when clients lack the capacity to provide informed consent, social workers should protect clients' interests by seeking permission from an appropriate third party, informing clients consistent with the clients' level of understanding. In such instances social workers should seek to ensure that the third party acts in a manner consistent with clients' wishes and interests. Social workers should take reasonable steps to enhance such clients' ability to give informed consent.

(d) In instances when clients are receiving services involuntarily, social workers should provide information about the nature and extent of services and about the extent of clients' right to refuse service.

(e) Social workers who provide services via electronic media (such as computer, telephone, radio, and television) should inform recipients of the limitations and risks associated with such services.

(f) Social workers should obtain clients' informed consent before audiotaping or videotaping clients or permitting observation of services to clients by a third party.

1.04 Competence

(a) Social workers should provide services and represent themselves as competent only within the boundaries of their education, training, license, certification, consultation received, supervised experience, or other relevant professional experience.

(b) Social workers should provide services in substantive areas or use intervention techniques or approaches that are new to them only after engaging in appropriate study, training, consultation, and supervision from people who are competent in those interventions or techniques.

(c) When generally recognized standards to not exist with respect to an emerging area of practice, social workers should exercise careful judgment and take responsible steps (including appropriate education, research, training, consultation, and supervision) to ensure the competence of their work and to protect clients from harm.

1.05 Cultural Competence and Social Diversity

(a) Social workers should understand culture and its function in human behavior and society, recognizing the strengths that exist in all cultures.

(b) Social workers should have a knowledge base of their clients' cultures and be able to demonstrate competence in the provision of services that are sensitive to clients' cultures and to differences among people and cultural groups.

(c) Social workers should obtain education about and seek to understand the nature of social diversity and oppression with respect to race, ethnicity, national origin, color, sex, sexual orientation, age, marital status, political belief, religion, and mental or physical disability.

1.06 Conflicts of Interest

(a) Social workers should be alert to and avoid conflicts of interest that interfere with the exercise of professional discretion and impartial judgment. Social workers should inform clients when a real or potential conflict of interest arises and take reasonable steps to resolve the issue in a manner that makes the clients' interests primary and protects clients' interests to the greatest extent possible. In some cases, protecting clients' interests may require termination of the professional relationship with proper referral of the client.

(b) Social workers should not take unfair advantage of any professional relationship or exploit others to further their personal, religious, political, or business interests.

(c) Social workers should not engage in dual or multiple relationships with clients or former clients in which there is a risk of exploitation or potential harm to the client. In instances when dual or multiple relationships are unavoidable, social workers should take steps to protect clients and are responsible for setting clear, appropriate, and culturally sensitive boundaries. (Dual or multiple relationships occur when social workers relate to clients in more than one relationship, whether professional, social, or business. Dual or multiple relationships can occur simultaneously or consecutively.)

(d) When social workers provide services to two or more people who have a relationship with each other (for example, couples, family members), social workers should clarify with all parties which individuals will be considered clients and the nature of social workers' professional obligations to the various individuals who are receiving services. Social workers who anticipate a conflict of interest among the individuals receiving services or who anticipate having to perform in potentially conflicting roles (for example, when a social worker is asked to testify in a child custody dispute or divorce proceedings involving clients) should clarify their role with the parties involved and take appropriate action to minimize any conflict of interest.

1.07 Privacy and Confidentiality

(a) Social workers should respect clients' right to privacy. Social workers should not solicit private information from clients unless it is essential to providing services or conducting social work evaluation or research. Once private information is shared, standards of confidentiality apply.

(b) Social workers may disclose confidential information when appropriate with valid consent from a client or a person legally authorized to consent on behalf of a client.

(c) Social workers should protect the confidentiality of all information obtained in the course of professional service, except for compelling professional reasons. The general expectation that social workers will keep information confidential does not apply when disclosure is necessary to prevent serious, foreseeable, and imminent harm to a client or other identifiable person. In all instances, social workers should disclose the least amount of confidential information necessary to achieve the desired purpose; only information that is directly relevant to the purpose for which the disclosure is made should be revealed.

(d) Social workers should inform clients, to the extent possible, about the disclosure of confidential information and the potential consequences, when feasible before the disclosure is made. This applies whether social workers disclose confidential information on the basis of a legal requirement or client consent.

(e) Social workers should discuss with clients and other interested parties the nature of confidentiality and limitations of clients' right to confidentiality. Social workers should review with clients circumstances where confidential information may be requested and where disclosure of confidential information may be legally required. This discussion should occur as soon as possible in the social worker-client relationship and as needed throughout the course of the relationship.

(f) When social workers provide counseling services to families, couples, or groups, social workers should seek agreement among the parties involved concerning each individual's right to confidentiality and obligation to preserve the confidentiality of information shared by others. Social workers should inform participants in family, couples, or group counseling that social workers cannot guarantee that all participants will honor such agreements.

(g) Social workers should inform clients involved in family, couples, marital, or group counseling of the social worker's, employer's, and agency's policy concerning the social worker's disclosure of confidential information among the parties involved in the counseling.

(h) Social workers should not disclose confidential information to third-party payers unless clients have authorized such disclosure.

(i) Social workers should not discuss confidential information in any setting unless privacy can be ensured. Social workers should not discuss confidential information in public or semipublic areas such as hallways, waiting rooms, elevators, and restaurants.

(j) Social workers should protect the confidentiality of clients during legal proceedings to the extent permitted by law. When a court of law or other legally authorized body orders social workers to disclose confidential or privileged information without a client's consent and such disclosure could cause harm to the client, social workers should request that the court withdraw the order or limit the order as narrowly as possible or maintain the records under seal, unavailable for public inspection.

(k) Social workers should protect the confidentiality of clients when responding to requests from members of the media.

(l) Social workers should protect the confidentiality of clients' written and electronic records and other sensitive information. Social workers should take reasonable steps to ensure that clients' records are stored in a secure location and that clients' records are not available to others who are not authorized to have access.

(m) Social workers should take precautions to ensure and maintain the confidentiality of information transmitted to other parties through the use of computers, electronic mail, facsimile machines, telephones and telephone answering machines, and other electronic or computer technology. Disclosure of identifying information should be avoided whenever possible.

(n) Social workers should transfer or dispose of clients' records in a manner that protects clients' confidentiality and is consistent with state statutes governing records and social work licensure.

(o) Social workers should take reasonable precautions to protect client confidentiality in the event of the social worker's termination of practice, incapacitation, or death.

(p) Social workers should not disclose identifying information when discussing clients for teaching or training purposes unless the client has consented to disclosure of confidential information.

(q) Social workers should not disclose identifying information when discussing clients with consultants unless the client has consented to disclosure of confidential information or there is a compelling need for such disclosure.

(r) Social workers should protect the confidentiality of deceased clients consistent with the preceding standards.

1.08 Access to Records

(a) Social workers should provide clients with reasonable access to records concerning the clients. Social workers who are concerned that clients' access to their records could cause serious misunderstanding or harm to the client should provide assistance in interpreting the records and consultation with the client regarding the records. Social workers should limit clients' access to their records, or portions of their records, only in exceptional circumstances when there is compelling evidence that such access would cause serious harm to the client. Both clients' requests and the rationale for withholding some or all of the record should be documented in clients' files.

(b) When providing clients with access to their records, social workers should take steps to protect the confidentiality of other individuals identified or discussed in such records.

1.09 Sexual Relationships

(a) Social workers should under no circumstances engage in sexual activities or sexual contact with current clients, whether such contact is consensual or forced.

(b) Social workers should not engage in sexual activities or sexual contact with clients' relatives or other individuals with whom clients maintain a close personal relationship when there is a risk of exploitation or potential harm to the client. Sexual activity or sexual contact with clients' relatives or other individuals with whom clients maintain a personal relationship has the potential to be harmful to the client and may make it difficult for the social worker and client to maintain appropriate professional boundaries. Social workers—not their clients, their clients' relatives, or other individuals with whom the client maintains a personal relationship—assume the full burden for setting clear, appropriate, and culturally sensitive boundaries.

(c) Social workers should not engage in sexual activities or sexual contact with former clients because of the potential for harm to the client. If social workers engage in conduct contrary to this prohibition or claim that an exception to this prohibition is warranted because of extraordinary circumstances, it is social workers—not their clients—who assume the full burden of demonstrating that the former client has not been exploited, coerced, or manipulated, intentionally or unintentionally.

(d) Social workers should not provide clinical services to individuals with whom they have had a prior sexual relationship. Providing clinical services to a former sexual partner has the potential to be harmful to the individual and is likely to make it difficult for the social worker and individual to maintain appropriate professional boundaries.

1.10 Physical Contact

Social workers should not engage in physical contact with clients when there is a possibility of psychological harm to the client as a result of the contact (such as cradling or caressing clients). Social workers who engage in appropriate physical contact with clients are responsible for setting clear, appropriate, and culturally sensitive boundaries that govern such physical contact.

1.11 Sexual Harassment

Social workers should not sexually harass clients. Sexual harassment includes sexual advances, sexual solicitations, requests for sexual favors, and other verbal or physical evidence of a sexual nature.

1.12 Derogatory Language

Social workers should not use derogatory language in their written or verbal communications to or about clients. Social workers should use accurate and respectful language in all communications to and about clients.

1.13 Payment for Services

(a) When setting fees, social workers should ensure that the fees are fair, reasonable, and commensurate with the services performed. Consideration should be given to clients' ability to pay.

(b) Social workers should avoid accepting goods or services from clients as payment for professional services. Bartering arrangements, particularly involving services, create the potential for conflicts of interests, exploitation, and inappropriate boundaries in social workers' relationships with clients. Social workers should explore and may participate in bartering only in very limited circumstances when it can be demonstrated that such arrangements are an accepted practice among professionals in the local community, considered to be essential for the provision of services, negotiated without coercion, and entered into at the client's initiative and with the client's informed consent. Social workers who accept goods or services from clients as payment for professional services assume the full burden of demonstrating that this arrangement will not be detrimental to the client or the professional relationship.

(c) Social workers should not solicit a private fee or other remuneration for providing services to clients who are entitled to such available services through the social workers' employer or agency.

1.14 Clients Who Lack Decision-Making Capacity

When social workers act on behalf of clients who lack the capacity to make informed decisions, social workers should take reasonable steps to safeguard the interests and rights of those clients.

1.15 Interruption of Services

Social workers should make reasonable efforts to ensure continuity of services in the event that services are interrupted by factors such as unavailability, relocation, illness, disability, or death.

1.16 Termination of Services

(a) Social workers should terminate services to clients and professional relationships with them when such services and relationships are no longer required or no longer serve the clients' needs or interests.

(b) Social workers should take reasonable steps to avoid abandoning clients who are still in need of services. Social workers should withdraw services precipitously only under unusual circumstances, giving careful consideration to all factors in the situation and taking care to minimize possible adverse effects. Social workers should assist in making appropriate arrangements for continuation of services when necessary.

(c) Social workers in fee-for-service settings may terminate services to clients who are not paying an overdue balance if the financial contractual arrangements have been made clear to the client, if the client does not pose an imminent danger to self or others, and if the clinical and other consequences of the current nonpayment have been addressed and discussed with the client.

(d) Social workers should not terminate services to pursue a social, financial, or sexual relationship with a client.

(e) Social workers who anticipate the termination or interruption of services to clients should notify clients promptly and seek the transfer, referral, or continuation of services in relation to the clients' needs and preferences.

(f) Social workers who are leaving an employment setting should inform clients of appropriate options for the continuation of services and of the benefits and risks of the options.

2. SOCIAL WORKERS' ETHICAL RESPONSIBILITIES TO COLLEAGUES

2.01 Respect

(a) Social workers should treat colleagues with respect and should represent accurately and fairly the qualifications, views, and obligations of colleagues.

(b) Social workers should avoid unwarranted negative criticism of colleagues in communications with clients or with other professionals. Unwarranted negative criticism may include demeaning comments that refer to colleagues' level of competence or to individuals' attributes such as race, ethnicity, national origin, color, sex, sexual orientation, age, marital status, political belief, religion, and mental or physical disability.

(c) Social workers should cooperate with social work colleagues and with colleagues of other professions when such cooperation serves the well-being of clients.

2.02 Confidentiality

Social workers should respect confidential information shared by colleagues in the course of their professional relationships and transactions. Social workers should ensure that such colleagues understand social workers' obligation to respect confidentiality and any exceptions related to it.

2.03 Interdisciplinary Collaboration

(a) Social workers who are members of an interdisciplinary team should participate in and contribute to decisions that affect the well-being of clients by drawing on the perspectives, values, and experiences of the social work profession. Professional and ethical obligations of the interdisciplinary team as a whole and of its individual members should be clearly established.

(b) Social workers for whom a team decision raises ethical concerns should attempt to resolve the disagreement through appropriate channels. If the disagreement cannot be resolved, social workers should pursue other avenues to address their concerns consistent with client well-being.

2.04 Disputes Involving Colleagues

(a) Social workers should not take advantage of a dispute between a colleague and an employer to obtain a position or otherwise advance the social workers' own interests.

(b) Social workers should not exploit clients in disputes with colleagues or engage clients in any inappropriate discussion of conflicts between social workers and their colleagues.

2.05 Consultation

(a) Social workers should seek the advice and counsel of colleagues whenever such consultation is in the best interests of the clients.

(b) Social workers should keep themselves informed about colleagues' areas of expertise and competencies. Social workers should seek consultation only from colleagues who have demonstrated knowledge, expertise, and competence related to the subject of the consultation.

(c) When consulting with colleagues about clients, social workers should disclose the least amount of information necessary to achieve the purpose of the consultation.

2.06 Referral for Services

(a) Social workers should refer clients to other professionals when the other professionals' specialized knowledge or expertise is needed to serve clients fully or when social workers believe that they are not being effective or making reasonable progress with clients and that additional service is required.

(b) Social workers who refer clients to other professionals should take appropriate steps to facilitate an orderly transfer of responsibility. Social workers who refer clients to other professionals should disclose, with clients' consent, all pertinent information to the new service providers.

(c) Social workers are prohibited from giving or receiving payment for a referral when no professional service is provided by the referring social worker.

2.07 Sexual Relationships

(a) Social workers who function as supervisors or educators should not engage in sexual activities or contact with supervisees, students, trainees, or other colleagues over whom they exercise professional authority.

(b) Social workers should avoid engaging in sexual relationships with colleagues when there is potential for a conflict of interest. Social workers who become involved in, or anticipate becoming involved in, a sexual relationship with a colleague have a duty to transfer professional responsibilities, when necessary, to avoid a conflict of interest.

2.08 Sexual Harassment

Social workers should not sexually harass supervisees, students, trainees, or colleagues. Sexual harassment includes sexual advances, sexual solicitation, requests for sexual favors, and other verbal or physical conduct of a sexual nature.

2.09 Impairment of Colleagues

(a) Social workers who have direct knowledge of a social work colleague's impairment that is due to personal problems, psychosocial distress, substance abuse, or mental health difficulties and that interferes with practice effectiveness, should consult with that colleague when feasible and assist the colleague in taking remedial action.

(b) Social workers who believe that a social work colleague's impairment interferes with practice effectiveness and that the colleague has not taken adequate steps to address the impairment should take action through appropriate channels established by employers, agencies, NASW, licensing and regulatory bodies, and other professional organizations.

2.10 Incompetence of Colleagues

(a) Social workers who have direct knowledge of a social work colleague's incompetence should consult with that colleague when feasible and assist the colleague in taking remedial action.

(b) Social workers who believe that a social work colleague is incompetent and has not taken adequate steps to address the incompetence should take action through appropriate channels established by employers, agencies, NASW, licensing and regulatory bodies, and other professional organizations.

2.11 Unethical Conduct of Colleagues

(a) Social workers should take adequate measures to discourage, prevent, expose, and correct the unethical conduct of colleagues.

(b) Social workers should be knowledgeable about established policies and procedures for handling concerns about colleagues' unethical behavior. Social workers should be familiar with national, state, and local procedures for handling ethics complaints. These include policies and procedures created by NASW, licensing and regulatory bodies, employers, agencies, and other professional organizations.

(c) Social workers who believe that a colleague has acted unethically should seek resolution by discussing their concerns with the colleague when feasible and when such discussion is likely to be productive.

(d) When necessary, social workers who believe that a colleague has acted unethically should take action through appropriate formal channels (such as contacting a state licensing board or regulatory body, an NASW committee on inquiry, or other professional ethics committees).

(e) Social workers should defend and assist colleagues who are unjustly charged with unethical conduct.

3. SOCIAL WORKERS' ETHICAL RESPONSIBILITIES IN PRACTICE SETTINGS

3.01 Supervision and Consultation

(a) Social workers who provide supervision or consultation should have the necessary knowledge and skill to supervise or consult appropriately and should do so only within their areas of knowledge and competence.

(b) Social workers who provide supervision or consultation are responsible for setting clear, appropriate, and culturally sensitive boundaries.

(c) Social workers should not engage in any dual or multiple relationships with supervisees in which there is a risk of exploitation of or potential harm to the supervisee.

(d) Social workers who provide supervision should evaluate supervisees' performance in a manner that is fair and respectful.

3.02 Education and Training

(a) Social workers who function as educators, field instructors for students, or trainers should provide instruction only within their areas of knowledge and competence and should provide instruction based on the most current information and knowledge available in the profession.

(b) Social workers who function as educators or field instructors for students should evaluate students' performance in a manner that is fair and respectful.

(c) Social workers who function as educators or field instructors for students should take reasonable steps to ensure that clients are routinely informed when services are being provided by students.

(d) Social workers who function as educators or field instructors for students should not engage in any dual or multiple relationships with students in which there is a risk of exploitation or potential harm to the student. Social work educators and field instructors are responsible for setting clear, appropriate, and culturally sensitive boundaries.

3.03 Performance Evaluation

Social workers who have responsibility for evaluating the performance of others should fulfill such responsibility in a fair and considerate manner and on the basis of clearly stated criteria.

3.04 Client Records

(a) Social workers should take reasonable steps to ensure that documentation in records is accurate and reflects the services provided.

(b) Social workers should include sufficient and timely documentation of records to facilitate the delivery of services and to ensure continuity of services provided to clients in the future.

(c) Social workers' documentation should protect clients' privacy to the extent that is possible and appropriate and should include only information that is directly relevant to the delivery of services.

(d) Social workers should store records following the termination of services to ensure reasonable future access. Records should be maintained for the number of years required by state statutes or relevant contracts.

3.05 Billing

Social workers should establish and maintain billing practices that accurately reflect the nature and extent of services provided and that identify who provided the service in the practice setting.

3.06 Client Transfer

(a) When an individual who is receiving services from another agency or colleague contacts a social worker for services, the social worker should carefully consider the client's needs before agreeing to provide services. To minimize possible confusion and conflict, social workers should discuss with potential clients the nature of the clients' current relationship with other service providers and the implications, including possible benefits or risks, of entering into a relationship with a new service provider.

(b) If a new client has been served by another agency or colleague, social workers should discuss with the client whether consultation with the previous service provider is in the client's best interest.

3.07 Administration

(a) Social work administrators should advocate within and outside their agencies for adequate resources to meet clients' needs.

(b) Social workers should advocate for resource allocation procedures that are open and fair. When not all clients' needs can be met, an allocation procedure should be developed that is nondiscriminatory and based on appropriate and consistently applied principles.

(c) Social workers who are administrators should take reasonable steps to ensure that adequate agency or organizational resources are available to provide appropriate staff supervision.

(d) Social work administrators should take reasonable steps to ensure that the working environment for which they are responsible is consistent with and encourages compliance with the *NASW Code of Ethics*. Social work administrators should take reasonable steps to eliminate any conditions in their organizations that violate, interfere with, or discourage compliance with the *Code*.

3.08 Continuing Education and Staff Development

Social work administrators and supervisors should take reasonable steps to provide or arrange for continuing education and staff development for all staff for whom whey are responsible. Continuing education and staff development should address current knowledge and emerging developments related to social work practices and ethics.

3.09 Commitments to Employers

(a) Social workers generally should adhere to commitments made to employers and employing organizations.

(b) Social workers should work to improve employing agencies' policies and procedures and the efficiency and effectiveness of their services.

(c) Social workers should take reasonable steps to ensure that employers are aware of social workers' ethical obligations as set forth in the *NASW Code of Ethics* and of the implications of those obligations for social work practice.

(d) Social workers should not allow an employing organization's policies, procedures, regulations, or administrative orders to interfere with their ethical practice of social work. Social workers should take reasonable steps to ensure that their employing organizations' practices are consistent with the *NASW Code of Ethics*.

(e) Social workers should act to prevent and eliminate discrimination in the employing organization's work assignments and in its employment policies and practices.

(f) Social workers should accept employment or arrange student field placements only in organizations that exercise fair personnel practices.

(g) Social workers should be diligent stewards of the resources of their employing organizations, wisely conserving funds where appropriate and never misappropriating funds or using them for unintended purposes.

3.10 Labor–Management Disputes

(a) Social workers may engage in organized action, including the formation of and participation in labor unions, to improve services to clients and working conditions.

(b) The actions of social workers who are involved in labor–management disputes, job actions, or labor strikes should be guided by the profession's values, ethical principles, and ethical standards. Reasonable differences of opinion exist among social workers concerning their primary obligation as professionals during an actual or threatened labor strike or job action. Social workers should carefully examine relevant issues and their possible impact on clients before deciding on a course of action.

4. SOCIAL WORKERS' ETHICAL RESPONSIBILITIES AS PROFESSIONALS

4.01 Competence

(a) Social workers should accept responsibility or employment only on the basis of existing competence or the intention to acquire the necessary competence.

(b) Social workers should strive to become and remain proficient in professional practice and the performance of professional functions. Social workers should critically examine and keep current with emerging knowledge relevant to social work. Social workers should routinely review the professional literature and participate in continuing education relevant to social work practice and social work ethics.

(c) Social workers should base practice on recognized knowledge, including empirically based knowledge, relevant to social work and social work ethics.

4.02 Discrimination

Social workers should not practice, condone, facilitate, or collaborate with any form of discrimination on the basis of race, ethnicity, national origin, color, sex, sexual orientation, age, marital status, political belief, religion, or mental or physical disability.

4.03 Private Conduct

Social workers should not permit their private conduct to interfere with their ability to fulfill their professional responsibilities.

4.04 Dishonesty, Fraud, and Deception

Social workers should not participate in, condone, or be associated with dishonesty, fraud, or deception.

4.05 Impairment

(a) Social workers should not allow their own personal problems, psychosocial distress, legal problems, substance abuse, or mental health difficulties to interfere with their professional judgment and performance or to jeopardize the best interests of people for whom they have a professional responsibility.

(b) Social workers whose personal problems, psychosocial distress, legal problems, substance abuse, or mental health difficulties interfere with their professional judgment and performance should immediately seek consultation and take appropriate remedial action by seeking professional help, making adjustments in workload, terminating practice, or taking any other steps necessary to protect clients and others.

4.06 Misrepresentation

(a) Social workers should make clear distinctions between statements made and actions engaged in as a private individual and as a representative of the social work profession, a professional social work organization, or the social worker's employing agency.

(b) Social workers who speak on behalf of professional social work organizations should accurately represent the official and authorized positions of the organizations.

(c) Social workers should ensure that their representations to clients, agencies, and the public of professional qualifications, credentials, education, competence, affiliations, services provided, or results to be achieved are accurate. Social workers should claim only those relevant professional credentials they actually possess and take steps to correct any inaccuracies or misrepresentations of their credentials by others.

4.07 Solicitations

(a) Social workers should not engage in uninvited solicitation of potential clients who, because of their circumstances, are vulnerable to undue influence, manipulation, or coercion.

(b) Social workers should not engage in solicitation of testimonial endorsements (including solicitation of consent to use a client's prior statement as a testimonial endorsement) from current clients or from other people who, because of their particular circumstances, are vulnerable to undue influence.

4.08 Acknowledging Credit

(a) Social workers should take responsibility and credit, including authorship credit, only for work they have actually performed and to which they have contributed.

(b) Social workers should honestly acknowledge the work of and the contributions made by others.

5. SOCIAL WORKERS' ETHICAL RESPONSIBILITIES TO THE SOCIAL WORK PROFESSION

5.01 Integrity of the Profession

(a) Social workers should work toward the maintenance and promotion of high standards of practice.

(b) Social workers should uphold and advance the values, ethics, knowledge, and mission of the profession. Social workers should protect, enhance, and improve the integrity of the profession through appropriate study and research, active discussion, and responsible criticism of the profession.

(c) Social workers should contribute time and professional expertise to activities that promote respect for the value, integrity, and competence of the social work profession. These activities may include teaching, research, consultation, service, legislative testimony, presentations in the community, and participation in their professional organizations.

(d) Social workers should contribute to the knowledge base of social work and share with colleagues their knowledge related to practice, research, and ethics. Social workers should seek to contribute to the profession's literature and to share their knowledge at professional meetings and conferences.

(e) Social workers should act to prevent the unauthorized and unqualified practice of social work.

5.02 Evaluation and Research

(a) Social workers should monitor and evaluate policies, the implementation of programs, and practice interventions.

(b) Social workers should promote and facilitate evaluation and research to contribute to the development of knowledge.

(c) Social workers should critically examine and keep current with emerging knowledge relevant to social work and fully use evaluation and research evidence in their professional practice.

(d) Social workers engaged in evaluation or research should carefully consider possible consequences and should follow guidelines developed for the protection of evaluation and research participants. Appropriate institutional review boards should be consulted.

(e) Social workers engaged in evaluation or research should obtain voluntary and written informed consent from participants, when appropriate, without any implied or actual deprivation or penalty for refusal to participate; without undue inducement to participate; and with due regard for participants' well-being, privacy, and dignity. Informed consent should include information about the nature, extent, and duration of the participation requested and disclosure of the risks and benefits of participation in the research.

(f) When evaluation or research participants are incapable of giving informed consent, social workers should provide an appropriate explanation to the participants, obtain the participants' assent to the extent they are able, and obtain written consent from an appropriate proxy.

(g) Social workers should never design or conduct evaluation or research that does not use consent procedures, such as certain forms of naturalistic observation and archival research, unless rigorous and responsible review of the research has found it to be justified because of its prospective scientific, educational, or applied value and unless equally effective alternative procedures that do not involve waiver of consent are not feasible.

(h) Social workers should inform participants of their right to withdraw from evaluation and research at any time without penalty.

(i) Social workers should take appropriate steps to ensure that participants in evaluation and research have access to appropriate supportive services.

(j) Social workers engaged in evaluation or research should protect participants from unwarranted physical or mental distress, harm, danger, or deprivation.

(k) Social workers engaged in the evaluation of services should discuss collected information only for professional purposes and only with people professionally concerned with this information.

(l) Social workers engaged in evaluation or research should ensure the anonymity or confidentiality of participants and of the data obtained from them. Social workers should inform participants of any limits of confidentiality, the measures that will be taken to ensure confidentiality, and when any records containing research data will be destroyed.

(m) Social workers who report evaluation and research results should protect participants' confidentiality by omitting identifying information unless proper consent has been obtained authorizing disclosure.

(n) Social workers should report evaluation and research findings accurately. They should not fabricate or falsify results and should take steps to correct any errors later found in published data using standard publication methods.

(o) Social workers engaged in evaluation or research should be alert to and avoid conflicts of interest and dual relationships with participants, should inform participants when a real or potential conflict of interest arises, and should take steps to resolve the issue in a manner that makes participants' interests primary.

(p) Social workers should educate themselves, their students, and their colleagues about responsible research practices.

6. SOCIAL WORKERS' ETHICAL RESPONSIBILITIES TO THE BROADER SOCIETY

6.01 Social Welfare

Social workers should promote the general welfare of society, from local to global levels, and the development of people, their communities, and their environments. Social workers should advocate for living conditions conducive to the fulfillment of basic human needs and should promote social, economic, political, and cultural values and institutions that are compatible with the realization of social justice.

6.02 Public Participation

Social workers should facilitate informed participation by the public in shaping social policies and institutions.

6.03 Public Emergencies

Social workers should provide appropriate professional services in public emergencies to the greatest extent possible.

6.04 Social and Political Action

(a) Social workers should engage in social and political action that seeks to ensure that all people have equal access to the resources, employment, services, and opportunities they require to meet their basic human needs and to develop fully. Social workers should be aware of the impact of the political arena on practice and should advocate for changes in policy and legislation to improve social conditions in order to meet basic human needs and promote social justice.

(b) Social workers should act to expand choice and opportunity for all people, with special regard for vulnerable, disadvantaged, oppressed, and exploited people and groups.

(c) Social workers should promote conditions that encourage respect for cultural and social diversity within the United States and globally. Social workers should promote policies and practices that demonstrate respect for difference, support the expansion of cultural knowledge and resources, advocate for programs and institutions that demonstrate cultural competence, and promote policies that safeguard the rights of and confirm equity and social justice for all people.

(d) Social workers should act to prevent and eliminate domination of, exploitation of, and discrimination against any person, group, or class on the basis of race, ethnicity, national origin, color, sex, sexual orientation, age, marital status, political belief, religion, or mental or physical disability.

Glossary

abuse   The infliction of physical or emotional injury through beatings, corporal punishment, persistent ridicule and degradation, or sexual maltreatment.

accommodation   Making environmental modifications in architecture, equipment, commercial structures, employment facilities, and so forth, to make them accessible to persons with disabilities.

ACSW   This acronym designates membership in the Academy of Certified Social Workers. This certification is available to members of NASW who have an MSW degree, two years of additional supervised social work practice, and who have passed the ACSW examination.

active treatment   Training, therapy, and services provided to people with disabilities to address any social, intellectual, or behavioral deficits and achieve the highest possible level of functioning.

activities of daily living   Those daily activities such as dressing, eating, and bathing that a person must be able to perform to maintain independence.

acute care   Health care facilities such as hospitals, outpatient clinics, and emergency rooms that provide immediate, short-term care.

acute traumatic stress   Overwhelming physical and psychological distress that occurs during and immediately following disasters.

adjudication   Decisions made by the juvenile court judge when a charge against a youth is reviewed. The court may decide to drop all charges, but if instead the youth is found guilty, sentencing follows.

advanced professional level   The highest level in the NASW classification system of social work personnel. Possession of a doctoral degree, the Diplomate in Clinical Social Work, or other certification of advanced practice competence is required. A social worker at this level may conduct social welfare and program evaluation research, practice in highly specialized clinical areas, or teach in college or university social work education programs.

adversarial court   A court setting in which there is opportunity for cross-examination by a prosecutor and a defense attorney. Although this procedure has been adopted in juvenile courts since the 1967 *Gault* decision, a much less formal court was envisioned when children's courts were first established.

advocacy   Representing and defending the rights of individuals, groups, or communities through direct intervention.

advocate   An advocate is someone who fights for the rights of others or fights to obtain needed resources.

AFDC   Aid to Families with Dependent Children: A government program authorized under the Social Security Act to provide income for dependent children of poor families and sometimes their parents. A means test and other eligibility criteria were required. Programs were administered by each state, and benefits varied by state. AFDC was eliminated in 1996.

affirmative action   Procedures used to ensure opportunities such as employment, advancement, or admission to professional programs to people who have been discriminated against, such as women and members of minority groups.

ageism   The practice of stereotyping people according to their age; frequently refers to prejudice against older adults.

alcohol abuse   The recurrent use of alcohol to the extent that repeated use results in an inability to fulfill normal role functions, or presents legal or social-interpersonal problems, or creates a hazard to self or others.

alcohol counselors   Formerly, recovering alcoholics or drug abusers (or both) whose expertise for their employment consisted of their life experience and ability to work with others; today most states require certification that persons hired for these positions have completed appropriate coursework and fieldwork.

alcohol dependence   The compulsive consumption of alcohol which, over a 12-month period, produces such symptoms as tolerance for alcohol, withdrawal symptoms, ineffective efforts to cut back on its use, and failure to change the drinking behavior despite evidence that it is causing serious difficulty.

alcoholism   The compulsive use of alcohol characterized by evidence of abuse or dependence, resulting in some level of personal and social malfunctioning.

almshouse   An institution or shelter, common before the twentieth century, to house and feed destitute families and individuals.

alternative schools   Schools that operate outside the regular public school system.

anxiety disorder   The term used by the *DSM–IV* to describe a large number of anxiety-related states; these tend to be chronic or recurring experiences arising from unknown or unrecognized perceptions of danger or conflict.

asylum   The protected legal status that is granted by the government only on a case-by-case basis to persons who can substantiate serious, possibly life-threatening political persecution. This status permits people to remain in the country for a specified period of time, but it may not afford them rights to citizenship.

basic professional level   The entry-level classification for social work professionals developed by the NASW. The required credential is a baccalaureate degree from a college or university social work program that is accredited by the Council on Social Work Education.

behavioral health care   A broad area of health care services often involving a combination of medication, various forms of psychotherapy or counseling, and patient education. Services are provided for persons with developmental disabilities, cognitive disorders, and mental illness or behavioral problems.

bilingual education   Education provided in two languages, usually including the language spoken by the majority culture and one spoken by a minority group.

block grants An increasingly common system used by the federal government and sometimes by state governments in their budgetary processes. Through consolidating health, education, and social welfare budget items, the governmental decision makers can avoid earmarking funds for specific programs, thus retaining considerable control over the expenditure of such funds without submitting them to the political process.

broker A professional role in which the social worker uses the processes of referral and follow-up to ensure that a family or person obtains needed resources.

BSW A baccalaureate-level social worker.

capital punishment A sentence of execution; the death penalty.

capitated plans Coordinated and managed, prepaid health care plans in which clients are not permitted to receive services outside the plan.

career ladder The imaginary upward-directed steps one must take, as on a ladder, to advance in a profession or occupation. In some fields, career advancement is based on performance, while in others additional academic credentials must be completed.

case advocacy Advocacy strategies used to attain social and economic justice on an individual basis.

case management Coordinating all helping activities on behalf of a particular client or group of clients.

case manager In social work, the combination of counselor/enabler, advocate, and broker roles plus responsibility for planning, locating, securing, and monitoring services for people who are unable to do this because of ill health or frailties. Should not be confused with the term "case management" that is used by insurance companies and health care organizations to designate a process that seeks to restrict access to care.

cause advocacy Advocacy strategies used to attain social and economic justice for whole groups of people.

Certified Social Work Case Manager An NASW certification (C-SWCM) for members who have completed at least one year of experience in appropriately supervised case management work, hold state licensure or certification at the BSW level (including passage of the ASWB exam), and submit supporting references.

charity The donation of goods and services to those in need.

children-at-risk Children born to or residing with families suffering significant problems—such as poverty, disability or absence of a parent, and substance abuse—that tend to increase the probability of abuse or neglect.

client An individual, family, group, organization, or community who brings an issue to a social worker for professional assistance.

clinical social worker A social worker qualified to engage in psychotherapy; formerly referred to as a *psychiatric social worker*. The MSW is the minimal credential required. Private practice in clinical social work requires at least the ACSW.

cloning The procedure whereby the nucleus of a single cell is used to reproduce an entirely new organism with identically the same genetic makeup as the organism that provided the original parent cell.

codependent A relationship between two or more people to meet reciprocal needs, which often are unhealthy psychological or social needs. In alcoholism, codependents may be friends or family members who, sometimes unconsciously, subtly encourage or aid an alcoholic to persist in consuming alcoholic beverages.

co-insurance The percentage of an overall medical bill that a person must pay in addition to what his or her health insurance pays.

community placement   Arranging supervised care for children and adults with special needs in small group and family care homes rather than in large custodial institutions.

community-based corrections   Programs, such as probation and parole, that provide an alternative to incarceration.

community-service sentencing   An alternative to imprisonment that requires work without pay in a human service organization for a specified period of time.

comparable worth   Also known as *pay equity,* this concept states that a person's wages or salary should be based solely on the value of the work performed rather than on other considerations. Recent comparable worth strategies have sought to correct the practice of paying low wages in occupations dominated by women.

conservative   A political perspective that is influenced by a desire to maintain the status quo and avoid change. The conservative view of human nature is pessimistic, that people will not work without economic insecurity and inequality to motivate them. Thus, conservatives tend to oppose government intervention in the economic market to aid poor people and, instead, may support tax breaks for the rich as incentives for investment.

contingency work   Jobs that are time-limited and devoid of any opportunity for ongoing, long-term employment. Although contingency work is more frequently associated with low wages, there are also highly paid consultants and other workers engaged in this employment sector.

continuum of care   Caretaking services that are coordinated to provide for a variety of client needs with minimal duplication or gaps in service.

corporal punishment   Physical punishment inflicted on the body, as in flogging, removal of a finger, or a sentence of hard physical labor.

correctional system   That part of the criminal justice system that seeks to change and improve the behaviors of convicted law offenders through imprisonment, parole, probation, and diverse community-based programs.

cost containment   Policies and procedures that seek to control rising costs. Health care organizations have been under considerable pressure from government and citizen groups to cut or at least stabilize health care costs.

counselor/enabler   The terms "counselor" and "enabler" tend to be used fairly interchangeably. The counselor or enabler role focuses on improving social functioning, affirming strengths, helping people to deal with feelings, to cope with stress, crises, or changing life circumstances.

court   Public tribunals existing at the federal, state, and local levels which are mandated to deal with offenses against the nation or the state or with controversies among individuals.

critical incident debriefing   A process used in social work intervention with trauma victims in which they are helped individually or in groups to talk about how the traumatic event has affected them; they are educated to understand the variety of normal and varied responses (physical, behavioral, and psychological) to traumatic events; and they are assisted in assessing and locating whatever services they might need to enable them to deal with the trauma.

cross-addiction   Addiction to two or more drugs. The combination of two or more drugs often results in more serious consequences than either drug would if used alone (this is known as *potentiation*).

cultural competency   The skill of communicating and working competently and effectively with people of contrasting cultures.

cultural pluralism   A model for understanding ethnic and racial diversity, in which difference is expected and respected.

culture   The customs, habits, values, beliefs, skills, technology, arts, science, and religious and political behavior of a group of people in a specific time period.

decision tree   A schematic diagram resembling a tree, used to demonstrate the steps of decision making that people engage in when making career choices.

deductible   The amount of money an insured person must pay up front before an insurer will pay the remaining amount of the bill.

deinstitutionalization   A policy promoting the use of alternatives to institutional care for people. The process of releasing people who are dependent for their physical and mental care from residential-custodial facilities, presumably with the understanding that they no longer need such care or can receive it through community-based services. Massive numbers of chronically mentally ill persons were discharged from mental health facilities in the 1960s as a result of this policy. While many were transferred to nursing homes and received adequate care, others were unsuccessfully supervised in the community and lived marginal lives, often as homeless street people.

delusions   Inaccurate but strongly held beliefs about reality, often with elements of persecution; delusional thinking suggests the presence of mental illness.

demographics   The study of population trends and statistics.

depressants   Drugs that depress the central nervous system.

detention   Placement in a juvenile jail facility.

detoxification   Medical treatment to remove or reduce dangerous levels of alcohol or drugs in the body and restore adequate physical and psychological functioning.

developmental disability   A condition that occurs as a result of disease, genetic disorder, or impaired growth pattern that is evidenced before adulthood. Such conditions include intellectual or cognitive disabilities, cerebral palsy, autism, orthopedic problems, hearing problems, epilepsy, traumatic brain injury, learning disabilities, fetal alcohol syndrome, cocaine exposed babies, and co-occurrence of disabilities.

diagnostic related groups (DRGs) plan   A plan, introduced by the federal government in 1983, that provides payment to hospitals based not on the number of days or services provided but on a predetermined dollar amount per diagnosis. Hospitals that are able to discharge patients expeditiously, without using the prescribed dollar amount, are permitted to retain these funds. Criticism of this form of cost containment occurs when patients suffer complications resulting from premature hospital discharge.

Diplomate in Clinical Social Work   A credential awarded by the NASW to social workers who have special qualifications for advanced clinical practice, including the MSW degree, five or more years of clinical practice, and successful completion of an advanced practice examination.

discharge planning   A social service provided by health care social workers (although sometimes performed by other members of the health care team) focusing on postdischarge planning for a patient. Family members are extensively involved, along with the patient, if possible. Discharge planning is routinely utilized with Medicare patients but may involve patients of any age.

disposition   Within the justice system, the carrying out of the court order; sentencing.

DSM-IV-TR   The fourth edition, revised, of the *Diagnostic and Statistical Manual of Mental Disorders* (American Psychiatric Association), a book providing comprehensive descriptions and classifications of various mental disorders, often used as a reference tool for diagnostic purposes.

dual diagnosis   The coexistence of mental illness and chemical dependence; this situation requires careful assessment and well-coordinated treatment between the substance abuse and mental health programs.

dual perspective   A conscious and nearly continuous process engaged in by people of minority cultures that requires them to be simultaneously alert to the values, attitudes, traditions, and behaviors of the dominant European American society as well as those derived from their own family and cultural community.

ecological perspective   A way of perceiving and thinking that takes account of the totality or pattern of relations between organisms and their environments.

ecosystems perspective   A perspective that maintains simultaneous focus on person and environment, and is attentive to their interactions and adaptations.

educator   A professional role involving teaching, coaching, or provision of information.

egg donor programs   The process by which the ovum (a human egg) of a donor is surgically implanted in another woman who is unable to produce her own ovum; the recipient may then be able to conceive a baby through sexual intercourse.

embryo transfer   The surgical implantation in a woman of another woman's egg that has already been fertilized by her husband's, partner's, or a donor's sperm.

emotional or behavioral disturbance   A condition characterized by inappropriate or harmful behavior leading to eligibility for special education services in a school setting. Eligible children demonstrate disturbed behavior in at least two or three environments: the school, the home, and/or the community.

employee assistance program   A counseling program provided by an employer as a fringe benefit. Some such programs provide only minimal counseling, focusing instead on the assessment of employees' needs and referral to other sources for counseling or other needed services. Social workers are often employed by—or they may develop and administer—employee assistance programs.

empowerment   A process through which people gain the strength to significantly impact the institutions that affect their lives.

English as a Second Language   A special method of instruction in public schools used to teach children who do not speak English. The goal is to bring children up to grade level in English and into regular classrooms as soon as possible.

entitlement program   A program providing services, goods, or money due to an individual by virtue of a specific status.

entrepreneurial organizations   Corporations or other organizations that are developed for the purpose of making a profit. Health care facilities today provide much less "charity" care than in the past, as many have evolved into entrepreneurial organizations. The for-profit corporation has recently entered the field of corrections.

equal employment opportunity   The right of all persons to work and advance on the basis of merit, ability, and potential.

Equal Rights Amendment (ERA)   An amendment to the U.S. Constitution prohibiting discrimination on the basis of gender and providing equal protection of all constitutional rights to women. Although it was passed by Congress in 1972, the amendment failed to achieve the ratification of a sufficient number of states and hence did not become law.

ethics   Behaviors prescribed by values.

ethnic group   A population group that shares certain cultural characteristics that distinguish it from others, characteristics such as customs, values, language, and a common history.

ethnic sensitive approaches   Strategies in social work practice that link knowledge of culture and ethnicity with understandings of social class differences; these approaches to practice reflect respect for and valuing of differences in people and communities.

ethnoconscious approach   A theoretical construct that links ethnic sensitive approaches with empowerment tactics that build upon appreciation for the strengths already existing in ethnically diverse communities.

extrapyramidal symptoms   The side effects of medication, generally psychotropic medication, that may include loss of balance, severe emotional reaction, nausea, or fatigue. Severe symptoms may require hospitalization and change of medication. The newer antipsychotic medications cause fewer negative side effects than pharmaceuticals used in the past.

facilitator   A professional role most frequently associated with group work; incorporates skills in convening groups, introducing members, promoting communication, and engaging members in planning, decision making, and goal attainment.

family care home   A foster care home where unrelated persons are cared for in a family-like setting.

felony   A serious criminal offense, generally punishable by a prison sentence. Murder, rape, and armed burglary are examples of felonies.

feminization of poverty   The increasing incidence of poverty among women, due to lower average wages than men and limited access to high-paying positions.

fetal alcohol syndrome (FAS)   A condition in which the fetus is damaged by the mother's alcoholism.

formal referral   This term is most frequently used in employee assistance work where it refers to a coercive form of referral to counseling by an employer or supervisor who stipulates, usually in writing, that failure to seek services will result in job termination or other disciplinary action.

frail elderly   Aged men and women who suffer from, or are vulnerable to, physical or emotional impairments and require services to ensure their well-being.

futurists   Persons who study global trends to predict the nature of life in the future.

gay   A person whose sexual orientation is homosexual. This term usually refers to homosexual men.

gene therapy   The introduction of new genetic material into the human body to modify or "fix" existing genes that may cause, or potentially already have caused, disease.

generalist   A professional social worker who engages in problem solving—discovering, utilizing, and making connections to arrive at unique, responsive solutions, involving intervention in systems of various sizes. Generalists are competent to work with or on behalf of individuals, families, groups, organizations, and communities.

generalist approach   An approach to social work practice drawn from social systems theory that uses an ecological perspective that is attentive to person and environment and their interactions. Generalist practice is based on research-guided knowledge and uses a planned change process to determine the level or levels of intervention—individual, family, group, organization, and/or community—appropriate to addressing the issues presented. It recognizes the profession's dual purpose and responsibility to influence social as well as individual change.

generalist social worker   A professional social worker who engages in a planned change process—discovering, utilizing, and making connections to arrive at unique, responsive solutions involving individual persons, families, groups, organizational systems, and communities. Generalist social workers respect and value human diversity. They identify and utilize the strengths existing in people and communities. Generalists seek to prevent as well as to resolve problems.

genetic testing   Tests to determine the existence or potential for genetically linked conditions such as cystic fibrosis, Huntington's disease, sickle-cell anemia, and some forms of ovarian, colon, and breast cancer. Testing that detects genetic mutations can alert people to the need for early and frequent cancer screening tests, such as mammograms, and can provide alternatives to disease management.

globalization   The interconnectedness of all regions and people of the world as a result of technological advances in communication and transportation; often thought of in terms of international commerce, this term also encompasses issues such as poverty and exploitation, religious movements, and terrorism.

guardian ad litem   A court-appointed attorney who represents the interests of a person considered incapable of managing his or her own affairs during litigation—for example, a minor child or an adult with mental retardation.

guilds   Fraternal organizations established during the Middle Ages to protect the interests of their members. Guilds were initiated by such occupational groups as craftspeople, artisans, and merchants. Over time, guilds began to provide death benefits to widows and orphans of deceased workers, and food and subsistence financial assistance to unemployed persons, thereby becoming the first form of employee assistance program. By the late Middle Ages, guilds had become a powerful political force in Europe.

habilitation   Services designed to help one achieve and maintain one's maximum level of functioning.

hallucinations   False perceptions of reality that result from mental illness, abuse of chemical substances, or damage to the brain. People who hallucinate sometimes respond to voices that they believe they hear; their behavior may be very inappropriate.

hallucinogens   A category of drugs that produce dreamlike experiences and hallucinations involving visual and/or auditory effects. The effects of such drugs are not always predictable; they sometimes include gross distortions of reality, frightening visualizations, and mental confusion. Heavy use can intensify underlying mental disorders. LSD, mescaline, and psilocybin are hallucinogens. Some hallucinogens come from mushrooms and cacti, but increasingly they are manufactured in home laboratories and are sold on the black market.

harm reduction model   A variety of alternative but controversial substance abuse treatment programs that seek to limit the hazards (such as overdose deaths, spread of disease, car accidents) that can occur while people are using chemical substances. It is based on the philosophy that people can be withdrawn more safely, effectively, and humanely from chemicals if this process is done slowly.

health maintenance organizations (HMOs)   Systems for delivering health care in which a corporation formed by health care providers contracts with employers to provide a wide range of health care services for employees for a set monthly fee. There are variations among HMOs regarding policies, procedures, costs, and quality of care.

Health Security Act   A proposal by the Clinton administration in 1991—ultimately withdrawn—to create a national health care system ensuring access to health care for all U.S. citizens.

hemodialysis A medical procedure in which the blood of a person with renal (kidney) disease is cleansed of toxins and impurities.

heterosexism The belief that people who are heterosexual are better in some way than people who are homosexual.

holistic The organic or functional relation between parts and wholes.

home health care Health care services, including social work, that are delivered to patients within their own homes.

homophobia The fear, dread, or hatred of people who are homosexual.

homosexual A person whose sexual orientation is toward members of that person's own gender.

hospice A program that cares for terminally ill people in an environment that is less restrictive than a hospital.

human diversity Normal variations among people reflecting differences in gender, genetics, ethnicity, cultural heritage, religious background, sexual preference, age, and the like.

Human Genome Project A research effort coordinated by the U.S. Department of Energy and the National Institutes of Health to determine the makeup of human DNA. Half of the data produced are not yet sufficiently refined to be applied but will have implications for health care and disease prevention through genetic engineering.

human services worker A person who does not have traditional professional academic credentials but who, through experience, training, or education, provides helping services.

hypothermia Extreme loss of body temperature; this condition can result in death if not treated immediately.

immigrant Someone who moves to another country for the purpose of settling there permanently.

income maintenance Social welfare programs designed to provide individuals with enough money or goods and services to maintain a predetermined standard of living.

independent professional level A level of classification of professional social work personnel which requires two years of appropriately supervised practice following completion of a master's degree from a program accredited by the Council on Social Work Education. Generally, social workers who obtain the ACSW are classified at this level.

indeterminate sentence A sentence imposing imprisonment for a time period that is not fixed by the court but that instead is left to the discretion of prison authorities, who, however, must comply with broad parameters set by the court.

indoor relief A historically important form of social welfare benefit in which the recipient was required to reside in an institution (almshouse or workhouse) in order to remain eligible.

industrial social work Social work that is conducted in or provides services to businesses, industry, governmental institutions, and/or unions.

in-home services Services provided to assist families that have special needs to remain living together in their own homes. Services include homemaker aides, home health care, day care services, and the like.

insurance A program designed to protect people from the full consequences of the risks to which they are vulnerable, such as disability, death of a breadwinner, medical needs, and financial problems in old age. Covered individuals are required to make regular contributions to a fund set aside to pay for the claims of those insured.

intensive probation   A specialized category of probation in which monitoring contacts occur very frequently and consistently, sometimes daily or at least several times a week. This form of probation is more cost-effective than imprisonment. It provides a relatively high level of community protection when used with discretion.

intervention process   A plan of action used by social workers to help create desired change involving several steps: engaging the client system, identifying and defining important issues, gathering and assessing data, identifying plans of action, contracting, implementing plans of action, evaluating outcomes, and terminating.

isms   Prejudices common to large segments of society.

jail   A correctional facility generally used for short sentences or for detaining persons while they await a court hearing. Prisons, by contrast, are used for lengthier sentences.

job coach   An employment specialist in a supported employment setting.

judgmental thinking   Drawing quick and possibly negative conclusions about clients based on their behavior.

juvenilization of poverty   The increasing incidence of poverty among children, related to the feminization of poverty.

kinship care   Care provided beyond the nuclear family to an inclusive family system that includes extended family members and also incorporates persons unrelated by blood or legal ties, persons related instead by strong affectional ties.

lady almoner   A forerunner of today's health care social worker. The original lady almoners were social workers from London's Charity Organization Society, who in the late 1800s interviewed patients at the Royal Free Hospital to determine which were eligible to receive free medical care. Lady almoners soon broadened their services to include advocacy, referral to other community resources, and patient education and counseling.

least restrictive environment   The setting that provides the least interference with normal life patterns and yet provides the most important and most needed services to a given client.

legal minor   A person too young to have the legal rights of an adult—usually a person under 18 years of age.

legal regulation   The control of certain activities, such as professional conduct, by government rule and enforcement; governmental controls that limit access to use of professional titles such as "social worker" or "psychologist."

legislative advocacy   The process of lobbying for more responsive legislation.

lesbian   A female whose sexual orientation is toward other females.

less eligibility   The concept, based on the belief that pauperism is voluntary, that the condition of a poor person receiving "relief" should be worse than the condition of the poorest self-supporting worker in the community.

levels of intervention   The systems with which social workers intervene or work: individual, family, group, organization, and community.

liberal   A political perspective that supports government intervention in the workings of the economic market to help "level the playing field" for disadvantaged groups such as women and minorities. Persons of this perspective tend to believe that people are inherently good, naturally industrious, and will work hard if conditions are humane. Liberals believe that it is conditions in the social environment that keep many poor people from achieving a decent standard of living.

lifestyle   An individual's manner of living, which includes one's choice of living single or coupled, one's orientation toward homosexual or heterosexual relationships, and the like.

long-term care Any combination of nursing, personal care, volunteer, and social services provided intermittently or on a sustained basis over a span of time to help persons with chronic illness or disability to maintain maximum quality of life.

mainstreaming In the context of educational policy, the term refers to a philosophy and practice in which children with disabilities—or children who are different from the majority in some special characteristic such as native language—should be educated in regular classrooms as much as possible.

managed health care The systematic administration of health care delivery that constrains costs by limiting the consumer's choice of health care providers to those who contract services at competitive rates, by requiring precertification for costly procedures or hospitalizations, and through effective marketing.

mandatory client Also known as an *involuntary client,* this is a person who does not seek out services voluntarily but instead is required by an authority (a court, for example) to obtain specified services. Persons on probation or parole are examples of mandatory clients.

means test Evaluation of a client's financial resources, using the result as the criterion to determine eligibility to receive a benefit.

Medicaid Title XIX of the Social Security Act, Medicaid is a federal program designed to provide health care for poor people of all ages.

medically indigent Persons who lack insurance coverage or other financial resources to cover the cost of treatment and follow-up care after hospitalization.

Medicare Title XVIII of the Social Security Act, Medicare is a federal program designed to provide health care for the elderly and for long-term disabled persons. Recent legislation has decreased Medicare coverage substantially, and older people especially are often surprised to learn how few hospital and nursing home bills are actually covered by Medicare.

mental disorder Impaired or dysfunctional cognitive or behavioral patterns that occur in individuals and that cause suffering, pain, or some level of disability.

Mental Health Bill of Rights Legislation that seeks to ensure consumers' rights to information, to a reasonable choice of providers and to emergency services, to participate in treatment decisions, to receive respectful care, and to appeal decisions of the mental health care plan.

Mental Health Parity Act of 1996 Legislation that sought to equalize mental health and physical health care in terms of access to and insurance coverage for care.

minority group A group that has less power than the majority group, so that members are relatively vulnerable to poverty and discrimination.

misdemeanor An offense that is considered to be relatively minor by the judicial system. Misdemeanors are generally punishable by fines, probation, or a short jail sentence. Misdemeanors are contrasted with felonies, which are more serious offenses.

mood disorder A commonly cited diagnostic category of *DSM–IV* that encompasses a broad range of dysfunctions of mood. The category includes very serious as well as relatively minimal dysfunctions such as depressive (low mood) and manic (abnormally high mood) states and bipolar states in which both depression and mania occur.

MSW A social worker at the master's degree level of the profession.

multidisciplinary team (M-team) A small, organized group of persons—each trained in different professional disciplines (for example, teaching, social work, psychology) and each possessing her or his own skills and orientations—working together to achieve a common goal.

mutual aid   Reciprocal aid among members of a family, ethnic group, organization, or some such community.

narcotics   Substances, either natural or synthetic, that are used medically to deaden pain. Heroin, morphine, and codeine are examples of narcotics.

national health insurance   A system that provides participation in comprehensive health care insurance for all citizens. The United States remains one of the few industrialized countries that has no national health insurance program.

national health service   A nation's ownership and administration of health care facilities and services that provide the complete range of health care to all citizens.

neglect   The failure of responsible persons to provide for the appropriate care of a dependent, including inadequate nutrition, improper supervision, and deficient health care.

neoconservative   A political perspective that arose in the mid-1970s that opposed government welfare programs for the poor and advocated ending entitlements to assistance under the Social Security Act for poor children and their parents. People of this perspective believe that public social welfare programs should be privatized.

neoliberal   Former liberals who decided that their best hope for election was to express more favorable attitudes toward big business and more caution about the role of big government.

neo-organs   The laboratory culture and growth of individual cells that will have the potential to be used as replacement organs for immediate or future use.

neurosis   A group of mental disorders characterized by persistent and recurring anxiety sometimes accompanied by somatic disorders. This term has been replaced in the *DSM–IV* by the term *anxiety disorder.*

nondiscrimination   Practices that avoid discrimination against minorities; laws that ban bias and require equal access to resources such as education and jobs.

normalization   Making available to persons with disabilities those conditions of everyday life that are as close as possible to the norms and patterns of mainstream society.

norms   Rules of behavior, both formal and informal, and expectations held collectively by a culture, group, organization, or society.

occupational social work   Also known as industrial social work. In this field of practice social workers provide service to businesses, industry, unions, or governmental institutions.

organ replacement   The removal of an organ or tissue from one body or part of a body followed by insertion of organ tissue from another body or body part.

organizer   A professional role most frequently associated with community intervention; incorporates skills in bringing together representatives of different groups or organizations to seek improvement in resources or to advance social justice. This role may also be used to effect policy changes within a social agency.

osteoporosis   A bone-thinning disease most commonly found in women over 50 years of age. Osteoporosis is a frequent cause of fractures in elderly persons.

outdoor relief   A form of welfare relief providing assistance outside of residential institutions (for example, in one's home).

out-of-home services   Services provided to assist needy children and their families when families are no longer able to care for their children in the home. Such services include foster care (both short-term and long-term), institutional care, and the like.

parole   The release of a prisoner by corrections officials before completion of the full sentence; supervision by persons designated by the court (often social workers) is generally required until the full sentence has been completed. Any violation of the terms of the parole agreement can result in return to prison for the remainder of the sentence (revocation).

pay equity   The policies and procedures used to ensure that sex and race discrimination are eliminated from wage-setting systems used by employers.

pension   A payment made regularly to an individual because of retirement, age, loss, or incapacitating injury or to dependents in the event of the holder's death.

pension plan   A plan or program designed to provide financial support for older adults who have retired from their former occupations.

permanency placement   Placement of children who, for whatever reason, cannot live with their biological parents, in permanent adoptive homes.

personal care home   A residential facility providing custodial care and supportive services such as assistance with meals, bathing, and dressing for elderly people. Nursing care provisions are limited or absent.

physical trauma   A wound caused by physical injuries. Fights, accidents, and rape cause physical trauma and may be accompanied by psychological pain.

point-of-service HMO   A model of managed health care designed to give patients access to health care providers or services outside the HMO in which they are enrolled. This model tends to be relatively expensive.

police social work   The practice of social work within police departments. Direct services are provided to persons accused of crime and to family members; some services may also be provided to victims and witnesses of crime and to police personnel, to help them deal with crises, trauma, and stress. Community education and crime prevention work are frequently an additional responsibility.

policy practice   Social work practice that involves participating in the political system to influence the direction and substance of social welfare policy to bring about systems change on behalf of people who are marginalized and disadvantaged.

political asylum   A protected legal status granted by the U.S. government on a case-by-case basis to persons who can demonstrate persecution.

populations-at-risk   Population groups at greater than average statistical risk of being poor or discriminated against socially or in job markets through no fault of their own. Children, women, the elderly, and members of racial and ethnic minority groups are examples of populations-at-risk.

posttraumatic stress disorder (PTSD)   Acute and overwhelming physical and psychological distress lasting for a prolonged time (beyond one month) following a traumatic life event. Unless it is treated, PTSD may impair children as well as adults, making it nearly impossible for them to study, work, sustain parenting responsibilities, or even maintain self-care.

potentiation   A dramatically increased potential for serious, even life-threatening hazards to health resulting from the combination of two or more chemical substances. Cross-addiction to tranquilizers and alcohol, for example, can result in loss of consciousness and body shutdown, requiring emergency medical attention.

poverty   The lack of resources to achieve a reasonably comfortable standard of living. When poverty is extreme, basic needs such as food and shelter are not met.

poverty line The amount of income determined to be the absolute minimum necessary to meet basic survival needs such as food and shelter. It is determined by the cost of food (as established by the U.S. Department of Agriculture) multiplied by three.

poverty turnover rate The rate produced by determining the number of families rising out of poverty in a given year and the number of families replacing them by falling below the poverty line.

practice concentration A concentration or focus (usually with advanced training) on a specific practice method, field of practice, or social problem area; characteristic of social workers with the MSW degree.

preferred practices Protocols or directives that set in place the specific practice to be followed for designated client problems; usually seen in short-term, highly focused interventions in mental health.

preferred-provider organization (PPO) A model of managed health care in which patients receive relatively low-cost care through a network of hospitals, doctors, and other health care providers linked by contractual agreements. Patients themselves pay all or most of the cost of care that they elect to receive outside the PPO.

prejudice Beliefs or opinions formed before the facts are known.

presentence investigation An investigation—ordered by the court before sentencing—into the life situation of a person convicted of a crime. Presentence investigations are conducted by probation officers; they are comprehensive and include information concerning the offender's social history, home and work environments, educational and employment experiences, and physical or mental health problems. This report typically concludes with a recommendation to the judge regarding sentencing.

primary alcoholism A condition in which the abuse of alcohol is not a function of another psychiatric disorder nor the result of a life crisis that preceded the heavy drinking.

primary social work setting A setting that has a fundamental social work purpose (such as enhancing social functioning) and in which the majority of the staff are social workers.

prison A correctional facility where persons convicted of a crime are confined. Generally prisons house persons whose sentences exceed one year, whereas jails hold persons who are awaiting trial or who have been sentenced for short durations.

private practice In social work, the autonomous provision of professional services by a licensed/qualified social worker who assumes responsibility for the nature and quality of the services provided to the client in exchange for direct payment or third-party reimbursement.

private trouble A trouble affecting a specific individual or family.

privatization The act of replacing government systems designed to meet the social welfare needs of people with private-sector services. In the United States growth of for-profit human service organizations has resulted from social policies that support privatization.

probation Suspension of a jail or prison sentence with an accompanying agreement that the offender will abide by all requirements of a court-appointed agent (often a social worker); violation of any terms of the probation agreement can result in return to court or incarceration.

professional roles The behaviors that are expected from persons who are sanctioned by society through education and legal certification to provide service in a specific profession.

prospective payment system (PPS) A system for paying hospitals a fixed amount regardless of the length of stay or the actual expense of caring for the patient.

protective services   Services—often including social, medical, legal, residential, and custodial care—that are provided to children whose caregivers are not providing for their needs.

psychological trauma   Shock or emotional pain that can have lasting effects if not treated promptly. Survivors of war or warlike life situations, automobile accidents, and rape are examples of persons who need assistance with psychological trauma.

psychosis   A group of major mental disorders, either organic or psychological in origin, that includes impaired thinking, perception, and emotional response as well as regressive behavior and possibly delusions and hallucinations.

psychotropic medications   Drugs prescribed by doctors to influence a patient's mental functioning, mood, or behavior. The symptoms of some forms of mental illness can now be well controlled by the use of psychotropic medications.

public assistance   A system of financial aid programs funded out of general tax revenues; people may receive benefits even if they have never paid any taxes. To qualify, one must fit a specific category (for example, "elderly," "blind," "disabled") and must also pass a means test.

public issue   An issue, such as poverty, that affects so many people in a society that people come to perceive the problem as beyond the "fault" of each affected individual. For example, during the Great Depression of the 1930s, the perception of poverty as a public issue rather than as just a private trouble led to the creation of many national public works programs to provide jobs for people out of work.

Qualified Clinical Social Worker (QCSW)   A credential acquired through the NASW that requires two years of full-time or 3,000 hours of part-time post-MSW or postdoctoral clinical social work practice. Additional requirements include evidence of ongoing continuing education.

qualitative research   Systematic research based on data gathered from interviews and field study with individuals, families, groups, organizations, or communities.

quantitative research   Systematic research based on statistical, numerical data gathering and analysis to arrive at valid, reliable conclusions.

racial group   A population with distinct physical or biological characteristics that distinguish it from other populations.

racial profiling   Police targeting of someone for investigation or arrest on the basis of that person's race, national origin, or ethnicity.

racism   The belief that one race is superior to others.

radical   A political perspective that, like the liberal, tends to believe that people are inherently good and naturally industrious. However, radicals do not believe that social justice can be achieved under a capitalist system but, rather, that society must be entirely restructured to redistribute wealth and power among all the people.

reactive alcoholism   A condition in which heavy use of alcohol occurs following a severe life crisis. Treatment should focus on the resolution of the crisis rather than on the abuse of alcohol.

reapportionment   The mandated redrawing of congressional districts when changes in population are determined following a government-conducted census.

recidivism   The tendency of criminal offenders to relapse to former behavior, thus bringing them again to the attention of the courts and probably to reincarceration. The term is sometimes also used to describe the rehospitalization of chronically mentally ill persons or to describe any return to institutional care.

refugees People who leave their country out of a fear of persecution based on religion, political affiliation, race, nationality, or membership in a particular group; they may be granted safety and legal approval to remain, at least temporarily, by another country.

rehabilitation Restoring someone to a healthy and useful capacity or to as satisfactory a condition as possible.

resident council Commonly found in nursing homes but also found in other institutional or residential settings, this is a group that represents all the residents; it engages in negotiation with administration to ensure that residents' needs are met.

resilience The ability to recover one's strength and good spirits after challenges and setbacks.

respite care Temporary personal care or short-term board away from home for people with disabilities, the frail elderly, or the terminally ill; this provides temporary rest and relief for their family caregivers.

restitution The act of restoring to a person something that was stolen, removed, damaged, or destroyed. An enlightened approach, most often seen in juvenile courts, is a restitution program in which the offender is required to repay or replace items stolen or damaged (such as a bicycle, an automobile, or a VCR). Face-to-face contact with the victim of the offense often helps the offender understand the depth of hurt caused by her or his actions. Restitution programs are often administered or staffed by social workers.

revocation A term used in corrections to describe the act of returning a paroled person to prison, thereby canceling parole. The right to revoke is granted to the parole agent by the legal system; revocation is used when there has been a serious violation or repeated less serious violations of the parole contract.

risk rating A system used in corrections that assesses and rates the risk of recidivism to determine the amount and frequency of supervision needed by a client.

sanction This terms has two quite different meanings: (1) the acknowledgment or permission by an established authority for an organization or entity to carry forward a plan or an action; thus, it can be said that social work is sanctioned by society; (2) a response that penalizes an individual for failure to conform to established policies or procedures; NASW, for example, can sanction a member who is found to have violated the *Code of Ethics.*

schizophrenia A serious form of mental disease in which the person has lost the capacity to function normally; disturbances in communication, perception, and affect are commonly associated with schizophrenia, although the disease has several different forms.

School Social Work Specialist (SSWS) A credential acquired through the NASW requiring completion of a minimum of two years' supervised school social work practice post-MSW or postdoctoral degree, satisfactory completion of a specialized test, and submission of professional evaluations and references, as well as evidence of continuing education.

secondary alcoholism A condition in which abuse of alcohol is related to a preceding and underlying psychiatric disorder, often depression. The primary mental illness must become the major focus of treatment.

secondary social work setting A setting in which social work services support the primary purpose of the setting. For example, the primary purpose of a school system is educational; the primary professionals who carry out that purpose are teachers.

self-determination An ethical principle of the social work profession which recognizes the right and need of clients to make their own choices and decisions.

self-referral   A person who seeks the help of a social worker, as contrasted with a mandatory client, who has been required by the courts, an employer, or some outside force to seek assistance.

Service Coordinator   A professional who provides case management services.

sexism   The belief that one gender is superior to the other, usually that males are superior to females.

sexual harassment   Abusive, discriminatory, or unwanted sexual behaviors.

sexual orientation   An individual's erotic orientation toward heterosexual, homosexual, or bisexual behavior.

sheltered workshop   A work environment that hires people with disabilities and provides special services enabling persons with handicaps to perform their work successfully.

shock probation   The practice of brief incarceration at the beginning of probation to frighten the offender into complying with the terms of the probation contract.

sickle-cell anemia   An inherited blood disorder most commonly, but not exclusively, found in African American people. In an acute phase this disease causes severe pain and may require blood transfusions to prevent death or serious complications.

single-payer system   A health insurance system where one governmental insurance plan pays all hospital and other health care expenses directly; the Canadian system is an example.

social and economic justice   Fairness among people, so that members of diverse population groups have an equal chance to achieve a reasonably comfortable standard of living.

social insurance   Government programs to protect citizens from the full consequences of the risks to which they are vulnerable, such as unemployment, disability, death of a breadwinner, and catastrophic medical care needs. Typically, the government requires covered individuals to make regular contributions to a fund that, theoretically, is set aside and used to reimburse those who are covered by the plan for any losses they suffer as a result of covered risks.

social service aide   An employee of a social agency hired not on the basis of academic credentials but for her or his unique life experiences. Social service aides may provide translation services, interpreting not only language but also cultural beliefs and practices. Aides typically assist clients with the completion of insurance and other complicated forms, provide other clerical duties, transport clients, and engage in community outreach efforts.

social service technician   A paraprofessional employee of a social service agency who has completed a two-year associate degree in community or human services work or who has completed a baccalaureate degree in a major other than social work. The technician assists clients in the completion of complex forms, helps with intake procedures, conducts noncomplex interviews, shepherds frail or disabled clients through financial aid applications, and processes some of the paperwork required by the agency.

social welfare   A nation's system of programs, benefits, and services that help people meet those social, economic, educational, and health needs fundamental to the maintenance of society.

social work   The major profession that delivers social services in governmental and private organizations throughout the world; persons educated for practice in this profession help people to prevent or to resolve problems in psychosocial functioning, to achieve life-enhancing goals, and to create a just society.

special education   Educational services and programs designed to meet the needs of children with special needs, such as physical disabilities, learning disabilities, emotional or behavioral disturbances, speech and language problems, or pregnancy.

specialized professional level   An NASW classification level of social work personnel. Professionals at this level are required to have a master's degree from a program accredited by the Council on Social Work Education. The social worker at this level should be able to engage in generalist practice and also should be competent to function as a specialist in more complex tasks.

staffings   Staff meetings, typically conducted on a regular basis, to assess, develop treatment plans, or monitor the care of clients.

status offense   A type of crime that is limited only to certain groups of persons, such as children. A violation of curfew, for example, is a crime for children, but there is no comparable crime for adults.

stimulants   Drugs that produce energy, increase alertness, and provide a sense of strength and well-being; one example is amphetamines.

strengths perspective   A viewpoint encouraging social workers to focus on finding and highlighting client strengths as opposed to problems and limitations.

subacute center   Health care facilities that provide intensive medical services for people who do not need to remain in the hospital but also may not need, or hopefully can avoid, long-term care.

subculture   A smaller variant of a particular culture.

subpoena   An order to appear in court on a specified date; failure to appear may result in a penalty.

subsidy   Monetary aid to assist in the purchase of needed goods or services, usually provided by governmental bodies to private organizations, programs, or persons according to specific eligibility guidelines.

supported employment   A vocational option providing individualized supports to people with disabilities so that they can achieve their goals in the workplace.

surrogate parenting   The process by which a woman agrees to be impregnated and to release the baby that she delivers to the person(s) who contracted with her for this purpose.

system   A whole consisting of interacting parts such that a change in one part affects all others.

Temporary Assistance for Needy Families (TANF)   A program authorized by the federal government under the Personal Responsibility and Work Opportunity Act of 1996. States are allowed but not required to assist poor parents for up to five years in a parent's lifetime. Parents are required to work after two years of assistance.

terrorism   The systematic use of fear, intimidation, and disruption of social systems, usually by politically motivated or criminal groups, to gain publicity or concessions. This is a violent form of social activism.

truancy   The failure to attend school as required by law.

underemployment   Employment at or near minimum wage, often part-time and without health insurance or other benefits.

universal coverage   The assurance of health care for all people in need.

universal health care   A government's policies and provisions that ensure health care benefits for all citizens at the same rate and without regard to their economic status.

utilization review   The term used to refer to decisions made by health care teams that relate strictly to access to medical care: no further knowledge of the social and psychological client issues is needed.

vagrants   People who wander from place to place with no permanent home or job.

values   Preferred ways of believing.

voucher   A coupon or stamp worth a certain amount of money only if spent on specified services or products.

welfare secretaries   Persons hired by industrial firms as early as the late 1800s to assist employees with housing (especially newly arrived immigrants), to improve sanitation and work conditions, and to administer any employee welfare programs.

work ethic   A societal attitude that work is good and laziness is "sinful."

workfare   A term used to describe social policies that require poor people to work in order to receive financial assistance.

workhouse   An "indoor relief" form of assistance common during the 18th century, in which poor people who received help had to live and work in special facilities.

working poor   Persons whose income from employment is not sufficient to meet their survival needs.

worldview   A comprehensive conception of the world especially from a specific standpoint (for example, as shaped by a particular culture).

zero tolerance   A government policy requiring schools to expel any student caught carrying a weapon. Some schools have adopted zero tolerance policies for other types of infractions as well.

Permissions

Chapter 1

(8–9) *Educational policy and accreditation standards,* Council on Social Work Education (2001). Used by permission of Council on Social Work Education.

(15–16) *Educational policy and accreditation standards,* Council on Social Work Education (2001). Used by permission of Council on Social Work Education.

(16) National Association of Social Workers, *Code of Ethics of the National Association of Social Workers,* NASW, 1996, pp. 5–6. Used with permission.

(17) National Association of Social Workers, *Code of Ethics of the National Association of Social Workers,* NASW, 1996, pp. 7–27. Used with permission.

(26) J. Rogers, M. Smith, J. Ray, G. Hull, C. Pike, V. Buchan et al., Information about first social work job. The revised BPD outcomes instrument report of findings: Total database (as of Oct. 1, 1999), paper presented at the 17th Annual Program Meeting of the Association of Baccalaureate Social Work Program Directors, St. Louis, MO., Association of Baccalaureate Social Work Program Directors, Nov. 1999, p. 5, 9. Used by permission of the authors.

(27) J. Rogers, M. Smith, J. Ray, G. Hull, C. Pike, V. Buchan et al., Information about first social work job. The revised BPD outcomes instrument report of findings: Total database (as of Oct. 1, 1999), paper presented at the 17th Annual Program Meeting of the Association of Baccalaureate Social Work Program Directors, St. Louis, MO., Association of Baccalaureate Social Work Program Directors, Nov. 1999, p. 5, 9. Used by permission of the authors.

(27) National Association of Social Workers, "Primary practice areas. Practice area. PRN datagram," *NASW Practice Research Network,* NASW, 2000. Used with permission.

(29) National Association of Social Workers, "1999 Social Work Income—Full Time Employment Only. PRN Datagram" *NASW Practice Research Network,* NASW, 2000. Used with permission.

(30) National Association of Social Workers, "1999 Full-Time Social Work Income by Primary Auspice. PRN Datagram," *NASW Practice Research Network,* NASW, 2000. Used with permission.

(35) National Association of Black Social Workers, *NABSW Code of Ethics,* NABSW, p. 2. Used with permission.

(36) International Federation of Social Workers, *Purposes of the International Federation of Social Workers* (IFSW), IFSW, July 17, 2001. Used by permission of International Federation of Social Workers.

Chapter 2

(19-20) *Educational policy and accreditation standards,* Council on Social Work Education (2001). Used by permission of Council on Social Work Education.

Chapter 3

(10) Excerpt from *Aging in Early Industrial Society: Work, Family, and Social Policy in Nineteenth Century England* by Jill Quadagno. Copyright © 1982 Elsevier Science (USA). Reprinted by permission of the publisher.

(35) War Resisters League, www.warresisters.org/piechart.htm. Used by permission of War Resisters League.

(37) National Association of Social Workers, "Welfare Reform Principles", *NASW Office of Government Relations,* NASW, March 1994. Used with permission.

Chapter 4

(7) Reprinted from the Washington Newsletter, No. 620, April 1998, published by the Friends Committee on National Legislation, www.fcnl.org. Used by permission of Friends Committee on National Legislation.

(8) From Arloc Sherman, *Poverty Matters: The Cost of Child Poverty in America,* Children's Defense Fund, 1997. Reprinted by permission of Children's Defense Fund.

From *Nickel and Dimed: On (Not) Getting By in America* by Barbara Ehrenreich. Copyright © 2001 by Barbara Ehrenreich. Reprinted by permission of Henry Holt & Co., LLC.

(15) From *Amazing Grace* by Jonathan Kozol. Copyright © 1995 by Jonathan Kozol. Used by permission of Crown Publishers, a division of Random House, Inc.

(15) From Arloc Sherman, *Poverty Matters: The Cost of Child Poverty in America,* Children's Defense Fund, 1997, p. 33. Reprinted by permission of Children's Defense Fund.

(37) International Federation of Social Workers, *Code of Ethics for Professional Social Workers,* IFSW, 1976. Used by permission of International Federation of Social Workers.

Chapter 5

(10) "Convention on the Rights of the Child," United Nations, 1990. Used by permission of the Secretary, United Nations Publications Board.

Chapter 6

(11) Reprinted with permission from the *Diagnostic and Statistical Manual of Mental Disorders,* Fourth Edition, Text Revision. Copyright © 2000 American Psychiatric Association.

(16) From *The Social Worker and Psychotropic Medication: Toward Effective Collaboration with Mental Health Clients, Families, and Providers,* 2nd edition, by K. J. Bentley and J. Walsh. Copyright © 2001 Thomson Learning. Reprinted with permission of Brooks/Cole, an imprint of the Wadsworth Group, a division of Thomson Learning.

(19) R. W. Mayden and J. Nieves, "Mental Health: Policy Statement Approved by the NASW Delegate Assembly, August 1999," *Social Work Speaks: National Association of Social Workers Policy Statements 2000–2003,* NASW Press, 2000, pp. 226–227. Used with permission.

M. D. Lerner and R. D. Shelton, "How Do People Respond During Traumatic Exposure?" *Acute Traumatic Stress Management,* The American Academy of Experts in Traumatic Stress, Inc., 2001. Used by permission of The American Academy of Experts in Traumatic Stress, Inc.

(26) A. Eng and E. F. Balancio, E. Lee, "Clinical Case Management with Asian Americans," *Working with Asian Americans: A Guide for Clinicians,* The Guilford Press, 1997, pp. 403–404. Used with permission.

(29) From *The Social Work Interview: A Guide for Human Service Professionals* by Alfred Kadushin and Goldie Kadushin. Copyright © 1997 Columbia University Press. Reprinted with the permission of the publisher.

National Association of Social Workers, "Mental Health Bill of Rights Project," *Joint Initiative of Mental Health Professional Organizations: Principles for the Provision of Mental Health and Substance Abuse Treatment Services,* www.naswdc.org/practice/mental.htm, NASW, Nov. 21, 1999. Used with permission.

Chapter 7

(11) R. W. Mayden and J. Nieves, "Policy Statement," *Social Work Speaks: National Association of Social Workers Policy Statements 2000–2003,* NASW Press, 2000, 5th ed. pp. 17, 152–153. Used with permission.

(12) National Association of Social Workers, "NASW Clinical Indicators for Social Work and Psychosocial Services in Nursing Homes," NASW, 1993. Used with permission.

(20) D. J. Butler and L. R. Beltran, "Functions of an Adult Sickle-Cell Group: Education, Task Orientation, and Support," *Health and Social Work,* NASW Press, 1993, 18 p. 51. Used with permission.

(34) United Nations Statistics Division, "Mortality Rates and Life Expectancy at Birth, by Sex, for Selected Countries, 2000," www.un.org/Depts/unsd/social/health.htm, United Nations Statistics Division. Used by permission of the Secretary, United Nations Publications Board.

(36) Robert Evans and Noralou P. Roos, "What is Right About the Canadian Health Care System," Physicians for National Health Plan (PNHP) Newsletter, Physicians for National Health Plan, March 2000. Used by permission of the authors.

(37) T. Mizrahi, R. Fasano, and S. M. Dooha, "Summary of Canadian Health Care System," *Health and Social Work,* NASW Press, 1993, 18 pp. 7–8. Used with permission.

Chapter 8
(11) J. V. O'Neill, "EAP's Offer Multitude of Internet Services," NASW News, NASW, Jan 2002, p. 14. Used with permission.

(14) J. Winkelpack and M. L. Smith, "The Formal Letter of Referral to an Employee Assistance Program," *Social Work in the Workplace,* Springer, 1988, pp. 57–58. Used with permission.

(15) IPRC: Injury Prevention Research Center, *Type 1 Criminal Intent, Workplace Violence: A Report to the Nation,* IPRC: Injury Prevention Research Center, Feb 2001, p. 5. Iowa City, IA: IPRC: Injury Prevention Research Center. Used by permission of IPRC: Injury Prevention Research Center.

(15) IPRC: Injury Prevention Research Center, *Type 2 Customer/Client, Workplace Violence: A Report to the Nation,* IPRC: Injury Prevention Research Center, Feb 2001, p. 7. Iowa City, IA: IPRC: Injury Prevention Research Center. Used by permission of IPRC: Injury Prevention Research Center.

(15) IPRC: Injury Prevention Research Center, *Type 3 Worker-on-Worker, Workplace Violence: A Report to the Nation,* IPRC: Injury Prevention Research Center, Feb 2001, p. 9. Iowa City, IA: IPRC: Injury Prevention Research Center. Used by permission of IPRC: Injury Prevention Research Center.

(15) IPRC: Injury Prevention Research Center, *Type 4 Personal Relationship, Workplace Violence: A Report to the Nation,* IPRC: Injury Prevention Research Center, Feb 2001, p. 11. Iowa City, IA: IPRC: Injury Prevention Research Center. Used by permission of IPRC: Injury Prevention Research Center.

(22) R. W. Mayden and J. Nieves, "Policy Statement," *Social Work Speaks: National Association of Social Workers Policy Statements 2000–2003,* NASW Press, 2000, 5th ed. pp. 17, 152–153. Used with permission.

Chapter 9
Scott Baldauf, "Schools Try Tuning Into Latino Ways," first appeared in *The Christian Science Monitor* on August 20, 1997, and is reproduced with permission. Copyright © 1997 The Christian Science Monitor (www.csmonitor.com). All rights reserved.

(24) Deena Morrow, "Social Work with Gay and Lesbian Adolescents," *Social Work,* Social Work, Nov. 1993, 38 pp. 655–660.

Chapter 10
(8) Reprinted with permission from the *Diagnostic and Statistical Manual of Mental Disorders,* Fourth Edition, Text Revision. Copyright © 2000 American Psychiatric Association.

(8) Reprinted with permission from the *Diagnostic and Statistical Manual of Mental Disorders,* Fourth Edition, Text Revision. Copyright © 2000 American Psychiatric Association.

(10) A. D. Polorny, B. A. Miller, and H. B. Kaplan, The Brief MAST: A Shortened Version of the Michigan Alcoholism Screening Test, *American Journal of Psychiatry, 129,* APPI, 1972, p. 344. Used with permission.

Chapter 11
(24) P. Metz, (1997), Staff Development for Working with Lesbian and Gay Elders, in J. K. Quam (Ed.), *Social Services for Senior Gay Men and Lesbians,* pp. 35–45. New York: Haworth Press. Used by permission of Haworth Press.

(31) R. R. Green, *Social Work with the Aged and Their Families,* Aldine de Gruyter, 1986, p. 177. Used with permission.

(35) Karen Bassuk and Janet Lessem, "Collaboration of Social Workers and Attorneys in Geriatric Community Based Organizations," *Journal of Gerontological Social Work, 34,* NAELA, 2001, pp. 103, 104. Used with permission.

(38) Kari Watson Culhane, "A Real Home," *Natural Health,* April 2000, p. 80. Used with permission.

Chapter 12
(25) E. Poe-Yamagata and M. A. Jones, "Figure 16: African American Proportion of Youth, And Justice for Some," www.buildingblocksforyouth.org/justice-forsome/jfs.pdf, May 17, 2000, p. 28. Used with permission.

(28) ICPS, "Incarceration Rate for Selected Nations", International Centre for Prison Studies (July 17, 2001). World Prison Brief of the International Centre for Prison Studies. <www.prisonstudies.org> Used by permission of the International Centre for Prison Studies.

Chapter 13
(18) AAMR, "AAMR Fact Sheet: What is Mental Retardation?" http://161.58.153.187/Policies/faq_mental_retardation.html, March 6, 2001. Used with permission.

(14) National Association of Social Workers, *NASW Standards for Service,* National Association of Social Workers. Used with permission.

Chapter 14
(9) M. Marien, "The New Age of Terrorism: Futurists Respond," *The Futurist,* World Future Society, Jan.–Feb. 2002, 36 pp. 16–22. Used with permission.

Index